T3-BGV-837

Econometric Model Performance

Econometric Model Performance

Comparative Simulation Studies of the U. S. Economy

Edited by LAWRENCE R. KLEIN
and
EDWIN BURMEISTER

University of Pennsylvania Press/1976

Library of Congress Catalog Card Number: 76-20145
ISBN: 0-8122-7714-7

Printed in the United States of America

CONTENTS

INTRODUCTION

By Edwin Burmeister and Lawrence R. Klein

No country has as many macro-econometric models as the United States. We do not refer to the long history of model building in which many attempts have been made to estimate equation systems for the U.S. economy; we mean on-going econometric models which are actually being used in repeated economic assessments to forecast or simulate alternative policies.

Models of the American economy exist in government, academe, research institutes, and private corporations. The new generation of contemporary economic analysts is turning increasingly to the use of models in whole or in part for their current assessments. By the time a new generation of analysts has completely replaced those functioning today, probably almost all forecasts and simulations will be model-based.[1] There will then be many more models of the U.S. economy.

Given the proliferation of modeling exercises, there is a need to take stock because the different models come from diverse inspirational sources or schools of thought. They may be saying quite different things about the economy, all at once. It is, in any event, a difficult and challenging problem to model a system as complex as the economy of the United States; accordingly the club of model builders or model proprietors gains much from periodic exchanges of information.

The Conference on Econometrics and Mathematical Economics (CEME), sponsored by the National Bureau of Economic Research and the National Science Foundation, provides a forum for bringing model builders together frequently for the purpose of making comparative studies. There are several national (inter-institutional) seminars sponsored by the conference on growth theory, general equilibrium theory, Bayesian inference, and a range of other subjects in econometrics and mathematical economics. The seminar on comparisons of econometric models has functioned since the inception of the conference and has been of significant help in the continuing effort at model building for this economy. The intent has been to bring together the major model builders or proprietors to exchange views and make standardized comparative studies. Some of the models are quarterly; others are annual or monthly, though the quarterly time unit is the most frequent. Some are demand oriented; others have major supply (input-output) sectors. Some are Keynesian; some are monetarist. Some use only observed, objective data; some use subjective, anticipatory data. Some are policy-oriented, while others

[1] See Vincent Su and Josephine Su, "An Evaluation of ASA/NBER Business Outlook Survey Forecasts," *Explorations in Economic Research* 2 (Fall, 1975), 588–618. The authors note an increasing tendency of participants in this survey to use econometric models in their forecasting operations—to the relative displacement of other methods.

concentrate more on forecasting. Both large and small models are included in the seminar's collection of systems.

There is great diversity, but in spite of the differences, we have cooperated well in trying to distill some common results and to trace differences to their root causes. In the course of these exercises, we have all learned a great deal about the individual models, some general principles about system design, some new techniques of analysis, and many characteristics of the American economy.

The results of the seminar on model comparison have been so attractive to outsiders that similar attempts have been taken up or placed under serious consideration elsewhere. Only one other country, Japan, has such a proliferation of models. The annual Rokko conference on econometrics took up the subject of Japanese model comparisons in their 1975 meetings. Canadian econometricians have been seriously studying the possibility of undertaking such comparative studies, and European groups have also looked into the possibilities, in their case of—across-countries comparisons.

The purpose of the present collection of articles is to let the model builder describe his system in his own words, using his own standards, set-up values, and inputs. Each model builder knows his own system best. The seminar meetings dwell on uniformity, however, and the results of more structured exercises are reported in the final summary chapter by Gary Fromm and Lawrence Klein. Also, Carl Christ's summary critique—from the outside—looks at the several models from a single viewpoint.

In further studies not yet ready for final report, the seminar is putting the models through a set of collective experiments at "optimal control" of the economy, replaying history and policy of the turbulent period 1966–1975. Many of these results were first presented to the public in a seminar-sponsored session at the meetings of the American Economic Association, in Dallas, in December 1975. That session attracted so much attention in the popular news media that the seminar members decided to spend a great deal more time unifying and strengthening the control calculations; the polished results are not yet available.

The model solutions reported in this volume are all retrospective. They include simulations of the models in their respective sample periods. Those in the Klein-Fromm chapter are uniform at starting and ending dates, but the separate chapters authored by model builders use diverse periods in which to look at the models retrospectively. The simulations also include extrapolations beyond the sample periods; these are called *ex post* forecasts, made after the event but not within the sample period.

Most of the models are used widely in *ex ante* forecasting, i.e., extrapolative simulations before the event. Results for some of these are included in several separate chapters, but the seminar members have de-emphasized that aspect of their own work when dealing with the issues of CEME comparisons. Some time was spent, however, in seminar deliberations to set out workable schemes of model comparison in *ex ante* forecasting. This has already been done to some extent by Stephen McNees in a series of studies at the Federal Reserve Bank of Boston.[2] Systematic reviews of *ex ante* forecasts may occupy seminar activities in the near future, but such studies are only lightly touched upon in the present volume.

Historical accuracy and system response characteristics (multiplier analysis)—these are the principal objectives of the analysis presented here. In future meetings, other approaches will be followed.

A Preview of the Contents

The Wharton Model has, for some time, been placed on a two-track system. There has always been a standard version expressed entirely in terms of objectively observed variables. Simultaneously, there has been an "anticipation" version using expected values for consumer sentiment and business capital spending. It also uses advance data on residential construction in the form of housing starts. The latter variable is not subjective; it is indicative of advanced commitments. The consumption and investment variables, however, are in some degree subjective. F. Gerard Adams and Vijaya Duggal find that the error performance of the Wharton Model appears to be better at all times and at turning points when anticipatory data are introduced and the system is simulated on the alternative track. They also find that the multipliers are somewhat smaller in the "anticipatory" version, but this is to be expected since some income-sensitive variables are replaced in important spending equations by the anticipation variables. In more recent versions of the Wharton Model completed after the symposium, the anticipatory variables are fully endogenized, which makes the multipliers obtained from this later generation more comparable with the conventional systems, i.e., the others in the present review.

Ray Fair examines the *ex ante* performance of a short-run forecasting model of the U.S. economy for the 1970.3 to 1973.2 period. Contrary to the prevailing view in the literature, Fair finds that reasonably accurate forecasts can be produced from a model that is not subjectively adjusted. In addition, his results show that the forecasting accuracy of the model is generally improved when the actual values of the exogenous variables are used in place of the *ex ante* forecasted values. In Fair's judgment, the overall results appear encouraging enough to suggest that his approach of no adjustment of equations be used in econometric forecasting. His systems differ from the others in the CEME seminar in that parameters are re-estimated as often as new data become available—every quarter. In some respects, frequent re-estimation does for Fair's systems what adjustment methods (in *ex ante* forecasting) do for others. His method, however, follows a fixed, objective rule.

Leonall C. Andersen and Keith Carlson evaluate the Federal Reserve Bank

[2] The latest study is Stephen K. McNees, "An Evaluation of Economic Forecasts," *New England Economic Review*, (November-December, 1975).

of St. Louis econometric model of which they are prominent architects. After summarizing the general nature of the model, its theoretical foundations and underlying research strategy, Andersen and Carlson review its projection record for the 1968 to 1973 period with outside sample projections using known values for the exogenous variables. They conclude with a checklist of successes and failures. Their model, like Ray Fair's, is small and readily manipulated, but it is distinct in being a "monetarist" model. Although much contemporary literature is devoted to the monetarists' mode of analysis, there is no workable monetarist econometric model besides that of Andersen and Carlson.

The Liu-Hwa model is different from all the others in this symposium because it is a *monthly* model. It is fascinating to contemplate the added richness of detail that we may gain by analyzing the dynamic economy through the medium of a monthly econometric model. The lag structure, business cycle dynamics, and quick forecasting possibilities should all be better analyzed on a monthly period if adequate monthly data on a comprehensive basis can be found. T. C. Liu and E. C. Hwa devote much attention to the construction of monthly series, especially in filling in inevitable gaps. In terms of historical performance measures, their first attempts are quite promising. Their error statistics compare favorably with the quarterly and annual models. They note, however, that the real test—yet to come—will be the difficult question of repetitive *ex ante* forecasting. This is surely an innovative and provocative contribution.

Howrey, Klein and McCarthy responded to the challenge given to econometricians by Ronald Cooper at a conference of model builders in 1969.[3] Being dissatisfied with Cooper's procedures in testing models on a comparative basis, Howrey, Klein and McCarthy attempt to lay down more acceptable procedures that, in their eyes, do not do violence to the models being examined. The paper presented here was discussed in some detail among all the members of the Seminar on Model Comparisons and had considerable influence in developing the kind of comparative program that lies behind the present volume. It sets up procedures for self-testing by the model builders.

Ando, Modigliani, Rasche and Turnovsky analyze the impact of expectations of price and technological change within the context of a "putty-clay" production function. They expect input and output prices to change over time, both in absolute terms and relative to each other. These expectations arise in part from prevailing anticipations of overall inflationary trends and in part from the anticipation of continued technological progress. In this case, however, the authors find the real rate of interest is not uniquely defined, and, in fact, the relevant real rate turns out to be that defined in terms of output price changes. They formulate their model as a "machine replacement problem" in which the eco-

[3] Ronald L. Cooper, "The Predictive Performance of Quarterly Econometric Models of the United States", *Econometric Models of Cyclical Behavior,* ed. Bert Hickman (New York: Columbia Univ. Press for N.B.E.R., 1972).

nomic life of the machine becomes an integral part of the optimization problem. The results of the statistical tests are not as conclusive as the authors might wish, due, perhaps, to the well-known difficulty of measuring inflationary expectations. In the present context, their specialized contribution takes on wider significance since their methods underlie the investment function of the MIT-Pennsylvania-Social Science Research Council (MPS) Model.

Continuing the analysis of the MPS model, Albert Ando takes up a simplified prototype of this model to look at questions of macro-economic stabilization policies and contrasts them with suggestions put forward by monetarists to deal with the same issues within their own model framework. An important contribution of this paper is that it adds to our understanding of how the MPS model works, since the analysis is of a greatly simplified version.

Duggal, Klein and McCarthy describe the principal structural elements and the performance characteristics of the Wharton Quarterly Econometric Forecasting Model Mark III. They show the theoretical roots for this model in the Keynesian system, through the well-known IS-LM curves. They show how a large, complicated system can be reduced to those two basic relationships in order to get a conceptual grasp of the working of the system. They present an extensive multiplier analysis and report historical *ex ante* error results for the period 1972.2 through 1974.1. On the basis of this analysis, Duggal, Klein and McCarthy develop guidelines for the construction of a successor model.

Following with a description of the Data Resources Model, Eckstein, Green and Sinai illustrate the model's properties with full dynamic simulations over the 1963.1 to 1972.4 period. They assert that the economy is stable in the absence of exogenous or random causes of fluctuations, and attribute sources of instability to (1) stock-flow adjustments in the consumption of automobiles; (2) producers' durable equipment expenditures, inventory investment, and housing; and (3) the wage-price mechanism, wide swings in monetary and fiscal policy, and the interactions between financial and real phenomena. In the DRI Model, complete system multipliers show the potency of both monetary and fiscal policies, the former with longer lags than the latter. Eckstein, Green and Sinai conclude that RMSE's for *ex post* simulations of varying lengths are low, while those for actual *ex ante* forecasts from 1969.4 to 1973.4 demonstrate the usefulness of the model as a forecasting tool.

The BEA Quarterly Model, examined by Hirsch, Grimm and Narasimham, is made to yield, in control solutions for different multiplier paths, alternatively a steady 6% and a steady 4% unemployment rate, accelerating demand near full capacity—with and without external supply constraints. The authors compare errors for *ex ante* forecasts with three stages of judgmental intrusion and four *ex post* forecasts, together with errors from post-sample simulations and Box-Jenkins type time-series extrapolations, all from a common time period. They study error growth over the extrapolation horizon and the contribution of judgment to the reduction of error. They find a result that has occurred in previous studies, namely that *ex post* extrapolations (without adjustment) are generally poorer than *ex ante* forecasts which have been improved by the superposition of judgment.

In an analysis of the Michigan Quarterly Model, authors Hymans and Shapiro examine the block structure of the model, the dynamic and structural properties of individual equations, the dynamics of the model as a simultaneous unity, and lastly, the model's *ex post* forecasting performance. They compute a variety of policy multipliers in different cyclical phases and find some of the same forecast error properties present in the other quarterly models. Finally, they indicate the lines that future research activities will follow.

Discussing an input/output system within the context of a macro-forecasting model, the Wharton Long Term Model, R. S. Preston shows how techniques are developed to model the adjustment of input coefficients in response to changing price and technology, resulting in a direct treatment of the problem of input/output coefficient change and price-induced substitution. Included for forty-nine final demand categories are estimates of the elasticity of substitution between inputs necessary to maintain given expenditure levels. Preston presents multipliers to show the distributional impact of monetary and fiscal policies, on both gross national product and manufacturing output.

This model is considerably larger than any of the others included in the symposium; it deals with a longer forecast horizon, and is based on annual data. The annual results are not fundamentally different from the yearly aggregation of quarterly results from many of the other models.

Like the Wharton Long Term Model, the Hickman-Coen Annual Model of the U.S. economy deals with a longer-run time horizon. It has a longer sample period and is designed for use in a longer simulation period. The model combines elements of the Keynesian and neo-classical traditions to analyze economic policy over periods of a decade or more. Authors Hickman, Coen and Hurd give an overview in tabular form of its block structure and principal variables. They go on to discuss in greater detail key relationships connecting firms' decisions on production, employment, investment, and prices, as well as the wage and housing sectors. Sample period prediction errors are given. Finally, the authors conclude with a presentation and analysis of responses of twelve key endogenous variables to five different fiscal and monetary policies in dynamic multiplier simulations covering a sixteen-year span.

George Schink subjects the Brookings Quarterly Model to various policy analyses over a fairly long time period—ten years—looking carefully at the time path of the various effects. These analyses are made from the model as it existed in June 1972, the last update period for it. The model used here is a condensed version. Schink examines the longer-run implications of policies that appear to be attractive in the short run. In some cases, perverse long-run side effects develop. Tax policy changes appear in this model to be better in the long run than public expenditure changes while combinations of tax, expenditures, and monetary policies may prove to be the best of all.

Carl Christ presents the first of two evaluative articles on model forecasting performance. Referring to the eleven models considered in the symposium, Christ argues that models must be tested against data that occurred *after* the models were specified. Otherwise, he claims, they cannot be relied upon for accurate predictions of time paths of effects of economic policies. Econometric forecasters, says Christ, usually predict GNP three quarters ahead to within 1% and six quarters ahead to within 2%. He points out that the models disagree strongly about paths of effects of monetary and fiscal policy. Evaluative computations are suggested, including post-model-specification forecasts, *ex ante* and *ex post,* with and without subjective adjustment, exact and stochastic, turning point errors, and twenty-year policy simulations. He finds a great deal of dispersion among the various models as regards their policy implications, in contrast to Fromm and Klein's feelings that there is a fair amount of uniformity of results from alternative policy exercises across models.

J. D. Sargan looks at econometric theory in relation to the building of large scale models. Although models are almost always estimated from small samples, Sargan concludes that asymptotic sampling theory still gives a good approximation to the distributions of estimates. He concentrates on the iterated instrumental variable type of estimates because this method accomodates the paucity of degrees of freedom very well in cases where the model is large, with many parameters, but the data base is small. In the appendix, he proves a theorem on the necessary sample size for full-information maximum-likelihood estimation, confirming a result previously introduced by Klein.

Suits, Mardfin, Paitoonpong and Yu complete the Symposium on Econometric Model Performance with an analysis of a growth model in which birth rates and female labor-force participation are endogenous. Their model is used to simulate economic development and the attendant demographic transition. In a second simulation, birth control is represented by modification of the birth rate equation. The authors compare the two simulations to yield estimates of $750 to $2,000 as the present value of preventing one birth in a poor country. In the model these authors develop, modification of the investment equation suggests that if investment is used to replace birth control, about $487 of additional investment is required to substitute for one prevented birth. The authors make comparisons with earlier results and conclude with suggestions for improvements for future models.

The work of the CEME seminar on econometric model comparisons and the symposium published in this volume bring the research through an important stage—one of careful line-up of diverse models under uniform conditions in which some consensus about structural characteristics of the economy can be reached. It is possible to go further in attaining uniformity, but such steps might bring only marginal new information. The new research directions taken by the seminar are to make systematic applications of control theory to difficult model solutions, to investigate the error structure (residuals) across models, to continue analysis of *ex ante* forecast errors among the various models, and possibly to combine the wealth of information in all the different models in a more general forecasting exercise. All these avenues are being explored in the seminar and could well form the basis for a sequel to the present volume.

One paper, not presented in the original symposium, but recognized by all participants in the CEME seminar, is a summary review of all the models by Gary Fromm and Lawrence Klein. At an earlier stage in the seminar's progress, Fromm and Klein presented a summary paper at the 1972 meetings of the American Economic Association.[4] In connection with the present symposium, Klein and Fromm revised, updated, and extended this summary analysis. They included error statistics for more variables, obtained more complete tabulations from each model builder, increased the degree of uniformity of exercise across models, and explained their analysis in more detail.

Conclusion

The emphasis in the CEME Seminar for research on model comparisons has been on achieving uniformity across models in initial conditions, simulation period, summary statistics, and model exercises. Uniformity has been taken a long way but is still not complete, and this aspect of research is still being investigated. Nevertheless, in spite of the degree of uniformity achieved in background conditions and methods of measurement, there is a fair amount of diversity in the results—not so much in the forecast-type exercises as in the dynamic multiplier calculations. Carl Christ, looking in from outside, finds a high degree of diversity in multiplier results that could form a basis for policy conclusions. The insiders—Fromm and Klein—on the other hand, knowing how hard it is to get the degree of cooperation achieved in the present study and to compare models, are more struck by similarity of results. Naturally, the St. Louis model and the Fair model are going to show multipliers vastly different from the rest. But this is readily seen, in advance, upon inspection of the models and their causal mechanisms. The other models show a stronger degree of similarity in their simulated trajectories, with, perhaps, the MPS model being something of an outsider. It is possible to agree with Christ's conclusion that, given the diversity of results found, the forecast ability does not, by itself, validate policy applications. However, the degree of success achieved so far in forecasting, especially when replicated, is surely evidence that suggests some measure of credibility. It would not be possible to do a decent forecasting job year in and year out, if the underlying model were far from the truth. Occasional successes would tend to be counterbalanced by significant failures, but the weight of evidence seems to be on the side of the consumer-type models.

[4] Gary Fromm and Lawrence R. Klein, " A Comparison of Eleven Econometric Models of the United States", *American Economic Review, Papers and Proceedings*, LXIII (May, 1973), 385–93.

1

ANTICIPATIONS VARIABLES IN AN ECONOMETRIC MODEL: PERFORMANCE OF THE ANTICIPATIONS VERSION OF WHARTON MARK III

By F. Gerard Adams and Vijaya G. Duggal[1]

The use of anticipatory data for prediction and, specifically, their inclusion in econometric models has many precedents.[2] But the question of how anticipations variables affect the multiplier and error properties of models has not been explored in depth. The Wharton Mark III model offers a unique opportunity to observe the effect of anticipatory data since the model is available, and is used for current prediction, in two variants: the Standard Version, which does not include anticipations data, and the Anticipations Version which makes use of the Michigan index of consumer sentiment, the BEA investment anticipations, and data on housing starts.[3]

The Anticipations Version introduces the anticipations structurally, as a step in the formation of economic behavior. It includes functions to explain the anticipations variables themselves. When observed values of anticipations are available, they are used; for forecast horizons for which no observed anticipations variables apply, the anticipations are estimated by the model. Consequently it is possible to distinguish between the effect on the model's properties of the structure including the anticipations and separately the effect of information embodied in the observed values of the anticipations variables. This paper is concerned with the properties of the Anticipations Version of Wharton Mark III. It focuses on the effects of anticipations variables on the multipliers and error properties of the model.

THE ANTICIPATIONS VARIABLES

Anticipations variables differ greatly in meaning, degree of firmness, and forecast lead time. We are concerned here with three variables which are not simply broad indicators of economic trends. They can be fitted structurally into behavioral equations.

The index of consumer sentiment (*CSI*) measures consumers' perception of the economic situation personally and nationally. Even though this variable

[1] The authors would like to thank Lawrence R. Klein and Dexter Rowell for many helpful suggestions.

Ida Green and Arthur Doud provided valuable research assistance.

[2] Anticipations data in models date from the use of stock market yields in Tinbergen's pioneering League of Nations model of the U.S. (see [4, (47)]). Of many models presently in use, Fair's model relies most heavily on anticipations variables.

[3] The Wharton Mark III model is described in M. D. McCarthy [3]. The properties of this model will be the subject of a future article in this series. An earlier version of the Anticipations Version of Wharton Mark III is summarized by F. Gerard Adams and Lawrence R. Klein in [**1**].

does not measure buying plans directly, it serves as an indicator of the consumers' feelings of job security and prospects about inflation and the income stream. The usefulness of consumer sentiment as a forecast variable has been documented at length.[4] But it is fair to note that in an elaborately specified consumption equation, the *CSI* variable has only a small effect, particularly on purchases of cars, with a forecast horizon of one to two quarters.

The BEA plant and equipment investment anticipations are somewhat more integral to the investment process. They represent survey responses about businessmen's investment expenditure expectations—presumably businesses plan future spending though survey questions never ask directly about the plan or its revision. The investment anticipations are linked closely to the data on actual investment; analogous survey questions call for information about planned investment and about investment which has taken place. And the responses to the latter question are the basis for BEA's calculation of investment spending in the national income and product accounts. The data considered here are for spending anticipations two quarters ahead—the so-called "first anticipations"—and for one quarter the "second anticipations."[5]

The housing starts statistics are anticipatory variables of still a different, perhaps more solid, sort. Starts represent a discernible step in the process of residential construction.[6] The national accounts statistics on construction are derived by placing a value on starts and by translating this value into construction put-in-place on the basis of a time phasing formula. Thus, the residential construction statistics are firmly linked to housing starts some months earlier.

Though quite different, each of these variables supplies advance information on the economy. The issue is whether such information improves the performance of the model.

THE ANTICIPATIONS EQUATIONS

The Anticipations Version of Wharton Mark III is identical to the Standard Version except for the 16 behavioral equations which build the anticipationary variables into the expenditure functions or which explain the anticipations data themselves.[7]

Consumption—Since the *CSI* variable is a supplement to income in explaining auto purchases, it has been substituted for the unemployment rate variable in the auto equation. In accord with the experience of previous research, *CSI* accounts for only a small improvement in the error statistics of this equation compared to the Standard Version. The coefficients of the other variables are not substantially changed by the addition of *CSI* to the equation. If *CSI* were

[4] The most recent appraisal is Saul Hymans [2].

[5] In recent years the BEA data also include anticipations for the remainder of the forecast year, these are not considered here.

[6] Actually, the housing starts data are themselves derived from an earlier step, reports on building permits granted. This step could also be modeled.

[7] A listing of equations is available from the authors on request.

used in addition to unemployment, it would have a smaller influence.[8]

The *CSI* variable itself is explained in terms of the inflation rate—consumer sentiment is adversely affected by inflation—and the change in the unemployment rate.

Business Fixed Investment—The equations to explain business fixed investment are cast in a realizations function mold. We view investment anticipations (I^a) as determined by the same variables which explain investment, i.e., current and past values of output, the user cost of capital and the price of output and the stock of capital. Investment may then be explained by adding the realizations equation to explain $I_t - I_t^a$. This scheme has been modified in our specification. In place of the formal realizations function, following Jorgenson, actual investment outlays have been made a distributed lag function of investment anticipations expressed at earlier time points.

Since investment plans may be modified after they have been made, it is appropriate also to introduce intervening variables, non-anticipatory variables which provide information on the period between the formulation of investment plans and their realization. The general functional form of the investment functions for manufacturing, regulated industry, and commercial is:

$$I_t = \alpha_0 + \alpha_1 \sum_{i=1}^{\infty} (\Theta_1)_i I^{a1}_{t-i-2} + \alpha_2 \sum_{i=1}^{\infty} (\Theta_2)_i I^{a2}_{t-i-1} + \sum_{i=0}^{1} \beta_{1,t-i} Z_{1,t-i} \cdots + \beta_{n,t-i} Z_{n,t-i}$$

where the anticipations (I^{a1} and I^{a2}) are introduced respectively with lags of at least two and one quarters, where Θ's are distributed lag weights, and where the Z's are non-anticipations variables for the period between the anticipations and the time investment is put in place. We assume that businessmen foresee capital equipment prices correctly.

The anticipations equations are formulated like investment equations. The functions for the "second" anticipations include the first anticipations as an explanatory variable; they may be seen as a form of "revision of anticipations" equations.

The equations explaining the first anticipations are quite similar with regard to coefficients and lag structure to the equations explaining investment in terms of only objective variables in the Standard Version of the model.

Residential Construction—The equation for residential construction, *IHT*, incorporates housing starts (single family and multiple family separated) with an empirical approximation of the time phasing which appears to be used to develop the residential construction values in the national accounts.[9] Once started, there is little likelihood that construction will be stopped or delayed. But current

[8] As we will see below, the elimination of the unemployment rate variable does significantly affect the behavior of the equation and of the system.

[9] The weighting for starts which appears to be used to prepare the official statistics assumes that 41% of a new home is put in place during the starting quarter, 49% during the next quarter, and the remaining 10% one quarter later. Weights obtained by estimating the function with distributed lags are:

(*Continued on next page*)

economic conditions may influence *IHT* by affecting "additions and alterations" which are not included in the housing starts but which do enter the overall *IHT* category. Average value per start may also reflect current economic forces. The equation for *IHT* includes, in addition to single and multiple housing starts, a proxy variable to measure financial availabilities, a price variable, and an income variable.

The housing starts are explained in terms of the variables usually found in housing equations, a mix of financial availability and demand variables. Since mortgage flows are not endogenous in the model, proxy variables—the difference between long and short interest rates, and a dummy variable for those unusual periods when the long rate exceeds the short rate—measure tightness of financial markets and the times of disintermediation. Real income and price have the expected impact. A time trend helps to catch the gradual shift from single family to multiple family dwellings. The vacancy rates in owner-occupied housing and in rental housing indicate the supply of unoccupied housing and represent a way of accomodating a stock variable in the housing starts equations. The vacancy rates themselves are explained endogenously. Reduced form equations to explain vacancy rates bring together variables representing demand for housing—income and price—and supply of new housing as measured by lagged starts.

The system of equations for housing thus explains the entire sequence from vacancies to starts and construction. The degree of explanation obtained by these equations is considerably higher than in the Standard Version of the housing equation.

ERROR PROPERTIES OF THE ANTICIPATIONS VERSION

The purpose of anticipatory data is, of course, to improve the forecasting performance of the model. In Table 1 we compare the error properties of alternative versions of the Wharton Model in one to eight quarter forecast simulations over the period 1961. 1 to 1967. 4. These are *ex-post* forecasts, within the sample period, without any equation adjustments, and using actual values of exogenous variables.

The comparison is between:

1. The *Standard Version* of Mark III.
2. The *Endogenous Anticipations Version*-with anticipations variables treated as endogenous variables.
3. The *Forecasting Anticipations Version* with exogenous anticipations data when it would normally be available to the forecaster (at other times anticipations must, of course, be treated as endogenous).

([9] *Continued*)

	Single family starts	Multiple family starts
Quarter t	.43	.29
t-1	.45	.35
t-2	.26	.26
t-3	.00	.11
t-4	−.14	−.01

TABLE 1

ROOT MEAN SQUARE ERRORS OF ALTERNATIVE VERSIONS OF WHARTON MODEL MARK III

Personal Consumption Expenditures on Automobiles, billions of 1958$ (*CA*)

Forecast Period[a]	1	2	3	4	5	6	7	8
Standard Version (1)	1.03	1.12	1.15	1.15	1.20	1.19	1.21	1.18
Endogenous Anticipations (2)	.92	.95	.98	1.03	1.12	1.13	1.16	1.16
Forecasting Anticipations (3)	.92	.91	.94	.99	1.08	1.14	1.17	1.19

Non-Residential Fixed Investment, billions of 1958$ (*IP*)

Forecast Period	1	2	3	4	5	6	7	8
Standard Version (1)	1.82	1.97	2.05	2.08	2.14	2.22	2.30	2.37
Endogenous Anticipations (2)	1.47	2.03	2.18	2.06	2.13	2.21	2.33	2.45
Forecasting Anticipations (3)	1.12	1.34	1.74	2.04	2.10	2.07	2.29	2.43

Fixed Investment on Residential Structures, billions of 1958$ (*IHT*)

Forecast Period	1	2	3	4	5	6	7	8
Standard Version (1)	1.57	1.57	1.67	1.79	1.87	1.95	2.01	2.03
Endogenous Anticipations (2)	.68	1.23	1.59	1.70	1.86	2.11	2.30	2.39
Forecasting Anticipations (3)	.49	.82	1.35	1.67	1.89	2.15	2.33	2.39

GNP, billions of 1958$ (*X*)

Forecast Period	1	2	3	4	5	6	7	8
Standard Version (1)	3.21	4.23	4.65	4.64	4.89	5.12	5.35	5.73
Endogenous Anticipations (2)	3.09	3.98	4.23	4.20	4.53	4.89	5.17	5.60
Forecasting Anticipations (3)	2.98	3.65	3.89	3.96	4.36	4.76	5.19	5.70

GNP, billions of $ (*GNP* $)

Forecast Period	1	2	3	4	5	6	7	8
Standard Version (1)	2.89	4.60	6.14	6.81	7.20	7.29	7.30	7.16
Endogenous Anticipations (2)	2.90	4.42	5.76	6.35	6.71	6.84	6.84	6.73
Forecasting Anticipations (3)	2.82	4.11	5.49	6.18	6.53	6.60	6.67	6.60

GNP Deflator, 1958=100.0 (*P*)

Forecast Period	1	2	3	4	5	6	7	8
Standard Version (1)	.28	.31	.37	.49	.62	.71	.81	.92
Endogenous Anticipations (2)	.28	.30	.35	.46	.59	.68	.77	.88
Forecasting Anticipations (3)	.29	.31	.36	.48	.60	.69	.78	.88

(*Continued on next page*)

[a] Error statistics under columns 1–8 are computed on the basis of 28 one to eight quarter ahead simulations respectively starting with 1961.1 and ending with 1967.4.

TABLE 1 (continued)

Unemployment Rate, Percent (*UN*)

Forecast Period	1	2	3	4	5	6	7	8
Standard Version (1)	.21	.39	.52	.57	.61	.63	.65	.66
Endogenous Anticipations (2)	.21	.39	.52	.57	.61	.64	.66	.68
Forecasting Anticipations (3)	.21	.38	.50	.56	.60	.63	.65	.66

The comparison between (1) and (2) indicates how the model with anticipations variables performs relative to the specification without them. We would hope for an improvement but there is little *a priori* reason why one should occur. The comparison between (2) and (3) focuses particularly on the question of whether the exogenous anticipations data contribute a net informational gain. Presumably such an improvement should be principally in the time period to which the anticipations variable applies but it may also affect performance in subsequent time periods.

The results of the calculations follow the expected pattern particularly for the variables influenced directly by the anticipations data: consumer purchases of autos and parts (*CA*), fixed business investment (*IP*), and residential construction (*IHT*). Forecast errors are substantially lower in the Anticipations Version (2) than in the Standard Version (1) for the one quarter ahead forecast. The current and future values of the anticipations variables are endogenous in Version (2). The improvement is particularly striking for *IHT* where the structure including the housing starts reduces errors by more than half in the first quarter and the improvement continues for the first five forecast quarters. The error in automobile purchases improves modestly with the Anticipations Version of the model for all eight quarter forecasts.

Comparing the version of the model which uses the exogenous information on anticipations, when it is available at the time of the forecast (Forecasting Anticipations Version 3), and the Endogenous Anticipations Version (2), there is a further gain in accuracy. The sharpest gain is in housing where introduction of the latest information on multiple and single family housing starts reduces errors, particularly for the first three quarters forecast, as we would expect. A similar improvement occurs in the forecast for investment as known data on the latest investment anticipations are introduced. Other components of aggregate demand, not directly connected with the anticipations equations, are also predicted more accurately.

Interestingly the improvements for the individual demand components do not simply carry through to the level of the aggregate economy. The improvement in error between Version 1 and Version 2 and between Version 1 and Version 3 is tabulated in Table 2. There is only small improvement for real GNP during the first quarter forecast in the Endogenous Anticipations (2) while there is a marginal increase in error in nominal GNP. The anticipations information introduced in Version 3 does however, yield a small payoff. In subsequent

TABLE 2

REDUCTION IN ERRORS OF REAL AND MONEY *GNP* IN THE ANTICIPATIONS MODEL FROM THE STANDARD MODEL

Standard Model (1) Error Minus Endogenous Anticipations (2) Error

Forecast Period	1	2	3	4	5	6	7	8
Real *GNP*	.12	.25	.42	.44	.36	.23	.18	.13
Money *GNP*	−.01	.18	.38	.46	.49	.45	.46	.43

Standard Model (1) Error Minus Forecasting Anticipations (3) Error

Forecast Period	1	2	3	4	5	6	7	8
Real *GNP*	.23	.58	.76	.68	.53	.36	.16	.03
Money *GNP*	.07	.49	.65	.63	.67	.69	.63	.56

quarters, the gain is more pronounced amounting to an error reduction of somewhat more than a half billion dollars (Version 3), still far from the gain obtained in the individual demand components. The improvements in the error statistics for the GNP deflator and for unemployment are very small. It is the negative covariance in errors among different components of demand that is responsible for the fact that the more accurate prediction of each of the separate components is not passed on as an equivalent improvement in the aggregate demand error. Each error statistic is calculated with a sample of 28 observations. For a particular sample point, some components must be doing worse in the Anticipations Versions (2 and 3) than in the Standard Version (1), making up for it at some other sample point where they do better while the remaining components do worse.

The root-mean-squared error analysis does not demonstrate whether one version of the model has a greater tendency to predict with a bias than the other version. Nor does it indicate whether the larger errors are due to a markedly poorer performance in a few forecasts or a consistently inferior performance in the entire sample period. In order to observe these characteristics of the different versions Theil diagrams were plotted for all forecasts. The horizontal axis measures actual percentage change over the forecast period. The vertical axis measures the percentage change in the predicted value for the same variable to its actual value observed when the forecast was made. A perfect forecast will place all points on the 45° line through the origin. The scatter of the 28 forecasts shows the error of the forecasts around the line of perfect prediction. Figure 1 shows the three scatters of one quarter ahead forecasts for nonfarm residential investment. Version 1 shows a tendency for substantial overestimation. In Version 3 the points lie closely on the 45° line. These three scatters convincingly show the superiority of Version 2 over Version 1 and of Version 3 over Version 2 for the residential construction variable. The use of available information on housing starts at the time of the forecast, when used within the framework of the complete model leads to the closest approximation to the line of perfect prediction.

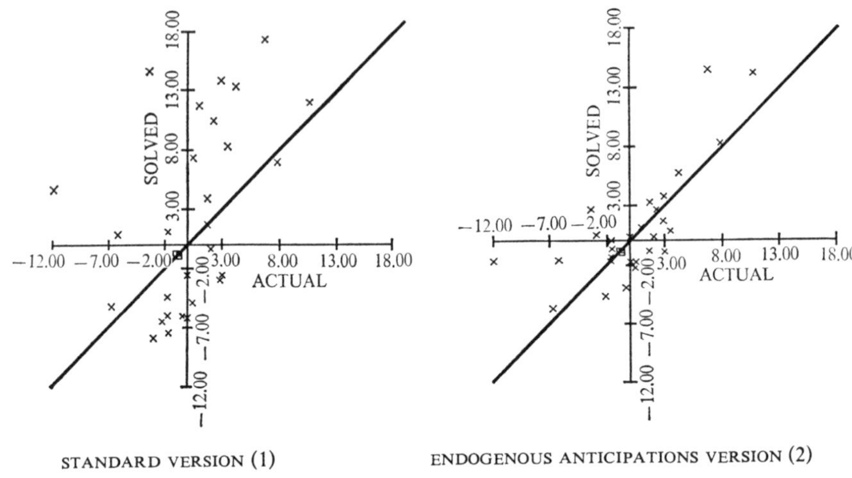

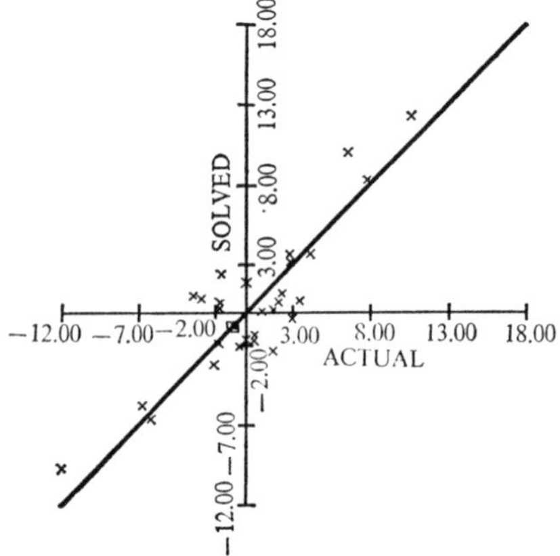

FIGURE 1

ONE QUARTER AHEAD FORECAST OF REAL FIXED INVESTMENT ON NONFARM RESIDENTIAL STRUCTURES (PERCENT CHANGES)

Unfortunately not all components of GNP have scatters that present so clearly the superiority of one version over another. A similar result is discernible in Figure 2 presenting the one quarter ahead scatter of investment in plant and equipment although it is less dramatic. In the scatter of changes in real GNP (not shown) it is difficult to compare visually. For all relevant variables we fitted least squares lines regressing actual percentage changes on predicted percentage changes. The results for one, two and six quarter forecasts, are tabulated in Table 3.

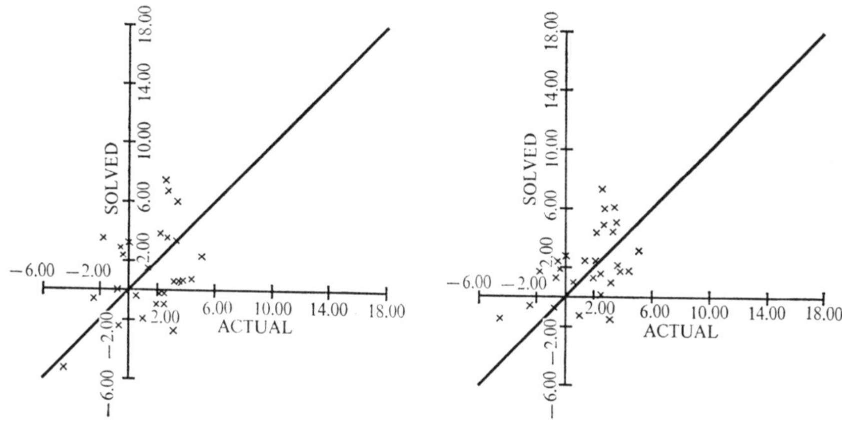

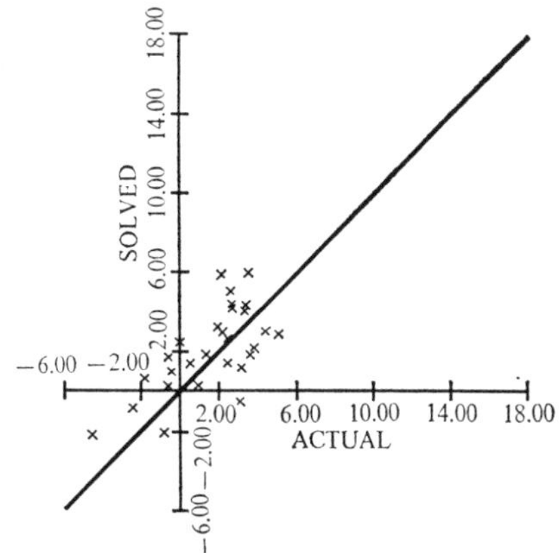

FORECASTING ANTICIPATIONS VERSION (3)

FIGURE 2

ONE QUARTER AHEAD FORECAST OF REAL NON-RESIDENTIAL FIXED INVESTMENT (PERCENT CHANGES)

The line of perfect prediction should have a zero intercept, and a regession coefficient of 1. The proximity of the two calculated values to their ideal values, together with the value of the $\bar{R}^2$ can be considered as three different statistics to compare the three versions of the model.

Looking vertically down each block of Table 3, $\bar{R}^2$ increases going from the Standard Version (1) to the Endogenous Anticipations Version (2) and to the Forecasting Anticipations Version (3). The improvement is considerably more pronounced, of course, for the one and two quarter forecasts than over a longer

TABLE 3

REGRESSIONS OF ACTUAL PERCENTAGE CHANGES ON PREDICTED PERCENTAGE CHANGES OF SELECTED VARIABLES[a]

	One Quarter Ahead			Two Quarter Ahead			Six Quarter Ahead		
	Constant	Slope	$\bar{R}^2$	Constant	Slope	$\bar{R}^2$	Constant	Slope	$\bar{R}^2$
Real Personal Consumption Expenditures on Automobiles (*CA*)									
Standard Version (1)	−0.04 (.0)	1.08 (7.0)	.64	− .12 (.1)	1.01 (7.3)	.66	−3.12 (2.7)	1.28* (14.3)	.88
Endogenous Anticipations (2)	−1.20 (1.7)	1.16 (8.8)	.74	−1.45 (1.8)	1.06 (9.6)	.77	−3.59 (3.1)	1.21* (14.4)	.88
Forecasting Anticipations (3)	−1.20 (1.7)	1.16 (8.8)	.74	−1.28 (1.7)	1.05 (10.2)	.79	−3.37 (2.8)	1.20* (13.7)	.87
Real Non-Residential Fixed Investment (*IP*)									
Standard Version (1)	1.23 (2.8)	.27* (1.9)	.09	.93 (1.2)	.72 (4.2)	.38	− .43 (.3)	1.02 (9.8)	.78
Endogenous Anticipations (2)	.55 (1.0)	.46* (2.8)	.20	.50 (.6)	.67 (4.0)	.35	− .96 (.7)	1.04 (10.0)	.78
Forecasting Anticipations (3)	.07 (.2)	.70 (4.6)	.42	− .66 (1.0)	.99 (7.6)	.68	− .75 (.6)	1.02 (10.7)	.81
Real Fixed Investment on Nonfarm Residential Structures (*IH*)									
Standard Version (1)	− .19 (.2)	.24* (2.4)	.16	− .91 (.7)	.56* (4.3)	.39	−1.69 (1.0)	.85 (4.4)	.40
Endogenous Anticipations (2)	− .38 (.6)	.69* (5.5)	.52	− .91 (.8)	.69* (5.4)	.51	−1.44 (.7)	.85 (3.2)	.26
Forecasting Anticipations (3)	− .05 (.13)	.86 (9.2)	.75	− .77 (1.0)	.92 (8.6)	.73	−1.54 (.8)	.81 (3.1)	.24
Nominal *GNP* (*GNP$*)									
Standard Version (1)	.25 (.8)	.86 (5.0)	.47	−1.37 (2.0)	1.35 (7.1)	.64	−3.3 (3.4)	1.30* (13.8)	.88
Endogenous Anticipations (2)	.34 (1.2)	.76 (5.3)	.50	− .99 (1.6)	1.21 (7.4)	.66	−3.3 (4.0)	1.29* (15.8)	.90
Forecasting Anticipations (3)	.35 (1.4)	.76 (5.5)	.52	− .94 (1.8)	1.2 (8.3)	.71	−3.3 (4.2)	1.29* (16.8)	.91
Real *GNP* (*X*)									
Standard Version (1)	.34 (1.3)	.70 (3.7)	.31	− .68 (1.4)	1.22 (6.9)	.63	−1.4 (2.6)	1.19* (16.0)	.90
Endogenous Anticipations (2)	.27 (1.1)	.70 (4.4)	.41	− .58 (1.4)	1.12 (7.8)	.69	−1.4 (2.7)	1.17* (16.6)	.91
Forecasting Anticipations (3)	.25 (1.1)	.72 (4.7)	.44	− .60 (1.7)	1.13 (9.0)	.75	−1.4 (2.8)	1.17* (17.1)	.91

[a] "*t*" statistics reported in parentheses.
* Significantly different from 1.0.

(*Continued on next page*)

TABLE 3 (continued)

	One Quarter Ahead			Two Quarter Ahead			Six Quarter Ahead		
	Constant	Slope	$\bar{R}^2$	Constant	Slope	$\bar{R}^2$	Constant	Slope	$\bar{R}^2$
GNP Deflator (*P*)									
Standard Version (1)	.23 (2.8)	.57* (3.8)	.33	− .01 (.1)	1.01 (7.1)	.64	−1.0 (2.1)	1.25 (7.9)	.69
Endogenous Anticipations (2)	.24 (3.0)	.57* (3.9)	.34	.01 (.1)	1.00 (7.5)	.67	−0.9 (2.1)	1.24 (8.4)	.72
Forecasting Anticipations (3)	.24 (3.0)	.57* (3.8)	.33	.01 (.1)	1.00 (7.3)	.66	− .90 (2.0)	1.23 (8.2)	.71
Unemployment Rate (*UN*)									
Standard Version (1)	− .13 (.2)	.54* (3.2)	.25	1.3 (.7)	.73 (3.0)	.23	2.16 (.7)	.72 (4.5)	.42
Endogenous Anticipations (2)	.18 (.2)	.58* (3.6)	.31	2.5 (1.3)	.83 (3.9)	.34	4.23 (1.4)	.77 (5.3)	.50
Forecasting Anticipations (3)	.21 (.3)	.59* (3.7)	.32	2.6 (1.4)	.85 (4.1)	.37	4.49 (1.5)	.79 (5.5)	.52

* Significantly different from 1.0.

forecast horizon. This corresponds with the results of the analysis of the root-mean-square errors above.

For investment and housing in the one and two quarter forecasts, the slope coefficients of these regressions are significantly improved in the Anticipations Versions 2 and 3 of the model. Where the slope coefficients differ significantly from unity in the Standard Version (1), for the Forecasting Anticipations Version (3), the coefficients are not significantly different from unity. There is similarly an improvement in the constants which tend to be closer to zero. It is interesting to note that the slope coefficient tends to be closer to unity, in all versions, over the longer term forecast in which the influence of short term movements is less pronounced.

For the aggregate economic variables there is also generally some improvement in $\bar{R}^2$ as a result of introducing anticipations, but as above, the improvement is much smaller and there is little systematic pattern to the constants and slope coefficients.

TURNING POINT ANALYSIS

Another important criterion for evaluating a model, is how well the model predicts turning points. Turning points are particularly critical periods for business decision making and they represent a particular challenge to the forecasters.

The Forecasting Anticipations Version (3) has been simulated over the NBER turning points from 1957 to 1970. For each turning point seven simulations, each starting in successive quarters, were generated to judge the performance of the model. In each case the earliest simulation examined represents a forecast made seven quarters before the turning point.[10]

Figures 3 to 7 illustrate the performance of the model over the five turning points during the sample period for real GNP. The graphs show that the model predicts most turning points. An example of a good prediction is depicted by the peak occurring in 1960. 1 (Figure 4). All seven simulations relevant for this peak simulate the peak exactly at the peak quarter. Not all simulations present such a clear cut picture. Take, for example, the trough of 1961. 1 (Figure 5). The forecasts made seven, six and five quarters preceding the turning point generate a trough three quarters before the actual turning point. Subsequent forecasts of this turning point require interpretation since the forecast line shows no turns. However, linking the first forecast value with the previous actual value, the line of "xs" (xxxx) in the graph shows that relative to the past experience the forecast does indeed represent a turning point. By this criterion the one, two, three and four quarter forecasts predict a trough, one, two, two and three quarters before the actual turning point, respectively.

In order to compare various versions of the model, we devised a recording procedure to determine whether or not a turning point was predicted and with what lead time.[11] Table 4 shows, for the various simulations of real GNP, the

FORECASTS OF REAL GNP AT TURNING POINTS (BILLIONS OF 1958 $)
WHARTON MODEL MARK III FORECASTING ANTICIPATIONS VERSION (3)

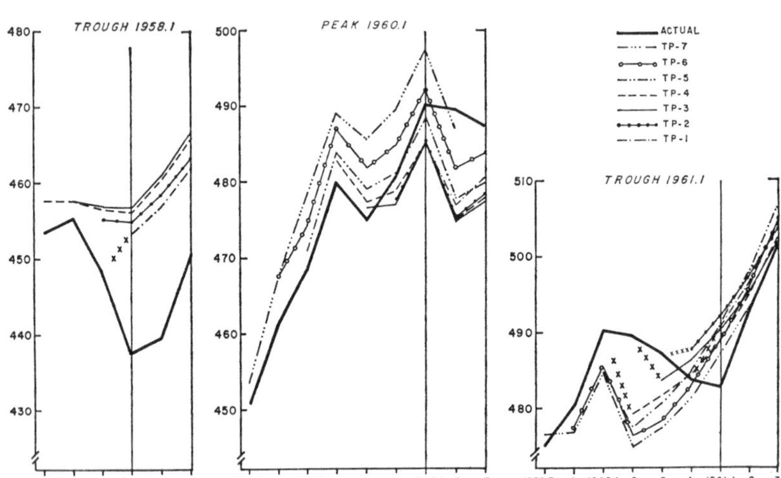

FIGURE 3 FIGURE 4 FIGURE 5

[10] Except for the peak of 1957.3 and the trough of 1958.1 where the earliest available forecasts start one quarter and four quarters before the turning points respectively.

[11] Predictions of turning points after the actual turning point are rejected. If there is more than one turning point during the forecast simulation, the one closest in time to the actual turning point is recognized. Changes in growth rates which correspond to turning points but do not qualify as true turning points are marked with an asterisk.

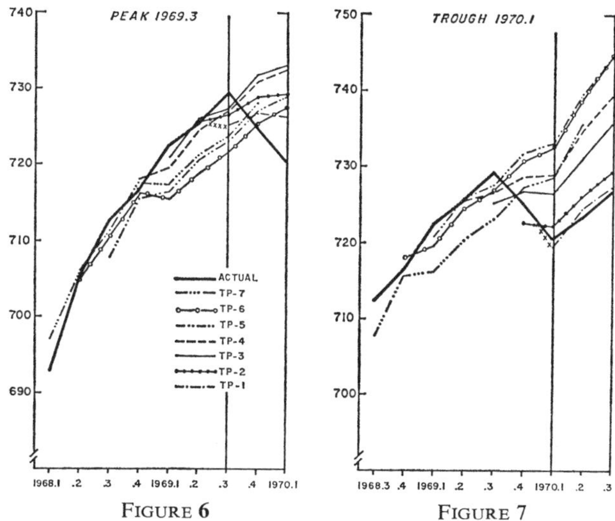

FIGURE 6 FIGURE 7

number of quarters the simulation turning point precedes the actual. For real GNP, turning points are predicted with considerable accuracy. All actual turns are predicted—though with a lead of up to three quarters in some cases—except a few predictions simulating the turning points of 1969. 3 and 1970. 1. In these cases the simulation did not show a turning point in the strict sense but there was a change in the rate of growth in the right direction.

We proceed to compare the intensity of the predicted turning point to the actual intensity. We have defined the intensity of a turning point as the algebraic difference between the percentage rate of growth moving into the turning point from the previous quarter and the corresponding percentage rate of growth moving out of the turning point. If TP is the time period at which the turn occurs and X is GNP then the measure of intensity

$$I = \frac{X_{TP} - X_{TP-1}}{X_{TP-1}} - \frac{X_{TP+1} - X_{TP}}{X_{TP}}.$$

For a peak, this measure will give a positive number and for a trough, it will be negative. If there is no change in rates of growth the "intensity" is zero. The greater the change in rate of growth, the greater the absolute value of the intensity measure. Such a computation is presented in Table 5 for the turning points recorded in Table 4.

The pattern described in Table 5 follows *a priori* expectations. Generally sharp changes are predicted as sharp changes, and less intense turns are predicted as mild changes. The closer to the turning point the forecast starts, with few exceptions, the closer is the predicted intensity to the actual intensity of the turn.

The turning point simulations were also done with the Standard Version (1).

TABLE 4

FORECASTING ANTICIPATIONS MODEL

Number of Quarters Predicted Turning point Precedes Actual

Turning point	Forecast Beginning[a]						
	TP-1	*TP*-2	*TP*-3	*TP*-4	*TP*-5	*TP*-6	*TP*-7
1957.3	0	n.a.	n.a.	n.a.	n.a.	n.a.	n.a.
1958.1	1	0	0	0	n.a.	n.a.	n.a.
1960.1	0	0	0	0	0	0	0
1961.1	1	2	2	3	3	3	3
1969.3	1	1*	1*	1*	3*	3	3
1970.1	0	0	0	0*	0*	0*	0*

TABLE 5

FORECASTING ANTICIPATIONS MODEL

Intensity of Predicted Turning Points vs. Intensity of Actual Turning Points

Turning point	Actual	Forecast Beginning[a]						
		TP-1	*TP*-2	*TP*-3	*TP*-4	*TP*-5	*TP*-6	*TP*-7
1957.3	1.98	1.21	n.a.	n.a.	n.a.	n.a.	n.a.	n.a.
1958.1	−2.84	−2.70	−0.92	−0.98	−0.98	n.a.	n.a.	n.a.
1960.1	2.14	2.48	3.65	3.63	3.73	3.71	3.64	3.70
1961.1	−2.34	−2.14	−0.51	−1.76	−2.81	−2.38	−2.65	−2.65
1969.3	1.03	0.55	0.32*	0.47*	0.38*	1.03*	0.88	0.91
1970.1	−1.04	−1.41	−0.58	−0.71	−0.81*	−0.78*	−0.75*	−0.68*

[a] $TP - i$, $i = 1, \ldots 7$: forecast starting *i* quarters before the turning point.
n.a. = not available.

* These are not turning points in the strict sense, since the growth rates predicted on both sides of the turning point are not opposite in sign. However, they may be considered to be indications of the turning point since the predicted growth rates change in the appropriate direction. We refer to them as quasi turning points.

The Standard Version does somewhat less well than the Forecasting Anticipations Version (3). Many turning points predicted in the Forecasting Anticipations Version show up in the Standard Version not as real turning points but as changes in the rate of growth.[12] Furthermore, the differential between the actual intensity and the predicted intensity is greater in the Standard Version (1).

MULTIPLIER SIMULATIONS

There is no accepted *a priori* standard by which econometric model multipliers can be judged. It is not realistic, after all, to assume that the multipliers

[12] In contrast to eight quasi turning points obtained with the Forecasting Anticipations Version (3), the Standard Version (1) generates 14 such quasi turning points.

should correspond to those obtained from analytic solutions of simple pedagogical models. Yet one's theoretical ideas about the varying impacts of different shocks on the economy are an aid in testing the feasibility of the model's structural properties. Multipliers were calculated with the Endogenous Anticipations Version (2) of the model. First, a control solution was simulated using actual values of the exogenous variables. Then multiplier simulations were generated using different autonomous changes which were maintained continuously over the solution period. Multipliers were obtained by normalizing differences between multiplier and control solution values.

The different multiplier simulations made were:

1. A nominal sustained increase in non-defense government expenditures of \$5 billion. It is assumed that 60 percent of the increase is spent on increased use of services at the exogenously fixed government wage rate.
2. Changes in non-defense government expenditures, wages and employment as in (1) above and a sustained increase in nonborrowed reserves of \$0.3 billion.[13]
3. An autonomous decrease in personal income tax of \$5 billion throughout the simulation.
4. An autonomous sustained increase in nominal exports of \$5 billion.
5. A sustained increase in nonborrowed reserves of \$0.5 billion.

Table 6 reports the multipliers[14] for real GNP obtained with the five alternative

TABLE 6

MULTIPLIER FOR REAL *GNP* OBTAINED WITH THE ENDOGENOUS ANTICIPATIONS VERSION (2)

Sustained change over quarters[a]	1	2	3	4	5	6	7	8	16	20
Government expenditure multiplier	1.09	1.38	1.56	1.68	1.74	1.79	1.82	1.83	1.69	1.55
Government expenditure multiplier with accomodating monetary policy	1.20	1.57	1.82	1.99	2.11	2.20	2.27	2.31	2.15	1.87
Personal income tax mutiplier	0.37	0.58	0.73	0.83	0.92	0.98	1.03	1.07	1.03	0.91
Export multiplier	1.49	1.78	2.03	2.16	2.30	2.39	2.42	2.42	1.61	1.18
Increase in nonborrowed reserves	0.37	0.57	0.73	0.84	0.96	1.05	1.17	1.28	1.34	1.18

[a] Quarter 1 corresponds to the first quarter of the exogenous multiplier change.

[13] The change in nonborrowed reserves is made to allow for accommodating monetary policy.

[14] Differences between the multiplier and the control solutions are normalized by the value of the autonomous change. In the case of an increase in an exogenous variable the procedure is clear cut. But when the shock consists of an autonomous change in a variable that is endogenous, such as personal income tax or exports, the final change in the variable is the net effect of the exogenous change and the endogenous feedbacks from the economic expansion generated by the autonomous change. The normalization was done using the autonomous change rather than the net result. Thus all nominal variables were normalized by dividing by 5. All real variables were divided by whatever the nominal \$5 billion were worth in real purchasing power, e.g., \$5

(*Continued on next page*)

policy configurations.

The government expenditure multiplier for real GNP in the first quarter of impact is small, the secondary effects being limited to 0.09 (Table 6). The feedback effects increase over time with a continued shock as the lagged adjustment processes start to work themselves out and reach a peak of 1.83 in the ninth quarter gradually reducing to a value of 1.55 after five years.

The second simulation that allows accommodating movements in money supply generates somewhat bigger increases in all components of GNP. The multiplier for real GNP peaks at a value of 2.35 in the 10th quarter and reduces to 1.87 after 5 years. The differential between the two multipliers (Simulations 1 and 2) increases over the first twelve quarters to a maximum of 0.5.

The tax multiplier (3) for real GNP is small as would be expected since the first impact of a tax stimulus on activity is via the increased consumption due to reduced taxes. The impact multiplier of 0.37 grows to a peak of 1.12 by the eleventh quarter and then gradually reduces to 0.91 after five years.

The export multiplier is significantly higher than the government expenditure multiplier. This is as it should be. All of the increase in exports has a first round effect on increased activity whereas more than half of the increased government expenditures are paid as government wages. Increased nondefense government expenditures do not have a direct impact in the model on either new orders or on gross output originating in the manufacturing sector. Inventory investment, which reacts to the difference between production and sales, as a result acts as a buffer in case of the government expenditures simulation. Exports, which do influence output in manufacturing durables have a positive impact on inventory accumulation for the first fourteen quarters of simulation. This contributes substantially to the differential between the government and the export multiplier. It points out problems with the structural specification of the equations for manufacturing output and for new orders in Wharton Mark III.

An increase in nonborrowed reserves of $0.5 billion leads to an increase in money supply of $2 to 3 billion. The monetary multiplier for real GNP normalized by the induced deflated money supply is 0.37 on impact, rising to a peak of 1.45 in the 12th quarter.

In order to determine the impact of the structural changes between the various versions of the model, control solution and multiplier simulations (simulation 1 only) were repeated with the Standard Version (1) and the Forecasting Anticipations Version (3). Table 7 compares the government expenditure multiplier for real GNP obtained with the three versions of the model.

Comparing rows 1 and 2 of Table 7, it can be seen that the government expenditure multiplier for real GNP is consistently lower in the Anticipations Version (2) than in the Standard Version (1). An impact difference of 0.2 be-

([14] *Continued*)
billion was divided by the implicit deflator for consumer expenditures to compute the exogenous real shock in the tax simulation. Monetary simulation multipliers were normalized by the generated increase in money supply.

TABLE 7

GOVERMENT EXPENDITURE MULTIPLIER FOR REAL GNP

Sustained change over quarters[a]	1	2	3	4	5	6	7	8	16	20
Standard Version (1)	1.28	1.60	1.84	2.00	2.12	2.21	2.29	2.35	2.22	1.65
Endogeneous Anticipations Version (2)	1.09	1.38	1.56	1.68	1.74	1.79	1.82	I.83	1.69	1.55
Forecasting Anticipations Version (3)	1.09	1.26	1.40	1.51	1.59	1.65	1.70	1.74	1.75	1.64

[a] Quarter 1 corresponds to the first quarter of the exogenous multiplier change.

tween the two versions increases to a differential of 0.5 at the end of 2 years.

The main reason for the lower multiplier has to do with the specification of the equation for consumer expenditures on automobiles. Replacement of the unemployment rate variable (Standard Version 1) by the consumer sentiment index (Anticipations Versions 2 and 3) makes automobile expenditures less cyclically sensitive. The latter specification also produces a stronger monetary influence with an almost unchanged coefficient for income. While the Standard Version multiplier for automobile expenditures is 0.11, the analogous multiplier in the Anticipations Version is 0.01. This differential impact on automobile spending leads to widening disparity in the overall GNP multiplier via its effects on orders, manufacturing output and therefore inventory investment. Automobile expenditures play a role in these equations which is even bigger than that of exports. A unit increase in automobile spending implies a unit increase in manufacturing output and positive inventory accumulation.[15]

The multipliers in the Forecasting Anticipations Version (3) are smaller than those of Endogenous Anticipations Version (2) in the first two years because the exogenous information available about the forecast period is not changed as the multiplier change is imposed.

CONCLUSIONS

The comparison of the Anticipations Version and the Standard Version of Wharton Mark III supports our *a priori* notions that anticipatory variables can make a valuable contribution to model accuracy. Incorporating anticipations variables tends to reduce error even in the case where no advance information is introduced. The gain is particularly marked for investment and residential construction for which the reduction in error is considerably greater than for GNP or other aggregate variables. The Forecasting Anticipations Version simulates more turning points as true turning points than does the Standard Version. The Anticipations Version also approximates the simulated intensity of

[15] Multipliers were computed with the Endogenous Anticipations Version (2) replacing the equation for automobile expenditures by the Standard Version specification. These multipliers were very close to those of the Standard Version. Thus this equation is chiefly responsible for the differences in multipliers between Version 1 and Versions 2 and 3.

the turn closer to the actual intensity. The multiplier sensitivity of the Anticipations Versions is lower than that of the Standard Version of Mark III. The factor chiefly responsible for the difference is the changed equation for consumer expenditures on automobiles which replaces the cyclically sensitive unemployment rate by the consumer sentiment index.

University of Pennsylvania

REFERENCES

[1] ADAMS, F. GERARD AND LAWRENCE R. KLEIN, "Anticipations Variables in Macro-Economic Models," in B. Strumpel *et al.* eds., *Human Behavior in Economic Affairs* (New York: Elsevier, 1972.)

[2] HYMANS, SAUL, "Consumer Durable Spending: Explanation and Prediction," in *Brookings Papers in Economic Activity*, 1970.

[3] MCCARTHY, MICHAEL D., *The Wharton Quarterly Econometric Forecasting Model, Mark III* (Philadelphia: Economics Research Unit, Department of Economics. Wharton School of Finance and Commerce, University of Pennsylvania, 1972).

[4] TINBERGEN, J., *Statistical Testing of Business Cycle Theories II* (Geneva: League of Nations, Economic Intelligence Service, 1939).

2

AN EVALUATION OF A SHORT-RUN FORECASTING MODEL

BY RAY C. FAIR

1. INTRODUCTION

AN IMPORTANT QUESTION in econometric model-building is how useful econometric models are likely to be for short-run forecasting purposes. The current practice of most model proprietors who issue regular forecasts is to adjust the forecasts from their models before the forecasts are released. The forecasts from the models can be adjusted by changing the values of the constant terms in the equations (including having the constant terms differ for different quarters in the forecast period) and by adjusting the values of the exogenous variables used for the forecasts. The studies of Evans, Haitovsky, and Treyz [**2**] and Haitovsky and Treyz [**7**] analyzing the Wharton and OBE models conclude that the adjusted forecasts of the model proprietors (the *ex ante* forecasts) are on average more accurate than the non-adjusted forecasts from the models. The *ex ante* forecasts are even more accurate than forecasts based on the actual values of the exogenous variables and on either no constant adjustments or on the same constant adjustments as were used for the *ex ante* forecasts.[1] The non *ex ante* forecasts from the two models are poor enough as to lead the authors to be pessimistic about the possibility of using econometric models in a mechanical way for forecasting purposes. In fact, Evans, Haitovsky, and Treyz go so far as to chide anyone as being naive who believes "that econometric models should not need any [constant-term] adjustments."[2] This view appears to be quite widespread, since the adjustment of constant terms is almost a universal practice among model proprietors, and model proprietors seldom release the unadjusted forecasts from their models in addition to the adjusted forecasts.[3]

One important consequence of this view is that it gives little incentive for trying to improve the specification of models and for trying to develop better estimation techniques. If it is felt that models will never be able to be used in a mechanical way and that forecasts from models will always be subjectively

[1] See Evans, Haitovsky, and Treyz [**2**, (1137–1138)] and Haitovsky and Treyz [**7**, Table 1, (319)]. For the OBE model, Evans, Haitovsky, and Treyz conclude that the *ex ante* forecasts are "no better or no worse" than the forecasts based on the actual values of the exogenous variables and on the *ex ante* constant adjustments (p. 1137). For the results in Table 1 in [7], however, the OBE *ex ante* forecasts are better than any of the other forecasts.

[2] Evans, Haitovsky, and Treyz [**2**, (957)].

[3] It is important to note the distinction between mechanical constant-term adjustments and other kinds of adjustments. Mechanical adjustments are adjustments for which rules can be made ahead of time, such as a rule that says adjust the constant term in an equation by the amount of the last observed error in the equation. Accounting for first-order serial correlation, as is done in the present model, can also be considered to be a form of mechanical constant-term adjustment. The discussion in this paper regarding constant-term adjustments is meant to refer only to the non-mechanical types of adjustments.

adjusted, the expected payoff in terms of increased forecast accuracy from model improvement is not likely to be very large.[4]

During 1968 and 1969 a short-run forecasting model of the United States economy was developed by the author. The model is described in Fair [5]. Since 1970 III, regular forecasts from the model have been released quarterly. No constant-term adjustments have ever been made for any of the forecasts. The main aim of this work has been to try to guage the likely forecasting accuracy of a model for which forecasts are not subjectively adjusted before being released. The purpose of this paper is to describe the results that have been obtained from the model for the 1970 III—1973 II period.

The model is described briefly in Section 2. Then in Section 3 the *ex ante* forecasts from the model are compared with two other sets of forecasts: one set using the same coefficient estimates as were used for the *ex ante* forecasts, but using the actual values of the exogenous variables instead of the *ex ante* predicted values (outside sample forecasts); and one set using the coefficient estimates obtained by estimating the model through 1973 II and using the actual values of the exogenous variables (within sample forecasts). The results provide an indication of how much of the forecast error is due to errors made in forecasting the exogenous variables and how much is due to having to make outside-sample forecasts rather than within-sample forecasts. These three sets of forecasts are also compared with the *ex ante* forecasts released from the ASA/NBER Survey of Regular Forecasters. These forecasts are the median forecasts from the survey of forecasters. The survey is primarily a survey of non-econometric forecasters.

2. THE MODEL

Since the model is described in detail in [5], it will only be briefly discussed here. Some of the features of the model are the following.

1. The model was designed primarily for short-run forecasting purposes, and use was made of expectational variables when they appeared to aid in the explanation of the endogenous variables. The model was also kept fairly small (14 stochastic equations and 5 identities).

2. The concept and measurement of "excess labor" played an important role in the explanation of employment. Disequilibrium considerations played an important role in the specification and estimation of the housing sector. The price-wage nexus was avoided by specifying a price equation that did not include any wage variables among the explanatory variables.

3. The primary estimation technique that was used accounted for both first-order serial correlation of the error terms and simultaneous equations bias. A method of estimating markets in disequilibrium was used to estimate the housing sector.

[4] This view has led Brunner [1, (930)] to quip that "The Evans procedure of 'sophisticated forecasting' . . . involves an abandonment of empirical science for a numerology similar to astrology."

TABLE 1

EQUATIONS OF THE MODEL BY SECTOR

Equation No. in [5]		$\hat{\rho}$	SE	$R\Delta^2$	No. of observations
	The Monthly Housing Starts Sector				
(8.23)	$HS_t = \sum_{l=1}^{11} \hat{d}_l DI_t + 2.70W_t + 112.95 - .0709 \sum_{i=1}^{t-1} HS_i$ (4.63) (2.46) (2.27)				
	2.07 + 113.36 − .0078 (4.69) (2.02) (0.48)	.841 (17.54)	8.98	.790	127
	$+ 8.48t - .127RM_{t-2} - .412/\Delta RM_t/$ (2.31) (1.45) (2.81)				
	+ 1.66 − .154 − .154 (0.82) (1.52) (1.25)	.919 (30.36)	9.87	.178	169
(8.24)	$HS_t = \sum_{l=1}^{11} \hat{d}_l' DI_t + 2.84W_t - 49.22 - .164t$ (4.42) (1.75) (2.63)				
	2.20 + 24.91 + .011 (4.39) (0.99) (0.12)				
	$+ .0541DSF6_{t-1} + .0497DHF3_{t-2}$ (8.07) (5.27)	.507 (6.64)	8.30	.822	127
	+ .0262 + .0166 (8.64) (2.23)				
	$+ .100RM_{t-1} - .412\backslash \Delta RM_t \backslash$ (2.67) (2.81)				
	+ .025 − .154 (0.61) (1.25)	.653 (11.21)	9.68	.213	169
	The Money *GNP* Sector				
(3.3)	$CD_t = -25.43 + .103GNP_t + .110MOOD_{t-1}$ (4.22) (39.78) (1.88)				
	−34.09 + .114 + .068 (4.99) (33.20) (1.22)	.648 (6.01)	1.125	.554	50
	$+ .092MOOD_{t-2}$ (1.54)				
	+ .148 (2.44)	.824 (11.37)	1.318	.606	61
(3.7)	$CN_t = .081GNP_t + .646CN_{t-1} + .147MOOD_{t-2}$ (5.40) (9.30) (4.67)	−.381 (2.47)	1.383	.550	36
	.067 + .738 + .065 (4.54) (11.49) (2.83)	−.077 (0.53)	1.649	.612	47
(3.11)	$CS_t = .022GNP_t + .945CS_{t-1} - .023MOOD_{t-2}$ (4.15) (47.77) (7.37)	−.077 (0.55)	.431	.891	50
	.025 + .931 − .022 (4.01) (40.27) (5.66)	.100 (0.78)	.547	.903	61
(4.4)	$IP_t = -8.50 + .063GNP_t + .687PE2_t$ (4.86) (8.87) (8.34)	.689 (6.72)	1.011	.633	50
	− 6.96 + .069 + .556 (3.94) (9.89) (6.63)	.774 (9.55)	1.061	.697	61

(*Continued on next page*)

TABLE 1 (*Continued*)

Equation No. in [5]		$\hat{\rho}$	SE	$R\Delta^2$	No. of observations
	The Money *GNP* Sector (*Continued*)				
(5.5)	$IH_t = -\underset{(2.31)}{3.53} + \underset{(13.12)}{.016}GNP_t + \underset{(5.37)}{.0242}HSQ_t$	.449 (3.01)	.582	.792	36
	$-\underset{(3.81)}{29.99} + \underset{(6.05)}{.043} \quad + \underset{(7.56)}{.0244}$				
	$+\underset{(4.45)}{.0230}HSQ_{t-1} + \underset{(1.66)}{.0074}HSQ_{t-2}$	.996 (25.75)	.687	.786	47
	$+\underset{(6.21)}{.0224} \quad + \underset{(3.11)}{.0108}$				
(6.15)	$V_t - V_{t-1} = -\underset{(4.09)}{114.76} + \underset{(4.27)}{.728}(CD_{t-1} + CN_{t-1})$				
	$-\underset{(0.86)}{9.38} + \underset{(1.30)}{.092}$				
	$-\underset{(3.94)}{.357}V_{t-1} + \underset{(0.42)}{0.95}(CD_{t-1} + CN_{t-1} - CD_t - CN_t)$	.791 (9.51)	2.540	.589	50
	$-\underset{(0.90)}{.043} \quad + \underset{(3.28)}{.496}$	.782 (9.80)	2.931	.329	61
(7.3)	$IMP_t = \underset{(8.70)}{.078}GNP_t$	1.0	.637	.437	45
	$\underset{(12.87)}{.106}$	1.0	.812	.651	53
Income identity	$GNP_t = CD_t + CN_t + CS_t + IP_t + IH_t + V_t - V_{t-1} - IMP_t + EX_t + G_t$				
	The Price Sector				
(10.5)	$GAP2_t = GNPR_t^* - GNPR_{t-1} - (GNP_t - GNP_{t-1})$				
(10.7)	$PD_t - PD_{t-1} = -\underset{(1.44)}{1.037}$				
	$+ \underset{(1.19)}{165.76} \dfrac{1}{\underset{(2.00)}{78.36} + \frac{1}{8}\sum_{i=1}^{8} GAP2_{t-i+1}}$	0	.183	.810	50
	$PD_t - PD_{t-1} = \underset{(16.32)}{1.280} - \underset{(7.89)}{.0247}\left(\frac{1}{20}\sum_{i=1}^{20} GAP2_{t-i+1}\right)$	0	.391	.501	64
(10.8)	$GNPR_t = 100\dfrac{GNP_t - GG_t}{PD_t} + YG_t$				
(10.9)	$Y_t = GNPR_t - YA_t - YG_t$				
	The Employment and Labor Force Sector				
(9.2)	$M_tH_t = \dfrac{1}{\alpha_t} Y_t$				
(9.8)	$\log M_t - \log M_{t-1} = -\underset{(3.44)}{.514} + \underset{(1.57)}{.0000643}t$				
	$-\underset{(4.48)}{.548} + \underset{(2.21)}{.0000720}$				

(*Continued on next page*)

TABLE 1 (*Continued*)

Equation No. in [5]		$\hat{\rho}$	SE	$R\Delta^2$	No. of observations
	The Employment and Labor Force Sector (*Continued*)				
	$-\underset{(3.41)}{.140}(\log M_{t-1} - \log M_{t-1}H_{t-1}) + \underset{(2.34)}{.121}(\log Y_{t-1}$				
	$-\underset{(4.46)}{.150} \qquad + \underset{(1.75)}{.073}$				
	$- \log Y_{t-2}) + \underset{(6.43)}{.298}(\log Y_t - \log Y_{t-1})$	.336 (2.52)	.00310	.778	50
	$+ \underset{(8.14)}{.297}$	.407 (3.56)	.00303	.783	64
(9.10)	$D_t = -\underset{(8.23)}{13014} - \underset{(6.15)}{71.10}t + \underset{(9.39)}{.358}M_t$	.600 (5.30)	181.4	.460	50
	$-\underset{(5.79)}{13246} - \underset{(4.84)}{86.40} + \underset{(6.68)}{.378}$	.773 (9.74)	202.3	.389	64
(9.9)	$E_t = M_t + MA_t + MCG_t - D_t$				
(9.11)	$\frac{LF_{1t}}{P_{1t}} = \underset{(652.38)}{.981} - \underset{(8.57)}{.000190}t$	.265 (1.94)	.00193	.447	50
	$\underset{(248.62)}{.990} - \underset{(6.43)}{.000326}$	.776 (9.84)	.00190	.114	64
(9.12)	$\frac{LF_{2t}}{P_{2t}} = \underset{(2.69)}{.180} + \underset{(4.97)}{.000523}t + \underset{(3.67)}{.447}\frac{E_t + AF_t}{P_{1t} + P_{2t}}$	.797 (9.32)	.00228	.373	50
	$\underset{(3.67)}{.225} + \underset{(5.92)}{.000774} + \underset{(3.03)}{.336}$	.905 (17.07)	.00203	.351	64
(9.14)	$UR_t = 1 - \frac{E_t}{LF_{1t} + LF_{2t} - AF_t}$				

Notes:

1. t-statistics in absolute value are in parentheses.
2. $\hat{\rho}$ = estimate of the serial correlation coefficient.
3. SE = estimate of the standard error of the regression.
4. $R\Delta^2$ = percent of the variance of the change in the left-hand-side variable explained by the regression except for equations (10.7) and (9.8), where it is simply the percent of the variance of the level of the left-hand-side variable explained by the regression.
5. For the first set of estimates, the values for $\hat{d}_I$ and $\hat{d}_I'$ are presented in Chapter 8 in [5].
6. α_t = production-function coefficient obtained by peak to peak interpolations.
7. Sample periods:

   127 obs. = June 1959—December 1969
   169 obs. = June 1959—June 1973
   50 obs. = 1956 I—1969 IV, excluding 1959 III, 1959 IV, 1960 I, 1964 IV, 1965 I, 1965 II
   61 obs, = 1956 I—1973 II, excluding 1959 III, 1959 IV, 1960 I, 1964 IV, 1965 I, 1965 II, 1970 IV, 1971 I, 1971 II
   36 obs. = 1960 II—1969 IV, excluding 1964 IV, 1965 I, 1965 II
   47 obs. = 1960 II—1973 II excluding 1964 IV, 1965 I, 1965 II, 1970 IV, 1971 I, 1971 II
   45 obs. = 1956 I—1969 IV, excluding 1959 III, 1959 IV, 1960 I, 1960 II, 1964 IV, 1965 I, 1965 II, 1965 III, 1968 IV, 1969 I, 1969 II, 1969 III

53 obs. = 1956 I—1973 II, excluding 1959 III, 1959 IV, 1960 I, 1960 II, 1964 IV, 1965 I, 1965 II, 1965 III, 1968 IV, 1969 I, 1969 II, 1969 III, 1970 IV, 1971 I, 1971 II, 1971 IV, 1972 I, 1972 II

64 obs. = 1956 I—1973 II, excluding 1959 III, 1959 IV, 1960 I, 1964 IV, 1965 I, 1965 II

8. The much lower $R\Delta^2$ for the second set of estimates of equations (8.23) and (8.24) is due in large part to the use of seasonally adjusted data for the second set of estimates. For the first set of estimates the seasonal dummy variables explain a large part of the variance of the non-seasonally-adjusted HS_t series.

TABLE 2

VARIABLES OF THE MODEL IN ALPHABETICAL ORDER BY SECTOR

The Monthly Housing Starts Sector

†$DHF3_t$ = Three-month moving average of the flow of advances from the Federal Home Loan Bank to Savings and Loan Associations in millions of dollars

†DI_t = Dummy variable I for month t, $I = 1, 2, \ldots, 11$

†$DSF6_t$ = Six-month moving average of private deposit flows into Savings and Loan Associations and Mutual Savings Banks in millions of dollars

HS_t = Private nonfarm housing starts in thousands of units

†RM_t = FHA mortgage rate series on new homes in units of 100

†W_t = Number of working days in month t

†$/\Delta RM_t/$ = [see equation (8.21) in [5]].

†$\backslash\Delta RM_t\backslash$ = [see equation (8.22) in [5]].

The Money GNP Sector

CD_t = Consumption expenditures for durable goods, SAAR

CN_t = Consumption expenditures for nondurable goods, SAAR

CS_t = Consumption expenditures for services, SAAR

†EX_t = Exports of goods and services, SAAR

†G_t = Government expenditures plus farm residential fixed investment, SAAR

GNP_t = Gross National Product, SAAR

HSQ_t = Quarterly nonfarm housing starts, seasonally adjusted at quarterly rates in thousands of units

IH_t = Nonfarm residential fixed investment, SAAR

IMP_t = Imports of goods and services, SAAR

IP_t = Nonresidential fixed investment, SAAR

†$MOOD_t$ = Michigan Survey Research Center index of consumer sentiment in units of 100

†$PE2_t$ = Two-quarter-ahead expectation of plant and equipment investment, SAAR

$V_t - V_{t-1}$ = Change in total business inventories, SAAR

The Price Sector and the Employment and Labor Force Sector

†AF_t = Level of the armed forces in thousands

D_t = Difference between the establishment employment data and household survey employment data, seasonally adjusted in thousands of workers

E_t = Total civilian employment, seasonally adjusted in thousands of workers

†GG_t = Government output, SAAR

(*Continued on next page*)

TABLE 2 (*Continued*)

$GNPR_t$ =	Gross National Product, seasonally adjusted at annual rates in billions of 1958 dollars
†$GNPR_t{}^*$ =	Potential GNP, seasonally adjusted at annual rates in billions of 1958 dollars
LF_{1t} =	Level of the primary labor force (males 25–54), seasonally adjusted in thousands
LF_{2t} =	Level of the secondary labor force (all others over 16), seasonally adjusted in thousands
M_t =	Private nonfarm employment, seasonally adjusted in thousands of workers
†MA_t =	Agricultural employment, seasonally adjusted in thousands of workers
†MCG_t =	Civilian government employment, seasonally adjusted in thousands of workers
M_tH_t =	Man-hour requirements in the private nonfarm sector, seasonally adjusted in thousands of man-hours per week
†P_{1t} =	Noninstitutional population of males 25–54 in thousands
†P_{2t} =	Noninstitutional population of all others over 16 in thousands
PD_t =	Private output deflator, seasonally adjusted in units of 100
UR_t =	Civilian unemployment rate, seasonally adjusted
Y_t =	Private nonfarm output, seasonally adjusted at annual rates in billions of 1958 dollars
†YA_t =	Agricultural output, seasonally adjusted as annual rates in billions of 1958 dollars
†YG_t =	Government output, seasonally adjusted at annual rates in billions of 1958 dollars

Notes: † Exogenous variable.
SAAR Seasonally adjusted at annual rates in billions of current dollars.

4. Different versions of the model were put through extensive tests before deciding on the final version. The stability of the estimated relationships over time was also examined in some detail, as was the sensitivity of the forecasting results to likely errors made in forecasting the exogenous variables.

The model is presented in Table 1, along with two sets of coefficient estimates. The first set is the set presented in Table 11–4 in [5] and consists of estimates through 1969 IV. The second set consists of estimates through 1973 II. Two changes have been made in the model since [5] was published. First, seasonal dummy variables are no longer used in equations (8.23) and (8.24), but instead HS_t, $DSF6_{t-1}$, and $DHF3_{t-2}$ are now seasonally adjusted before estimation. Second, the price equation (10.7) is now linear and has a lag length of 20 quarters rather than of 8 quarters. The variables of the model are listed in alphabetical order by sector in Table 2.

The model is structured as follows. Monthly housing starts are determined from the supply and demand equations in the monthly housing starts sector. The predicted value of monthly housing starts, HS_t, is taken to be the average of the predicted values from the two equations. The predicted values of HS_t

are averaged across time to obtain predicted values of quarterly housing starts, HSQ_t. Given HSQ_t, current dollar *GNP* and seven components are determined in the money *GNP* sector, which is a linear, simultaneous block. Given GNP_t, the price level and then constant dollar *GNP* are determined in the price sector. After real output is determined, employment, the labor force, and the unemployment rate are determined in the employment and labor force sector. The price and employment and labor force sectors are nonlinear, but are recursive, and the predicted values from these sectors do not feed back into the money *GNP* sector. There is no monetary sector: the mortgage rate and deposit flows are exogenous to the housing sector. There is likewise no income side: *GNP* enters as the income variable in the consumption equations.

In Chapter 12 in [**5**] the stability[5] of the coefficient estimates to additions of observations to the sample period was examined for the 1965 III—1969 IV period. The results in Table 1 can be considered to be an extension of this analysis. The conclusion in [**5**] was that the most unstable equations are the two monthly housing starts equations (8.23) and (8.24), the inventory equation (6.15), the price equation (10.7), and the labor force participation equation for secondary workers (9.12). This conclusion is also true of the results in Table 1. In addition, the results in Table 1 are characterized by generally larger estimates of the serial correlation coefficients for the latest set of estimates.

3. A COMPARISON OF THE FORECASTS

Between July 21, 1970, and April 23, 1973, twelve sets of forecasts from the model were released. The number of periods ahead forecast was either four or five, depending on the time of the year. Error measures for these forecasts are presented in the first row of Table 3 for each variable. These forecasts are denoted *ex ante*/*ex ante*. Both mean absolute errors for levels (*MAE*) and mean absolute errors for changes (*MAE*Δ) are presented. The actual data used for the comparisons are the most recent data as of July 21, 1973. To make the forecasts comparable to the most recent data, the level of each forecast value for each variable was adjusted in the following way. Consider a forecast made at the beginning of period $t + 1$ for period $t + 1$ and beyond, where preliminary estimates of the actual values for period t are available. For a variable y, let y_t^0 denote the estimate of y for period t available at the beginning of period $t + 1$, and let y_t^a denote the most recent (as of July 21, 1973) estimate of y for period t. Then the forecasts of y made at the beginning of period $t + 1$ for periods $t + 1$ and beyond were adjusted by adding $y_t^a - y_t^0$ to them before they were compared to the actual data (i.e., to the actual data as of July 21, 1973).

In the second row of Table 3 for each variable, error measures are presented for forecasts generated using the same coefficient estimates as were used for the *ex ante* forecasts, but using the actual values of the exogenous variables. All of the

[5] "Stability" in this context refers to how much or little the coefficient estimates of an equation change as the sample period is lengthened.

TABLE 3

ERROR MEASURES FOR THE DIFFERENT SETS OF FORECASTS
MAE = MEAN ABSOLUTE ERROR FOR LEVELS
*MAE*Δ = MEAN ABSOLUTE ERROR FOR CHANGES

	MAE Quarters Ahead					*MAE*Δ Quarters Ahead				
	1 (12 obs.)	2 (11 obs.)	3 (10 obs.)	4 (9 obs.)	5 (4 obs.)	1 (12 obs.)	2 (11 obs.)	3 (10 obs.)	4 (9 obs.)	5 (4 obs.)
GNP_t										
1. *Ex Ante/Ex Ante*	4.38	9.20	12.73	14.72	17.88	4.38	5.50	4.96	4.70	5.75
2. *Ex Ante/Ex Post*	4.17	5.92	6.99	9.42	9.55	4.17	5.03	4.49	4.41	5.17
3. *Ex Post/Ex Post*	3.82	5.16	5.68	7.65	8.40	3.82	4.26	4.27	4.25	5.47
4. ASA/NBER *Ex Ante*	3.98	6.49	8.79	10.58	12.80	3.98	4.04	4.39	3.73	3.45
CD_t										
1. *Ex Ante/Ex Ante*	1.84	2.91	3.66	4.29	4.00	1.84	1.76	1.74	1.84	1.10
2. *Ex Ante/Ex Post*	1.84	2.51	3.37	3.86	3.80	1.84	1.68	1.57	1.61	0.78
3. *Ex Post/Ex Post*	1.59	1.62	2.01	2.11	1.61	1.59	1.45	1.32	1.47	1.30
4. ASA/NBER *Ex Ante*	2.35	3.36	4.75	6.13	6.47	2.35	2.16	2.21	2.06	0.75
CN_t										
1. *Ex Ante/Ex Ante*	1.80	3.26	4.06	4.64	5.48	1.80	2.05	1.80	1.92	2.10
2. *Ex Ante/Ex Post*	1.69	2.95	3.85	4.19	4.34	1.69	1.79	1.70	1.78	1.84
3. *Ex Post/Ex Post*	1.55	2.34	2.74	2.73	2.80	1.55	1.69	1.60	1.64	1.64
CS_t										
1. *Ex Ante/Ex Ante*	0.70	0.97	0.98	1.26	1.58	0.70	0.67	0.69	0.56	0.63
2. *Ex Ante/Ex Post*	0.66	0.87	0.71	0.65	0.61	0.66	0.68	0.63	0.50	0.44
3. *Ex Post/Ex Post*	0.63	0.84	0.98	1.25	1.23	0.63	0.66	0.67	0.50	0.34
IP_t										
1. *Ex Ante/Ex Ante*	1.15	2.71	3.87	4.67	5.60	1.15	1.81	1.54	1.72	1.43
2. *Ex Ante/Ex Post*	1.35	1.83	1.91	2.09	1.62	1.35	1.20	1.07	0.96	1.58
3. *Ex Post/Ex Post*	1.18	1.63	1.89	1.88	1.76	1.18	1.11	1.13	1.02	1.54

(Continued on next page)

TABLE 3 (*Continued*)

	MAE Quarters Ahead					*MAEΔ* Quarters Ahead				
	1 (12 obs.)	2 (11 obs.)	3 (10 obs.)	4 (9 obs.)	5 (4 obs.)	1 (12 obs.)	2 (11 obs.)	3 (10 obs.)	4 (9 obs.)	5 (4 obs.)
IH_t										
1. *Ex Ante/Ex Ante*	1.78	4.45	7.13	9.44	11.58	1.78	2.62	2.47	2.23	1.83
2. *Ex Ante/Ex Post*	1.62	3.35	4.82	6.25	8.22	1.62	1.85	1.54	1.46	1.44
3. *Ex Post/Ex Post*	1.03	1.69	2.70	3.52	4.24	1.03	1.07	1.08	1.15	0.66
$V_t - V_{t-1}$										
1. *Ex Ante/Ex Ante*	3.59	4.33	4.98	6.00	6.65	3.59	2.18	2.49	2.59	1.23
2. *Ex Ante/Ex Post*	2.91	3.36	4.07	5.03	5.38	2.91	2.10	2.16	2.21	1.37
3. *Ex Post/Ex Post*	1.76	2.09	2.52	2.20	1.87	1.76	1.80	1.87	1.87	1.29
4. ASA/NBER *Ex Ante*	2.10	2.77	2.83	3.22	3.38	2.10	1.76	1.85	2.08	1.35
IMP_t										
1. *Ex Ante/Ex Ante*	1.56	2.95	3.80	4.59	5.92	1.56	1.81	1.91	2.08	2.40
2. *Ex Ante/Ex Post*	1.46	2.56	3.21	3.80	5.12	1.46	1.54	1.67	1.84	2.20
3. *Ex Post/Ex Post*	1.36	2.24	2.22	1.61	2.13	1.36	1.33	1.40	1.50	1.77
HSQ_t										
1. *Ex Ante/Ex Ante*	12.02	19.58	25.24	29.53	32.25	12.02	10.67	11.72	9.11	6.24
2. *Ex Ante/Ex Post*	9.55	13.05	12.98	15.49	15.35	9.55	8.58	10.82	9.94	9.22
3. *Ex Post/Ex Post*	9.84	13.10	12.72	12.36	10.62	9.84	13.88	16.37	16.62	21.50
4. ASA/NBER *Ex Ante*	13.68	19.37	24.90	29.46	25.69	13.68	14.94	13.80	14.06	18.52
PD_t										
1. *Ex Ante/Ex Ante*	0.58	0.84	0.98	1.00	0.96	0.58	0.60	0.58	0.62	0.73
2. *Ex Ante/Ex Post*	0.58	0.84	1.00	0.95	0.94	0.58	0.60	0.57	0.60	0.71
3. *Ex Post/Ex Post*	0.55	0.73	0.86	0.87	0.89	0.55	0.55	0.55	0.59	0.80
$GNPD_t$										
1. *Ex Ante/Ex Ante*	0.60	0.87	1.02	1.16	1.08	0.60	0.64	0.57	0.64	0.70
2. *Ex Ante/Ex Post*	0.58	0.83	0.98	0.92	0.91	0.58	0.59	0.56	0.59	0.71
3. *Ex Post/Ex Post*	0.53	0.71	0.83	0.83	0.87	0.53	0.54	0.53	0.58	0.80
4. ASA NBER/*Ex Ante*	0.51	0.86	1.02	0.88	0.82	0.51	0.60	0.65	0.54	0.59

(*Continued on next page*)

TABLE 3 (*Continued*)

	MAE Quarters Ahead					*MAE*Δ Quarters Ahead				
	1 (12 obs.)	2 (11 obs.)	3 (10 obs.)	4 (9 obs.)	5 (4 obs.)	1 (12 obs.)	2 (11 obs.)	3 (10 obs.)	4 (9 obs.)	5 (4 obs.)
$GNPR_t$										
1. *Ex Ante/Ex Ante*	3.52	5.22	6.22	8.72	8.12	3.52	3.63	2.81	3.74	6.22
2. *Ex Ante/Ex Post*	4.79	7.52	8.29	10.60	5.92	4.79	5.55	5.41	5.81	6.82
3. *Ex Post/Ex Post*	3.89	4.94	5.62	7.20	6.94	3.89	4.72	4.85	5.06	7.60
5. ASA/NBER *Ex Ante*	2.78	2.95	4.83	6.26	6.97	2.78	3.25	3.47	3.69	4.80
M_t										
1. *Ex Ante/Ex Ante*	198	296	368	471	397	198	188	114	122	147
2. *Ex Ante/Ex Post*	244	351	398	461	452	244	249	173	149	165
3. *Ex Post/Ex Post*	211	296	300	327	269	211	204	185	146	197
D_t										
1. *Ex Ante/Ex Ante*	294	353	301	364	544	294	228	217	198	245
2. *Ex Ante/Ex Post*	309	364	392	473	658	309	242	235	208	265
3. *Ex Post/Ex Post*	200	262	193	212	312	200	202	213	188	225
E_t										
1. *Ex Ante/Ex Ante*	147	283	455	608	824	147	171	182	163	242
2. *Ex Ante/Ex Post*	196	278	416	484	620	196	180	175	170	216
3. *Ex Post/Ex Post*	214	265	329	351	473	214	157	164	179	255
LF_{1t}										
1. *Ex Ante/Ex Ante*	58	89	110	122	189	58	53	59	58	72
2. *Ex Ante/Ex Post*	86	145	186	206	228	86	58	60	51	71
3. *Ex Post/Ex Post*	48	65	72	76	90	48	51	58	53	68
LF_{2t}										
1. *Ex Ante/Ex Ante*	125	161	147	77	201	125	129	126	149	242
2. *Ex Ante/Ex Post*	157	205	190	140	191	157	176	172	171	264
3. *Ex Post/Ex Post*	171	181	152	173	171	171	167	179	186	191

(*Continued on next page*)

TABLE 3 (*Continued*)

	MAE Quarters Ahead					*MAEΔ* Quarters Ahead				
	1 (12 obs.)	2 (11 obs.)	3 (10 obs.)	4 (9 obs.)	5 (4 obs.)	1 (12 obs.)	2 (11 obs.)	3 (10 obs.)	4 (9 obs.)	5 (4 obs.)
UR_t										
1. *Ex Ente/Ex Ante*	.0018	.0034	.0044	.0041	.0028	.0018	.0018	.0009	.0006	.0011
2. *Ex Ante/Ex Post*	.0030	.0051	.0068	.0078	.0075	.0030	.0023	.0015	.0013	.0013
3. *Ex Post/Ex Post*	.0017	.0033	.0044	.0058	.0071	.0017	.0018	.0016	.0016	.0013
4. ASA/NBER *Ex Ante*	.0008	.0015	.0026	.0033	.0028	.0008	.0012	.0010	.0010	.0008

Notes: 1. $GNPD_t = GNP$ deflator, seasonally adjusted in units of 1 00

$$= 100\left(\frac{GNP_t}{GNPR_t}\right).$$

2. *Ex Ante/Ex Ante* = *Ex ante* forecasts released.
Ex Ante/Ex Post = Forecasts generated using *ex ante* coefficient estimates but actual data on the exogenous variables.
Ex Post/Ex Post = Forecasts generated using coefficient estimates through 1973 II and actual data on the exogenous variables.
ASA/NBER *Ex Ante* = ASA/NBER *ex ante* forecast released.

3. Let $\hat{y}_t^{(j)}$ denote the j-quarter-ahead forecast of y for quarter t (the forecast being made in quarter $t - j$), and let y_t denote the actual value of y for quarter t. Then MAE and $MAE\Delta$ for the j-quarter-ahead forecast are:

$$MAE = \frac{1}{T}\sum_{t=1}^{T} |y_t - \hat{y}_t^{(j)}| \qquad MAE\Delta = \frac{1}{T}\sum_{t=1}^{T} |(y_t - y_{t-1}) - (\hat{y}_t^{(j)} - \hat{y}_{t-1}^{(j-1)})| ,$$

where in the second expression $\hat{y}_{t-1}^{(j-1)}$ is the $(j - 1)$-quarter-ahead forecast of y for quarter $t - 1$. The forecasts $\hat{y}_t^{(j)}$ and $\hat{y}_{t-1}^{(j-1)}$ are made at the same time (in quarter $t - j$), and so the difference in these two forecasts is the j-quarter-ahead forecast of the change in y for quarter t. For the one-quarter-ahead forecast, MAE and $MAE\Delta$ are the same.

4. Forecast periods:
12 obs. = 1970 III—1973 II
11 obs. = 1970 IV—1973 II
10 obs. = 1971 I—1973 II
9 obs. = 1971 II—1973 II
4 obs. = 1971 IV, 1972 II, 1972 IV, 1973 II

data used for these results, including data on the lagged endogenous variables needed to begin the forecasts, were the data as of July 21, 1973. A more detailed description of the procedure used to obtain these forecasts is presented in the Appendix. These forecasts are denoted *ex ante/ex post*. In the third row of Table 3 for each variable, error measures are presented for forecasts generated using the second set of coefficient estimates in Table 1 (estimates through 1973 II) and the actual values of the exogenous variables. These forecasts are denoted *ex post/ex post*. Finally, in the fourth row of Table 3 for relevant variables, error measures are presented for the *ex ante* forecasts released from the ASA/NBER Survey of Regular Forecasters. These forecasts are denoted ASA/NBER *ex ante*. The same level adjustments were made for these forecasts as were made for the *ex ante* forecasts from the present model.

Consider the GNP_t results in Table 3 first.[6] The *ex ante/ex post* forecasts are obviously better than the *ex ante/ex ante* forecasts, and the *ex post/ex post* forecasts are obviously better than the *ex ante/ex post* forecasts. Both of these results are what one would expect for a model, but the first result is contrary to what Evans, Haitovsky, and Treyz [**2**] and Haitovsky and Treyz [**7**] found for the Wharton and OBE models. Here, knowing the actual values of the exogenous variables certainly improves the accuracy of the forecasts. The gain in improved accuracy on this score is greater than the gain in using *ex post* coefficients rather than *ex ante* coefficients.

The housing starts sector depends heavily on hard-to-forecast exogenous variables (the mortgage rate and especially deposit flows), which is reflected in the results for HSQ_t in Table 3. The *ex ante/ex post* forecasts are considerably better than the *ex ante/ex ante* forecasts for HSQ_t, a conclusion which is then also true for housing investment, IH_t. An important variable in the equation explaining nonresidential fixed investment, IP_t, is $PE2_t$, the two-quarter-ahead expectation of plant and equipment investment, and data other than proxies for this variable are only known two quarters ahead. This characteristic of $PE2_t$ is reflected in the results for IP_t in Table 3, where the *ex ante/ex post* forecasts are much better than the *ex ante/ex ante* forecasts for three quarters ahead and beyond. The unstable nature of the coefficient estimates of the inventory equation is reflected in the results for $V_t - V_{t-1}$ in Table 3, where the *ex post/ex post* forecasts are much better than the *ex ante/ex post* forecasts.

Consider next the price and employment and labor force sectors. The price equation does not depend directly on any exogenous variable except potential *GNP*, $GNPR_t^*$, and because of the long lag length in the equation, the price forecasts are not very sensitive to recent forecasts of current dollar and constant dollar *GNP*. Consequently, the *ex ante/ex ante* and *ex ante/ex post* forecasts of the private output deflator, PD_t, and the *GNP* deflator, $GNPD_t$, are of about the same accuracy. Real *GNP*, $GNPR_t$, is the ratio of GNP_t and $GNPD_t$, and since the *ex ante/ex post* forecasts of GNP_t are more accurate than the *ex ante/ex ante*

[6] The discussion in this section will concentrate on the *MAE* results in Table 3. The *MAEΔ* results are similar to the *MAE* results, although the *MAEΔ* values are generally closer to each other.

forecasts (with the different forecasts of $GNPD_t$ being of about the same accuracy), one would also expect the *ex ante/ex post* forecasts of $GNPR_t$ to be more accurate than the *ex ante/ex ante* forecasts. This is not true for all but the five-quarter-ahead results, however, which turns out to be caused by fortunate error cancellation for the *ex ante/ex ante* forecasts. For the *ex ante/ex ante* forecasts, errors made in forecasting GNP_t were offset to some extent by errors made in forecasting $GNPD_t$, which was not true as much for the *ex ante/ex post* forecasts.

The variables in the employment and labor force sector are not dependent on any hard-to-forecast exogenous variables, and for all of these variables except the unemployment rate, UR_t, the *ex ante/ex ante* and *ex ante/ex post* results are close. On average, the *ex ante/ex ante* forecasts are slightly better, which is at least in part caused by the more accurate *ex ante/ex ante* forecasts of $GNPR_t$. The better *ex ante/ex ante* forecasts of UR_t must again be caused by fortunate error cancellation, since the forecasts of the employment and labor force variables are close for the two sets of forecasts.

Consider now the ASA/NBER *ex ante* forecasts. For GNP_t, the *ex ante/ex post* and *ex post/ex post* forecasts are generally better than the ASA/NBER forecasts, but the *ex ante/ex ante* forecasts are worse. For consumer durable expenditures, CD_t, the ASA/NBER forecasts are always the worst. For $V_t - V_{t-1}$, the *ex post/ex post* forecasts are better than ASA/NBER, but ASA/NBER is better otherwise. For HSQ_t, the *ex ante/ex ante* and ASA/NBER forecasts are about the same, with the *ex ante/ex post* and *ex post/ex post* forecasts being much better. For $GNPD_t$, the results are all fairly close, and for $GNPR_t$, ASA/NBER does better except for the five-quarter-ahead forecasts. For UR_t, ASA/NBER is the best. Overall, the *ex ante/ex ante* forecasts are not quite as accurate as the ASA/NBER forecasts.

The results in Table 3 can also be used to pinpoint those areas where improved specification would be likely to yield the most gain in forecasting accuracy. The model does not, for example, do well in forecasting the unemployment rate. The employment equation (equation (9.8) explaining M_t) is one of the best equations of the model, but the equations involved in going from the forecasts of M_t to the forecasts of UR_t are not accurate enough to yield forecasts of UR_t that are as good as, say, the ASA/NBER forecasts. More work is clearly needed in this sector, especially regarding the explanation of the secondary labor force, LF_{2t}, and possibly also regarding the link between establishment-based employment, M_t, and household-survey employment, E_t. The *ex ante* forecasting accuracy of the model is also likely to be greatly increased if good equations can be developed or better ways found for forecasting $PE2_t$ and deposit flows.

4. CONCLUSION

The results in Table 3 show that the model as it now stands leads to the production of *ex ante* forecasts that are almost as good as the ASA/NBER *ex ante* forecasts[7] and that the forecasting accuracy of the model is generally improved when the actual values of the exogenous variables are used in place of the forecast values and when more recent coefficient estimates are used. The results are thus contrary to the view that forecasts from models have to be adjusted in order to produce at all accurate results. The results are also encouraging as to the possibility of being able to increase forecasting accuracy by improving model specification and by developing better estimation techniques. The fact that the accuracy of the model is generally improved when the actual values of the exogenous variables are used and when more recent coefficient estimates are used makes it seem likely that any improvement in the model, such as the addition of a good equation explaining a hard-to-forecast exogenous variable or the replacement of an equation with an equation that has better properties, will lead to improved forecasting accuracy.[8]

The main conclusion of this paper is thus that it does appear possible to build econometric models that can be used in a mechanical way and still produce reasonably accurate results. There is clearly a long way to go to the attainment of the goal of building highly accurate models, and the present model is by no means put forth as being anywhere close to this goal. But the results do look encouraging enough to warrant the suggestion that a more scientific approach be taken to econometric model-building and forecasting.

The main conclusion of this paper should not be interpreted to mean that the author believes that no subjectivity is involved in forecasting. Clearly subjectivity is involved in the choice of the model in the first place and in the choice of the forecasts of the exogenous variables. For the *ex ante* forecasts evaluated in this paper, subjectivity was also involved, as can be seen from the discussion in the Appendix, in the choice of which price and labor force participation equations to use, of whether to use seasonally adjusted or unadjusted data in the housing sector, and of how to adjust for the effects of the auto and dock strikes.

One of the reasons why the present model performs as well as it does is probably the use of more advanced techniques to estimate the model than have been used previously. The results of two recent studies, [**3**] and [**4**], indicate that substantial gain in prediction accuracy can be achieved by the use of more advanced estimation techniques, and in the present case it seems likely that improved forecasting accuracy can be achieved in the future by the use of an even more advanced technique than the one currently used.

Princeton University

[7] In a recent analysis of the *ex ante* forecasts of ASA/NBER, Chase, DRI, Wharton, and the present model, McNees [**8**, (23)] concluded that the accuracy of the ASA/NBER forecasts was on average about the same as the accuracy of the Chase, DRI, and Wharton forecasts. The ASA/NBER forecasts thus appear to be a good benchmark from which to make comparisons of forecasting accuracy. The conclusion of McNees regarding the *ex ante* forecasts from the present model is similar to the conclusion reached in this paper, namely that the *ex ante* forecasts are on average not quite as accurate as the *ex ante* forecasts of the others.

[8] An example of an equation with better properties would be an equation with a better fit and more stability of the coefficient estimates to changes in the sample period. Another example of an improvement in the model would be the use of an alternative estimation technique that led to more accurate within-sample predictions and more stability of the estimates to changes in the sample period.

APPENDIX

DETAILS ON THE GENERATION OF THE FORECASTS

The release dates of the twelve sets of forecasts analyzed in this paper are: 1) July 21, 1970, 2) October 20, 1970, 3) January 20, 1971, 4) April 20, 1971, 5) July 21, 1971, 6) October 25, 1971, 7) January 24, 1972, 8) April 21, 1972, 9) July 24, 1972, 10) November 9, 1972 11) January 22, 1973, and 12) April 23, 1973. A new set of forecasts was always made right after the preliminary national-income-accounts data were released for the previous quarter. The forecast dated November 9, 1972, was delayed until after the 1972 election. For all forecasts except 3), 4), and 5), the model was reestimated before the forecasts were generated. Most equations of the model were not reestimated for forecasts 3), 4), and 5) because of the auto strike in 1970 IV. When the entire model was begun to be reestimated again for forecast 6), observations for 1970 IV, 1971 I, and 1971 II were excluded from the sample periods for the expenditure equations. The following are the changes that were made to the model during the three year period under consideration.

For the *ex ante/ex ante* forecasts (the actual forecasts released), the length of lag in the price equation was gradually changed from 8 in [**5**] to 20 currently. For forecast 1) the lag was 12, for forecast 2) the lag was 14, for forecast 3) the lag was 16, for forecasts 4)—10) the lag was 18, and for forecasts 11) and 12) the lag was 20. The nonlinear version of the price equation was used for forecasts 1)—4), and the linear version was used thereafter. The price equation to be used for a particular forecast was chosen on grounds of goodness of within-sample fit, with more weight being given to the accuracy of the equation for the more recent quarters. For the generation of the *ex ante/ex post* forecasts, the same price equation was used for each set of forecasts as was used for the *ex ante/ex ante* forecasts. For the generation of the *ex post/ex post* forecasts, the (current) linear price equation with a lag of 20 was used for all sets of forecasts.

The variables $DHF3_t$ and $DSF6_t$ were seasonally adjusted for the first time for forecast 5) (to make it easier to forecast these variables exogenously without having to be concerned with seasonal fluctuations), and HS_t was seasonally adjusted and the seasonal dummy variables dropped from the two housing starts equations for the first time for forecast 10). For the generation of the *ex ante/ex post* forecasts, this same timing was used to switch from seasonally unadjusted to seasonally adjusted data. For the generation of the *ex post/ex post* forecasts, seasonally adjusted data were always used.

For forecasts 2)—9) a different equation than (9.12) was used to forecast LF_{2t}. The results in [**6**] suggest that the real wage rate is important in explaining the labor force participation of some age-sex groups other than prime-age males. Because of these results, a distributed lag of a money wage variable, $WAGE_t$, and a distributed lag of the private output deflater, PD_t, were added to the equation explaining LF_{2t}/P_{2t}.[1] In addition, the equation was estimated in log form, as was done for the work in [6]. The $WAGE_t$ variable was treated as exogenous and was exogenously forecast. The equation was eventually dropped in favor of equation (9.12) because of the difficulty of forecasting $WAGE_t$ accurately and because of the sensitivity of the forecasts of LF_{2t} to the forecasts of PD_t (and thus to errors made in forecasting PD_t). For the generation of the *ex ante*/*ex post* forecasts, this new LF_{2t} equation was used for forecasts 2)—9), and equation (9.12) was used for the others. For the generation of the *ex post*/*ex post* forecasts, equation (9.12) was always used.

The 1970 auto strike had a pronounced effect on *GNP* and at least two of its components for 1970 IV. For forecast 3), which was made after the strike was over and after the preliminary data for 1970 IV were released, the 1970 IV values of seven variables were changed from the published data before the forecasts for 1971 I and beyond were generated. The model had no way of knowing that the low values for 1970 IV were due to a special factor and were likely to be made up in large part in 1971 I, and so some of the 1970 IV values were raised. The values of CD_t and IP_t for 1970 IV were raised by two thirds of the difference between the predicted values from forecast 2) and the published values. $GNPD_t$ was lowered by .40 points because part of the increase in $GNPD_t$ in 1970 IV was due to the auto strike. Using these three adjustments, the values for GNP_t, $GNPR_t$, PD_t, and Y_t were adjusted accordingly. For forecast 4), the 1970 IV values of four variables were changed. The values for CD_t and GNP_t for 1970 IV were taken to be the average of the published values for 1970 III and 1971 I, rather than the actual published values. The values for $GNPR_t$ and Y_t were then adjusted accordingly. For forecast 5), the 1970 IV value of GNP_t was changed to be the average of the 1970 III and 1971 I values, and then the values for $GNPR_t$ and Y_t were changed accordingly. The 1971 dock strike had a pronounced effect on imports for 1971 IV, and for forecast 7) the published 1971 IV value of imports was changed to be the value predicted by forecast 6). The two strikes were thus handled by adjusting the lagged values of a few of the variables before generating the forecasts. For the generation of both the *ex ante*/*ex post* and *ex post*/*ex post* forecasts, these same adjustments were used.

Since forecasts 1) and 2) were not adjusted in any way to try to account for the auto strike, the predicted values of GNP_t, CD_t, IP_t, and $GNPR_t$ for 1970 IV for these two forecasts were not compared to the actual values in computing the error measures in Table 3. Rather, they were compared to the average of the actual values for 1970 III and 1971 I. Likewise, the *ex ante*/*ex post*, *ex post*/*ex post*, and ASA/NBER *ex ante* forecasts were compared to the adjusted values. For ASA/NBER, the comparison with the adjusted values rather than the actual values had the effect of raising the one-quarter-ahead errors for GNP_t and CD_t slightly, but lowering the one-quarter-ahead error for $GNPR_t$ and the two-quarter-ahead errors for all three variables. The adjustment was not relevant for the three-quarter-ahead errors and beyond. The actual 1971 IV value of imports

[1] A truncated Pascal distribution with lag length of 8 was used for this equation.

was also changed to be the average of the 1971 III and 1972 I values before comparing the predicted values to it.[2]

Two important adjustments were made in the CD_t and IH_t equations for the generation of the *ex ante/ex post* forecasts. Consider, for example, the IH_t equation. The important explanatory variables in this equation are the housing starts variables. Over the three year period under consideration here the (NIA) data on IH_t have been revised upward, but the (non-NIA) data on housing starts have not. Consequently, when the *ex ante* coefficient estimates are used to forecast IH_t, the forecast is really more a forecast of the nonrevised IH_t data than of the revised IH_t data. The fact that the revised data on IH_{t-1} and on the other lagged values are used for the forecast is less important than the fact that the data on housing starts have not been revised. This problem is also important in the CD_t equation, where the (non-revised) consumer sentiment variable is an important explanatory variable. In order to account for this problem for the *ex ante/ex post* forecasts, the constant terms in the CD_t and IH_t equations were adjusted for each set of forecasts by adding to them $y^a_{t-1} - y^0_{t-1}$, where y^a_{t-1} is the current estimate of y for period $t - 1$ and y^0_{t-1} is the estimate of y for period $t - 1$ at the time the forecast (for periods t and beyond) was made. This general problem of data comparability makes it difficult to compare *ex ante/ex ante* and *ex ante/ex post* forecasts, and in the end one must attempt to reach some sort of a compromise. In the present case, the fact that none of the other equations were adjusted aside from the CD_t and IH_t equations probably biases the results somewhat against the *ex ante/ex post* forecasts. For the *ex post/ex post* forecasts no adjustments are needed because the coefficient estimates are obtained from the same data base as is used to generate the forecasts.

Problems of data comparability also arise for the *ex ante/ex post* forecasts in deciding what values of potential GNP, $GNPR^*_t$, and what values of α_t to use. These two series change slightly for each set of forecasts, and for the *ex ante/ex post* forecasts it was decided to use the same series as were used for the *ex ante/ex ante* forecasts rather than to use the latest series. In this case, however, it made little difference to the final results which series were used. The $WAGE_t$ data used for forecasts 2)—9) were also revised substantially during the period, while the labor force data were not, and so it was decided for the *ex ante/ex post* forecasts to use the same data as were used for the *ex ante/ex ante* forecasts rather than to use the latest data. Otherwise, all of the data used for the *ex ante/ex post* forecasts were the latest data.

REFERENCES

[1] Brunner, Karl, Review of Bert Hickman, ed. *Econometric Models of Cyclical Behavior, Journal of Economic Literature,* XI (September, 1973), 927–933.

[2] Beginning in 1972, the household-survey data were benchmarked to the 1970 Census data, which had a small effect on some of the variables in the model. Consequently, the forecasts of these variables for 1972 made prior to the benchmark date were compared to estimates of what the actual values would have been had there been no new benchmark. These corrections were all fairly minor.

[2] EVANS, MICHAEL K., YOEL HAITOVSKY, AND GEORGE I. TREYZ, assisted by Vincent Su, "An Analysis of the Forecasting Properties of U.S. Econometric Models," in Bert Hickman, ed., *Econometric Models of Cyclical Behavior* (New York: National Bureau of Economic Research, 1972), 949–1139.

[3] FAIR, RAY C., "A Comparison of Alternative Estimators of Macroeconomic Models," *International Economic Review*, XIV (June, 1973), 261-277.

[4] ———, "A Comparison of FIML and Robust Estimates of a Nonlinear Macroeconometric Model," Research Report, NBER Computer Research Center, October, 1973.

[5] ———, *A Short-Run Forecasting Model of the United States Economy* (Lexington, Mass.: D.C. Health and Co., 1970).

[6] ———, "Labor Force Participation, Wage Rates, and Money Illusion," *The Review of Economics and Statistics*, LIII (May, 1971), 164-168.

[7] HAITOVSKY, YOEL AND GEORGE TREYZ, "Forecasts with Quarterly Macroeconometric Models: Equation Adjustments, and Benchmark Predictions: The U.S. Experience," *The Review of Economics and Statistics*, LIV (August, 1972), 317-325.

[8] MCNEES, STEPHEN K., "The Predictive Accuracy of Econometric Forecasts," *New England Economic Review*, (September/October, 1973), 3-27.

3

ST. LOUIS MODEL REVISITED

By Leonall C. Andersen and Keith M. Carlson

During the early 1960's a framework of economic analysis stressing the role of monetary aggregates was developed at the Federal Reserve Bank of St. Louis. Originally this framework depended on the "chart" as a tool of analysis, but by the late 1960's efforts had been directed toward the addition of the use of regression techniques in the analysis of economic data. Some of these quantitative research efforts were consolidated in 1970 with the publication of what has come to be known as the "St. Louis model" [**4**].

1. ORIGIN AND DEVELOPMENT OF ST. LOUIS MODEL

1.1. Purpose of the model. The purpose of publishing research results in the form of an empirically estimated model was threefold. First, and foremost, a model with a monetarist foundation was sought for purposes of assisting in the development and evaluation of stabilization policies. Second, there was a desire to add a monetarist model to the existing set of Keynesian econometric models. Third, the model was offered as a challenge to other monetarists to produce empirical statements of their views.

The purposes of the model can be emphasized by noting some of the purposes for which it was *not* designed. First, the model was not designed for exact quarter-to-quarter forecasting. Its purpose, rather, was to indicate the general nature of the differential response of certain key economic variables to alternative courses of monetary and fiscal action. Second, the model was not offered as a substitute for existing macroeconometric models, though to the extent that it differed in methodology and carried different implications it was offered as a challenge to the models of others. Third, the model was not designed to provide information on allocative detail, which was a reflection of the belief that aggregative behavior can be analyzed quite independently of the behavior of individual sectors.

1.2. Theoretical foundation. The primary theoretical consideration underlying the development of the model was the modern quantity theory of money.[1] The focus of the modern quantity theory is on the behavior of economic units in response to changes in the money stock. Money is an asset which provides services to its holder as do all other assets. Furthermore, the existing stock of money must be held by someone. As a result, a change in the stock of money will induce a discrepancy between actual and desired holdings of money, which will cause shuffling of the wealth portfolio. Included in this adjustment is a change in spending on goods and services.

A second theoretical consideration which was implicit in the construction of

[1] See [**13**] and [**19**].

the model, though not explicitly recognized by the model builders at the time, was the effect of search and information costs on economic behavior.[2] Information about equilibrium prices is not costless to gather, and thus economic units must search for equilibrium prices by sampling the market. As a result, prices do not necessarily adjust instantaneously to their new equilibrium level in response to a change in the pace of total spending.

As a result of these theoretical considerations, the relative impact of monetary and fiscal actions requires a careful assessment. This assessment includes differentiating between short-run effects and long-run effects, as well as paying special attention to the method of financing government expenditures.

1.3. Research strategy. Construction of the St. Louis model was guided by four major principles. As always, an underlying theoretical foundation was considered essential. For the most part, this theoretical frame of reference was the quantity theory as it had been applied by the St. Louis Bank over the years to the analysis of economic developments. Furthermore, analysis relating to the timing of response of economic variables like prices and output to monetary and fiscal actions was consistent with the theory of search and information costs.

A second principle, reflecting the objectives of the model builder, was that the model have primarily a policy orientation. With this primary interest in economic stabilization, the aim was not to forecast economic events, but rather, to assess the impact of alternative monetary and fiscal policies. Though considerations of forecasting could not be ignored, the emphasis was on capturing the timing and magnitude of the effect of monetary and fiscal actions. As has been demonstrated with other models, a model need not contain policy variables in order to forecast well.[3] Such forecasting models, almost by definition, are of little direct use to policymakers.

A third principle, which might be considered a subprinciple of the policy-orientation principle, is the use of a reduced form approach. The impact of monetary and fiscal actions cannot be accurately gauged by assuming that such actions affect economic activity via only certain assumed channels. The choice of appropriate monetary policy cannot be formulated by examining only its effect on the economy through, say, interest rate changes or wealth effects. A reduced form approach is not without its dangers, but the results based on this approach represent an important addition to the results of existing models.

Finally, a small model approach serves as the fourth guiding principle. For purposes of policy formulation, primary interest is focused on a few key economic variables. By keeping the model small and limited in scope, research resources can be concentrated on a few important relationships. Underlying this small model methodology is the belief that sectoral detail is not required to produce an accurate assessment of the aggregative impact of monetary and fiscal actions.

[2] As a general reference, see [**18**]. For a specific interpretation of the St. Louis model from the viewpoint of information costs, see [**8**]. More recent research results at the Federal Reserve Bank of St. Louis, which take into account information costs, are summarized in [**7**].

[3] For further discussion of this point, see [**11**]. For a comparison of the St. Louis model with a forecasting model which places little emphasis on policy variables, see [**15**].

2. SUMMARY OF MODEL

This section summarizes the model and some of its properties. The algebraic form of the model has not changed since the model was published in 1970. This is not to say that some changes in specification would not have been appropriate, but with the initial development of the model, a trial period was considered necessary in order to gain a better understanding of the performance of the model in light of its original purposes.

2.1. Equations of the model. The model is summarized in algebraic form in Table 1. This summary provides only the essential features of the model, ignoring problems of dimensionality and lag length. The exact form of the equations and two sets of statistical estimates of coefficients are given in the Appendix.

TABLE 1

ALGEBRAIC FORM OF ST. LOUIS MODEL

(1) Total Spending Equation

$$\Delta Y_t = f_1(\Delta M_t \cdots \Delta M_{t-n}, \Delta E_t \cdots \Delta E_{t-n})$$

(2) Price Equation

$$\Delta P_t = f_2(D_t \cdots D_{t-n}, \Delta P_t^A)$$

(3) Demand Pressure Identity

$$D_t = \Delta Y_t - (X_t^F - X_{t-1})$$

(4) Total Spending Identity

$$\Delta Y_t = \Delta P_t + \Delta X_t$$

(5) Interest Rate Equation

$$R_t = f_3(\Delta M_t, \Delta X_t \cdots \Delta X_{t-n}, \Delta P_t, \Delta P_t^A)$$

(6) Anticipated Price Equation

$$\Delta P_t^A = f_4(\Delta P_{t-1} \cdots P_{t-n})$$

(7) Unemployment Rate Equation

$$U_t = f_5(G_t, G_{t-1})$$

(8) GNP Gap Identity

$$G_t = \frac{X_t^F - X_t}{X_t^F}$$

Notation:

Endogenous Variables

- ΔY_t = change in total spending (nominal GNP)
- ΔP_t = change in price level (GNP price deflator)
- D_t = demand pressure
- ΔX_t = change in output (real GNP)
- R_t = market interest rate
- ΔP_t^A = anticipated change in price level
- U_t = unemployment rate
- G_t = GNP gap

Exogenous Variables*

- ΔM_t = change in money stock
- ΔE_t = change in high-employment Federal expenditures
- X_t^F = potential (full-employment) output

* Other than lagged variables

One set of coefficients is for the sample period ending fourth quarter 1968 and the other is based on data through second quarter 1973.

Equation (1) in Table 1 is the total spending (nominal GNP) equation. The quarterly change in total spending (ΔY) is specified as a function of current and past changes in money stock (ΔM) and current and past changes in high-employment Federal expenditures (ΔE).

Equation (2) specifies the quarterly change in the price level (ΔP) as a function of current and past demand pressures (D) and anticipated price changes (ΔP^A).[4] Demand pressure is defined in equation (3) as the change in total spending minus the potential increase in output ($X^F - X$). This price equation is essentially a short-run Phillips curve extended to include changes in total spending and anticipated prices.[5]

Equation (4) is a definition of changes in total spending in terms of its components. With ΔY determined by equation (1), and ΔP by equation (2), ΔX can be derived from equation (4).

Equation (5) gives the market rate of interest (R) as a function of current changes in the money stock (ΔM), current and past changes in output (ΔX), current price change (ΔP), and anticipated price change (ΔP^A). Anticipated price change is assumed to depend on past price changes.

Equation (7) is the unemployment rate equation and is a transformation of the GNP gap (G), as defined in equation (8), into a measure of unemployment relative to the labor force. This transformation is based on "Okun's Law."[6]

2.2. Workings of the model. The St. Louis model is described as a reduced form model, but such a description is not completely accurate in describing each of the equations of the model. However, due to the recursive nature of the model, the reduced-form label is accurate as a general label.

The fundamental relationship of the model is the total spending equation. Total spending is determined by monetary and fiscal (federal spending financed by taxes or borrowing from the public) actions, though no direct information is provided as to how such actions affect spending.

The change in total spending is combined with an estimate of potential output to provide a measure of demand pressure. An estimate of anticipated price change (with the weights on past price changes taken from the long-term interest rate equation) is combined with demand pressure to determine the change in the price level.

The total spending identity provides the determination of the change in output, given the change in total spending and the change in prices. This procedure differs from standard practice in other econometric models, where output and prices are determined separately, then combined to determine total spending.

The changes in output, prices, anticipated prices and in the money stock de-

[4] For a critique of this price equation, see [**14**].

[5] For a discussion of the St. Louis model in the context of the Phillips curve controversy, see [**5**].

[6] See [**16**].

termine market interest rates. Interest rates do not exercise a direct role in the model in the determination of spending, output and prices.

To determine the unemployment rate, the change in output is first combined with the estimate of potential output to determine the GNP gap. The GNP gap is then transformed into the unemployment rate.

2.3. Properties of the model. To describe the model, its characteristics are summarized in relation to four key monetarist propositions.[7] These propositions are:

(1) Monetary actions are the dominant factor contributing to economic fluctuations.

(2) Monetary actions have little, if any, lasting effect on real variables, with lasting effects on only nominal variables.

(3) Fiscal actions, defined as changes in Federal spending with a given money stock, have only a transitory impact on economic activity.

(4) The private economy is inherently stable.

Monetary actions as dominant impulse. The St. Louis model, as designed and estimated, is consistent with the proposition that monetary actions are the major factor contributing to economic fluctuations. Though not designed as a model depicting the cyclical movements of the economy, operating via the total spending equation, a change in the growth rate of money gives rise to cyclical variation in real GNP and unemployment. The total spending equation does not permit forces other than monetary and fiscal actions to change the growth in total spending, but analysis of the error term in that equation indicates that such a specification is not unwarranted.[8]

The model does not provide direct evidence disconfirming the hypothesis that nonpolicy influences are instrumental in causing economic fluctuations. However, direct evidence is provided relating to the contribution of monetary as opposed to fiscal actions as a factor contributing to cyclical movements in economic activity.

Monetary impact on nominal variables. Simulations of the St. Louis model indicate that after a considerable period of time a change in the rate of monetary expansion influences only nominal magnitudes, namely, total spending (GNP), the price level, and nominal interest rates. Real magnitudes, notably the growth of output and employment, are unaffected. Following short-run responses to a change in monetary growth, total spending and the price level grow at rates determined by the rate of increase in the money stock. Output and employment grow at rates determined by growth of natural resources, capital stock, labor force, and productivity.

Transitory impact of fiscal actions. Fiscal actions are measured by the change in high-employment Federal expenditures. This choice for a fiscal variable is designed to capture the effects of changes in Federal spending when financed by borrowing or taxation. According to the model fiscal actions have short-run

[7] For further discussion of these propositions, see [**1**] and [**9**].

[8] See the appendix to [**6**].

TABLE

ST. LOUIS MODEL PROJECTIONS*

NOMINAL

(Annual Rates of Change from Initial

INITIAL

	4-68		1-69		2-69		3-69		4-69		1-70		2-70		3-70		4-70	
Terminal quarter	Act.	Proj.	Act.	Proj.	Act.	Proj.	Act.	Proj.	Act.	Proj.	Act.	Proj.	Act.	Proj.	Act.	Proj.	Act.	Proj.
1-69	7.8	8.1																
2-69	7.6	7.8	7.5	7.3														
3-69	7.8	7.5	7.8	7.1	8.1	7.0												
4-69	6.6	7.2	6.2	6.8	5.6	6.5	3.1	6.2										
1-70	6.1	6.9	5.7	6.5	5.1	6.3	3.6	6.1	4.1	5.6								
2-70	5.9	7.1	5.6	6.8	5.1	6.7	4.1	6.7	4.6	6.7	5.1	7.7						
3-70	6.1	7.1	5.8	6.9	5.5	6.9	4.9	6.9	5.4	7.0	6.1	7.6	7.1	7.7				
4-70	5.6	7.1	5.2	6.9	4.9	6.9	4.2	6.9	4.5	7.0	4.7	7.4	4.4	7.5	1.8	7.2		
1-71	6.6	7.1	6.4	6.9	6.3	6.8	6.0	6.9	6.5	6.9	7.2	7.3	7.8	7.2	8.2	6.9	15.1	6.6
2-71	6.7	7.3	6.6	7.2	6.5	7.2	6.2	7.3	6.8	7.4	7.3	7.7	7.9	7.6	8.1	7.6	11.4	8.0
3-71	6.7	7.8	6.6	7.7	6.5	7.8	6.3	7.9	6.7	8.1	7.2	8.5	7.6	8.6	7.7	8.7	9.8	9.2
4-71	6.8	7.9	6.7	7.9	6.6	7.9	6.5	8.1	6.9	8.2	7.3	8.6	7.7	8.7	7.8	8.9	9.3	9.1
1-72	7.1	7.9	7.0	7.8	7.0	7.9	6.9	8.1	7.3	8.2	7.7	8.5	8.1	8.5	8.3	8.6	9.6	8.8
2-72	7.4	7.9	7.4	7.9	7.3	7.9	7.3	8.1	7.7	8.1	8.1	8.4	8.5	8.3	8.7	8.4	9.9	8.6
3-72	7.5	7.9	7.5	7.8	7.5	7.9	7.4	8.0	7.8	8.1	8.2	8.3	8.5	8.3	8.7	8.3	9.7	8.3
4-72	7.7	8.0	7.7	8.0	7.7	8.1	7.7	8.2	8.1	8.3	8.5	8.5	8.8	8.4	9.0	8.5	10.0	8.6
1-73	8.2	8.1	8.2	8.1	8.2	8.2	8.2	8.3	8.6	8.3	9.0	8.5	9.4	8.5	9.6	8.6	10.5	8.7
2-73	8.3	8.1	8.3	8.1	8.3	8.2	8.3	8.3	8.7	8.3	9.1	8.5	9.4	8.5	9.6	8.6	10.5	8.6
3-73*p*	8.4	8.0	8.4	8.0	8.5	8.1	8.5	8.2	8.8	8.2	9.2	8.3	9.5	8.3	9.7	8.4	10.5	8.3

* Projections in each column are based on regressions using actual data through the quarter expenditures. The figures in each column are compounded annual rates of change from p—3-73 actual is preliminary.

effects, but for periods of a year of more, the net effect is much smaller. When first estimated, the long-run fiscal multiplier on nominal GNP was about zero. Estimated with data through second quarter 1973, the value of the multiplier is about .5, but still not significantly different from zero.

Inherent stability of the economy. The St. Louis model does not provide evidence on the proposition that the economy is inherently stable in the sense of Brunner [**9**]. However, simulations of the St. Louis model demonstrate properties which are consistent with a corollary to the inherent stability proposition, that monetary and fiscal actions are a source of instability.[9] When the model is shocked by changing any one of the three exogenous variables (change in

[9] For results of a similar exercise with a large econometric model, the Data Resources Model, see [**12**].

2

COMPARED WITH ACTUAL

GNP

Quarter to Terminal Quarter)

QUARTER

1–71		2–71		3–71		4–71		1–72		2–72		3–72		4–72		1–73		2–73	
Act.	Proj.	Act.	Proj.	Act.	Proj.	Act.	Proj.	Act.	Proj.	Act.	Proj.	Act.	Proj.	Act.	Proj.	Act.	Proj.	Act.	Proj.
7.9	10.7																		
7.2	11.1	6.5	11.7																
7.5	10.4	7.3	10.4	8.0	8.6														
8.3	9.8	8.4	9.6	9.4	8.2	10.9	7.7												
8.9	9.5	9.1	9.1	10.0	8.0	11.0	7.7	11.2	8.0										
8.8	9.0	9.0	8.7	9.7	7.5	10.2	7.1	9.9	6.8	8.7	5.9								
9.2	9.3	9.5	9.0	10.1	8.2	10.6	8.1	10.5	8.3	10.2	8.5	11.7	10.3						
10.0	9.3	10.3	9.0	10.9	8.3	11.5	8.2	11.7	8.5	11.9	8.8	13.5	9.7	15.2	9.3				
10.0	9.2	10.2	8.9	10.8	8.2	11.2	8.0	11.3	8.3	11.3	8.5	12.2	9.2	12.5	8.6	9.8	8.0		
10.0	8.8	10.3	8.6	10.7	7.8	11.1	7.7	11.2	7.8	11.2	8.0	11.8	8.5	11.8	7.9	10.1	7.2	10.4	6.4

heading each column, assuming subsequent actual changes in money and high-employment the initial quarter to the terminal quarter.

money stock, change in high-employment Federal expenditures, and potential output), simulations indicate an initial period of oscillation followed by a return to a steady long-run growth path.[10]

3. EVALUATION OF MODEL

The St. Louis model was developed in various stages over the period 1968 to 1970. Once published in 1970, its basic form was kept unchanged so as to permit more accurate assessment of its usefulness and validity than if frequent changes in specification were made. Though the fundamental specification of

[10] For a summary of these simulations as well as further discussion of the properties of the model, see [2]. For further discussion of the inherent stability issue and a contrasting interpretation of the St. Louis model, see [**17**].

TABLE

ST. LOUIS MODEL PROJECTIONS*

GNP PRICE

(Annual Rates of Change from Initial

INITIAL

	4-68	1-69	2-69	3-69	4-69	1-70	2-70	3-70	4-70
Terminal quarter	Act. Proj.	Act. Proj.	Act. Proj.	Act. Proj.	Act. Proj.	Act. Proj.	Act. Proj.	Act. Proj.	Act. Proj.
1-69	4.2 4.4								
2-69	4.9 4.4	5.5 4.4							
3-69	5.3 4.4	5.8 4.5	6.1 4.8						
4-69	5.3 4.5	5.7 4.5	5.8 4.8	5.5 5.2					
1-70	5.5 4.5	5.9 4.5	6.0 4.8	5.9 5.2	6.3 5.3				
2-70	5.4 4.5	5.6 4.5	5.6 4.8	5.5 5.2	5.5 5.2	4.6 5.5			
3-70	5.2 4.5	5.4 4.5	5.3 4.8	5.1 5.2	5.0 5.2	4.3 5.5	4.1 5.2		
4-70	5.3 4.4	5.5 4.4	5.5 4.8	5.4 5.2	5.3 5.2	5.0 5.5	5.2 5.1	6.4 4.8	
1-71	5.4 4.4	5.5 4.4	5.5 4.7	5.4 5.2	5.4 5.2	5.1 5.4	5.3 5.1	5.9 4.7	5.5 4.9
2-71	5.3 4.4	5.4 4.4	5.4 4.7	5.3 5.2	5.3 5.1	5.1 5.4	5.2 5.0	5.6 4.7	5.2 4.8
3-71	5.1 4.4	5.2 4.4	5.1 4.7	5.0 5.2	4.9 5.1	4.7 5.4	4.7 5.0	4.9 4.7	4.4 4.8
4-71	4.8 4.4	4.8 4.3	4.7 4.7	4.6 5.2	4.5 5.1	4.2 5.4	4.1 5.0	4.2 4.7	3.6 4.8
1-72	4.8 4.3	4.9 4.3	4.8 4.7	4.7 5.2	4.6 5.1	4.4 5.3	4.4 5.0	4.4 4.6	4.0 4.7
2-72	4.6 4.3	4.6 4.3	4.6 4.6	4.4 5.1	4.3 5.1	4.1 5.3	4.0 4.9	4.0 4.6	3.6 4.7
3-72	4.5 4.3	4.5 4.3	4.4 4.6	4.3 5.1	4.2 5.0	3.9 5.3	3.9 4.9	3.8 4.5	3.5 4.6
4-72	4.4 4.3	4.4 4.3	4.3 4.6	4.2 5.1	4.1 5.0	3.9 5.2	3.8 4.8	3.8 4.5	3.5 4.5
1-73	4.5 4.3	4.5 4.2	4.5 4.6	4.3 5.0	4.2 4.9	4.1 5.1	4.0 4.7	4.0 4.4	3.8 4.4
2-73	4.6 4.3	4.7 4.2	4.6 4.5	4.5 5.0	4.5 4.9	4.3 5.1	4.3 4.6	4.3 4.3	4.1 4.3
3-73*p*	4.8 4.2	4.8 4.2	4.7 4.5	4.7 4.9	4.6 4.8	4.5 5.0	4.5 4.6	4.5 4.3	4.3 4.2

* Projections in each column are based on regressions using actual data through the quarter expenditures. The figures in each column are compounded annual rates of change from
p—3-73 actual is preliminary.

the model has been kept unchanged, the model has been reestimated as new data have become available. Consequently, despite unchanged form, the nature and properties of the model have changed somewhat since first published in 1970.

This section gives a summary of the projection record of the model. This summary is based on simulations of the model outside the sample period. Then some observations are made about the model in the form of apparent "successes" and "failures" of the model to date.

3.1. Projection record. The projection record for the key economic variables in the St. Louis model is given in Tables 2 to 7. These projections, even though they are beyond the sample period, can be described as *ex post* because they are generated using known values for the exogenous variables as they existed in late 1973. The projections do *not* include intercept adjustments, add factors, or

3

COMPARED WITH ACTUAL

DEFLATOR

Quarter to Terminal Quarter)

QUARTER

1-71		2-71		3-71		4-71		1-72		2-72		3-72		4-72		1-73		2-73	
Act.	Proj.	Act.	Proj.	Act.	Proj.	Act.	Proj.	Act.	Proj.	Act.	Proj.	Act.	Proj.	Act.	Proj.	Act.	Proj.	Act.	Proj.
4.9	5.2																		
3.8	5.2	2.8	5.1																
3.0	5.2	2.1	5.1	1.3	4.4														
3.7	5.2	3.3	5.1	3.5	4.4	5.7	3.6												
3.2	5.2	2.8	5.0	2.8	4.3	3.6	3.5	1.6	3.9										
3.2	5.1	2.8	4.9	2.8	4.2	3.3	3.4	2.2	3.8	2.8	3.4								
3.2	5.1	2.9	4.9	2.9	4.1	3.3	3.3	2.6	3.7	3.1	3.4	3.3	3.3						
3.5	5.0	3.4	4.8	3.4	4.0	3.9	3.2	3.4	3.7	4.0	3.3	4.7	3.3	6.0	3.3				
4.0	4.9	3.8	4.7	4.0	3.8	4.4	3.2	4.2	3.6	4.8	3.3	5.5	3.2	6.7	3.3	7.3	3.8		
4.2	4.8	4.1	4.6	4.3	3.7	4.8	3.1	4.6	3.5	5.2	3.2	5.8	3.2	6.7	3.2	7.0	3.7	6.7	4.0

heading each column, assuming subsequent actual changes in money and high-employment the initial quarter to the terminal quarter.

tender loving care, except to the extent that mechanical reestimation with most recent data is given such an interpretation. Furthermore, strike variables are not used, nor is there any use of autoregression in the residuals.

The interpretation of Tables 2 to 7 is as follows: the numbers along the main diagonal indicate actual (act.) and projected (proj.) values one quarter ahead; the projections are based on coefficients estimated with data through the quarter heading each column. Similarly, the second diagonal represents the actual average and the average of the projection for two quarters ahead, the third diagonal for three quarters ahead, etc.

With respect to the variables of the model, primary interest is focused on the average projection for several quarters ahead. Experience with the St. Louis model indicates that it is not suitable for exact quarter-to-quarter forecasting, or even for periods of two or three quarters. The projection record, as summarized in these tables, provides a basis for attempting to determine what ho-

TABLE

ST. LOUIS MODEL PROJECTIONS*

REAL

(Annual Rates of Change from Initial

INITIAL

	4-68	1-69	2-69	3-69	4-69	1-70	2-70	3-70	4-70
Terminal quarter	Act. Proj.	Act. Proj.	Act. Proj.	Act. Proj.	Act. Proj.	Act. Proj.	Act. Proj.	Act. Proj.	Act. Proj.
1-69	3.3 3.7								
2-69	2.6 3.3	1.9 2.8							
3-69	2.4 3.0	1.9 2.6	1.9 2.1						
4-69	1.2 2.6	0.5 2.2	-0.2 1.7	-2.2 1.0					
1-70	0.5 2.3	-0.2 2.0	-0.8 1.4	-2.2 0.8	-2.1 0.3				
2-70	0.5 2.5	0.0 2.3	-0.5 1.8	-1.3 1.4	-0.8 1.4	0.5 2.1			
3-70	0.9 2.6	0.4 2.4	0.2 2.0	-0.3 1.6	0.4 1.7	1.7 2.1	2.9 2.4		
4-70	0.2 2.6	-0.2 2.4	-0.6 2.0	-1.1 1.6	-0.8 1.7	-0.4 1.9	-0.8 2.3	-4.3 2.3	
1-71	1.1 2.6	0.9 2.4	0.7 2.0	0.5 1.6	1.1 1.7	1.9 1.8	2.4 2.1	2.2 2.1	9.1 1.6
2-71	1.3 2.9	1.1 2.8	1.0 2.4	0.9 2.0	1.4 2.2	2.1 2.2	2.5 2.5	2.4 2.8	6.0 3.1
3-71	1.5 3.3	1.3 3.3	1.3 3.0	1.2 2.6	1.7 2.9	2.4 3.0	2.7 3.4	2.7 3.9	5.1 4.3
4-71	1.9 3.4	1.8 3.4	1.8 3.1	1.8 2.8	2.3 3.0	3.0 3.1	3.4 3.6	3.5 4.1	5.5 4.2
1-72	2.2 3.4	2.1 3.4	2.1 3.1	2.1 2.8	2.6 3.0	3.2 3.0	3.6 3.4	3.7 3.9	5.4 4.0
2-72	2.7 3.5	2.6 3.5	2.7 3.2	2.7 2.8	3.3 3.0	3.9 2.9	4.3 3.3	4.5 3.7	6.1 3.8
3-72	2.9 3.5	2.8 3.4	2.9 3.2	3.0 2.8	3.5 2.9	4.1 2.9	4.5 3.3	4.7 3.6	6.0 3.6
4-72	3.2 3.6	3.2 3.6	3.3 3.4	3.4 3.0	3.9 3.2	4.4 3.1	4.8 3.6	5.0 3.9	6.3 4.0
1-73	3.5 3.7	3.5 3.7	3.6 3.5	3.7 3.1	4.2 3.3	4.8 3.3	5.2 3.7	5.4 4.0	6.5 4.1
2-73	3.4 3.8	3.4 3.8	3.5 3.5	3.7 3.2	4.1 3.4	4.6 3.3	4.9 3.7	5.1 4.1	6.1 4.1
3-73*p*	3.4 3.7	3.5 3.7	3.5 3.5	3.6 3.1	4.1 3.3	4.5 3.2	4.8 3.7	5.0 4.0	5.9 4.0

* Projections in each column are based on regressions using actual data through the quarter expenditures. The figures in each column are compounded annual rates of change from *p*—3-73 actual is preliminary.

rizon is appropriate for this model. Any conclusions, however, are subject to the usual warnings, in that they reflect the peculiarities of the particular period under review. With a small model, however, continual monitoring of the model's performance is possible with a relatively small amount of effort.

Tables 2–7 are based on full model simulations rather than equation by equation estimates. Because of the recursive nature of the model, total spending projections would be the same in either case. Before summarizing these results by calculating mean absolute errors along the diagonal for each of the variables, a few comments are offered relating to each of the variables.

Total spending. The results in Table 2 for total spending indicate that for the full nineteen-quarter-ahead period from 1968 to 1973, the projected average annual rate of increase for GNP was in error by .4 of a percentage point. The period as a whole consisted of two subperiods which tended to offset each other.

4

COMPARED WITH ACTUAL

GNP

Quarter to Terminal Quarter)

QUARTER

1-71		2-71		3-71		4-71		1-72		2-72		3-72		4-72		1-73		2-73	
Act.	Proj.	Act.	Proj.	Act.	Proj.	Act.	Proj.	Act.	Proj.	Act.	Proj.	Act.	Proj.	Act.	Proj.	Act.	Proj.	Act.	Proj.
2.9	5.3																		
3.2	5.7	3.6	6.3																
4.4	5.0	5.1	5.1	6.6	4.1														
4.5	4.4	5.0	4.3	5.7	3.7	4.8	4.0												
5.5	4.1	6.1	3.9	7.0	3.6	7.1	4.1	9.5	4.0										
5.5	3.7	6.0	3.6	6.7	3.2	6.7	3.6	7.6	2.9	5.8	2.5								
5.9	4.1	6.4	4.0	6.9	4.0	7.0	4.6	7.8	4.4	6.9	5.0	8.1	6.8						
6.2	4.2	6.7	4.1	7.2	4.3	7.3	4.9	8.0	4.8	7.5	5.3	8.4	6.3	8.6	5.9				
5.8	4.1	6.2	4.1	6.5	4.2	6.5	4.8	6.8	4.6	6.2	5.1	6.3	5.8	5.5	5.2	2.4	4.1		
5.6	3.9	5.9	3.9	6.2	4.0	6.1	4.5	6.3	4.3	5.7	4.6	5.6	5.2	4.8	4.6	3.0	3.4	3.5	2.3

heading each column, assuming subsequent actual changes in money and high-employment the initial quarter to the terminal quarter.

The first subperiod, from fourth quarter 1968 to fourth quarter 1971, consisted of an overestimate of 1.1 percentage point, while the second subperiod, from fourth quarter 1971 to third quarter 1973, was an underestimate of 3.4 percentage points. In fact, for each of the last seven quarters the model underestimated the increase in GNP. By comparison only three of the previous 12 quarters were underestimated, and one of those was a post-strike quarter. The problem with the total spending equation is one of capturing the changes in velocity during the period, though for the full period the average increase in velocity was apparently captured with a fair degree of accuracy.

Prices. The price projections reflect to some extent the errors in the projection of GNP, though the lag structure of the model is such that total spending error is reflected more in real GNP projections. The price equation has long lags because of the anticipated price term, so quarter-to-quarter errors are to be

TABLE

ST. LOUIS MODEL PROJECTIONS*

UNEMPLOYMENT

(Average Level from Initial

INITIAL

	1-69	2-69	3-69	4-69	1-70	2-70	3-70	4-70	1-71
Terminal quarter	Act. Proj.	Act. Proj.	Act. Proj.	Act. Proj.	Act. Proj.	Act. Proj.	Act. Proj.	Act. Proj.	Act. Proj.
1-69	3.4 3.7								
2-69	3.4 3.7	3.4 3.7							
3-69	3.5 3.7	3.5 3.8	3.6 3.9						
4-69	3.5 3.8	3.5 3.8	3.6 4.0	3.6 4.0					
1-70	3.6 3.8	3.7 3.9	3.8 4.1	3.9 4.2	4.2 4.5				
2-70	3.8 3.9	3.9 4.0	4.0 4.2	4.2 4.3	4.5 4.7	4.8 5.0			
3-70	4.0 4.0	4.1 4.1	4.3 4.3	4.4 4.4	4.7 4.8	5.0 5.1	5.2 5.3		
4-70	4.2 4.1	4.4 4.1	4.5 4.3	4.7 4.5	5.0 4.8	5.3 5.2	5.5 5.3	5.8 5.4	
1-71	4.4 4.1	4.6 4.2	4.7 4.4	4.9 4.6	5.2 4.9	5.4 5.3	5.7 5.4	5.9 5.5	6.0 6.1
2-71	4.6 4.2	4.7 4.3	4.9 4.5	5.1 4.7	5.3 5.0	5.5 5.4	5.7 5.5	5.9 5.5	5.9 6.1
3-71	4.7 4.2	4.8 4.3	5.0 4.5	5.2 4.7	5.4 5.1	5.6 5.4	5.8 5.6	5.9 5.6	5.9 6.2
4-71	4.8 4.2	4.9 4.3	5.1 4.6	5.3 4.8	5.5 5.1	5.7 5.4	5.8 5.6	5.9 5.6	6.0 6.1
1-72	4.9 4.3	5.0 4.3	5.2 4.6	5.3 4.8	5.5 5.1	5.7 5.5	5.8 5.6	5.9 5.6	5.9 6.1
2-72	5.0 4.3	5.1 4.3	5.2 4.6	5.4 4.8	5.5 5.2	5.7 5.5	5.8 5.6	5.9 5.6	5.9 6.1
3-72	5.0 4.3	5.1 4.4	5.2 4.6	5.4 5.9	5.5 5.2	5.7 5.6	5.8 5.6	5.8 5.6	5.8 6.2
4-72	5.0 4.3	5.1 4.4	5.2 4.6	5.4 4.9	5.5 5.2	5.6 5.6	5.7 5.7	5.8 5.6	5.8 6.2
1-73	5.0 4.3	5.1 4.4	5.2 4.6	5.3 4.9	5.5 5.3	5.6 5.6	5.7 5.7	5.7 5.6	5.7 6.2
2-73	5.0 4.3	5.1 4.4	5.2 4.7	5.3 5.0	5.4 5.3	5.5 5.6	5.6 5.7	5.6 5.6	5.6 6.2
3-73*p*	5.0 4.3	5.1 4.4	5.2 4.7	5.3 5.0	5.4 5.3	5.5 5.7	5.5 5.7	5.6 5.6	5.5 6.2

* Projections in each column are based on regressions using actual data through the period and high-employment expenditures. The figures in each column are averages of the rates

p—3-73 actual is preliminary.

expected given the nature of quarter-to-quarter variation in prices as measured by the GNP deflator and the treatment of government pay increases in the national income accounts. In addition, governmental interference with the operation of the price system and worldwide economic conditions are factors to be considered in interpreting Table 3.

Looking at the period before wage-price controls, from fourth quarter 1968 to second quarter 1971, the model projected inflation at a 4.4 percent average annual rate; the actual increase was at a 5.3 percent average rate. However, the price equation is a learning equation in the sense that reestimation with most recent data quickly captured the inflation experience of the period. For example, for the last year prior to the controls the model projected price advances at a 5.0 percent increase which compared with an actual increase of 5.2 percent.

Despite the inapplicability of the price equation during the period of controls,

TABLE

ST. LOUIS MODEL PROJECTIONS*

CORPORATE

(Average Level from Initial

INITIAL

	1–69		2–69		3–69		4–69		1–70		2–70		3–70		4–70		1–71	
Terminal quarter	Act.	Proj.	Act.	Proj.	Act.	Proj.	Act.	Proj.	Act.	Proj.	Act.	Proj.	Act.	Proj.	Act.	Proj.	Act	Proj.
1–69	6.7	6.5																
2–69	6.8	6.7	6.9	6.9														
3–69	6.9	6.8	7.0	7.0	7.1	7.2												
4–69	7.0	6.9	7.1	7.1	7.3	7.2	7.5	7.3										
1–70	7.2	7.0	7.3	7.1	7.5	7.3	7.7	7.3	7.9	7.3								
2–70	7.4	7.0	7.5	7.1	7.6	7.3	7.8	7.4	8.0	7.4	8.1	7.5						
3–70	7.5	7.0	7.6	7.2	7.8	7.3	7.9	7.4	8.1	7.4	8.2	7.6	8.2	7.8				
4–70	7.5	7.1	7.7	7.2	7.8	7.3	7.9	7.4	8.0	7.5	8.1	7.6	8.1	7.8	7.9	7.9		
1–71	7.5	7.1	7.6	7.2	7.7	7.3	7.8	7.5	7.9	7.5	7.9	7.7	7.8	7.8	7.6	7.9	7.2	7.9
2–71	7.5	7.1	7.6	7.2	7.7	7.3	7.8	7.5	7.8	7.5	7.8	7.7	7.7	7.8	7.5	7.9	7.3	7.8
3–71	7.5	7.1	7.6	7.2	7.7	7.4	7.7	7.5	7.8	7.5	7.8	7.7	7.7	7.8	7.5	7.9	7.4	7.8
4–71	7.5	7.1	7.6	7.3	7.6	7.4	7.7	7.6	7.7	7.6	7.7	7.8	7.6	7.9	7.5	8.0	7.4	7.9
1–72	7.5	7.2	7.5	7.3	7.6	7.4	7.6	7.6	7.7	7.6	7.6	7.8	7.6	7.9	7.4	8.0	7.4	7.9
2–72	7.5	7.2	7.5	7.3	7.6	7.4	7.6	7.6	7.6	7.6	7.6	7.8	7.5	7.9	7.4	7.9	7.3	7.9
3–72	7.4	7.2	7.5	7.2	7.5	7.4	7.6	7.6	7.6	7.6	7.6	7.8	7.5	7.8	7.4	7.9	7.3	7.8
4–72	7.4	7.1	7.5	7.2	7.5	7.4	7.5	7.6	7.5	7.5	7.5	7.7	7.5	7.8	7.4	7.8	7.3	7.7
1–73	7.4	7.1	7.5	7.2	7.5	7.4	7.5	7.6	7.5	7.5	7.5	7.7	7.4	7.7	7.4	7.8	7.3	7.7
2–73	7.4	7.1	7.4	7.2	7.5	7.4	7.5	7.5	7.5	7.5	7.5	7.7	7.4	7.7	7.3	7.7	7.3	7.6
3–73*p*	7.4	7.1	7.4	7.2	7.5	7.3	7.5	7.5	7.5	7.5	7.5	7.6	7.4	7.6	7.4	7.6	7.3	7.5

* Projections in each column are based on regressions using actual data through the period and high-employment expenditures. The figures in each column are averages of the rates

p–3–73 actual is preliminary.

Given the construction of the model, output projections are residually determined and thus reflect fully errors in the projections of total spending and prices.

Unemployment. Projections of unemployment display the property of greater accuracy over short periods than for long periods (Table 5). Relevant to the assessment of the model's performance in connection with unemployment is that the period contained a recession followed by a slow recovery. As a result, a tendency to underestimate the rise in unemployment during recession shows up as a continuing error on an average basis as long as the unemployment rate does not quickly return to its pre-recession level. The estimates for unemployment reflect the learning characteristics of the price equation; that is, the price equation is important because it is the key factor in determining how much total spending is reflected in real output growth, which is the chief determinant of

5

COMPARED WITH ACTUAL

RATE

quarter to Terminal Quarter)

QUARTER

2-71		3-71		4-71		1-72		2-72		3-72		4-72		1-73		2-73		3-73	
Act.	Proj.	Act.	Proj.	Act.	Proj.	Act.	Proj.	Act.	Proj.	Act.	Proj.	Act.	Proj.	Act.	Proj.	Act.	Proj.	Act.	Proj.
5.9	5.7																		
5.9	5.7	6.0	5.8																
5.9	5.6	6.0	5.7	6.0	5.9														
5.9	5.6	5.9	5.7	5.9	5.9	5.9	5.7												
5.9	5.6	5.9	5.8	5.8	5.9	5.8	5.7	5.7	5.7										
5.8	5.7	5.8	5.8	5.8	6.0	5.7	5.7	5.6	5.7	5.6	5.3								
5.7	5.7	5.7	5.8	5.7	6.0	5.6	5.8	5.5	5.8	5.4	5.4	5.3	5.2						
5.7	5.7	5.6	5.9	5.6	6.0	5.5	5.7	5.4	5.7	5.3	5.3	5.2	5.1	5.0	4.9				
5.6	5.7	5.5	5.9	5.5	6.0	5.4	5.7	5.3	5.7	5.2	5.3	5.1	5.0	5.0	4.9	4.9	4.6		
5.5	5.7	5.5	5.9	5.4	6.0	5.3	5.7	5.2	5.7	5.1	5.2	5.0	5.0	4.9	4.8	4.9	4.6	4.8	4.7

preceding the quarter heading each column, assuming subsequent actual changes in money from the initial quarter to the terminal quarter inclusive.

actual experience did not depart substantially from what the model projected. From second quarter 1971 to third quarter 1973 the model projected a 4.6 percent average annual rate compared to the actual increase of 4.1 percent. And it could be that the general price level has not yet fully adjusted to a level consistent with the long-run trend of monetary growth.

Output. Given the nature of the price equation, that is, a long lag on past price change and a sticky response to changes in aggregate demand, projections of output tend to mirror projections of total spending. Table 4 indicates that on a quarter-to-quarter basis the pattern of error for output is essentially the same as for total spending–overestimating in the early part of the period and underestimating in the later part.

Over the full period, there are some differences. In particular, for the period as a whole output was overestimated while total spending was underestimated.

6

COMPARED WITH ACTUAL

AAA RATE

Quarter to Terminal Quarter)

QUARTER

2-71		3-71		4-71		1-72		2-72		3-72		4-72		1-73		2-73		3-73	
Act.	Proj.	Act.	Proj.	Act.	Proj.	Act.	Proj.	Act.	Proj.	Act.	Proj.	Act.	Proj.	Act.	Proj.	Act.	Proj.	Act.	Proj.
7.5	7.8																		
7.5	7.9	7.6	7.9																
7.4	8.0	7.4	8.0	7.3	7.9														
7.4	8.0	7.4	8.0	7.3	7.8	7.2	7.5												
7.4	7.9	7.3	7.9	7.3	7.6	7.3	7.3	7.3	7.2										
7.3	7.9	7.3	7.8	7.3	7.5	7.2	7.2	7.2	7.1	7.2	7.0								
7.3	7.8	7.3	7.7	7.2	7.4	7.2	7.1	7.2	7.0	7.2	7.0	7.1	6.9						
7.3	7.8	7.3	7.6	7.2	7.3	7.2	7.0	7.2	7.0	7.2	6.9	7.2	6.8	7.2	6.9				
7.3	7.7	7.3	7.6	7.2	7.2	7.2	6.9	7.2	6.9	7.2	6.8	7.2	6.7	7.3	6.7	7.3	6.7		
7.3	7.6	7.3	7.5	7.3	7.1	7.3	6.8	7.3	6.8	7.3	6.7	7.3	6.6	7.4	6.6	7.4	6.7	7.6	6.7

preceding the quarter heading each column, assuming subsequent actual changes in money from the initial quarter to the terminal quarter inclusive.

unemployment.

Interest rates. Interest rate projections are especially difficult to interpret as a part of full model simulations because they represent the end of the recursive chain, though this could mean that offsetting errors in the arguments can work to provide an accurate projection on average. Accuracy on average seems to be the case for interest rates in the model (Tables 6 and 7). Projections of the average commercial paper rate for the full period are in error by .4 of a percentage point. Projections of the corporate bond rate are even closer, showing an error of .3 of a percentage point for the full period.

Summary. Table 8 gives the mean absolute error for each of the diagonals in Tables 2–7. The mean absolute errors are not adjusted for the number of differences used in the calculation, yet the inverse relationship between the number of observations and the number of the diagonal is relevant for inter-

TABLE

ST. LOUIS MODEL PROJECTIONS*

COMMERCIAL

(Average Level from Initial

INITIAL

	1-69		2-69		3-69		4-69		1-70		2-70		3-70		4-70		1-71	
Terminal quarter	Act.	Proj.	Act.	Proj.	Act.	Proj.	Act.	Proj.	Act.	Proj.	Act.	Proj.	Act.	Proj.	Act.	Proj.	Act.	Proj.
1-69	6.7	5.7																
2-69	7.1	5.9	7.5	6.3														
3-69	7.6	6.2	8.0	6.6	8.5	7.0												
4-69	7.8	6.4	8.2	6.7	8.6	7.1	8.6	7.6										
1-70	8.0	6.4	8.3	6.7	8.6	7.1	8.6	7.5	8.6	7.4								
2-70	8.0	6.4	8.3	6.7	8.5	7.0	8.4	7.4	8.4	7.2	8.2	7.2						
3-70	8.0	6.4	8.2	6.6	8.3	7.0	8.2	7.4	8.2	7.3	8.0	7.3	7.8	7.5				
4-70	7.8	6.4	7.9	6.6	8.0	6.9	7.9	7.3	7.7	7.2	7.4	7.3	7.1	7.4	6.3	7.5		
1-71	7.4	6.3	7.5	6.5	7.5	6.8	7.3	7.2	7.1	7.2	6.7	7.2	6.2	7.3	5.4	7.3	4.6	6.5
2-71	7.2	6.2	7.2	6.4	7.2	6.7	7.0	7.1	6.7	7.0	6.4	7.0	5.9	7.0	5.3	6.9	4.8	6.1
3-71	7.0	6.2	7.1	6.4	7.0	6.7	6.9	7.1	6.6	6.9	6.3	7.0	5.9	7.0	5.4	6.9	5.1	6.1
4-71	6.9	6.2	6.9	6.4	6.8	6.7	6.7	7.1	6.4	7.0	6.1	7.1	5.8	7.1	5.3	7.0	5.1	6.3
1-72	6.7	6.2	6.7	6.4	6.6	6.7	6.4	7.1	6.2	7.0	5.9	7.1	5.5	7.0	5.1	6.9	4.9	6.3
2-72	6.5	6.2	6.5	6.4	6.4	6.6	6.2	7.0	6.0	6.9	5.7	6.9	5.4	6.9	5.1	6.8	4.8	6.1
3-72	6.4	6.2	6.4	6.3	6.3	6.6	6.1	6.9	5.9	6.8	5.6	6.8	5.3	6.7	5.0	6.8	4.9	5.9
4-72	6.3	6.2	6.3	6.3	6.2	6.5	6.1	6.9	5.8	6.7	5.6	6.8	5.3	6.6	5.1	6.5	4.9	5.9
1-73	6.3	6.2	6.3	6.4	6.2	6.6	6.1	6.9	5.9	6.7	5.7	6.7	5.4	6.6	5.2	6.5	5.1	5.9
2-73	6.4	6.2	6.4	6.4	6.3	6.5	6.2	6.8	6.0	6.7	5.8	6.7	5.6	6.6	5.4	6.5	5.3	5.8
3-73*p*	6.6	6.2	6.6	6.4	6.5	6.5	6.4	6.8	6.3	6.6	6.1	6.6	5.9	6.5	5.8	6.4	5.7	5.8

* Projections in each column are based on regressions using actual data through the period and high-employment expenditures. The figures in each column are averages of the rates *p*—3-73 actual is preliminary.

preting Table 8. The calculation of mean absolute error for the main diagonal is based on 19 observations whereas the 19th diagonal represents only one observation. In other words, there are 19 one-quarter-ahead projections and one 19-quarters-ahead projection.

For the variables which are projected in rate of change form (nominal GNP, GNP deflator, and real GNP), the mean absolute error declines sharply as you initially move to higher numbered diagonals. But the extent of decline for these rate of change variables tends to fall off after the 3rd or 4th diagonal. Even though the mean absolute error reaches a minimum along the 15th to 17th diagonal, this result does not imply that 15 to 17 quarters ahead represents the optimal projection horizon. These results are based only on this particular sequence of economic events. Repeated experiments would be required to shed light on the best projection horizon. What seems to be clear with respect to the

7

COMPARED WITH ACTUAL

PAPER RATE

Quarter to Terminal Quarter)

QUARTER

2–71	3–71	4–71	1–72	2–72	3–72	4–72	1–73	2–73	3–73
Act. Proj.	Act. Proj.	Act. Proj.	Act. Proj.	Act. Proj.	Act. Proj.	Act. Proj.	Act. Proj.	Act. Proj.	Act. Proj.
5.0 5.9									
5.4 6.3	5.7 6.3								
5.3 6.6	5.4 6.6	5.1 6.6							
5.0 6.5	5.0 6.5	4.6 6.2	4.1 5.5						
4.9 6.4	4.9 6.2	4.6 5.8	4.3 5.2	4.6 5.0					
4.9 6.3	4.9 6.1	4.7 5.5	4.5 5.0	4.8 4.9	4.9 5.0				
5.0 6.3	5.0 6.0	4.8 5.4	4.7 5.0	4.9 5.0	5.1 5.1	5.3 5.3			
5.1 6.3	5.1 6.0	5.0 5.5	5.0 5.0	5.3 5.1	5.5 5.3	5.8 5.5	6.3 5.8		
5.4 6.3	5.4 6.0	5.4 5.4	5.4 5.0	5.7 5.1	6.0 5.3	6.4 5.4	6.9 5.6	7.5 7.5	
5.8 6.3	5.9 6.0	5.9 5.4	6.1 5.0	6.4 5.1	6.8 5.3	7.2 5.5	7.9 5.6	8.7 7.5	9.9 6.4

preceding the quarter heading each column, assuming subsequent actual changes in money from the initial quarter to the terminal quarter inclusive.

rate of change variables is that projections several quarters ahead are more reliable than those only one or two quarters ahead. Smoothing the data on rates of change brings them in line with the averaging process implicit in ordinary least squares regression techniques.

Mean absolute errors calculated for variables expressed in level form (unemployment and interest rates) show a substantially different pattern as you move to higher numbered diagonals. These results suggest that projection errors for "level" variables cannot be interpreted in the same way as those for rate of change variables. In the case of the unemployment rate, the minimum mean absolute error for this period was along the fourth diagonal, though this error was essentially unchanged for the first five diagonals. In the case of interest rates, the error was essentially unchanged for the first six or seven diagonals and then declined to a minimum along the 15th to 17th diagonal.

TABLE 8

MEAN ABSOLUTE ERROR

(Average Absolute Difference of Percents in Tables 2–7)

Diagonal	Nominal GNP	GNP Price Deflator	Real GNP	Unemployment Rate	Commercial Paper Rate	Corporate AAA Rate
Main	2.85	1.46	2.49	.21	1.01	.35
2nd	2.37	1.23	1.77	.20	1.01	.36
3rd	1.89	1.12	1.55	.19	1.07	.35
4th	1.54	.91	1.61	.18	1.04	.35
5th	1.47	.89	1.63	.19	1.03	.37
6th	1.40	.90	1.61	.23	1.03	.39
7th	1.27	.89	1.52	.28	.96	.36
8th	1.11	.83	1.53	.32	.94	.33
9th	.93	.76	1.43	.34	.84	.29
10th	.92	.66	1.34	.32	.82	.25
11th	.93	.54	1.20	.37	.74	.22
12th	.75	.53	.99	.35	.69	.19
13th	.61	.50	.87	.43	.57	.16
14th	.43	.40	.68	.45	.45	.15
15th	.26	.22	.48	.48	.30	.12
16th	.20	.18	.28	.55	.27	.18
17th	.23	.30	.20	.63	.03	.23
18th	.30	.45	.30	.70	.20	.25
19th	.40	.60	.30	.70	.40	.30

Conclusions regarding these calculations of mean absolute error for the St. Louis model are mixed. The characteristics of the time series of each variable, as well as the distinction between levels and rates of change, have to be considered in an attempt to judge what horizon is appropriate for the model. Each variable requires analysis both in isolation and in the broader context of the model as a whole.

3.2. A checklist of successes and failures. These calculations for the St. Louis model indicate that projections have to be carefully interpreted. Since the model was not formulated primarily as a forecasting device, it should not be judged solely on this basis. Yet, significant departures from experience raise questions about the validity of the model's application for whatever purposes it was designed. In this general spirit, the model is evaluated in a judgmental fashion, giving emphasis on its possible influence on economic thinking and its possible role in the formulation of stabilization policy. The listing is in terms of successes and failures, but it should be emphasized that this checklist is highly subjective in character.

Successes. With respect to "successes," there is no way of knowing whether these developments would have occurred in the absence of the formulation of the St. Louis model. So the following list is more representative of consistencies with trends in economic thinking than of definite contributions to those trends.

(1) Demonstrated short-run vs. long-run effects of stabilization policy.

The St. Louis model yielded short-run properties which differed substantially from its long-run properties. These varying properties are reflected mainly in the short-run vs. long-run response of real product, prices, unemployment and interest rates.

(2) Demonstrated the importance of monetary actions in determination of movements in economic activity.

(i) The reduced form approach to estimating the impact of monetary actions provoked consideration of the limitations of standard models which, until quite recently, restricted the channel of monetary influence to interest rates. Some standard models have moved more recently in the direction of including real balance effects in spending functions.

(ii) The direct approach to estimating the impact of monetary actions has been associated with a change in thinking about the quickness of response of GNP. Until recently the estimated lag in the effect of monetary actions was very long, reflecting in part the restriction of channels of influence to interest rates.

(3) Demonstrated indirectly the role of costs of information in stabilization analysis.

The results of the St. Louis model were consistent with the notion that changes in total demand are reflected initially in real product and only later in prices. The model traces the process whereby there is a short-run trade-off between inflation and unemployment which vanishes in the long-run. These results are consistent with the developing literature on costs of information and search.

(4) Called attention to an alternative framework of analysis.

Prior to 1968 there were virtually no empirically estimated alternatives to the econometric model constructed on a Keynesian foundation. With a substantially different framework of analysis, many of the conventional results relating to the impact of policy actions were differently analyzed.

(5) Demonstrated the usefulness of small models in capturing the aggregative impact of stabilization actions.

Prior to 1968 the trend was toward greater sectoral detail in econometric model building. Now there is a question in the minds of some people whether it is necessary to build a large model with allocative detail in order to gain some notion about the general course of economic developments.

Failures. Similarly, the "failures," or short-comings of the model can be assessed in a subjective manner.

(1) Failed to educate policymakers on the long-run effects of their short-run decisions.

One of the purposes of the model, given its properties of varying effects for the short-run compared to the long-run, was to show the longer-run consequences of short-run actions. The recent experience of the U.S. economy with recession, inflation and experiments with price controls serves as ample evidence indicating that the model has failed in this objective.

(2) Failed to capture short-run movements in velocity.

One of the shortcomings of the model, as indicated in Table 2, is that short-run movements in velocity are not successfully captured by the model. This remains an area of further research.

(3) Failed to shed light on price developments during periods of governmental controls and worldwide inflation.

The St. Louis model was in no way able to predict the actions of the Cost of Living Council during the period of controls beginning in third quarter 1971. Similarly, there are exogenous factors which affect economic activity in the short-run, and the model is limited in the information it can provide on the consequences of these factors.

(4) Failed to cope successfully with large variations in government spending and in the money stock and to anticipate revisions in the money stock data.

With the monetary and fiscal variables fundamental in their role for the model, any variation beyond historical experience or revisions in the data can give rise to large errors in the short-run. It is this inability to anticipate variations in monetary growth or revisions in the data which accounts for the procedure of giving model projections in terms of assumed steady growth rates of money. Since such steady growth rates are seldom, if ever, realized, projections of the model based on this assumption should not be interpreted as forecasts in the same sense as in other models.[11]

4. CONCLUSIONS AND FUTURE RESEARCH

The course of action for the St. Louis model is indicated by the list of failures. Some considerations are beyond the purview of the model, but such a list serves as a set of guidelines. For example, the problem of velocity as well as the timing of economic response to monetary and fiscal actions are continuing topics of study at the Federal Reserve Bank of St. Louis.[12]

Another direction expected for research relating to the model is toward the formulation and testing of hypotheses. Propositions have been developed and tested relating to magnitude and timing of the impact of monetary and fiscal actions, but little has been done on testing propositions relating to the *modus operandi* of monetary and fiscal actions.[13] Development of results along these

[11] For a full discussion and interpretation of the sources of projection error in the St. Louis model, see [3] and [**10**].

[12] See [7].

[13] For further discussion, see [**11**].

theoretical lines would help in clarifying an understanding of the foundations of the monetarist propositions, which, in turn, would provide a firmer foundation for policy formulation.

Federal Reserve Bank of St. Louis

APPENDIX

Estimated Equations of the St. Louis Model*

I. Total Spending Equation

A. Sample period: I/1953 – IV/1968 — $R^2 = .632$

$\Delta Y_t = 2.30 + 5.35\,\Delta M_{t-i} + .05\,\Delta E_{t-i}$ — S.E. = 3.948

(2.69) (6.69) (.15) — D–W = 1.741

B. Sample period: I/1953 – II/1973 — $R^2 = .683$

$\Delta Y_t = 1.52 + 5.30\,\Delta M_{t-i} + .54\,\Delta E_{t-i}$ — S.E. = 5.169

(1.59) (8.10) (1.36) — D–W = 1.894

II. Price Equation

A. Sample period: I/1955 – IV/1968 — $R^2 = .788$

$\Delta P_t = 2.95 + .09\,D_{t-i} + .73\,\Delta P_t^A$ — S.E. = 1.072

(6.60) (9.18) (5.01) — D.E. = 1.415

B. Sample period: I/1955 – II/1973 — $R^2 = .748$

$\Delta P_t = 2.46 + .09\,D_{t-i} + .96\,\Delta P_t^A$ — S.E. = 2.350

(5.03) (6.00) (12.92) — D–W = 1.408

III. Unemployment Rate Equation

A. Sample period: I/1955 – IV/1968 — $R^2 = .915$

$U_t = 3.94 + .06\,G_t + .26\,G_{t-i}$ — S.E. = .307

(67.42) (1.33) (6.15) — D.W. = .596

B. Sample period: I/1955 – II/1973 — $R^2 = .918$

$U_t = 3.90 + .04\,G_t + .29\,G_{t-i}$ — S.E. = .293

(77.00) (1.00) (8.20) — D–W = .647

IV. Long-Term Interest Rate

* Constraints and lag structures correspond to those set forth in the original article discussing the St. Louis model. See Andersen and Carlson, [**4**]. Coefficient values on lagged variables (subscripted "$t-i$") are sums of the coefficients for current and lagged quarters. Figures enclosed by parentheses under the coefficients are "t" statistics.

A. Sample period: I/1955 – IV/1968 $R^2 = .854$

$R_t^L = 1.28 - .05\dot{M}_t + 1.39\,Z_t + .20\dot{X}_{t-i} + .97\dot{P}/(U/4)_{t-i}$ S.E. = .306

(4.63)(−2.40) (8.22) (2.55) (11.96) D-W = .564

B. Sample period: I/1955 – II/1973 $R^2 = .954$

$R_t^L = 1.44 - .04\dot{M}_t + 1.50\,Z_t + .12\dot{X}_{t-i} + .99\dot{P}/(U/4)_{t-i}$ S.E. = .320

(5.46)(−2.11)(12.03) (1.67) (21.81) D-W = .652

V. Short-Term Interest Rate Equation

A. Sample period: I/1955 – IV/1968 $R^2 = .839$

$R_t^S = -.84 - .11\dot{M}_t + .50\,Z_t + .75\dot{X}_{t-i} + 1.06\dot{P}/(U/4)_{t-i}$ S.E. = .443

(−2.43)(−3.72)(2.78) (9.28) (12.24) D-W = .593

B. Sample period: I/1955 – II/1973 $R^2 = .827$

$R_t^S = -.44 - .12\dot{M}_t + .89\,Z_t + .54\dot{X}_{t-i} + 1.16\dot{P}/(U/4)_{t-i}$ S.E. = .679

(−1.02)(−3.23)(3.66) (5.18) (13.23) D-W = .495

Symbols are defined as:

ΔY = dollar change in total spending (GNP in current prices)
ΔM = dollar change in money stock
ΔE = dollar change in high-employment federal expenditures
ΔP = dollar change in total spending (GNP in current prices) due to price change
$D = Y - (X^F - X)$
X^F = potential output
X = output (GNP in 1958 prices)
ΔP^A = anticipated price change (scaled in dollar units)
U = unemployment as a percent of labor force
$G = ((X^F - X)/X^F) \cdot 100$
R^L = Moody's seasoned corporate AAA bond rate
$\dot{M}$ = annual rate of change in money stock
Z = dummy variable (0 for I/1955 – IV/1960) and (1 for I/1961 – end of regression period)
$\dot{X}$ = annual rate of change in output (GNP in 1958 prices)
$\dot{P}$ = annual rate of change in GNP price deflator (1958 = 100)
$U/4$ = index of unemployment as a percent of labor force (base = 4.0)
R^S = four- to six-month prime commercial paper rate.

References

[1] Andersen, L., "A Monetarist View of Demand Management: The United States Experience," Federal Reserve Bank of St. Louis *Review*, LIII (September, 1971), 3–11.

[2] ———, "Properties of a Monetarist Model for Economic Stabilization," in Proceedings of the First Konstanzer Seminar, *Kredit und Kapital*, Beiheft 1 (1972).

[3] ———, "The St. Louis Model Revisited," Paper given at the Economic Outlook at Midyear Conference of the Chicago Chapter of the American Statistical Association, Chicago, Illinois (June 7, 1973).

[4] ——— AND K. CARLSON, "A Monetarist Model for Economic Stabilization," Federal Reserve Bank of St. Louis *Review*, LII (April, 1970), 7-25.

[5] ——— AND ———, "An Econometric Analysis of the Relation of Monetary Variables to the Behavior of Prices and Unemployment," in O. Eckstein, ed., *The Econometrics of Price Determination*, Conference sponsored by Board of Governors of the Federal Reserve System and Social Science Research Council, Washington, D. C. (October 30-31, 1970), 166-183.

[6] ——— AND J. JORDAN, "Monetary and Fiscal Actions: A Test of Their Relative Importance in Economic Stabilization," Federal Reserve Bank of St. Louis *Review*, L (November, 1968), 11-24.

[7] ——— AND D. KARNOSKY, "The Appropriate Time Frame for Controlling Monetary Aggregates: The St. Louis Evidence," in *Controlling Monetary Aggregates II: The Interpretation*, Conference sponsored by Federal Reserve Bank of Boston, Melvin Village, New Hampshire (September, 1972), 147-177.

[8] BAIRD, C., *Macroeconomics: An Integration of Monetary, Search, and Income Theories* (Chicago: Science Research Associates, 1973).

[9] BRUNNER, K., Review of B. Hickman, ed., *Econometric Models of Cyclical Behavior*, *Journal of Economic Literature*, XI (September, 1973), 927-933.

[10] CARLSON, K., "Projecting with the St. Louis Model: A Progress Report," Federal Reserve Bank of St. Louis *Review*, LIV (February, 1972), 20-27.

[11] ———, "Monetary and Fiscal Actions in Macroeconomic Models: Towards a Clarification of the Issues," Paper presented at the Fourth Annual Konstanzer Conference on Monetary Theory and Policy, Konstanz, West Germany (June, 1973).

[12] ECKSTEIN, O., "Instability in the Private and Public Sectors: Some Model Simulations," *Swedish Journal of Economics*, LXXV (March, 1973), 19-26.

[13] FRIEDMAN, M., *The Optimum Quantity of Money and Other Essays* (Chicago: Aldine Publishing Company, 1969).

[14] GORDON, R., "Discussion of Papers in Session II," in O. Eckstein, ed., *The Econometrics of Price Determination*, Conference sponsored by Board of Governors of the Federal Reserve System and Social Science Research Council, Washington, D. C. (October 30-31, 1970), 202-211.

[15] MCNEES, S., "A Comparison of the GNP Forecasting Accuracy of the Fair and St. Louis Econometric Models," Federal Reserve Bank of Boston, *New England Economic Review* (September/October, 1973), 29–34.

[16] OKUN, A., "Potential GNP: Its Measurement and Significance," *1962 Proceedings of the Business and Economic Statistics Section of the American Statistical Association*, 98-104.

[17] ———, "Fiscal-Monetary Activism: Some Analytical Issues," *Brookings Papers on Economic Activity*, 1 (1972), 123-163.

[18] PHELPS, E., *et al.*, *Microeconomic Foundations of Employment and Inflation Theory* (New York: W. W. Norton and Company, Inc., 1970).

[19] WARBURTON, C., *Depression, Inflation and Monetary Policies, Selected Papers 1945-53* (Baltimore: Johns Hopkins University Press, 1969).

4

A MONTHLY ECONOMETRIC MODEL OF THE U.S. ECONOMY

BY TA-CHUNG LIU AND ERH-CHENG HWA[1]

GIVEN THE LIMITED AVAILABILITY OF MONTHLY DATA, opinions may differ whether it is feasible to construct a monthly econometric model of the U.S. economy at the present time. There may also be different views regarding the method of constructing a monthly model on time series data. Few economists, however, would disagree with the desirability of having a monthly model if it could be constructed satisfactorily.[2]

The advantages of having a monthly econometric model are numerous. First, important government policy decisions have often been influenced by the latest change in monthly economic data. A more systematic and rigorous analysis of monthly data through the construction of a monthly econometric model would reduce the hazard in using monthly data in an *ad hoc* manner as is ususally done. Second, short term forecasts are likely to be more accurate if they are made on a monthly model than on equally good quarterly or annual models. If this is true, then a monthly model can contribute to policy formulation in a way in which quarterly and annual models cannot. Third, the application of the Cowles Foundation maximum likelihood simultaneous equation estimating procedures [**11**] or Theil's k-class estimators [**19**] to small samples is of uncertain merit, especially with regard to statistical efficiency.[3] The Cowles and k-class estimates of the regression coefficients in a system of simultaneous equations merely have the desirable property of consistency for large samples. In a monthly model, there would be much less simultaneity involved in the system of economic relationships than in quarterly or annual models so that the estimation of monthly recursive relationships by the ordinary least squares method would suffer little in inconsistency but would perhaps gain in efficiency.

Finally but perhaps more importantly, a recursive monthly model, compared to quarterly and annual models, may involve the least specification error concerning causal directions; and at the same time, it may not give rise to greater serial correlations in the disturbance terms than those involved in models of longer unit periods of observation. This point was argued strongly by one of the authors of the present paper, but it may not be shared by others.[4]

A test of the feasibility of constructing a monthly econometric model was

[1] The authors are grateful to the National Science Foundation for the support of this research.

[2] This is far from saying that the monthly model presented in this paper, estimated on the 1954–1971 sample, is satisfactory from all important points of view; in fact, it is not. As explained below, a revised but still preliminary version of the model, with the 1972 data added to the sample, has been estimated and the predictive capabilities are being analyzed.

[3] See, for instance, Christ [**2**], Klein [**10**], McCarthy [**14**], Nagar [**15**], Richardson [**17**], and Theil [**19**].

[4] See Section 1 of Liu [**12**], Engle and Liu [**4**], and also the discussion of serial correlations in the residuals of estimated equations involving distributed lag structures in Section 2 of this paper.

made by Liu [**12**] in 1969. The test was intended to throw light on the following questions. (1) Is it possible to generate all the monthly data necessary to build a monthly econometric model for the United States for making forecasts and policy recommendations? (2) On account of the inertia and continuity of almost all economic processes and activities, lagged magnitudes of the dependent variable are logically required to be included as explanatory variables for the current magnitude of the same variable in an economic relationship of a short unit period of observation, say, a monthly relationship. High serial correlations in practically all economic variables are plainly observable. Can *other* explanatory variables of theoretical relevance and importance still take on plausible and significant regression coefficients when they are included, together with the lagged magnitudes of the dependent variable itself, in an equation to explain a given variable? (3) Would not the serial correlation in the disturbance term of a monthly relationship be so high that, with lagged magnitudes of the dependent variable included as explanatory variables, consistent and efficient estimates of the regression coefficients in the relationship could not be obtained? The results obtained in [**12**] appear to give affirmative answers to the first two questions and tend to dispel our qualms about the third.

A second attempt was made by the authors in 1971 to estimate a monthly model, containing all major sectors of the economy, for the sample period 1954–1970; the predictive properties of this version, however, have not been analyzed. After data for 1971 became available, this model was re-estimated for the sample period 1954–1971; and some of its predictive properties have been reported in Fromm and Klein [**5**]. The present paper reports in some detail the structure and the characteristics of a revised and enlarged version of the model, constructed again on the data for 1954–71. The preliminary version of a still larger model has been estimated for the sample period 1954–72; but its predictive characteristics have not yet been analyzed. There are some interesting features in the *changes* in the regression coefficients as the sample period of the model lengthens from 1954–1970, through 1954–1971, to 1954–1972. Space limitation, however, precludes a presentation of the model for the three consecutive sample periods and of an analysis of the changes in the structural coefficients.

In addition to being more comprehensive in the coverage of the different sectors of the economy, the monthly model reported here represents an improvement over that in Liu [**12**] in two major aspects. The first has to do with the generation of certain monthly series. For the construction of a monthly model, the data that are lacking are mainly those for GNP and its components. The steps involved in obtaining these required monthly data are described in [**12**]. The same procedure is used in the present model except for the following improvement. Instead of the ordinary least squares method used in [**12**], the best linear unbiased method of deriving interpolation and extrapolation of time series by related series, developed by Chow and Lin [**1**], is used in generating the monthly data in the present model.

The second improvement lies in the technique used in estimating the recursive relationships. Since serial correlations exist in the disturbance terms, a two-stage method was used in [**12**] to make approximate corrections for the asymptotic biases of the estimated regression coefficients. This method admittedly falls short of consistency.[5] The computer program developed by Hendry [**6**], for estimating relations with lagged dependent variables and autoregressive errors, is used in constructing the model presented here. Under certain assumptions, Hendry's method produces maximum likelihood estimates of the regression coefficients and the serial correlation coefficients in the residuals simultaneously.

1. THE MODEL AND THE LAG STRUCTURES

The model presented here determines the current magnitudes of 100 dependent variables by a system of 100 equations. Fifty one of the relationships are stochastic, the others being identities or definitions. In addition, there are 31 other less important identities necessary to close the model. Thus, the model consists of 131 equations.

The equations and the definitions of symbols are presented in the Appendix. Space does not allow a full discussion of the theoretical considerations underlying the specification of the equations. The special features of the specification can best be presented by pointing out the major aspects in which the model differs from the latest published versions of the Wharton Mark III quarterly model [**14**] and of the quarterly model constructed by the Bureau of Economic Analysis (BEA) of the U.S. Department of Commerce [**7**] and [**8**].[6] The three models are of roughly comparable sizes.

After the major differences in the explanatory variables (other than the lagged dependent variables) included in this model and the two well known quarterly models are discussed, the simple lag structures used in the model are explained.

In estimating the stochastic equations presented in the Appendix, two decision rules are strictly followed. (a) After an equation is theoretically specified and estimated, the variables with economically implausible signs attached to their respective regression coefficients are dropped and the equations are re-estimated only once.[7] Since our equations are relatively simple, it has been our good fortune that the re-estimated equations no longer contain implausible signs for the regression coefficients of the remaining variables. (b) Those theoretically plausible and important variables, which have regression coefficients with the expected signs but are insignificant on conventional statistical standards, are retained. The sample period covers only eighteen years (1954–71). The use of seasonally adjusted monthly data does not increase the annual sample by twelve times or the quarterly sample by four times; the monthly sample used in this paper remains small. The statistical insignificance is likely due to the small size

[5] See, for instance, Christ [**2**], Dhrymes [**3**], Malinvaud [**13**] and Sargan [**18**].

[6] The other special features of the model have been mentioned: (a) it is a monthly model; (b) the equation system is practically diagonally recursive (see the Appendix); (c) the regression coefficients and the serial correlation coefficients are simultaneously and consistently estimated by the Hendry program [**6**].

[7] The only experimental fittings permitted have to do with the lengths of the moving averages involved in the distributed lag functions for investment goods. See footnote 10 below.

of the sample rather than the incorrect specification of the theoretical relationships.

1.1. *The structural equations.* The functions for consumers' expenditures on nondurable goods, services, automobiles, and other durable goods (equations (1) to (4) in the Appendix) are formulated on the basis of classical consumer demand theory. Apart from the lagged dependent variables, the explanatory variables are disposable personal income, initial liquid assets (representing a proxy for total wealth, if one so prefers), relative prices, and, in the case of durable goods, initial stocks. Initial liquid assets are found to be important in all equations except that for automobiles, whereas this variable is absent from the equations for nondurables and services in the BEA model and from that for nondurables in the Wharton model. The relative price variable is present in our model in all equations except that for nonauto consumers' durable goods; but it is absent also from the equations for nondurables and services in the BEA model and from the relationships for automobiles and services in the Wharton model.[8] The initial stock variables are either weak or absent in the equations for durable consumers' goods in all three models.

In both the BEA and the Wharton quarterly models, the functions for business fixed investment have not been disaggregated into those for plant and for equipment.[9] Yet these two important components of fixed investment behaved very differently indeed over the sample period. Separate functions are estimated for plant and for equipment (equations (5) and (6)) in our model along the neoclassical user cost approach developed by Jorgenson [**9**]. In addition, the ratio of unfilled orders to shipments is included as a proxy for capacity utilization; it turns out to be significant in the equation for equipment.

The specification of the nonfarm residential housing investment function is very similar in the Wharton and the Liu-Hwa model (equation (7)). The BEA model contains a fairly elaborate set of equations for the housing sector, but this set of equations has not been used in the BEA complete model simulations [**7**, (25)]; instead, a single equation explaining housing investment, similar to the Wharton and the Liu-Hwa model but with disposable personal income absent from the equation, replaces the elaborate set of equations in the simulations.

The BEA model disaggregated the inventory function into two relationships respectively for auto and nonauto, whereas the Wharton model separates manufacturing from nonmanufacturing in its inventory sector. Neither model, however, includes a variable representing the short term interest rate in real terms as the Liu-Hwa model does. In spite of its present statistical insignificance, this variable may be expected to play an increasingly important role in the future.

The specifications of the functions for manufacturers' new orders, shipments and unfilled orders are generally quite similar in the three models (equations

[8] The relative price variable, however, is present and very significant in the equation for durables except automobiles in the Wharton model.

[9] The Wharton Mark III model, however, disaggregated the fixed investment function into three separate functions respectively for manufacturing, the regulated industries, and the commercial sector.

(9)–(11) in the Liu-Hwa model).

The private manhours function (equation (12a)) is transformed from an estimated CES production function. While this function simulates well for short periods of time, errors accumulate more quickly in simulations for longer periods. However, a linear form of the function with employment as the dependent variable (equation (12b)) yields better results for longer period simulations. The ratio of gross private product to business capital serves as a proxy for capacity utilization in the weekly hours function (equation (14)). The supply of civilian labor force depends significantly upon the wage rate (equation (15)). These features appear different from their counterparts in the BEA and the Wharton models.

The specification of the equations in the relatively simple financial sector (equation (17)–(41)) is different from the BEA and the Wharton models mainly in the following aspects. First, currency, demand deposits, savings and time deposits, and savings and loan association shares are disaggregated into those held by household, business, and government in the Liu-Hwa model. Second, the influence of the rate of change of the consumer price level on household holdings of currency and demand deposits appears discernible even though it is statistically insignificant in the small sample used.

The functions for various types of income (equations (42)–(44)) and the equations for the several variables leading from GNP to disposable personal income (equations (45)–(65)) are straightforward.

The implicit price deflator for gross private product (equation (66)) depends upon private unit labor cost and the ratio of gross private product to private business capital (a proxy for capacity utilization), representing respectively the cost-push and the demand-pull influences on the general price level. Other price deflators hinge on the gpp deflator and the private wage rate (equations (67)–(76) and (78)). The manufacturers' wholesale price level depends upon the gpp deflator and the ratio of unfilled orders to shipments (equation (77)). Adjustment in the private wage rate (equation (79)) is determined by a modified Phillips curve relationship which, in addition to the rate of unemployment, includes changes in the consumer price level and corporate profits. The model is closed by a simple foreign trade sector (equations (85)–(89)). The identities and definitions (equations (90)–(131)) are self-explanatory.

1.2. *The distributed lag structures.* The lag structure used in the consumption functions is the same modified Koyck-Nerlove lag discussed in detail in Liu [**12**]. The investment functions are formulated on a "double" Koyck-Nerlove lag distribution on the ground that the investment process involves two steps: planning and the actual implementation of the plan. The capital stock desired at the end of a period is a simple Koyck-Nerlove distributed lag function of a vector of pertinent determining variables, denoted simply by x.

$$K_t(\text{planned}) = \frac{1-\theta}{1-\theta L} a' x_{t-1}$$

where L is the lag operator, θ is the geometrically declining ratio, and a is the vector of long-run propensities attached to x.

Planned investment in a given period is

$$I_t \text{ (planned gross)} = K_t - K_{t-1} + dK_{t-1}$$

where d is the rate of depreciation.

Investment actually put in place is then assumed to be another Koyck-Nerlove distributed lag function of planned investment as follows:

$$I_t \text{ (actual gross)} = b\frac{1-\gamma}{1-\gamma L}[(1-\theta)a'x_{t-1} - (1-\theta-d)K_{t-1}]^{**} + u_t$$

where the symbol double asterisks (**) indicates moving averages of various lengths[10] and u_t the disturbance term. It follows that

$$I_t \text{ (actual gross)} = b(1-\gamma)[(1-\theta)a'x_{t-1} - (1-\theta-d)K_{t-1}]^{**} + \gamma I_{t-1} + v_t$$

where

$$v_t = u_t - \gamma u_{t-1}\,.$$

Thus, the dependent investment variable lagged by one period appears in the investment functions in the model presented (see equations (5)–(8) in the Appendix). On the assumption that u_t is serially correlated as follows

$$\begin{aligned} u_t &= ru_{t-1} + e_t \\ E(e_t) = 0\,, \quad Ee_te_{t-s} &= \sigma^2\,, && \text{for } s = 0 \\ &= 0\,, && \text{for } s \neq 0\,. \end{aligned}$$

The covariance of v_t and v_{t-1} can be shown to be the following:

$$\begin{aligned} E(v_t, v_{t-1}) &= \frac{(r-\gamma)(1-r\gamma)}{1-r^2}\,\sigma^2 \\ &= 0 && \text{if } r = \gamma \\ &< 0 && \text{if } r < 0 \text{ or } 0 < r < \gamma\,. \end{aligned}$$

The covariance is small if γ is close to r.

A similar analysis of this covariance function was given in Liu [**12**] for the disturbance term of the simple Koyck-Nerlove distributed lag function. A large number of the first order serial correlation coefficients, estimated consistently by the Hendry computer program [**6**], turn out to be either insignificantly different from zero, or negative, or of small positive magnitudes. (See the magnitudes of the α's given in the Appendix.) This tends to indicate that the simple lag structures used in the model presented here may not be poor approximations to the true relationships. Space limitation does not permit further analysis of the mean lags and other properties of the estimated distributed lag functions.

[10] It was found that for the investment functions for plant, equipment and residential housing moving averages of twelve months yield sharper estimates for the regression coefficients than those of other lengths of time. This is a welcome result, as the use of twelve month moving averages avoids certain pitfalls in the use of seasonally adjusted data. See Nerlove [**16**].

2. THE PREDICTIVE PERFORMANCE OF THE MODEL

The predictive capabilities of an econometric model can be summarized by the root mean square error (*RMSE*) represented by the following formula:

$$RMSE = \sqrt{\frac{1}{T}\sum_{t}(F_t - A_t)^2}$$

where F_t and A_t are respectively the predicted and the actual values of the i-th observation and T the number of observations.

Since the different variables have very different magnitudes, the ratios of the *RMSE*'s to the sample means of the different variables are better indicators of the prediction errors than the *RMSE*'s. In addition, it is well known that the mean square error (*MSE*) can be decomposed into a bias component $(\bar{F} - \bar{A})$ and a variance component[11] as follows:

$$MSE = (\bar{F} - \bar{A})^2 + S^2_{F-A}\,.$$

If the *MSE* of a variable has a large and significant bias component, it would be a justifiable procedure to correct the outside-sample period predictions of that variable by the estimated bias during the sample period.

The Seminar on Econometric Model Comparisons, under the leadership of Lawrence R. Klein and jointly sponsored by the National Science Foundation and the National Bureau of Economic Research, has made comparisons of the predictive properties of a number of U.S. models both within and outside the sample periods of the different models. (See Fromm and Klein [**5**]). The comparisons are made essentially on the basis of the root mean square errors. Since the different models have different sample periods, the within-sample period comparisons are made for a common period 1961–1967 inclusive. We have therefore computed the within-sample period error statistics of our model for a large number of predicted variables first for the two sub-sample periods 1961.01–1967.12 and 1968.01–1971.12, and then for the entire sample period as a whole.

The four statistics (the *RMSE*'s, the ratios of the *RMSE*'s to the sample means, the standard deviations and the biases) for the first sub-sample period 1961.01 to 1967.12 have been submitted to the NSF-NBER Seminar on Comparisons of Econometric models and will be analyzed with those of the other U.S. models in a paper by Fromm and Klein. Space limitation does not permit a complete presentation of these statistics for the second sub-sample period and those for the entire sample period (1954.01–1971.12).[12] However, from the error statistics, it is observed that two features well known to exist in other econometric models are also present in our model. First, the *RMSE*'s of some of the aggregates are less than the respective sums of the *RMSE*'s of the components. Thus, for consumption in constant 1958 prices, the *RMSE*'s for total consumption are respectively 4.34 and 4.58 for the two sub-sample periods 1961.01–1967.12 and 1968.01

[11] The variance of the error around the average, S^2_{F-A}.

[12] Some of the error statistics are compared with those of two quarterly models in Tables 1 and 2 below.

to 1971.12; whereas the respective sums of the *RMSE*'s of the components of total consumption are 6.42 and 6.78. There is therefore a tendency of errors to offset among components of some of the aggregates. Second, in general, the *RMSE*'s grow in magnitude as the prediction horizon lengthens. For within-sample period predictions, this is the result of the accumulation of the prediction errors of lagged endogenous variables which are used more extensively as the prediction horizon lengthens. It is important, however, to note that the tendency of the *RMSE*'s to increase with the prediction period is negligible or even absent in the predictions of the *changes* in GNP in current and constant dollars in our model.

In a large number of cases, biases account for significant portions of the *RMSE*'s in the sample period. They can therefore be used systematically to adjust the post-sample period predictions; such adjustments, however have not been done in the post-sample period predictions presented later.

It is difficult to evaluate the predictive capacities of any model, including the monthly model presented here, without a comparison with other models. Comparable data from other models are available only for the *RMSE*'s and for a small number of variables in Fromm and Klein [**5**] for the sub-sample period 1961–67. A rather interesting result emerges in that comparison: the monthly model ranks first among all models in predicting the *first differences* of GNP in both current and constant dollars. *First differences are short term changes.* The implication of this comparison is apparent; a monthly model may be the best among econometric models for the purpose of making short term predictions. To make short term forecasts is of course precisely one primary purpose of constructing a monthly model.

It is possible to make another comparison of the short run forecasting performance of the Liu-Hwa model with that of the recently published Wharton Mark III quarterly model for a larger number of variables than those included in Fromm and Klein [**5**]. In [**14**,(93)], the *RMSE*'s of the within-sample period predictions of a number of key variables in the Wharton model are calculated for prediction horizons of one to four quarters for the period 1960.I to 1970.I.[13] We have computed similar *RMSE*'s for prediction horizons of one to eight months for the entire sample period of our model, 1954.01 to 1971.12. In Table 1, the Wharton *RMSE*'s of a number of variables for one-quarter prediction horizons are compared with our three-month *RMSE*'s and the averages of one-, two- and three-month *RMSE*'s. Similarly, the Wharton *RMSE*'s for two-quarter prediction horizons are compared with our six-month *RMSE*'s and the averages of four-, five- and six-month *RMSE*'s. Table 1 shows that there are comparative advantages for the Wharton Mark III quarterly model for the short term predictions of the implicit price deflator, the unemployment rate,[14] compensation

[13] For the computation of the RMSE's for overlapping intervals of a given prediction horizon, see Hirsh [7, (25)] and several papers on simulation studies in the two volume set edited by Hickman cited in [**4**].

[14] It should be noted that the civilian labor force is exogenous in the Wharton Mark III complete model simulations; whereas it is endogenous in the Liu-Hwa simulations.

of employees, and consumption expenditure on automobiles in 1958 dollars. On the other hand, the monthly model has scored better for GNP in current and constant dollars, total consumption expenditures, nonfarm residential investment, plant and equipment investment, corporate profits, Moody's average domestic yield, and the 4–6 month commercial paper rate.

There is some evidences, therefore, that a monthly model may have advantages in short term forecasting. It is rather surprising that a monthly model may also be more accurate in making longer run predictions. The following comparison is an indication of this possibility. The Bureau of Economic Analysis of the U.S. Department of Commerce has released the current version of its quarterly model [**8**] and has analyzed its predictive properties [**7**]. In [**7**], Hirsch has published the root mean square errors of a larger number of variables for a part

TABLE 1

A COMPARISON OF THE ROOT MEAN SQUARE ERRORS OF CERTAIN SHORT TERM FORECASTS FROM THE WHARTON MARK III QUARTERLY MODEL AND THE LIU-HWA MONTHLY MODEL

	Wharton Quarterly Mark III (1960.I–1970.I) one quarter predictions	Liu-Hwa Monthly (1954.01–1971.12)	
		3-month predictions	average of 1–3 month predictions
GNP in current dollars	3.76	3.68	3.32
GNP in 1958 dollars	3.57	3.22	2.85
Consumption expenditures, 1958 dollars	2.14	1.96	1.84
Consumption of autos, 1958 dollars	1.10	1.30	1.18
Nonfarm residential investment 1958 dollars	1.42	0.55	0.44
Plant and equipment investment 1958 dollars	1.64	1.63	1.60
Implicit deflator for GNP, 1958 = 100	0.25	0.42	0.40
Unemployment rate in percent[1]	0.23	0.45	0.36
Compensation of employees billions of dollars	1.85	2.89	2.73
Corporate profits and inventory valuation adjustments, billions of dollars	3.04	2.48	2.20
Moody's average domestic yield in percent	0.14	0.14	0.11
4-6 month commercial paper rate in percent	0.35	0.32	0.27

Source: McCarthy [**14**, (93)].

[1] Civilian labor force is exogenous in the Wharton Mark III model simulations, but is endogenous in the Liu-Hwa model simulations.

(*Continued on next page*)

TABLE 1 (*Continued*)

	Wharton Quarterly Mark III (1960.I–1970.I) 2 quarter predictions	Liu-Hwa Monthly (1954.01–1971.12)	
		6-month predictions	Average of 4–6 month predictions
GNP in current dollars	5.30	4.47	4.25
GNP in 1958 dollars	4.50	3.91	3.83
Consumption expenditures, 1958 dollars	2.51	2.20	2.16
Consumption of autos, 1958 dollars	1.21	1.38	1.34
Nonfarm residential investment, 1958 dollars	1.44	0.75	0.71
Plant and equipment investment, 1958 dollars	1.80	1.75	1.72
Implicit deflator for GNP, 1958 = 100	0.39	0.52	0.48
Unemployment rate in percent[1]	0.39	0.67	0.59
Compensation of employees billions of dollars	3.01	3.47	3.36
Corporate profits and inventory valuation adjustments, billions of dollars	3.28	2.83	2.85
Moody's average domestic yield in percent	0.23	0.18	0.18
4–6 month commercial paper rate in percent	0.49	0.39	0.36

[1] Civilian labor force is exogenous in the Wharton Mark III model simulations, but is endogenous in the Liu-Hwa model simulations.

of the sample period of the BEA model from the first quarter of 1955 to the fourth quarter of 1968. However, Hirsch's prediction horizons cover only one to six quarters; he has not published the *RMSE*'s for the sample period of the BEA model as a whole. Our sample period is 1954.01 to 1971.12, longer by four years than that used by Hirsch in his calculations of *RMSE*'s. However, we have made calculations for the *RMSE*'s only for prediction horizons of one to eight months and for our sample period as a whole. In Table 2, the *RMSE*'s of the BEA model for its longest prediction horizon (six quarters) are compared with the corresponding *RMSE*'s of our model for a prediction horizon of the 18 years from 1954 to 1971 inclusive. The *RMSE*'s generally have a tendency to increase with the horizon of prediction. Moreover, the larger magnitudes of the variables during 1959–1971 are included in our sample but not in the BEA model; these large magnitudes perhaps tend to result in larger *RMSE*'s than the small magnitudes of the variables for the one year 1954, which magnitudes are in our calculation but not in that done by Hirsch. This comparison should tend, therefore, to show favorable results for the BEA model. Nevertheless, as shown

TABLE 2

A COMPARISON OF ROOT MEAN SQUARE ROOT ERRORS OF GNP AND ITS COMPONENTS IN THE BEA QUARTERLY AND THE LIU-HWA MONTHLY MODELS

	The BEA model	The Liu-Hwa Model
	Prediction Horizon	
	6-Quarters during 1955.I–1968.IV	Entire Sample Period 1954.01–1971.12
In Current Dollars		
GNP	13.65	11.64
Change in GNP	4.25	3.18
Personal consumption expenditures	7.10	6.02
Fixed nonresidential investment	4.50	3.02
Residential structures	1.72	2.95
Change in business inventories	3.74	4.45
In 1958 Dollars		
GNP	11.83	9.02
Change in GNP	*	2.91
Personal consumption expenditures	5.92	4.52
Automobile and parts	1.74	2.47
Nonauto durables	1.01	1.22
Nondurables	2.59	2.27
Nonhousing services	0.63	1.00**
Housing services	1.23	
Fixed nonresidential investment	4.02	2.27
Residential structures	1.46	2.14
Change in business inventories	3.60	4.58

Source: [**8**, (27)].
* Not reported.
** Not separated into housing and nonhousing.

in Table 2, our model stands up fairly well in a comparison of GNP and its components. Among 14 comparable variables, the monthly model yields smaller *RMSE*'s for 8 variables, including the aggregate variable GNP and its change, in spite of the factors discussed above in favor of the BEA model.

Post sample-period statistics on the *RMSE*'s, the ratios of the *RMSE*'s to the respective sample means, the standard deviations and the biases of prediction errors of a large number of variables have been computed for prediction horizons of one to eight months and for the twelve months of the entire post-sample year 1972. Space limitation, however, does not permit a full presentation of these statistics. These post-sample period error statistics are computed using the true magnitudes of the exogenous variables; therefore, they are not *ex ante* predictions in the more rigorous sense of the term. Moreover, the period (the twelve months of 1972) for which the post-sample period statistics have been computed is rather short. Since preliminary equations have been estimated for our model for the longer sample period 1954–1972, consideration of time and resource allocation dictates that we concentrate on the completion of the new model and the making of true *ex ante* forecasts from the new model rather than on further analysis of the model presented here. Nevertheless, these limited post-sample period forecasts indicate that the model constructed using the data for 1954–1971 predicts reasonably well for 1972. For instance, the ratios of the *RMSE*'s to sample means for GNP in current and constant dollars vary within a range from 0.35 to 1 percent. There is also somewhat less tendency for the errors to grow as the prediction horizon lengthens during 1972 than within the sample period 1954–1971. This is somewhat surprising, but it may be due to the short length of the post-sample period tested.

As an indication of the errors of post-sample period predictions relative to those within the sample period, the ratios of post-sample period and within-sample period calculations of the statistic *RMSE*/sample mean are computed for prediction horizons of one to eight months and for the sample period and the post-sample year 1972 as a whole. The results are presented in Table 3. These ratios compare favorably with similar results given in Table 3 in [**7**, (27)] for the BEA model. This favorable result for the monthly model may be due to the fact that the post-sample period in the BEA model (1969.I–1971.II) is 2.5 times as long as ours (1972.01–1972.12).

TABLE 3

POST-SAMPLE PERIOD (1972.01–1972.12) RATIOS OF *RMSE*'S TO SAMPLE MEANS COMPARED WITH THE CORRESPONDING RATIOS WITHIN THE SAMPLE PERIOD (1954.01–1971.12)

Unit: Ratios of Post-Sample Period Ratios to Within-Sample Period Ratios

Variables	Number of Predicted Periods								Entire Within-and Post-Sample Periods
	1	2	3	4	5	6	7	8	
GNP (billions of current $)	1.10	0.90	0.88	0.87	0.81	0.63	0.47	0.45	0.27
ΔGNP (change in GNP)	0.68	0.63	0.76	0.65	0.63	0.61	0.62	0.62	0.63
gnp (billions of 1958 $)	1.52	1.56	1.37	1.59	1.36	1.22	1.33	1.22	0.59
Δgnp (change in gnp)	0.76	0.74	0.71	0.78	0.79	0.68	0.76	0.74	0.50
c (Total consumption, billions of 1958 $)	1.46	1.22	1.19	0.98	1.00	1.40	1.00	1.10	0.74
bc + *eq* (Investment: plant and equipment, billions of 1958 $)	0.56	0.55	0.58	0.58	0.55	0.55	0.48	0.42	0.39

(*Continued on next page*)

TABLE 3 (*Continued*)

Variables	Number of Predicted Periods								Entire Within-and Post-Sample Periods
	1	2	3	4	5	6	7	8	
h (Investment: housing, billions of 1958 $)	1.08	1.17	1.08	1.26	0.97	1.04	0.85	0.96	0.46
v (Investment: inventory, billions of 1958 $)	2.10	2.06	2.25	2.21	2.12	2.06	2.19	2.16	1.64
rs (4-6 month commercial paper rate, %)	1.17	1.16	1.11	1.07	1.01	0.96	1.04	0.93	0.80
rL (Average corporate bonds yield, %)	0.58	0.62	0.63	0.77	0.63	0.81	0.89	0.59	0.59
CPIV (Corporate profits before tax, billions of current $)	2.31	1.83	1.27	1.58	1.35	1.12	1.31	1.15	0.78
MS (Money supply, billions of current $)	1.90	1.45	1.83	1.14	1.44	1.02	1.20	1.14	0.27
hr (Average weekly hours, manufacturing)	0.88	0.83	0.63	0.67	0.42	0.50	0.41	0.43	0.34
ur (Unemployment rate, %)	0.96	1.33	1.82	0.75	1.62	1.86	1.61	1.37	1.29
pgnp (GNP deflator, 1958 = 100)	1.09	1.31	1.08	1.22	1.18	1.11	1.22	1.02	0.38
W (Employee compensation, billions of current $)	0.80	0.71	0.82	0.60	0.55	0.55	0.45	0.46	0.20
WR (Private non-farm wage rate, $/hour)	0.86	0.86	1.01	0.94	0.76	0.91	1.03	0.85	0.36
YP (Personal income, billions of current $)	1.42	1.47	1.88	1.53	0.99	1.99	1.21	1.24	0.47

3. DYNAMIC MULTIPLIER ANALYSIS

For applications of econometric models to economic policy formulation, an analysis of the multipliers of important government instruments through time is of great reference value. Since our model is highly nonlinear, simulation studies are probably the only way to obtain information on multipliers for a sufficiently long period of time. Computer simulations of a monthly model are of course much more expensive than those of models of longer unit periods of observation. Up to this time, we have simulated the model for multiplier effects only for forty months. While some information is obtained through this exercise, it is clear that the cyclical properties of the model are not sufficiently revealed. The new model constructed using data from the longer sample period of 1954–72 will, in the future, be simulated for a period of 120 months for the purpose of multiplier analysis.

Multiplier simulations have been made for the following four important policy instruments: government expenditures, personal taxes, exports and nonborrowed reserves. The simulations are again made for the two sub-sample periods 1961–67 and 1968–71. While the entire sample period is so divided in order to supply to the NSF-NBER Seminar on Comparisons of Econometric Models the information required for the first sub-period for uniform comparison with other models, this division is also economically meaningful. The rate of unemployment was high (6.7 percent) and capacity utilization very low in 1961. The reverse is true in 1968; the rate of unemployment was then merely 3.6 percent. Thus, the two simulations yield information on the multipliers with opposite initial conditions. One would expect the multipliers to be greater during the first than the second sub-period.

Tables 4a and 5a present the effect of a sustained $1 billion increase in government expenditures on the economy for the two sub-sample periods. It is immediately observed that, as expected, the GNP multipliers in both current and constant prices are greater during 1961–67 than 1968–71. Within the forty month period simulated, the GNP multiplier in current dollars rises above two, even though the multiplier for the 1968–1971 period increases only at a decreasing rate toward the end of the simulation. On the other hand, the GNP multiplier in real tearms starts to decline from a peak of 1.69 in the twenty-fifth month during the first sub-sample period 1961–67; and it declines from a peak of 1.14 in the seventeenth month during the second sub-sample period 1968–71.[15] If the simulations had been carried further, the "perverse effect" described in Fromm and Klein [**5**, (393)] might indeed have occurred.[16] This possibility is supported by the multiplier effects on the unemployment rate given in Tables 4a and 5a. Increases in government expenditures reduce the unemployment rate; but during the 1961–67 sub-sample period the reduction in the unemployment rate starts to diminish, also starting with the 25th month, and during the 1968–1971 sub-sample period, the unemployment rate actually increased after the 25th month. This phenomenon suggests an explanation of the "perverse effect" pointed out but unexplained in Fromm and Klein [**5**]. Sustained increases in government expenditures could result in higher wage rates and, hence, would in time lead to less employment; and the increased rate of unemployment would also almost immediately reduce the demand for automobiles (see equation (3) in the Appendix) which constitutes an important sector of the economy. These

[15] While the second figure does not appear in Table 5a because not all monthly figures are included there, it can be inferred from the figures for the 15th and the 20th month.

[16] To quote Fromm and Klein [**5**, (393)] "Conventional textbook expositions generally depict real expenditure multipliers approaching positive asymptotes. In fact, most of the models here show such multipliers reaching a peak in two or three years and then declining thereafter in fluctuating paths. At the end of five to ten years, some of the models show that continued sustained fiscal stimulus has ever-increasing perverse impacts."

direct and indirect effects would be adverse to further increases in real output due to increases in government expenditures and in time might more than cancel the favorable effects of increases in government expenditures on GNP. Tables 4a and 5a also give a part of the distribution of the multiplier effects among the final demand categories.

The multipliers of a $1 billion decrease in personal taxes are presented in Tables 4b and 5b. The different initial conditions of the two sub-sample periods lead to even more conspicuous differences in their effects on the multipliers of reductions of personal taxes than in the case of increases in government expenditures. Starting with high unemployment and low capacity utilization in 1961, a reduction in personal taxes results in increases in GNP in real terms *more rapidly* than in money terms, whereas the reverse is true during the second sub-sample period which starts with low unemployment and high capacity utilization. The decline in the GNP multiplier in real terms is again observed during the second sub-sample period; in this case, it occurrs in the fortieth month. During the entire forty months simulated, the magnitudes of the multipliers of a sustained $1 billion reduction in personal taxes are smaller than those of a a sustained $1 billion increase in government expenditures. The multipliers of a sustained increase in exports (Tables 4c and 5c) are very similar to those of a sustained increase in government expenditures.

Tables 4d and 5d show that the stimulating effects of a $0.5 billion increase in non-borrowed reserves are very strong indeed. This may reflect the several important roles played by liquid assets, interest rates and the spread between the long and the short term rates of interest in the equations for the components of gross private product (see the Appendix).

4. CONCLUDING REMARKS

The monthly model presented here is probably the youngest among econometric models of similar sizes and hence has been subjected to only limited tests of its predictive performance. Nevertheless, it shows promise for short term forecasting. Analysis of the forecasting capacities of the model, with the sample period extended from 1954–1971 to 1954–1972, is underway. Monthly industrial sector models have been constructed for manufacturing (both durable and non-durable), chemicals, petroleum and coal, rubber and plastic products, primary metals, machinery, and transportation equipment. Similar sub-models will be developed for other industries. Tests will be made to see whether monthly changes in these disaggregated sectors can be predicted with reasonable accuracy.

The real test of the monthly model will come with repeated applications to ex ante forecasting. It will be interesting to see whether the ex ante forecasts to be obtained from the next version of this model, constructed on the data for the longer sample period 1954–1972, can perform as well as, or better than, the existing group of quarterly models that are used for regular forecasting exercises. There is often a large difference between ex ante and ex post forecast performance.

TABLE 4a

CHANGE IN SELECTED VARIABLES FOR $1.0 BILLION (IN CURRENT $) INCREASE IN GOVERMENT EXPENDITURES: SUB-SAMPLE PERIOD 1961.01–1967.12

No. of months after the action	*Δgnp* (GNP 58 $)	*ΔGNP* (Money GNP)	*Δur* (Un-employ ment rate %)	*Δc* (Con-sump-tion, 58 $)	*Δ(bc+eq)* (Invest-ment in plant & equip-ment, 58 $)	*Δv* (Non-farm inven-tory invest-ment, 58 $)	*Δrs* (4–6 month com-mercial paper rate)	*Δnei* (Bal-ance of trade, 58 $)	*ΔMS* (Money supply, current $)
1	0.39	0.41	−0.01	0.00	0.00	−0.55	0.00	0.00	0.00
2	0.55	0.57	−0.02	0.01	0.00	−0.39	0.00	−0.01	0.00
3	0.71	0.73	−0.03	0.03	0.01	−0.23	0.01	−0.03	0.00
4	0.87	0.88	−0.04	0.05	0.02	−0.08	0.01	−0.05	0.00
5	1.01	1.02	−0.05	0.07	0.03	0.04	0.01	−0.07	0.00
6	1.13	1.13	−0.06	0.09	0.04	0.14	0.00	−0.09	0.00
7	1.23	1.23	−0.07	0.12	0.05	0.22	0.00	−0.10	0.00
8	1.32	1.32	−0.08	0.14	0.07	0.28	0.00	−0.11	0.00
9	1.40	1.39	−0.08	0.16	0.09	0.33	0.00	−0.13	0.01
10	1.46	1.46	−0.09	0.18	0.11	0.36	0.00	−0.14	0.01
11	1.51	1.51	−0.10	0.20	0.13	0.38	0.00	−0.15	0.01
12	1.55	1.56	−0.10	0.22	0.16	0.38	0.00	−0.15	0.02
15	1.63	1.69	−0.11	0.28	0.23	0.36	0.01	−0.17	0.04
20	1.69	1.86	−0.12	0.36	0.31	0.27	0.01	−0.18	0.09
25	1.69	2.02	−0.12	0.46	0.35	0.19	0.01	−0.19	0.15
30	1.66	2.20	−0.10	0.54	0.37	0.13	0.02	−0.19	0.22
35	1.65	2.40	−0.08	0.62	0.37	0.08	0.02	−0.19	0.29
40	1.64	2.63	−0.04	0.70	0.37	0.06	0.02	−0.19	0.36

TABLE 4b

CHANGE IN SELECTED VARIABLES FOR $1.0 BILLION (IN CURRENT $) DECREASE IN PERSONAL TAXES: SUB-SAMPLE PERIOD 1961.01–1967.12

No. of months after the action	*Δgnp* (GNP 58 $)	*ΔGNP* (Money GNP)	*Δur* (Un-employ ment rate %)	*Δc* (Con-sump-tion, 58 $)	*Δ(bc+eq)* (Invest-ment in plant & equip-ment, 58 $)	*Δv* (Non-farm inven-tory invest-ment, 58 $)	*Δrs* (4–6 month com-mercial paper rate)	*Δnei* (Bal-ance of trade, 58 $)	*ΔMS* (Money supply, current $)
1	0.00	0.00	0.00	0.00	0.00	0.00	0.00	0.00	0.00
2	0.02	0.02	0.00	0.04	0.00	−0.02	0.00	0.00	0.00
3	0.06	0.05	0.00	0.11	0.00	−0.06	0.00	−0.01	0.00
4	0.11	0.10	0.00	0.20	0.00	−0.09	0.00	−0.01	0.00
5	0.18	0.16	−0.01	0.27	0.00	−0.09	0.00	−0.02	0.00
6	0.24	0·22	−0.01	0.32	0.00	−0.08	0.00	−0.05	0.00
7	0.31	0.28	−0.01	0.36	0.01	−0.05	0·00	−0.07	0.00
8	0·38	0.34	−0.02	0.40	0.01	−0.02	−0.01	−0.08	0.00
9	0.45	0.40	−0.02	0.44	0.02	0.01	−0.01	−0.10	0.00
10	0.52	0.46	−0.03	0.47	0.02	0.04	0.00	−0.11	0.00
11	0.58	0.51	−0.03	0.50	0.03	0.07	0.00	−0.12	0.00
12	0.65	0.57	−0.03	0.53	0.04	0.10	0.00	−0.13	0.00
15	0.81	0.70	−0.05	0.61	0.07	0.16	0.01	−0.16	0.00
20	1.01	0.86	−0.06	0.73	0.14	0.18	0.01	−0.18	0.01
25	1.16	0.97	−0.07	0.83	0.20	0.17	0.01	−0.18	0.03
30	1.26	1.06	−0.07	0.92	0.24	0.14	0.01	−0.18	0.05
35	1.34	1.14	−0.07	1.00	0.27	0.11	0.02	−0.18	0.07
40	1.42	1.21	−0.07	1.08	0.29	0.10	0.02	−0.18	0.10

TABLE 4c

CHANGE IN SELECTED VARIABLES FOR $1.0 BILLION (IN CURRENT $) INCREASE IN EXPORTS: SUB-SAMPLE PERIOD 1961.01–1967.12

No. of months after the action	Δgnp (GNP 58 $)	ΔGNP (Money GNP)	Δur (Un-employ ment rate %)	Δc (Con-sump-tion, 58 $)	$\Delta(bc+eq)$ (Invest-ment in plant & equiq-ment, 58 $)	Δv (Non-farm inven-tory invest-ment, 58 $)	Δrs (4–6 month com-mercial paper rate)	Δnei (Bal-ance of trade, 58 $)	ΔMS (Money supply, current $)
1	0.41	0.43	−0.01	0.00	0.00	−0.59	0.00	0.99	0.00
2	0.63	0.65	−0.02	0.01	0.00	−0.37	0.00	0.98	0.00
3	0.80	0.81	−0.03	0.03	0.01	−0.21	−0.01	0.96	0.00
4	0.93	0.94	−0.04	0.06	0.02	−0.10	−0.01	0.95	0.00
5	1.05	1.05	−0.05	0.08	0.03	0.07	−0.01	0.92	0.00
6	1.15	1.15	−0.06	0.10	0.04	0.08	0.00	0.91	0.00
7	1.24	1.23	−0.07	0.12	0.05	0.14	0.00	0.90	0.00
8	1.32	1.31	−0.08	0.15	0.07	0.20	0.00	0.88	0.01
9	1.39	1.38	−0.08	0.17	0.09	0.24	0.00	0.87	0.01
10	1.45	1.46	−0.09	0.19	0.10	0.27	0.00	0.87	0.02
11	1.51	1.52	−0.10	0.21	0.12	0.30	0.00	0.85	0.02
12	1.56	1.58	−0.10	0.23	0.14	0.31	0.01	0.85	0.03
15	1.68	1.74	−0.11	0.30	0.20	0.33	0.01	0.82	0.04
20	1.77	1.96	−0.13	0.40	0.27	0.30	0.01	0.82	0.08
25	1.77	2.12	−0.13	0.48	0.31	0.23	0.02	0.80	0.13
30	1.74	2.32	−0.10	0.55	0.32	0.14	0.02	0.81	0.18
35	1.71	2.55	−0.07	0.63	0.31	0.09	0.02	0.81	0.24
40	1.72	2.83	−0.03	0.73	0.30	0.07	0.02	0.79	0.30

TABLE 4d

CHANGE IN SELECTED VARIABLES FOR $0.5 BILLION (IN CURRENT $) INCREASE IN NONBORROWED RESERVES: SUB-SAMPLE PERIOD 1961.01–1967.12

No. of months after the action	Δgnp (GNP 58 $)	ΔGNP (Money GNP)	Δur (Un-employ ment rate %)	Δc (Con-sump-tion, 58 $)	$\Delta(bc+eq)$ (Invest-ment in plant & equip-ment, 58 $)	Δv (Non-farm inven-tory invest-ment, 58 $)	Δrs (4–6 month com-mercial paper rate)	Δnei (Bal-ance of trade, 58 $)	ΔMS (Money supply, current $)
1	0.00	0.00	0.00	0.00	0.00	0.00	−0.14	0.00	0.00
2	0.00	0.00	0.00	0.00	0.00	−0.01	−0.25	0.00	0.01
3	0.00	0.00	0.00	0.00	0.00	−0.03	−0.34	0.00	0.04
4	0.02	0.02	0.00	0.01	0.00	−0.07	−0.41	0.00	0.09
5	0.05	0.06	0.00	0.02	0.00	−0.11	−0.47	0.00	0.17
6	0.15	0.13	0.00	0.05	0.01	−0.14	−0.51	0.00	0.26
7	0.23	0.23	−0.01	0.09	0.01	−0.18	−0.55	−0.01	0.36
8	0.37	0.38	−0.01	0.16	0.02	−0.21	−0.58	−0.01	0.47
9	0.56	0.58	−0.02	0.25	0.03	−0.23	−0.60	−0.02	0.59
10	0.80	0.82	−0.03	0.36	0.04	−0.23	−0.61	−0.04	0.78
11	1.09	1.11	−0.04	0.49	0.06	−0.24	−0.62	−0.05	0.83
12	1.42	1.45	−0.06	0.65	0.08	−0.22	−0.63	−0.08	0.95
15	2.68	2.74	−0.13	1.26	0.17	−0.03	−0.64	−0.18	1.33
20	5.20	5.36	−0.29	2.51	0.45	0.67	−0.62	−0.43	1.94
25	7.43	7.99	−0.43	3.77	0.86	1.32	−0.57	−0.69	2.53
30	8.70	10.47	−0.28	4.97	1.29	1.51	−0.52	−0.90	3.19
35	9.80	13.56	0.05	6.39	1.64	1.24	−0.47	−1.06	4.03
40	10.87	15.70	0.11	7.77	1.89	1.07	−0.45	−1.18	4.69

TABLE 5a

CHANGE IN SELECTED VARIABLES FOR $1.0 BILLION (IN CURRENT $) INCREASE IN GOVERNMENT EXPENDITURES: SUB-SAMPLE PERIOD 1968.01–1971.12

No. of months after the action	Δgnp (GNP 58 $)	ΔGNP (Money GNP)	Δur (Unemployment rate %)	Δc (Consumption, 58 $)	$\Delta(bc+eq)$ (Investment in plant & equipment, 58 $)	Δv (Nonfarm inventory investment, 58 $)	Δrs (4–6 month commercial paper rate)	Δnei (Balance of trade, 58 $)	ΔMS (Money supply, current $)
1	0.32	0.37	−0.01	0.00	0.00	−0.44	0.00	0.00	0.00
2	0.47	0.55	−0.01	0.01	0.00	−0.29	0.00	−0.09	0.01
3	0.60	0.69	−0.02	0.02	0.01	−0.16	0.00	−0.02	0.01
4	0.69	0.79	−0.03	0.04	0.01	−0.07	0.00	−0.04	0.01
5	0.78	0.89	−0.04	0.06	0.02	0.00	0.00	−0.06	0.02
6	0.85	0.97	−0.04	0.08	0.03	0.06	0.00	−0.07	0.02
7	0.91	1.04	−0.05	0.09	0.04	0.11	0.00	−0.08	0.03
8	0.97	1.11	−0.05	0.11	0.05	0.15	0.00	−0.09	0.03
9	1.00	1.17	−0.05	0.12	0.07	0.18	0.00	−0.09	0.04
10	1.04	1.23	−0.06	0.13	0.08	0.20	0.00	−0.10	0.05
11	1.07	1.29	−0.05	0.14	0.10	0.21	0.00	−0.11	0.06
12	1.09	1.34	−0.05	0.15	0.11	0.22	0.01	−0.11	0.06
15	1.13	1.50	−0.04	0.19	0.15	0.21	0.01	−0.12	0.09
20	1.12	1.72	−0.01	0.26	0.20	0.16	0.01	−0.13	0.15
25	1.11	1.92	0.00	0.36	0.22	0.09	0.01	−0.13	0.20
30	1.10	2.12	0.02	0.42	0.22	0.05	0.01	−0.13	0.24
35	1.08	2.27	0.01	0.45	0.21	0.04	0.01	−0.13	0.28
40	1.04	2.37	0.01	0.45	0.21	0.04	0.02	−0.13	0.31

TABLE 5b

CHANGE IN SELECTED VARIABLES FOR $1.0 BILLION (IN CURRENT $) DECREASE IN PERSONAL TAXES: SUB-SAMPLE PERIOD 1968.01–1971.12

No. of months after the action	Δgnp (GNP 58 $)	ΔGNP (Money GNP)	Δur (Unemployment rate %)	Δc (Consumption, 58 $)	$\Delta(bc+eq)$ (Investment in plant & equipment, 58 $)	Δv (Nonfarm inventory investment, 58 $)	Δrs (4–6 month commercial paper rate)	Δnei (Balance of trade, 58 $)	ΔMS (Money supply, current $)
1	0.00	0.00	0.00	0.00	0.00	0.00	0.00	0.00	0.00
2	0.01	0.02	0.00	0.03	0.00	−0.02	0.00	0.00	0.00
3	0.05	0.06	0.00	0.09	0.00	−0.05	0.00	0.00	0.00
4	0.10	0.12	0.00	0.17	0.00	−0.07	0.00	0.00	0.00
5	0.16	0.19	−0.01	0.23	0.00	−0.08	0.00	−0.01	0.00
6	0.22	0.26	−0.09	0.28	0.00	−0.06	0.00	−0.01	0.00
7	0.29	0.33	−0.01	0.33	0.01	−0.04	0.00	−0.02	0.00
8	0.35	0.40	−0.02	0.36	0.01	−0.01	0.00	−0.02	0.01
9	0.41	0.68	−0.02	0.39	0.01	0.02	0.00	−0.03	0.01
10	0.41	0.54	−0.02	0.41	0.02	0.05	0.00	−0.04	0.01
11	0.52	0.61	−0.03	0.44	0.02	0.08	0.00	−0.04	0.02
12	0.57	0.67	−0.03	0.46	0.03	0.10	0.00	−0.05	0.02
15	0.70	0.85	−0.03	0.52	0.06	0.15	0.01	−0.06	0.03
20	0.82	1.10	−0.03	0.61	0.11	0.16	0.01	−0.08	0.05
25	0.88	1.32	−0.03	0.71	0.15	0.13	0.01	−0.09	0.09
30	0.92	1.51	−0.02	0.78	0.17	0.09	0.01	−0.10	0.12
35	0.92	1.68	−0.01	0.83	0.18	0.07	0.01	−0.10	0.16
40	0.90	1.81	−0.01	0.84	0.18	0.05	0.02	−0.11	0.19

TABLE 5c

CHANGE IN SELECTED VARIABLES FOR $1.0 BILLION (IN CURRENT $) INCREASE IN EXPORTS: SUB-SAMPLE PERIOD 1968.01–1971.12

No. of months after the action	Δgnp (GNP 58 $)	ΔGNP (Money GNP)	Δur (Un-employment rate %)	Δc (Con-sumption, 58 $)	Δ(bc+eq) (Invest-ment in plant & equiq-ment, 58 $)	Δv (Non-farm inven-tory invest-ment, 58 $)	Δrs (4–6 month com-mercial paper rate)	Δnei (Bal-ance of trade, 58 $)	ΔMS (Money supply, current $)
1	0.42	0.44	−0.01	0.00	0.00	−0.58	0.00	1.00	0.00
2	0.62	0.72	−0.02	−0.01	0.00	−0.37	0.00	0.99	0.00
3	0.76	0.87	−0.03	−0.02	0.01	−0.21	0.01	0.97	0.00
4	0.85	0.97	−0.04	−0.03	0.02	−0.09	0.01	0.94	0.01
5	0.91	1.04	−0.04	−0.03	0.03	−0.01	0.01	0.92	0.01
6	0.97	1.11	−0.05	−0.02	0.04	0.04	0.00	0.91	0.01
7	1.03	1.18	−0.06	−0.01	0.05	0.06	0.00	0.12	0.00
8	1.07	1.25	−0.06	0.01	0.06	0.11	0.00	0.89	0.00
9	1.12	1.31	−0.06	0.01	0.07	0.13	0.00	0.89	0.00
10	1.15	1.37	−0.06	0.01	0.09	0.15	0.00	0.89	0.01
11	1.18	1.43	−0.06	0.02	0.10	0.17	0.00	0.89	0.01
12	1.20	1.49	−0.06	0.02	0.12	0.19	0.00	0.88	0.01
15	1.25	1.66	−0.04	0.03	0.16	0.21	0.01	0.87	0.03
20	1.18	1.85	−0.01	−0.03	0.19	0.21	0.01	0.87	0.06
25	1.01	1.88	0.01	−0.09	0.20	0.12	0.01	0.88	0.08
30	0.78	1.82	0.04	−0.16	0.18	0.01	0.01	0.89	0.08
35	0.76	1.95	0.04	−0.04	0.14	−0.10	0.00	0.91	0.10
40	0.94	2.29	0.03	0.08	0.12	−0.01	0.00	0.89	0.12

TABLE 5d

CHANGE IN SELECTED VARIABLES FOR $0.5 BILLION (IN CURRENT $) INCREASE IN NON-BORROWED RESERVES: SUB-SAMPLE PERIOD 1968.01–1971.12

No. of months after the action	Δgnp (GNP 59 $)	ΔGNP (Money GNP)	Δur (Un-employment rate %)	Δc (Con-sumption, 58 $)	Δ(bc+eq) (Invest-ment in plant & equiq-ment, 58 $)	Δv (Non-farm inven-tory invest-ment, 58 $)	Δrs (4–6 month com-mercial paper rate)	Δnei (Bal-ance of trade, 58 $)	ΔMS (Money supply, current $)
1	0.00	0.00	0.00	0.00	0.00	0.00	−0.10	0.00	0.00
2	0.00	0.01	0.00	0.00	0.00	0.00	−0.18	0.00	0.00
3	0.02	0.02	0.00	0.00	0.00	0.00	−0.25	0.00	0.00
4	0.04	0.05	0.00	0.01	0.00	0.02	−0.30	0.00	0.01
5	0.09	0.10	0.00	0.02	0.00	−0.03	−0.35	0.00	0.02
6	0.15	0.18	0.00	0.04	0.01	−0.05	−0.38	0.00	0.04
7	0.24	0.28	−0.01	0.07	0.01	−0.06	−0.40	−0.01	0.08
8	0.36	0.42	−0.01	0.12	0.02	−0.08	−0.43	−0.02	0.12
9	0.50	0.59	−0.02	0.19	0.02	−0.09	−0.44	−0.02	0.18
10	0.68	0.80	−0.03	0.27	0.04	−0.10	−0.46	−0.03	0.27
11	0.89	1.05	−0.03	0.37	0.05	−0.09	−0.47	−0.05	0.37
12	1.11	1.34	−0.05	0.49	0.06	−0.08	−0.47	−0.07	0.51
15	2.04	2.50	−0.09	0.92	0.13	0.05	−0.48	−0.14	1.11
20	3.82	4.80	−0.14	1.88	0.33	0.51	−0.46	−0.32	2.55
25	5.51	7.35	−0.20	2.89	0.62	0.93	−0.43	−0.51	4.31
30	6.88	9.14	−0.19	3.87	0.94	1.11	−0.39	−0.67	6.43
35	7.69	12.13	−0.17	4.72	1.21	1.05	−0.36	−0.80	7.70
40	7.99	14.03	−0.16	5.34	1.40	0.77	−0.33	−0.87	9.47

APPENDIX

The Model and Definitions of Symbols

(I) Components of gpp

(1) Consumers' Nondurable Goods

$$cn = \underset{(0.014)}{0.043}y^*_{-1} + \underset{(0.008)}{0.019}Lh^*_{-1} - \underset{(8.770)}{32.671}\frac{pcn}{pc} + \underset{(0.049)}{0.798}cn_{-1} + \underset{(10.738)}{43.933} \qquad \alpha = \underset{(0.075)}{-0.237} \quad R^2 = 0.998$$

(2) Consumers' Services

$$cs = \underset{(0.006)}{0.004}y^*_{-1} + \underset{(0.003)}{0.012}Lh^*_{-1} - \underset{(5.169)}{2.885}\frac{pcs}{pc} + \underset{(0.026)}{0.922}cs_{-1} + \underset{(0.008)}{0.019}t + \underset{(5.601)}{6.911} \qquad \alpha = \underset{(0.069)}{-0.241} \quad R^2 = 0.999$$

(3) Consumers' Durable Goods: Automobiles and Parts

$$ca = \underset{(0.006)}{0.046}(y - trp)^*_{-1} - \underset{(2.529)}{11.663}\frac{pca}{pc} - \underset{(0.022)}{0.001}kca_{-1} - \underset{(0.107)}{0.420}ur^*_{-1} + \underset{(0.045)}{0.361}h^*_{-1} + \underset{(0.176)}{2.567}ds + \underset{(0.044)}{0.464}ca_{-1} + \underset{(0.676)}{1.491}dfz1 + \underset{(2.693)}{2.024} \qquad \alpha = \dagger \quad R^2 = 0.985$$

(4) Other Consumers' Durable Goods

$$cod = \underset{(0.010)}{0.018}(y - trp)^*_{-1} + \underset{(0.005)}{0.008}\,Lh^*_{-1} + \underset{(0.079)}{0.811}cod_{-1} - \underset{(1.310)}{2.335} \qquad \alpha = \underset{(0.091)}{0.742} \quad R^2 = 0.999$$

(5) Gross Private Domestic Investment in Business Construction

$$bc = \underset{(0.002)}{0.007}gpp^{**}_{-1} - \underset{(0.020)}{0.060}\left(\frac{uccbc}{p}10^4\right)^{**}_{-1} - \underset{(0.005)}{0.006}kbc^{**}_{-1} + \underset{(0.029)}{0.877}bc_{-1} + \underset{(0.242)}{0.068}dfz2 + \underset{(0.256)}{0.938} \qquad \alpha = \dagger \quad R^2 = 0.985$$

(6) Gross Private Domestic Investment in Producers' Durable Equipment

$$eq = \underset{(0.014)}{0.080}gpp^{**}_{-1} - \underset{(0.125)}{0.532}\left(\frac{ucceq}{p}10^4\right)^{**}_{-1} + \underset{(10.019)}{29.230}\left(\frac{uo}{sm}\right)^{**}_{-1} + \underset{(0.114)}{0.344}eq_{-1} + \underset{(0.711)}{1.786}dfz2 + \underset{(3.003)}{8.340} \qquad \alpha = \underset{(0.077)}{0.757} \quad R^2 = 0.998$$

NOTE: The structural equations are estimated for the sample period, 1954–71. The numbers in parentheses are standard errors of the respective regression coefficients. α is the estimated first order serial correlations coefficients of the residuals. In the simulations studies presented in this paper, the equations are transformed to take into consideration the serial correlations involved in the residuals. Theoretically relevant variables are retained in the equations if their respective regression coefficients have the expected signs even when they are statistically insignificant on conventional standards. The superscripts $*$, ∇, and $**$ represent 3-month, 6-month and 12-month moving averages respectively. † indicates serial correlation coefficients too small and ad statistically insignificant to be taken into consideration.

(7) Gross Private Domestic Investment in Residential Housing Construction

α R^2

$$h = \underset{(0.004)}{0.008}(y - trp)^{**}_{-1} + \underset{(0.186)}{0.835}(rL - rs)^{**}_{-1} - \underset{(0.660)}{2.071}\left(\frac{ph}{pr}\right)^{**}_{-1}$$

$$- \underset{(0.004)}{0.001}kh^{**}_{-1} + \underset{(0.062)}{0.785}h_{-1} + \underset{(1.344)}{4.241} \qquad \underset{(0.078)}{0.738} \quad 0.989$$

(8) Change in Nonfarm Business Inventories

$$v = \underset{(0.015)}{0.066}s_{-1} - \underset{(0.036)}{0.583}(s - s_{-1}) - \underset{(0.067)}{0.042}(rs - \dot{p})^{*}_{-1} + \underset{(0.154)}{0.589}(uo - uo_{-1})_{-1}$$

$$- \underset{(0.038)}{0.161}kv_{-1} + \underset{(0.036)}{0.748}v_{-1} + \underset{(0.317)}{1.870}dv - \underset{(0.903)}{2.677} \qquad \dagger \quad 0.851$$

(II) Manufacturers' New Orders, Sales and Unfilled Orders

(9) Manufacturers' New Orders

$$nom = \underset{(0.187)}{0.572}(c - cs)^{*}_{-1} + \underset{(0.327)}{0.466}(bc + eq + h)^{*}_{-1} + \underset{(0.433)}{0.417}x^{*}_{-1}$$

$$+ \underset{(0.156)}{0.330}\left\{\left[\frac{GSL + GF}{pg}100\right] - gg\right\}^{*}_{-1} - \underset{(0.245)}{0.933}kv^{*}_{-1}$$

$$+ \underset{(0.043)}{0.834}nom_{-1} + \underset{(1.458)}{9.815}dnom - \underset{(7.505)}{3.859} \qquad \dagger \quad 0.991$$

(10) Manufacturers' Shipments

$$sm = \underset{(0.038)}{0.240}nom^{*}_{-1} + \underset{(0.039)}{0.754}sm_{-1} + \underset{(0.858)}{9.490}dsm + \underset{(2.095)}{4.177} \qquad \dagger \quad 0.995$$

(11) Manufacturers' Unfilled Orders

$$uo = uo_{-1}\left(\frac{pm_{-1}}{pm}\right) + nom - sm$$

(III) Employment, Hours and Labor Force

(12a) Private Man-Hours

$$Ln(mhp) = \underset{(0.026)}{0.245}Ln(gpp) - \underset{(0.024)}{0.194}Ln\left(\frac{WR}{p}100\right) + \underset{(0.035)}{0.711}Ln(mhp)_{-1}$$

$$+ \underset{(0.089)}{0.024} \qquad \underset{(0.076)}{-0.077} \quad 0.990$$

(12b) Private Civilian Employment

$$e = eg + \underset{(0.002)}{0.013}gpp - \underset{(0.330)}{1.396}\left(\frac{WR}{p}100\right) + \underset{(0.023)}{0.913}(e - eg)_{-1} + \underset{(0.900)}{4.934} \qquad \underset{(0.068)}{-0.174} \quad 0.996$$

(13) Private Business Capital

$$k = kbc + keq$$

(14) Average Weekly Hours

$$hr = \underset{(0.006)}{0.024}(gpp_{-1} - gpp_{-2}) + \underset{(0.779)}{2.775}\left(\frac{gpp_{-1}}{k_{-2}}\right) + \underset{(0.021)}{0.044}WR_{-1} + \underset{(0.062)}{0.717}hr_{-1} + \underset{(1.595)}{7.786}$$

$\alpha = \underset{(0.081)}{-0.232}$ $\quad R^2 = 0.865$

(15) Civilian Labor Force

$$L = \underset{(0.240)}{0.935}WR + \underset{(0.039)}{0.833}e_{-1} + \underset{(0.045)}{0.805}(L - e)_{-1} + \underset{(0.108)}{0.310}[(L - e)_{-1} - (L - e)_{-2}] + \underset{(0.002)}{0.007}t + \underset{(2.127)}{9.223}$$

$\alpha = \underset{(0.080)}{-0.166}$ $\quad R^2 = 0.998$

(16) Civilian Unemployment Rate

$$ur = \left(\frac{L - e}{L}\right)100$$

(IV) Financial Sector

(17) Household Holdings of Currency and Demand Deposits

$$curddh = \underset{(0.002)}{0.006}yp^{*}_{-1} - \underset{(0.078)}{0.117}rL^{*}_{-1} - \underset{(0.054)}{0.098}rs^{*}_{-1} - \underset{(0.287)}{0.209}\dot{p}c^{*}_{-1} + \underset{(0.011)}{0.984}curddh_{-1} - \underset{(0.430)}{0.111}$$

$\alpha = \dagger$ $\quad R^2 = 0.997$

(18) Change in Household Holdings of Savings Deposits and Savings and Loan Association Shares

$$\Delta sah = \underset{(0.005)}{0.011}y^{*}_{-1} + \underset{(0.847)}{3.150}(rL - rs)^{*}_{-1} + \underset{(0.128)}{0.407}(\Delta sah)_{-1} - \underset{(1.981)}{2.105}$$

$\alpha = \dagger$ $\quad R^2 = 0.342$

(19) Change in Household Holdings of Commercial Bank Time Deposits

$$\Delta tdh = \underset{(0.040)}{0.119}y^{*}_{-1} + \underset{(0.584)}{1.473}(rL - rs)^{*}_{-1} - \underset{(0.097)}{0.259}tdh_{-1} + \underset{(0.068)}{0.677}(\Delta tdh)_{-1} - \underset{(7.817)}{24.154}$$

$\alpha = \underset{(0.090)}{-0.179}$ $\quad R^2 = 0.500$

(20) Financial and Non-Financial Business Holdings of Currency and Demand Deposits

$$curddb = \underset{(0.001)}{0.001}\left(bc + eq + h + \frac{W - WG}{p}100\right)^{*}_{-1} - \underset{(0.030)}{0.123}rs^{*}_{-1} + \underset{(0.017)}{0.951}curddb_{-1} + \underset{(1.151)}{2.828}$$

$\alpha = \dagger$ $\quad R^2 = 0.981$

(21) Change in Financial and Non-Financial Business Holdings of Commercial Bank Time Deposits

$$\Delta tdb = \underset{(0.027)}{0.027}\left(\frac{GcpIV - DIV - TC}{p}100\right)^{*}_{-1} + \underset{(0.163)}{0.125}(rL - rs)^{*}_{-1} - \underset{(0.065)}{0.085}tdb_{-1} + \underset{(0.080)}{0.736}(\Delta tdb)_{-1} - \underset{(0.870)}{0.600}$$

$\alpha = \dagger$ $\quad R^2 = 0.617$

(22) Government Holdings of Currency and Demand Deposits in Current Dollars

$$CURDDG = \underset{(0.011)}{0.043}(GF + GSL)_{-1} + \underset{(1.679)}{9.149} \qquad \alpha = \underset{(0.029)}{0.918} \quad R^2 = 0.914$$

(23) Government Holdings of Commercial Bank Time Deposits in Current Dollars

$$TDG = \underset{(0.012)}{0.023}(GF + GSL)_{-1} + \underset{(0.064)}{0.866}TDG_{-1} - \underset{(1.043)}{1.704} \qquad \alpha = \underset{(0.218)}{0.944} \quad R^2 = 0.999$$

(24) Household Holdings of Savings Deposits and Savings and Loan Association Shares

$$sah = sah_{-1} + \frac{\Delta sah}{12}$$

(25) Household Holdings of Commercial Bank Time Deposits

$$tdh = tdh_{-1} + \frac{\Delta tdh}{12}$$

(26) Household Holdings of Liquid Assets

$$Lh = curddh + sah + tdh$$

(27) Household Holdings of Currency and Demand Deposits in Current Dollars

$$CURDDH = curddh\left(\frac{pc}{100}\right)$$

(28) Household Holdings of Savings Deposits and Savings and Loan Association Shares in Current Dollars

$$SAH = sah\left(\frac{pc}{100}\right)$$

(29) Household Holdings of Commercial Bank Time Deposits in Current Dollars

$$TDH = tdh\left(\frac{pc}{100}\right)$$

(30) Household Holdings of Liquid Assets in Current Dollars

$$LH = CURDDH + SAH + TDH$$

(31) Financial and Non-Financial Business Holdings of Commercial Bank Time Deposits

$$tdb = tdb_{-1} + \frac{\Delta tdb}{12}$$

(32) Financial and Non-Financial Business Holdings of Currency and Demand Deposits in Current Dollars

$$CURDDB = curddb\left(\frac{p}{100}\right)$$

(33) Financial and Non-Financial Business Holdings of Commercial Bank Time Deposits in Current Dollars

α R^2

$$TDB = tdb\left(\frac{p}{100}\right)$$

(34) Money Supply

$$MS = CURDDH + CURDDB + CURDDG$$

(35) Total Demand Deposits

$$\underset{}{DD} = \underset{(0.010)}{0.662MS} + \underset{(1.553)}{17.904} \qquad \underset{(0.055)}{0.562} \quad 0.991$$

(36) Total Time Deposits

$$TD = TDH + TDB + TDG$$

(37) Required Reserves

$$RR = \underset{(0.013)}{0.035}\,[\gamma(DD) + (1-\gamma)TD] + \underset{(181.08)}{18.906} \quad \text{where,} \quad \gamma = \frac{zdd}{zdd + ztd} \qquad \underset{(0.079)}{0.999} \quad 0.993$$

(38) Free Reserves

$$RF = NBR - RR$$

(39) Ratio of Free Reserves to Required Reserves in %

$$ef = \left(\frac{RF}{RR}\right)100$$

(40) Short Term Rate of Interest (Prime Papers, 4–6 Months)

$$rs = \underset{(0.043)}{0.188rd} - \underset{(0.010)}{0.051ef} + \underset{(0.007)}{0.006\dot{p}_{-1}} + \underset{(0.003)}{0.006v_{-1}} + \underset{(0.033)}{0.808rs_{-1}} + \underset{(0.054)}{0.100} \qquad \dagger \quad 0.986$$

(41) Long Term Rate of Interest (Moody's Average)

$$rL = \underset{(0.013)}{0.010rs_{-1}} + \underset{(0.026)}{0.033(rs_{-1} - rs_{-2})} + \underset{(0.002)}{0.004(bc + eq + h)^{*}_{-1}}$$

$$- \underset{(0.016)}{0.959rL_{-1}} - \underset{(0.068)}{0.103} \qquad \underset{(0.072)}{0.455} \quad 0.997$$

(V) Proprietors', Rental and Personal Interest Incomes

(42) Proprietors' Income

$$PRI = \underset{(0.002)}{0.004W_{-1}} + \underset{(0.007)}{0.017GCPIV_{-1}} + \underset{(0.036)}{0.907PRI_{-1}} + \underset{(0.882)}{2.173} \qquad \underset{(0.076)}{0.165} \quad 0.998$$

(43) Rental Income of Persons

$$REN = \underset{(0.00041)}{0.00039}\left(kh\,\frac{pr}{100}\right) + \underset{(0.014)}{0.992REN_{-1}} + \underset{(0.062)}{0.026} \qquad \underset{(0.068)}{0.036} \quad 0.999$$

(44) Personal Interest Income

$$INP = \underset{(0.005)}{0.057YP_{-1}} + \underset{(0.159)}{0.467rL_{-1}} + \underset{(20.125)}{20.106} \qquad \underset{(0.002)}{0.997} \quad 0.999$$

(VI) Relationships Leading From GNP to Disposable Personal Income

α R^2

(45) Capital Consumption Allowances

$$D = \underset{(0.001)}{0.062}KD - \underset{(0.611)}{4.575} \qquad \underset{(0.293)}{0.971} \quad 0.999$$

(46) Total Private Capital

$$KD = kbc\frac{pbc}{100} + keq\frac{peq}{100} + kh\frac{ph}{100}$$

(47) Indirect Business Tax and Nontax Liability

$$IT = f\left(gpp\frac{p}{100}\right)$$

Different functions were estimated for different sub-periods of our sample due to changes in tax laws.

(48) Gross Corporate Profits and Inventory Valuation Adjustment

$$GCPIV = \underset{(0.007)}{0.291}gpp_{-1} + \underset{(15.639)}{68.713}uf_{-1} + \underset{(2.208)}{1.925}dfz1 - \underset{(27.646)}{163.853} \qquad \underset{(0.341)}{0.791} \quad 0.992$$

(49) Ratio of Price to Unit Cost

$$uf = \frac{p/100}{\left(\dfrac{W - WG + IT}{gpp}\right)}$$

(50) Corporate Depreciation Allowances

$$DC = \underset{(0.001)}{0.076}KC - \underset{(0.548)}{2.541} \qquad \underset{(0.063)}{0.983} \quad 0.999$$

(51) Corporate Capital Stock

$$KC = kbc\left(\frac{pbc}{100}\right) + keq\left(\frac{peq}{100}\right)$$

(52) Corporate Profits and Inventory Valuation Adjustment

$$CPIV = GCPIV - DC$$

(53) Contributions for Social Insurance

$$SI = f(YP - TRP + SIP)$$

Different functions were estimated for different sub-periods of our sample period due to change in tax laws.

(54) Government Transfer Payments to Persons

$$TRGP = \underset{(0.259)}{2.666}\left(ur\frac{L}{100}\right)_{-1} + \underset{(0.001)}{0.033}\left[\frac{(YP - TP)}{N}10^3\right]_{-1} - \underset{(1.700)}{49.038} \qquad \underset{(0.072)}{0.933} \quad 0.996$$

(55) Dividends

$$DVD = \underset{(0.005)}{0.013}(GCPIV - TC)^*_{-1} + \underset{(0.019)}{0.938}DVD_{-1} + \underset{(0.058)}{0.083} \qquad \underset{(0.065)}{-0.329} \quad 0.996$$

(56) Personal Contributions for Social Insurance

α R^2

$SIP = f(SI)$

Different functions were estimated for different sub-periods of our sample period due to changes in tax laws.

(57) Personal Tax and Nontax Payments

$TP = f(YP - TRP + SIP)$

Different functions were estimated for different sub-periods of our sample period due to changes in tax laws.

(58) Corporate Profit Tax Liability

$TC = f(CPIV)$

Different functions were estimated for different sub-periods of our sample period due to changes in tax laws.

(59) Transfer Payments to Persons

$$TRP = \underset{(0.162)}{0.371}\left(\frac{ur}{100}L\right)_{-1} + \underset{(0.001)}{0.004}\left(\frac{YP - TP}{N}10^3\right)_{-1} + \underset{(0.037)}{0.884}TRP_{-1} - \underset{(1.923)}{6.532} \qquad \underset{(0.063)}{-0.425} \quad 0.993$$

(60) Personal Income Derived from GNP

$$YP = GNP - D - IT + SUB - CPIV - SI - WA + TRGP + INGP + DVD - SD$$

(61) Disposable Personal Income

$$Y = YP - TP$$

(62) Disposable Personal Income in 1958 Dollars

$$Y = \frac{Y}{pc}100$$

(63) Wage and Salary Disbursements Other Than Employer Contributions for Social Insurance

$$WI = W - SIB$$

(64) Employer Contributions for Social Insurance

$$SIB = SI - SIP$$

(65) Statistical Discrepancy

$$SD = YP - WI - PRI - REN - DVD - INP - TRP + SIP$$

(VII) Prices, Wages and Labor Cost

(66) Implicit Price Deflator, Gross Private Product

$$p = \underset{(2.514)}{11.227}uLc^{*}_{-1} + \underset{(0.455)}{1.421}\left(\frac{gpp}{k}\right)^{*}_{-1} + \underset{(0.016)}{0.938}p_{-1} - \underset{(0.128)}{0.355}dfz1 - \underset{(0.477)}{1.384} \qquad \underset{(0.035)}{0.295} \quad 0.999$$

(67) Implicit Price Deflator, Personal Consumption Expenditures

$$pc = \underset{(0.052)}{0.436p} + \underset{(0.057)}{0.386pc_{-1}} + \underset{(0.055)}{0.159pc_{-2}} - \underset{(0.095)}{0.217dfz1} + \underset{(1.853)}{2.354} \qquad \alpha = \underset{(0.048)}{0.954} \quad R^2 = 0.999$$

(68) Implicit Price Deflator, Consumer Services

$$pcs = \underset{(0.012)}{0.065pc} + \underset{(0.016)}{0.003pr} + \underset{(0.196)}{0.543WR} + \underset{(0.067)}{1.093pcs_{-1}} - \underset{(0.063)}{0.158pcs_{-2}}$$

$$- \underset{(0.078)}{0.257dfz1} - \underset{(0.674)}{1.162} \qquad \alpha = \dagger \quad R^2 = 0.999$$

(69) Implicit Price Deflator, Consumer Nondurables

$$pcn = \underset{(0.033)}{0.288pf} + \underset{(0.063)}{0.268pc} + \underset{(0.057)}{0.245pcn_{-1}} + \underset{(0.051)}{0.159pcn_{-2}} + \underset{(1.166)}{4.161} \qquad \alpha = \underset{(0.048)}{0.887} \quad R^2 = 0.999$$

(70) Implicit Price Deflator, Automobiles and Parts

$$pca = \underset{(0.091)}{0.150WR} + \underset{(0.055)}{1.545pca_{-1}} - \underset{(0.055)}{0.563pca_{-2}} + \underset{(0.676)}{1.507} \qquad \alpha = \dagger \quad R^2 = 0.994$$

(71) Implicit Price Deflator, Other Consumer Durable Goods

$$pcod = \underset{(0.002)}{0.004pc} + \underset{(0.052)}{1.629pcod_{-1}} - \underset{(0.053)}{0.634pcod_{-2}} - \underset{(0.103)}{0.096dfz1} + \underset{(0.450)}{0.036} \qquad \alpha = \dagger \quad R^2 = 0.999$$

(72) Implicit Price Deflator, Business Construction

$$pbc = \underset{(0.244)}{0.309WR} + \underset{(0.096)}{1.447pbc_{-1}} - \underset{(0.098)}{0.449pbc_{-2}} - \underset{(0.330)}{0.298} \qquad \alpha = \underset{(0.100)}{-0.304} \quad R^2 = 0.999$$

(73) Implicit Price Deflator, Producers' Durable Equipment

$$peq = \underset{(0.005)}{0.017p} + \underset{(0.060)}{1.440peq_{-1}} - \underset{(0.059)}{0.456peq_{-2}} - \underset{(0.151)}{0.405dfz1} + \underset{(0.168)}{0.024} \qquad \alpha = \dagger \quad R^2 = 0.999$$

(74) Implicit Price Deflator, Housing Construction

$$ph = \underset{(0.430)}{1.666WR} + \underset{(0.057)}{1.470ph_{-1}} - \underset{(0.058)}{0.534ph_{-2}} - \underset{(0.217)}{0.402dfz1} + \underset{(0.967)}{3.344} \qquad \alpha = \dagger \quad R^2 = 0.999$$

(75) Implicit Price Deflator, Government Purchases of Goods and Services

$$pg = \underset{(0.043)}{1.168p} + \underset{(0.004)}{0.006}\left(\frac{WG}{eg}10^3\right) - \underset{(2.492)}{50.799} \qquad \alpha = \underset{(0.081)}{0.951} \quad R^2 = 0.999$$

(76) Consumer Price Index, Rent

$$pr = \underset{(0.006)}{0.033pc} + \underset{(0.071)}{1.451pr_{-1}} - \underset{(0.066)}{0.487pr_{-2}} + \underset{(0.101)}{0.369} \qquad \alpha = \underset{(0.071)}{-0.479} \quad R^2 = 0.999$$

(77) Manufacturers' Wholesale Price Index, All Commodities

$$pm = \underset{(0.014)}{0.032p} + \underset{(1.023)}{3.682}\left(\frac{uo}{sm}\right)^*_{-1} + \underset{(0.120)}{0.747pm_{-1}} + \underset{(0.112)}{0.218pm_{-2}}$$

$$- \underset{(0.788)}{0.406} \qquad \alpha = \underset{(0.113)}{0.399} \quad R^2 = 0.999$$

(78) Implicit Price Deflator, General Government

$$pgg = \underset{(0.0002)}{0.0240}\left(\frac{WG}{eg}10^3\right) - \underset{(1.638)}{32.655} \qquad \alpha = \underset{(0.263)}{0.960} \quad R^2 = 0.999$$

(79) Adjustment of Money Wage Rate

$$waj = \underset{(1.539)}{5.081}\left(\sum_{i=1}^{12}\gamma_i ur_{-i}\right)^{-1} + \underset{(0.064)}{0.134}pcaj_{-1}$$

$$+ \underset{(0.005)}{0.011}\left(\frac{GCPIV_{-1} - GCPIV_{-13}}{GCPIV_{-13}}100\right) + \underset{(0.052)}{0.804}waj_{-1}$$

$$- \underset{(0.452)}{0.327}dfz1 - \underset{(0.074)}{0.423} \qquad \alpha = \underset{(0.074)}{-0.311} \quad R^2 = 0.79$$

$$\gamma_i = \begin{cases} \frac{4}{30} & i = 1, 2, 3 \\ \frac{3}{30} & i = 4, 5, 6 \\ \frac{2}{30} & i = 7, 8, 9 \\ \frac{1}{30} & i = 10, 11, 12 \end{cases}$$

(80) Money Wage Rate

$$WR = WR_{-1} + \frac{waj}{100}(WR_{-12})$$

(81) Adjustment of Consumer Price Index

$$pcaj = \frac{(pc - pc_{-12})}{pc_{-12}}100$$

(82) Wage and Salary Disbursements

$$W = (WR)(mhp)(52.14) + WG$$

(83) Unit Labor Cost

$$uLc = \frac{W - WG}{gpp}$$

(84) Gross National Product, General Government

$$gg = \frac{WG}{pgg}100$$

(VIII) Foreign Trade Sector

(85) Exports of Goods and Services in 1958 Dollars

$$x = \underset{(0.008)}{0.041}(wtx)^{\nabla}_{-1} + \underset{(5.079)}{14.412}\left(\frac{pwtx}{px}\right)^{\nabla} - \underset{(0.453)}{1.765}dock + \underset{(0.311)}{1.200}dsuz$$

$$+ \underset{(0.362)}{0.774}daut + \underset{(0.057)}{0.557}x_{-1} + \underset{(0.008)}{0.044}t - \underset{(5.236)}{11.017} \qquad \alpha = \dagger \quad R^2 = 0.99$$

(86) Imports of Goods and Services in 1958 Dollars

$$m = \underset{(0.009)}{0.076} gpp^*_{-1} - \underset{(7.387)}{8.808}\left(\frac{pim}{p}\right)^*_{-1} - \underset{(0.176)}{1.648} dock + \underset{(0.052)}{0.293} m_{-1} - \underset{(8.803)}{8.826} \qquad \alpha = \underset{(0.018)}{0.961} \qquad R^2 = 0.99$$

(87) Balance of Trade in 1958 Dollars

$$nei = x - m$$

(88) Implicit Deflator for Exports

$$px = \underset{(0.034)}{0.084} p - \underset{(0.569)}{0.171} dfz1 + \underset{(0.125)}{0.550} px_{-1} + \underset{(0.098)}{0.341} px_{-2} + \underset{(1.907)}{2.617} \qquad \alpha = \underset{(0.125)}{0.310} \qquad R^2 = 0.99$$

(89) Balance of Trade in Current Dollars

$$NEI = x\frac{px}{100} - m\frac{pim}{100}$$

(XI) GNP Definitions

(90) Gross National Product in Current Dollars

$$GNP = cs\frac{pcs}{100} + cn\frac{pcn}{100} + ca\frac{pca}{100} + cod\frac{pcod}{100} + bc\frac{pbc}{100} + eq\frac{peq}{100} + h\frac{ph}{100} + v\frac{p}{100} + VF + NEI + GSL + GF$$

(91) Gross Private Product in 1958 Dollars

$$gpp = cs + cn + ca + cod + bc + eq + h + v + vf + nei + [(GSL+GF)/pg]100 - gg$$

(92) Final Sales in 1958 Dollars

$$s = gpp - cs - v - vf$$

(93) Gross Private Product in Current Dollars

$$GPP = gpp\frac{p}{100}$$

(94) Implicit Price Deflator for Gross National Product

$$pgnp = \frac{GNP}{gnp}100$$

(95) Consumption in 1958 dollars

$$c = cn + cs + ca + cod$$

(X) Capital Stocks

(96) Net Capital Stock of Plant

$$kbc = kbc_{-1} + \frac{bc}{12} - 0.005kbc_{-1}$$

(97) Net Capital Stock of Equipment

$$keq = keq_{-1} + \frac{eq}{12} - 0.012keq_{-1}$$

(98) Net Capital Stock of Housing

$$kh = kh_{-1} + \frac{h}{12} - 0.002kh_{-1}$$

(99) Net Stock of Automobiles

$$kca = kca_{-1} + \frac{ca}{12} - 0.026kca_{-1}$$

(100) Net Stock of Inventories

$$kv = kv_{-1} + \frac{v}{12.0}$$

(XI) Other Identities

(101) $y^* = \sum_{i=0}^{-2} y_i/3$

(102) $Lh^* = \sum_{i=0}^{-2} Lh_i/3$

(103) $ur^* = \sum_{i=0}^{-2} ur_i/3$

(104) $gpp^{**} = \sum_{i=0}^{-11} gpp_i/12$

(105) $(y - trp)^* = \sum_{i=0}^{-2} (y - trp)_i/3$

(106) $\left(\frac{pbc}{peq}\right)^{**} = \sum_{i=0}^{-11} \left(\frac{pbc}{peq}\right)_i \Big/ 12$

(107) $(rL - rs)^{**} = \sum_{i=0}^{-11} (rL - rs)_i/12$

(108) $\left(\frac{ph}{pr}\right)^{**} = \sum_{i=0}^{-11} \left(\frac{ph}{pr}\right)_i \Big/ 12$

(109) $(rs - \dot{p})^* = \sum_{i=0}^{-2} (rs - \dot{p})_i/3$

(110) $kbc^{**} = \sum_{i=0}^{-11} kbc_i/12$

(111) $kh^{**} = \sum_{i=0}^{-11} kh_i/12$

(112) $(y - trp)^{**} = \sum_{i=0}^{-11} (y - trp)_i/12$

(113) $rL^* = \sum_{i=0}^{-2} rL_i/3$

(114) $rs^* = \sum_{i=0}^{-2} rs_i/3$

(115) $(\dot{p}c)^* = \sum_{i=0}^{-2} (\dot{p}c)_i/3$

(116) $(rL - rs)^* = \sum_{i=0}^{-2} (rL - rs)_i/3$

(117) $\dot{p} = \left(\frac{p - p_{-1}}{p_{-1}}\right)1200$

(118) $uLc^* = \sum_{i=0}^{-2} uLc_i/3$

(119) $(GCPIV - TC)^* = \sum_{i=0}^{-2} (GCPIV - TC)_i/3$

(120) $c = \sum_{i=0}^{-2} c_i/3$

(121) $\dot{p}c = \left(\frac{pc - pc_{-1}}{pc_{-1}}\right)100$

(122) $trp = \left(\frac{TRP}{pc}\right)100$

(123) $(c - cs)^* = \sum_{i=0}^{-2} (c - cs)_i/3$

(124) $(bc + eq + h)^* = \sum_{i=0}^{-2} (bc + eq + h)_i/3$

(125) $(g - gg)^* = \sum_{i=0}^{-2} (g - gg)_i/3$

(126) $x^* = \sum_{i=0}^{-2} x_i/3$

(127) $\left(\frac{uo}{sm}\right)^* = \sum_{i=0}^{-2} \left(\frac{uo}{sm}\right)_i \Big/ 3$

(128) $(wtx)^\triangledown = \sum_{i=0}^{-5} (wtx)_i/6$

(129) $\left(\frac{pwtx}{px}\right)^\triangledown = \sum_{i=0}^{-5} \left(\frac{pwtx}{px}\right)_i \Big/ 6$

(130) $\left(\frac{pim}{p}\right)^* = \sum_{i=0}^{-2} \left(\frac{pim}{p}\right)_i \Big/ 3$

(131) $yp^* = \sum_{i=0}^{-2} \left(\frac{Yp}{pc} 100\right)_i \Big/ 3$

DEFINITIONS OF SYMBOLS

Those with the symbol # preceding them are assumed to be exogenous. All flow variables are in terms of annual rates.

bc	Gross private domestic investment in business construction, billions of 1958 dollars
c	Personal consumption expenditures, billions of 1958 dollars
ca	Personal consumption expenditures, automobiles and parts, billions of 1958 dollars
cn	Personal consumption expenditures, nondurables, billions of 1958 dollars
cod	Personal consumption expenditures, durables other than automobiles and parts, billions of 1958 dollars
cs	Personal consumption expenditures, services, billions of 1958 dollars
curddb	Financial and non-financial business holdings of currency and demand deposits, end of month, billions of 1958 dollars
CURDDB	Financial and non-financial business holdings of currency and demand deposits, end of month, billions of dollars
curddh	Household holdings of currency and demand deposits, end of month, billions of 1958 dollars
CURDDH	Household holdings of currency and demand deposits, end of month, billions of dollars
CURDDG	Government holdings of currency and demand deposits, end of month, billions of dollars
CPIV	Corporate profits and inventory valuation adjustment, billions of dollars
D	Capital consumption allowances, billions of dollars
#*daut*	Dummy for U.S.-Canada Auto Pact; 1956.01–65.12=0.5, 1966.01–71.12 = 1.0; otherwise 0.0
DC	Capital consumption allowances, corporate, billions of dollars
DD	Demand deposits, total, billions of dollars, end of month
#*dfz*1	Dummy for wage and price control: 1971.08 = 0.5; 1971.09–1971.11 = 1.0; 1971.12 = 0.5
#*dfz*2	Dummy for wage and price control: 1971.09 = 0.5; 1971.10–1971.12 = 1.0
#*dnom*	Steel strike dummy: 1956.08 = 3.162, 1956.09 = −3.971, 1959.01 = 1.4, 1959.02 = 1.9, 1959.03 = 0.0, 1959.04 = 0.4, 1959.05 = −0.4, 1959.06 = 0.0, 1959.07 = −0.5, 1959.08 = −2.0, 1959.09 = 0.8, 1959.10 = 0.2, 1959.11 = −1.1, 1959.12 = 2.0; other wise, 0.0
#*dock*	Dummy for dock strike: 1965.01–65.03 = 0.5, 1965.04–65.06 = −0.5, 1969.01–69.03 = 1.0, 1969.04–69.06 = −1.0; otherwise, 0.0
#*ds*	Dummy for auto strike: 1956.08–56.09 = −1.0, 1956.10–56.12 = 1.0, 1957.01–59.10 = 0.5, 1959.11 = −1.5, 1959.12 = −1.0, 1960.01 = 1.0, 1964.09 = 1.0, 1964.10 = −2.2, 1964.11 = −1.0, 1964.12 = 1.0, 1966.03 = 1.0, 1966.04 = −1.0, 1966.05 = −1.5,

	1966.06 = −0.5, 1966.07 = 0.5, 1967.09 = 1.0, 1967.10 = −1.0, 1967.11 = −0.5, 1967.12 = −0.3, 1968.01 = 0.5, 1970.10 = −2.0, 1970.11 = −2.5, 1970.12 = −1.5, 1971.01 = 1.0, 1971.02–71.03 = 0.8; otherwise; 0.0
♯*dsm*	Strike dummy: 1956.07 = −2.57, 1956.08 = 3.6, 1959.09 = −1.56, 1959.06 = −0.4, 1959.07 = −2.1, 1959.08 = −2.1, 1959.09 = −0.3, 1959.10 = 0.0, 1959.11 = 0.3, 1959.12 = 2.2, 1960.01 = 1.5, 1964.10 = −1.0, 1964.11 = 0.6, 1964.12 = 1.6, 1967.09 = −1.5; otherwise, 0.0
♯*dsuz*	Dummy for Suez canal crisis: 1953.01–55.12 = 0.0, 1956.01–57.09 = 1.0; otherwise, 0.0
♯*dv*	Strike dummy used in inventory investment function: 1958.12 = 1.0, 1959.01 = −1.0, 1959.02 = 0.4, 1959.03 = 0.0, 1959.04 = 2.4, 1959.05 = −1.0, 1959.06 = 1.0, 1959.07 = −0.4, 1959.08 = −1.5, 1959.09 = −1.7, 1959.10 = 1.5, 1959.11 = −0.4, 1959.12 = 3.0, 1960.01 = −0.5, 1964.09 = 1.5, 1964.10 = −2.0, 1964.11 = 1.5, 1964.12 = 1.8, 1965.01 = 0.5, 1967.08 = 1.2, 1967.09 = −1.2, 1967.10 = 1.3, 1967.11 = 0.2; otherwise, 0.0
DVD	Dividends, billions of dollars
e	Total civilian employment, millions
♯*eg*	General civilian government employment, millions
ef	Ratio of free reserves to required reserves, percent
eq	Gross private domestic investment in producers' durable equipment, billions of 1958 dollars
GCPIV	Gross corporate profits and inventory valuation adjustment, billions of dollars
♯*GF*	Federal government purchases of goods and services, billions of dollars
gg	Gross national product, general government, billions of 1958 dollars
GG	Gross national product, general government, billions of dollars
gnp	Gross national product, billions of 1958 dollars
GNP	Gross national product, billions of dollars
♯*GSL*	State and local government purchases of goods and services, billions of dollars
h	Gross private domestic investment in residential structures, billions of 1958 dollars
hr	Average weekly hours of manufacturing sector
INP	Personal interest income, billions of dollars
♯*INGP*	Interest paid by government (net) and by consumers, billions of dollars
IT	Indirect business tax and nontax liability, billions of dollars
k	Private net capital stock, plant and producers' durable equipment, end of month, billions of 1958 dollars
kbc	Private net stock, business construction, end of month, billions of 1958 dollars
kca	Net stock, automobile and parts, end of month, billions of 1958 dollars

KC	Net stock, plant and equipment of corporations, end of month, billions of dollars
KD	Net stock, plant, equipment and residential structures, end of month, billions of dollars
keq	Net stock, equipment, billions of 1958 dollars
kh	Net stock, residential structures, end of month, billions of 1958 dollars
kv	Stock of nonfarm inventories, end of month, billions of 1958 dollars
L	Civilian labor force, 16 years of age and over, millions
Lh	Liquid assets held by households at end of month (currency, bank deposits, and savings and loan association shares), billions of 1958 dollars
LH	Liquid assets held by households at end of month (currency, bank deposits, and savings and loan association shares), billions of dollars
m	Imports of goods and services, billions of 1958 dollars
mhp	Private man-hours (civilian employment, millions, multiplied by average weekly hours of manufacturing sector)
MS	Money supply, end of month, billions of dollars
♯*N*	Total civilian resident population, millions
♯*NBR*	Nonborrowed Reserves, billions of dollars
NEI	Balance of trade (exports minus imports), billions of dollars
nei	Balance of trade (exports minus imports), billions of 1958 dollars
nom	Manufacturers' new orders, billions of 1958 dollars
p	Implicit price deflator for gross private product, 1958 = 100
pbc	Implicit price deflator for business construction, 1958 = 100
pc	Implicit price deflator for personal consumption expenditures, 1958 = 100
pca	Implicit price deflator for automobiles and parts, 1958 = 100
pcaj	Percentage adjustment in implicit price deflator for gross private product
pcn	Implicit price deflator for nondurable consumers' goods, 1958 = 100
pcod	Implicit price deflator for durable consumers' goods other than automobiles and parts, 1958 = 100
pcs	Implicit price deflator for consumers' services 1958 = 100
peq	Implicit price deflator for producers' durable equipment, 1958 = 100
♯*pf*	Consumer price index on food, 1958 = 100
pg	Implicit price deflator for government purchases of goods and services, 1958 = 100
pgg	Implicit price deflator for gross national product, general government, 1958 = 100
pgnp	Implicit price deflator for gross national product, 1958 = 100
ph	Implicit price deflator for residential construction, 1958 = 100
♯*pim*	Implicit price deffator for imports, 1958 = 100
pm	Wholesale price index, manufactured goods, 1958 = 100
pr	Consumer price index on rent 1958 = 100
PRI	Proprietors' income, billions of dollars

#pwtx	Index of world price (exports), 1958 = 100
px	Implicit deflator for exports, 1958 = 100
#rd	Discount rate, N. Y. Federal Reserve Bank, end of month, percent
REN	Rental income of persons, billions of dollars
rL	Domestic corporate (Moody's) average bond yield, percent
$R\bar{F}$	Free Reserves, billions of dollars
RR	Required reserves, billions of dollars
rs	Open market rates, N. Y. City, commercial paper (prime, 4–6 months), percent
s	Final sales, billions of 1958 dollars
sah	Household holdings of savings deposits and savings and loan association shares, billions of 1958 dollars
Δsah	Incremental household holdings of savings deposits and savings and loan association shares, billions of 1958 dollars
SAH	Household holdings of savings deposits and savings and loan association shares, billions of dollars
SI	Contributions for social insurance, billions of dollars
SIB	Employer contributions for social insurance, billions of dollars
SIP	Personal contributions for social insurance, billions of dollars
SD	Statistical discrepancy in national income accounts
sm	Manufacturers' shipments, billions of 1958 dollars
#SUB	Subsidies less current surplus of government enterprises, billions of dollars
#t	Time trend (starting period = 1)
TD	Time deposits, total, billions of dollars, end of month
tdb	Financial and Non-Financial business holdings of commercial bank time deposits, end of month, billions of 1958 dollars
TDB	Financial and Non-Financial business holdings of commercial bank time deposits, end of month, billions of dollars
tdh	Household holdings of commercial bank time deposits, end of month, billions of 1958 dollars
TDH	Household holdings of commercial bank time deposits, end of month, billions of dollars
TDG	Government holdings of commercial bank time deposits, end of month, billions of dollars
TP	Personal income tax and nontax liability, billions of dollars
TRP	Transfer payments to persons, billions of dollars
TRGP	Government transfer payments to persons, billions of dollars
uccbc	Users cost of capital, business construction
ucceq	Users cost of capital, producers' durable equipment

Where:

$$uccbc = \frac{pbc}{100} \cdot \left(\frac{rL}{100} + Dbc\right) \cdot (1 - u \cdot Zbc)/(1 - u)$$

$$ucceq = \frac{peq}{100} \cdot \left(\frac{rL}{100} + Deq\right) \cdot [1 - k - u \cdot Zeq \cdot (1 - k')]/(1 - u)$$

and,

Dbc = depreciation rate for plant; a value of 0.0584 is assumed

Deq = depreciation rate for equipment; a value of 0.135 is assumed

$$\begin{aligned} Zbc &= a \cdot 2\Big/\left(\frac{rL}{100} \cdot Tbc\right) \\ &\quad \times \left\{1 - \left[1 - \exp\left(-\frac{rL}{100} \cdot Tbc\right)\right]\Big/\left(\frac{rL}{100} \cdot Tbc\right)\right\} \\ &\quad + (1 - a) \cdot \left[1 - \exp\left(-\frac{rL}{100} \cdot Tbc\right)\right]\Big/\left(\frac{rL}{100} \cdot Tbc\right) \end{aligned}$$

$$\begin{aligned} Zeq &= a \cdot 2\Big/\left(\frac{rL}{100} \cdot Teq\right) \\ &\quad \times \left\{1 - \left[1 - \exp\left(-\frac{rL}{100} \cdot Teq\right)\right]\Big/\left(\frac{rL}{100} \cdot Teq\right)\right\} \\ &\quad + (1 - a) \cdot \left[1 - \exp\left(-\frac{rL}{100} \cdot Teq\right)\Big/\left(\frac{rL}{100} \cdot Teq\right)\right] \end{aligned}$$

a = proportion of plant and equipment depreciated by acceleration methods (%)

u = corporate income tax rate (%) = $\frac{TC}{CPIV}$

#k = effective rate of tax credit against equipment purchases (%)

#k' = effective rate of tax credit to be deducted from depreciation base (%)

#Tbc = assumed lifetime of plant for tax purposes

#Teq = assumed lifetime of equipment for tax purposes

ur	Unemployment rate of all civilian workers, percent
uLc	Unit labor cost in fractions (cost in current dollars; output in 1958 dollars)
uo	Manufacturers' unfilled orders, billions of 1958 dollars
v	Nonfarm inventory investment, billions of 1958 dollars
#$V\bar{F}$	Farm inventory investment, billions of dollars
#*vf*	Farm inventory investment, billions of 1958 dollars
W	Compensation of employees, billions of dollars
#*WA*	Wage accruals less disbursements, billions of dollars
waj	Percentage adjustment of money wage rate

#*WG*	Wages, compensation of general government employees, billions of dollars
WR	Wage rate ($/man-hour)
#*wtx*	Index of world trade (exports), 1958 = 100
WI	Wages and salaries plus other labor income, billions of dollars
x	Exports of goods and services, billions of 1958 dollars
Y	Disposable personal income, billions of dollars
y	Disposable personal income, billions of 1958 dollars
YP	Personal income, billions of dollars
#*zdd*	Reserve requirement against member bank demand deposits (%)
#*ztd*	Reserve requirement against member bank time deposits (%)

Cornell University

REFERENCES

[1] CHOW, G. C. AND A. L. LIN, "Best Linear Unbiased Interpolation, Distribution, and Extrapolation of Time Series by Related Series," *The Review of Economics and Statistics*, LIII (November, 1971), 372-375.

[2] CHRIST, C., *Econometric Models and Methods* (New York, London and Sydney: Wiley and Sons, 1966).

[3] DHRYMES, P. J., *Econometrics* (New York, Evanston and London: Harper and Row, 1970).

[4] ENGLE, R. F. AND T. C. LIU, "Effects of Aggregation over Time on Dynamic Characteristics of an Econometric Model," in B. G. Hickman, ed., *Econometric Models of Cyclical Behavior*, Volume II (New York and London: Columbia University Press, 1972), 673-733.

[5] FROMM, G. AND L. R. KLEIN, "A Comparison of Eleven Econometric Models of the United States," *The American Economic Review, Papers and Proceedings*, LXIII (May, 1973), 385-393.

[6] HENDRY, D. F., "User's Manual for the Estimation of Linear Equations with Lagged Dependent Variables and Autoregressive Errors," London School of Economics, (August, 1970).

[7] HIRSCH, A. A., "The BEA Quarterly Model as a Forecasting Instrument," *Survey of Current Business*, Volume LIII (August, 1973), 24-38.

[8] ———, LIEBENBERG, M. AND GREEN, G. R., *The BEA Quarterly Econometric Model*, BEA Staff Paper No. 22, (Washington, D. C.: U.S. Department of Commerce, July, 1973).

[9] JORGENSON, D. W., "Capital Theory and Investment Behavior," *American Economic Review, Papers and Proceedings*, LIII (May, 1963), 247-254.

[10] KLEIN, L. R., "The Efficiency of Estimation in Econometric Models," in R. W. Pfouts, ed., *Essays in Economics and Econometrics in Honor of Harold Hotelling* (Chapel Hill: University of North Carolina Press, 1960), 216-232.

[11] KOOPMANS, T. C. AND W. C. HOOD, "The Estimation of Simultaneous Linear Economic Relationships," in W. C. Hood and T. C. Koopmans, eds., *Studies in Econometric Methods* (New York: John Wiley and Sons, 1953), 112-199.

[12] LIU, T. C., "A Monthly Recursive Econometric Model of the United States: A Test of Feasibility," *The Review of Economics and Statistics*, LI (February, 1969), 1-13.

[13] MALINVAUD, E., *Statistical Methods of Econometrics* (Chicago: Rand McNally, 1966).

[14] MCCARTHY, M. D., *The Wharton Quarterly Econometric Forecasting Model, Mark III* (Philadelphia: Economics Research Unit, Department of Economics, Wharton School of Finance and Commerce, University of Pennsylvania, 1972).

[15] NAGAR, A. L., "The Bias and Moment Matrix of the General *k*-class Estimators of the Parameters in Simultaneous Equations," *Econometrica*, XXVII (October, 1959), 575-595.

[16] NERLOVE, M., "Spectral Analysis of Seasonal Adjustment Procedures," *Econometrica*, XXXII (July, 1964), 241-286.

[17] RICHARDSON, D. H., "The Exact Distribution of a Structural Coefficient Estimator," *Journal of the American Statistical Association*, XLIII, (December, 1968), 1214-1226.

[**18**] SARGAN, J. D., "The Maximum Likelihood Estimation of Economic Relationships with Autoregressive Residuals," *Econometrica*, XXIX (July, 1961), 414-426.
[**19**] THEIL, H., *Economic Forecasts and Policy* (Amsterdam: North-Holland, 1961).

5

NOTES ON TESTING THE PREDICTIVE PERFORMANCE OF ECONOMETRIC MODELS

By E. Philip Howrey, Lawrence R. Klein and Michael D. McCarthy

INTRODUCTION

The past decade has seen the development of a number of large scale econometric models.[1] It was the intention of the authors of these models that they be useful tools in the analysis of the economic impacts of a wide range of policy alternatives, thereby making possible more informed policy choices. Inevitably, models such as these were also used as economic forecasting tools. Attention was focused on the set of policy alternative under serious consideration at the moment and on the future implications of these policies. Due to the policy orientation, the large scale models are all stated as specific structural hypotheses. For example, the way that personal taxes are assumed to enter the demand equations for consumption goods is explicitly stated; the way that corporate taxes affect the various business relationships and the role of monetary controls in the money demand and supply relationships is also stated explicitly.

Inevitably and appropriately, questions were raised as to which of the various models (various competing hypotheses) was best, and a number of studies have recently been completed which purport to shed light on this question. One of these studies was conducted by Ronald L. Cooper [**2**] and a recent paper by R. J. Gordon [**9**] is also available. Papers by Zarnowitz, Boschan and Moore [**18**] and Evans, Haitovsky and Treyz [**5**] also deal with aspects of testing alternative models. The Cooper study merits special consideration because it attempts to construct a framework for general application based on an explicit testing methodology. Briefly, his study seeks to introduce uniformity among models by re-estimating each model (by an "appropriate" method) using the same body of data. Tests of the competing models (hypotheses) were then performed. The models were also tested against autoregressive (naive) models. The naive models made the simple assumption that each economic variable depends only on lagged values of itself.

Two types of tests of the models were undertaken. First, the performance of the models over the sample used for estimation (1949–1960) was examined. Specifically, using the actual values of the exogenous variables, one quarter forecasts were generated for the variables explained by the different models. Variable by variable, squared forecast errors were calculated, and compared, model by model. Second, a parallel set of one quarter forecast tests were performed using data beyond the estimation sample period. These data were from the period 1961–1965. The conclusion of the Cooper study was that, on the basis of his tests the simple autoregressive schemes seemed to perform at least as well from

[1] Some of the better known models that are currently operational are listed in Fromm and Klein [**7**].

the viewpoint of squared error considerations as the structural policy models.

The purpose of this paper is to consider what can reasonably be inferred from the Cooper study. More generally, our purpose is to explore alternative ways to assess the potential contribution of econometric models to prediction and public policy formation. Whether or not the Cooper study sheds light on this problem hinges crucially on the credibility of his conclusions. Credibility, in turn, depends on the evidence that his tests of hypotheses were in some sense good tests. If the Cooper study fails the credibility tests, we are still left with the very important issues associated with the design of tests of significance of econometric models.

The first part of this paper is devoted to a brief review of the Cooper study. Although the study is an admirable and heroic first effort, it raises a number of important questions since the test procedures employed deal with only limited aspects of model building. Model building consists of four interrelated activities:

(i) specification,
(ii) sample selection,
(iii) estimation, and
(iv) application, including prediction, simulation, and cyclical analysis.

Cooper attempts to test specification mainly by single period prediction analysis. The other dimensions of model building and analysis are left untouched. Even on the narrow issue of specification his approach is too restrictive. A priori information is not rich enough to provide us with complete specification. The precise nature of the lag structures, nonlinearities, the degree of aggregation, and the selection of exogenous variables are not fixed a priori. They can only be ascertained by experimental study of particular samples. The interaction of specification and estimation has certain implications for the tests that are proposed by Cooper. In Part 2 of this paper, some guidelines for tests of alternative models are presented.

A. *The Cooper study: a review.* In deciding on the credibility of Cooper's conclusions, (or on the conclusions of any such study) we really focus on the issue whether the tests of different models were good tests. We seek evidence that (1) taking the model structure as given, appropriate methods of estimation were used; (2) that adequate use was made of prior knowledge in specifying the model structures to be estimated, and (3) assuming (1) and (2) are satisfied, that the tests applied to the competing models seem to be good tests. We begin with an examination of the estimation procedure that was employed.

1. ESTIMATION METHOD

Structural econometric models are inevitably nonlinear in the endogenous and exogenous variables, yet feasible textbook estimation techniques are designed for linear systems. There is a presumption that estimation of non-linear structural models by an appropriate method will give such models an advantage over the purely autoregressive schemes that they would not otherwise have had in a statistical horse race. The method Cooper used to estimate the different structural models is called repeated reduced form estimation (RR). The method, attributed to Jorgenson, has been analyzed by Klein [**12**] within the context of a linear model.[2] Although the method has been shown to have certain desirable properties in the linear-model framework, it is not readily apparent that a straight forward extension of this method to nonlinear models is appropriate.

In order to investigate the applicability of the RR method of parameter estimation to a nonlinear model, assume that each dependent variable of the model can be written as a unique function of the exogenous variables and the other dependent variables in the system. For simplicity, suppose that the T observations on the variables in the i-th equation can be expressed as

$$(1\text{–}1) \qquad y_i = F_i(Y_i)\alpha_i + XB_i + \eta_i$$

where $y_i' = [y_{1i}\ y_{2i}\ \cdots\ y_{Ti}]$ is the vector of observations on the i-th dependent variable, $Y_i' = [Y_{1i}\ Y_{2i}\ \cdots\ Y_{Ti}]$ with Y_{ti} denoting the row vector of observations on the dependent variables (other than the i-th) which appear in the i-th equation, and

$$F_i(Y_i) = \begin{bmatrix} F_{i1}(Y_{1i}) & F_{i2}(Y_{1i}) & \cdots & F_{iG}(Y_{1i}) \\ \vdots & \vdots & & \vdots \\ F_{i1}(Y_{Ti}) & F_{i2}(Y_{Ti}) & \cdots & F_{iG}(Y_{Ti}) \end{bmatrix}$$

where the $F_{ij}(.)$ are known functions of the rows of Y_i. The term α_i is an appropriately ordered vector of unknown coefficients and η_i is a vector of disturbances with the usual properties including nonautocorrelation.[3] The matrix X denotes the matrix of observations on all the exogenous variables in the model and B_i is the associated vector of coefficients. Generally, several of the elements in B_i will be zero in which case it is convenient to write

$$(1\text{–}2) \qquad XB_i = x_i\beta_i$$

where β_i is a column vector of the nonzero elements of B_i and x_i is a matrix of the exogenous variables which appear in the i-th equation. Thus equation (1–1) may also be written as

$$(1\text{–}3) \qquad y_i = F_i(Y_i)\alpha_i + x_i\beta_i + \eta_i.$$

Writting $y = [y_1\ y_2 \cdots y_p]$, $F = [F_1\ F_2 \cdots F_p]$, $B = [B_1\ B_2 \cdots B_p]$, $\eta = [\eta_1\ \eta_2 \cdots \eta_p]$ and

$$A = \begin{bmatrix} \alpha_1 & 0 & \cdots & 0 \\ 0 & \alpha_2 & \cdots & 0 \\ \cdot & \cdot & & \cdot \\ \cdot & \cdot & & \cdot \\ \cdot & \cdot & & \cdot \\ 0 & 0 & & \alpha_p \end{bmatrix}$$

[2] Variations of this method were examined at an early stage by Houthakker, Theil, and Nagar.

[3] Problems created by autocorrelation will be treated below.

the entire system of $p \cdot T$ equations takes the form

$$y = F(Y)A + XB + \eta. \tag{1-4}$$

Note that this model, like the models estimated by Cooper, is nonlinear in the economic variables.

The RR method of estimation is a two-step procedure in which consistent estimates $\hat{\alpha}_i$ and $\hat{\beta}_i$ are first obtained for α_i and β_i $(i = 1, 2, \ldots, p)$. We will assume that some such method exists. Given estimates $\hat{A}$ and $\hat{B}$ of A and B, an equation system of the form

$$y = F(Y)\hat{A} + X\hat{B} \tag{1-5}$$

is then solved for y, yielding the solution[4]

$$\hat{y} = H(\hat{A}, \hat{B}, X). \tag{1-6}$$

Next, for each equation, estimates $\hat{F}_i$ of $F_i(Y)$ are computed as $\hat{F}_i = F_i(\hat{Y}_i)$, and second-stage estimates are then obtained by applying least squares to an equation of the form

$$y_i = F_i(\hat{Y}_i)\alpha_i + x_i\beta_i + v_i \tag{1-7}$$

where

$$\begin{aligned} v_i &= \eta_i + [F_i(Y_i) - F_i(\hat{Y}_i)]\alpha_i \\ &= \eta_i + f_i\,. \end{aligned} \tag{1-8}$$

The estimates are calculated as

$$\begin{aligned} \begin{bmatrix} \hat{\alpha}_i \\ \hat{\beta}_i \end{bmatrix} &= \begin{bmatrix} \hat{F}_i'\hat{F}_i & \hat{F}_i'x_i \\ x_i'\hat{F}_i & x_i'x_i \end{bmatrix}^{-1} \begin{bmatrix} \hat{F}_i'y_i \\ x_i'y_i \end{bmatrix} \\ &= \begin{bmatrix} \alpha_i \\ \beta_i \end{bmatrix} + \begin{bmatrix} T^{-1}\hat{F}_i'\hat{F}_i & T^{-1}\hat{F}_i'x_i \\ T^{-1}x_i'\hat{F}_i & T^{-1}x_i'x_i \end{bmatrix}^{-1} \begin{bmatrix} T^{-1}\hat{F}_i'\eta_i + T^{-1}\hat{F}_i'f_i \\ T^{-1}x_i'\eta_i + T^{-1}x_i'f_i \end{bmatrix}. \end{aligned} \tag{1-9}$$

The most obvious difficulty with this particular method of estimation is that due to the nonlinear nature of the functions in $F_i(Y_i)$, terms of the form $T^{-1}\hat{F}_i'f_i$ and $T^{-1}x_i'f_i$ will possess zero probability limits only under strong assumptions.[5] Hence this application of RR may not yield consistent estimates.

There are variants of the RR method which tend to alleviate this problem. In particular, an instrumental variable formulation would yield estimates of α_i and β_i of the form[6]

[4] A fixed point in the neighborhood of Y_{t-1} appears to be typical for the class of models under consideration.

[5] This is essentially the point raised by Goldfeld [**8**] in connection with this version of the RR estimation procedure.

[6] The instrumental variable method is essentially the same (without iteration) as that proposed by Dutta and Lyttkens [**4**]. It was also taken up by Brundy and Jorgenson [**1**] modifying Jorgenson's original proposals cited above.

$$
(1\text{-}10)\qquad \begin{bmatrix}\hat{\alpha}_i\\ \hat{\beta}_i\end{bmatrix}=\begin{bmatrix}\hat{F}_i'F_i & \hat{F}_i'x_i\\ x_i'F & x_i'x_i\end{bmatrix}^{-1}\begin{bmatrix}\hat{F}_i'y_i\\ x_i'y_i\end{bmatrix}
=\begin{bmatrix}\alpha_i\\ \beta_i\end{bmatrix}+\begin{bmatrix}T^{-1}\hat{F}_i'F_i & T^{-1}\hat{F}_i'x_i\\ T^{-1}x_i'F_i & T^{-1}x_i'x_i\end{bmatrix}^{-1}\begin{bmatrix}T^{-1}\hat{F}_i'\eta_i\\ T^{-1}x_i'\eta_i\end{bmatrix}.
$$

Consistency requires that the probability limits of both $T^{-1}\hat{F}_i'\eta_i$ and $T^{-1}x_i'\eta_i$ vanish.[7] The latter probability limit causes no difficulty under the usual assumptions. In view of the way in which $\hat{F}_i'$ is defined, $T^{-1}\hat{F}_i'\eta_i$ can be written as $T^{-1}H_i(\hat{A}, \hat{B}, X)\eta_i$ where H_i is, in general, a nonlinear function in X. It appears likely that the probability limit of this term will be zero in any practical situation although there may be some pathological cases in which this is not true. In any event it is clear that instrumental variable estimators defined in (1–10) do not have the obvious problem exhibited by the two-stage least-squares estimator defined in (1–9).

It should be noted that due to nonlinearity, the consistency problems just discussed also arise in the first stage of the estimation procedure unless care is exercised at this stage. One device for circumventing the problem would be to calculate $\hat{F}_i$ as the predicted value from the regressions F_i on each of the columns of x_i and on appropriate linear and nonlinear functions of other exogenous variables.[8] That consistency is preserved is seen from a straightforward extension of arguments made by Fisher [**6**], Kloek and Mennes [**13**] and others.

This analysis indicates that the estimation procedure employed by Cooper does not in general yield consistent estimates of the parameters in nonlinear models. This certainly detracts from the prediction error tests that were performed with the re-estimated models. However, it should be noted that there is no guarantee that the small-sample mean squared prediction errors would have been smaller had a consistent estimator been used instead of the inconsistent estimator. Nor is it necessarily true that the prediction errors generated by the re-estimated models are larger than the errors generated by the original models. Indeed, the original models were frequently estimated by inconsistent methods, and the inappropriate estimators used in the original studies may have led to an acceptance of erroneous structural hypotheses.

2. USE OF PRIOR KNOWLEDGE IN SPECIFYING THE STRUCTURE.

In testing competing hypotheses, it is desirable for the tests to be applied to comparable bodies of data. The Cooper study satisfies this requirement, but much more is required. In particular, in estimating a structural model, the sample data must be drawn from the same population. If samples are drawn from different populations, the estimates (and forecasts) can be expected to be biased. One thing that seems certain is that because of factors such as technical change, strikes, government economic policies, and wars, the structure of economic

[7] It is assumed that the matrix $T^{-1}[\hat{F}_i x_i]'[F_i x_i]$ possesses a nonsingular probability limit.

[8] See Kelejian [**11**] for a further discussion of this point.

models shifts over time. An uncritical pooling of time series observations will surely involve sampling from different populations. Hence it is necessary to include known shifts in economic structure in the model.

The quarterly sample used in Cooper's study covered the period 1949 through 1960. Over this period a war occurred, and tax laws also changed. It is difficult to accept the single unchanging set of regression estimates for tax and transfer payment functions that was postulated. A minimal requirement in an econometric application is to change these functions as statutes change. This is of great importance. Moreover, it is likely that, due to strikes and technical progress, production functions, and hence investment demand functions, as well as price mark-up relations shift. These shifts need not be of a simple exponential sort. The shifts in the tax laws can also be expected to affect functions other than the equations for government tax receipts. Depreciation equations shift, and investment incentives are affected. This is only the beginning of a very long list of complications due to structural shifts.

It should be clear that building a good forecasting model involves a great deal of care. The economist begins by specifying an initial structural hypothesis; a prior or null hypothesis. This prior hypothesis involves a statement about the form of the structural equations, a statement of what knowledge is available concerning structural shifts, a statement of all prior knowledge about coefficient signs and magnitudes, and some statement about the error properties of the model. Finally, an explicit design of an appropriate sampling and estimation method is required. (Typically, the prior hypothesis implicitly involves a statement that some of the equations have stable structures.) The model is then estimated and some effort is then made to improve on it. This involves an examination of the initial estimates in the light of the prior hypotheses. If, for example, the original state of knowledge dictated that a coefficient was positive, and using an "appropriate" estimator, a significantly negative estimate was obtained, there are grounds for rejecting (revising) some part of the prior hypothesis (or of the estimation and sampling procedure). If the prior hypothesis specified that the error of the structural equations were non-autocorrelated and the calculated residuals of the estimated equations show strong systematic behavior over time, this too would be justification for rejecting (revising) the prior hypothesis. Sometimes attention is focused on the form of the equations; variables may have been omitted or included in an inappropriate fashion. New knowledge (additional data and information) typically suggest an answer. In reconsidering the prior hypotheses attention is often focused on structural shifts not originally hypothesized. Here too, new knowledge (information not available in the initial data set) is required.[9]

[9] It is noted that the above discussion has a certain Bayesian flavor. However, the formal analytic Bayesian framework is not present. It will, in fact, probably never be present. From a Monte Carlo viewpoint, the situation is akin to that of the decision maker who (1) has freedom to draw additional samples, but (2) who has only limited control over the characteristics of the sample, and (3) who has a certain amount of prior knowledge about the signs and magnitudes

(*Continued on next page*)

Unfortunately, in the Cooper paper there is little evidence that anything was done other than to estimate mechanically the various models using a consistent body of data; this is of course no small task. In view of the fact that the body of data used for the study differed (because of data revision and because the author chose a different sample period) from the bodies of data used by the original authors, some attention to prior knowledge is certainly called for. What is lacking is evidence that in constructing the models the author gave the same tender loving care (TLC) to each one that the authors of the earlier studies gave in constructing their models. Suppose the sign of a particular coefficient was obviously wrong, or that due to pooling of data from periods in which there were different structures, the calculated residuals of some equations showed strong systematic behavior. No one would consider using equations with such difficulties in a forecasting exercise. At this point we merely note that if TLC is lacking there is a *presumption* that the models tested will yield seriously biased *ex post* and *ex ante* forecasts.

In view of the great amount of work involved in estimating a structural model, and in view of the large number of competing models that Cooper was testing, it is reasonable to infer that applications of TLC to all of them would have been too much for any one investigator (or several). Suppose, on the other hand, that it was feasible to apply TLC. It is just possible that none of the models would have made it to the final squared error tests in a form that would be recognized by the original authors. Some of them would have been rejected even after taking "proper account" of strikes, wars and other structural shifts. The signs of many estimators may turn out wrong, and strong systematic behavior in the calculated residuals may lead to the conclusion that the earlier models were hopelessly misspecified. Even without the applications of TLC in the estimation process, some of the models might be rejected as being in obvious contradiction with the economic structure and institutions generating the data. Anyone who has carefully read *National Income 1954*, the volume which documents the construction of the NIA accounts (prior to revision), can cite numerous equation "specifications" in existing models which are completely at odds with the procedures used by the agency generating much of the data. In a slightly different vein a casual review of the inventory "theory" incorporated in many (perhaps all) of the models studied by Cooper will lead either to complete rejection or substantial revision of the inventory equations. The point is that had Cooper attempted to apply TLC he would possibly never have been content to race any of the old models against the autoregressive rabbit (our thanks to Goldfeld [**8**]); he would have raced his own model or models fortified by TLC. (This is not to say that the old models do so badly in the race, when properly fortified.)

(Continued)
of the coefficients. Such a decision maker could be expected to omit samples deemed to be outliers in terms of his prior knowledge. The investigator might well wish to examine the distribution of an estimator obtained by allowing for the exclusion of outliers. The statistical properties of such estimators would be close to the properties of the estimators used in a good forecasting model.

3. TESTS OF HYPOTHESES

As noted above the tests applied to the various models examined by Cooper were based on equation-by-equation comparisons of the mean squared error of one-quarter "forecasts" over the sample period (1949–1960) as well as mean squared errors calculated over the post-sample period (1961–1965). Unfortunately, classical hypothesis-testing procedures cannot be employed since the small-sample properties of the mean squared error statistics are generally unknown. It is therefore necessary to resort to more or less straightforward descriptive comparisons. Three types of comparisons immediately suggest themselves. First, the sample mean squared errors can be compared across models to determine which of the models achieves the closest fit to the data. Second, the post-sample MSE can be compared with the sample MSE in an attempt to ascertain the temporal stability of a given model. Finally, the post-sample MSE can be compared across models to determine which model has the samllest one-period forecast error. Of particular interest in all of these cases is a comparison of the MSE of a simple autoregressive model with the MSE of various structural models, the presumption being that the predictive accuracy of the structural model should at least equal if not surpass that of the autoregressive model in order to justify its use in forecasting. Each of these types of comparisons will now be considered in some detail in order to see what valid inferences can be drawn from such mean squared error comparisons.

3.1. *Sample-period mean squared error comparisons.* The major problems associated with the interpretation of sample-period mean squared error statistics become readily apparent in connection with a comparison of an autoregressive model with a structural model. Suppose that the null hypothesis is that the variable y_t is generated by an autoregressive process of order p; that is,

$$y_t = \sum_{i=1}^{p} b_i y_{t-i} + N_t \,. \tag{3–1}$$

For a sample of $T + 1$ observations, the null hypothesis can be written as

$$y = Z_2 B_2 + N \tag{3–2}$$

where

$$y = \begin{bmatrix} y_t \\ y_{t-1} \\ \vdots \\ y_{t-T} \end{bmatrix}, \qquad Z_2 = \begin{bmatrix} y_{t-1} & y_{t-2} & \cdots & y_{t-p} \\ y_{t-2} & y_{t-3} & \cdots & y_{t-p-1} \\ \vdots & & & \\ y_{t-T-1} & y_{t-T-2} & \cdots & y_{t-T-p} \end{bmatrix}$$

$$B_2 = \begin{bmatrix} b_1 \\ b_2 \\ \vdots \\ b_p \end{bmatrix}, \quad \text{and} \quad N = \begin{bmatrix} N_t \\ N_{t-1} \\ \vdots \\ N_{t-T} \end{bmatrix}. \tag{3–3}$$

The competing (structural) hypothesis is that y also depends on current and lagged exogenous variables and other lagged endogenous variables. In a linear framework, the alternative hypothesis is,

$$(3\text{–}4)\qquad \begin{aligned} y &= Z_1B_1 + Z_2B_2 + \xi \\ &= ZB + \xi \end{aligned}$$

where Z_1 is a matrix of observations on exogenous and other lagged endogenous variables, B_1 is a vector of parameters, and ξ is a vector of disturbances.

Now the sum of squared errors obtained from the autoregressive model is,

$$(3\text{–}5)\qquad \begin{aligned} S_1 &= [y - Z_2\hat{B}_2]'[y - Z_2\hat{B}_2] \\ &= y'[I - Z_2[Z_2'Z_2]^{-1}Z_2']y \end{aligned}$$

where $\hat{B}_2 = [Z_2'Z_2]^{-1}Z_2'y$ is the least squares estimate of B_2. Similarly, the sum of squared errors for the structural model is given by

$$(3\text{–}6)\qquad \begin{aligned} S_2 &= [y - Z\hat{B}]'[y - Z\hat{B}] \\ &= [y - Z\hat{B}_L - Z(\hat{B} - \hat{B}_L)]'[y - Z\hat{B}_L - Z(\hat{B} - \hat{B}_L)] \end{aligned}$$

where $\hat{B}_L = [Z'Z]^{-1}Z'y$ is the least squares estimate of B and $\hat{B}$ is a consistent simultaneous-equation estimate of B. It is not difficicult to verify that

$$(3\text{–}7)\qquad S_2 = S_1 - A + C$$

where

$$(3\text{–}8)\qquad A = y'\hat{Z}_1[\hat{Z}_1'\hat{Z}_1]^{-1}\hat{Z}_1'y$$

$$(3\text{–}9)\qquad C = (\hat{B} - \hat{B}_L)'Z'Z(\hat{B} - \hat{B}_L)$$

$$(3\text{–}10)\qquad \hat{Z}_1 = [I - Z_2[Z_2'Z_2]^{-1}Z_2']Z_1.$$

We now note the following:

1. Both A and C are nonnegative.
2. Since $\hat{Z}_1$ is the matrix of residuals obtained from a regression of Z_1 on Z_2', it follows that if Z_1 and Z_2 are highly correlated within the sample, the calculated residuals will be small in absolute value and A will therefore be small relative to S_1. In other words, if Z_1 and Z_2 are highly correlated, the reduction in the sum of squares achieved by the introduction of the additional regressors Z_1 will be small and S_2 will not be significantly smaller than S_1 despite the fact that more regressors are used to obtain S_2.
3. The term C is larger the greater the deviation of $\hat{B}$ from $\hat{B}_L$. The effect of such deviation is to make S_2 larger than S_1. Since the structural model may involve restrictions on some of the elements of B, $\hat{B}$ and $\hat{B}_L$ will generally differ. For example, the structural model may impose zero restrictions on some of the elements of B_2. The effect on C of high order (nonsense) lags obtained by least squares autoregression without regard to these restrictions is obvious. Another potentially important source of deviation of $\hat{B}$ from $\hat{B}_L$

is the case in which the error term exhibits serial correlation. In this case it is easy to show that the least squares estimates are biased; the bias resulting from the fact that lagged values of the dependent variable explain to some extent the movement of the error term. The effect of this bias is to increase the value of C since the least squares fit has the advantage of getting a lower MSE due to autocorrelated errors whereas the restricted reduced form if estimated by consistent methods, can never expect this advantage (in large samples).

These observations lead to the conclusion that sample-period mean squared error comparisons of the autoregressive and structural models are not powerful tests for at least two reasons. First, because many exogenous variables exhibit autocorrelation and because of the joint dependency of lagged values of y and lagged values of the other dependent variables in the system, lagged values of y serve as good substitutes for Z_1 for purposes of one quarter forecasts. This is true both within the sample used to estimate the parameters and outside the sample. Second, the squared errors of the structural model will be inflated due to the fact that the restricted reduced form estimate $\hat{B}$ will not be a least squares estimate. One problem here is that by expanding the regressor matrix sufficiently, arbitrarily close least-squares fits to the data can be obtained. Unless some "degrees of freedom" adjustment is made, it is extremely difficult to know what inferences to draw from the mean squared error comparisons. Unfortunately, the nature of an appropriate adjustment for degrees of freedom is not known. Even under the null hypothesis that the autoregressive model is true, the exact small sample moments of the sample MSE are not known in general. The first order case could possibly be handled by an extension of the work of Takeuchi [**17**] or Richardson [**16**] on the exact small sample moments of least squares estimates of two-dependent variable econometric models; however, the general case appears to be intractable. Still some adjustment is appropriate, and the expectation is that the autoregressive one quarter MSE is biased downward. The structural model MSE may also be similarly downward biased, though it seems unlikely that the structural MSE would be as seriously affected, since the structural estimation techniques do not lend themselves to error minimization in the same straightforward way that least squares autoregression does.

It has been suggested by Goldfeld [**8**], McCarthy [**14**], BEA [**10**], and others that a more adequate test of structural estimation might be obtained if the models' MSE of forecasts with longer lead times were compared. The reason that multiperiod forecast comparisons might be more powerful is that in the case of long term forecasts, the term Z_1 can be shown to contain variables from many periods beyond the periods represented in Z_2. In such a case Z_2 can be expected to do less well in explaining Z_1, and A can be expected to be larger. Moreover, the dependence of future errors on Z_2 is likely to be significantly less. This would be reflected in a smaller expected value for C. The longer period forecasts take away the advantage that the autoregressive scheme has in the short run.

A striking example of how multiperiod forecast comparisons yield results that are at odds with those reported by Cooper can be found in an experiment recently conducted by the BEA staff [**10**] and summarized in Table 1. It can be seen that the real GNP forecasts produced by the OBE model are more accurate than the autoregressive predictions even in the one quarter case. But the advantage of the structural model is considerably more striking in the case of forecasts with longer lead times.

TABLE 1

AVERAGE ABSOLUTE ERRORS IN REAL GNP OVER THE 40 QUARTERS 1955: I THROUGH 1966: IV

Billions of $		
	"Best" Autoregressive Equation	OBE Model*
One quarter forecasts	3.60	2.35
Two quarter forecasts	6.93	3.58
Three quarter forecasts	9.55	4.47
Fourth quarter forecasts	11.39	4.92
Fifth quarter forecasts	13.17	5.42
Sixth quarter forecasts	14.43	5.82

* Adjusted for first order serial correlation of residuals.

Another way in which the power of forecast error comparisons might be increased is to place more weight on those periods during which the economy is undergoing unusual changes. The ability of a model to track turning points, for example, might be more important than the average error over the entire sample period. The potential increase in the power of turning point comparisons again derives from the fact that when the economy is undergoing such adjustments, there is likely to be more independent variation in the exogenous variables and hence Z_2 will not provide as good a proxy for Z_1 as during periods of steady growth.

The following example illustrates this point. Using the time period 1949–1964, roughly the period covered by Cooper's study, we found the "best" autoregressive equation for real GNP to be,

$$\text{(3–11)} \qquad \begin{aligned} x &= \underset{(4.02)}{1.68} + \underset{(.11)}{1.44}X_{-1} - \underset{(.11)}{.44}X_{-2} \\ SE &= \text{Standard deviation} = 5.09. \end{aligned}$$

(The numbers in parentheses are estimated standard errors.) This relationship may be rewritten as[10]

$$\text{(3–12)} \qquad \Delta X = 1.68 + .44\Delta X_{-1}\,.$$

In this form it is clear why this particular autoregressive scheme would not perform well around turning points. Such a model would forecast a decline in X

[10] This equation is reminiscent of Orcutt's [**15**] single autoregressive equation used to represent all the dependent variables in Tinbergen's first U. S. Model.

only if the initial change (ΔX_{-1}) were negative and large enough in absolute value. If ΔX_{-1} were positive, the model would never forecast a downturn. In particular such an autoregressive model would have missed completely the recent downturn in economic activity (1969–1970) as shown by the estimated forecast beginning in 1969.3 and extending to 1970.2 presented in Table 2. For comparison, the Wharton model post release control forecasts made in August 1969 are also presented along with the actual figures.

TABLE 2

FORECASTS OF THE RECENT RECESSION (GNP, BILLIONS OF 1958 DOLLARS)

	69.3	69.4	70.1	70.2
Autoregression	730.0	733.1	736.2	739.2
Wharton*	729.1	727.2	728.1	732.5
Actual	730.9	729.2	723.8	724.9

* Source: Wharton-EFA, Inc., August 25, Post Release Control Solution

3.2. *Post-sample mean squared error comparisons.* The difficulties associated with comparisons of mean squared error statistics within the sample period indicate that such comparisons must be interpreted with caution. The question we now consider is whether post-sample mean squared error comparisons are subject to similar difficulties. As mentioned previously, post-sample statistics can be used in two ways: to test for temporal stability of a given model and to evaluate the predictive performance of alternative models.

The post-sample tests performed by Cooper create the presumption that the models that were analyzed were subject to temporal instability since the post-sample MSE typically exceeded the sample-period MSE. This result should occasion no surprise among those who have used econometric models for economic forecasting.[11] Indeed, it is generally agreed that mechanistic extrapolation of an econometric model frequently yields unsatisfactory results. One interpretation of this is that the sample-period mean squared error statistics are not good estimates of the variances of the residual process. This should simply serve to remind us of a point that is often lost sight of in model building; namely, the econometrician is attempting to estimate the variance-covariance matrix of the disturbance process as well as the coefficients of the model. The elements of the variance-covariance matrix are parameters of the model in the same sense that the coefficients of the model are parameters and the objective is to obtain a good estimate of this matrix and not necessarily to minimize its diagonal elements. A fact of life is that estimates of the variance-covariance matrix may leave us in the uncomfortable position that standard tolerance interval statements that should accompany simulations are very large. If one simply follows mechanical rules for model estimation and application, appropriate error and interval

[11] A more careful procedure for evaluation of post-sample errors is discussed in Dhrymes, *et al.* [3].

calculations may deprive the applied economist of any useful role whatsoever. The intervals are frequently so wide that almost anything from explosion to disaster can happen to the economy within their ranges.

We hasten to add, however, that this does not necessarily mean that it is impossible to derive from econometric models meaningful results for business or public policy use. It simply means that the contribution of econometric models to applied economics is increased substantially when it is used together with *a priori* information on error values to help reduce residual variance. And the intelligent user of econometric models would contend that there is a substantial amount of information that can be used to improve predictive performance. Many of the structural shifts that take place in the economy can be foreseen a quarter or more in advance; tax law changes and important strikes are examples. In preparing forecasts, the intelligent model user would surely have included the effect of these shifts in the forecast. Even in the case of those shifts that were not foreseen, the model forecaster would surely have learned by experience: having observed that some of his structural equations had begun to exhibit large errors, he could be expected to take corrective measures. In such a case, the forecast MSE would be expected to be much lower than the beyond-sample errors calculated by simple extrapolation of the model. In short, the fact that the beyond-sample errors yielded evidence of structural shifts precludes their use as measures of forecasting ability unless we are to believe that the model builder will do nothing about such shifts. The significance of the evidence of structural change lies in the fact that in a realistic forecasting environment many structural shifts can not be foreseen. Structural change does erode forecasting performance, but to the extent that structural shifts are correctly anticipated or rapidly detected, the actual forecast error will not be as large as the MSE obtained by simple extrapolation of the model.

In summary, the following point emerges in connection with post-sample mean squared error comparison. If the post-sample MSE is significantly larger than the sample MSE for a given model, then the post-sample MSE may be a poor measure of the forecasting performance of the model. For in this case, a judicious use of prior and posterior (i.e., error analysis) information may well yield a measurable increase in forecast accuracy. It follows that in order to interpret the post-sample MSE correctly, it is necessary to isolate the way in which temporal instability manifests itself.

3.3. *Remarks on ex ante forecasts.* Fortunately, the economist is not forced to make a once and for all decision based on sample period statistics. These statistics dictate the model he uses for an initial forecast. However, after the results are in, the decisions may be reviewed. The new data may be pooled with the old, and new sample tests performed. (Some day, years from now, convergence in probability may actually take place to a degree that the small sample problems discussed above may be ignored.) The major appeal of the *ex ante* forecast test is that it avoids the Monday Morning Quarterback aspects of the historical period tests. In this context, historical curve fitting buys the forecaster nothing. In a true *ex ante* forecast, models which have been "forced" to a close sample period fit may be expected to be poor performers. The autoregressive forecasters by choice make no use of exogenous variables, and hence are surely subject to error in an *ex ante* framework. The structural model forecaster must extrapolate the exogenous variables. On the other hand, in the near term, a good deal of intelligence is available on future values of these variables. For instance tax law changes are often legislated years ahead. Also the structural models, if correctly specified, provide a framework within which good exogenous information might be used. In other respects the competing forecasting models seem to be on equal grounds in the *ex ante* forecasts. Their managers are free to make use of past errors in attempts to improve future forecasts.

B. *Summary: some guidelines for future testing.* In pointing out deficiencies in Cooper's testing procedures and conclusions, we do not intend to negate the possibility of testing models. We do firmly believe that if this form of analysis is properly done, it can shed light on model credibility, validation, and improvement. We shall try to outline in this section what we would regard as suitable model testing procedures. Our recommended procedure will be far from the simple mechanistic approach followed by Cooper and will, in fact, be a more difficult, time-consuming process than that used in his study.

A guiding principle of our approach will be that the available information should be used efficiently—as efficiently as possible. Since economic samples are small and much less revealing than we would like, a great deal of TLC must be applied to all studies or nothing useful will be accomplished. The Model Tester should put himself in the position of the Model Builder and try to build the best possible structural model prior to testing; otherwise, he will be testing empty propositions.

Sample data: There is much to be said for choosing a fixed sample for fitting and extrapolation, common to all models being tested. It is not absolutely necessary to have the same sample for all models. In some cases it may not be possible, but for the most part homogeneity of sample appears to be desirable.

Within a fixed historical sample, the problem of data revision should not arise. It is not ruled out, however, because economic data are never "true," and measurement errors may affect different models in different ways. The best procedure, however, seems to be to choose a common sample period and fix the data for the whole set of test calculations.

Another caveat with respect to homogeneity of samples is the question of degrees of freedom. Alternative models and alternative methods of estimation have different requirements for degrees of freedom. This could be a factor in relaxation of the principle of sample homogeneity.

Specification: Economic theory and knowledge of the world around us can suggest a list of variables and some general parametric relationships. It cannot, however, set out in advance what the precise lag structure is nor all the departures from linearity. *That is a matter of sample experimentation and not purely a matter of specification.*

The model to be tested should be estimated, either by the tester or original model builder, with TLC to get as good a system as possible. We would have preferred that Cooper built his own structural models with TLC. This will be especially important for within-sample tests, for it is well known that sufficient work done on lag structure, a wide range of variable selection, or use of additional parameters can markedly improve the fit. An efficient search of the parameter space will not necessarily drive a complete system to close fit in simultaneous equation solution, but it often can improve the fit considerably. The autoregressive test equations are driven, equation by equation, towards close fit by experimenting with the lag structure and similar experimentation is needed for the structural model, subject of course, to *a priori* information about the nature of the overall relationship and the general shape of the lag distributions incorporated in the model.

Because we lack information on exact small sample properties, historical period results are of limited value. Some thought should be given to designing tests of forecasting performance in a true *ex ante* framework.[12]

Estimation: Since different model structures have different degrees of freedom, within a given sample, and since methods of estimation are not equally sensitive to limitations of degrees of freedom it is not clear that all models to be tested should be estimated by the same technique. Each model should be estimated by a method that will give the best performance for that system. Best performance might be determined by simulation testing within the sample used for fitting. This is all part of TLC. Brookings-type models are so large that they cannot be estimated by maximum likelihood methods. Whether the other models likely to be considered can be so estimated or not is an open question, but this comparison illustrates that estimation methods must be tailored to the model.

Collinearity is as important as shortage of degrees of freedom in making estimation difficult or inefficient. Models differ as to degree of collinearity. Nonlinearity differences and identification differences provide additional reasons why estimation methods should not be made uniform.

Many models may, in fact, be well suited to the RR method used by Cooper, but if this method is to be used for each model to be tested, it should not be applied in the manner suggested by Cooper (or Jorgenson). The method consists of first estimating a model by some consistent method such as ordinary TSLS, indirect least squares, instrumental variables, or modified TSLS, where the first stage regressors are some selected subset of instrumental variables in the whole system.[13] In the final stage of the RR method, regressors are constructed in each structural equation using computed values of dependent variables from the restricted reduced forms of the system (estimated at the earlier stage) and the included predetermined variables in each individual equation. As noted above, care must be taken at both stages of this process if consistency is to be

[12] Cooper's extrapolation period tests should definitely not be viewed as *ex ante* tests, but as tests of structural stability with limited significance.

[13] We have recently come to the view that the first round estimater used not be consistent, and OLS might be a good starting choice. Jorgenson and Brundy, in a later paper, suggest one extra iteration following an inconsistent (OLS) start.

preserved.

Since this process could be iterated, as in the work of Dutta and Lyttkens [4], but is usually stopped after the first or second iteration, the set of parameter estimates used will depend heavily on the value from the first round. It is, therefore, imperative to estimate the first round with much TLC and using an efficient selection procedure for obtaining instruments when there is a shortage of degrees of freedom. If there are enough degrees of freedom, the first round estimates to be used for getting the restricted reduced forms may well make use of all available instruments. If there are not enough degrees of freedom we recommend the data-reduction procedure of choosing appropriate principal components of predetermined variables or perhaps following the suggestions of Fisher [6]. Since system simulation performance depends on the choice of instruments, some experimentation may be called for.

Some parameter estimates may be manifestly unsatisfactory. The system should be re-specified and re-estimated until the investigator is sure that all coefficients are satisfactory. This is estimation with TLC. Often only one or two poor equation estimates can be readily modified and change a poorly behaving system into a well behaving system.

The final stage of the RR method should use an estimate of the first stage that a model builder would be willing to accept in deriving regressors for the second stage from system solutions of the first stage, i.e., from estimated restricted reduced forms if the system is linear. Again, however, TLC must be applied, for all estimates in the final stage regressions will not necessarily turn out to be satisfactory. It is simply a fact of life that estimation or re-estimation of models in new or modified samples changes a few parameter estimates from being reasonable to being unreasonable. By respecifying and re-estimating, these changes can be effectively dealt with. In some cases, re-normalization is all that is needed. Since the TSLS or RR method depends on units normalization and since the normalization rules are arbitrary, such applications of TLC must be made. It has been found that iteration of the Wharton Model estimate (TSLS with principal components of predetermined variables) can produce within sample simulations that reduce root-mean-squared error of GNP by $3–4 billion if one production function estimate is renormalized and restricted to have constant returns to scale. Otherwise there would be no improvement in simulation error. Why should a model tester throw away such valuable information simply because he wants to adhere to a strict mechanical rule?

Application: A rounded set of applications should be made in testing a model. Prediction performance should be tested, but both multi- as well as single-period predictions should be considered. Autoregressive or even more general autoregressive-moving average schemes are known to generate rapidly increasing prediction error as the time horizon of extrapolation lengthens; therefore, tests should not be biased by being confined to single period prediction.

If major exogenous events occur in the extrapolation period that were not present in the sample period, and if these events could, in principle, have been known in advance of prediction, they should be quantified and introduced in the ex-post prediction tests. Statutory changes in tax, transfer, reserve, and other laws that form structural restrictions on the system must be introduced in the testing period as they occurred in actual economic life. This was not done in Cooper's tests. The *ex ante* prediction performance of models, in the hands of model builders using TLC, takes these events into account. That is an important reason why ex ante prediction records with models are so much better in terms of performance accuracy than mechanically applied ex post records. Although it takes painfully long to build up statistical samples of systematically applied ex ante forecast records, we feel that they are as revealing (perhaps even more so) in the validation of a model as are ex post prediction tests.

Some standards must be set on the variables to be tested. There is no unique way of writing a given model, for definitional identities can be added indefinitely. The generation of additional forecasts from a given solution has no bounds. There are actually only as many predictions of variables as there are stochastic equations of a system. Prediction tests often score points on accuracy of the GNP deflator, GNP in current prices, GNP in constant prices; yet these three variables are nonstochastically related in the identity

$$pX = GNP\,.$$

It may be of descriptive interest to see how well all three variables are predicted, but the error analysis does not constitute three independent pieces of test information. By judicious invention of additional identities, test scores may be drastically altered; therefore testing should be confined to as many dependent variables of a system as there are stochastic equations.

Prediction at turning points is of unusual importance, and these should be separately tested. The entire cyclical or frequency response characteristics of a model should be tested. The standard tests are in the time domain, but model performance in the frequency domain is of equal importance.

The growth characteristics of a model should also be tested. The short run models may need amplification for this form of testing and the corresponding naive model may be different from the pure autoregressive, but this aspect of testing should not be overlooked.

In general policy simulation, the naive models have no content. If they are modified to include exogenous policy variables, they may cease to be naive alternatives. Without comparing models to the naive case, suitably built models may well be compared with one another in respect to response in alternative policy simulations. This could constitute another form of test and has been the procedure in the working seminar that gave rise to this symposium [7].

University of Michigan
University of Pennsylvania
Case Western Reserve University

REFERENCES

[1] BRUNDY, J. AND D. JORGENSON, "Efficient Estimation of Simultaneous Equations by Instrumental Variables," *Review of Economics and Statistics*, LIII (August, 1971), 207–224.

[2] COOPER, RONALD L., "The Predictive Performance of Quarterly Econometric Models of the United States," in B.G. Hickman, ed., *Econometric Models of Cyclical Behavior,* Studies in Income and Wealth, No. 36 (New York: Columbia University Press for NBER, 1972).

[3] DHRYMES, PHOEBUS J. *et al.*, "Criteria for Evaluation of Econometric Models," *Annals of Economic and Social Measurement*, I (Summer, 1972), 291–324.

[4] DUTTA, M. AND E. LYTTKENS, "Iterative Instrumental Variables Method and Estimation of a Large Simultaneous System," Discussion paper No. 7, Rutgers University, 1970.

[5] EVANS, MICHAEL K., YOEL HAITOVSKY, AND GEORGE TREYZ, "An Analysis of the Forecasting Properties of U. S. Econometric Models," in B. G. Hickman ed., *Econometric Models of Cyclical Behavior*, Studies in Income and Wealth, No. 36. (New York: Columbia University Press for NBER, 1972).

[6] FISHER, FRANKLIN M., "Dynamic Structure and Estimation in Economy Wide Econometric Models," in J. Duesenberry *et al.*, eds., *The Brookings Quarterly Econometric Model of the United States* (Chicago: Rand McNally, 1965).

[7] FROMM, G. AND L. R. KLEIN, "A Comparison of Eleven Econometric Models of the United States," *American Economic Review, Papers and Proceedings*, LXIII (May, 1973), 385–393.

[8] GOLDFELD, STEPHEN M., "The Predictive Performance of Quarterly Econometric Models of the United States: Comments," in B. G. Hickman ed., *Econometric Models of Cyclical Behavior*, Studies in Income and Wealth, No. 36 (New York: Columbia University Press for NBER, 1972).

[9] GORDON, R. J., "Large Scale Econometric Models: An Introduction and Appraisal for Non-Econometricians," unpublished mimeograph, February, 1970.

[10] GREEN, G. R., M. LIEBENBERG, AND A. A. HIRSCH, "The Predictive Performance of Quarterly Econometric Models of the United States: Comments," in B. G. Hickman ed., *Econometric Models of Cyclical Behavior*, Studies in Income and Wealth, No. 36 (New York: Columbia University Press for NBER, 1972).

[11] KELEJIAN, HARRY H., "Two-Stage Least Squares and Econometric Systems Linear in Parameters but Nonlinear in the Endogenous Variables," *Journal of the American Statistical Association*, LXVI (June, 1971), 373–374.

[12] KLEIN, LAWRENCE R., *An Essay on the Theory of Economic Prediction*, Helsinki, 1968. Distributed by the Academic Bookstore, Helsinki. Enlarged U. S. edition (Chicago: Markham, 1971).

[13] KLOEK, T AND L. B. M. MENNES, "Simultaneous Equation Estimation Based on Principal Components of Predetermined Variables," *Econometrica*, XXVIII (January, 1960), 45–61.

[14] MCCARTHY, MICHAEL D., "The Predictive Performance of Quarterly Econometric Models of the United States: Comments," in B. G. Hickman ed., *Econometric Models of Cyclical Behavior*, Studies in Income and Wealth, No. 36 (New York: Columbia University Press for NBER, 1972).

[15] ORCUTT, G. H., "A Study of the Autoregressive Nature of the Time Series Used for Tinbergen's Model of the Economic System of the United States, 1919–1932," *Journal of the Royal Statistical Society*, Series B, X (1948), 1–53.

[16] RICHARDSON, D. H., "The Exact Distribution of a Structural Coefficient Estimate," *Journal of the American Statiscal Association*, LXIII (December, 1968), 1214–1226.

[17] TAKEUCHI, K., "Exact Sampling Moments of the Ordinary Least Squares, Instrumental Variable, and Two Stage Least Squares Estimator," *International Economic Review*, XI (February, 1970), 1–12.

[18] ZARNOWITZ, VICTOR, CHARLOTTE BOSCHAN, AND GEOFFREY H. MOORE, "Business Cycle Analysis of Econometric Model Simulations," in B. G. Hickman ed., *Econometric Models of Cyclical Behavior*, Studies in Income and Wealth, No. 36 (New York: Columbia University Press for NBER, 1972).

6

ON THE ROLE OF EXPECTATIONS OF PRICE AND TECHNOLOGICAL CHANGE IN AN INVESTMENT FUNCTION

By Albert K. Ando, Franco Modigliani, Robert Rasche, and Stephen J. Turnovsky[1]

1. INTRODUCTION

It is a simple tautology that, when prices of inputs and outputs are not expected to remain constant during the planning horizon, real rates of interest and the money rate of interest are not the same. While the investment decision must depend upon a "real" rate of interest, the monetary authority can at best control directly the money rate of interest. Furthermore, the notion of a real rate of interest is itself ambiguous since there are three alternative real rates, namely, in terms of output, of capital goods, and of labor. Therefore, in order to evaluate the effects of monetary policy on investment decisions, it is crucial to specify the way in which the money rate of interest and the expected rate of change of prices both enter the cost of capital which in turn directly influences investment decisions.

To answer this question requires the formulation of an investment function. The purpose of this paper is to investigate this problem, both theoretically and empirically, in the context of the investment function developed by Bischoff [**1**, **2**], which is based on the assumption of a "putty-clay" production function. In this model the equipment in which the investment at any given point of time is embodied is characterized by fixed proportions, and in particular by a fixed output labor ratio, although the proportions embodied in the equipment can be chosen from a set of alternatives describable by an *ex ante* production function allowing for continuous factor substitution. Bischoff has shown that under these conditions the investment function takes the general form

$$I_t = \hat{k}_t \Delta X_t^c \tag{1}$$

where I_t and ΔX_t^c denote respectively gross investment and the gross increment to capacity which firms wish to provide for in period t, both for expansion and for replacement, and $\hat{k}_t$ is the optimum (cost minimizing) capital output ratio in the same period t, as determined by the relative prices of relevant inputs prevailing then, and expected to prevail over the relevant future.

In his original contribution Bischoff derived an expression for $\hat{k}_t$ but his analysis was based, in part, implicitly on two rather restrictive, interrelated,

[1] We are grateful to Dale Jorgenson for his comments on an earlier draft of this paper and to Robert Shiller for his comments on the theoretical section and especially for his help in the derivation in Section 2.2. We also wish to thank Al Hoffman for his excellent research assistance. Finally, we owe special thanks to Charles Bischoff on whose work we have drawn freely and whose advice was especially helpful in the final revision of the manuscript.

simplifying assumptions. First, he assumed that input prices were expected to remain constant over the life span of the currently acquired equipment. He assumed further that the equipment remained in service until it completely depreciated physically, an assumption which, as we shall see, can be justified if, but only if, the first assumption holds.

Our task is to generalize his analysis by allowing explicitly for the fact that, in general, input (and output) prices will be expected to change over time, both in absolute terms and relative to each other. These expectations will arise in part from prevailing anticipations of *overall inflationary or deflationary trends* and in part from the anticipation of *continued technological progress*.

Thus far, expectational elements have received little attention in either the theory or the empirical estimation of investment functions.[2] One previous attempt to deal with this question is in two papers by Jorgenson and Siebert [**13**, **14**] which are based on the assumption of a putty-putty technology. They show that under this assumption the relevant real rate of interest is the rate measured in terms of capital goods. However, in the putty-putty model even already installed capital is instantaneously malleable and thus factor proportions are free to adjust in response to changes in relative prices as they occur. This implies a myopic investment rule, depending only on the *current* real rate of interest and hence only on the expected rate of change of prices for the current period. Their equations estimated over the period 1949–63 provide some evidence that the incorporation of a measure of the expected rate of change of prices of capital goods leads to some improvement in the quality of the results.

In a putty-clay model, however, since all existing capital is characterized by fixed proportion over its economic life, a myopic rule will, in general, not be optimal. The current choice of technology must depend instead on the current as well as expected future "real" rate of interest and real wage rate, and, therefore, on the expected future course of money wages and prices, as well as on expected technological change over the life of the investment (and even beyond—see below).[3] A somewhat counter-intuitive result of our analysis is that, in the putty-clay model, the relevant rate of interest is the real rate in terms of output rather than of capital goods (or labor).

A further complication arises from the fact that the expected service life can no longer be taken as determined exogenously by technological properties. On

[2] For a recent extensive and enlightening review of econometric estimates of investment functions, see Jorgenson [**12**].

[3] Even in the conventional putty-putty model the optimality of the myopic rule ceases to hold if one assumes the existence of "adjustment costs" so that, for example, the cost of installed capital goods is an increasing function of the rate of investment, as suggested, in particular, by Eisner and Strotz [**6**], (see also the references cited by Jorgenson [**12**, (1142)]); this has been shown, for example, by Gould [**8**]. In our analysis, we have not explicitly introduced adjustment costs related to the rate of investment. Note, however, that our putty-clay model does explicitly allow for the cost of adjusting the existing stock of capital to changes in relative prices—a cost which is, in fact, indefinitely large. Because of this cost, a putty-clay model can readily account for the slow adjustment of the stock of capital to changes in relative prices, suggested by the empirical evidence, without recourse to the somewhat *ad hoc* notion that the cost of capital goods depends on the rate of growth of the stock of capital, gross or net.

the contrary, the expectations of forthcoming technological progress and changes in relative prices may lead to the expectation that it will be advantageous to discard the current equipment before it is physically obsolete. As is well known, this will occur once the marginal cost of producing with the current equipment exceeds the average cost for the latest available vintage. Thus the determination of the "economic service life" of the present investment becomes itself an integral part of the optimization problem which interacts with the choice of the optimum capital-output ratio and thus affects the form of the investment function.

In the light of the above consideration it appears that the derivation of the investment function must be cast in the framework of a "machine replacement problem." That is, given some output X to be produced throughout the indefinite future, and given a (consistent) set of expectations about future prices and technological progress, there is an optimal sequence of machines that minimizes the present value of expected costs. The currently purchased equipment must then be viewed as the first link in this optimal chain.

The rest of this paper is divided into three parts. In 2, we endeavor to establish which are the variables, current and expectational, that determine the optimum capital output ratio $\hat{k}_t$, at any given date, and to derive the parametric form of the function relating $\hat{k}_t$ to these variables. In 3 the results of 2 are utilized to derive an empirically testable investment function, making due allowance for the relevant response lags, and for the nature of the available data. Finally, in 4 we proceed to test the model and estimate its parameters.

The results of our statistical tests are not as clear cut as one might wish, due in part to the well known difficulty of measuring the expectation of the rate of change of prices. However, it is hoped that the theoretical and empirical analysis presented here will provide a useful basis for further research on the difficult problem of explaining the behavior of aggregate investment.

2. THE EFFECT OF EXPECTED TECHNOLOGICAL AND PRICE CHANGES ON THE OPTIMAL CAPITAL OUTPUT RATIO

2.1. *Assumptions.* Since the empirical work in this paper is based on the Cobb-Douglas production function, this shall be assumed throughout.[4] We further assume that Harrod neutral technical progress occurs at the constant rate g, and that firms (correctly) anticipate the indefinite continuation of this progress. Thus at date t the *ex ante* (putty) production function, assumed to be homogeneous of degree one can be denoted by:

$$X_t = AI_t^{1-a}(e^{gt}E_t)^a$$

where,

X = flow of gross output
I = putty content of capital equipment
E = man hours per unit time

[4] The considerations that justify this assumption as a useful approximation in an econometric analysis of investment data are discussed in footnote 29.

g = the rate of "Harrod neutral" (embodied) technical progress[5]
t = the point in time when I is installed.

Since we shall eventually apply our formulation to the explanation of investment in producers' equipment in the economy as a whole, it is more natural to think of I not as one machine but as a collection of machines. We make the following additional assumptions:

(a) A proportion d of all existing equipment becomes physically incapacitated and scrapped per year.
(b) As machines get older, the required labor increases at the rate m per year for surviving machines.
(c) Demand for the output of new machines is exogenously given and firms expect that it will continue indefinitely.
(d) Producers expect that over the "relevant" future, the money wage rate, W, will rise at the constant proportional rate w, the money interest rate, r, will remain constant and the price of capital goods (putty), Q, relative to the price of output, P, will increase at a constant proportional rate q^*. (In the special case of a "one sector" model q^* would of course be zero.)
(e) Finally, as in Bischoff's original formulation, we assume that the output price is set by applying an oligopolistic mark up, M, determined by entry preventing considerations, to the minimum cost achievable, given current and expected technology and factor prices. We further postulate that firms assume that the mark up policy will remain constant over the relevant future. However, in view of the dynamic nature of our analysis the assumed mark-up policy is specified as follows: the price at any date t is such that, given that the same price *policy* will apply at all future dates, the present value of revenue derived from a constant stream of output must be M times the present value of the minimized cost of the same stream of output.

2.2. *Derivation of the optimal capital—output ratio.* As indicated in Section 1, the derivation of the investment function requires determining the current investment I_0 that is optimal for a given output X in the sense that, together with an optimal sequence of later investments, it minimizes the present value (PV) of costs of producing the perpetual stream X. The task of determining the optimal sequence can be accomplished by relying on fairly standard methods; however, since it turns out to be rather lengthy and tedious we shall here merely sketch out the derivation, highlighting those steps which have a bearing on later developments.[6]

In the first place it can be shown that, under our "constant expectations" assumption, the optimal life of each machine in the chain is the same and is independent of the point of time at which the chain starts. The problem can then be conveniently attacked in two stages. We first determine the capital output and labor output ratio that minimize the present value of costs for *given* service

[5] The analysis developed in the text assumes that all technological progress is embodied. It can, however, be readily generalized to the case where some constant portion of g is disembodied.
[6] A detailed derivation is available on request from the authors.

life, T. The solution to this suboptimization problem can then be used to express the PV of costs in terms of T and, hence, finally to determine the cost minimizing value of T, which we denote by $\hat{T}$.

When T is given, it follows from assumptions (a), (b) and (d) that the present value of costs of the stream of output resulting from the initial investment can be expressed as

$$(2) \qquad C_0(X, T) = Q_0 I_0 + E_0 W_0 \int_0^T e^{-(r-w+d-m)s}\, ds$$

where X is the initial capacity of the equipment and I_0, E_0, must satisfy the initial production function constraint, $X = A(I_0)^{1-a}(E_0)^a$. The cost in (2) consists of the initial purchase cost of the equipment together with the present value of the payments to labor employed on that machine throughout its life.

Let us define:

p = the proportional rate of change of output price

$R = r - p + d$; $L = m + w - p$; $R^* = r - m - w + d = R - L$

$B(s, T) = \dfrac{1 - e^{-sT}}{s}$ for all s and T $s > 0, T > 0$.

Note that $r - p$ is the "real" rate of interest in terms of output, R is the "real" rental rate in terms of output, and L is the rate of increase in the real labor cost of operating machines of a given vintage, as those machines grow older.

From the above definition and (2) it follows that the PV of cost *per unit* of initial capacity X, can be written as

$$(3) \qquad \chi_0(T) = \frac{C_0(X, T)}{X} = Q_0\left(\frac{I_0}{X}\right) + W_0 B(R^*, T)\left(\frac{E_0}{X}\right).$$

Now, let $(\hat{I}_0/X)$ and $(\hat{E}_0/X)$ denote the capital output and the capital labor ratio that minimize $\chi_0(T)$, subject to the production function constraint, and let $\hat{\chi}_0(T)$ denote the minimized value of $\chi_0(T)$, or

$$\hat{\chi}_0(T) = Q_0\left(\frac{\hat{I}_0}{X}\right) + W_0 B(R^*, T)\left(\frac{\hat{E}_0}{X}\right).$$

Relying on standard methods of constrained minimization one finds that

$$(4a) \qquad \left(\frac{\hat{I}_0}{X}\right) = A^{-1}\left[\frac{(1-a) W_0 B(R^*, T)}{aQ_0}\right]^a$$

$$(4b) \qquad \left(\frac{\hat{E}_0}{X}\right) = A^{-1}\left[\frac{(1-a) W_0 B(R^*, T)}{aQ_0}\right]^{a-1}.$$

One can then establish that our assumption about the expected course of W, r, and P/Q and about the constancy of the mark up have the following implications:

i) The minimized PV of costs per unit of capacity expected to result from a machine installed at any later date t, and computed as of that date, must be expected to grow in time at a constant rate, or

(5a) $$\hat{\chi}_t(T) = \hat{\chi}_0(T)e^{pt}$$

where[7]

(6) $$p = w - g + q^*(1 - a)/a\,.$$

Similarly, the price set on output must also be expected to rise at the same rate p, or

(5b) $$P_0(t) = P_0e^{pt}$$

where $P_0(t)$ is the price which, in period 0, is expected to rule t periods later. (Note that for $q^* = 0$ (6) reduces to the familiar formula, $p = w - g$.)

ii) The minimized PV of cost per unit of producing a constant output X over the infinite horizon starting at time 0, given that service life is T, can be expressed as

$$\hat{c}_0(T) = \frac{\hat{\chi}_0(T)}{(r-p)B(R,T)} = \frac{1}{(r-p)B(R,T)} \times \left[Q_0\left(\frac{\hat{I}_0}{X}\right) + W_0B(R^*,T)\left(\frac{\hat{E}_0}{X}\right)\right].$$

Substituting for $\hat{I}_0/X$ and $\hat{E}_0/X$ from equation (4) we finally obtain

(7) $$\hat{c}_0(T) = \frac{[(1-a)B(R^*,T)]^{(a-1)}}{A(r-p)a^a}\,Q_0^{1-a}W_0$$

which gives the unit cost associated with any service life T, when factor intensities are chosen optimally for that T. The optimal T, $\hat{T}$, is then that value which minimizes the right-hand side of (7); it must satisfy the first order minimum condition[8]

(8) $$\frac{ae^{-R^*T}}{B(R^*,T)} - \frac{e^{-RT}}{B(R,T)} = 0\,.$$

Hence from equation (4a) we can conclude that the currently optimum capital output ratio, k_0 is given by the right-hand side of that equation with T replaced by $\hat{T}$. That equation, however, expresses k_0 in terms of the ratio of the wage rate to capital good prices, W_0/Q_0 which cannot be taken as an exogenous parameter in our model. Indeed, what our model assumes as exogenously given is

[7] Since by assumption the price of capital goods relative to the price of output is expected to change at the constant rate q^*, it follows that the price of capital goods itself is expected to grow at the constant rate $q = p + q^*$. Note that the conclusion that cost must be expected to rise at a constant rate could be reached without recourse to the assumption of a constant mark up by starting out with the assumption that Q is expected to grow at the constant rate q. With this assumption, cost can readily be shown to grow at the constant rate $(1-a)q + a(w-g)$. Alternatively, (5) could be established by defining q^* as the growth of Q relative to unit cost. In either case the assumption of a constant mark up would still be needed to establish the constancy of the rate of growth of output price and its equality to the rate of growth of unit cost.

[8] It can be verified that the second order condition, $d^2c_0/dT^2 > 0$, is also satisfied as long as $m + g > 0$ and hence $L > 0$. An approximate explicit solution of (8) for $\hat{T}$ is given in the footnote to Table 2.

the ratio of capital goods to output prices or Q_0/P_0. Hence

$$\frac{Q_0}{W_0} = \left(\frac{Q_0}{P_0}\right)\frac{P_0}{W_0},$$

is determined by P_0/W_0 which, in turn, depends on the mark-up policy. Our mark-up policy assumption (cf. assumption (e)) can now be formally expressed as

$$PV \text{ of Revenue per unit} = M\hat{c}_0(\hat{T}) . \qquad (9)$$

But from equation (5b) it follows that

$$PV \text{ of Revenue per unit} = \int_0^\infty P_0(t)e^{-rt}dt = P_0\int_0^\infty e^{-(r-p)t}dt = \frac{P_0}{r-p} .$$

Substituting this result in the left hand side of (9) and making use of (7) we can therefore write

$$P_0 = \frac{M[(1-a)B(R^*, \hat{T})]^{a-1}}{Aa^a} Q_0^{1-a} W_0{}^a .$$

Multiplying both sides by $P_0^{(a-1)}$ and solving for P_0, we finally obtain:

$$P_0 = \frac{1}{a}\left(\frac{M}{A}\right)^{1/a}\left[\frac{(1-a)B(R^*, \hat{T})}{q_0}\right]^{(a-1)/a} W_0 \qquad (10)$$

expressing the price in terms of its "ultimate" determinants: the parameters of the production function, a, A; the factor prices, W_0, R^* and the exogenously given q_0; and the mark-up factor, M.

From (10), we can infer:

$$\frac{Q_0}{W_0} = q_0\frac{P_0}{W_0} = \frac{1}{a}\left(\frac{M}{A}\right)^{1/a}[(1-a)B(R^*, \hat{T})]^{(a-1)/a}q_0^{1/a}$$

and substituting this result for W_0/Q_0 in (4a) yields our final expression for the current optimal capital output ratio:

$$k_0 = \left(\frac{\hat{I}_0}{X}\right) = \frac{1-a}{Mq_0}B(R^*, \hat{T}) = \frac{1-a}{M}\frac{P_0}{Q_0}\frac{1-e^{-(r-p+d)\hat{T}}}{r-p+d} . \qquad (11)$$

This equation is remarkably similar in form to that originally derived by Bischoff. It actually differs from that equation in only two respects, both having to do with the last factor. In the first place, in the denominator Bischoff's money rate r is replaced by the "real rate", $r - p$. We have thus established that, at least under our assumptions, *the real rate of interest relevant to the investment decision is the "own" rate measured in terms of output.*[9] The other difference is

[9] It is interesting to observe that this result differs substantively from that obtained for the conventional "putty-putty" model where it turns out that the real rate of interest should be

(*Continued on next page*)

the term, $e^{-(r-p+d)\hat{T}}$ appearing in the numerator and which brings in the effect of the "economic service life." This term did not appear in Bischoff because, under his simplifying assumptions, $\hat{T}$ could, essentially, be taken as indefinitely large (though, of course, even in his model the capacity of each vintage is dwindling toward zero through the decay factor d). This last term, unfortunately, confronts us with somewhat of a problem. We know that $\hat{T}$ is the solution for T of equation (8) so that to complete our derivation of $\hat{k}_0$ we should, in principle, replace this solution for $\hat{T}$ in the right hand side of (11). The difficulty is that equation (8) does not yield an explicit analytical solution.

One way around this difficulty is to secure some approximation to $\hat{T}$, or possibly to the whole numerator of the last factor, $1 - e^{-R\hat{T}}$. To this end we may note that, given Bischoff's estimate of d as .16, any realistic value of the real rate implies a value of R of no less than .20. Hence, if $\hat{T}$ were to be reasonably large, say somewhere above 10, $e^{-R\hat{T}}$ would be a rather small number compared with unity. But then, especially if $\hat{T}$ turned out to be not very sensitive to variations in $r - p$, the quantity $1 - e^{-R\hat{T}}$ might well be approximated by a constant close to one. These considerations led us to investigate the properties of $\hat{T}$ through the numerical solution of equation (8), for a range of "reasonable" values of the relevant parameters and for a realistic range of values of the real rate $r - p$. Selected results of these calculations are reproduced in Table 1.

Inspection of (8) shows that T is independent of the mark-up factor M, but depends on the coefficient a of the production function and on R and R^*, or equivalently R and L (since $R^* = R - L$). We chose for a a range of .65 to .75, though we regard the neighborhood of the lower bound as somewhat more realistic. It is harder to guess a reasonable range for L, which by definition equals $m + w - p$. However, using (6), this expression can be written more usefully in the alternative form $m + g - ((1 - a)/a)q^*$. For the United States, the rate of technical progress, g, can be estimated at close to 3 percent but we have no direct measure of m. As for the ratio of Q/P, q^*, it has had some tendency to increase at a very modest rate, though this may largely reflect errors of measurement. In the table we present results for a range of L from.03 to .05.

An inspection of the table suggests the following summary conclusions:

i) The only parameter to which $\hat{T}$ is sensitive is L. As might be expected $\hat{T}$ is a decreasing function of L; the faster machines deteriorate (m), and the faster the rate of technological progress (g), the shorter the economic life. In fact, as can be verified by inspection of (8) as L tends to zero (Bischoff's implicit assumption), T approaches infinity (if equipment does not accumulate inferiority with respect to new equipment, it never pays to discard it). It is also apparent from (11) that a larger value of L, (and hence m

(continued)
measured in terms of capital goods. Of course, in the special case $q^* = 0$, and hence $p = q = w - g$ (see (6)), the real rate in terms of output coincides with that in terms of capital goods (putty), and also with the real rate in terms of labor measured in "efficiency" units. Similarly for the general case $q^* \neq 0$, since $p = (1 - a)q + a(w - g)$, we can also say that what matters is the real rate in terms of a "basket," consisting of $(1 - a)$ units of putty and a units of labor in efficiency units.

TABLE 1

VALUE OF $\hat{T}$ AS A FUNCTION OF a, d, L, AND $r - p$

a	d	L	$r-p$	T
.65	.16	.03	.02	20
			.06	19
			.10	18
		.04	.02	16
			.06	15
			.10	14
		.05	.02	13
			.06	13
			.10	12
.75	.16	.03	.02	14
			.06	14
			.10	13
		.04	.02	11
			.06	11
			.10	10
		.05	.02	9
			.06	9
			.10	9
.65	.10	.03	.02	21
			.06	20
			.10	19
		.04	.02	17
			.06	16
			.10	15
		.05	.02	14
			.06	13
			.10	13

and g), by reducing the service life, tends to *decrease* the capital output ratio, as it results in a higher "rental cost."

ii) For the neighborhood of the parameters which we regard as most realistic for the U.S. economy of the postwar period, the value of $\hat{T}$ is in the neighborhood of 15 years ± 2 years, or a little lower if a is closer to .75.

iii) $\hat{T}$ is a *decreasing* function of the real rate $r - p$, but in the relevant range of the parameters, it is clearly very insensitive to variations in this variable.[10]

[10] The finding that $\hat{T}$ tends to fall with R is rather surprising and counter-intuitive. Indeed, the literature on optimal equipment replacement policy suggests that a higher interest rate generally works toward postponing replacement and thus larger $\hat{T}$. Our results come about because as R rises, the optimal labor capital ratio rises, which makes for a decreasing $\hat{T}$. It can be verified that if this ratio were unaffected by R then, in general, $d\hat{T}/dR$ would indeed tend to be positive (although even in this case $d\hat{T}/dR < 0$ is not impossible if the labor capital ratio is large enough and L is large relative to R).

TABLE 2

	(1)	(2)
$r - p$	Elasticity of $\frac{1 - e^{-(r-p+d)\hat{T}}}{r - p + d}$ with respect to $(r - p)$[1]	Elasticity of $\frac{1}{r - p + d}$ with respect to $(r - p)$
.02	−0.103	−0.111
.06	−0.253	−0.273
.10	−0.357	−0.385

[1] In computing this elasticity we relied on the following approximations to T, which is close for $\hat{T}$ sufficiently large:

$$T = \frac{\ln R - \ln R^* - \ln c}{L},$$

where c is a constant. The values of T were obtained from Table 1, under the assumption $L = .04$, $a = .65$, and $d = .16$.

These observations in turn suggest that, in the relevant range of $r - p$, the last factor on the right hand side of (11), $(1 - e^{-R\hat{T}})/R$ might well be replaced by the very convenient approximation: D/R, D a constant. As a further check on this approximation, we provide in Table 2 a comparison between the elasticity with respect to $r - p$ of $(1 - e^{-R\hat{T}})/R$ and of the proposed approximation, D/R.[11] These elasticities are seen to be quite close, though that of the approximation is, of course, systematically slightly higher. This suggests that a better approximation might be $D/(R + c)$ where c is some small positive constant. This is the approximation we have actually employed, with c estimated from the data.

2.3. *Allowing for the effect of taxes.* Before we can utilize (11), or its approximation, for empirical tests we must make proper allowance for the effect of major tax provisions: the corporate income tax, depreciation provisions and investment tax credit. In this respect our treatment is analogous to that of previous authors (see e.g., Bischoff [**2**], Hall and Jorgenson [**10**], Jorgenson [**11**]), so that again we need only summarize the results.

Taking tax considerations into account, the present value (at time zero) of the "tax adjusted" cost per unit of initial capacity, resulting from the investment I_0—i.e., the right hand side of (3)—must be modified to:

$$(1 - u)\frac{E_0}{X} W_0 B(R^*, T) + Q_0 \frac{I_0}{X}(1 - k - uz')$$

where

u = rate of direct taxation of business income

$z = \int_0^J e^{-rs} D(s) ds$

J = lifetime of the machine for tax purposes

$D(s)$ = proportion of the original cost of an asset of age s that can be deducted from taxable income

k = rate of tax credit on investment
$z' = (1 - k')z$, k' = rate of tax credit that can be deducted from original cost to obtain the depreciation base.

Also, in order to make proper allowances for taxes, our mark-up rule is modified to:

$$PV \text{ of tax adjusted revenue per unit} \equiv \frac{(1-u)P_0}{r-p} = M \cdot PV \text{ of minimized tax adjusted cost per unit.}$$

Then a step-by-step repetition of the derivation in 2.2 leads to the following generalization of (11)

$$k_0 \equiv \left(\frac{\hat{I}_0}{X}\right) = \frac{(1-a)(1-u)P_0}{MQ_0(1-k-uz')} \cdot \frac{1-e^{-(r-p+d)\hat{T}}}{r-p+d}.$$

This equation is again similar to (3.6) of Bischoff [**1**, (73)] from which it differs again only in the last factor. It can also be readily verified that the optimal economic life is totally unaffected by the kind of taxes we have allowed for and hence $\hat{T}$ is again given by the solution of equation (8). It follows that our arguments supporting the approximation of the last factor by $D/(R+c)$ remain valid. We thus conclude that the optimal capital-output ratio implied by our model can be approximated by

$$\hat{k}_t = \frac{(1-a)}{M}\left(\frac{(1-u)}{1-k-uz'}\right)\left(\frac{P}{Q}\right)\left(\frac{D}{r-p+d+c}\right). \tag{12}$$

This result, it should be acknowledged, depends on a number of rather stringent assumptions. However, some of these assumptions can be considerably relaxed. In particular, it should be apparent from our derivation that, given the constancy of g and q^*, our results remain valid even if r and w are expected to change, as long as $r - w$ (the real rate in terms of labor) is expected to remain constant. Finally, while we have developed the theory for the Cobb-Douglas production function, the crucial proposition in our derivation, namely that prices and unit costs both rise at the same constant rate p, generalizes for any production function homogeneous of degree 1, provided $p = q$, i.e., in essence, for a single sector model.

3. DERIVATION OF THE INVESTMENT FUNCTION

3.1. *Short-run adjustments.* Equation (1), with $\hat{k}_t$ defined by (12), gives the static equilibrium relationship among I, ΔX^c, P/Q, and $r - p$. Since actual data are generated by the economy in which these variables are continuously changing, we must modify (12) in order to accommodate adjustment processes. This is one of the problems thoroughly discussed by Bischoff. In this paper, we will simply list the more important considerations which led Bischoff to his formulation of the dynamic adjustment.

(a) In our theoretical discussion we did not distinguish among decisions to add to capacity, placement of orders for, and shipment of equipment, and actual additions to capacity. In actual practice, these are clearly distinct actions which take place sequentially. After the need for addition to capacity is recognized, specifications for the equipment required for this addition to capacity corresponding to anticipated relative prices are drawn up. The order containing these specifications is then placed, and the equipment is finally produced, shipped and installed. We have no information on the timing of decisions to add to capacity, but we feel that the timing relationship between the decision to add to capacity and orders for equipment is much less variable over business cycles than that between orders and shipments. We therefore take orders for equipment as the dependent variable for our investment equation. The relationship between orders and the national income definition of expenditures on producers durable equipment will be discussed in Section 3.4.

(b) Orders reflect recent past decisions, and decisions are based on the anticipated need for additions to capacity and anticipated relative prices. Like Bischoff, we assume that anticipated relative prices are functions of past relative prices, and that anticipated need for capacity is proportional to anticipated output which is, in turn, a function of past outputs.

These considerations, together with a variety of statistical reasoning, led Bischoff to the following specifications:

$$OPD_t = \sum_{i=0}^{n} \alpha_i VPD_{t-i-1} XB_{t-i} + \sum_{i=1}^{n+1} \beta_i VPD_{t-i} XB_{t-i} \tag{13}$$

where n is the length of the orders lag, OPD denotes orders for producers durable equipment, XB is gross domestic business product (our approximation to X), and

$$VPD \equiv A' \frac{1-u}{1-k-uz'} \frac{PXB}{PPD} \frac{1}{d+\rho^*+c} \tag{13'}$$

is our operational empirical approximation to $\hat{k}$ of equation (12).[11,12] The

[11] It should be readily apparent that this formulation of the investment function is broadly consistent with the findings about the determinants of replacement expenditure reported by Feldstein and Foot [7]. Our dependent variable is (order for) *gross* investment, and we make nowhere use of the assumption that replacement expenditure is proportional to the stock of capital. Furthermore, our distributed lags of past sales can, at least in principle, account for the variables that are found to affect replacement expenditure, except for "available funds" whose role in *total* expenditure, however, cannot be inferred from the equation for replacement alone.

[12] As has been pointed out by Gould [9], the use of actual output XB as the independent variable in (13) is not altogether satisfactory. It would be clearly preferable to use a variable like orders booked, since, strictly speaking, actual output must be regarded as an endogenous, "optimizing" response of the firm to orders received. Unfortunately, there seems to be at present no feasible alternative to XB at the level of aggregation with which we deal in the present paper. Indeed, there exists no comprehensive series of aggregate orders corresponding to XB, and even the partial series available cannot be readily utilized because they involve a great deal of duplication. In any event, while the (attenuation) bias resulting from the use of actual output could be serious in dealing with individual firms, or even very disaggregated industry totals, it is unlikely to be very significant at the very aggregate level of our analysis, especially since the output variable that finally determines orders is an average of some twelve terms.

constant A' stands for the factor $(1 - a)D/M$, PXB is the deflator for XB, (our approximation to p) and PPD is the NIA price index for producers durable goods (our approximation to Q). Finally, ρ^* denotes a measure of the required real rate of return, or cost of capital, which we have denoted by $r - p$ in Section 2. It is only with respect to the measurement of this variable that our procedure differs significantly from Bischoff's.[13]

3.2. *The measurement of the cost of capital.* Following Modigliani-Miller [**15** and **16**], Bischoff proposed to measure ρ^* as

$$\rho^* = \rho(1 - ul)$$

where ρ is the market capitalization rate of an unlevered stream, and l is the target leverage or ratio of debt to debt-plus-equity. Note that since he did not explicitly face the problem of price expectations he did not need to specify whether this measure was an approximation to r or to $r - p$.

According to Modigliani-Miller $(M - M)\rho$ itself can be inferred from market data as

$$\rho = \frac{\hat{Z}(1 - u)}{S + D - uD} G$$

where D is the (market) value of firms' debt, S the market value of equity, Z the expected stream of before tax returns from current assets and G an adjustment factor for special growth opportunities incorporated in the market valuation of equity, S. Denoting by i the average rate of interest on outstanding debt and by $\Pi = (1 - u)[Z - (iD)]$ net of tax profits, we can rewrite $\hat{Z}(1 - u)$ as $\hat{\Pi} + (1 - u)(iD)$. Expected net profits $\hat{\Pi}$ is unobservable, but Bischoff suggested approximating it from dividends (Div) by relying on the hypothesis that dividend payments are proportional to expected profits, or $\Pi = Div/\delta$ where δ is the "target" payout ratio. We can then approximate ρ by

$$\rho \simeq b_1 i + b_2 \frac{Div}{S} \tag{14}$$

$$b_1 \equiv \frac{G(1 - u)D}{S + (1 - u)D}, \quad b_2 \equiv \frac{G}{\delta} \frac{S}{S + (1 - u)D}. \tag{14$'$}$$

Bischoff next assumed that G, δ and S/D are reasonably stable over time, justifying treating b_1 and b_2 as constants. He further approximated Div/S and i respectively by a linear function of an index of dividend yields, RDP, and of corporate bond yields, RCB. He was thus led to measure ρ, by a linear function of RCB and RDP, say

$$\rho' = c_0 + c_1 RCB + c_2 RDP. \tag{15}$$

Accordingly, in (13′), he used the approximation

[13] Eisner and Nadiri have raised certain objections against the specification (13), (see [**4**, footnote 30]). These objections are discussed in footnote 17.

(16) $$d + \rho^* = d + (c_0 + c_1 RCB + c_2 RDP)(1 - ul)$$

(the constant c_0 does not appear in Bischoff since it is related to our approximation to e^{-RT}). He further assumed l to be constant (0.2) and estimated the coefficients c_0, c_1, c_2, simultaneously with the coefficients α_i and β_i of (13) by the method of maximum likelihood.

One striking feature of Bischoff's results is that his estimate of c_1 was consistently quite large relative to c_2, typically about one and a half times as large. Taken at face value, these estimates would seem to be inconsistent with (14), since, as is apparent from (14′), the ratio c_1/c_2 should be of the order of $b_1/b_2 = (1 - u)\delta D/S$. With the corporate tax rate u around .5, the dividend pay out ratio δ also in the order of .5 and since D/S is certainly less than one, c_1/c_2 should be less than 1/4, instead of over 1.5. His results, however, might be accounted for by the consideration that ρ' of equation (15) is a measure of ρ subject to errors on at least two counts: i) because dividends are an imperfect measure of expected profits $\hat{\Pi}$ and ii) because the growth component G may be subject to variations in time. At the same time, the long rate RCB also contains important information about ρ. Indeed the required return on equity capital, ρ, should differ from the long rate only by a "risk premium." If this premium were constant—or more generally a linear function of the long rate—then the long rate would be a perfect proxy for ρ. Thus, one might think of RCB as an alternative measure of ρ subject to error, this time error resulting from variation in time in the risk premium. Under these conditions the weights c_1 and c_2 may be expected to reflect in part the relative informational content of the two variables ρ' and RCB with respect to the non-directly observable variable ρ.[14]

However, our analysis of Section 2 shows that the appropriate measure of the required rate of return ρ^* is not the money rate of return r, but rather the real rate $(r - p)$. Now, as is well known, the capitalization rate of profits, $\hat{\Pi}/S$ is a real rate, and hence RDP itself can be regarded as a measure of the real rate up to proportionality factor.[15] However, RCB is a money rate. These considera-

[14] A possible additional explanation for the large relative weight of RCB is that the *MM* measure may be directly relevant for firms having reasonable access to the equity markets, while for other investors the required rate might be some linear function of the long rate. The cost of capital would then be an average of the *MM* measure and the long rate.

[15] This statement is only approximately valid. While it is correct to say that ρ, the capitalization rate for an *unlevered* stream, is a real rate, in the sense that it should be unaffected by the rate of inflation p, this is not strictly valid in the case of the capitalization rate for a levered stream, $\hat{\Pi}/S$. It was shown in [**16**, (equation (12c))], that $\hat{\Pi}/S = \rho + (1 - u)D/S(\rho - i)$. This equation can be shown to remain valid also in the presence of inflation, if D is expected to remain constant, while if one assumes, more reasonably, that the target leverage *ratio* remains constant in the face of inflation, then the right side should contain an additional term $-u(Dp/S\hat{i})\rho$, where $\hat{i}$ is the "real" rate of interest. Thus, in principle, $\hat{\Pi}/S$ is a (decreasing) function of the expected rate of inflation, p, because the last term contains p explicitly, and because, even in the absence of this term, it depends on the money rate which, in turn, will tend to increase with p. However, since D/S is quite small (around .2, as already noted) and u is roughly .5, the effect of p on $\hat{\Pi}/S$ should be quite small as long as p remains moderate. Some numerical calculations based on NIA and Flow of Funds data, fully confirmed this conjecture and lead to the conclusion that this effect could be safely disregarded, for the period of observation, and for foreseeable rates of inflation.

tions lead us to approximate $d + \rho^* + c$ by

$$d + \rho^* + c = d + [c_0 + c_1(RCB - p) + c_2 RDP](1 - ul) + c\,. \tag{17}$$

p measures the expected rate of change of prices, as in Section 2.[16,17]

3.3. *The measurement of the expected rate of inflation.* Unfortunately, the estimation of p in equation (17) poses a very difficult problem because what is needed is a subjective, anticipated rate of change of prices for which there are no direct data. One possibility, which has been used extensively in earlier work, is to rely on a weighted average of the past actual rate of change of prices as a proxy. However, it did not seem feasible to estimate the weights as a part of the estimation of the investment equation due to the severe non-linearity of the equation. We were thus led to attempt to approximate the expected rate of change by the following weighted average of past cited price changes:

$$p_s = 400 \frac{1}{\sum_{j=0}^{11} (.87)^j} \sum_{j=0}^{11} (.87)^j \frac{PXB_{t-j} - PXB_{t-j-1}}{PXB_{t-j-1}}\,. \tag{18}$$

The weights are taken from a paper by Modigliani and Shiller [**17**], in which they have estimated a set of weights similar to the one in the above equation

16 In the actual estimation of (13) the last constant c was dropped. This is because l is assumed constant and u has had no significant changes in the period of estimation. Under these conditions it would be impossible to secure reliable separate estimates of the constants c_0 and c. The estimated value of the constant c_0 reported in Table 3A below must thus be regarded as standing for $c_0 + c/(1 - ul)$, and since the first term should be close to zero, we should expect this estimated value to be positive, or at least non-negative.

17 This measure of the cost of capital should be immune to the criticism levied by Eisner and Nadiri [**4**, (373–74)], against a somewhat related measure used in some of Jorgenson's work in computing the rental price of capital (c_1), namely the earning price ratio. This ratio, they argue, is "an implicit measure of expected future profits," rather than the desired measure of the ratio of *expected* earnings to market value. They further suggest that the latter ratio should tend to be more or less proportional to the interest rate. Accordingly the influence of the cost of capital on investment could be more reliably estimated by using the interest rate rather than the earning price ratio. Indeed the association of the latter variable with investment might reflect the role of expectations rather than the true effect of the cost of capital.

In our measure of the cost of capital we have replaced earnings with dividends which we regard as a better measure of expected future profit. At the same time, we acknowledge that even the dividend price ratio will not provide a perfect measure of the ratio of expected profit to price. On the other hand, as indicated in the text, the (real) interest rate will also not provide a perfect indicator—except if the risk premium is constant. There is no justification for such an assumption on a priori ground or in the light of the post-war experience. This period was characterized by a *declining* trend in the earning and dividend ratio, at least until the early 60's and a *rising* trend in interest rates, strongly suggesting a declining trend in the risk premium. (These opposite trends, incidentally readily explain the negative correlation between Jorgenson's c_1 and c_2 measures which so puzzled Eisner and Nadiri in [**5**, (220, Footnote 17)]. Since both the (real) interest rate and the dividend price ratio contain some, but only some, information about the true cost of capital, the measure we have used is a weighted average of these two. Finally, since the estimated weight of the interest rate turns out to be twice as large as that of the dividend-price ratio, there seems very little danger of significant upward bias in our estimate of the effect of the cost of capital, of the type suggested by Eisner and Nadiri for Jorgenson's c_1.

as a by-product of their study of the term structure of interest rates. We are not on very firm ground in transplanting the weights obtained in the estimation of a term structure equation to the investment equation, but we could not come up with a better alternative to it. Under the circumstances, we have tried to locate some information, however indirect, on the accuracy of this approximation.

The only continuous time series covering the period of 1950–1969 related to the price expectations of business decision makers that we have been able to locate is a semi-annual survey of so-called business economists conducted by Mr. J. A. Livingston of the *Philadelphia Bulletin*. In his survey, Mr. Livingston asks his respondents to state what they think the level of Consumer Price Index (CPI) and Wholesale Price Index (WPI) will be six months and twelve months after the date of the survey. Since the questionnaire used in the survey provides the latest figures on these indices, we can interpret the responses to these questions as giving the respondents' idea of the expected rate of change of these indices.

There are several serious difficulties in using these time series of expectations generated by Mr. Livingston's surveys. First, they are on the WPI and CPI, while what we need for our purposes is the expectation of the rate of change of *PXB*, domestic private business output in the national income accounts. Second, Livingston's data are expectations for the period of one year or less from the time when the survey is conducted, while what we need are much longer run expectations; short run expectations of prices may be influenced much more by very recent special circumstances than the longer period expectations would be.

To get around the first of these two difficulties, we have calculated the weighted average of the past actual rate of change of CPI in the same way as in equation (18) above, and compared the resulting series with the Livingston data on expectations of the rate of change of the CPI for a period of a year from the time when the survey is given.[18] This comparison is shown in Figure 1.

All we can say about Figure 1 is that the Livingston expectations and our proxy move in broadly similar patterns, though the levels are different, after 1962 or so, while the two series have totally different patterns before 1960. Perhaps all we can conclude from this comparison is that, for the period since 1965, any series based on the past rate of change of prices catches the broad pattern of the movements of the price expectations, while it does not provide much reliable information about price expectations before 1960.

Under the circumstances, we conclude that we have to be very cautious in using equation (18) as the mechanism generating price expectations, and that we should not be surprised if it served as a very rough approximation since 1965 but did not work at all before.

We would like to make a final comment on the measurement of p. It is quite possible that some of the decision makers do not pay much attention to the expected rate of change of prices unless their recent experience indicates that it

[18] Since the Livingston data are only six-monthly, we have interpolated them to give quarterly predictions.

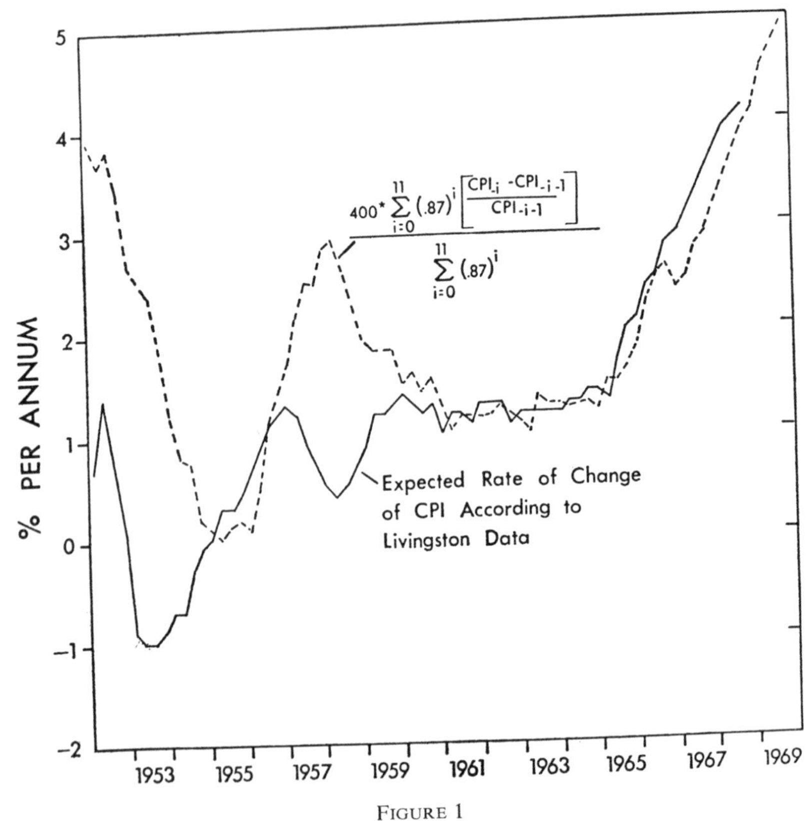

FIGURE 1

COMPARISON OF EXPECTED RATE OF CHANGE OF CPI ACCORDING TO THE LIVINGSTON SURVEY AND A WEIGHTED AVERAGE OF PAST VALUES OF CPI

is quite important to do so. If the actual rate of change of prices has been very small in the recent past, those decision makers who did not correct for the rate of change of prices in their calculation of cost of capital find that, *ex post*, they have not been seriously wrong, and they may then continue to ignore the rate of change of price in their calculation of the cost of capital in their current decisions. If a substantial proportion of the decision makers behaved this way, then at any point of time, some proportion would take account of the expected rate of change of prices while the remainder would assume that it is either zero or a small constant, the proportionality depending on the recent actual rate of change of prices.

To take this kind of consideration explicitly into account would be an impossible task since the estimation of our investment function already involves fairly complex non-linearities. We shall attempt to account for this possibility by supposing that if some fraction of the decision makers adjust the money interest rate for the rate of change of prices and the rest do not, then this is similar, in effect, to a situation in which all decision makers adjust only partially.

Thus we hypothesize that the rate of interest that enters the cost of capital in our investment equation is a weighted average of the form:

$$w_1 RCB + w_2(RCB - p) = RCB - w_2 P$$
$$w_1 + w_2 = 1.0$$

where w_2 depends on the recent past actual rate of change of prices. We have experimented with the following approximations for w_2:

$$w_2 = \frac{1}{12}\sum_{i=0}^{11} D_i$$

(19)

$$D_i = \begin{cases} 0 & \text{if} \\ 1 & \text{otherwise} \end{cases} \qquad \frac{PXB_{t-i} - PXB_{t-i-1}}{PXB_{t-i-1}} \leq C .$$

We shall refer to w_2 as defined above as "threshold weights."

3.4. *New orders and their relation to expenditure on producer durables.* We have noted that *OPD*, the dependent variable in equation (13), represents (net) orders for producers' durable goods. Unfortunately, data for this variable do not exist at present. We have, therefore, constructed a time series for this variable based on current and later expenditure on producers' durables (*EPD*) as given in the national income accounts, orders for machinery and equipments, and shipments of machinery and equipments.[19] This constructed series is used as the dependent variable in (13).

The variable *OPD* plays an important direct role in the FMP model, particularly in the inventory equation and in the price equation. However, for our present purpose interest centers on actual expenditure, *EPD*. We hypothesize that *EPD* can be accounted for by a distributed lag of current and past values of *OPD*, with the weights reflecting the prevailing time required for execution of different types of orders. We also allow for the possibility of a variable lag because the time required to process an order might tend to change over the business cycle, depending on the volume of orders outstanding, relative to existing capacity. Lacking an explicit measure of capacity of the equipment industry we have approximated the last mentioned effect by the ratio of unfilled orders (*OUPD*) to deliveries, or *EPD*.

Thus our investment expenditure equation takes the form:

(20a)
$$EPD = \sum_{i=0}^{5}\left[a_i + b_i\left(\frac{OUPD}{EPD}\right)_{-(1+i)}\right] OPD_{-i} .$$

The coefficients of this equation have been estimated subject to the constraint that

$$\sum_{i=0}^{5} a_i = 1 , \quad \sum_{i=0}^{5} b_i = 0$$

[19] A detailed description of the procedure used for generating the *OPD* data and a discussion of the reliability of the data so generated is available from the authors.

to insure that, given time enough, deliveries must match orders. The estimated value of coefficients and other characteristics of this equation are:

$a_0 = .4357$	$b_0 = -.5378$
$a_1 = .3378$	$b_1 = -.1752$
$a_2 = .2102$	$b_2 = -.0768$
$a_3 = .0290$	$b_3 = .2181$
$a_4 = -.0145$	$b_4 = .2489$
$a_5 = -.0521$	$b_5 = .1691$
$R^2 = .9261$	Sample period: 54.3–66.4
$\sigma_\varepsilon = .8462$	
$D.W. = 1.14$	

Unfilled orders, *OUPD*, are in turn given by the perpetual inventory formulation

$$OUPD = .25(OPD - EPD) + OUPD_{-1}\,. \tag{20b}$$

In interpreting the coefficients of equation (20), it is helpful to note that the average value of the ratio $OUPD/EPD$ over the sample period is roughly .37.[20] Thus, the pattern of the b_i coefficients of equation (20) implies that, as $OUPD/EPD$ rises, the weight of the most recent orders declines, while the weight of orders placed further back correspondingly rises, lengthening the average delivery period.

It is apparent from the content of this section that there are two ways in which one can judge the performance of our model. One method consists in comparing the actual values of *OPD* with the values generated by (13). This test, however, is of limited value in that the series for *OPD* is our own construction, and, furthermore, because of the method used to construct it, the current and very recent values of this series are subject to large revisions. A more telling test is how well (13) together with (20) can account for actual expenditure, *EPD*. In this test, the results of which are reported below, *EPD* is always computed from (20), using the values of *OPD*, current and lagged, generated by (13).

4. ESTIMATION AND TESTS

Table 3 reports the results of our estimation of equation (13), with the cost of capital given by (17), for alternative periods of estimation and alternative specifications of the crucial variable p.[21] Part A provides summary measures of

[20] It should be remembered that *EPD* is measured at an annual rate, while *OUPD*, being a stock concept, is not affected by the length of period. This accounts for the coefficient .25 in (20b).

[21] The estimates were carried out before the revision of the National Income data in summer '71, '72 and '73. Since the period of estimation extends at most through 1968, and the revision did not affect the pre-1967 data, and affected 1968 to a relatively minor extent, we can safely conclude that revised data would not perceptibly affect the estimates reported in Table 3. The data used in the extrapolation tests of Table 4 are also unrevised, and here the effect of the revisions is considerably more serious, as the revisions for more recent years are non-negligible and affect not only *EPD* and *OPD*, but also the independent variables used in the extrapolation of (13). Some comments on the implications of the revised data are provided in footnotes 27 and 28.

TABLE 3

PART A

SUMMARY CHARACTERISTICS OF ALTERNATIVE SPECIFICATION

	Sample Period: 1953 : 1—1965 : 4			Sample Period: 1953 : 1—1968 : 4		
	(1)[6]	(2)[7]	(3)[8]	(4)[9]	(5)[10]	(6)[11]
R^2[1]	.979	.968 (.974)	.974 (.977)	.984 (.987)	.987 (.990)	.910 (.982)
Se[2,4]	1.095	1.370 (1.238)	1.227 (1.169)	1.397 (1.273)	1.253 (1.143)	3.234 (1.517)
DW[3,4]	1.71	1.29 (1.75)	1.27 (2.07)	1.25 (1.77)	1.232 (1.915)	0.32 (2.00)
λ[4]	0	.35	.35	.45	.40	.96
c_0[5]	0	.37494	.30465	0	0	—
c_1[5]	3.64316	3.49123	6.83889	2.35035	2.08971	—
c_2[5]	2.28964	5.81559	−.66020	1.82362	1.38398	—

1. The ratio of explained variance to total variance adjusted for the degrees of freedom.
2. Standard error of estimate, adjusted for degrees of freedom.
3. Durbin-Watson Statistic of the residual.
4. λ represents the first order serial correlation of residuals. The estimation program does not minimize the residual sum of squares with respect to λ. We have, therefore, followed the procedure in which we first estimate parameters assuming λ to be zero, and calculate the serial correlation of residual, and then re-estimate the equation assuming the true serial correlation to be equal to the one so calculated. The second round estimates almost always gave residuals whose serial correlation was very close to zero. Whenever λ is other than zero, for R^2, Se, and DW, we report, *without* parenthesis, their values calculated with $\lambda = 0$, which are, for present purpose, the relevant statistics to judge goodness of fit. For the sake of completeness we also show in parenthesis the values obtained allowing for the estimated value of λ as reported in the table.
5. c_0, c_1, and c_2 are, respectively, the constant and the coefficients of *RCB-p* and *RDP* in the cost of capital terms. See equation (17) in the text.
6. Estimated under the assumption that p is constant.
7. p is assumed to be given by (21a).
8. p is assumed to be given by (21c).
9. p is assumed to be zero for the period 1954–64, and given by (21a) for the period 1965–68. Because of the way the depreciation rate, d, and c_0 enter the cost of capital, this could be reinterpreted to mean that p is a constant $\bar{p}$, for 1953–64, and it is $p_s - 1.2 + \bar{p}$ for 1965–1968.
10. p is assumed to be zero for the period 1953–1964, and given by (21b) for 1965–68. The same comment as in footnote 13 applies to this case.
11. *VPD* is assumed constant throughout the straight acceleration model.

PART B

ESTIMATED STEADY STATE ELASTICITIES OF *OPD* WITH RESPECT TO *RCB-p* AND *RDP*

	(1)		(2)		(3)		(4)		(5)	
	RCB-p	*RDP*	*RCB-p*	*RDP*	*RCB-p*	*RDP*	*RCB-p*	*RDP*	*RCB-p*	*RDP*
1953, 1st quarter	−.34	−.38	−.05	−.37	−.42	.05	−.28	−.38	−.29	−.34
1958, 1st quarter	−.41	−.32	−.08	−.32	−.36	.05	−.35	−.33	−.35	−.29
1963, 1st quarter	−.50	−.25	−.19	−.23	−.35	.04	−.42	−.25	−.41	−.22
1965, 1st quarter	−.53	−.22	−.20	−.20	−.33	.04	−.44	−.22	−.42	−.20

TABLE 3

PART C

PERCENT APPROACH TO EQUILIBRIUM

Changes in *XB*	(1)	(2)	(3)	(4)	(5)
1	310	138	270	284	230
2	262	160	280	275	235
3	230	169	273	263	234
4	209	168	252	247	227
5	195	161	224	229	215
6	185	150	192	209	199
7	175	137	161	188	179
8	164	126	133	167	187
9	150	116	112	146	136
10	135	108	98	127	117
11	118	103	94	112	104
12	100	100	100	100	100
Changes in *V*					
1	0	0	0	0	0
2	18	87	49	20	28
3	38	143	80	38	54
4	59	173	98	54	75
5	78	183	107	67	91
6	92	181	109	78	103
7	103	170	108	86	110
8	108	153	106	92	112
9	110	135	103	96	111
10	107	119	101	99	107
11	103	107	100	100	103
12	100	100	100	100	100

fit as well as the estimated value of the three coefficients c_0, c_1, and c_2 of (17). When, as in column (1), the value of c_0 is given as zero, the estimation was carried out constraining this coefficient to be zero. This was done because the unconstrained estimation tended to yield a large negative value of c_0 which cannot be readily reconciled with *a priori* specifications.[22] It also implied an implausibly high value of the elasticity of the capital output ratio, and hence of investment, with respect to the long-run cost of capital. In every instance imposing this constraint increased but slightly the sum of squared residuals while yielding much more plausible estimates of the elasticities. The long-run elasticities implied by the estimates are shown in Part B of the table for each component

[22] Cf. footnote 16.

of the cost of capital, namely *RDP* and the "real" interest rate, *RCB-p*. Since these elasticities are not constant under our specifications, we report the values computed for four representative periods; we recall here that, over the period of observation, *RDP* has tended on the whole to decline, especially till the mid 60's, while *RCB* has tended to rise steadily. It should also be observed that in the steady state, *RDP* can be expected to change roughly in proportion to the real rate of interest; hence, the overall longest-run effect of a change in the real interest rate, both directly and indirectly through *RDP*, is roughly equal to the sum of the elasticities for each component.

The coefficients α_i and β_i of the distributed lag of equation (13) were estimated, as in Bischoff [**1**] by Almon's method using third degree polynomials. We do not report the values of the individual coefficients α_i, β_i, because they are not easy to interpret economically. Instead we report in Part C, the essential economic implication of the estimated pattern. Specifically we show in the upper part of the table the time path of response to a step change in output, *XB*, as a percentage of the steady state response; this steady state response is simply the rate of investment which is needed to *maintain* the additional capacity, installed in response to the change in *XB*. The initial response on the other hand shows the path of investment through which the *additional* capacity, needed to produce the incremental output is provided for; in other words, it shows the time path of the "accelerator." As did Bischoff, we assume that the process of providing the additional capacity is completed within three years. Our model, like most others, implies that the entries in the upper half should rise to a peak (which could occur in the very first quarter) and then decline monotonically toward the steady state value, which is normalized to be 100.

The lower part of Table 3C gives the path of response of orders to a step change in the optimal capital output ratio, *VPD* (the counterpart of $\hat{k}$ of Section 2), whatever the source of change in *VPD*, (cost of capital, *P/Q*, or tax provisions). The entries show the implicit response in quarter *j* after the step change, as a percentage of the long-run response. (In the long run, we recall, investment is unit elastic with respect to *VPD*). As shown by Bischoff, it is an essential implication of the putty-clay model that this response should rise monotonically from zero to 100. By contrast the putty-putty hypothesis implies an "accelerator type" path, greatly overshooting the steady state response and reflecting investment expenditure for the purpose of modifying the capital intensity of the stock of capital *already in place*.

In columns (1) to (3) of Table 3A the parameters were estimated over the sample period 1953 through 1965. 1953 was chosen as the beginning of the sample period so as to avoid the severe disturbances due to the Korean war, and we terminated the sample period at 1965 so as to exclude the period of increasingly inflationary expectations that began in 1966. The last three equations based on the period 1953–1968, incorporate the more recent inflationary episode.

In column (1) we have assumed *p* to be zero; the resulting equation is thus a replication of Bischoff's original equation, except for the effect of revisions in the data. This equation is seen to perform quite well in terms of R^2 and DW, though the implied elasticity of investment with respect to RDP and RCB given in Part B are rather higher than the *a priori* values computed in Table 2. The pattern of dynamic response in Part C also conforms reasonably well with *a priori* specification. To be sure, there is a slight overshooting in the response to a change in VPD, but it is small enough to be consistent with an "almost" putty-clay hypothesis.[23]

In columns (2) and (3) we have tested two alternative specifications of p. Our intention was to test three possible specifications, to wit:

$$p = p_s - 1.2 \tag{21a}$$

$$p = w_2 p_s \tag{21b}$$

$$p = p_L - 1.2 \tag{21c}$$

where p_s is defined by equation (18), w_2 is defined by equation (19), and p_L is the one year expected rate of change of the CPI taken from the Livingston survey data. The reason for subtracting 1.2 will be discussed a little later. Unfortunately, we were unable to obtain estimates using specification (21b), as the non-linear estimation program ran into a singular matrix in the process of minimization, presumably reflecting multicollinearity of the variables. Estimates using the definitions (21a) and (21c) are reported in columns (2) and (3) respectively.

It is readily apparent that explicit introduction of p, in either specification, worsens the result in every aspect. In columns (2) and (3) the standard errors of residuals are 35% and 20% larger than that in column (1). Furthermore, the Durbin-Watson statistic has deteriorated sufficiently that we felt it necessary

[23] In [4, (footnote 30)], Eisner, commenting on a similar result reported by Bischoff in a paper presented at the 1966 San Francisco meetings of the Econometric Society, has hypothesized that he "obtained his results in support of the putty-clay role of relative prices from the particular constraints introduced into the Almon lag estimator." Although the nature of these biassing constraints is not specified in [4], Bischoff has kindly informed us that Eisner objected to the fact that in the distributed lag there was no term in current VPD, a specification which is also retained in our equation (13). Eisner conjectured that a very different pattern of coefficients would be obtained if one added, to the second summation, the term $VPD_t XB_t$.

This objection has already been largely invalidated by the results reported by Bischoff in [2, (362, Section III)]. He showed that using the very same method of estimation employed by Eisner and Nadiri in [4], even though this method is not entirely appropriate under a putty-clay hypothesis, one obtains a set of estimated coefficients for VPD and for XB which "are in accord with the suggestion of the "putty-clay" hypothesis", (p. 365) that the change "in relative prices operates more slowly than... ...changes in output", (p. 366, cf. also Table 5, columns (4) and (5)). Bischoff has also kindly made available to us the results of a recent test in which he relied on the specification (13) used also in his original contribution [1] but, following Eisner's suggestion, he added the term $\beta_0 VPD_t XB_t$. For the purpose of this test he used the specification of VPD underlying column (5) which is our preferred specification (see below) and a period of observation only slightly different from that used in column (5), 1954.1 to 1968. IV. Since our putty-clay hypothesis implies that the coefficient β_0 should be close to zero, it could not be expected to lie on the 3rd degree polynomial on which the weights β_i, $i = 1$ to 11 were required to lie. Accordingly, this coefficient was estimated freely. The point estimate of β_0 is negative but numerically small (less than 10% of the steady state response), and statistically insignificant (t ratio of 0.7), and, contrary to Eisner's conjecture, the remaining coefficients, and hence the approach to equilibrium, are essentially unchanged.

TABLE 4

DYNAMIC SIMULATION ERRORS OF SELECTED EQUATIONS[1]

PART A *OPD*

	OPD ACTUAL ($, bill.)[2] (0)	Simulation Error					
		(1)	(1a)[3]	(1b)[4]	(2)	(4)	(5)
1965 I	44.2	0	0	0	0	−.9	.1
II	45.3	.1	0	−.2	−2.5	−1.0	−.3
III	46.6	−.6	−.9	−1.5	−4.5	−2.0	−1.3
IV	49.9	.7	.2	−.8	−3.2	−.8	−.3
1966 I	52.8	2.3	1.7	.2	−1.5	.5	.9
II	54.1	4.3	3.4	1.7	0	1.9	2.1
III	54.4	3.7	2.2	.4	−.9	.6	.6
IV	51.8	3.7	1.4	−.5	−.7	−1.0	−.8
1967 I	48.4	3.0	−.2	−2.1	−1.3	−2.1	−2.2
II	49.9	5.2	1.1	−1.3	.3	−.4	−1.1
III	51.5	7.2	2.2	−.8	1.5	1.1	−.3
IV	51.5	7.9	2.1	−1.5	.5	1.1	−.8
1968 I	51.3	7.2	.6	−3.8	−.8	−.2	−2.4
II	51.7	7.9	.5	−4.3	2.2	−.3	−2.4
III	54.1	10.9	3.0	−2.1	5.1	1.7	−.5
IV	57.3	14.8	6.3	.8	7.6	4.4	1.6
1969 I	58.3	16.4	7.1	.6	7.3	4.9	.8
II	59.5	18.3	8.3	1.2	8.7	6.2	1.4
III	58.0	17.7	7.1	−.5	9.3	5.1	.4
IV	58.0	19.6	8.8	1.0	11.7	7.0	2.3
1970 I	56.0	19.8	9.2	1.6	12.1	7.5	3.1

1. Dynamic Simulation of equations (13), (20a) and (20b) together starting in the first quarter of 1958.
2. The actual and computed figures reported in part A and B of this table are based on the data available at the time the estimation was carried out, basically those reported in the July 1970 issue of the Survey of Current Business. Since then the data have been repeatedly and substantially revised. The effect of these revisions is taken up in footnote 28.
3. The difference between actual *OPD* (*EPD*) and its simulated value, using the estimate given in column (1), Table 3, and assuming that p is zero for 1953–64 and given by (21a) thereafter.
4. The difference between actual *OPD* (*EPD*) and its simulated value, using the estimate given in column (1), Table 3, and assuming that p is zero for 1953–64 and given by (21b) thereafter.
5. Actual values of *EPD* (same as "Investment in Producers' Durable Equipment; Billions of 1958 dollars" as reported in Table 1.2, National Income Accounts). The effect of the recent revision of the *EPD* figures for the comparisons made in the table is briefly touched upon in footnote 28.

TABLE 4

DYNAMIC SIMULATION ERRORS OF SELECTED EQUATIONS[1]

PART B *EPD*

	Actual Value ($, bill.)[5] (0)	Simulation Error					
		(1)	(1a)[3]	(1b)[4]	(2)	(4)	(5)
1965 I	42.1	.3	.3	.3	−.4	−.4	.3
II	42.7	−.2	−.2	−.3	−1.4	−1.1	−.4
III	45.0	.7	.6	.4	1.1	−.3	.4
IV	46.4	.6	.4	0	−1.9	−.6	.1
1966 I	48.1	.7	.4	−.3	−2.2	−.6	0
II	49.4	.9	.5	−.5	−2.5	−.7	−.2
III	50.9	1.4	.7	−.6	−2.4	−.6	−.2
IV	52.0	2.5	1.3	−.2	−1.7	−.3	0
1967 I	49.8	1.0	−.8	−2.5	−3.4	−2.5	−2.4
II	51.1	3.3	.8	−1.2	−1.3	−1.0	−1.0
III	50.6	3.8	.5	−1.8	−1.1	−1.1	−1.5
IV	50.8	5.1	1.0	−1.8	−.5	−.5	−1.4
1968 I	52.7	7.7	2.7	−.5	1.3	1.4	.1
II	51.5	7.0	1.2	−2.6	.6	0	−1.6
III	52.6	8.6	2.0	−2.2	2.2	.9	−1.0
IV	54.3	10.9	3.6	−1.1	4.2	2.3	.1
1969 I	55.4	12.5	4.5	−.7	5.3	3.0	.3
II	57.0	14.7	6.0	.2	6.8	4.3	1.0
III	57.3	15.8	6.3	−.1	7.4	4.5	.7
IV	57.8	17.4	7.4	.4	8.8	5.5	1.3
1970 I	56.5	17.7	7.2	−.1	8.9	5.4	.9

3, 4. See bottom of Part A.

to reestimate these equations allowing for first order serial correlation of residuals. In column (3), c_2 has the "wrong" sign, so that the elasticity of *OPD* with respect to *RDP* is positive (though it also is negligibly small). In column (2), the elasticities are not altogether unreasonable, but the dynamic reaction pattern shown in Part C of the table does not seem to be sensible. The acceleration seems to be unusually weak, and the overshooting of the reaction to changes in *VPD* is very large.[24]

However, if we extrapolate these equations into the period of rapidly rising prices and uncommonly high interest rates beginning with 1966, the results turn out to be quite different from those obtained over the period of fit, and are altogether rather disquieting. This can be verified from Table 4. In Part A of

[24] If the true nature of the production function is putty-putty, the over-shooting in the response to changes in *XB* and *VPD*, should roughly be the same, and this possibility cannot be ruled out completely. However, our experiences in the past suggest that strong overshooting in response to changes in *VPD* leads to an unrealistic degree of instability of the full model.

this table, column (0) gives the actual value of *OPD*, from 1965 through the first quarter of 1970. The remaining columns—except for (1a) and (1b) to be discussed presently—show the difference between this value and the value computed from the corresponding estimated equation. Similarly, in Part B column (0) gives the actual value of *EPD* while the remaining columns show the difference between this value and that computed from (13) and (20).[25]

It is seen that equation (1) begins to underestimate *OPD* seriously immediately following the sample period; and this underestimate, in turn, generates a similar error in *EPD* beginning a few quarters later. By 1970 the underestimate for both equations approach the 20 billion level!

We do not present results of extrapolating equation (3) based on the Livingston measure of p, both because this equation is inconsistent with our model and because, in any event, this series is supposed to measure short-run expectations of the cost of living rather than long-run expectations of output prices. However, the extrapolation of equation (2), shown in the corresponding column of Table 4 is rather instructive. Despite its inferior performance through 1965, this equation manages to go through the middle of 1968 with errors which are not significantly different from those of the sample period. It is only in the third quarter of 1968 that it begins to significantly underestimate both *OPD* and *EPD*. But, once it begins, it becomes rapidly worse, reaching $12 billion for *OPD* and $9 billion for *EPD* by the first quarter of 1970.

A possible clue to this rather puzzling set of results might be found in the Livingston survey data. As we argued in our earlier discussion of these data, they suggest that there was a break in the formation of expectations in the mid 1960's. Indeed, an earlier study (Turnovsky [**18**]) concluded that before 1965, expectations could be regarded as rather constant, averaging about 1.2% per annum, and it was only after the early 1960's that they were found to be closely related to actual price changes.

To pursue this clue that a radical change in the prevailing mechanism of formation of price expectation on the part of firms might have occurred around 1965–1966, we began by carrying out the following experiment. We took equation (1) which, it will be recalled, is estimated through 1965 assuming that p was zero, and we extrapolated it from 1966 on by replacing *RCB* by *RCB-p* with p defined by equation (21a). Because there is a long lag in the reaction of *OPD* to *VPD*, we have replaced *RCB* by *RCB-p* in the first quarter of 1965 so that by the first quarter of 1966 some of the effect of this replacement will be felt. The resulting predictions of *OPD* and *EPD* are given in columns (1a) of Table 4. This result is very similar to that given in column (2), though generally somewhat superior. To the extent that the dynamic reaction pattern of (1.a) is more plausible than that of (2), this result provides some support for the hypothesis that one should explicitly allow for a break in the mechanism of price expectation formation around the mid-sixties, instead of assuming that the same mechanism was operating through the whole period, as specified in equation (2).

[25] These so-called "extrapolations" reported in Table 4B are dynamic simulations of equations (13), (20a), and (20b) starting from the first quarter of 1958.

The experiment was also repeated using the alternative specification of p given by (21b) and the results, reported in column (1b) are striking. The fit remains remarkably good down to the very end of the period.

Encouraged by these results we have reestimated two versions of equation (13) incorporating in it formally the hypothesis of a break in expectations by specifying that p is a constant through 1964 and is given by either (21a),—equation 4 or by (21b)—equation (5). The period of estimation in both cases is 1953 to the end of 1968. Turning first to Table 3, we find that the fit of both equations is rather good, especially that of (5). It is, in fact, comparable to that of equation (1), when we allow for the generally higher level of *OPD* in the more recent period. The estimated elasticities in Part B of Table 3 are generally somewhat lower, which is in the right direction, though even the elasticities of (5), which are the lowest, remain above the *a-priori* values of Table 2. The dynamic response characteristics in Part C are again broadly consistent with the putty-clay formulation, though (5) implies a slight overshooting. But, in terms of extrapolation for the five quarters following the period of fit (5) performs distinctly better. Indeed this equation performs roughly as well in the post 1966 period as in earlier periods. To illustrate, the ratio of the root mean square error to the mean value of *OPD* is 2.8% for the period 1966–69, as compared with 3.1% for the entire period '58–'69. In the case of *EPD* the relative errors are 2% and 2.1% respectively[26]

On the whole then equation (5) appears to be the most satisfactory in that it is consistent with the *a-priori* specifications of the model and is also capable of accounting for the behavior of *EPD* throughout the postwar period. It should be added that since the completion of the calculation given in Table 4, the National Income Account estimates of *EPD*, and of other series relevant to the estimation of our series of *OPD*, have been significantly revised. On the whole, these revisions have tended to make the errors of extrapolation for *EPD* appreciably smaller than those reported in Table 4B.[27] Equation (5) (together with (20)) also appears to account rather well for the behavior of *EPD* since 1969, down to the very present (1973.I), though this conclusion must be regarded as somewhat tentative because the National Income Account estimates of *EPD* are subject to surprisingly large revisions, at least up to three years back. For the years 1969–70, which are by now unlikely to undergo significant revisions, the computed series tracks remarkably well the actual series, including its flat peak in the second half of 1969, and its subsequent rapid decline: indeed the RMS is only about 1 billion or less than 2%. For the most recent nine quarters the RMS is substantially higher, around 2.6 billion or over 4%. Most of this error can be traced to substantial underestimates in 1971 and the first quarter of 1972,

[26] It will also be noted that (5) implies a more plausible initial response of investment to changes in output. Even in the case of (5) this response may appear suspiciously large in the first few quarters, suggesting the possibility of some simultaneous equation bias. While this possibly cannot be excluded, it is most unlikely to be serious because as dependent variable we use not investment but new orders, which have a relatively small feedback on current sales.

[27] The errors implied by the latest revision of the data (July 1973) are reported in the table in footnote 28.

averaging over three billion, whereas for the latest four quarters the error again averages below one billion (see footnote 28). Even the relatively large underestimates for 1971, cannot, in our view, be reliably assessed at this time, and for two reasons. In the first place, this period was affected by a series of abnormal circumstances which our model is not designed to handle, including, in the first half of the year, the aftermath of the automobile strike at the end of 1970, and, in the second half, the uncertainty over the reinstatement of investment credit and its "buy American" clause, and the introduction of wage and price controls. In the second place, as already noted, the data for *EPD* are still subject to substantial revisions as far back as 1971, and past experience indicates that such revisions (as well as the usually smaller revisions of the independent variables used in the *OPD-EPD* equations), typically reduce the error, sometimes rather dramatically.[28]

[28] This conclusion is supported by the following table which reports the error of *EPD*, from 1969 to date, as calculated from the data provided in successive July issues of the Survey of Current Business, following the July 1970 issue underlying the estimation through 1968, and the extrapolation through 1970.I, reported in Table 4B:

Error of *EPD* calculated from the data in *SCB* of:

YEAR and Quarter	July 1971 (1)	July 1972 (2)	July 1973 (3)
69.I	−.6	.6	.7
II	−.4	−.5	−.4
III	−.5	−.5	−.3
IV	.3	−.2	.1
70.I	−.9	−.8	−.9
II	.5	.5	.2
III	3.2	2.7	2.5
IV	1.6	−.1	−.1
71.I	4.7	2.5	2.6
II	6.8	4.1	3.8
III		3.7	3.0
IV		4.8	4.0
72.I		4.5	3.4
II		2.9	.9
III			−1.2
IV			−.8
73.I			−.7

It is readily apparent that the errors based on the latest revision, in column (3), for the five quarters 1969.I to 1970.I, are generally smaller than those reported in column (5) of Table 4B, and substantially so in three of the five quarters. For the remaining quarters the latest error is also uniformly smaller than that implied by the first available estimates, with reductions ranging up to 3 billion. It is also generally smaller than that implied by the first revision of the data.

Before concluding brief mention should be made of one more test, the outcome of which is reported in column (6) of Table 3. The major effect of switching the specifications of p from a constant up to 1965 to (21b) beginning in 1965 is that of offsetting, to some extent, the unprecedented rise in the corporate bond rate *RCB* which has occurred in the post 1965 period. Under these conditions one could suspect that our procedure has primarily the effect of preventing the occurrence of large changes in the cost of capital term and, hence, in *VPD*. If so, might we not obtain at least as good a fit by taking *VPD* as a constant, i.e., with the straight accelerator model? We have carried out this test and, as can be seen from column (6) the answer is rather unequivocally negative. The root means square error of (6) for the entire period 1953–68 is nearly three times as large as that of specification (5), and the errors exhibit very high serial correlation, as evidenced by the value of DW and by the estimate of the autoregression coefficient of .96. Clearly, allowing for variations in the optimal capital output ratio makes a very substantial contribution to the explanation of *EPD*.[29]

This completes the survey of the empirical results that we have been able to obtain so far on the ability of our investment function to explain the behavior of aggregate data under several alternative assumptions concerning the behavior of the cruical, but unobserved variable, the expected rate of change of prices.

[29] This test compares only two very specific alternatives; a zero elasticity of capital with respect to relative prices (E_p) versus a unit steady state elasticity, implicit in our maintained hypothesis of a Cobb Douglas. The empirical validity of the latter specification has been questioned in a well known contribution of Eisner and Nadiri [**4**]. From an extensive analysis of the data used by Jorgenson, they have concluded that "Results contradict Jorgenson's assumption of a Cobb-Douglas production function" though "they are generally consistent with the implications of a CES production function with elasticities of substitution nearer zero than unity" (p. 381). This serious indictment of the Cobb Douglas has been challenged by Bischoff [**2**] who has shown that "with an improved stochastic specification the result does not contradict the Cobb-Douglas assumption" although the point estimate of the elasticity E_p of capital with respect to relative prices (our *VPD*) is typically well below unity. He has also shown, however, that a similar analysis of data for producers durable equipment—the data used in our analysis—yields point estimates of both E_p and E_q (the elasticity with respect to output), numerically close to, and not significantly different from, unity—(cf. Section 3 and Tables 3, 4). Besides this test, both Bischoff and ourselves have, in the past, worked with the variant of (13) implied by a *CES* production function, and endeavored to estimate the elasticity of substitution without prior constraint. We have consistently found that the estimated E_p was close to unity and that the difference from unity was not very robust. More recently, Bischoff has carried out one further test relying on the specification of *VPD* used in our preferred variant, that underlying column (5) of Table 3—but replacing specification (13) with a specification analogous to that employed by Eisner and Nadiri in [**4**] namely

$$\log OPD_t = \sum_{i=0}^{7} w_i \log VPD_{t-i} + \sum_{i=0}^{7} v_i \log XB_{t-i} + \sum_{i=1}^{2} q_i \log OPD_{t-i} + u_t \, .$$

E_p is then given by $\quad \sum_{i=0}^{7} w_i \Big/ \left(1 - \sum_{i=1}^{2} q_i\right)$ and $E_q = \sum_{i=0}^{7} v_i \Big/ \left(1 - \sum_{i=1}^{2} q_i\right)$.

The resulting estimates are found to be $E_p = 1.17$, $E_q = .92$, quite representative of similar results obtained in earlier tests. Also the fit is somewhat poorer than that of (5) as the standard error is 3.7%. On the whole we suggest that imposing the assumption of a Cobb-Douglas and constant returns to scale, $E_p = E_q = 1$, involves at most a modest specification bias, and is preferable to trying to estimate E_p and E_q from the data, along with the other parameters.

The conclusion of our survey is fairly clear: the hypothesis that is capable of accounting for the behavior of the aggregate data within the overall framework of our investment function is that the expected rate of change of prices was roughly constant and close to zero until about 1964, and thereafter is given by equation (21b). Within our theoretical framework, we have not been able to find any other formulation that can account for the behavior of *EPD* and *OPD* for the period 1953–69 as a whole.

Our evidence, of course, is far short of establishing that the estimate given under column (5) in Table 3, is the best specification and estimate of the investment equation for the next several years. For one thing, the threshold weights are a bit too arbitrary to accept blithely without much more careful tests against alternative weighting structures. Such tests cannot be readily performed in the context of our investment function because the estimation of this function, even without a complex lag structure in the price expectations, is a difficult enough non linear estimation problem. Furthermore, some plausible alternative explanation of the investment behavior in 1966–69 could be found. One such alternative hypothesis, which does not require serious changes in our theoretical construct, would say that p is constant before 1964, given by (21a) thereafter, and in addition, there was an unusually high level of investment in public utilities beginning around 1968–69. In order to test an alternative such as this, however, we need detailed data on investment by industries. Very recent data on *EPD* are subject to substantial revision, and as *EPD* is revised, *OPD* will change further back as we have indicated earlier. The more detailed the data are, the more subject to revision they tend to be. Thus, we do not feel that the time is ripe, in terms of data availability, to undertake a detailed study of investment behavior during the post 1968 period, and unfortunately, the choice between columns (4) and (5) must be largely based on their performance in this later period.

We, therefore, conclude our discussion at this time by accepting specification (5) as the best working hypothesis available within our framework for the explanation of investment behavior, and hope to be able to reach a more definitive judgment in the coming years, as more and sounder data on investment become available for the more recent period and especially if we also manage, in the near future, to bring the rate of inflation back to levels prevailing before 1966.

University of Pennsylvania
Massachusetts Institute of Technology
Michigan State University
The Australian National University

REFERENCES

[1] Bischoff, C. W., "A Study of Distributed Lags and Business Fixed Investment," unpublished Ph.D. dissertation, Massachusetts Institute of Technology, (1968).

[2] ———, "Hypothesis Testing and the Demand for Capital Goods," *The Review of Economics and Statistics*, LI (August, 1969), 354–68.

[3] ———, "The Effects of Alternative Lag Distribution," in G. Fromm, ed., *Tax Incentives and Capital Spending* (Washington, D. C.: The Brookings Institution, 1971).

[4] EISNER, E. AND M. I. NADIRI, "Investment Behavior and Neoclassical Theory," *Review of Economics and Statistics*, L (August, 1968), 369–82.

[5] ——— AND ———, "Neoclassical Theory of Investment Behavior: A Comment," *Review of Economics and Statistics*, LII (May, 1970), 216–22.

[6] ——— AND R. STROTZ, "Determinants of Business Investment," in *Impacts of Monetary Policy*, Research Study Two, prepared for the Commission on Money and Credit (Englewood Cliffs, N. J.: Prentice-Hall, Inc., 1963).

[7] FELDSTEIN, M. S. AND D. K. FOOT, "The Other Half of Gross Investment: Replacement and Modernization Expenditure," *Review of Economics and Statistics*, LIII (February, 1971), 49–58.

[8] GOULD, J. P., "Adjustment Costs in the Theory of Investment of the Firm," *Review of Economic Studies*, XXXV (January, 1968), 47–55.

[9] ———, The Use of Endogenous Variables in Dynamic Models of Investment," *Quarterly Journal of Economics*, LIII (November, 1969), 580–99.

]10] HALL, R. E. AND D. W. JORGENSON, "Tax Policy and Investment Behavior," *American Economic Review*, LVII (June, 1967), 391–414.

[11] JORGENSON, D. W., "Capital Theory and Investment Behavior," *American Economic Review*, LIII (May, 1963), 247–59.

[12] ———, "Econometric Studies of Investment Behavior: A Survey," *Journal of Economic Literature*, IX (December, 1971), 1111–47.

[13] ——— AND C. D. SIEBERT, "A Comparison of Alternative Theories of Corporate Investment Behavior, *American Economic Review*, LVIII (September, 1968), 681–712.

[14] ——— AND ———, "Optimal Capital Accumulation and Corporate Investment Behavior," *Journal of Political Economy*, LXXVI (November-December, 1968), 1123–51.

[15] MODIGLIANI, F. AND M. H. MILLER, "The Cost of Capital, Corporation Finance and the Theory of Investment," *American Economic Review*, XLVIII (June, 1958), 261–97.

[16] ——— AND ———, "Corporate Income Taxes and the Cost of Capital: A Correction," *American Economic Review*, LIII (June, 1963), 433–42.

[17] ——— AND R. SHILLER, "Price Expectations and the Term Structure of Interest Rates," *Economica*, new series, XL (February, 1973), 12–43.

[18] TURNOVSKY, S. J., "Some Empirical Evidence on the Formation of Price Expectations," *Journal of the American Statistical Association*, LXV (December, 1970), 1441–54.

7

SOME ASPECTS OF STABILIZATION POLICIES, THE MONETARIST CONTROVERSY, AND THE MPS MODEL

By Albert Ando[1]

1. INTRODUCTION

In the past several years, economists' knowledge of the impacts of fiscal and monetary stabilization policies on the macro-economic conditions of a country has been called into question. In the early sixties, it was hoped that improved empirical knowledge of behavioral functions that constitute macro-economic models would improve our understanding of how stabilization policies work. It is, at least in part, in pursuit of this goal that econometric models discussed in this symposium have been built. Of course, any conclusion that one may derive from an estimated econometric model is dependent, among other things, on the theoretical specification of the model, and more recently, these models have been subject to some criticisms that deficiencies of their underlying theoretical structure make any analysis of policy alternatives based on these models suspect. Since these econometric models are the only means at the disposal of economists for quantitatively analyzing impacts of alternative stabilization policies, these criticisms are very serious indeed.

Some disputes on theoretical structure are at least easy to define. If the consumption function in a particular model is not in accordance with the critic's view of how the consumption function should be formulated, we know the exact point of dispute, and it should not be too difficult, under most circumstances, for the critic to substitute his own specification of the consumption function for the one in the model while leaving the rest of the structure of the model undisturbed.

One of the more difficult problems faced by econometricians working on macro-economic models has been the question of exactly how econometric models should be modified in order to accommodate points stressed by "monetarists." For some years, the theoretical framework which monetarists had in mind appeared so different from that used in formulating existing macro econometric models that any attempt to construct a more general model that could accommodate both theoretical structures seemed all but impossible. Without the possibility of constructing a general model which is acceptable to both sides except for well defined differences, the prospect of making progress towards meaningful analysis of relative merits of the two theories were very slight.

[1] As in all publications originating in the MPS Model Project, the content of this paper has been developed in the process of cooperative work among main participants in the project. While Ando has written this paper and therefore takes the responsibility for it, contributions of Franco Modigliani of MIT and Jared Enzler of the Federal Reserve Board are close to that of co-authors. Professors Christopher Higgins, Karl Shell, and Robert M. Solow read an earlier draft and provided valuable comments. Support of the National Science Foundation under Grant GS-32383X for the preparation of this paper is gratefully acknowledged.

Recent writings of Professor Friedman and others, however, suggest that the situation is not quite so hopeless. What monetarists consider to be the critical question appears to be the treatment of shifts in the LM curve induced by monetary and fiscal policy actions. Provided that this question is handled to their satisfaction, it appears possible that the remaining structure of at least some currently existing models can be made acceptable to monetarists without drastic overhauls. Even so, it must be recognized that the central issues involved in the analysis of stabilization policies in general and the monetarist controversy in particular are interactions among effective demands, conditions of financial markets, and the forces determining the level of prices and wages, and that a model in which these issues can be explicitly discussed and resolved will have to contain the specifications of all these sectors and hence be fairly large and complex.

We are aware that, with good reason, theorists resist working with large models, but this is one of the rare situations where the nature of the questions raised demands a larger and more complex system than theorists are accustomed to dealing with. One of the reasons why so much confusion has been generated in the literature on stabilization policies is the insistence of many theorists that impacts of these policies be analyzed within the context of small, simple models containing no more than four or five equations and a few identities. I shall give some illustrative cases for this assertion later in this paper.

The theory embedded in the structure of the MPS Model is sufficiently comprehensive to serve as the framework for discussing most questions of stabilization policies, and, in view of more recent writings of monetarists, to discuss most of their contentions. But here the difficulty is that, in order to accommodate the reality of the economy and to provide sufficient details for actual policy-making purposes, the MPS Model is so large and complex that its basic theoretical structure is obscured for all but a few who work with it intimately. Most of the institutional details incorporated into the MPS Model are not needed for the discussion of qualitative consequences of alternative monetary and fiscal policies.

In this paper, we shall present a theoretical model which is as simple as possible but which contains features that are essential for the discussion of stabilization policies. In constructing this model, we have attempted to maintain the parallel between the structure of this model and that of the MPS Model so that we can call upon the empirical estimates of the MPS Model when such empirical estimates are needed in this paper. In addition, for readers who are interested in using the MPS Model for more detailed studies, the model of this paper should serve as a convenient guide.[2]

We shall first describe the model, and then discuss some questions of stabilization policies in its context.

[2] Much more extensive analysis of the macro-economic model underlying the MPS Model is being prepared as a part of the forthcoming book on the MPS Model by Ando and Modigliani. What is presented here is a simplified summary taken from the draft of this book.

TABLE 1

SIMPLIFIED MACRO-ECONOMIC MODEL

I. Demand for Output
Definition of Net National Product

(1) $$X = C + I + G$$

Consumption Function

(2) $$C = w_1 a_1 Y + w_2 a_1 L(Y_{-1}) + a_2 A\,; \quad w_1 + w_2 = 1$$

Investment Function

(3) $$I = I(X, \rho_k;\ [X_{-i}], [\rho_{k_{-i}}], \tau)$$

Government Expenditure

(4) $$G = G_f + G_s(C, N, \rho_k)$$

II. Income Identities, Taxes, and Market Value of Assets
Definition of Disposable Income

(5) $$PY = PX + r_s D - PT$$

Tax Function

(6) $$PT = T(PX + r_s D,\ WE;\ \tau)$$

Definition of Net Worth

(7) $$A = V + \frac{M+D}{P}$$

Definition of Saving

(8) $$\Delta(PA) = P_{-1}Y_{-1} - P_{-1}C_{-1} + \Delta^*(PV)$$

Market Value of Capital

(9) $$PV = \frac{\Pi^e}{\rho_k}$$

Expected Income from Capital

(10) $$\Pi^e = \Pi^e\left(\Pi,\ PL\left(\frac{\Pi_{-1}}{\rho_{-1}}\right)\right)$$

Definition of Income from Capital

(11) $$\Pi = PX - WE - T_e(PX - WE)$$

Capital Gains on Existing Capital

(12) $$\Delta^*(PV) = \Delta(PV) - P_{-1}I_{-1}$$

III. Labor Market and Determination of Prices and Wages
Demand for Labor

(13) $$E = E(X;\ [\rho_{k_{-i}}], [\xi_{-i}])$$

(*Continued on next page*)

TABLE 1 (*Continued*)

Supply of Labor and the Definition of Unemployment Rate

(14) $$u = u(E, N)$$

Determination of Money Wage Level

(15) $$\frac{W - W_{-1}}{W_{-1}} = w\left(u, L\left(\frac{P_{-1} - P_{-2}}{P_{-2}}\right)\right)$$

Determination of Real Wage Rate and Price Level

(16) $$P = WF\left(L\left(\frac{E}{X}\right), \mu; u, P_{-1}\right)$$

IV. Financial Markets
Demand for Real Assets

(17) $$f_v(\rho_k^h, \rho_s)A = V$$

Demand for Short-term Money, Fixed Assets and the Equilibrium Condition

(18) $$f_s(\rho_k^h, \rho_s)A = \frac{M + D}{P}$$

Demand for Money and the Equilibrium Condition

(19) $$f_m(r_s, PX) = M$$

Relation Between Real and Nominal Short-term Interest Rates

(20) $$r_s - \frac{P^e - P}{P} = \rho_s$$

Relation Between the Holding Rate and the Capitalization Rate

(21) $$\rho_k^h = \rho_k - \frac{\overset{e}{\rho_k} - \rho_k}{\rho_k}$$

Generation of Expected Rate of Change of Prices

(22) $$\frac{P^e - P}{P} = P^e\left(L\left(\frac{P - P_{-1}}{P_{-1}}\right)\right)$$

Generation of Expected Rate of Change of ρ_k

(23) $$\frac{\overset{e}{\rho_k} - \rho_k}{\rho_k} = \rho^e\left(L\left(\frac{\rho_k - \rho_{k-1}}{\rho_{k-1}}\right)\right)$$

V. Budget Identity for Government

(24) $$\Delta M + \Delta D = P_{-1}G_{-1} + r_{s_{-1}}D_{-1} - P_{-1}T_{-1}$$

VI. Financial Sector in the Reduced Form

(19) $$f_m(r_s, PX) = M$$

(25) $$\rho_k = \sum_{i=0}^{T} \beta_i r_{s_{-i}} + \sum_{i=0}^{T} \gamma_i\left(\frac{P_{-i-1} - P_{-i-2}}{P_{-i-2}}\right) + f_\rho\left(\frac{V}{A} - \frac{M + D}{PA}\right).$$

(*Continued on next page*)

TABLE 1 (*Continued*)

Endogenous Variables

A : Net Worth of Consumers
C : Consumption in Constant Dollars
D : Government Debt (assumed to be one-period bonds) Held By Private Sector
$\Delta^*(PV)$: Real Capital Gain on Existing Real Assets in Current Dollars
E : Employment in Manhours
G : Total Government Expenditures in Constant Dollars
I : Net Investment in Constant Dollars
P : Price Level for Output
P^e: Price Level Expected to Prevail in the Next Period
Π : Income from Real Assets in Current Dollars
Π^e: Expected Income from Existing Real Assets in Current (not future) Dollars
r_s : Nominal Rate of Interest on One Period Debt of Government
ρ_k : Capitalization Rate (in real terms) Applicable to the Real Assets
ρ_k^e : Level of ρ_k Expected to Prevail in the Next Period
ρ_k^h : One Period Holding Rate (in real terms) Applicable to the Real Asset
ρ_s : Real Rate of Interest on One Period Debt of Government
T : Tax in Constant Dollars
u : Unemployment Rate
V : Market Value of Existing Real Assets in Constant Dollars
W: Nominal Wage Rate Per Manhour
X : Net National Product in Constant Dollars
Y : Disposable Income in Constant Dollars

Exogenous Variables

G_f: Federal Government Expenditure in Constant Dollars
M: Money Supply in Current Dollars, to be Interpreted Here as Currency Plus Reserves
N : Vector Expressing Total Population and Its Structure
μ : Standard Mark-up Factor, i.e., the Ratio of Price of Output to its Minimized Cost of Production Expected to Prevail Under Normal Employment Conditions
τ : Vector of Tax Rates
ξ : Rate of (Harrod neutral) technical progress

Special Notations

We omit the subscript "t" to denote current period. Hence, the subscript "-1" means the value of the variable in the period immediately preceding the current period.

$$\Delta Z \equiv Z - Z_{-1}$$

(*Continued on next page*)

TABLE 1 (*Continued*)

$L(Z)$ denotes weighted average of lagged values of Z where weights sum to one, i.e.,

$$L(Z) = \sum_{i=0}^{T} l_i Z_{-i};$$

$$\sum_{i=0}^{T} l_i = 1$$

$[Z_{-i}]$ denotes the vector of past values Z, i.e.,

$$[Z_{-i}] = [Z_{-1}, Z_{-2}, \ldots, Z_{-T}].$$

2. DESCRIPTION OF THE MODEL

The model with which we shall work is given in Table 1, and briefly discussed in this section. Before we proceed with our discussion, however, a few general comments may be helpful. We have formulated the model in discrete time rather than continuous time. For analytical purposes, the use of continuous time would have simplified a few aspects of the model, but we have found that the boundary conditions can be specified more naturally and intuitively in discrete form. Also, the correspondence between this model and the MPS Model is more apparent when this model is formulated in discrete form since the MPS Model, being empirically implemented, is necessarily a discrete time model. Stock variables without time subscript refer to the beginning of the period stock. The physical quantity of stock at the beginning of the period is completely determined by activities in the previous period, but their market values are at the prices of the current period, so that some of beginning of period stocks are genuine endogenous variables. These points will become clearer as we deal with concrete cases.

2.1. *Demands for real output.* The first four equations in Table 1 describe the demand for real output. We neglect the external sector in this model, and take federal government expenditure in terms of consumption goods, G_f, as exogenous.[3]

Equation (4) defines total government expenditure as the sum of federal govern-

[3] In the real economy as well as in the MPS Model, there are a number of complex issues related to G. First of all, purchases of goods and payment of wages to government workers enter the economy differently, and they are separately treated in the MPS Model. Second, the question of whether government purchases in constant dollars or those in current dollars should be treated as exogenous does not have an obvious answer, and the MPS Model enables its users to choose between these two alternatives. The reality probably lies between the two extremes. Third, some purchases of government, for example, heavy defense equipment, are ordered many quarters before they are actually delivered and show up as a component of G in the national income statistics. In these cases, what can be treated as exogenous are orders. When deliveries are made, inventories of firms delivering them fall by precisely the same amount as increase in G, thus creating artificial negative correlation between G and inventory investment simply due to the treatment of these transactions in the national income statistics. All these problems are discussed in detail in our forthcoming book [**4**].

ment expenditure, which is exogenous, and state and local government expenditure, which is endogenous. State and local government expenditure appears to respond fairly strongly to cyclical conditions of the economy and the incentives provided by the federal government, so that it is difficult to justify treating it as exogenous. More importantly, there are some fundamental differences between the behavior of state and local government and that of the federal government, since the federal government has unlimited taxing power while state and local governments do not (at least effectively), and the federal government has the sole monetary authority. Thus, in a more detailed model such as the MPS Model, it is essential to treat the federal government and state and local governments separately. In this paper, to keep the model as simple as possible, we shall proceed as though there is a single government in the country whose expenditure is partly exogenous and partly endogenous.

Equation (2) is the consumption function. It is derived from the life cycle hypothesis of saving, and its properties and its role in the MPS Model have been discussed elsewhere [**14**]. Here we merely note one feature of this function that is not the same as the earlier formulation [**3**] of this function. In the earlier formulation, the main income variable was expected labor income, while in this version it is expected total disposable income, approximated by a distributed lag of actual disposable income. This was done for two reasons. First, it is extremely difficult to estimate imputed personal income tax applicable to labor income alone, and since the MPS Model is specifically meant to be a model for analysis of alternative stabilization policies, we wished to use a concept of income for which the income tax liability was well defined. Second, in the original formulation, the coefficient of net worth was in principle a function of the rate of return, and it appears that by using total income rather than labor income, we can more readily justify the assumption of the constancy of the coefficient of net worth.[4]

It may be worth while to note the response of this function to a short run change in the rate of return. In the short run, a change in the rate of return has two conflicting impacts on consumption. If the rate of return is increased while

[4] Consider the basic aggregate implication of life cycle hypothesis

(a) $$C = a_1' YL + a_2' A$$

where YL is labor income. Computations carried out by Modigliani and Brumberg reported in Table 1 of Ando and Modigliani and our past empirical findings [**3**] suggest that it is not too unrealistic to suppose a_1' to be constant and about .65 while a_2' can be approximated by

(b) $$a_2' = .05 + .6(.01)\rho$$

where ρ is the rate of return in percent. We can then rewrite (a) as

(c) $$C = .65 YL + .6(.01)\rho A + .05A$$
$$C = .65\left(YL + \frac{.6}{.65}(.01)\rho A\right) + .05A\,.$$

Since $.6/.65(.01)\rho A$ is very close to long term average income from assets, it seems reasonable to approximate the consumption function by

(d) $$C = a_1 YD^e + a_2 A, \qquad a_1 \simeq .65, \qquad a_2 \simeq .05$$

where YD^e is expected disposable income in constant dollars.

the value of assets is unchanged, than A is constant while Y increases, so that consumption will increase. On the other hand, if the rate of return is increased while the income from assets is unchanged, Y remains constant while A decreases, so that consumption will decline. Which one of these two cases is relevant for a particular situation depends on the reasons why the rate of return is changed in that situation, and we cannot make any unequivocal statement without specifying the type of situation under consideration.[5]

The MPS Model contains seven investment functions: investment in producers' equipment, investment in producers' structures, investment in consumer durables, investment in single family and multi-family dwelling units, investment by state and local governments, and net inventory investment.

The theoretical basis for our investment functions for producers' durable equipment and structures is quite complex, but we have published a paper dealing with this question [**6**], and the reader is referred to it for the details. Here, we confine our comments to the comparison of our formulation to a very elegant theory of investment currently popular in theoretical literature, which we shall refer to as the Tobin-Foley-Sidrauski theory of investment [**11**].

This theory proceeds roughly as follows. The production of producers physical capital depends on the comparison of the reproduction cost of the physical capital and the sales price of the capital, which in turn must be equal to the market value of the existing capital. The market value of the existing capital is in turn determined by the capitalization of the stream of net income expected to be generated by the existing capital. The expected stream of net income associated with the existing capital must be determined by the demand conditions for output, the size of the existing stock of capital, and the expected wage cost. The fundamental advantage of this theory is that the decision process for investment in capital goods is clearly dichotomized into the determination of the market value of existing capital on one hand, and production of capital goods given market value of existing capital of the other. Thus, if we have observation on market value of existing capital and on the cost of producing capital, no other information is needed in order to determine the production of capital goods except for the short-run adjustment process.

Unfortunately, this theory breaks down when the assumption of perfect malleability of physical capital is dropped. Under the assumption of ex ante substitutability, expost fixed proportions, if technology and relative prices of factors of production are not held constant, the reproduction cost of existing capital is not a meaningful concept. Investment decisions must instead be based on the comparison of the present value of the expected stream of income generated by the investment and the cost of investment under the assumption that the capital market is well functioning and therefore the cost of capital is well defined.

[5] When Y is increasing at a constant rate, η, for a long time, it is easy to show that the steady state asset income ratio, $(A/Y)^*$, is given by

$$\left(\frac{A}{Y}\right)^* = \frac{1 - a_1}{\eta + a_2}$$

and therefore independent of the rate of return.

The paper referred to earlier describes the derivation of the investment function in this framework, and the result is incorporated into the MPS Model [6].

In the case of investment in residential structures, the Tobin-Foley-Sidrauski theory is basically valid. This is because houses, in production of housing services, do not require any other factor of production, so that the reproduction cost of a unit of housing that generates a given amount of housing service is well defined. The difficulty in implementing it in the case of housing investment arises from the unavailability of data on market value of existing houses. Hence, we start our formulation of housing investment with the framework very similar to the Tobin-Foley-Sidrauski theory, but are forced to eliminate the market value of existing houses through substitution. The resulting equations are then modified to allow for non-price rationing effects that seem to be important in the mortgage market, and we arrive at two housing start equations contained in the MPS Model.

The investment in consumer durables should be similar to that in housing in principle, except that the rate of depreciation of durables is fast enough so that producers of durables can set the sales price of these goods as a mark-up on the minimized average cost, and produce to the expected demand at this price. Thus, the equation for the investment in consumer durables in the MPS Model is a fairly conventional one, and we need not comment on it here.

We assume that the construction expenditures of state and local government depend to a large extent on the needs for facilities and the subsidies from the federal government, and the capital cost influences these expenditures only marginally. We would have liked to have had a more elegant theory for these important expenditures, but we could not find support for doing so in available data.

Finally, our equation for net inventory investment reflects influence of three quite different forces on inventory. First, inventory moves positively with the expected level of consumption expenditure, but it can decline with sudden increase in consumption. Second, when orders for producers' durables increase, inventory increases as these equipments are produced, and then decline as they are delivered. Third, a similar reasoning applies also to the orders for defense goods, except that the exact timing pattern is quite different.

In order to keep the model in this paper within manageable size and complexity, we let our equation (3) represent all investment discussed above, except the construction expenditure of state and local government which is included in G. We do so at the cost of neglecting different responses of components discussed above, and this is particularly serious in the short run time pattern of response of investment to the conditions of the economy.[6]

[6] A few additional comments may be helpful here. First, the Tobin-Foley-Sidrauski theory of investment can be easily reduced into the general form of equation (3) by solving out the market value of existing capital and physical stock of capital as functions of past values of output and the cost of capital. Second, most investment functions, including those used in the MPS Model explain gross investment. In putty-clay models such as those used in the MPS Model, it is not even possible to define net investment unambiguously. But I do not see how I

(*Continued on next page*)

2.2. *Income identities, taxes, and the market value of assets.* Equation (5) is the definition of disposable income in current dollars. The comment required here is that *PY* excludes real capital gains on existing real assets. While this is unsatisfactory theoretically, it is in accordance with the standard practice of national income accounting and with most econometric work using a concept of disposable income. For our purposes here, the choice is not of major significance provided that the definition of saving given below is consistent with it.

Equation (6) is the summary tax function. *PT* should be interpreted as total tax receipt less all transfer payments. In the MPS Model, there are some fourteen separate tax and transfer payment functions, and it is difficult to summarize them into a single equation. The particularly difficult tax to handle in this way is the corporate profit tax, since it has substantially different impact on the economy from all other taxes and it is in recognition of the special nature of this tax that *T* includes *WE* among its arguments. While we cannot treat all taxes explicitly in this model, it should be remembered that they are in the background in our subsequent analysis.

Equation (7) is the definition of net worth of households. When the accounts of the various sectors of the economy are consolidated, households own all assets in the economy directly or indirectly. In the MPS Model, we distinguish those assets owned by households directly, such as consumer durables and residential houses, and thóse held indirectly, mostly assets of corporations owned through equity shares and corporate bonds. Here we merge them all into one variable, *V*. We have also netted out all financial assets and liabilities in the economy. Thus, *D* should be thought of as government debts outside of government agencies and the Federal Reserve System, and *M* should be interpreted as currency plus reserves.[7]

Equation (8) defines the change in the value of net worth, or saving. As we mentioned earlier, since disposable income is defined not including capital gains on real assets, this item must be taken care of here. We shall discuss the nature of this capital gain a few paragraphs below.

Maıket value of real assets, *PV*, is obtained by capitalizing expected stream of income from existing assets as indicated in equation (9). The expected stream of income is in turn a function of past, actual income, as shown in equation (10). It should be noted that all income from assets are measured in dollars of current period, not in dollars of past or future periods, and that expected stream of income refers to that from existing assets, not from assets expected to be acquired

(*Continued*)
can describe the depreciation process here without introducing serious additional complexities into the model, so I deviate here from the MPS Model and avoid the problems of depreciation by pretending as though it is possible to deal with net investment. Finally, various tax provisions, including tax treatment of depreciation, affect investment in a very complex manner, and I avoid dealing with it explicitly here by simply introducing a vector of tax parameters, τ into equation (3). For all these points, the reader is referred to [**4**] and [**6**].

[7] There is a serious problem of how to handle the implied equity of households in the social security system. For this model, we have ignored it. Thus, contribution to the social security system is treated as a tax, and benefits are treated as transfer payments.

in the future.[8] Equation (11) defines current actual income from real assets, and we gloss over the detailed question raised by the existence of corporate profit tax by writing corporate profit tax as a function of profits before tax.

In the case of capital owned through corporations, the formulation contained in equations (9) through (11) reflects the essence of the mechanism through which market valuation of capital takes place. To the extent that V also includes assets owned directly by housholds, such as houses and durables, it is a little artificial. The MPS Model does allow for this distinction.

The value of PV changes from one period to the next for three reasons. First, Π^e will rise to reflect net addition to real assets equal to PI, and PV will rise accordingly. Second, the expected stream of income from the existing assets may change due to changing economic conditions, and if this happens PV will change to reflect it. Third, the capitalization rate ρ_k, can change, and PV will change accordingly. Finally, the price level, P, will change both PV and Π^e. Equation (12) defines all these changes in PV other than PI as the capital gains on real assets.

2.3. *Labor market and determination of wage and price.* Since we assume that producers' durable equipment is in the form of putty-clay, the observed relationship between the employment and output is not the production function out of which the investment function is derived. At any point in time, there exists in the economy a collection of machines, whose labor-output ratios were determined by the technology and the relative prices at the time each machine was produced. These machines will be used in production, from the most efficient to the least given the relative prices of the current period, until all output desired in the current period is produced. In order to describe the nature of existing machines produced in past periods, in equation (13) we include among arguments of E the past values of the cost of capital $[\rho_{k_{-i}}]$ and the history of technical progress $[\xi_{-i}]$. In the MPS Model, in place of $[\xi_{-i}]$, a weighted average of a time trend and $L(E/X)$ was used. Equation (13) dipicts this short-run relationship between the output and labor, modified by the presence of overhead labor which is independent of output in the short run.

What is determined by (13) is required manhours for production. In order to translate manhours to employment, hours worked per man must be determined. It is also well known that the labor force itself is quite responsive to employ-

[8] There is one really complex problem glossed over in this paper but discussed in detail in the forthcoming book on the MPS Model [**4**]. Mark-up on minimized cost pricing allows for the existence of oligopoly profits. If there are oligopoly profits, then there will be present value of future oligopoly profits included in the net worth of households. While new physical assets must be produced and acquired at price and hence income that will accure to them will not be capitalized to be added to net worth of consumers, increase in oligopoly profits due to increase in the scale of the economy will accure to the present producers without any cost, and this will be capitalized and included in the value of net worth. It is not possible to treat these questions explicitly in this paper, but the formulation of the model under discussion here can allow for the consequences of the presence of oligopoly profits. For the proof of this assertion and the detailed analysis, the reader is referred to [**4**].

ment conditions, given the size and characteristics of population such as sex and age distribution. We have compressed all these considerations into equation (14) which gives the unemployment rate as a function of manhours and population characteristics.

Equation (15) is a fairly conventional equation for the rate of change of wages. We leave the question of whether or not the partial derivative of this function with respect to $L[(P_{-1} - P_{-2})/P_{-2}]$ should be equal to unity or not as an open one.

Equation (16) is the equation which determines the level of price of output given the level of money wage. It was derived together with the investment function, and contains the hypothesis that the price is determined by a markup on the minimized average cost. For a detailed discussion of this equation, the reader is referred to [**4**] and [**6**]. In principle, the level of price will vary proportionately with the level of money wage, and the reciprocal of the long-run productivity. We shall approximate the latter by $L(E/X)$ and assume that the partial derivative of F with respect to $L(E/X)$ is unity. F also contains μ, the mark-up factor. u is present in F indicating that in the short run the mark-up may vary with utilization of capacity, and P_{-1} is in F suggesting that the adjustment of price to it basic determinants may not be immediate.

2.4. *Financial markets.* We have discussed the problems of modelling the financial market at some length in a recent paper [**5**], and we adopt the formulation presented in that paper here.

Let us suppose that there are three assets in the economy, money, M, government debt, D, and real assets, V. D is assumed to be fixed in money value, and it is all in the form of one-period bonds. This set-up satisfies the condition of the Appendix to [**5**], and hence the demand for money is strictly transactions demand and depends only on the nomial interest rate on D, and on a measure of transaction. This conclusion, which is proved in the Appendix to [**5**], enables us to write equation (19). The supply of M is assumed to be exogenous. The argument in the Appendix to [**5**] also suggests that the conditions under which the demand for $D+M$ is independent of M is likely to be satisfied, and therefore the demand for $D + M$ can be written in the form of equation (18). Equation (17) is the demand for real assets.

Equations (17) and (18), together with the definition of net worth equation (7), appear to be the same as the model used by Tobin in [**17**], except the treatment of the demand for money is simplified using the proposition proved in the Appendix to [**5**]. However, there is one important modification.

In Tobin's formulation, it is not clearly specified whether ρ_k^h, the rate of return on V, is a one-period holding rate or a capitalization rate. Since the return on D, ρ_s, is the rate of interest on one-period bond, it is clear that the rate of return on V that enters equations (17) and (18) must also be a one-period holding rate, and we have so specified. But then we must specify the relationship between the one-period holding rate and the capitalization rate, ρ_k, which was used in equation (7) and the investment equation (3). It is given by

(21a) $$\rho_k^h = \rho_k + \frac{V^e - V}{V}$$

where V^e is the expected value of currently existing assets in current period price in the next period. It is not the same as expected market value of real assets in the next period, since the latter will be greater than the former by the net investment during the current period.

Because of the definition (9), the last term in the above equation can be approximated by

(e) $$\frac{V^e - V}{V} = -\frac{\rho_k^e - \rho_k}{\rho_k} + \frac{(\Pi^e)^e - \Pi^e}{\Pi^e}$$

where ρ_k^e is the value of ρ_k expected to prevail in the next period, and $(\Pi^e)^e$ is the expected income from currently existing real assets expected to prevail during the next period. But Π^e and $(\Pi^e)^e$ are expectations of the same stream of income and the only reason that they might differ from each other is that current, actual income is substantially out of line for some special reason. Hence, the last term in equation (e) above must be very close to zero under most conditions, and for this reason, we approximate (e) by equation (21) in our model.

Equation (20) defines the relationship between the nominal interest rate on D and the corresponding real rate, and equations (22) and (23) then introduce a simple hypothesis of the formation of expectations.

In view of the definition of A given by equation (7), equations (17) and (18) are not independent. Let us divide both equations by A, and subtract (18) from (17) obtaining

(f) $$f_r(\rho_k^h, \rho_s) - f_s(\rho_k^h, \rho_s) = \frac{V}{A} - \frac{M + D}{PA}.$$

We then substitute equations (20) and (21) into (f), and further substitute (22) and (23) into the resulting equation, and we finally arrive at equation (25), which is a term structure equation containing the term

$$f_\rho\left(\frac{V}{A} - \frac{M + D}{PA}\right).$$

Equation (25) corresponds to two equations in the MPS Model, namely, the term structure equation relating the long term bond rate to current and past short term rate of interest, and the equation that relates the market required rate of return on equity (a weighted average of the dividend-price ratio and the earnings-price ratio) to the long term bond rate and past rates of change of price. We have always recognized that a term like

$$f_\rho\left(\frac{V}{A} - \frac{M + D}{PA}\right)$$

should appear in at least one of these equations, but we have never been able statistically to detect its presence. We recognize that this is an important shortcoming of the MPS Model, and we shall have an occasion to dicuss the point again later in this paper.[9]

One point must be stressed. It is often said that a term structure equation is a reduced form of a more complete system such as equations (7), (17), and (18). This proposition is correct provided that a relation such as (21) and some hypothesis on expectations such as (22) are assumed to exist in the background. Without them, the system such as (7), (17), and (18) is an incomplete system, since it contains V and V depends on ρ_k, while functions f_v and f_s contain ρ_k^h. The system consisting of (7), (17), and (18) is a single independent equation in two unknowns, and it cannot determine both variables by itself. To this extent, the proposition that the term structure equation is a reduced form of a system such as (7), (17), and (18) is at best a misleading statement.

2.5. *General comment on the model.* While there are 23 equations in the model we have discussed so far, because equations (17) and (18) are not independent of each other in view of (7), we have 22 independent equations in the system, and 22 variables, as listed in Table 1. We have indicated in our discussion of the financial sector that equations (17) through (23) can be reduced to two equations, resulting in equations (19) and (25) as shown in Table 1 as "Financial Sector in Reduced Form." Equations (1) through (16) plus (19) and (25) constitute the system of 18 equations. Variables eliminated from the list given in Table 1 are ρ_k^h, ρ_s, P^e, and ρ_k^e. In our discussion in the remainder of this paper, we shall use whichever version is most convenient for the purpose at hand.

While even the reduced system is fairly large and not suitable for taking partial derivatives necessary for formal comparative static analysis, we shall show that the model has the virtue of making obvious some of the points raised in the recent discussion on stabilization policies. Answers to some of the questions turn out to depend on numerical values of parameters, but here we have the advantage that the MPS Model is the empirical counterpart of this model and hence we can call on the estimates contained in the MPS Model. We now turn to the discussion of specific issues raised in recent discussions of stabilization policies.

[9] There is one serious difficulty in the empirical implementation of equation (25). Both V and A are functions of ρ_k, and hence we cannot estimate (25) treating the term

$$f_\rho\left(\frac{V}{A} - \frac{M + D}{PA}\right)$$

as though it is exogenously given. We have tried a variety of ways of getting around this difficulty, but we cannot exclude the possibility that this difficulty is one of the reasons for our not having been able statistically to detect the presence of a term like

$$f_\rho\left(\frac{V}{A} - \frac{M + D}{PA}\right)$$

in our term structure equations.

3. SOME STABILIZATION PROBLEMS

3.1. *Government budget constraint and its role in stabilization.* This question can be very quickly disposed of. Carl Christ [**8**] and [**9**], has repeatedly stressed that government deficit must equal change in government debt plus money supply, and that any conclusion concerning impacts of stabilization policies based on the model which neglects this budget constraint is suspect.

The government budget constraint does not appear in our model explicitly. However, it can be derived from several of the equations in our model. To see this, multiply both sides of equation (7) by P, and take the first difference. Then substitute the resulting expression for $\Delta(PA)$ and equation (12) into equation (8). Next, substitute equation (1) into equation (5) to eliminate X from equation (5), move the time subscript back by one in the resulting equation, and use this expression to eliminate $P_{-1}Y_{-1}$ in (8). Appropriate cancellations and rearrangement of terms then yield the government budget constraint, shown in Table 1 as equation (24).

Since all the identities used to derive equation (24) have their counterparts in the MPS Model, it follows that the MPS Model contains the government budget constraint implicitly, and it is not subject to Christ's criticisms.[10] This result is by no means surprising. We are dealing with two sector accounts, government sector and private sector, and any model that contains the private sector accounting identities and also requires that transactions between the private and government sectors be fully recorded must automatically satisfy government sector accounting identities.

The more interesting question is the reasons why attention was focused on the government budget constraint in the discussion of stabilization policies. Here again, one superficial point can be disposed of simply. It might appear that an increase in government deficit without a corresponding increase in money supply will increase the volume of government debts that must be absorbed in the financial market, and this will necessarily increase the level of interest rates, other things equal. Thus, an increase in government deficit without a corresponding increase in money supply, in addition to the usual expansionary effect on the expenditure side, has a contractionary effect through increased debt issues, and this side effect tends to be neglected unless the government budget constraint

[10] Christ later acknowledged this point, with a reservation. His reservation was that, in its generation of net worth, the MPS Model fails to take into account capital gains on government bonds, and to this extent, the government budget constraint implied by the MPS Model is incorrect. The MPS Model does take account of capital gains and losses in government bonds due to changes in the general price level, but it does fail to allow explicitly for capital gains and losses on government bonds due to changes in market rates of interest. This is due to the lack of any data concerning market value of government debts, and the MPS Model carries government bonds at its nominal face value *both for the private sector and for the government.* Thus, the MPS Model is perfectly consistant. If there is any problem, it is not that the implied government balance constraint is incorrect, but rather that net worth of consumers is somewhat misstated. We do not feel that this is a serious problem since government debts are mostly in short term securities, and the difference between the face value and the market value is not very arge. The discount bonds, such as treasury bills, are recorded at their market value.

is shown explicitly in the model. This proposition in this naive form is clearly false. From the above discussion showing that our model contains the government budget implicitly, it is clear that an increase in government deficit will be accompanied by an increase in the saving in the private sector of exactly the same amount, so that, in the financial market, there will be exactly the same increase in the demand as well as supply of funds, and there is no reason to expect the level of interest rates to rise or fall.[11]

The more sophisticated argument is that the proportion of government bonds in total assets available in the market must increase as a result of additional issue of debts, and this must have consequences on the level and the structure of interest rates. This is true, and it now appears that this point is closely related to the mechanism for the "crowing out" effects which monetarists have in mind. We shall consider this problem a little later in this paper, but we wish to clear up somewhat different problems before we come to the monetarists controversy.

3.2. *First round effects and ultimate effects.* We seem to use expressions such as the above, and the phrases "long run" and "short run" very causally in macro economics and we seem to get ourselves into some very confusing arguments due to the lack of precision on these phrases. Let us start our discussion with an example. Christ **[9]**, and following him Blinder and Solow **[7]**, work with a model in which the only apparent dynamic element is the change in government debt and money supply appearing in the government budget constraint. Taking advantage of this special feature of their model, they define the "steady state," or "long run" solution to be that in which the rate of change of government debt and money supply is equal to zero.[12] This is a strange definition of steady

[11] It may be noted that many existing econometric models do not contain equation (7) and define savings excluding capital gains, and hence they do not contain the government budget constraint implicitly. However, even in those models, it is true that savings in the economy is equal to the sum of investment and government deficits, and hence increase in government deficits will automatically be matched by the same increase in saving. Thus, there is no presumption that the level of interest rates will increase as a result of increased deficits, other things equal.

In reality, an increase in government deficits is always accompanied by increased income and output through the standard multiplier effects, other things equal. Given the money supply, this will cause an increase in the level of interest rates, so that we may observe government deficits and the level of interest rates moving together. Perhaps this is the reason why some economists are convinced that there must be some direct link between the size of deficits and the level of interest rates. To see that the link must be through income, consider a conceptual experiment in which government expenditure is decreased, and the taxes are decreased more than expenditure in such a way that, taking advantage of the balanced budget multiplier mechanism, the level of income is left unchanged. There will be an increase in deficits. But it will be matched by the same increase in saving, because it is this increase in saving that makes the balanced budget multiplier work. The reader can then see that there should be no presumption that the level of interest rates must rise or fall in this situation.

[12] We take up works of Christ and Blinder and Solow for our criticism not because these works have more serious defects than others, but because these authors deserve and receive the highest respect from all of us, and hence their writings are most influential in our profession.

It may be that they are led to this definition of steady state because, in terms of our model, they write explicitly equation (25) and treat equation (8) to be redundant, and hence the rate of change of net worth does not explicitly appear in their model.

state, since they do not require the rate of change of net worth of consumers to be zero, and assets may still be accumulating either in the form of real net investment, or in the form of capital gains (or losses). Blinder and Solow recognize this particular point, and remedy it in the second part of their paper by requiring that net investment also be zero in the steady state. But this raises another set of serious problems. If Blinder and Solow are concerned with "crowding out" effects as the economy moves from one stationary state to another in response to a change in fiscal policies, by requiring that net investment be zero in both states, they are requiring that the crowding out takes place entirely at the expense of consumption, unless they have some specific response of depreciation of capital in mind. If, on the other hand, they are concerned with stabilization policies in general, the assumption of zero net investment introduces serious distortion because the responses of investment and consumption to fiscal actions are quite different from each other and therefore the response of the total demand depends on the relative size of investment and consumption.

From their requirement that government deficits must be zero in the steady state, both Christ and Blinder and Solow conclude that the steady state multiplier on government expenditure must be equal to the reciprocal of the marginal tax rate. Blinder and Solow state that this result is "independent of all functional relations in the model except the tax function" [7, (326)]. The only way income and output can be increased to the level defined by this multiplier is through the presence of net worth in the consumption function which keeps rising so long as there are government deficits, and/or by a much more indirect channel, in which the supply of money is increased by the increased deficits which reduces the interest rate through the demand for money function, and this in turn increases investment through the presence of the interest rate in the investment function. But we can increase M and D in such a way that the interest rate will remain constant. Hence, unless net worth is present in the system, there is no way income and output can be increased to the level specified by the steady state multiplier obtained from the tax function alone. This means that, unless the functional relations in the model are specified appropriately, there is no way the system can reach the new stationary state defined by the long run multiplier.

But this is the least of the problems associated with the steady state, or "long run" analysis of Blinder and Solow. Since they assume that the price level is constant, the increase in income and output generated by the increase in government expenditure must be real output. But this must then be accompanied by a decrease in unemployment, as clear from the model in Table 1. The conclusion that one can draw from this observation depends on whether one believes in some Phillips Curve trade-off, or in the natural rate of unemployment hypothesis. If we accept the possibility of Phillips Curve trade-off, then, in the initial equilibrium the rate of unemployment must have been such that it was consistent with the rate of change of the price level of zero, since otherwise, given that the rate of change of money supply is zero in equilibrium and the rate of output is constant, the rate of interest could not be held constant (see equation (19) in our model). But the higher level of output at the new equilibrium implies higher employment and a lower level of unemployment, and hence, through equations (15) and (16) of our model, a higher rate of change of prices. Since the rate of change of prices in the original equilibrium was zero, this must mean that in the new equilibrium the rate of change of prices is positive. But this is inconsistent with the requirement that the rate of change of money supply be zero in any equilibrium. Thus, if the original equilibrium did exist, the new one cannot.

Suppose on the other hand that we accept the natural rate of unemployment hypothesis. Then in equilibrium output is basically given by the supply of labor,[13] and hence the increase in income defined by the steady state multiplier must be almost entirely due to an increase in prices. Thus, *PX* will be increased by $\Delta G/\tau$ where τ is the marginal tax rate, while M is increased by the accumulated deficits. Since these increases are the same proportion of *PX* and of M only by an accident, this would imply a change in r_s through equation (19), and this, together with a change in

$$\left[\frac{V}{A} - \frac{M + D}{A}\right],$$

would imply a change in ρ_k through equations (17) and (18). This in turn implies a change in demand for real output, but the supply of real output was fixed through the supply of labor except for a change in labor capital ratio due to the change in ρ_k. When we work through the model in Table 1 formally, we can see that the solution with the multiplier equal to the reciprocal of the marginal tax rate is not possible, unless we are prepared to mix an increase in money supply and that in government debts in exactly the right proportions.

Surely, this complex analysis is not what Christ and Solow and Blinder had in mind when they announced that the long run multiplier of government expenditure is the reciprocal of tax rate. In our view, their difficulty arises from their attempt to get an answer to a very complex problem using a simple, inadequate model. Because of their insistence that the model be simple, they avoided specifying critical relations needed for their analysis, in this case the labor market and determination of wages and prices. They then proceed to define a steady state in the context of their model, having forgotten that, in the background, they were making strong assumptions on variables that they were not prepared to deal with explicitly.

The only meaningful long run equilibrium is something close to a golden age path, on which all intensive variables remain constant and all extensive variables increase proportionately.[14] The MPS Model and the model given in Table 1 is, by design, capable of generating such a path provided that some minor adjust-

[13] Except for changes due to capital-labor ratio, which will be discussed a little later.

[14] This statement is inaccurate. There must be proper allowance for the difference in the rate of growth of current dollar variables and that of constant dollar variables, and still another rate for labor variables to allow for the technical change. In the following paragraphs, it should be understood that these qualifications are always allowed for.

ments are made and exogenous variables are set properly.[15] But on such a path, almost by definition, unemployment rate will be constant, or, if there is the Phillips Curve trade-off even in the long run, must be consistent with the rate of change of price level which in turn must be consistent with the rate of growth of money supply. In any case, on such a path, real output is largely determined from the supply side and stabilization policies are not concerned with such paths under normal conditions. It is true that alternative fiscal and monetary policies will generate different golden age paths, and one can ask a number of complex and important questions in the form of comparing among these alternative golden age paths.[16] Whatever the merit of such comparative analysis of alternative golden age paths, it is not what we usually mean by the analysis of stabilization policies, unless it turns out that the economy is so stable around such golden age paths that it never deviates far from them.[17] But we know that the U.S. economy is not that stable. Our analysis of the MPS Model indicates that the historical path of the U.S. economy is very substantially away from any conceivable golden age path.

Nor do we think that Professor Friedman is referring to the shift from one golden age path to another resulting from a change in monetary and fiscal policy when he talks of "ultimate effects." Since, as we have pointed out earlier, output on these paths is determined almost entirely by supply conditions, the conclusion that a change in government expenditure is largely off-set by corresponding changes in private expenditure, and that a change in money supply will almost entirely be reflected in a change in price level is quite obvious.[18,19]

At the other extreme, I am sure no one is suggesting that analysis of stabilization policies should focus almost exclusively on the immediate, impact effect in

[15] The most important adjustment concerns the federal personal income tax function. The elasticity of personal income tax with respect to total personal income is close to 1.5, largely because of the personal exemption. In generating a golden age path, we handle this problem by the device of letting personal exemption rise with money income, thus enabling personal income tax to increase more or less proportionately with income in the long run, while retaining 1.5 elasticity with respect to personal income in the short run and hence strong stabilizing effects on the economy.

[16] Such an analysis is currently underway using the MPS Model, and will be reported elsewhere. See Ando and Modigliani [**4**] and Corrado [**10**].

[17] It is not enough that the economy is stable around these paths in an ordinary sense, since it is not good enough that the economy, after moving away from such paths far and wide for 30 or 50 years, eventually returns to them.

[18] In [**12**] and [**13**], Friedman appears to say that real output and the real interest rate are basically independent of fiscal and monetary policies, while the prices and the nominal rate of interest is determined almost entirely by the monetary policy. These propositions are acceptable to most economists as a rough approximation if they are meant to apply to golden age paths. The basic point of Professor Friedman may be that, in his view, the economy is capable of always staying very close to a golden age path without any intervention from monetary and fiscal policies and the role of monetary and fiscal policies is to move the economy from one golden age path to another.

[19] I say "almost" instead of "completely" in this paragraph, because some aspects of fiscal policy, particularly the equilibrium size of national debts and some tax policies such as corporate profit tax can induce the real rate of return on the economy to change and hence the labor-capital ratio and output. See, for instance, Phelps and Shell [**15**] and Ando and Modigliani [**4**].

the first few months following the initiation of the policy change.

We therefore suggest that, when analyzing the impacts of stabilization policies, we should be concerned with the time path of the effects of a policy change over some specific length of time, say one to three years, and should not be overly concerned with such abstract a question as whether the effects are first round or ultimate. Such distinctions are unlikely to be well defined in any case. Once this is admitted, however, we are no longer entitled to ignore detailed time response characteristics of each behavioral equation in our model. Stability characteristics of some truncated system, in which some critical variables are taken as exogenous and distributed lag structures of some important behavioral equations are omitted, are irrelevant for our purposes.[20]

We shall now turn our attention to an outline of channels through which fiscal and monetary policies work in the Model of Table 1, and a discussion of some aspects of monetarists controversy.

3.3. *Fiscal and monetary policies in the MPS Model and some aspects of monetarists controversy.* Let us now look at the consequences of an exogenous increase in government expenditure, G, in the model in Table 1. We shall specify the monetary side of the policy a little later. Conceptually, as the initial condition for our experiment, we visualize the situation in which the economy has been moving along a golden age path, with all extensive variables growing at a constant rate and intensive variables remaining constant. Thus, whenever we speak of an "increase" or "decrease" in any variable, we mean an increase or decrease relative to the base path.

An increase in G will increase X by the same amount through identity (1). In addition, it will increase Y but by less than the increase in G since T will also respond to a change in X. These increases will induce increases in C and I, since equations (2) and (3) contain Y and X respectively. But because Y and X enter equations (2) and (3) through long distributed lags, the initial response of C and I are quite small, increasing only gradually. The increase in X will lead to an increase in employment, E, and a decrease in the unemployment rate, u. This in turn will cause a higher rate of change of wages, and hence a higher rate of change of prices and a higher level of prices.

Now suppose that we adopt the monetary policy of keeping the short term nominal rate of interest, r_s, constant. This means increasing M in proportion to PX. Under normal conditions, this means that only a small fraction of the deficit will be financed through an increase in M, the remaining part being financed through an increase in D.[21] In addition, let us for the moment assume that expected rate of change of prices is independent of actual rate of change of prices; in other words, we suspend equation (22) for the time being and assume that P^e is given exogenously. Let us further suppose that the characteristics of

[20] For example, it is difficult to interpret the conclusions that Blinder and Solow derive from the stability properties of their model around its steady state solutions.

[21] It should be recalled that, because we have netted the banking system with the private sector, M should be thought of as currency plus reserves. Hence, M is somewhat less than one-tenth of nominal GNP.

functions f_v and f_s in equations (17) and (18) are such that the term

$$f_\rho\left(\frac{V}{A} - \frac{M+P}{PA}\right)$$

in equation (25) is absent. Under these assumptions, the real rate of return on capital, ρ_k, will remain unchanged.

Returning now to the conditions of income and output, we expect V to rise because Π/P, and hence Π^e/P, will increase as a result of the increase in X and ρ_k is unchanged due to the set of assumptions we have made in the financial side. $M + D$ will increase by the amount of new deficit, and since the increase in P will occur only with a delay, we expect $(M + D)/P$ to increase initially. However, P will eventually begin to rise, and $(M + D)/P$ can be larger or smaller than the original value depending upon the relative changes of $M + D$ on the one hand and P on the other.[22] The net effect of these considerations is to increase consumption beyond what is expected from the standard multiplier-accelerator model, because the capital gains in V dominate the change in $(M + D)/P$ due to both increased deficits and changes in P.

In the meanwhile, the taxes, T, must be rising both because the real income has increased and also because prices have risen. The elasticity of PT is substantially greater than unity with respect to PX,[23] so that even after the real income has ceased to rise, so long as prices are rising, taxes in constant dollars as a proportion of real output will continue to rise. But prices will continue to rise so long as unemployment rate is less than it was initially, and the unemployment rate will stay below the initial level so long as the real output is above the initial level. Hence, as time goes on, there is an inherent tendency in the system to return to the original level of output at higher prices. However, it is an empirical question how quickly this tendency will overcome the initial expansionary impact of the increase in government expenditure. It may even

[22] The increase in $M + D$ is the increase in nominal saving that is the counterpart of the increased deficit of government. The decrease in $(M + D)/P$ due to increase in P is the Pigou effect on the existing government debts and money. Christ and Blinder and Solow appear to be neglecting the Pigou effect in their analysis by assuming prices to be constant.

In any case, I do not wish to exaggerate the importance of either increased $M + D$ due to new government deficits or the Pigou effect on consumption, in the context of the present analysis, that is, analysis with a two or three year horizon. A $10 billion increase in government expenditure at an annual rate over a three year period might generate, taking into account the response of taxes, a maximum of $15 billion in government debts, which would increase consumption by roughly $.7 billion. This is a very small change in consumption relative to that generated by the standard multiplier process. Similarly, since the part of government debts that is relevant to the Pigou effects is roughly $400 billion, a ten percent increase in prices will cause the real capital loss of $40 billion, and generate a reduction of consumption of $2 billion. A 10% change in prices in any year is much more than even the current rate of inflation. These figures should be compared with the impact of a 10% fall in the stock market, which is not uncommon, that should cause a $5 billion reduction in consumption since the total value of corporate shares is currently roughly $1,000 billion. These computations are based on the estimates of the parameters of the consumption function incorporated into the MPS Model.

[23] Empirically, it is much greater than 1.5 in the very short run and then becomes somewhat less than 1.5, because of the way personal income tax and corporate profit tax respond to changes in output and prices.

be that the system is not stable and hence the real demand will increase without limit until it is constrained from the production side, or that the contractionary forces due mostly to the tax system will be strong enough to overshoot on the negative side. The indications from experiments using the MPS Model are that, operated under the assumptions we have imposed in above paragraphs, the system is stable, and it reaches the maximum impact and then gradually declines, but very slowly.

Let us now remove the assumption that the term

$$f_\rho\left(\frac{V}{A} - \frac{M + D}{PA}\right)$$

in equation (25) is absent, while retaining all other simplifying assumptions. As I indicated earlier, this appears to be the critical element in the monetarist argument. Monetarists deemphasize the direct role of interest rates and stress the readjustment of the portfolio among real and financial assets in response to the changes in the supply of money and government debts as the more important channel through which impacts of monetary and fiscal policies are felt. The model in Table is one of the simplest models which enables us to deal with this mechanism explicitly.

When the government increases the supply of $M + D$ at any particular point in time, it must have the effect of increasing the supply of $M + D$ relative to that of V (more accurately, we should say the supply of Π^e/P rather than of V since V is determined in the process of financial market equilibrium while Π^e/P is given to it). Now the structure of equations (17) and (18) and hence of equations (25), together with the usual assumptions about the own and cross price elasticities, must lead us to the conclusion that, when the relative supply of $M + D$ is increased, its return must increase relative to that of V. Since, by our assumption ρ_s is given, this means that ρ_k must fall. But this has an expansionary effect on the demand for real goods, both because I depends negatively on ρ_k, and because, given Π^e/P, a fall in ρ_k will increase V, and an increase in V will increase C.

Of course, when the increase in P in response to the increase in G is taken into account, the increase in supply of $(M + D)/P$ is less than that of $M + D$ itself, and hence the expansionary effect described in the preceding paragraph is somewhat less. But an increase in P will increase PG given G, and hence make the increase in $M + D$ greater, unless the increase in P is so great that the increase in PT becomes larger than that of PG. Thus, while the increase in $(M+D)/P$ will be less than that in $M+D$ itself, it is unlikely that $(M+D)/P$ will decrease rather than increase.

This conclusion appears to be in conflict with the impression one gets from reading works of monetarists.[24] They seem to assert that the portfolio readjust-

[24] The case under discussion is not exactly the one stressed by monetarists, since we are letting both M and D change in order to accommodate new deficits. We shall discuss the case in which M is held constant a little later in this paper. However, it should be emphasized that our conclusion concerning the specific role of the portfolio readjustment process applies equally to both cases.

ment process in response to an increase in government expenditure should be contractionary, so much so that it is capable of canceling out the expansionary impact of the government expenditure increase.

There is one possibility of modifying the model of Table 1 which makes the portfolio readjustment process contractionary rather than expansionary. In the model in Table 1, it is assumed that all government debts are issued in the form of one period bonds with the nominal rate of interest on them given with certainty. Suppose we change this arrangement and assume instead that all government debts are in the form of perpetuity, and the rate of return on them is equal to that on V, ρ_k. In such a model, money serves not only as the means of transaction but also as an item in the portfolio. It is no longer possible to write the demand functions for money in the form of (19) and there are no short term rates, r_s and ρ_s. Nevertheless, without going into the details, it is easy to see that an increase in the supply of government bonds given the supply of money must decrease the price of government bonds and PV relative to that of M, i.e., increase the rate of return of ρ_k. Thus, the portfolio readjustment process becomes contractionary.[25]

I do not believe that this alternative formulation is a reasonable one. In the first place, a large part of government debts is in fact in the form of one period bonds. In the second place, suppose that we generalize the model to allow government debts to take forms of both one period bonds and long term bonds. Let us also recognize the distinction between long term government bonds and real assets or private equity, and their respective rates of return. Then it can be shown, provided that all the price elasticities for the demands for short and long term government bonds and for equity are all of expected signs, (i) that the short term nominal rate of interest will be determined by the volume of transactions and the money supply through an equation like (19) independent of portfolio considerations (see Appendix to [**5**]), (ii) that an increase in the supply of short term goverment debts will decrease ρ_k and is therefore expansionary, and (iii) that an increase in the supply of long term government debts may increase or decrease ρ_k depending upon whether long term debts are a closer substitute for equity or for short term government debts. The case in which the additional deficits is financed by long term debts and long term debts are a closer substitute for equity than for short term debts, the only case in which ρ_k will rise and therefore contractionary, is the least likely case in practice. Therefore, the mone-

[25] It is probably this model that Solow and Blinder had in mind when they wrote their paper [**7**]. But their model is in fact quite different because in it, the government bond as perpetuity has its value determined through the division of coupon payment by the market rate of interest, while the value of capital is *independent* of interest rate. Yet, the government bonds and capital apparently yield the same rate of return in their model. This formulation may be reasonable if the economy always remains on a golden age path, since on a golden age path the value of capital must be equal to its reproduction cost. But as soon as the economy is off a golden age path, it is difficult to see how the value of capital can be independent of the market rate of return. Blinder and Solow should have allowed the value of capital to depend on the rate of interest in their analysis of the stability of their model around the stationary state, since their conclusions about the stability of the model depend on the behavior of the system off the stationary state.

tarists' contention that, somehow, the portfolio readjustment process in response to government expenditure increase is so contractionary that it explains almost complete "crowding out" has no foundation, unless they have a portfolio theory that is very much different from the standard one in financial literature and yet to be presented publicly.

In the MPS Model, we allow for both one period bonds and long term bonds to be issued by the government, and private equity shares. We also allow for private bonds and other financial instruments, but the basic question is the role of a term like

$$f_\rho\left(\frac{V}{A} - \frac{M + D}{PA}\right)$$

in equation (25). After fairly extensive efforts to estimate the impact of a term like

$$f_\rho\left(\frac{V}{A} - \frac{M + D}{PA}\right)$$

in the context of the MPS Model, we had to conclude that it was not at all significant. Since the nature of the term makes it very difficult to handle statistically (see footnote 8), this does not mean that our result is necessarily conclusive, and we shall make another try at it in the context of the flow of funds submodel of the MPS Model currently being developed. However, the implications of our analysis in this paper should be clearly understood: if our failure to find the statistical evidence for the presence of this term is due to some bias of our procedure, the result has been to bias our estimates of the impact of fiscal actions towards zero, and not the other way around.

Let us now change our assumption concerning the monetary policy, and suppose that, instead of keeping the nominal short rate, r_s, constant, money supply is kept constant, meaning that it is the same both in the base and shocked paths. All additional deficits are financed by issuing additional government debts. We shall retain one assumption, that the expected rate of change of prices is exogenously given; we shall discuss the consequences of dropping this assumption a little later. Now suppose that we undertake the same government expenditure increase that we have been discussing, and consider the consequences under this altered monetary rule. All the comments we have made concerning the behavior of output, employment, prices, and taxes still apply in this case. But, unlike under the policy of maintaining the constant r_s, as soon as PX begins to rise, r_s must rise also. Our estimates incorporated into the MPS Model suggest that the elasticity of r_s with respect to PX is quite large, around three, and that the response is quite rapid. Moreover, so long as the change in X is positive, unemployment is lower than before, and hence the prices will keep on rising, which pushes r_s higher and higher.

r_s itself does not influence demands for real output. But, under our assumption that the expected rate of change of prices is given, the rise in r_s does increase the real short rate, ρ_s. This in turn must increase the crucial capitalization rate, ρ_k, through equation (25). The distributed lags involved in the response of ρ_k to ρ_s are such that a part of the response, roughly one-quarter of the total, takes place fairly quickly, and the remaining part of the response will occur much more slowly. This will be partially off-set by the portfolio rearrangement effects through the term

$$f_\rho\left(\frac{V}{A} - \frac{M + D}{A}\right)$$

if this term has significant impact, but in practice this off-set appears not to be significant.

An increase in ρ_k has powerful impacts on output through two channels. The first, and more conventional one, is through its role in the cost of capital, and hence, investment. Second, it reduces the market value of real assets, V, through equation (9); this, through identity (7), reduces net worth of consumers, and finally consumption. This tendency will persist so long as the value of ρ_k is higher than that which prevailed without the increase in government expenditure. But ρ_k will stay higher so long as PX is higher as the result of the increased government expenditure. Since P is at a higher level than before, even when X returns to the level without the government expenditure increase, PX is larger, and ρ_k will be higher, and the pressure for lower output will continue. Thus, under this set of policies, not only does the complete "crowding out" occur, but total output at some point in the response path may become even lower than what would have prevailed without the government expenditure increase.

However, this lower level of output cannot be maintained. As soon as X becomes less that what would have prevailed without the government expenditure, the unemployment rate also becomes higher than before, and the rate of increase of P becomes lower. Eventually, PX also becomes less than what would have prevailed without the increase in government expenditure, and finally brings ρ_k back to the original level and even lower.

The foregoing discussion suggests that, under the constant money supply rule, the response of the economy, as represented by the MPS Model as well as the model in Table 1, to an increase in government expenditure is likely to be a cyclical one, and numerical analysis with the MPS Model indicates that it indeed is. However, in the absence of the response of the expected rate of change of prices to the actual rate of change of prices, the pattern of response is quite damped, and the system returns eventually to a path on which total demand for output is the same as on the original path, although the composition of total demand has changed.

We thus have a situation in which the complete "crowding out" effects do occur. But the mechanisms involved in bringing this about are not very exotic ones. They are fairly familiar ones of tax system and the higher interest rates brought about by higher output and prices and the constant money supply. The only element in our model that has not been stressed in the traditional literature is perhaps the role of the market value of real assets in consumption.

The important question at this point is how long does it take for the complete "crowding out" effects to occur. The answer to this question depends on the detailed dynamic characteristics of the system, and cannot be given on a purely theoretical basis. The MPS Model, with current estimates of all its parameters, indicates that it will take roughly 30 to 40 quarters, or 8 to 10 years before complete "crowding out" effects take place. It takes even longer for PX to return to its original level. This result contrasts sharply with that given by the St. Louis Model, in which complete "crowding out" effects in current dollar terms take place within four quarters.[26] We shall comment more on this point a little later in this paper.

Let us now finally drop the assumption that the expected rate of change of prices is independent of actual rate of change of prices, and inquire how the scenario discussed in the foregoing paragraphs will be changed when this linkage is added. The initial increase of X, and P and hence PX, in response to the increase in government expenditure is exactly as before, and the response of r_s is also unchanged. However, since the actual rate of change of prices has now been increased, the expected rate of change of prices, $(P^e - P)/P$, must also become larger through equation (22). Thus, it is no longer guaranteed that ρ_s will rise in response to the rise in r_s. It will depend upon numerical values of parameters, in particular, those in functions (13) through (16) and (22) which determine the size and speed of the response of the expected rate of change of prices to an increase in output, and those in equation (19) which determine the response of r_s to a change in PX. It may be helpful to look at equation (25) which is the reduced form derived from all equations in the financial sector other than equation (19). The direction of response of ρ_k to an increase in output depends on the relative magnitudes and speeds of responses of r_s and $(P - P_{-1})/P_{-1}$ to an increase in output, and also on the pattern of coefficients β_i and γ_i. The response of r_s depends on the movement of prices and on the characteristics of the demand for money given by equation (19) while that of $(P - P_{-1})/P_{-1}$ depends on the characteristics of the demand and supply of labor and the wage and price equations. The pattern of coefficients β_i and γ_i, on the other hand, depends on the response of expectations of the future short rates to the current and past short rates, and of expectations of the future rate of change of prices to the current and past rates of change of prices.

The response of ρ_k to an increase in government expenditure (or tax reduction) and the consequent increase in output thus involves very complex empirical questions, and cannot be settled on a theoretical basis alone. In particular, the response of expected rate of change of prices to actual rate of change of prices is a very much unsettled empirical question, and the estimates of this process incorporated in the MPS Model are probably among the least reliable of all estimates in it. This is partly because it is extremely difficult to obtain any

[26] See [**1**] and [**2**]. It should be noted that, throughout this paper and most of the literature, "crowding out" refers to the demand in real terms, while in the St. Louis Model, it specifically refers to the demand in nominal terms. See also [**14**] for comparison of the St. Louis Model and the MPS Model.

reliable data on expectation of rates of change of prices that are relevant for our analysis.

Moreover, even if we had reliable estimates of all parameters of behavioral equations involved, we would still not be able to make unconditional statements on the response of ρ_k to a change in output. This is because some of the functions involved are highly nonlinear, and the response of ρ_k to a change in output depends critically on the relevant initial conditions.[27]

For these reasons, the possibility that the economy will plunge itself into a hyper-inflationary situation in response to a fiscal stimulus, even when the supply of money is kept constant, cannot be ruled out. Of course, the constant money supply rule is not the limit of restrictive monetary policies. It is always possible to go further and reduce the money supply, thereby increasing r_s further. If we knew the movement of the expected rate of change of prices, it is possible even to devise a policy to move r_s sufficiently to counteract it, so that ρ_k always moves countercyclically. The difficulty is that we seldom know the movement of the expected rate of change of prices, even approximately, let alone exactly. It should be emphasized that it is not the actual rate of change of prices, but the expected rate of change of prices that we must counteract. Thus, it becomes very critical to design the fiscal aspects of the stabilization policy judiciously. Not only is it possible for some fiscal actions to cause an unstable response from the economy. Once the economy begins to exhibit serious instability, under some circumstances, only well designed further fiscal actions are capable of bringing the economy under control. Monetary actions may not be sufficient to control the economy under such conditions.[28]

Because this is one of the critical issues in the discussion of stabilization policies, and it is frustrating to say that the resolution of this issue depends on the empirical estimates of the response of the expected rate of change of prices to actual rate of change of prices which is hard to come by, it is tempting to look for some short-cut way of resolving this issue which does not involve empirical estimates of the response of the expected rate of change of prices to the actual rate of change of prices. One of the short-cuts suggested is the following:

[27] Consider, for instance, a situation where, due to the past monetary and fiscal policies, the unemployment rate is kept fairly high, the rate of change of prices relatively low, and the nominal short term interest rate relatively high. In this situation, an increase in government expenditure and a consequent increase in real income and output will raise unemployment but the response of the rate of change of prices is likely to be quite mild due to the nonlinear character of the wage equation. On the other hand, the response of r_s is likely to be substantial in absolute terms, thus dominating the response of ρ_k. In the opposite situation, if the initial conditions are such that unemployment is quite low and the rate of change of prices is substantial, while r_s was kept fairly low, then, with the same estimates of all the parameters involved, there is good chance that the response of ρ_k is dominated by the change in the expected rate of change of prices.

[28] The condition which the Keynesian "liquidity trap" was meant to describe may be thought of as a special case of this proposition. Suppose that, given the fiscal policy, the value of ρ_k required to bring about reasonable employment conditions is a very low value, say ρ_k^0. Now suppose that expected rate of change of prices is negative, and its absolute value is greater than ρ_k^0. Then, since the lowest value that r_s can take is zero, there is no way the monetary policy can bring about the required value of ρ_k.

Suppose, for whatever the reason, that expected rate of change of prices is equal to the actual rate of change of prices. This seems reasonable as a property of the economy if it stays on a golden age path for a long time, although it is a dubious proposition when the economy is not on a golden age path. Based on this assumption, let us replace the expected rate of change of prices in the model in Table 1 by the current actual rate of change of prices. Then the system will be greatly simplified, and the uncertainty about the empirical estimates of critical parameters is greatly reduced, making it much easier to arrive at some conclusions concerning the conditions under which the response of the economy to a fiscal stimulus is stable or unstable. But conclusions based on such a procedure are of no use in dealing with the real economy. The stability of the real economy depends most critically on the time pattern of response of the expected rate of change of prices to the actual rate of change of prices. To suppose that the expected rate responds immediately and fully to changes in the actual rate is to confine ourselves to the most unstable limiting case, and it is not surprising that individuals who follow such reasoning appear to conclude that the U.S. economy is much more unstable than most of us believe it to be.

The second, more elaborate short-cut appears to be embedded in the theoretical structure used by monetarists.[29] They simply assert that the real rate of return is given by the marginal productivity of capital, and it is basically constant over time. They also assert that the nominal rate of interest is simply equal to the real rate of return plus the expected rate of change of prices, and since the real rate of return is a constant, by observing changes of the nominal rate over time, we can observe the changes in the expected rate of changes of prices over time.

I do not know on what basis one can assert that the real rate of return is constant over time. If it is indeed constant and independent of monetary policy, the real demand must be independent of monetary policy. Sometimes, monetarists do indeed appear to accept this interpretation of their argument [**3**]. Suppose we accept this position for the moment, and inquire how the nominal rate of interest can always be equal to this constant rate plus the expected rate of change of prices. In view of the proposition that we have proven elsewhere [**5**], this must mean that the monetary authority always knows exactly what the expected rate of change of prices is, and provides just enough money supply to bring about the level of the short rate equal to the sum of the constant real rate of return and the expected rate of change of prices.

The monetarists' proposition is perfectly reasonable if we are concerned only with steady, golden age paths discussed earlier in this paper. Then, the real rate of return is indeed constant and equal to the marginal productivity (except for the effects of taxes and monopolistic powers of some groups), and monetary policy, in order not to disturb the economy, must be such that nominal rate of interest is equal to the sum of the real rate of return and the expected rate of change of prices. Perhaps, then, this is the basic difference between monetarists

[29] See Friedman [**12**] [**13**].

and those of us who are not monetarists as the term is conventionally understood. Monetarists believe that the economy is very stable around golden age paths, so that the role of fiscal and monetary policies is to move the economy from one golden age path to another, mainly affecting the price level and nominal rates of interest. We believe, on the other hand, that the economy is sufficiently unstable, especially in the presence of exogenous random shocks, so that it requires active fiscal and monetary policies to keep it fairly close to a golden age path. It would be useful to know if monetarists will agree with this interpretation or not, because it will clarify a great deal of confusion in the profession, and I do not think I am the only one among non-monetarist economists who finds surprising the above interpretation of the differences between monetarists and others.

4. CONCLUDING REMARKS

A large part of recent discussion on the theory of economic stabilization is concerned with the monetarist controversy, and yet, even at this late date, we are not at all sure what are the basic behavioral assumptions which lead monetarists to their central conclusion, i.e., that nominal income is almost completely determined by the nominal money supply, and fiscal actions have very little effect on nominal income. One assumption that clearly leads to this conclusion, namely, that the demand for money is a function of nominal income alone and is independent of the rate of interest, has been explicitly disowned by Friedman. There have been many vague references to the portfolio readjustments by the public in response to changes in money supply and in government deficits, but, to the best of my knowledge, the description of the portfolio readjustment process has not been clearly articulated in the context of a complete macroeconomic model.

In an earlier paper [**14**], Modigliani indicated that the impacts of monetary policies implied by the MPS Model were of a similar order of magnitude to those indicated by the St. Louis Model though there were important differences of detail. On the other hand, estimates of the impacts of fiscal policy actions based on the MPS Model are vastly different from those suggested by the St. Louis Model. Does this mean that the theoretical structure of the MPS Model is different in some critical way from that underlying the St. Louis Model, and if so, exactly what are the differences? We cannot tell because the St. Louis Model consists of a set of reduced form equations rather than of structural equations.

In this paper, we have presented the basic theoretical structure of the MPS Model, taking special care to describe the process of portfolio readjustment in response to changes in money supply and government deficits incorporated into the MPS Model. We have argued that the portfolio readjustment process built into the MPS Model is in general accordance with the standard one apparently acceptable to both monetarists and non-monetarists. A careful analysis of the role played by this process in the transmission of stabilization policies leads to the conclusion that it strengthens, rather than weakens, the impacts of fiscal policy actions on both real and nominal income and output. It will contribute greatly to our understanding if monetarists are to specify exactly how their model of income determination differs from the one presented in this paper.

The model we have presented in this paper also serves as a framework within which to analyze several theoretical questions related to economic stabilization raised by some authors. We have tried to show how some misleading conclusions have been presented in the literature primarily because some authors analyzed stabilization questions using partial models which ignore some important aspects of macroeconomic systems. Such models may enable us to obtain clear cut analytical results, but at the expense of losing any correspondence to the real economy. While it gives us less aesthetic satisfaction to work with a complex model and to conclude that many important conclusions depend on numerical estimates of parameters, in the analysis of economic stabilization, there is no alternative but to accept this conclusion and to engage in the hard and unglamorous task of obtaining best estimates for numerical values of those critical parameters.

As complex as the model presented in this paper may be, it is a grossly simplified version of the theoretical structure underlying the MPS Model. For example, treatment of imperfection in various markets which increases the complexity of the MPS Model very substantially was completely left out from the model in Table 1. We think, however, that this model does contain most elements that are essential for general discussion of stabilization policies. It enables the user to distinguish those aspects of stabilization analysis which can be pursued without reference to empirical estimates from those aspects which are critically dependent on empirical estimates. Those impacts of stabilization policies that can be deduced without reference to empirical estimates are severely limited, and we have called on estimates contained in the MPS Model to arrive at our conclusions whenever necessary in this paper. Estimates of some parameters in the MPS Model are subject to serious doubt, but the only alternative is to obtain better estimates. To avoid facing this conclusion, and to resort to estimation of reduced form equations or to models which omit critical aspects of the macroeconomic system will not advance our understanding of stabilization problems.

University of Pennsylvania

REFERENCES

[1] ANDERSON, L. C., "A Monetarist View of Demand Management: The U. S. Experience," *Federal Reserve Bank of St. Louis Review*, LIII (September, 1971), 3-11.

[2] ——— AND K. M. CARLSON, "A Monetarist Model for Economic Stabilization," *Federal Reserve Bank of St. Louis Review*, LII (April, 1970), 7-25.

[3] ANDO, A. AND F. MODIGLIANI, "The Life Cycle Hypothesis of Saving: Aggregate Implications and Tests," *American Economic Review*, LIII (March, 1963), 55-84. Reprinted with corrections in R. A. Gordon and L. R. Klein, eds., *AEA Readings in Business Cycles* (Homewood, Ill.: Richard D. Irwin, Inc., 1965).

[4] ——— AND ———, *The MPS Econometric Model: Its Theoretical Foundation and Empirical Findings*, forthcoming in 1976.

[5] ——— AND ———, "Some Reflections on Describing Structure of Financial Sectors," in Gary Fromm and Lawrence R. Klein, eds., *The Brookings Model: Perspective and Recent Developments* (Amsterdam: North Holland Co., 1975).

[6] ———, ———, R. RASCHE, AND S. J. TURNOVSKY, "On the Role of Expectations of Price and Technological Change in an Investment Function," chapter 7 in this volume.

[7] BLINDER, A. S. AND R. M. SOLOW, "Does Fiscal Policy Matter?" *Journal of Public Economics*, II (November, 1973), 319-338.

[8] CHRIST, C. F., "Econometric Models of the Financial Sector," *Journal of Money, Credit, and Banking*, IV (May, 1972), 419-449.

[9] ———, "A Simple Macroeconomic Model with a Government Budget Restraint," *Journal of Political Economy*, LXXVI (January-February, 1968), 53-67.

[10] CORRADO, C., "The Long Run Properties of the MPS Model and its Relation with Stabilization Policies," unpublished Ph. D. dissertation, University of Pennsylvania, (1976).

[11] FOLEY, D. K., AND M. SIDRAUSKI, *Monetary and Fiscal Policy in a Growing Economy* (London: The Macmillan Co., 1971).

[12] FRIEDMAN, M., "A Monetary Theory of Nominal Income," *Journal of Political Economy*, LXXIX (March-April, 1971), 323-337.

[13] ———, "A Theoretical Framework of Monetary Analysis," *Journal of Political Economy*, LXXVIII (March-April, 1970), 193-238.

[14] MODIGLIANI, F., "Monetary Policy and Consumption: Linkages via Interest Rates and Wealth Effects in the MPS Model," in *Consumer Spending and Monetary Policy: The Linkages Conference Series*, No. 5 (Boston: The Federal Reserve Bank of Boston, 1971).

[15] PHELPS, E. S. AND K. SHELL, "Public Debt, Taxation, and Capital Intensiveness," *Journal of Economic Theory*, I (October, 1969), 330-346.

[16] SPECIAL ISSUE ON MONETARY THEORY, *Journal of Political Economy*, LXXX (September-October, 1972).

[17] TOBIN, J., "A General Equilibrium Approach to Monetary Theory," *Journal of Money, Credit, and Banking*, I (February, 1969), 15-29.

8

THE WHARTON MODEL MARK III: A MODERN IS-LM CONSTRUCT

By Vijaya G. Duggal, Lawrence R. Klein and Michael D. McCarthy[1]

INTRODUCTION

This paper describes the principal structural elements and the performance characteristics of the Wharton Mark III, the version of the Wharton Quarterly Model used for forecasting and simulation from 1971 to 1974.[2]

1. MARK III—THE BASIC STRUCTURE

The equation structures of large econometric models appear to be extremely complex. In fact the equation system of Wharton Mark III can be decomposed into two relatively simple broad groupings—real product supplies and demands, and financial sector supply and demands. The model can be seen as an elaborate IS-LM scheme. This is true of most of the large macro forecasting systems for the U.S. economy.

1.1. *The I-S Curve—commodity and factor demands and supplies.* Mark III has been described as a demand oriented model; Hurd [**9**]. It will be seen that the point is not strictly correct; sectoral short run and long run marginal cost curves can be inferred from the equation structure of Mark III; it is true, however, that the degree of aggregation on the production sector level is much greater than we would like particularly for treating a complex situation like the energy crisis. Part of the solution in such a case is to seek more detailed production sector disaggregation.

In the Brookings Model [**4**] and the predecessor Wharton Model [**6**] the equations might have given the appearance of being piecemeal work. There were the "labor equations," "price equations," "capital demand equations," etc. In the Brookings Model different research groups were given responsibilities for the development of the different equation "blocks." We note that there are potential pitfalls in such a strategy. However, it proved fruitful at a pioneering stage, in generating many research leads that might not have been uncovered. In construcing Mark III an attempt was made at the outset to give an integrated treatment of commodity and factor supplies and demands. We began by considering a simple single production sector and assumed some degree of mo-

[1] The authors wish to thank F. Gerard Adams for his generous help with preparation of this paper. George R. Green provided the analysis of forecast performance. The authors wish to acknowledge significant research support provided by the Cleveland Federal Reserve Bank and Wharton E.F.A., Inc.

[2] An earlier article in this volume (Adams and Duggal [**1**]) discussed the properties of the "Anticipations Version" of Wharton Mark III.

nopoly power. The production function for this sector was of the form:

(1) $Q_t = Ae^{\lambda t}L_t^{\alpha}K_t^{1-\alpha}$ where Q_t = output at time period t; L_t and K_t are labor and capital respectively; $A > 0$; $\lambda > 0$, and $0 < \alpha < 1$.[3] Demand for the sector output was given by

(2) $P_t = BQ_t^{\delta}$ where P_t = price; $B > 0$, and $-1 < \delta < 0$. Next letting w_t and r_t be the labor costs and capital costs total profit was given by

(3) $\pi_t = P_tQ_t - w_tL_t - r_tK_t$. It was assumed that the sector determined L_t, K_t, Q_t and hence P_t in a manner that would maximize π_t. The solution led to the following first order equilibrium conditions (or decision rules).

(4a) $$L_t = A^{-1/\alpha}e^{-(\lambda/\alpha)t}K_t^{(\alpha-1)/\alpha}Q_t^{1/\alpha}$$

(4b) $$Q_t = B^{-1/\delta}P_t^{-1/\delta}$$

(4c) $$P_t = [\alpha(1 + \delta)]^{-1}\frac{w_t \cdot L_t}{Q_t}$$

(4d) $$K_t = (1 - \alpha)(1 + \delta)\frac{P_t \cdot Q_t}{r_t}.$$

Substitution of (4a) into (4c) yields a relation between P_t and Q_t which has a ready interpretation (taking K_t as given) of a short run marginal cost markup curve, the markup factor being $(1 + \delta)^{-1}$. Also substitution of L_t and K_t from (4c) and (4d) into (4a) yields

$$P_t = [(1 + \delta)Ae^{\lambda t}]^{-1}[\alpha^{\alpha}(1 - \alpha)^{1-\alpha}]^{-1}[w_t^{\alpha}r_t^{1-\alpha}]$$
$$= (1 + \delta)^{-1}LRMC$$

where

$$LRMC = [Ae^{\lambda t}]^{-1}[\alpha^{\alpha}(1 - \alpha)^{1-\alpha}]^{-1}[w_t^{\alpha}r_t^{1-\alpha}]$$

that is, long run marginal cost. Again $(1 + \delta)^{-1}$ is the markup factor. The model need not be considered deficient on the supply side simply because it does not explicitly include short run (and long run) marginal cost curves. Lack of production sector detail may still pose problems, however.

For an analysis of the adequacy of the equation structure of Mark III, the equation system (4) provides a convenient framework. One ought to be able to point to equations on a sector by sector basis that are analogous to (4). In the case of Mark III, the endogenous production sectors are manufacturing (and mining) (*MM*) the regulated sector (*R*) and the commercial sector (*C*). Let us begin with (4a). The equations for manhours (and employment) have the general forms:

[3] The assumption of constant returns to scale is not essential to the main argument but simplifying from an estimation and presentation point of view.

(5)
$$\begin{aligned} MH_{it} &= f(t, Q_{it}, K_{it}, MH_{it-1}) \text{ and} \\ E_{it} &= h(t, Q_{it}, K_{it}, E_{it-1}) \text{ where} \\ MH_{it} &= \text{Manhours employed in sector } i, \text{ period } t. \\ E_{it} &= \text{Employees in sector } i, \text{ period } t. \\ Q_{it} &= \text{Output originating in sector } i, \text{ period } t. \\ K_{it} &= \text{Capital stock in sector } i, \text{ period } t. \end{aligned}$$

The manufacturing and mining manhours equation, for example is of the form

(5a)
$$\begin{aligned} \Delta \ln MHMM = \underset{(.957)}{.1594} - \underset{(18.3)}{.60637} \ln XMM - \underset{(7.02)}{.37466} \ln XMM_{-1} \\ - \underset{(4.50)}{.2199} \ln MHMM_{-1} - \underset{(4.50)}{.2199{*}.547} \ln KMF_{-1} \\ + \text{time trend dummy variables.} \end{aligned}$$

The manhours equations for the other sectors are similar with the exception that the capital stock variable was not included; for a short term forecasting model such as Mark III this is a minor fault. The Cobb-Douglas framework underlying the manhours equations should be obvious. These equations are simply log linear versions of Kuh's short term production functions [**10**].

The "sector price" equations in the model, see McCarthy [**11**], are unit labor cost markup equations as in (4c) (with distributed lags), and the Jorgenson type investment demand equations are in conformity with (4d). Equation (4b) is, of course, an over-simplification; variables other than prices enter demand equations. Very briefly, the main counterparts of (4b) in Mark III are fairly conventional Keynesian consumption functions, and the neoclassical business plant and equipment demand equations commonly found in modern macro models. These are supplemented by functions for the foreign sector and by public sector demands. This statement requires only one modification. Net inventory investment is treated in a novel way. In the earlier Wharton Model there are explicit inventory demand equations. A review of the rationale for these inventory equations suggests that the authors were thinking of a finished goods inventory scheme. Manufacturing inventory changes were taken as depending on recent (previous quarter) manufacturing sales, changes in unfilled orders, and previous inventory stocks (in the earlier Wharton Model). Unfilled orders, in turn, were contemporaneously related to manufacturing sales and government defense expenditures.

There are at least two problems with this approach. First, it fails to recognize explicitly that an important component of net inventory change is the work-in-process inventory change underlying the business plant and equipment investment cycle. This consideration suggests that high order lags in user costs of capital should influence inventory movements. Second, the approach does not explicitly recognize the fact that inventories serve as a buffer between production (P) and deliveries (D). Inventory change $= \Delta II = P - D$. The exact data on P (production) and D (deliveries) for this identity are not readily available. Proxy variables are available, however. P can be expected to be positively related to manufacturing production (XMF) and D to be positively related to the delivery items in the national income accounts (consumption expenditures on goods, (CG), plant and equipment investment expenditures (IP), residential housing (IH), and government purchases of goods (GG). Mark III uses such a statistical approximation of an inventory change identity. The actual equation estimated for Mark III was of the form:

$$\Delta II = \alpha_0 + \alpha_1 XMF + \alpha_2 CG + \alpha_3 IP + \alpha_4 IH + \alpha_5 GG \,.$$

Where $\alpha_1 > 0$ and $\alpha_2, \alpha_3 \cdots \alpha_5 < 0$. The next step to close the model was to introduce an explicit output decision function. This function related XMF to production-to-stock items such as CG, and to a distributed lag in manufacturers' new orders (MNO). The lags attempt to recognize that a major component of XMF is production related to the plant and equipment investment cycle. Two refinements in the XMF equation were the inclusion of a distributed lag on the inventory sales ratio and the separate treatment of government defense orders in the form of a distributed lag on defense gross obligations incurred ($GOI\$$), deflated by the manufacturing wholesale price index (PMF). Finally MNO was assumed to depend on current order type variables such as $GOI\$$, and also on distributed lags in past changes in the sales of consumption goods and past changes in user costs of capital (divided by the wholesale price index of manufactured goods).[4]

In the above we have noted that supply equations (or more accurately, marginal cost equations) are implicitly present in Mark III on a production sector basis. They are, of course, not present in the form of explicit supply equations for national income account (NIA) final demand components such as consumption expenditures and plant and equipment investment expenditures. Labor supply, is however, exogenous in current applications of Mark III though labor force participation equations are being developed. Supply is also introduced through the impact of unemployment on the wage rate (Phillips curve) and through the impact of capacity utilization on sectoral prices. On the price side, the NIA implicit deflators are derived from simple regression linkages of NIA prices to sectoral prices.

Given wages, prices, and real demand, output and factor inputs we can calculate current price results for the wage bill, GNP, corporate profits, tax receipts and so on.

1.2. *The LM Curve—money supply and demand.* In the preceding discussion interest rates and user costs of capital were taken as given; to this point we have in effect been describing an IS curve. The structure of money demand and supply side in Mark III relies heavily on the MPS (MIT-Pennsylvania-SSRC)[5] Model. Briefly, the private demand deposit equation ($DDP\$$) is a conventional

[4] This equation system has significant promise but the difficulty of properly measuring and explaining some of the variables, $GOI\$$ and MNO, sometimes causes difficulties in prediction or simulation applications.

[5] See Modigliani [**12**] or for an earlier version [**3**].

structure which relates money demand to current price GNP and to short term interest rates, with a distributed lag. The money supply equation relates private demand deposits positively to non-borrowed reserves of Federal Reserve member banks, negatively to the Federal Reserve rediscount rate, and positively to market interest rates. Supply and demand equations are also developed for time deposits, certificates of deposit, and business loans.

2. SAMPLE PERIOD ERROR ANALYSIS

The Wharton Model has been simulated over eight quarter periods starting in successive quarters with 1961.1 and ending with 1967.4. Error statistics listed in column 8 of Table 1, for instance, are computed using the 28 available eight quarter ahead simulations.

The one quarter ahead root mean square error for real Gross National Product is $3.21 billion.[6] The error rises by one billion dollars in a two quarter ahead simulation but from a two to an eight quarter ahead projection, the build-up of error is slower. The error calculated from eight quarter ahead simulations is less than double the error of one quarter ahead projections. In no major component of real GNP does the error double as we move from a one quarter ahead to an eight quarter ahead simulation. This is unfortunately not true in sample period simulation of prices. The deflator for Gross National Product is

TABLE 1

WHARTON MODEL MARK III SAMPLE PERIOD ERROR ANALYSIS
1961.1—1967.4

Root Mean Square Errors
(Billions of Dollars)

Variable	Type	Simulation Period[1]							
		1	2	3	4	5	6	7	8
Gross National Product	Current $	2.89	4.60	6.14	6.81	7.20	7.29	7.30	7.16
	1958 $	3.21	4.23	4.65	4.64	4.89	5.12	5.35	5.73
Personal Consumption Expenditures	Current $	1.92	2.53	3.30	3.87	4.23	4.52	4.66	4.80
	1958 $	2.00	2.46	2.76	2.88	3.00	3.16	3.24	3.22
Nonresidential Fixed Investment	Current $	1.96	2.25	2.44	2.49	2.53	2.54	2.53	2.52
	1958 $	1.82	1.97	2.05	2.08	2.14	2.22	2.30	2.37
Fixed Investment on Residential Structures	Current $	1.84	1.89	2.02	2.14	2.17	2.21	2.24	2.27
	1958 $	1.57	1.57	1.67	1.79	1.87	1.95	2.01	2.03
Inventory Investment	Current $	3.45	3.64	3.74	3.68	3.72	3.72	3.77	3.86
	1958 $	3.32	3.50	3.58	3.51	3.53	3.53	3.57	3.65
Unemployment Rate	(%)	0.21	0.39	0.52	0.57	0.61	0.63	0.65	0.66
GNP Price Deflator	1958=100	0.28	0.31	0.37	0.49	0.62	0.71	0.81	0.92

[1] Error statistics under columns 1-8 are computed on the basis of 28 one to eight quarters ahead simulations respectively starting with 1961.1 and ending with 1967.4.

[6] This starting point error would be greatly reduced with appropriate constant adjustments for serially correlated errors. No adjustments were made here.

TABLE 2

CROSS CORRELATION OF ERRORS OF ESTIMATED EQUATIONS
(1961.1—1967.4)

	FE	*CA*	*IH*	*IPMM*	*IPR*	*IPC*	*IIMF**	*IIN*	*XMF*	*WRMM*	*PMF*	*IS*	*IL*
FE	1.0000												
CA	−0.1297	1.0000											
IH	−0.1156	0.5507	1.0000										
IPMM	−0.1999	−0.0953	−0.4024	1.0000									
IPR	0.0635	0.2049	0.1401	0.2923	1.0000								
IPC	−0.3297	0.3263	0.2683	0.5004	0.1805	1.0000							
*IIMF**	0.1437	−0.2187	−0.2685	0.3899	−0.0257	0.3608	1.0000						
IIN	−0.0295	0.0534	0.1820	−0.1833	0.1343	−0.0646	−0.5323	1.0000					
XMF	−0.0638	−0.2202	−0.3324	−0.0652	−0.2407	0.0892	0.0747	0.2692	1.0000				
WRMM	0.5274	−0.2157	−0.1934	−0.0561	0.0564	−0.2691	0.0629	0.0362	−0.0994	1.0000			
PMF	−0.1769	0.3465	0.4530	0.2005	0.4634	0.4956	0.2058	−0.2066	−0.4055	−0.1064	1.0000		
IS	0.1114	−0.6859	−0.6490	0.3019	−0.1007	−0.2919	0.1341	−0.1740	0.1683	0.0380	−0.2625	1.0000	
IL	0.0409	0.0332	−0.0058	−0.0427	0.3480	−0.2019	−0.3215	−0.0857	−0.0807	−0.1109	0.0458	0.3952	1.0000

Variable Definitions See Table 3.

TABLE 3

CROSS CORRELATION OF ERRORS OF ONE QUARTER AHEAD SIMULATIONS
(1961.1—1967.4)

	FE	*CA*	*IH*	*IPMM*	*IPR*	*IPC*	*IIMF**	*IIN*	*XMF*	*WRMM*	*PMF*	*IS*	*IL*
FE	1.0000												
CA	−0.0239	1.0000											
IH	0.1005	0.5388	1.0000										
IPMM	−0.3438	−0.0119	−0.3874	1.0000									
IPR	0.1633	0.2555	0.1371	0.3069	1.0000								
IPC	−0.2966	0.3810	0.2843	0.5137	0.2009	1.0000							
*IIMF**	−0.0630	−0.4864	−0.8081	0.1421	−0.3032	−0.2437	1.0000						
IIN	−0.0225	−0.0304	0.0310	−0.2044	0.0323	−0.0659	0.0763	1.0000					
XMF	−0.1156	0.1948	−0.1765	0.2271	0.0730	0.2772	0.4838	0.4243	1.0000				
WRMM	0.4703	−0.3888	−0.2858	−0.0652	−0.1115	−0.3216	0.1524	−0.0135	−0.1333	1.0000			
RMF	−0.0703	0.2804	0.3614	0.3125	0.4395	0.5027	−0.4619	−0.3792	−0.1667	−0.0953	1.0000		
IS	−0.0202	−0.4110	−0.3676	0.1750	0.0975	−0.0513	0.2998	0.1850	0.1610	0.2579	−0.0707	1.0000	
IL	−0.0217	−0.1311	−0.1348	−0.0183	0.2294	−0.2662	0.0802	0.0640	0.1493	0.0267	0.0226	0.6373	1.0000

Variable Definitions:

FE	U.S. exports of goods and services
CA	Personal consumption expenditures on automobiles
IH	Fixed investment on nonfarm residential structures
IPMM	Fixed investment in manufacturing and mining
IPR	Fixed investment in regulated industries
IPC	Fixed investment in commercial and other industries
*IIMF**	Change in manufacturing inventories
IIN	Change in nonmanufacturing inventories
XMF	Gross product originating in manufacturing
WRMM	Wage rate in manufacturing and mining
PMF	Sector deflator for manufacturing
IS	Interest rate, 4-6 month prime commercial paper
IL	Moody's total corporate bond yield

predicted with an error of only .28 (on a base of 100) for the one quarter ahead projection, but the average error for an eight quarter ahead simulation is .92. It is because of the relative inaccuracy of the price prediction that the nominal Gross National Product which is predicted with an error of \$2.89 billion in a one period simulation, has an error of more than \$7 billion in an eight quarter ahead simulation.

Tables 2 and 3 present cross-correlations of errors among major economic variables explained by behavioral equations. The statistic (r_{ij}) computed is

$$\frac{\Sigma(e_i - \bar{e}_i)(e_j - \bar{e}_j)}{[\Sigma(e_i - \bar{e}_i)^2 \Sigma(e_j - \bar{e}_j)^2]^{1/2}}$$

where e_i and e_j in Table 2 are the errors of the estimated equations for variables i and j. Table 3 reports the correlation of errors generated for the variables i and j in one quarter ahead simulations of the simultaneous model. These are system errors in comparison to single equation errors reported in Table 2. A large value for r_{ij} in Table 2 implies that the equation errors of variables i and j are related. This may suggest that the excluded variables being picked up by the error terms are related. A major increase in r_{ij} moving from Table 2 to Table 3 suggests that the simultaneous solution of the model reinforces the error inter-relation because of the feedbacks embedded in the equations.

The cross-correlation of errors of the estimated equations (Table 2) are in general remarkably small. There are only six cross-correlations that are bigger than .5 in absolute magnitude and the maximum cross-correlation is .68.

There are apparently few important changes in the cross-correlation of errors moving from Table 2 to Table 3. The number of cross-correlations greater than .5 in absolute magnitude are now reduced to five. While there does not appear to be much build-up of error because of feedback effects, there is no consistent gain from offsetting errors either. The correlation for the short and the long term interest rates in Table 2 is .39 hinting that the same kind of excluded variables affect both rates. The corresponding cross-correlation increases in Table 3 to .64. This is, of course, because the short interest rate enters the equation for the long term interest rate. Not all differences in cross-correlations are so simple to explain. The cross-correlation of error between the short term rate and consumer expenditures on automobiles is −.68 in Table 2 and −.41 in Table 3. This suggests that factors which have not been accounted for influence interest rates and automobile purchases. Some aspect of liquidity may be responsible.

3. MULTIPLIER PROPERTIES OF MARK III

Macro-econometric models are subjected to extensive multiplier analysis for at least two reasons. First, if the model is accepted as correct (true), the multipliers reveal many of its economic policy control properties. Second, the multiplier results may reveal mathematical properties of the model that sometimes suggest needed respecification of structural characteristics. Experiments studying the sensitivity of the model to exogenous policy changes frequently locate problem areas of the model. Eight different policy experiments have been undertaken. All the exogenous policy changes presented involved a sustained stimulus in current dollars.

The assumptions underlying the alternative multiplier simulations are as follows:

Policy I. A sustained increase in nominal government defense expenditures of $5.0 billion devoted entirely to purchase of goods from the private sector. Defense expenditures (*GD*$) were increased $5.0 billion, together with an equal increase in defense gross obligations incurred (*GOI*$).

Policy II. A sustained increase in nominal government defense expenditures of $5.0 billion devoted entirely to purchases of services.[7]

Policy III. A sustained increase in nominal nondefense government expenditures of $5.0 billion, with 60 percent of the increase devoted to increased purchases of services.[8]

Policy IV. Same as Policy III, except that the expenditure increase is accompanied by an accomodating monetary policy in the form of a sustained increase in nonborrowed reserves of $0.3 billion.

Policy V. A sustained decrease of $5.0 billion in the intercept of the Federal personal income tax equation, holding the slope (or marginal income tax rate) fixed at base solution levels.

Policy VI. A balanced budget multiplier experiment. Government expenditures are increased as in Policy III. The slope (or marginal income tax rate) in the Federal personal income tax equation is held fixed at control solution levels and the intercept is adjusted from period to period to sustain the Federal deficit (surplus) at its control solution levels.[9]

Policy VII. A sustained increase in nonborrowed reserves of $1.0 billion.

Policy VIII. Same as Policy VII, except that the simulation was undertaken

[7] In Policies II, III, IV and VI, the policy changes were made in a manner that kept the average government wage rate fixed at its historical level.

[8] We tried a variation of this policy (Policy A) in which government expenditures were increased by $5 billion but the increase was sustained for only one quarter. In a linear system with constant coefficients, the cumulative effect of a single period impulse should be the same as the current effect of the sustained impulse of the same magnitude in exogenous variables. The multipliers calculated for this alternative by integrating the effects of the single period impulse differed little from Policy III results. It appears that the non-linearities in the system do not significantly affect these results. As such Policy A is tabulated in only two of the multiplier tables.

[9] The required intercept adjustments to the personal income tax equation from the 1st to the 16th quarter in this simulation were, in billions of dollars:

1	4.0416	9	3.7240
2	3.9608	10	3.7841
3	3.8629	11	3.7535
4	3.8160	12	3.7363
5	3.7214	13	3.7443
6	3.7214	14	3.7175
7	3.7059	15	3.7602
8	3.6939	16	3.7615

TABLE 4

MULTIPLIERS FOR GROSS NATIONAL PRODUCT (CURRENT PRICES)
Alternative Policy Configurations

Sustained Change Over Quarters[1]	Policy I	Policy II	Policy III	Policy IV	Policy V	Policy VI	Policy VII	Policy VIII	Policy A[2]
1	.8786	1.5442	1.2568	1.3351	.3959	.9487	1.3154	.9851	1.2568
2	1.0236	1.9058	1.4998	1.6456	.6333	1.0213	2.4556	1.8179	1.5172
3	1.1590	2.1896	1.7000	1.9040	.8109	1.0991	3.4356	2.5391	1.7208
4	1.2424	2.3826	1.8332	2.0801	.9316	1.1542	4.1500	3.1621	1.8593
5	1.3524	2.4932	1.9458	2.2359	1.0333	1.2052	4.8666	3.6160	1.9806
6	1.4780	2.6490	2.0437	2.3779	1.1184	1.2525	5.5982	4.2490	2.0877
7	1.6214	2.7802	2.1281	2.5011	1.1886	1.2958	6.2398	4.8008	2.1770
8	1.7764	2.9142	2.2074	2.6125	1.2483	1.3399	6.7642	5.3350	2.2572
9	1.9454	3.0290	2.2755	2.7082	1.2976	1.3771	7.2120	5.7510	2.3236
10	2.1314	3.1552	2.3506	2.8091	1.3428	1.4178	7.6250	6.1709	2.3838
11	2.3192	3.2404	2.4137	2.8909	1.3712	1.4627	7.9130	6.4670	2.4319
12	2.5346	3.3412	2.4623	2.9485	1.3806	1.5082	8.1016	6.7439	2.4745
13	2.7318	3.4172	2.4443	2.9144	1.3787	1.5187	7.8462	6.8660	2.5075
14	2.9310	3.4978	2.4844	2.9533	1.3692	1.5697	7.8994	6.9751	2.5369
15	3.1204	3.5520	2.5076	2.9663	1.3516	1.6072	7.7182	7.0801	2.5539
16	3.2894	3.6024	2.5174	2.9588	1.3142	1.6463	7.5406	7.2070	2.5612

[1] Quarter 1 corresponds to the first quarter of the exogenous multipler change in Tables 4 through 12.

[2] The change in government expenditures in Policy A is sustained for only one quarter. Multipliers reported in this column are the cumulated effect of the single period impulse in Tables 4 and 11.

at a different starting point in time. A further explanation is given below.

The multiplier simulations for the policies described above differ among themselves in interesting ways. Simulations for the first set of policies (I, II, VIII)[10] were initialized at the first quarter of 1965, a period at which the unemployment rate was 4.9%. In the second set (Policies III through VII) the simulations were initialized at 1962.1, at which time the unemployment rate was 5.6%. Since Policies VII and VIII are identical except for the starting point, we have an opportunity to see the effect of the model's nonlinearities on the multipliers. All the $5.0 billion changes in government expenditures and in personal taxes have been "normalized" to per-unit expansion ratios in the multiplier tables.

Table 4 reports the multipliers for current price Gross National Product with

[10] These simulations were chosen from McCarthy [**11**], the other calculations were made especially for the present study. (A few of the equations in the version of Mark III used to make the second set of simulations were reestimated due to minor data revisions (in the sample), but the coefficient changes were minimal.)

TABLE 5

MULTIPLIERS FOR TOTAL CONSUMPTION EXPENDITURES (CURRENT PRICES)
Alternative Policy Configurations

Sustained Change Over Quarters	Policy I	Policy II	Policy III	Policy IV	Policy V	Policy VI	Policy VII	Policy VIII
1	−.0002	.4292	.2724	.3269	.2854	.0433	.9160	.7290
2	.0154	.6352	.4060	.5003	.4279	.0671	1.5940	1.2341
3	.0528	.7776	.4964	.6218	.5170	.0940	2.1148	1.6091
4	.0934	.8990	.5689	.7176	.5821	.1215	2.5004	1.9438
5	.1418	1.0026	.6245	.7946	.6321	.1415	2.8574	2.2529
6	.1976	1.1072	.6785	.8705	.6747	.1716	3.2198	2.5540
7	.2654	1.2110	.7317	.9421	.7134	.1987	3.5253	2.8381
8	.3404	1.3190	.7858	1.0114	.7496	.2279	3.7744	3.1610
9	.4234	1.4152	.8392	1.0790	.7839	.2547	4.0030	3.4009
10	.5122	1.5272	.9008	1.1552	.8196	.2854	4.2348	3.6780
11	.6044	1.6252	.9540	1.2206	.8469	.3178	4.4244	3.9309
12	.7020	1.7238	1.0023	1.2785	.8662	.3521	4.6088	4.1340
13	.8110	1.8300	1.0483	1.3333	.8836	.3851	4.7568	4.3110
14	.9254	1.9440	1.0889	1.3796	.8943	.4184	4.8370	4.4751
15	1.0398	2.0424	1.1266	1.4188	.9034	.4465	4.8364	4.6230
16	1.1568	2.1512	1.1658	1.4583	.9074	.4803	4.9648	4.7830

alternative policy configurations. The results in current prices for total consumption expenditures, capital outlays for fixed plant and equipment, inventory accumulation and fixed investment in residential housing are presented in Tables 5 to 8 respectively. Tables 9, 10 and 11 report changes in the commercial paper rate, corporate bond yield and the implicit deflator for GNP. Table 12 presents multipliers for real Gross National Product.

The results are substantially in accordance with what theoretical analysis would lead us to expect. Expansionary governmental fiscal and monetary policies lead to an expansion in current price GNP and in its major components. The impact effect on prices is negative as productivity increases with expansionary policies. It is only after the exogenous stimulus is sustained for a few quarters that the inflationary impact of the policies can be noticed. The interest rate changes reveal increased interest rates in the case of fiscal expansion and decreases in the case of monetary expansion (Policies VII and VIII). In longer run fiscal multiplier calculations the higher values induced for interest rates may in time tend to bring down GNP multipliers below their peak values. In fact, multipliers for real GNP peak within the time horizon of these experiments. With most policies, multipliers for real GNP grow until the 11th or 12th quarter, after which they decline slowly.

Policies I, II and III differ from each other in that different types of government expenditures are increased in each case. The multipliers for GNP obtained

TABLE 6

MULTIPLIERS FOR FIXED PLANT AND EQUIPMENT EXPENDITURES (CURRENT PRICES)
Alternative Policy Configurations

Sustained Change Over Quarters	Policy I	Policy II	Policy III	Policy IV	Policy V	Policy VI	Policy VII	Policy VIII
1	.0500	.0252	.0227	.0253	.0116	.0135	.0422	.0470
2	.1072	.0970	.0810	.0938	.0544	.0375	.2128	.1870
3	.1576	.1710	.1404	.1660	.0976	.0630	.4268	.3580
4	.1946	.2434	.1974	.2368	.1399	.0875	.6602	.5500
5	.2168	.2976	.2469	.3003	.1784	.1082	.8916	.7270
6	.2430	.3558	.2902	.3580	.2126	.1265	1.1312	.9330
7	.2582	.3918	.3190	.4001	.2361	.1389	1.3526	1.1150
8	.2722	.4182	.3367	.4296	.2511	.1468	1.5476	1.2840
9	.2906	.4340	.3445	.4472	.2689	.1501	1.7080	1.4430
10	.3228	.4504	.3480	.4592	.2627	.1514	1.8460	1.5910
11	.3690	.4664	.3492	.4676	.2636	.1520	1.9596	1.7300
12	.4380	.4894	.3472	.4704	.2604	.1523	2.0432	1.8700
13	.4788	.4982	.3457	.4714	.2552	.1546	2.0936	1.9800
14	,5218	.5040	.3434	.4702	.2484	.1572	2.1232	2.0720
15	.5600	.5008	.3399	.4664	.2393	.1603	2.1254	2.1390
16	.5988	.4922	.3350	.4591	.2276	.1636	2.1006	2.1980

with Policy I (defense expenditures increase) are consistently smaller than those for Policy II (increase in wage payments). The one quarter impact multipliers for nominal GNP with Policy I and II are .88 and 1.54 respectively. In Policy I there is no immediate consumption response; production does expand, but not fast enough to prevent a drain on inventories. The one-quarter multiplier for inventories is −0.16. Because of the strong inertia in the manhours and employment equations, whatever increase in output that does take place results in only small increases in disposable income.

The relatively high one quarter GNP multiplier in Policy II is not difficult to explain. Policy II amounts to a pure government employment increase with a fixed government wage rate; this immediately contributes $1.0 billion to the multiplier, since the higher wage cost is counted as production. Also the wage increase is translated immediately into increased disposable income; the short run marginal propensity to consume is .37, giving a $.37 billion contribution to the multiplier. In this case of consumption-oriented expansion, production delays appear to be short, and there is a modest inventory change of $.14 billion. All other final demand changes are miniscule.

The multipliers for current price GNP (Table 4) in Policy III (balanced increase in nondefense government expenditures and wages) are consistently lower than those for Policy II (pure increase in government wage payments due

TABLE 7

MULTIPLIERS FOR INVENTORY ACCUMULATION (CURRENT PRICES)
Alternative Policy Configurations

Sustained Change Over Quarters	Policy I	Policy II	Policy III	Policy IV	Policy V	Policy VI	Policy VII	Policy VIII
1	−.1604	.1418	−.0238	−.0002	.0724	−.0817	.3984	.3090
2	−.0364	.2766	.0684	.1146	.1335	−.0373	.7784	.6010
3	.0280	.3800	.1354	.1972	.1810	−.0061	1.0440	.7950
4	.0386	.4098	.1487	.2120	.1936	−.0002	1.0706	.8020
5	.1012	.4484	.1605	.2250	.2046	.0057	1.0940	.8330
6	.1680	.4698	.1739	.2423	.2138	.0138	1.1628	.7940
7	.2518	.5106	.1985	.2623	.2231	.0228	1.2546	.8640
8	.3384	.5320	.2034	.2820	.2318	.0317	1.3368	1.0960
9	.4228	.5158	.2182	.2990	.2393	.0410	1.3740	1.2280
10	.5024	.5072	.2342	.3160	.2454	.0515	1.3902	1.3300
11	.5784	.4860	.2432	.3268	.2448	.0609	1.4166	1.3880
12	.6296	.4406	.2442	.3283	.2360	.0691	1.4346	1.4140
13	.6948	.3938	.2344	.3155	.2192	.0729	1.4046	1.3990
14	.7532	.3484	.2311	.3071	.2029	.0828	1.1446	1.3050
15	.8032	.2954	.2257	.2922	.1841	.0918	.9662	1.1530
16	.8282	.2348	.2055	.2511	.1543	.0944	1.0292	.9480

to increases in employment). This reflects largely a greater impact on inventory accumulation.[11]

Comparing Policies III and IV, the differences in these cases reflect only the impact of accomodating monetary policy. Policy IV shows a greater production expansion. It is especially interesting to note that the interest rate changes are virtually zero in Policy IV (Tables 9 and 10). The depressing effects of interest rate increases on fixed investment present in Policy III are removed in Policy IV, since interest rate increases are cancelled by the $.3 billion increase in non-borrowed reserves.

The tax multipliers (Policy V) for GNP, are, of course, considerably smaller than the corresponding expenditure multipliers. The impact tax multiplier is only .39. The induced increase in consumption with a billion dollar reduction in the personal income tax is .28 on impact. The multiplier for consumption risesto .91 after 16 quarters. The tax multiplier for GNP rises above unity in the

[11] Notice that the long run *GNP* multipliers are uniformly lower for Policy III by nearly $.8 billion after only 10 quarters. Some of this difference is due to the fact that the simulations were initialized at different points in time. However, the most important source of difference is that in Mark III there is no structural mechanism for translating nondefense government purchases of goods ($2.0 billion) into manufacturers new orders and increased production. Since inventories are determined in Mark III as the difference between inflow and deliveries the impact on inventories is unduly depressed.

TABLE 8

MULTIPLIERS FOR FIXED INVESTMENT IN RESIDENTIAL HOUSING (CURRENT PRICES)
Alternative Policy Configurations

Sustained Change Over Quarters	Policy I	Policy II	Policy III	Policy IV	Policy V	Policy VI	Policy VII	Policy VIII
1	.0050	.0224	.0139	.0146	.0270	−.0078	.0104	.0100
2	−.0252	.0142	−.0008	−.0090	.0186	−.0227	−.0153	−.0050
3	−.0254	.0124	−.0092	.0082	.0167	−.0220	.0162	.0510
4	−.0162	.0104	−.0059	.0021	.0176	−.0193	.1284	.2080
5	−.0062	.0092	−.0013	.0152	.0197	−.0162	.2662	.3780
6	−.0076	.0108	−.0032	.0198	.0191	−.0178	.3722	.6390
7	−.0098	−.0142	−.0055	.0218	.0180	−.0194	.4400	.7460
8	−.0092	−.0156	.0052	.0245	.0177	−.0189	.4766	.6660
9	−.0060	.0160	−.0050	.0284	.0172	−.0188	.5342	.6170
10	−.0016	.0316	−.0047	.0322	.0167	−.0187	.5906	.5690
11	.0028	.0408	−.0014	.0342	.0174	−.0158	.5688	.5170
12	.0084	.0534	.0048	.0362	.0195	−.0112	.5004	.4330
13	.0154	.0672	.0103	.0372	.0213	−.0073	.4260	.3390
14	.0200	.0746	.0180	.0435	.0246	−.0020	.6446	.3200
15	.0208	.0726	.0202	.0457	.0251	−.0005	.6700	.3670
16	.0178	.0648	.0217	.0459	.0249	.0009	.3932	.4680

fifth quarter.

The expenditure and the tax multipliers differ from each other by less than one in the first quarter of impact. Starting with the second quarter, the difference is greater than one. It is important to note that the difference between these two multipliers is not equivalent to a balanced budget multiplier since the expenditure multiplier generates some endogenous increase in taxes. Policy VI is an exercise in computing the balanced budget multiplier in which the increase in government expenditures is exactly equal to the increase in taxes (endogenously generated supplemented by exogenous increases). With relatively simple Keynesian schemes, balanced increases in taxes and government expenditures lead to increased production; in the simplest case, the balanced budget multiplier is unity. This tidy result begins to elude us when even simple refinements are added to the Keynesian system. For example, see Musgrave [**13**] Salant [**14**] and Duggal [**5**]. When a financial sector is incorporated with the standard Keynesian multiplier model, qualitative analytical results become difficult to deduce. Whether or not the positive balanced budget multiplier survives these generalizations becomes an empirical question.

The balanced budget multiplier for money GNP is greater than one starting with the second quarter. This should not be surprising. The required tax intercept increase is less than the $5 billion government expenditure increase because

TABLE 9

CHANGE IN THE 4–6 MO. COMMERCIAL PAPER RATE*
Alternative Policy Configurations

Sustained Change Over Quarters	Policy I	Policy II	Policy III	Policy IV	Policy V	Policy VI	Policy VII	Policy VIII
1	.0120	.0190	.0138	.0000	.0041	.0106	−.0452	−.0660
2	.0260	.0430	.0328	−.0003	.0113	.0242	−.1078	−.1400
3	.0380	.0630	.0493	−.0007	.0191	.0350	−.1622	−.2020
4	.0470	.0790	.0629	−.0010	.0264	.0434	−.2062	−.3680
5	.0580	.2120	.0735	−.0007	.0327	.0497	−.2390	−.3080
6	.0620	.1050	.0810	−.0004	.0377	.0540	−.2618	−.3270
7	.0630	.1050	.0987	.0000	.0476	.0652	−.3174	−.3300
8	.0640	.1050	.1072	.0015	.0530	.0703	−.3400	−.3270
9	.0660	.1050	.1057	.0031	.0532	.0689	−.3304	−.3250
10	.0610	.0940	.1033	.0041	.0527	.0672	−.3200	−.2910
11	.0610	.0910	.1018	.0052	.0523	.0661	−.3122	−.2800
12	.0710	.1030	.1073	.0077	.0552	.0698	−.5508	−.3040
13	.0850	.1190	.1157	.0095	.0597	.0756	−.3462	−.3400
14	.1070	.1480	.1142	.0088	.0589	.0752	−.3442	−.4030
15	.1110	.1500	.1100	.0076	.0563	.0729	−.3338	−.3920
16	.1040	.1390	.1113	.0082	.0564	.0744	−.5644	−.4580

* These results are not multipliers, simply changes.

of the internally generated tax revenues. This alone should hint to a smaller depressing effect on consumption. Finally, the depressing interest rate effects appear to be slight; a good share of that part of the multiplier above one is accounted for by fixed plant and equipment investment after 8 quarters. In short, strength in consumption and fixed investment appear to be the major factors, making the multiplier greater than one. It should be noted that the intercept adjustment should be interpreted as a change in tax provisions whose effect on tax receipts does not depend on the level of income. It is also possible to undertake a balanced budget study using adjustments to the slope, but that has not been done in this study.

Turning now to the monetary policy multipliers, we should note that a $1 billion increase in nonborrowed reserves is not equivalent to a $1 billion increase in federal spending. The monetary multipliers cannot simply be compared to fiscal multipliers. Moreover the impact mechanisms and lags of monetary policy are quite different. Monetary expansion directly affects interest rates and these in turn affect fixed investment decisions. However, in the case of fixed investment, production increases and increases in work in process inventories are observed long before increases in deliveries of the fixed investment items are observed. The inventory response (in Policies VII and VIII) as a percent of the

TABLE 10

CHANGE IN MOODY'S AVERAGE DOMESTIC BOND YIELD*
Alternative Policy Configurations

Sustained Change Over Quarters	Policy I	Policy II	Policy III	Policy IV	Policy V	Policy VI	Policy VII	Policy VIII
1	−.0005	−.0030	−.0031	−.0055	−.0024	−.0012	−.0078	−.0090
2	−.0008	−.0020	−.0043	−.0107	−.0033	−.0017	−.0214	−.0266
3	−.0070	.0030	−.0022	−.0104	−.0029	.0001	−.0390	−.0470
4	−.0040	.0110	.0024	−.0156	.0014	.0036	−.0592	−.0840
5	.0000	.0340	.0086	−.0161	.0010	.0079	−.0808	−.1100
6	.0060	.0460	.0158	−.0157	.0040	.0130	−.1028	−.1350
7	.0130	.0570	.0250	−.0144	.0081	.0191	−.1282	−.1570
8	.0190	.0670	.0349	−.0121	.0126	.0259	−.1528	−.1780
9	.0260	.0780	.0442	−.0092	.0169	.0321	−.1738	−.1940
10	.0330	.0870	.0513	−.0057	.0211	.0382	−.1912	−.2040
11	.0390	.0950	.0613	−.0019	.0248	.0437	−.2058	−.2130
12	.0470	.1040	.0691	.0014	.0282	.0492	−.2448	−.2230
13	.0550	.1150	.0791	.0073	.0331	.0558	−.2562	−.2360
14	.0670	.1300	.0875	.0119	.0369	.0616	−.2670	−.2530
15	.0770	.1420	.0946	.0158	.0400	.0666	−.2756	−.2690
16	.0870	.1540	.1018	.0203	.0430	.0718	−.3080	−.2890

* These results are not multipliers, simply changes.

total GNP response is really not appreciably different after, say, 10 quarters than in Policies I to IV. On the other hand, we note a sharp drop in inventory investment for Policies VII–VIII beginning at the 14th quarter. This drop continues and inventory accumulation becomes negative after the 20th quarter. As deliveries increase, observed inventory accumulation declines and eventually becomes negative. We are not certain of the extent to which the price distortions cited below are a factor in this case.

It is of interest to note that the expansionary effect of an exactly equivalent monetary shock is stronger when the economy is in a slack position with a higher unemployment rate (Policy VII) than when the economy is closer to full employment (Policy VIII).

The main conclusion that we draw from Table 8 is that fiscal expansion has virtually no influence on residential housing investment. This is not implausible. Fiscal expansion does lead to increased disposable income, but this positive factor is completely offset by negative tight money effects. On the other hand, in the cases of monetary expansion, the effects of increased purchasing power and lower interest rates reinforce each other, and a significant increase in residential housing construction is observed.

The price responses of the expansionary policies tabulated in Table 11 reveal

TABLE 11

CHANGE IN THE IMPLICIT DEFLATOR FOR GROSS NATIONAL PRODUCT*
Alternative Policy Configurations
(1958=1.0)

Sustained Change Over Quarters	Policy I	Policy II	Policy III	Policy IV	Policy V	Policy VI	Policy VII	Policy VIII	Policy A
1	.0000	.0000	−.0002	−.0003	−.0002	.0001	−.0004	.0000	−.0002
2	−.0010	−.0010	−.0009	−.0011	−.0004	−.0004	−.0006	−.0001	−.0010
3	−.0020	−.0010	−.0013	−.0015	−.0005	−.0006	−.0020	−.0001	−.0014
4	−.0020	−.0010	−.0014	−.0017	−.0005	−.0006	−.0012	−.0001	−.0016
5	−.0020	.0000	−.0014	−.0018	−.0006	−.0006	−.0014	−.0001	−.0017
6	−.0020	.0000	−.0013	−.0018	−.0005	−.0005	−.0016	−.0001	−.0017
7	−.0020	.0010	−.0012	−.0017	−.0005	−.0004	−.0018	−.0001	−.0016
8	−.0020	.0020	−.0010	−.0014	−.0004	−.0001	−.0018	−.0001	−.0014
9	−.0020	.0030	−.0007	−.0012	−.0003	.0001	−.0009	−.0001	−.0011
10	−.0010	.0040	−.0003	−.0008	−.0002	.0004	−.0008	.0000	−.0008
11	−.0010	.0050	.0001	−.0004	−.0002	.0008	−.0008	−.0001	−.0004
12	.0000	.0060	.0005	.0000	−.0001	.0012	−.0008	−.0001	−.0000
13	.0010	.0080	.0011	.0006	.0003	.0017	−.0008	.0000	.0004
14	.0010	.0090	.0017	.0013	.0005	.0022	−.0008	.0000	.0008
15	.0020	.0100	.0023	.0020	.0006	.0027	−.0008	.0000	.0013
16	.0030	.0120	.0030	.0026	.0007	.0033	−.0009	.0000	.0018

* These results are not multipliers, simply changes.

a persistent negative, (though generally quite small), initial response. The inflationary impact of the various policies tested begins to appear by the sixth quarter.

Many economists and model builders have expressed concern that the price change effects should at any time be negative. This concern stems in large part from the sorts of factors recently noted by Harrod [**8**]. The result is counter to accepted Keynesian views of the 1930's (or of the 1950's). But Mark III and the other modern econometric models are not static Keynesian systems. There is strong inertia (on a quarterly basis) in employment responses to increases in aggregate demand. There is also inertia in the response of wage rates to the unemployment rate (in a modified Phillips Curve scheme). The price equations in Mark III are based on a mark-up on unit labor cost. The lag in the response of manhours and employment to increases in demand appears as short term increase in productivity. This in turn results in short run downward pressures on prices.

The above are the mechanistic reasons for the dominant short run productivity effect on prices. If wages are slow to move, a short run productivity increase will produce a fall in prices in the case of an expansionary multiplier simulation.

TABLE 12

MULTIPLIERS FOR REAL GROSS NATIONAL PRODUCT (1958 $)
Alternative Policy Configurations

Sustained Change Over Quarters	Policy I	Policy II	Policy III	Policy IV	Policy V	Policy VI	Policy VII	Policy VIII
1	.9314	1.6341	1.2766	1.3646	.4126	.9429	1.4014	1.0549
2	1.2098	2.0968	1.6000	1.7664	.6686	1.0663	2.6548	1.9729
3	1.4140	2.4383	1.8379	2.0709	.8560	1.1646	3.7158	2.7568
4	1.5404	2.6485	1.9960	2.2806	.9810	1.2292	4.4882	3.4089
5	1.6784	2.7236	2.1184	2.4532	1.0820	1.2798	5.2402	3.8210
6	1.8187	2.8289	2.2140	2.5994	1.1632	1.3206	6.0010	4.3689
7	1.9696	2.9171	2.2875	2.7166	1.2279	1.3515	6.6586	4.8281
8	2.1146	2.9787	2.3507	2.8181	1.2792	1.3749	7.1738	5.2478
9	2.2583	3.0091	2.3950	2.8948	1.3194	1.3858	7.5992	5.5032
10	2.4155	3.0379	2.4322	2.9597	1.3530	1.3915	7.9712	5.7400
11	2.5884	3.0355	2.4544	3.0034	1.3702	1.3959	8.2128	5.8889
12	2.7871	3.0324	2.4583	3.0185	1.3763	1.4006	8.4086	5.9541
13	2.9542	2.9804	2.3676	2.9056	1.3227	1.3520	8.0888	5.9050
14	3.1113	2.9015	2.3281	2.8604	1.2946	1.3369	8.0458	5.8191
15	3.2584	2.7552	2.2831	2.8052	1.2592	1.3119	7.8736	5.7000
16	3.3489	2.5630	2.2187	2.7237	1.4863	1.2803	7.7632	5.5869

Whether or not, this is a realistic or plausible result requires further consideration and sensitivity experiments with respecified price equations. However one need not exclude the possibility that in the early stages of an expansionary monetary or fiscal policy, the only observed price adjustments will be in the stock and bond markets if unemployment is initially relatively high. Only after employment has been stimulated for sufficiently long will we observe adjustments in commodity prices.

Table 12 presents multipliers for real GNP for the expansionary policies. Multipliers for all policies with the exception of Policy I peak around the 11th or 12th quarter.[12] A possible reason for the real multiplier to peak may be that the sustained increase in all policies is held fixed in current dollars. The real stimulus is decreasing over time due to rising prices. The early peaking may also be due to the fact that Mark III treats variables such as labor force and government wage rate exogenously. For short term forecasting purposes this may be expedient, but for an extrapolation or multiplier experiment of 12 or more quarters, it cannot be considered realistic. Holding labor force unchanged from the base solution in the expansionary simulations fails to account for the "encouraged worker" effect on labor force participation as new employment opportunities become available. As a result, the fall in the unemployment rate

[12] Multiplier for real GNP obtained with Policy I peaks in the 19th quarter [**11**].

is too large in the long run. The long run price (and real) distortions that result from this simplifying assumption can be seen in the multiplier results reported in [7]. The idea that a $1.0 billion increase in current price government expenditures in 1962.1 could lead to an increase in the implicit deflator for GNP of more than .64 (on a base of 100) after 40 quarters seems implausible. In the 16 quarter results reported here, we are beginning to witness the effect of an unduly rapid rate of inflation in depressing the real multipliers.

The exogenous treatment of average government wage rate generates additional bias to the real multipliers. Our failure to adjust government wage rates in the multiplier experiments depresses the government deflator (at least in the long run) and may overstate the real increase in constant price government purchases of goods and services (*G*). This in turn results in an understatement of the real GNP multipliers, which are calculated by dividing the real change in GNP by the change in real government expenditures.

4. FORECASTING EXPERIENCE WITH MARK III: 1971.2–1974.1

The Wharton Mark III Model has been used for three years for forecasting purposes, from February 1971 to the present. This three year period was a very difficult period for the economic forecaster. In terms of cyclical movements, the period started with an unemployment rate close to 6%, then rapid economic growth with a low unemployment rate near 4.5% in the latter part of 1973 followed by a wave of consumer pessimism, the Arab oil embargo, a sharp decline in real output in the first quarter of 1974. New economic policies were introduced including wage and price controls and freezes, various fiscal policy measures, devaluations of the dollar, increases in interest rates to record high levels, and substantial world-wide increases in the prices of agricultural and petroleum products. Some of the major developments which took place in this period were not at all represented in the sample period over which the equations were fit.

One would suspect that the structural parameters of the model would be unstable in the light of such unusual developments and that the model will not prove to be a useful tool for forecasting and for policy analysis. In fact, however, Mark III was used and produced useful and realistic descriptions of the general pattern of economic development. Besides the a priori constant adjustments that are regularly made to the structural equations to get them in line with current developments, special adjustments had to be made to accomodate the effects of the new economic policies. For example, during the devaluation periods, a carefully calculated adjustment was made to the foreign trade equation effectively to increase the price elasticities in these equations for that part of the price movement associated with the devaluation period.

The two rounds of devaluations were accompanied by substantial movements in import prices. The treatment of the pass through from increases in import prices to the domestic price structure in Mark III appeared to be inadequate in the context of large movements in import prices. The manufacturing price

TABLE 13

WHARTON MODEL MARK III EX-ANTE FORECAST ERROR ANALYSIS
1971.2—1974.1
Root Mean Square Errors of Predicted Changes
(Billions of Dollars)

Variable	Type	Forecast Period[1]								1st Year Average
		1	2	3	4	5	6	7	8	
Gross National Product	Current $	4.81	6.21	6.69	7.48	9.51	10.47	12.19	9.50	4.81
	1958 $	3.18	4.90	5.70	6.91	8.85	9.73	10.35	8.91	2.44
Personal Consumption Expenditures	Current $	3.09	5.62	4.25	4.48	4.37	5.39	6.20	7.10	2.10
	1958 $	2.86	3.93	4.68	6.02	6.41	7.58	7.41	7.46	2.67
Nonresidential Fixed Investment	Current $	2.34	1.89	1.66	1.73	1.59	1.32	1.50	1.40	0.87
	1958 $	1.70	1.44	1.44	1.46	1.43	1.31	1.54	1.26	0.79
Fixed Investment in Residential Structures	Current $	1.68	2.25	2.26	2.47	2.55	2.96	2.99	3.23	1.30
	1958 $	0.98	1.28	1.27	1.43	1.49	1.69	1.74	1.99	0.58
Government Purchases	Current $	2.52	2.50	2.51	2.59	3.48	3.10	2.38	3.10	0.65
Disposable Income	Current $	3.19	6.01	7.62	8.62	8.54	10.91	10.16	5.38	3.12
	1958 $	2.04	4.67	6.59	8.51	8.37	10.73	10.63	8.33	2.45
Unemployment Rate	(%)	0.11	0.16	0.15	0.17	0.19	0.23	0.19	0.17	0.07
GNP Price Deflator	1958=100	0.46	0.82	1.25	1.31	1.37	1.47	1.47	1.50	0.74

[1] Error statistics under column 1 are computed on the basis of 12 one quarter ahead forecasts; error statistics under column 2 are computed on the basis of 11 two quarter ahead forecasts, etc.

equation was re-estimated with an import price term in order to allow for this effect in the forecast period. The inventory equations were also re-estimated.

The forecasting performance of the Mark III version of the Wharton Model is summarized in Table 13. Column 1 shows the root mean squared error of 12 available one quarter ahead forecasts with the model. Column 2 tabulates the error for the 11 available two quarter ahead forecasts etc. The errors for predicted changes shows that over this period, we have made a smaller error in forecasting real GNP than in predicting nominal GNP. The errors are partly due to the errors in exogenous assumptions. One of the most important exogenous assumptions driving the model is government purchases of goods and services. The error in government purchases tabulated in Table 13 is external to the model but it substantially contributes to the error in the endogenous variables. The error in the GNP price deflator is quite large; this in particular reflects the unusual nature of the recent inflationary period.

5. LESSONS FOR MARK IV

The simulation properties of Mark III revealed in multiplier and error analysis are important trouble shooters for showing main directions in which the system is to be improved in its next version.

The anomalous results discussed in connection with a multiplier analysis in which expansion effects lead to price reductions because of initial productivity gains are probably the result of associating price changes too closely with current unit-labor-costs, which involve both a wage and productivity factor. If prices are made to depend on both *current* and *long-run* unit-labor-costs, with some added emphasis on the latter, there will be a much reduced tendency for immediate productivity gains to be translated into price decrease.

This is not the total suggested revision to the price equations. There must be nonlinear effects of capacity utilization, so that added pressure for price increases occur as the economy approaches full utilization rates. If this is done on a more detailed sector or industry basis, there may be some realistic pressures on prices where utilization rates are high. In addition, import price increases must be allowed to work their way through the economy to domestic price increases. This is especially important for catching the effects of fuel and other basic commodity price rises. In many respects, price forecasts have been subject to larger error than is tolerable because import price rises have not been properly allowed for.

The idea of transforming prices by sector of production to estimates for GNP deflators through use of input-output weights was pioneered in the Brookings Model and will be incorporated in the new version of the Wharton Model. These changes, together with respecification of the basic price equations as indicated above, should improve the multiplier response characteristics and the accuracy of price forecasts.

Inventory change is estimated in an interesting way in Mark III, from empirical estimates of the production-shipments identities. This approach, however, suffers the consequences of all residual estimates; they tend to have low precision in extrapolation. Direct estimates of inventory investment equations, unemployment, profits, and other residual variables will be incorporated in Mark IV in such a way as not to violate basic identities, but to improve estimates of the strategic residual quantities. The multiplier response of residual inventory estimates in Mark III is not a cause for seeking change in specification; it is primarily a matter of forecast accuracy.

Labor supply is troublesome. In the long run, it is a smooth trend variable moving mainly with demographic factors, but short-run variations in measured work force can be sharp and unexpected. There are sampling and definitional errors in determining "who are actively seeking employment," but more careful statistical investigation of demographic subgroups, better treatment of special institutional factors, and use of standard variables like real wages and labor market conditions should lead to improved estimates. In any event, labor supply will have to be given full endogenous treatment in applications of Mark IV.

Finally, expansionary multipliers for exports are unsatisfactory because they are based on crude assumptions about the movement of world trade and its prices. The foreign trade equations being estimated for Mark IV have much longer lags for relative price effects than has been the case with earlier estimates. This change will have no bearing on the standard multiplier or error tabulations that we are discussing in this paper, but it will be important for analyzing the effect of changes in exchange rates or trade policies, multipliers that are important but not covered in this study at this time.

In traditional single-country exercises, there is no attempt to account for induced effects in trade volume or prices. The U.S. economy is so large by itself and often moves in concert with some other large economies that its feedback effects cannot be ignored. These facts were impressed on us forcefully in trying to analyze the effects of grain shipments to the USSR in 1972–73 and the oil embargo of 1973–74. In the first case, U.S. exports so depleted home stocks that domestic prices rose as a consequence of the trade expansion. This means that some strategic price equations will have to take account of both home and foreign market supply-demand pressures. This is again relevant to considerations for revising the price equations to eliminate the tendency for prices to fall under the impact of expansion with cyclical productivity gains.

To get the full multiplier effects of joint world expansion or to take account of U.S. export expansion on the total volume of world trade, an internationally linked export multiplier calculation will have to be made. That calls for integration of Mark IV in a world system and, of course, that is done in Project LINK. The international multiplier is indeed amplified in that system when there is simultaneous movement in several countries together.

University of Pennsylvania
University of Pennsylvania
Case Western Reserve University

REFERENCES

[1] ADAMS, F. GERARD AND VIJAYA G. DUGGAL, "Anticipations Variables in an Econometric Model: Performance of the Anticipations Version of Wharton Mark III," chapter 1 in this volume.

[2] DARLING, PAUL G. AND MICHAEL C. LOVELL, "Factors Influencing Investment in Inventories," in J. S. Duesenberry *et al.*, eds., *The Brookings Quarterly Econometric Model of the United States* (Chicago: Rand McNally and Co., 1965), 131–162.

[3] DE LEEUW, FRANK AND EDWARD GRAMLICH, "The Federal Reserve-MIT Econometric Model," *Federal Reserve Bulletin*, LIV (Washington D. C.: Board of Governors of the Federal Reserve System, January, 1968), 11–40.

[4] DUESENBERRY, J. S.; G. FROMM; L. R. KLEIN; AND E. KUH, eds., *The Brookings Quarterly Econometric Model of the United States* (Chicago: Rand McNally and Co., 1965).

[5] DUGGAL, VIJAYA GULHATI, "Fiscal Policy and Economic Stabilization," in Gary Fromm and Lawrence R. Klein, eds., *The Brookings Model: Perspective and Recent Developments* (Amsterdam: North Holland, 1975).

[6] EVANS, MICHAEL K. AND LAWRENCE R. KLEIN, *The Wharton Econometric Forecasting Model* (Philadelphia: Economics Research Unit, Wharton School of Finance and Commerce, University of Pennsylvania, 1968).

[7] FROMM, GARY AND LAWRENCE R. KLEIN, "A Comparison of Eleven Econometric Models of the United States," *The American Economic Review*, LXIII (May, 1973), 385–393.

[8] HARROD, SIR ROY, "A Reassessment of Keynes' Views on Money," *The Journal of Political Economy*, LXXVIII (July/August, 1970), 617–625.

[9] HURD, MICHAEL D., "Review: The Wharton Quarterly Econometric Forecasting Model—Mark III," *Journal of the American Statistical Association*, LXVIII (December, 1973), 1025–1027.

[10] KUH, EDWIN, "Income Distribution and Employment over the Business Cycle," in J.S.

Duesenberry *et al.*, eds., *The Brookings Quarterly Econometric Model of the United States* (Chicago: Rand McNally and Co., 1965), 227–280.

[**11**] MC CARTHY, MICHAEL D., *The Wharton Quarterly Econometric Forecasting Model—Mark III* (Philadelphia: Economics Research Unit, Wharton School of Finance and Commerce, University of Pennsylvania, 1972).

[**12**] MODIGLIANI, FRANCO, "The Dynamics of Portfolio Adjustment and the Flow of Savings Through Financial Intermediaries," in Edward M. Gramlich *et al.*, eds., *Savings Deposits, Mortgages, and Housing* (Lexington, Mass.: D.C. Heath, 1972), 63–102.

[**13**] MUSGRAVE, RICHARD A., "Alternative Budget Policies for Full Employment," *The American Economic Review*, XXXV (June, 1945), 387–400.

[**14**] SALANT, WILLIAM A., "Taxes, Income Determination and the Balanced Budget Theorem," *Review of Economics and Statistics*, XXXIX (May, 1957), 152–161.

9

THE DATA RESOURCES MODEL: USES, STRUCTURE, AND ANALYSIS OF THE U. S. ECONOMY

By Otto Eckstein, Edward W. Green, and Allen Sinai[1]

1. INTRODUCTION

The Data Resources (DRI) quarterly econometric model of the United States economy is the major component in a national economic information system. Through time-sharing computer and communications technology, the model is accessed by private and public organizations for use in their economic studies and forecasts. Users also apply the answers developed by the model to drive satellite models of their own markets or of other microeconomic variables needed for decisions.

The model's role as the centerpiece of the DRI national economic information system imposes certain requirements on it. First, the model must be designed to minimize forecasting error. This criterion favors the selection of time series with high information content and low measurement error. It also requires annual re-estimation of the model following the government's July revisions of the National Income Accounts. Forecasting accuracy is also advanced by the use of supplementary econometric data filters and systematic error analysis in the management of the model forecasts.

Second, the model must provide sufficient possible points of contact for satellite models so that the analyst in a micro-economic unit can obtain the necessary inputs for his model building and forecasts. At some level of detail, activity must be decentralized to achieve an optimal division of analytical labor. But experience is suggesting that the dividing line between the central forecasting activity and the work in the separate microunits should be drawn at a rather fine level of disaggregation.

Third, the model must be highly structural, explicitly displaying a great many economic processes. An explicit structure permits the model to absorb a large amount of information as it becomes available, thereby improve forecasting accuracy. It also allows for testing the micro-implications of macro-forecasts and the macro-implications of micro-forecasts.

Fourth, the model must possess detailed policy levers that make it possible for public agencies to analyze the economic implications of highly specific policy alternatives. These include instruments that represent tax rates, Federal govern-

[1] Besides the present authors, several individuals participated in the construction of the DRI model: Martin Feldstein on the basic design of the financial sector; Samuel Rea and Lester Thurow on the equations for the structure of unemployment; V. Sundararajan on the construction of the initial industry block and Peter Jones on its subsequent development; Gary Fromm on the mortgage market sector. Rosanne Hersh played an important role in putting the model together initially. Robert Lacey developed the interactive model program that embeds the model in the DRI national economic information system. Numerous other individuals helped to bring the model to its present state.

ment expenditures, open market operations, ceiling interest rates, housing agency activities, price controls and investment tax credits. The model must also contain a set of endogenous rules for the policy levers in order to search for optimal policies and to simplify the simulation activity.

Finally, the model must exhibit both the cyclical and trend characteristics of the economy. It must reflect the stock-flow relations, financial-real interactions, lag structures, and non-linearities which business cycle theory has long identified as the causes of fluctuations. While the model's endogenous structure should display the strongly damped oscillatory character that the economy seems to possess, it must also capture the impact of various types of exogenous shocks that can realistically occur. A proper specification of the economy's trend characteristics is necessary if the model is to be used for more than a few quarters of forecasting. In macro-modeling, the short-run appears to be no more than a year. Changes in population, capital stocks and technology significantly affect the short-run parameters rather quickly.

2. STRUCTURE OF THE DRI MODEL: OVERVIEW

The DRI model follows the income-expenditure approach pioneered by Keynes [**12**] and initially applied in econometric models of the U. S. by Tinbergen [**17**] and Klein [**14**]. The circular flow of income and expenditures, as measured in the national income accounts, relates the spending and income variables. The financial sector and wage-price mechanism are simultaneous with the expenditure block. Many of the individual equations embody the consensus of current theory, such as a neoclassical investment function, employment-adjustment functions for productivity, and a price-cost relationship for profits.

In some regards, the model differs from its predecessors. Any model-building team will have ideas of its own. Also, annual reestimation, based on new data and each year's forecasting experience, leads to a continuous process of revision and extension. Thus, while the general structure has been retained, the 1973–1974 version of the DRI model contains few specifics from the 1969–1970 edition. Some of the more novel features in the DRI model which survive from the original 1969 version include:

1) a set of social indicator equations which relate the composition of unemployment by race, age, and sex to the macro-economy;
2) a wholly endogenous, behavioral, state and local government sector which relates various revenues and expenditures to macro-conditions, to demographic factors and to the financial condition of the sector's budget;[2]
3) a two-market model of interest rates, in which the long-term capital market is mainly affected by inflation expectations and the supply of liquidity, along with portfolio considerations;[3]
4) a set of industry bridge models which extend the time-series approach to input-output analysis so that it includes trend, cycle, and mix corrections

[2] See Henderson [**9**], Gramlich [**7**], and Eckstein and Halvorsen [**4**].

[3] The long-term bond rate equation is based on work by Feldstein and Eckstein [**5**].

of the coefficients;[4]

5) consumption functions for some components expressed in current dollar terms in order to overcome the measurement error created by price deflation, and explicit modeling of the links between housing activity and the sale of housing-related durables;
6) a housing equation which stresses demographic factors;[5]
7) an inventory equation which models the unintended stock variations

TABLE 1

DRI MODEL-SUMMARY OF EQUATIONS

Sector	Behavioral	Identities and Minor Relations	Total
I. *Final GNP Demands*	40	89	129
A. Consumption	13	44	57
B. Investment	15	21	36
C. Government	10	20	30
D. Foreign	2	4	6
II. *Incomes*	11	6	17
III. *Financial*	68	44	112
A. Monetary and Reserve Aggregates	7	12	19
B. Interest Rates	22	1	23
C. Commercial Bank Loans	5	3	8
D. Stock Prices, Price Expectations, Misc.	5	2	7
E. Flow-of-Funds: Households	16	14	30
F. Mortgage Activity	13	12	25
IV. *Supply, Capacity, Operating Rates*	5	2	7
V. *Employment, Unemployment and the Labor Force*	10	0	10
VI. *Prices, Wages and Productivity*	34	12	46
VII. *Industry*	309	68	377
A. Production, Generated Output	112	4	116
B. Sales, Generated Sales	72	0	72
C. Profits, Taxes	22	44	66
D. Dividends, Depreciation	44	0	44
E. Capacity, Capital Stock, Operating Rates	10	10	20
F. Employment	29	0	29
G. Investment	20	10	30
Total	477	221	698
Plus Exogenous Variables			184
Total Variables			882

[4] Stemming from the pioneering work of Arrow and Hoffenberg [**1**].

[5] The classic early work on housing starts is by Maisel [**15**].

caused by surprising changes in sales.

As the model has been revised each year, it has moved increasingly toward the explicit treatment of demographic factors and physical stocks, and to an increasingly detailed modeling of the interactions between financial and real flows. Some of the newer features are:

1) the relation of housing to household portfolio choice, mortgage and financial flows, along with demography;
2) a stage-of-processing approach to price equations and a wage equation reflecting an inflation-severity concept;
3) a highly detailed specification of the U.S. financial sector including models of the mortgage market and the household sector's flow-of-funds;[6]
4) some consumer spending equations that include household financial assets, consumer debt and repayment burdens, and the age structure of the population. These factors somewhat deemphasize the traditional role of income in consumption functions, while providing links to monetary policy and to the financial position of households and demography.

To illustrate the nature of the model, a few of the key equations are presented below. The model's structure is summarized in Table 1.

3. STRUCTURE OF THE DRI MODEL: SOME EXAMPLES

3.1. *Housing sector, mortgage market and household flow-of-funds.* The theory underlying the housing sector can be sketched as follows. Suppose that the long-run desired housing stock is determined as part of a household portfolio which contains consumption goods, financial assets and liabilities, and housing. Defining household net worth (HNW) as the total of household financial assets, the actual housing stock, and the stock of consumer goods less household liabilities, the aggregate of the desired stock of housing can be written as

$$(1) \qquad KH^* = f(N22^+, HNW)$$

where KH^* is the long-run demand for housing and $N22^+$ is population of age 22 and over. The presence of $N22^+$ results from aggregating over all households and reflects the important role of demography in housing demand.

Let VAC be the number of vacancies in the housing market and a measure of disequilibrium. Then

$$(2) \qquad VAC = g[KH^*, KH]$$

where KH is the existing housing stock. Given KH^* and the actual stock of housing, the adjustment of KH toward KH^* depends on the supply of housing starts, $HUSTS$. Substituting for KH^* in equation (2), we obtain

$$(3) \qquad VAC = g(N22^+, HNW, KH), \ \frac{\partial VAC}{\partial N22^+} < 0; \ \frac{\partial VAC}{\partial HNW} > 0; \ \frac{\partial VAC}{\partial KH} > 0.$$

[6] Virtually all contemporary work on large-scale model financial sectors stems from De Leeuw [**2**]. The DRI mortgage sector builds on the work of Jaffee [**10**].

The supply of housing starts is

$$(4) \qquad HUSTS = h(VAC^*, r^*, F, SUB), \frac{\partial HUSTS}{\partial VAC^*} < 0; \frac{\partial HUSTS}{\partial r^*} < 0;$$

$$\frac{\partial HUSTS}{\partial F} > 0; \frac{\partial HUSTS}{\partial SUB} > 0,$$

where VAC^* is expected vacancies and is defined as a weighted average of actual previous VAC's; r^* is the expected real financial cost of housing starts defined as the nominal mortgage rate less expected inflation in residential construction prices; F is the supply of mortgage funds from commercial banks and nonbank financial intermediaries; and SUB is an exogenous variable which measures the extent of government subsidies for low-income housing. Builders are assumed to supply starts in response to their expectations of vacancies and costs, but also as a result of the availability of mortgage funds.

The real mortgage rate depends on the interest rates and prices that are developed simultaneously in the complete model. Other important influences arise from the supply of mortgages and the marginal cost of lendable funds available to financial institutions.

The supply of mortgage funds depends on the mortgage market activity of the financial institutions who actively participate in the mortgage market. Let

$$(5) \qquad F \equiv \sum_{j=1}^{n} F_j$$

and

$$(6) \qquad F_j = v[\underline{INF}_j, \underline{i}_j, \underline{MTG}_j, \underline{POL}]$$

where F_j is the contribution of the j-th type of financial institution to the total supply of mortgage funds, $\underline{INF}_j$ is a vector of j's inflow of investable funds, $\underline{i}_j$ is a vector of j's alternative investment returns, $\underline{MTG}_j$ is the j-th financial institution's beginning of period stock of mortgages, and $\underline{POL}$ is an exogenous vector of mortgage market policy instruments.

Each institution allocates a share of its investable funds, primarily deposits and mortgage repayments, to the acquisition of mortgages. The share depends on the volume of available funds, the lending and investment opportunities that exist in the mortgage and other markets, the initial portfolio position in mortgages, and policy support from various government agencies.

The inflow of investable funds and the alternative market rates of interest are, of course, beyond the control of each institution. $\underline{INF}_j$ depends on a set of household sector portfolio decisions which determine the amount of personal saving and the pattern of households' flow-of-funds. The vector of interest rates, $\underline{i}_j$, is determined by the capital markets, the Federal Reserve, and by institutional factors such as ceilings on deposit rates. Briefly stated,

$$(7) \qquad \underline{INF}_j = m[YD, \underline{i}_k, \underline{A}_k],$$

where *YD* is disposable personal income, i_k is the vector of k interest rates open to households, and A_k is the vector of k portfolio holdings at the beginning of the period.

This theoretical structure has properties that make it suitable for a simulation model designed to possess cyclical and trend characteristics of the economy. First, the trend in the number of housing units to be built is set by adult population growth and the growth of real financial assets. Any deviation affects the housing stock so that future starts bring the stock back to trend through the action of the vacancy rate. Second, the impact of monetary policy is modeled explicitly, rather than through *adhoc* proxies. A tight money policy creates interest rate differentials that produce disintermediation, a sharp reduction in the supply of mortgages, and a rise in the mortgage rate. Housing starts fall and the adjustment of *KH* to *KH** is interrupted. Should monetary policy be easy, too many funds filter through the financial system into mortgages, creating an above-trend housing stock, a high vacancy rate and a subsequent correction of building activity.

The empirical implementation of the theoretical structure requires considerable further specification. The relevant interest rates for the portfolio behavior of financial institutions must be selected. Institutional constraints limit their range of portfolio choice. The mortgage creation process must be structured from the new commitments stage to the closing of mortgage loans, in order to more correctly specify the lags that affect housing. The behavior of the household sector must be described by a complete model of household flow-of-funds so that the interaction between all of the households' balance sheet items is reflected. The appropriate lags in adjustment and in the formation of expectations also must be included. The housing equations have to go beyond total starts to an allocation among single and multiple units and mobile homes. The average value of each type of unit has to be estimated, and the time profile of the construction process has to be estimated to derive the GNP component, residential construction.

It is impossible to reproduce here all the regressions and empirical derivations for the housing sector, mortgage market, and household flow-of-funds specifications. Some of the main equations of the housing sector, however, are

$$
\begin{aligned}
(8)\quad HUSTSTOT = {} & \underset{(.18)}{2.60} - \underset{(.00007)}{.001}\left[\sum_{i=0}^{3} VACR_{-i} * N22^{+}\right] \\
& - \underset{(.0003)}{.0007}[(RMMTGNNS - PICREXP) * N22^{+}] \\
& + \underset{(.0131)}{.0558}[\Delta MTGCOM/PICR] + \sum_{i=0}^{2} a_i[\Delta MTG_{-i}/PICR] \\
& + \underset{(.0015)}{.0089}\, SUB_{-1},
\end{aligned}
$$

$$\bar{R}^2 = .987 \qquad DW = 2.02 \qquad \sum_{i=0}^{2} a_i = \underset{(.007)}{.179}$$

$SEE = .057$ Almon PDL, 1961 : 1 to 1973 : 2

where $HUSTSTOT$ is housing starts plus mobile home shipments; $VACR$ is the vacancy rate; $RMMTGNNS$ is the effective conventional mortgage rate on new homes; $PICREXP$ is the expected rate of inflation for residential construction; $MTGCOM$ is outstanding mortgage commitments at Savings and Loan Associations ($S\&L$'s), Mutual Savings Banks (MSB's), and Life Insurance Companies (LIC's); $PICR$ is the implicit deflator for residential construction; MTG is the total of outstanding mortgages at $S\&L$'s, MSB's, LIC's, and Commercial Banks (CB's); and SUB is Federal government subsidized units.

$$(9) \quad \underset{}{VACR} = \underset{(5.1)}{63.1} - \underset{(2.54)}{40.3} \ln (N22^{+}) + \underset{(.035)}{.038}\, RU_{-1} + \sum_{i=1}^{12} a_i \ln [HFA/PC]_{-i} + \sum_{j=2}^{4} b_j \ln (KQHUSTS_{-i})$$

$\bar{R}^2 = .973$ $DW = 1.58$ $\sum_{i=1}^{12} a_i = \underset{(2.6)}{-10.2}$

$SEE = .085$ Almon PDL, 1960 : 1 to 1973 : 1

$\sum_{j=2}^{4} b_j = \underset{(4.4)}{48.9}$

where HFA is household financial assets, RU is the unemployment rate, and $KQHUSTS$ is the stock of houses. HFA is a flow-of-funds series defined as the sum of household money, deposits, bonds, and the book value of equity.

$$(10) \quad MTGCOMS\&LNEW = \underset{(.96)}{-11.02} + \underset{(.141)}{.807}[RRF@DS\&L] + \underset{(.287)}{.921}[\Delta RRF@DS\&L] + \underset{(.159)}{1.683}[MTGRPYS\&L] - \underset{(.138)}{1.048}[MTGS\&L(-1)] + \underset{(.005)}{.045}[RMMTGNNS(-1) * RRF@DS\&L] - \underset{(.003)}{.006}[RMGBS3NS(-1) * RRF@DS\&L] + \underset{(.633)}{.875}[FHLMCCOMNEW]$$

$\bar{R}^2 = .991$ $DW = 1.51$

$SEE = 1.108$ OLS, 1959 : 1 to 1973 : 1

where $MTGCOMS\&LNEW$ is new mortgage commitments by $S\&L$'s; $RRF@DS\&L$ is effective deposits at $S\&L$'s, defined as $S\&L$ deposits less liquidity requirements; $MTGRPYS\&L$ is mortgage repayments at $S\&L$'s; $MTGS\&L$ is outstanding mortgages at $S\&L$'s; and $FHLMCCOMNEW$ is new mortgage commitments by the Federal Home Loan Mortgage Corporation.

$$\text{(11)} \quad \frac{(DS\&L - DS\&L(-1))}{HFA(-1)} = \underset{(.004)}{-0.016} + \underset{(.006)}{.023}[YD/HFA(-1)]$$

$$+ \underset{(.086)}{.162}[(YD - YD(-1))/HFA(-1)] + \underset{(.001)}{.002}[RMS\&L - RMSD]$$

$$+ \underset{(.0003)}{.002}[RMS\&L - RMGBS3NS]$$

$\bar{R}^2 = .538$ $\qquad DW = 1.17$

$SEE = .001$ $\qquad TSLS$, 1956 : 1 to 1972 : 4

where $DS\&L$ is deposits at $S\&L$'s; $RMS\&L$ is the effective interest rate on deposits at $S\&L$'s; $RMSD$ is the effective yield on deposits at commercial banks, and $RMGBS3NS$ is the average market yield on U. S. Government 3-month bills.

3.2. *The consumption sector.* The DRI model disaggregates consumer spending into 13 categories, relating them to pertinent concepts of disposable income, demography, physical stocks, household finanical assets, debt and prices.

A key equation in this sector, with its associated regression statistics, is[7]

$$\text{(12)} \quad CDA58 = \underset{(37.2)}{-94.2} + \underset{(.043)}{.106}[(YD - VG)/PC] + \underset{(.038)}{.114}[HFA/PC]_{-1}$$

$$- \underset{(0.30)}{1.14}\, KCARS_{-1} + \underset{(0.51)}{1.12}\, N16^{+} - \underset{(82)}{247}(CIC/YD)_{-1}$$

$$+ \underset{(0.81)}{3.43}\, DMY1 + \underset{(0.80)}{2.32}\, DMY2$$

$\bar{R}^2 = .953$ $\qquad DW = .753$

$SEE = 1.615$ $\qquad TSLS$, 1956 : 1 to 1973 : 3

where $CDA58$ is consumer durable purchases of automobiles in 1958 dollars, YD is disposable income, VG is government transfer payments to persons, PC is the implicit deflator for personal consumption expenditures, HFA is household financial assets, $KCARS$ is the stock of autos, $N16^{+}$ is the number of individuals 16 years of age and over, CIC is repayments of consumer installment credit, $DMY\,1$ is a strike dummy, and $DMY\,2$ is a dummy for the 1968 tax surcharge. All the variables are in real terms because the underlying data are in physical units.

Auto sales depend positively on real income other than transfers, real household financial assets, and the driving age population. Car sales are reduced by the existing stock of cars and the fraction of disposable income required for repayment of installment credit. The surcharge dummy reflects spending adjustments to temporary disposable income changes.

Several theoretical characteristics of the automobile sales equation should be noted. First, the long-run equilibrium demand for cars is hypothesized to de-

[7] See Suits [**16**] for an early study of the effects of consumer credit on auto sales.

pend on demography, income and household financial assets. Second, deviations from equilibrium are self-corrective. After a period of high sales, the rising stock of autos exerts a negative effect on demand, the credit burden becomes high, and household financial assets decline as a result of balance sheet adjustments in the stronger economy. Third, relative prices are not in the equation explicitly because they do not emerge statistically in this specification, but there is an implicit price elasticity of −0.35 in complete model simulations.

To complete the auto sector, equation (9) is supplemented by relations that divide sales between domestic new cars, foreign new cars, and used cars. There are also equations for tires, mobile homes, and light and heavy duty trucks. Changes in the auto stock affect spending on tires, parts, car repairs, and gasoline and oil.

4. THE BASELINE SIMULATION: A STABLE GROWTH PATH

Throughout our industrial history, the economy has experienced business cycle fluctuations. To portray the main mechanisms of instability, we begin with a simulation where many of the exogenous and random causes of fluctuations have been removed, and in which the economy operates in a zone where stability is self-sustaining. Figure 1 shows a comparison between a full dynamic simulation (BASE) of the DRI model over the historical period, given actual values for the main exogenous variables, and a simulation (STABLE GROWTH PATH or SGP) where the growth rates of real government expenditures, Federal transfers, prime military contract awards, tax rates, nonborrowed reserves and reserve requirements are held constant. In addition, all strike dummy variables are set at zero.

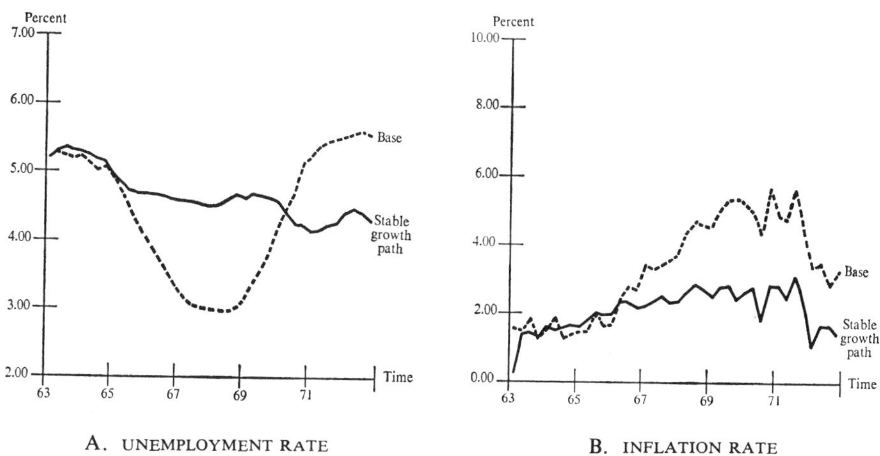

FIGURE 1

DRI MODEL SIMULATION: STABLE GROWTH PATH VS. BASE

Figures 1. A and 1. B′ show that a relatively smooth path is produced in the DRI model by excluding some of the major exogenous shocks that actually occurred in history. The unemployment rate stabilizes at 4–1/2% after two years, compared with the extremes of 3% and 6% in the BASE simulation. The rate of inflation in the late 1960's is 2% lower per year. The standard deviation of real GNP from its trend is only $3.5 billion in SGP compared to $18.8 billion in BASE. Although not shown in the charts, the amplitudes of the fluctuations in housing, automobiles, and inventory investment are substantially less than in the BASE.

5. DEPARTURES FROM THE STABLE GROWTH PATH

5.1. *Stock-flow adjustments as a source of instability.* To illustrate the stock-flow adjustment process as a source of cyclical variation, a model simulation was developed to isolate this factor. Personal taxes were reduced by $30 billion per quarter relative to the SGP simulation, but the repercussions through the financial and price-wage sectors were aborted by exogenizing the principal

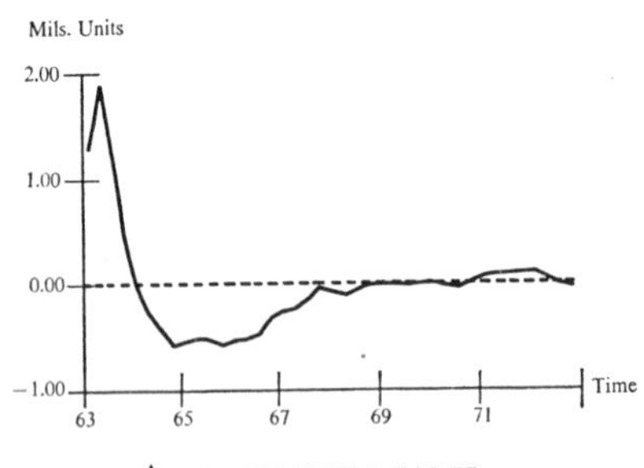

A. AUTOMOBILE SALES

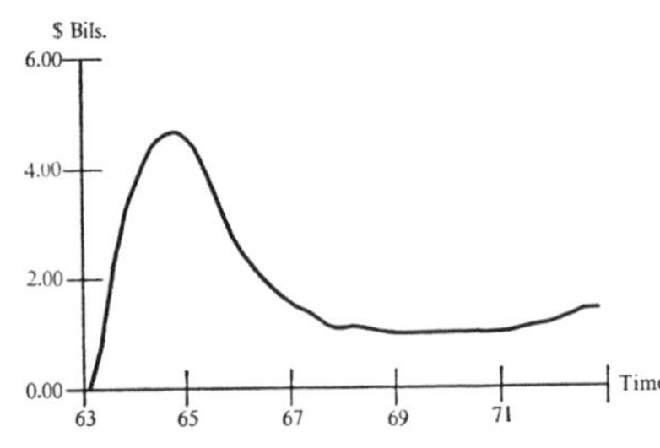

C. REAL PRODUCERS DURABLE EQUIPMENT

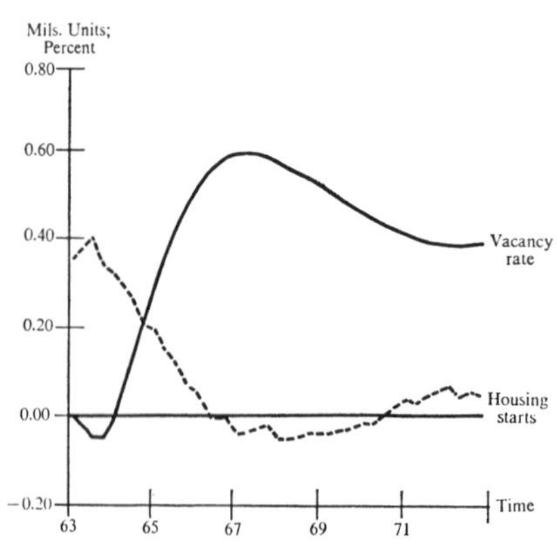

B. HOUSING AND THE VACANCY RATE

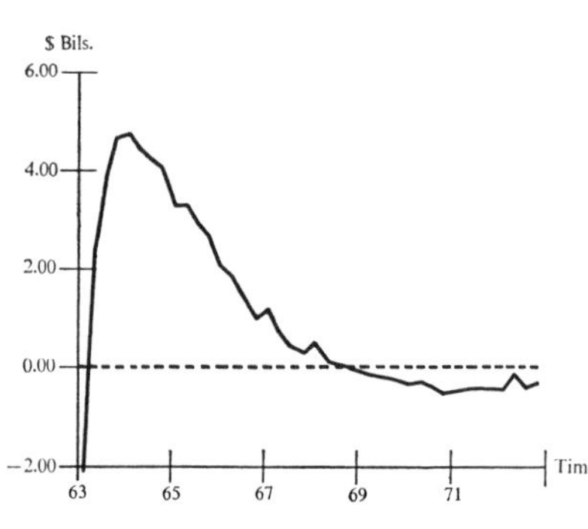

D. INVENTORY INVESTMENT

FIGURE 2

STOCK-FLOW ADJUSTMENTS RESULTING FROM A $30 BILLION PERSONAL TAX CUT

interest rates, prices, and wages. The results for the variables that are characterized by the most significant stock-flow reactions are shown in Figure 2. The graphs show the deviations in these variables relative to the SGP simulation.

Figure 2.A shows that under the stimulus of personal tax reduction, the stock-flow cycle in automobiles is strong and quick. Automobile sales rise 1.9 million units by the second quarter. The automobile stock increases one million units by the fourth quarter. This rising stock and the greater debt burden have a negative effect on auto sales and, as a result, the benefit from the tax stimulus disappears by the fifth quarter. Subsequently, there is a mild 4-year down-cycle in car sales.

The response of housing to the tax cut shows a more extended cyclical swing (see Figure 2.B). The income stimulus raises the desired housing stock as unemployment declines and household financial assets rise with the additional flow of saving. Deposit flows to commercial banks and nonbank financial intermediaries rise, mortgage credit becomes more ample, the supply of housing starts is enhanced, and the adjustment of actual to desired housing stock is accelerated. With interest rates arbitrarily (or perhaps by policy) left unaffected, the volume of housing activity rises by 401,000 units in the third quarter and remains above the base line values for 14 quarters. Thereafter, the enlarged housing stock and a substantially higher vacancy rate create a mild down-cycle for housing, but the negative values are quite small.

Business expenditures on producers durable equipment also enter a cycle as a result of the added stimulus (see Figure 2.C). Additional sales in the economy induce an extra $4.7 billion of real durable equipment spending after two years. Subsequently, the accelerator effects dissipate and the negative impact of the increase in the cost of capital lowers the increment of investment expenditures to $1 billion.

An inventory cycle of desired and undesired accumulation is also created by the tax stimulus (see Figure 2.D). In the initial quarter, inventories decline by $2.1 billion as a result of undesired decumulation in response to strong sales. The stimulus of added consumer and business expenditures creates a desire for more inventories, producing a cycle which peaks at $4.8 billion after five quarters.

5.2 *The wage-price mechanism as a source of instability.* Even with other things equal, a higher inflation rate produces instability in the real economy. To illustrate this process, price and wage levels were initially raised by 5% over the stable growth path solution. Interest rates were kept at their SGP values. Figure 3 shows the effects on the economy of this one-time, extra burst of inflation.

The extra inflation hurts the economy. The inflation-severity factor in the wage equation comes into play accelerating the initial 5% price shock to a peak of 17.5% after 26 quarters.[8] The real value of GNP is cut mainly through less

[8] See Eckstein and Brinner [3] for a discussion of the inflation severity factor in wage determination.

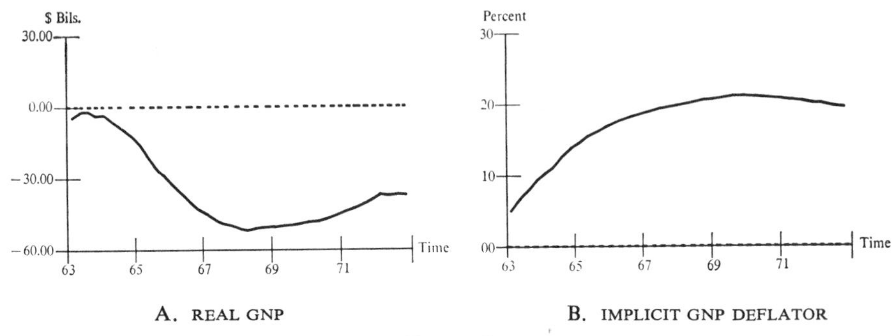

A. REAL GNP B. IMPLICIT GNP DEFLATOR

FIGURE 3

INFLATION AS A SOURCE OF INSTABILITY: 5% INITIAL SHOCK TO PRICES AND WAGES

real consumer spending. In due time, the loss of real GNP reduces pressure on wages through a higher unemployment rate and on prices through a lower operating rate. Ultimately, the rate of inflation goes below that in the SGP and the gap in real GNP relative to BASE begins to close (see Figure 3.A). The instability resulting from the additional inflation would have been greater if the price effects on interest rates had been allowed to work their way through the economy.

5.3. *Financial-real interactions as a source of instability.* The financial system has long been recognized as a source of instability. Besides the independent effects of stock market fluctuations on wealth and expectations, the financial system is the main channel through which monetary policy affects the economy. A simulation was run in which the monetary authorities inject an additional $1 billion of nonborrowed bank reserves through open market operations, and then sustain the nonborrowed reserves at that higher level compared with the SGP solution. The results of this simulation illustrate the channels from monetary policy to the real economy.

Figure 4 shows the main channel through which an easing of monetary policy affects the economy in the DRI model. The linkage is to housing from interest rates, deposit flows to nonbank financial intermediaries, and mortgage sector activity.

Figure 4.A shows the impacts of the easier monetary policy on the two key interest rates in the financial sector. The 90-day Treasury bill rate drops immediately by 120 basis points and then, with some interruptions due to feedback effects from the real economy, heads toward a new equilibrium that is about 35 basis points below the SGP solution. The immediate decline in the yield on new issues of high-grade corporate bonds is much less, but it is still 50 basis points. Subsequently, the new issue rate rises as the "income effect" of easier monetary policy offsets its "liquidity effect." After three years, the inflation effects cause the long-term bond rate to rise to its SGP level.

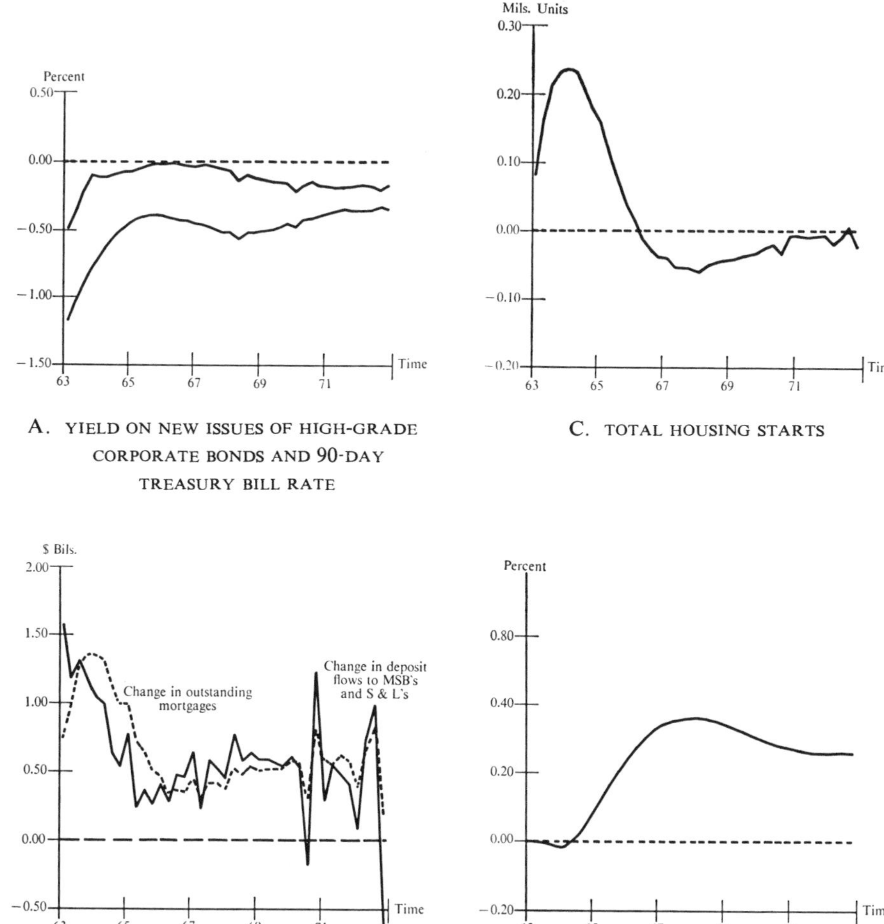

A. YIELD ON NEW ISSUES OF HIGH-GRADE CORPORATE BONDS AND 90-DAY TREASURY BILL RATE

C. TOTAL HOUSING STARTS

B. DEPOSIT FLOWS AND MORTGAGE ACTIVITY

D. VACANCY RATE

FIGURE 4

FINANCIAL-REAL INTERACTION ON HOUSING: $1 BILLION INCREASE IN NONBORROWED RESERVES

Figure 4.B illustrates that deposit flows to Mutual Savings Banks (*MSB*'s) and Savings and Loan Associations (*S&L*'s) rise sharply for almost two years as a result of the easier monetary policy. The major reason is the sharp drop in the 90-day Treasury bill rate relative to the yields on deposits, which are slow to react. Households adjust their portfolios, acquiring deposits and disposing of other assets whose rates of return have become relatively less attractive. Subsequently, deposit flows at *MSB*'s and *S&L*'s decline toward their SGP values as the stronger economy causes short-term interest rates to rise.

Mortgage activity rises sharply with the easing of monetary policy. New and outstanding mortgage commitments increase with the higher deposit flows. After some lags, mortgage acquisitions and outstanding mortgages rise. This increase in mortgage supply contributes to a decline in mortgage rates.

Figures 4.C and 4.D show the effects on housing of the easier monetary policy. Housing starts respond sharply to the increased supply of mortgages and lower mortgage rates. A lower vacancy rate, which stems from the income-induced increase in the demand for housing, also stimulates starts. The peak of the response occurs after five quarters, when total housing starts are 237,000 units above the SGP solution. Thereafter, a stock-flow adjustment produces a higher vacancy rate, bringing new housing starts below the stable growth path. However, the 10-year cumulative effect of easy money is a net positive increase in housing.

Figure 5 illustrates a second channel for monetary policy, through a link from the real value of household financial assets to consumer expenditures. Household financial assets were defined following equation (9).

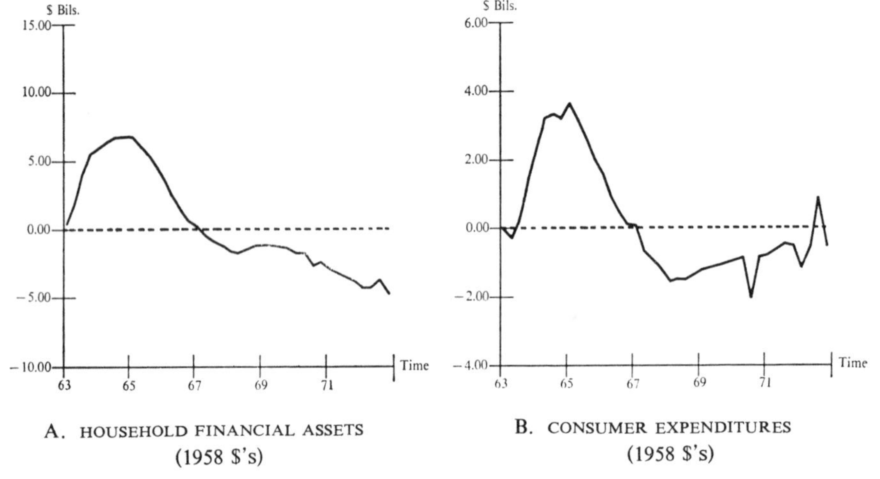

A. HOUSEHOLD FINANCIAL ASSETS (1958 $'s)

B. CONSUMER EXPENDITURES (1958 $'s)

FIGURE 5

FINANCIAL-REAL INTERACTION ON CONSUMPTION: $1 BILLION INCREASE IN NONBORROWED RESERVES

When the monetary authority injects reserves, the economy is stimulated, disposable income rises, and the volume of savings increases. This introduces adjustments in household portfolios. Market interest rates fall relative to the rates paid on time and savings deposits. As a result, household deposits at commercial banks, *S&L*'s and *MSB*'s increase sharply. Household money and equity also rise. Household bond holdings decline, but by considerably less than the increase in the other financial assets.

The net effect is a sharp rise in the real value of household financial assets

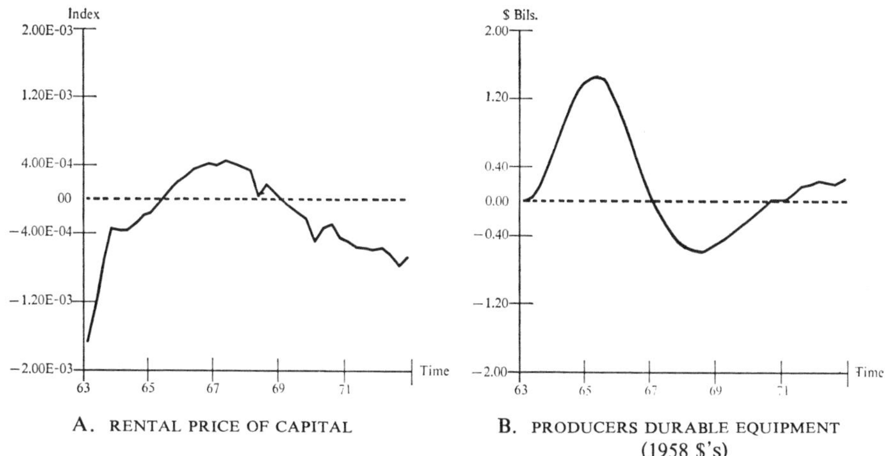

A. RENTAL PRICE OF CAPITAL

B. PRODUCERS DURABLE EQUIPMENT (1958 $'s)

FIGURE 6

FINANCIAL-REAL INTERACTION ON FIXED INVESTMENT: $1 BILLION INCREASE IN NONBORROWED RESERVES

during the first two years of the easier monetary policy (see Figure 5.A). This increase and a rising disposable income stimulate durable and related consumption expenditures (see Figure 5.B). The fluctuations in consumption that appear after two years stem from stock-flow adjustments in autos and residential construction.

Figure 6 shows the linkage from the financial sector to business fixed investment. DRI incorporates the rental price of capital along with impacts from cash flow and sales changes in the equation for producers durable equipment.[9] The direct link from the financial sector to investment is through the effect of the long-term bond rate on the rental price of capital.

The rental price of capital declines sharply with the ease in monetary policy, contributing to an increase in producers durable equipment expenditures. In part, the rise in equipment purchases stems from the accelerator and cash flow effects of the stronger economy. The later decline of this form of invenstment is due to the higher rental price of capital goods and the cycle in the economy.

5.4. *Fiscal stimulus as a source of instability.* The effect of a fiscal stimulus in creating added income and instability is shown in Figure 7. A $5 billion increase in real nonmilitary government expenditures is sustained for 40 quarters.

The increase in income from the fiscal stimulus immediately leads to a burst in expenditures on the highly income-elastic durable items, particularly automobiles (see Figure 7.A). As durables are purchased, the ratio of consumer installment credit repayments to disposable income becomes larger, and the stock of

[9] For a discussion of the neoclassical approach to capital accumulation and the rental price of capital, see Jorgenson [**11**] and Hall-Jorgenson [**8**].

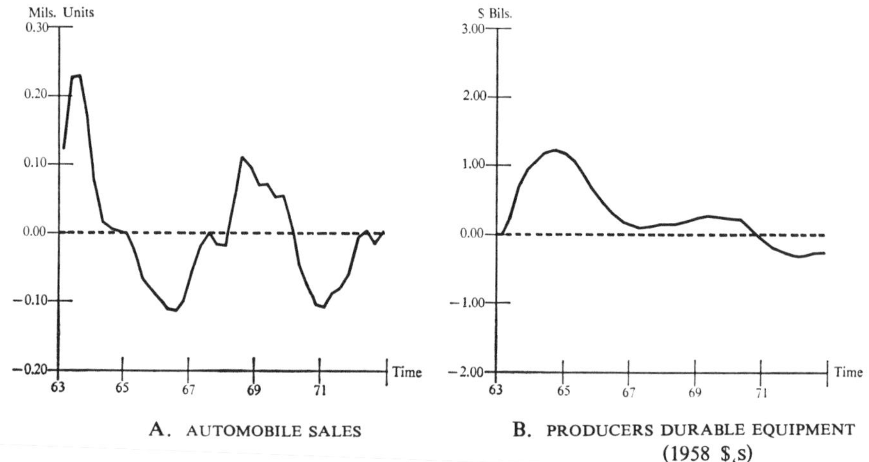

A. AUTOMOBILE SALES

B. PRODUCERS DURABLE EQUIPMENT (1958 $,s)

FIGURE 7

FISCAL STIMULUS AND ECONOMY INSTABILITY: $5 BILLION RISE IN REAL NONMILITARY GOVERNMENT EXPENDITURES

automobiles rises above the underlying demographic trend. Auto sales retreat from their peak in the fifth quarter of the simulation, swinging far below the trend values by the 11th quarter. A second cycle ensues, with only a slightly lower amplitude than the first.

The extra growth of demand and rising cash flow creates a spurt in producers durable equipment. Subsequent declines result from the restraining effect of higher interest rates and the fall in the economy's growth rate (see Figure 7.B). The fiscal stimulus has an impact on the financial sector, on investment, and on housing. The long-term bond rate is raised by higher inflation expectations and

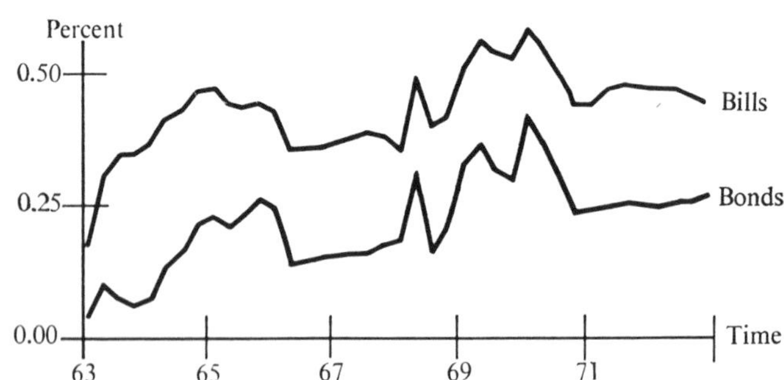

90-DAY TREASURY BILL RATE AND NEW ISSUE RATE ON HIGH-GRADE CORPORATE BONDS

FIGURE 8

INTEREST RATE EFFECTS: $5 BILLION INCREASE IN REAL NONMILITARY GOVERNMENT EXPENDITURES

greater bond financing needs (see Figure 8). This slows business equipment expenditures through an increase in the rental price of capital.

To some extent, the additional government expenditures crowd out housing. Higher short-term interest rates cause a loss of deposits, a drop in mortgage activity, and a loss of almost 100,000 starts (see Figure 9).

TOTAL HOUSING STARTS

FIGURE 9

THE EFFECT OF HIGHER INTEREST RATES ON HOUSING STARTS: $5 BILLION INCREASE IN REAL NON-MILITARY GOVERNMENT EXPENDITURES

6. COMPLETE SYSTEM MULTIPLIERS[10]

A series of simulations were run, applying policy stimuli to the SGP solution.

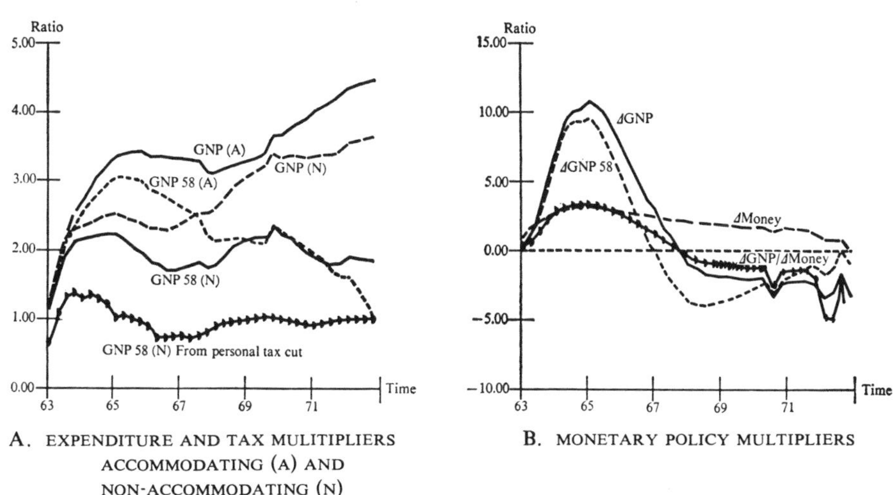

A. EXPENDITURE AND TAX MULITIPLIERS ACCOMMODATING (A) AND NON-ACCOMMODATING (N)

B. MONETARY POLICY MULTIPLIERS

FIGURE 10

IMPACT AND DYNAMIC MULTIPLIERS: $5 BILLION INCREASE IN REAL GOVERNMENT EXPENDITURES AND $1 BILLION RISE IN NONBORROWED RESERVES

10 See Fromm and Taubman [6] for a detailed discussion of policy multipliers.

Different multipliers would be produced depending upon the level of of activity; they tend to be lower when the economy is strong and suffering from inflation. Figure 10 shows the results.

6.1. *Government expenditures multipliers: accommodating monetary policy.* Figure 10.A shows the multipliers resulting from a $5 billion sustained increase in real federal purchases of goods and services. Interest rates are kept unchanged. The real GNP multiplier reaches a peak of 3.1 after ten quarters. Gradually, the extra activity produces more inflation, which brings the multiplier down to 2.1 after 24 quarters and to 1.0 after 40 quarters.

6.2. *Government expenditure multipliers: non-accommodating monetary policy.* If the growth of bank reserves is left unchanged, the extra real activity produces higher interest rates, less financial flows to housing and other negative effects. The real GNP multiplier peaks at 2.3 after ten quarters and then remains near 2.0 through the 40 quarters. It is interesting that the fiscal stimulus has a more prolonged effect without accommodating monetary policy.

6.3. *Personal tax multiplier.* A $5 billion personal tax cut portrays a generally similar time profile as expenditures, but the values are lower by one. Thus, the balanced budget multiplier of unity advanced in static macro theory seems to be verified.

6.4. *Monetary policy multipliers.* An injection of $1 billion of nonborrowed bank reserves leads to a multiplier in GNP which reaches a peak value of 10.8 after nine quarters and then begins to fall (see Figure 10.B). The multiplier turns negative after 17 quarters, as the impact of extra inflation more than offsets the earlier stimulus of lower interest rates, and the stock adjustment of houses and cars cuts demand. The implicit money multiplier in the model reaches a peak of 3.3 by the 8th quarter of the simulation.

7. FORECASTING PROPERTIES

What kind of forecasting accuracy can reasonably be expected from a highly structural, disaggregated, largely endogenous model? The most common measures in the literature have related to ex-post model simulations spanning the period of fit. Table 2 summarizes a set of such exercises for the DRI model.

A full dynamic simulation of the model was run from 1963 to 1972. The model stays near the actual path over this period. Also, simulations for shorter intervals were run within the same period. The errors are not dramatically larger as the period lengthens. This is partly because the model has self-correcting properties, and also because of the emphasis in the model's design on long-term simulation properties.

While good ex-post simulation and "forecasting" properties are a necessary condition for validating a model, they are not sufficient. Only a genuine ex-ante forecasting record—where the exogenous variables are not known but other

TABLE 2
ERROR ANALYSIS IN THE DRI MODEL
(1963–1972)

Full 10 year Dynamic Simulation	*RMSE*	*SRMSE* (%)	Bias	*SE*	*Eight Quarters Ahead*	*RMSE*	*SRMSE* (%)	Bias	*SE*
GNP	7.7	.9	– .5	7.7	GNP	7.1	.8	.2	7.1
Real GNP	10.5	1.6	4.8	9.3	Real GNP	7.3	1.1	1.9	7.0
Real Consumption	6.5	1.5	4.0	5.1	Real Consumption	4.6	1.0	1.1	4.5
Real Business Fixed Investment	3.0	4.2	1.3	2.7	Real Business Fixed Investment	2.0	2.8	.7	1.9
Real Residential Construction	2.5	10.1	– .1	2.5	Real Residential Construction	2.1	8.6	– 0	2.1
Profits Before Tax	7.5	9.4	4.6	5.9	Profits Before Tax	4.7	5.9	.6	4.7
Implicit Price Deflator (1958=100)	1.7	1.4	– .9	1.4	Implicit Price Deflator (1958=100)	.78	.6	– .28	.73
Compensation Index (1967=100)	1.6	1.5	–1.1	1.1	Compensation Index (1967=100)	.56	.5	– .1	.56
Money	2.6	1.3	–1.8	1.8	Money	1.9	1.0	– .5	1.8
New High Grade Corporate Bond Rate (%)	.44	7.2	– .12	.42	New High Grade Corporate Bond Rate (%)	.41	6.7	– .10	.40
Treasury Bill Rate (%)	.47	10.2	– .21	.43	Treasury Bill Rate (%)	.42	9.1	– .03	.42
Four Quarters Ahead					*One Quarter Ahead*				
GNP	7.2	.9	.3	7.2	GNP	5.0	.6	.5	5.0
Real GNP	5.2	.8	.9	5.1	Real GNP	3.8	.6	.5	3.8
Real Consumption	3.6	.8	.7	3.5	Real Consumption	3.0	.7	.7	2.9
Real Business Fixed Investment	1.8	2.6	.3	1.8	Real Business Fixed Investment	1.3	1.8	.1	1.3
Real Residential Construction	1.3	5.4	– 0	1.3	Real Residential Construction	.7	2.9	.1	.7
Profits Before Tax	2.6	3.2	.2	2.6	Profits Before Tax	2.2	2.7	.1	2.1
Implicit Price Deflator (1958=100)	.59	.5	– .1	.57	Implicit Price Deflator (1958=100)	.32	.3	–.02	.32
Compensation Index (1967=100)	.55	.5	–.06	.55	Compensation Index (1967=100)	.38	.4	–.02	.38
Money	1.8	.9	– .3	1.7	Money	1.4	.7	–.1	1.4
New High Grade Corporate Bond Rate (%)	.34	5.7	–.07	.34	New High Grade Corporate Bond Rate (%)	.29	4.7	–.06	.28
Treasury Bill Rate (%)	.40	8.7	–.05	.40	Treasury Bill Rate (%)	.29	6.2	–.02	.29

$RMSE = \sqrt{\left(\sum_{i=1}^{n}(P-A)^2\right)/N}$ where:

Bias $= \bar{P} - \bar{A}$ — A = Actuals; $\bar{A}$ = mean of A

$SRMSE = (RMSE/\bar{A})*100$ — P = Predicted; $\bar{P}$ = mean of P

$RMSE^2 = BIAS^2 + SE^2$ — N = Number of Observations

information about the future is available—can serve as an evaluation criterion.[11] Table 3 shows the full history of actual DRI model forecasts, from 1969 to 1973, covering 17 quarters. The forecasts for real GNP and long-term interest rates have errors that are about the same as in the ex-post simulations. The model forecasting activity appears to be projecting quite well the basic movements of the real business cycle and its composition. The forecasting of prices, and hence of nominal GNP, has not been as successful. Initially, the model's wage-price sector was too simple. It has been respecified to include the role of commodities through a stage-of-processing approach, along with a role for expectations and the inflation-severity factor in the basic wage-price mechanism. The errors in short-term interest rates are mainly due to inability to predict the exact timing of Federal Reserve policy.

TABLE 3

ERROR ANALYSIS OF FORECASTS WITH THE DRI MODEL
FORECASTS OF 1969, FOURTH QUARTER,
THROUGH 1973, FOURTH QUARTER

Root Mean Squared Errors

	Quarter Ahead							
	1	2	3	4	5	6	7	8
GNP (current $)	4.3	7.9	12.4	15.1	17.8	18.5	21.0	26.4
RMSE as % of mean	.4	.7	1.1	1.3	1.5	1.5	1.8	2.2
GNP (1958 $)	3.1	5.6	7.8	7.7	10.0	9.1	9.1	13.1
RMSE as % of mean	.4	.7	1.0	1.0	1.2	1.2	1.1	1.6
Treasury Bill Rate (Percent)	.17	.87	1.29	1.58	1.67	1.68	1.83	1.82
New High Grade Bond Rate (Percent)	.12	.36	.32	.27	.28	.40	.42	.39

Note: *RMSE*'s were calculated with the first forecast after each quarter's GNP release. DRI updates its forecast monthly. The levels of forecasted nominal and real GNP were adjusted for data revisions. Calculation for interest rates was begun with forecasts for 1970, fourth quarter.

DATA Resources, INC.

REFERENCES

[1] Arrow, K. and M. Hoffenberg, *A Time Series Analysis of Inter-Industry Demands* (Amsterdam: North Holland, 1959).
[2] DeLeeuw, F., "A Model of Financial Behavior," in J. S. Duesenberry, G. Fromm, L. R. Klein and E. Kuh, eds., *The Brookings Quarterly Econometric Model of the United States* (Chicago: Rand McNally, 1965), 465–532.
[3] Eckstein, O. and R. Brinner, "The Inflation Process in the United States", Study prepared for the Joint Economic Committee of the United States (Washington, D. C.: U. S. Government Printing Office, 1972).

[11] Zarnowitz [**18**] has an extensive summary of the record for alternative forecasting methods prior to 1972.

[4] ECKSTEIN, O. AND R. HALVORSEN, "A Behavioral Model of the Public Finances of the State and Local Sector," in *Essays in Honor of R. A. Musgrave* (Amsterdam: North Holland, 1974).

[5] FELDSTEIN, M. S. AND O. ECKSTEIN, "The Fundamental Determinants of the Interest Rate," *Review of Economics and Statistics*, LII (November, 1970), 363-375.

[6] FROMM, G. AND P. TAUBMAN, *Policy Simulations with an Econometric Model* (Washington, D. C.: Brookings, 1968).

[7] GRAMLICH, E. M., "State and Local Governments and Their Budget Constraints," *International Economic Review*, X (June, 1969), 163-182.

[8] HALL, R. E. AND D. W. JORGENSON, "Application of the Theory of Optimum Capital Accumulation," in G. Fromm, ed., *Tax Incentives and Capital Spending* (Washington, D. C.: Brookings, 1971), 9-60.

[9] HENDERSON, J. M., "Local Government Expenditures: A Social Welfare Analysis," *Review of Economics and Statistics*, L (May, 1968), 156-163.

[10] JAFFEE, D. M., "An Econometric Model of the Mortgage Market," in E. M. Gramlich and D. M. Jaffee, eds., *Savings Deposits, Mortgages, and Housing* (Lexington, Mass.: D. C. Heath, 1972).

[11] JORGENSON, D. W., "Capital Theory and Investment Behavior," *American Economic Review*, LIII (May, 1963), 247–269.

[12] KEYNES, J. M., *The General Theory of Employment, Interest, and Money* (New York: Macmillan, 1936).

[13] KLEIN, L. R., *Economic Fluctuations in the United States*, 1921-1941 (New York: John Wiley & Sons, 1950).

[14] ——— AND A. S. GOLDBERGER, *An Econometric Model of the United States*, 1929-52 (Amsterdam: North Holland, 1955).

[15] MAISEL, S., "A Theory of Fluctuations in Residential Construction Starts," *American Economic Review*, LIII (June, 1963), 359-383.

[16] SUITS, D., "The Demand for Automobiles in the United States, 1929–1956," *Review of Economics and Statistics*, XL (August, 1958), 273–280.

[17] TINBERGEN, J., *Business Cycles in the United States of America*, 1919-1932, Vol. II of *Statistical Testing of Business-Cycle Theories* (Geneva: League of Nations, 1939).

[18] ZARNOWITZ, V. "Forecasting Economic Conditions: The Record and the Prospect," in V. Zarnowitz, ed., *The Business Cycle Today*, National Bureau of Economic Research (New York: Columbia University Press, 1972).

10

SOME MULTIPLIER AND ERROR CHARACTERISTICS OF THE BEA QUARTERLY MODEL

By Albert A. Hirsch, Bruce T. Grimm, and Gorti V. L. Narasimham[1]

1. INTRODUCTION

Multipliers and prediction errors based on simulations with the Bureau of Economic Analysis (BEA) quarterly model have previously been submitted for analysis by the National Bureau of Economic Research and National Science Foundation (NBER–NSF) seminar on comparison of U.S. econometric models. This paper—after outlining the structure of the model—presents additional multiplier simulations of changes in Government expenditures and taxes and further analysis of model prediction errors.

For purposes of the seminar, in order to achieve a maximum degree of comparability among models, specific restrictions were placed on the nature of the simulations: multiplier paths were derived using as the control solution a dynamic simulation over the period 1962–71, with historical values of the exogenous variables; prediction errors were derived using a specific version of the model over a specified sub-sample period and a post-sample period for which actual data had been observed, with no more than mechanical adjustments of constant terms based on autoregressive characteristics of equation errors.

Because the decade 1962–71 encompasses both periods of economic slack and of high employment, the multiplier simulations were not controlled for the cyclical state of the economy—a factor making for differences in multipliers in nonlinear systems. Thus, we show here results of several multiplier simulations, each under a different cyclical condition. More specifically, multipliers are obtained using control solutions which maintain, alternatively, substantial unemployment, moderate unemployment, and rapid growth near full employment, with and without external supply constraints.

The NBER–NSF post-sample simulations are restrictive inasmuch as they do not reveal the error tendencies of the model under the kinds of conditions and procedures used in forecasting.[2] In particular, forecasting almost invariably involves a substantial degree of judgment on the part of the model user, not only in projecting exogenous variables, but also in ways that modify otherwise mechanical solutions. Here, we show summary error statistics for predictions made with varying degrees of judgmental intrusion. Results based on the model are also compared with a relatively sophisticated naive benchmark.

[1] The authors wish to thank Fannie M. Hall, Irene M. Mattia, and Judith K. White for computational and clerical assistance.

[2] We recognize that forecasting use is not the only purpose for which it is desirable to analyze model prediction errors; it is just that from this point of view such tests are inadequate.

2. MAIN STRUCTURAL FEATURES OF THE BEA MODEL

The most recent version of the BEA quarterly model[3] has, in its most complete form, 117 equations of which 67 are stochastic equations. Its formulation is geared to the twin objectives of short-term forecasting and quantitative analysis of policy alternatives. Final demand equations, which—except for imports—are expressed in real (i.e., deflated) terms exist for six consumption components, residential and nonresidential fixed investment, two inventory components, and two import categories. Government purchases and exports of goods and services are made exogenous. An option exists for using a purely endogenous formulation of an equation for nonresidential fixed investment or either of two realization functions using, respectively, one-quarter ahead or two-quarter ahead expectations based on the BEA Survey of Plant and Equipment Expenditures.

A unique feature of the model is in the specification of the output-employment relationship. A Cobb-Douglas production function relating potential output to capital stock, potential employment, and a "normal" workweek is estimated from a corresponding function relating actual inputs and outputs. Following Fair [**3**], "actual" man-hours differ from measured man-hours. Thus, different and separate equations are used to determine measured employment and hours worked. These variables are related to output in ways that reflect the quasi-fixed nature of employment over the cycle (which in turn reflects transactions costs of hiring and firing) and the role of hours worked as a partial buffer variable between employment and labor requirements; but they are constrained to lie on the production-function surface when output is at its potential level. The ratio of actual to potential output is also used to determine (in an empirical relationship) the Wharton index of capacity utilization (the latter is more cyclically sensitive than the former); the Wharton index occurs in equations for nonresidential fixed investment, imports, and prices.

Equations for the private-sector wage rate, implicit price deflators, nonwage income components, taxes and transfers, and a financial sector complete the model. The procedure for price determination represents a compromise between minimizing the disadvantages of estimating the overall deflator from an equation that does not reflect changes in mix among GNP final demand components, on the one hand, and avoiding reliance on direct prediction of component deflators, on the other; theoretically meaningful equations for the latter are not readily obtained. Since there are stochastic equations for all income components, an adjustment procedure incorporating pre-set limits on the per-

[3] The model has been updated since the submission of simulation results to the NBER-NSF seminar. Updating, however, has been largely parameter re-estimation: the new sample period is 1954-1-1971.4; for the earlier version, it is 1953.2-1968.4. The latter version is documented in [**9**] and represents, in turn, a substantial revision of the first published BEA (then Office of Business Economics) model [**11**]. Perhaps the most significant specification change in the latest version is in the equation for nonresidential fixed investment; the latter no longer includes cash flow, a variable that was dropped reluctantly mainly for reasons of multicollinearity. This makes for a substantial difference in multipliers of changes in corporate income taxes; the user cost of capital is the only vehicle for this factor, and its impact on investment is not strong.

missible level and change in the statistical discrepancy is used to enforce the income-product identity. The fiscal sector includes an option for deriving personal tax payments from tax liability, quarterly estimated tax payments, and net year-end settlements—balance-due less refunds; this option was, however, not used in the simulations discussed in the present paper.

The imposition of limits on the statistical discrepancy illustrates the use of boundary conditions on the model. Other boundary conditions are imposed on certain variables in specific equations. We have also experimented with two other kinds of boundary conditions of more substantial significance: (1) a ceiling on the growth of real output, given the initial level of capacity utilization,[4] and (2) a (institutional) limit on the permissible level of net borrowed Federal Reserve member bank reserves. The first of these boundary conditions, when effective, results in lower aggregate output levels and higher prices than would obtain in an unconstrained solution. This constraint provides the basis of one of the multiplier variants discussed below. The second, when effective, serves to exert full control over the money supply and yields a smaller money supply and higher interest rates than the unconstrained solution.

3. MULTIPLIER SIMULATIONS

Multiplier paths can vary for the same model under different initial conditions and time paths of exogenous variables and for different-sized shocks because of nonlinearities in the system.[5] In this section, multiplier paths are shown for two types of inputs—a permanent increase of $1 billion in Government goods purchases and a permanent decrease of $1 billion in personal taxes—under four different kinds of controlled conditions; these multipliers are also compared with the historically based NBER-NSF multipliers.

A key nonlinearity in the system, and thus a major cause of variation in the size of multipliers, is the hyperbolic relationship of money wage-rate changes to the level of the unemployment rate.[6] A change in government purchases will have a different impact at low than at high levels of unemployment. In order to test the magnitude of such differences, control simulation paths were obtained by adjusting government purchases[7] to yield alternatively an unemployment rate of 4 percent and 6 percent in each quarter. Initial conditions were those of 1965.4 and exogenous variables, other than Federal nondefense purchases, were

[4] See Hirsch [7, Section 4] and Hirsch and Narasimham [**10**].

[5] This fact was recognized by Goldberger [**5**] in his multiplier simulations with the Klein-Goldberger model; there, the problem was dealt with by linearizing the reduced form of the model, with nonlinear components set at their sample-mean values.

[6] Another important nonlinearity is the multiplicative interaction of quantities and prices in the GNP identity. The direct real impact of a $1 billion increase varies both within a single dynamic multiplier simulation over time as the price level of government purchases rises and among different multiplier paths with different rates of price increase. Since the rate of price increase is functionally related to the unemployment rate, we did not control separately for this source of variation.

[7] Specifically, Federal nondefense goods purchases were used; however, any other exogenous final demand component would have served as well.

set at actual values for the 1966–70 period.

A third control path was obtained by letting Federal defense purchases rise more rapidly after 1965 than they did in reality (The increase from a $50 billion to a $79 billion level was telescoped from three years to two years). This was done in order to achieve an extremely rapid growth of demand from an initial state of high capacity utilization. The rapid rate of growth brings into focus another source of variation in multiplier behavior; namely, the rate growth in labor productivity. Accelerated growth of output tends to increase productivity growth and by thus holding down unit labor cost, to reduce the rate of inflation. More important, given the high initial capacity utilization level, such rapid demand growth must realistically come into collision with short-run supply constraints which limit output growth and raise prices. Hence, comparable sets of multiplier runs were made with external supply constraints imposed.[8]

3.1. *Results.* Table 1 presents dynamic multiplier paths, by quarter, for a $1 billion increase in Government goods purchases. Results are shown for the historical NBER–NSF simulation as well as for the four control paths described above.[9]

The current-dollar gross national product (GNP) multipliers (Table 1A) differ relatively little except for the case with supply-constrained accelerated demand. Since unemployment was near 6 percent at the beginning of the NBER–NSF simulation, the trivial differences between the second and third columns are not surprising. The similarity lasts over the first 20 quarters, despite the fact that in the NBER–NSF case the unemployment rate has dropped to 4 percent by that time, primarily because of the long lags from unemployment, via the wage rate, to the price level.

In the constant 4 percent unemployment case, the current-dollar GNP multiplier reaches a substantially higher level by the twelfth quarter than those in the NBER–NSF and 6 percent unemployment cases, as larger positive price multipliers (Table 1C) more than offset smaller real GNP multipliers (Table 1B). The latter reflect smaller real purchases associated with a constant amount of current-dollar purchases. The reversals in the real GNP multipliers in each of the first four variants are due to negative accelerator feedbacks and diminishing inputs of real government purchases as their price level rises.

Despite the presence of the wage rate and demand pressure variables in the model's overall price level equation, price multipliers are weaker in the

[8] The multipliers for the accelerated demand simulations with and without supply constraints are reproduced from Hirsch and Narasimham [**10**]. The methodology for imposing constraints and adjusting prices is also explained in the appendix of that paper.

[9] In order to achieve comparability with the NBER–NSF results, the earlier version of the model was used consistently. The actual inputs were a $5 billion change in purchases for the NBER–NSF and constant unemployment runs and $3 billion for the accelerated demand runs. (Technical problems in solving the model under supply constraint occurred when $5 billion inputs were tried.) The differences between corresponding alternate and control values were, accordingly, divided by 5 and 3. Results for the accelerated demand versions are only available for twelve quarters. The NBER–NSF results differ somewhat from those reported by Fromm and Klein [**4**] because the latter involve a mix of goods and services in the expenditure input.

TABLE 1

DYNAMIC MULTIPLIERS FOR $1 BILLION INCREASE IN GOVERNMENT GOODS PURCHASES

1A. Change in gross national product, billions of dollars.

Quarters of Change	NBER-NSF	Constant Unemployment		Accelerated Demand	
		6 pct.	4 pct.	NSC[a]	SC[b]
1	.86	.87	.87	.85	.72
2	1.48	1.45	1.46	1.30	.64
3	1.94	1.84	1.88	1.64	1.08
4	2.23	2.07	2.16	1.88	1.28
5	2.34	2.19	2.33	2.01	1.36
6	2.43	2.26	2.49	2.11	1.64
7	2.40	2.32	2.66	2.21	1.60
8	2.35	2.38	2.84	2.31	1.81
12	2.04	2.31	3.10	2.68	1.65
16	2.13	2.35	2.92	n.a.	n.a.
20	2.57	2.52	2.94	n.a.	n.a.

1B. Change in gross national product, billions of 1958 dollars.

Quarters of Change	NBER-NSF	Constant Unemployment		Accelerated Demand	
		6 pct.	4 pct.	NSC[a]	SC[b]
1	.82	.79	.77	.76	−.20
2	1.41	1.34	1.29	1.18	−.31
3	1.83	1.70	1.59	1.48	−.33
4	2.06	1.87	1.69	1.66	−.35
5	2.13	1.93	1.65	1.74	−.37
6	2.10	1.90	1.54	1.74	−.38
7	2.00	1.86	1.44	1.74	−.05
8	1.86	1.80	1.37	1.72	.13
12	1.19	1.30	.71	1.29	.00
16	.76	1.08	.17	n.a.	n.a.
20	.50	.58	−.28	n.a.	n.a.

(*Continued on next page*)

case of accelerated demand with no supply constraint than with steady 4 percent unemployment: the productivity effect dominates the excess-demand effect.

When the supply boundary condition is imposed, it is effective for the first six quarters of the simulation. Accordingly, the increment of government pur-

TABLE 1 (*Continued*)

1C. Change in GNP implicit price deflator, (Index, 1958=100).

Quarters of Change	NBER-NSF	Constant Unemployment		Accelerated Demand	
		6 pct.	4 pct.	NSC[a]	SC[b]
1	.00	.00	.00	.00	.16
2	.00	.00	.01	.00	.16
3	.00	.00	.02	.00	.24
4	.01	.00	.04	.00	.27
5	.02	.01	.07	.01	.29
6	.03	.03	.12	.02	.33
7	.05	.04	.16	.03	.26
8	.06	.06	.20	.05	.26
12	.13	.13	.34	.17	.25
16	.22	.19	.41	n.a.	n.a.
20	.32	.26	.45	n.a.	n.a.

[a] NSC - Without supply constraint
[b] SC - With supply constraint

chases has no positive effect on total real output.[10] Higher real Government purchases displace real private expenditures. Since, under the constraint procedure, prices are raised in response to the short supply, the price multipliers are in this case higher (through the first eight quarters) than in any of the others. Continuation of weak real GNP multipliers in the period after the constraint is effective (i.e., the seventh through twelfth quarters) reflects investment accelerator response to the lack of positive output changes during the earlier period.

Table 2 contains similar multipliers for a $1 billion decrease in personal taxes. (The control solution paths are the same as for the increase in government purchases.) The current-dollar GNP multipliers are uniformly smaller than the corresponding Government purchases multipliers for all variants. This result is expected in Keynesian models because of the savings leakage in the first round. The differences in multipliers are, however, less than unity—the value derived from simple Keynesian models.

Real GNP multipliers for a tax decrease are also smaller than corresponding Government purchases multipliers at least through eight quarters for all cases except that with supply constraint. The multipliers fall less rapidly from their peak values, however, both because there is less negative accelerator feedback and because the real value of the tax change is less diminished by price increases.

Comparisons among cases are qualitatively similar to those for Government

[10] In fact, the impact is slightly negative because the boundary condition is given in terms of the Wharton utilization index rather than real GNP; and the equation relating them involves other variables.

TABLE 2

DYNAMIC MULTIPLIERS FOR $1 BILLION DECREASE IN PERSONAL TAXES

2A. Change in gross national product, billions of dollars.

Quarters of Change	NBER-NSF	Constant Unemployment		Accelerated Demand	
		6 pct.	4 pct.	NSC[a]	SC[b]
1	.42	.42	.41	.41	.35
2	.76	.74	.74	.72	.39
3	1.03	.97	.97	.95	.79
4	1.24	1.14	1.15	1.15	.96
5	1.41	1.29	1.32	1.32	1.10
6	1.52	1.41	1.48	1.45	1.34
7	1.59	1.52	1.66	1.56	1.30
8	1.63	1.62	1.85	1.66	1.48
12	1.62	1.76	2.20	1.93	1.44
16	1.64	1.76	2.28	n.a.	n.a.
20	1.87	1.92	2.36	n.a.	n.a.

2B. Change in gross national product, billions of 1958 dollars.

Quarters of Change	NBER-NSF	Constant Unemployment		Accelerated Demand	
		6 pct.	4 pct.	NSC[a]	SC[b]
1	.40	.39	.38	.38	−.05
2	.74	.70	.67	.67	−.09
3	.98	.90	.84	.87	−.05
4	1.16	1.04	.93	1.03	−.04
5	1.30	1.15	.98	1.16	−.03
6	1.36	1.20	.99	1.22	−.04
7	1.38	1.25	1.01	1.27	.13
8	1.37	1.29	1.04	1.29	.27
12	1.12	1.13	.75	1.01	.16
16	.82	.82	.35	n.a.	n.a.
20	.54	.60	.09	n.a.	n.a.

(*Continued on next page*)

purchases multipliers for basically similar reasons. Quantitatively, the differences are less sharp, however, largely because the differences in price multipliers are smaller. In particular, price multipliers are substantially smaller in the 4 percent unemployment case where—except for the supply constraint case—the effect of additional demand on the price level is greatest.

TABLE 2 (*Continued*)

2C. Change in GNP implicit price deflator, (Index, 1958=100).

Quarters of Change	NBER-NSF	Constant Unemployment		Accelerated Demand	
		6 pct.	4 pct.	NSC[a]	SC[b]
1	.00	.00	.00	.00	.07
2	.00	.00	.00	.00	.08
3	.00	.00	.01	.00	.14
4	.00	.00	.02	.00	.16
5	.00	.00	.03	.00	.18
6	.01	.01	.06	.01	.22
7	.02	.02	.08	.02	.18
8	.03	.03	.10	.02	.18
12	.07	.08	.20	.10	.19
16	.12	.12	.26	n.a.	n.a.
20	.20	.18	.31	n.a.	n.a.

[a] NSC - Without supply constraint
[b] SC - With supply constraint

In the supply-constraint case, real GNP multipliers with respect to the personal tax reduction are only slightly negative. Because of the constraint, consumers' attempts to spend more in response to the tax decline is frustrated. In this instance, there is, therefore, no crowding out (in real terms) of other final demand components.

4. PREDICTION ERRORS[11]

Root mean square errors (RMSE) of prediction that were submitted to the NBER-NSF seminar were derived from multiperiod model solutions using known values of exogenous variables and (revised) values of lagged variables as initial conditions and (at most) mechanical methods of adjusting constant terms on the basis of autoregressive properties of equation residuals. For within-sample periods, such statistics represent goodness-of-fit measures for system outputs analogous (apart from the dynamic aspect) to the standard error of estimate for a single equation. The post-sample estimates are more genuinely predictive tests since they pertain to data not used in fitting the equations. As indicators of the comparative usefulness of different models for forecasting, however, these data are by themselves inadequate since: (1) models vary in the number and kinds of exogenous variables (The more comprehensive the exogenous variables, the better the fits will tend to be); (2) these tests do not simulate

[11] In the following discussion "prediction" is used in a generic sense to include post-sample model simulations, forecasts, and time-series extrapolations.

the typical forecasting situation in which data for initial conditions are preliminary and numerous judgemental elements are introduced in addition to judgmental projection of exogenous variables; and (3) they do not provide comparisons with alternative forecasting procedures.

In this section, we give experimental results that take these elements into account. Specifically, we present RMSE's for eight model variables using six kinds of post-sample predictions: mechanical simulations, such as were done for the NBER–NSF seminar, but using the more recent version of the BEA model and for a later period; *ex ante* forecasts with three stages of judgmental intrusion (as detailed below); *ex post* forecasts, i.e., predictions that replicate actual *ex ante* forecasts, except that observed values of exogenous variable replace originally projected values; and predictions generated by the time-series methodology of Box and Jenkins [**1**] (also briefly described below). The latter serves as a benchmark for judging whether the specification and estimation of models based on economic theory aids prediction relative to sophisticated, but purely empirical extrapolation technique. We feel that only a joint and comparative examination of such statistics can provide the basis of an adequate evaluation of a model as a forecasting device.[12] Unfortunately, the observations are derived from overlapping dynamic predictions and their number is very limited; therefore, the conclusions to be drawn are at best tentative.

4.1. *Constant adjustments used in forecasts.* Since mid–1970, our econometric forecasting group has maintained two sets of forecasts, based on intermediate stages of judgmental intrusion, alongside the "final" versions that were circulated as representing our best forecasts. The first stage involves best projections of exogenous variables, but constant adjustments based on a formula —also used in the post-sample predictions—involving past residuals:

$$\delta_{t+i} = \frac{1}{2} r^i[(e_t - \bar{e}_{-1:8}) + r(e_{t-1} - \bar{e}_{-1:8})] + \bar{e}_{-1:8} \tag{4.1}$$

where δ_{t+i} is the amount added to the constant term in the (normalized) equation in question in the i-th quarter of the prediction period; e_t is the observed residual in the initial quarter (first quarter prior to the prediction period; e_{t-1} is the residual in the previous quarter; r is the estimated first-order autocorrelation coefficient; and $\bar{e}_{-1:8} = (1/8) \sum_{i=1}^{8} e_{t-i}$. Since invariably $0 < r < 1$, δ_{t+i} converges toward $\bar{e}_{-1:8}$, which represents a longer-run adjustment that allows for the possibility of a "permanent" shift in the equation residuals after the sample period.[13] Exceptions to the use of automatic adjustments are made to allow for such objective special factors as the direct effects of the General

[12] A similar study of the BEA model has been recently reported by Hirsch [**8**]. The present study differs in that: (1) an updated version of the model (see footnote 3) is used to provide the post-sample predictions; (2) a later, but common, period is examined for all variants; (3) results with intermediate stages of forecasts are included; and (4) the Box-Jenkins methodology replaces simple second-order autoregressive equations as an empirical extrapolation benchmark.

[13] A shift may be due partly to data revisions between the time of estimation and forecasting use of the model.

Motors strike in late 1970 and changes in the tax laws.

In the second-stage forecasts, many automatic adjustments are replaced by judgmental ones. However, such adjustments are based only on *a priori* considerations. Most of such adjustments are made on the basis of observed residuals, but according to a pattern that is subjectively superior to that given by equation (4.1); an obvious basis for different adjustment occurs, for example, if the residuals have a significant trend. Sometimes special factors accounting for the behavior of past residuals are taken into account. Similarly, special factors, such as strikes, that are expected to affect specific equations in the future are incorporated. Specifically excluded, however, are adjustments based on judgmental evaluation of preliminary model outputs.[14]

The "final" forecasts include further adjustments made after examining initial results. There are two kinds of considerations underlying such adjustments: (1) partial information pertaining to the first quarter of forecast, which is usually well in progress at the time of making the forecast, and (2) subjective judgments based on "reasonableness and consistency." A tally of reasons for making various kinds of adjustments shows that the proportion of nonautomatic adjustments made at the final forecast stage is relatively small—about 14 percent for the period analyzed.

4.2. *Selection of forecasts and computation of errors.* Whenever more than one forecast was made in any quarter or if there are multiple versions of a specific forecast, only one forecast version for that quarter was selected for analysis. Several principles underlay the selection. First, wherever possible, the forecast chosen was one made after the final national income and product account estimates for the previous quarter had been completed, but before substantial two-month information for the quarter was available. Second, in the case of multiple versions representing different degrees of endogeneity, the version with maximum endogeneity was selected. Third, where more than one fiscal policy or strike variant was available, the variant whose assumption most closely approximated the actual outcome was selected.

Data revisions create a problem for measuring forecasting error since the levels of forecast variables depend heavily on initial conditions and, for most variables, revisions are positively autocorrelated. On the assumptions that revisions are perfectly autocorrelated and that forecasts are to be judged in terms of cumulative changes from initial levels, the solution is straight-forward for a linear system. To compute the adjusted error for any variable in period $t + i$, calculate the adjusted forecast level in $t + i$ by adding the cumulative change originally forecast from t to $t + i$ to the revised initial level; the revised actual level in $t + i$ is then subtracted from the adjusted forecast level:

$$(4.2) \qquad e_{t+i} = F^r_{t+i} - A^r_{t+i} = (A_t^r + F^u_{t+i} - A_t^u) - A^r_{t+i},$$

where e_{t+i} is the adjusted error, A and F are, respectively, actual and forecast

[14] Note that the runs using mechanical adjustments can be (and are) made independently, i.e., not as a prior step to the second-stage forecasts.

values, and the superscripts r and u indicate, respectively, revised and unrevised values. This formula is used for all variables analyzed in this paper except change in business inventories (where serial correlation of revisions is low), despite lack of perfect autocorrelation of revisions and existence of nonlinearities in the system.

4.3. *Time-series predictions.* As a benchmark for comparison of various prediction methods, extrapolations were made using a relatively sophisticated time-series technique. Following the procedures developed by Box and Jenkins [**1**], optimal time-series—more specifically, autoregressive integrated moving average (ARIMA)—models were derived for each of the eight series for which model prediction errors are analyzed. The general form of the ARIMA model for stationary processes is

$$(4.3)\qquad \begin{aligned}(1 - B^d)(1 - \phi_1 B - \phi_2 B^2 - \cdots - \phi_p B^p)y_t \\ = (1 - \theta_1 B - \theta_2 B^2 - \cdots - \theta_q B^q)u_t\,,\end{aligned}$$

where y is the time-series variable, B is the lag operator (i.e., $B^p y_t = y_{t-p}$), p is the order of the autoregressive process, q is the order of the moving average process, d is the order of difference applied to the original data, u is a random deviate with zero mean and constant variance. The model used was generalized still further by adding a trend term. A "best" (in the least-squares sense) model is obtained by searching over the (ϕ, θ) parameter space for different combinations of p, d, and q. A chi-square test is used to determine goodness of fit, and the residuals are examined to ensure that there are no remaining autoregressive pattern. Extrapolations are made using the lagged errors as determined by the estimated time-series model.

4.4. *Results.* Root mean square errors of prediction are presented for the six procedures shown in Table 3. They are given for eight model variables: GNP in current and constant dollars; personal consumption expenditures, nonresidential fixed investment, change in business inventories—all in constant dollars; corporate profits; the GNP implicit price deflator; and the unemployment rate. The RMSE is calculated for prediction horizons up to six quarters.

The prediction procedure variants are arranged from left to right in the table in an order which reflects a generally increasing degree of judgmental involvement. Thus, the purely empirically based Box-Jenkins (ARIMA) results are given in the second column. This is followed by the post-sample model simulations (PSS), which are based on an essentially *a priori* specified structure. Next, are the *ex ante* forecasts with mechanical constant adjustments (EAF(1)). These differ from the post-sample simulations in that projections of exogenous variables occur in place of known values; also, initial conditions are given by preliminary, rather than revised data and the models used in individual forecasts do not represent a constant model version or a constant degree of exogeneity.[15] Error

[15] In connection with the last point, it should be noted that in forecasts made after August 1971, the wage rate was generally made exogenous to concur with the new incomes-policy announced at that time; prices were also made exogenous in 1971.4 to reflect the Phase I freeze.

TABLE 3

ROOT MEAN SQUARE ERRORS FOR SELECTED MODEL VARIABLES, 1970.3–1973.2

3A. Gross national product, billions of dollars.

Horizon (quarters)	ARIMA[a]	PSS	EAF(1)	EAF(2)	EAF(3)	EPF
1	10.80	8.71	5.54	4.51	3.23	6.45
2	18.78	12.78	9.95	8.61	6.99	8.90
3	26.90	12.70	14.05	11.22	8.39	14.22
4	36.76	12.31	17.71	12.46	12.82	16.02
5	45.98	16.66	20.16	12.92	16.49	13.89
6	57.91	19.82	28.63	16.02	15.24	13.55

[a] $(p, d, q) = (2, 2, 1)$

3B. Gross national product, billions of 1958 dollars.

Horizon (quarters)	ARIMA[b]	PSS	EAF(1)	EAF(2)	EAF(3)	EPF
1	8.73	7.86	4.26	3.35	2.50	5.35
2	12.78	10.59	4.98	5.19	4.70	8.27
3	17.21	10.79	6.75	6.06	5.16	11.74
4	23.39	11.43	9.91	7.82	8.18	14.76
5	28.84	14.85	12.75	9.30	9.29	12.72
6	36.22	16.69	16.22	9.81	7.19	9.18

[b] $(p, d, q) = (1, 1, 1)$

3C. Personal consumption expenditures, billions of 1958 dollars.

Horizon (quarters)	ARIMA[c]	PSS	EAF(1)	EAF(2)	EAF(3)	EPF
1	4.63	3.40	3.35	2.95	3.31	5.16
2	7.66	5.39	5.76	5.38	5.35	7.54
3	10.32	7.02	6.93	7.03	7.73	10.32
4	13.74	9.21	10.04	9.11	9.73	12.71
5	17.61	11.42	11.89	11.74	12.30	14.20
6	22.33	13.10	12.85	11.16	11.03	13.55

[c] $(p, d, q) = (2, 1, 1)$ *(Continued on next page)*

statistics in columns headed EAF(2) and EAF(3) are, respectively, for second-stage and final forecasts, which, as previously noted, involve progressively higher degrees of judgement. The final column, which gives results for *ex post* forecasts (EPF), represents less judgmental involvement than does EAF(3) since actual exogenous variables are used in place of projections, but is placed there because of its direct comparability with the EAF(3) results.

TABLE 3 (*Continued*)

3D. Nonresidential fixed investment, billions of 1958 dollars.

Horizon (quarters)	ARIMA[d]	PSS	EAF(1)	EAF(2)	EAF(3)	EPF
1	2.43	2.30	1.89	1.39	1.47	1.78
2	3.95	3.69	2.57	2.60	2.41	2.40
3	4.40	3.71	2.04	2.42	2.57	1.75
4	8.06	5.03	2.36	2.71	3.26	2.64
5	6.61	6.91	2.95	3.62	4.22	3.15
6	7.53	8.15	2.28	3.51	3.60	3.13

[d] $(p, d, q) = (1, 1, 1)$

3E. Change in business inventories, billions of 1958 dollars.

Horizon (quarters)	ARIMA[e]	PSS	EAF(1)	EAF(2)	EAF(3)	EPF
1	2.01	5.56	4.32	2.76	2.46	2.82
2	2.86	7.78	5.99	4.71	4.11	5.17
3	2.09	8.27	6.00	5.10	3.91	5.20
4	3.84	8.03	6.51	5.64	4.60	6.19
5	4.25	8.07	6.69	6.24	4.50	6.12
6	4.58	8.20	4.31	3.85	3.59	5.02

[e] $(p, d, q) = (1, 1, 1)$

3F. Corporate profits and inventory valuation adjustment, billions of dollars.

Horizon (quarters)	ARIMA[f]	PSS	EAF(1)	EAF(2)	EAF(3)	EPF
1	4.67	6.44	4.70	5.08	4.32	7.34
2	7.20	9.81	7.67	7.88	6.63	11.76
3	9.30	11.25	7.78	9.60	6.55	6.98
4	12.28	13.22	7.19	8.68	6.54	10.47
5	13.79	17.26	6.35	9.08	6.03	9.64
6	16.73	19.48	7.19	10.45	6.51	8.68

[f] $(p, d, q) = (1, 1, 0)$

(*Continued on next page*)

The period covered is 1970.3–1973.2.[16] In the cases of the ARIMA and PSS predictions, there are, accordingly, 12 observations for one-quarter predictions,

[16] Since the sample period for the model used in the PSS predictions extended through 1971, these are not strictly post-sample simulations. However, we felt it more important to have a common period for comparing various prediction results than to avoid use of any within-sample observations. The alternative of using fewer Box-Jenkins and forecast observations was equally unattractive.

TABLE 3 (*Continued*)

3G. GNP implicit price deflator (Index, 1958=100).

Horizon (quarters)	ARIMA[g]	PSS	EAF(1)	EAF(2)	EAF(3)	EPF
1	.75	.59	.45	.47	.48	.50
2	1.32	.61	.70	.83	.84	.96
3	2.11	.56	1.21	1.38	1.37	1.30
4	2.82	.69	1.73	1.91	1.89	1.53
5	3.05	1.05	1.77	1.72	1.74	1.72
6	3.85	1.42	1.38	1.29	1.08	1.99

[g] $(p, d, q) = (1, 2, 1)$

3H. Unemployment rate, civilian labor force (percent).

Horizon (quarters)	ARIMA[h]	PSS	EAF(1)	EAF(2)	EAF(3)	EPF
1	.23	.34	.19	.13	.09	.46
2	.51	.42	.23	.18	.15	.46
3	.73	.45	.23	.20	.16	.41
4	.91	.51	.29	.26	.27	.43
5	1.01	.62	.33	.27	.31	.30
6	1.06	.76	.33	.30	.31	.25

[h] $(p, d, q) = (2, 1, 1)$

11 for two-quarter predictions, · · ·, and 7 for six-quarter predictions. There are somewhat fewer observations for forecasts.[17] Some major generalizations concerning the results follow.

First, there is near consistency in the tendency for the RMSE in all variants to increase with the prediction horizon. This tendency reflects accumulation of errors through lagged variables, which—after the first quarter—also contain prediction errors. It is especially pronounced in the Box-Jenkins extrapolations—with the notable exception of inventory investment—where the autoregressive nature of the model is dominant. In the forecasts, there is sometimes a reversal in the sixth quarter; but this must be discounted because of the paucity of observations for that horizon.

Second, there is a substantial superiority in the model predictions during the observed period relative to the Box-Jenkins extrapolations. Beyond the first quarter, this reflects the greater tendency for the RMSE in the time-series pre-

[17] The forecast made during 1971.3 was omitted since, because of extreme uncertainty regarding the implications of the New Economic Policy at that time, it was not possible to produce meaningfully distinct EAF(1) and EAF(2) forecasts. Furthermore, forecasts were not made with six-quarter horizons each time. Thus the number of observations ranges from eleven for one-quarter horizons to five for six-quarter horizons.

dictions to increase with horizon length, but for most variables, they are also greater in the first quarter. Exceptions to the general rule are found in the case of inventory investment. For corporate profits, the Box-Jenkins predictions are also more accurate than the post-sample simulations.[18]

Third, the post-sample simulations usually gave poorer predictions than the *ex ante* forecasts at all three stages of judgmental intrusion. With respect to the EAF(1) forecasts, this inferiority cannot be attributed to an ameliorative role of judgmental elements since the constant adjustments are mechanical and unrevised initial data and projections of exogenous variables were used in the latter. The difference is most likely due to offsetting of errors between exogenous variables on the one hand and model equation errors on the other. This explanation is corroborated by a tendency for greater errors in EPF than in EAF(3) forecasts. It must be remembered, however, that there are other factors of difference between the PSS and EAF(1) runs.[19]

An exception occurs for current-dollar GNP: EAF(1) errors are larger than PSS errors. This apparently reflects a similar exception in the case of the implicit GNP price deflator.

Fourth, forecasts generally improve with increasing degrees of judgmental intrusion, as is seen by the tendency to diminishing error from EAF(1) to EAF(2) to EAF(3) forecasts. There are, of course, exceptions. For nonresidential fixed investment, errors become progressively larger going from EAF(1) to EAF(3) forecasts. For corporate profits, EAF(2) errors are larger than corresponding EAF(1) errors, but EAF(3) errors are again sufficiently reduced in magnitude to be smaller than EAF(1) errors. Judgmental intrusions neither help nor hurt significantly forecasts of real consumption, the price level, and —after the third quarter—the unemployment rate.

Fifth, as previously noted, *ex post* forecasts are generally poorer than corresponding EAF(3) *ex ante* forecasts. Where that is the case, it is usually also true that the PSS errors are greater than EAF(1) errors, indicating that the cause is an offsetting of the effects of errors in exogenous variables and stochastic error in the model structure. To the extent that PSS errors are smaller than EAF(1) errors where EPF errors are larger than EAF(3) errors, there is evidence for the suggestion of Evans, Haitovsky, and Treyz **[2]** that econometric forecasters adjust constants so as systematically to offset the errors caused by exoge-

[18] These results represent a clearer victory for the model over mechanical extrapolations than was indicated in [**8**], where only final *ex ante* forecasts and extrapolations using simple second-order autoregressive equations were compared. In that article, in cases where the model performed better, the superiority was less pronounced, and the price level and corporate profits were less accurate in the model forecasts. It is difficult, however, to pinpoint the reason for the different comparative behavior, especially since the periods analyzed are not the same. Perhaps the policy actions that have occurred since August, 1971, have caused sufficient structural change to harm substantially the quality of the time-series predictions. (In the earlier article the period analyzed ended in 1971.2)

[19] Particularly notable is the superiority of the EAF(1) forecasts of non-residential fixed investment for horizons longer than three quarters. This may reflect the substantial change in functional specification for that variable; since the later version was used throughout in the PSS case, it apparently yielded relatively poor predictions for this particular period.

nous variables. In the present study, this happens too infrequently and sporadically to give support to that view.[20]

U.S. Department of Commerce, Washington, D.C.

REFERENCES

[1] Box, G. E. P. and G. M. Jenkins, *Time Series Analysis, Forecasting, and Control* (San Francisco: Holden Day, Inc., 1970).

[2] Evans, M. K., Y. Haitovsky, and G. I. Treyz, "An Analysis of the Forecasting Properties of U.S. Econometric Models" in B. G. Hickman, ed., *Econometric Models of Cyclical Behavior*, Studies in Income and Wealth, No. 36 (New York: National Bureau of Economic Research, 1972), 949-1139.

[3] Fair, R. C., *The Short-run Demand for Workers and Hours* (Amsterdam: North-Holland Publishing Company, 1969).

[4] Fromm, G. and L. R. Klein, "A Comparison of Eleven Econometric Models of the United States," *American Economic Review*, LXIII (May, 1973), 385–393.

[5] Goldberger, A. S., *Impact Multipliers and Dynamic Properties of the Klein-Goldberger Model* (Amsterdam: North-Holland Publishing Company, 1959).

[6] Haitovsky, Y. and G. I. Treyz, "Forecasts with Quarterly Macroeconometric Models, Equation Adjustments, and Benchmark Revisions," *Review of Economics and Statistics*, LIV (August, 1972), 317-325.

[7] Hirsch, A. A., "Price Simulations with the OBE Econometric Model" in O. Eckstein, ed., *The Econometrics of Price Determination* (Washington: Board of Governors, Federal Reserve System, 1972), 237-276.

[8] ———, "The BEA Quarterly Model as a Forecasting Instrument," *Survey of Current Business*, LIII (August, 1973), 24-38.

[9] ———, M. Liebenberg, and G. R. Green, "The BEA Quarterly Econometric Model," Bureau of Economic Analysis Staff Paper No. 22, U.S. Department of Commerce (July, 1973).

[10] ——— and G. V. L. Narasimham, "Simulation Paths and Multipliers in an Econometric Model With and Without Supply Constraints," Paper delivered at North American Meetings of the Econometric Society, Toronto, (December, 1972).

[11] Liebenberg, M., A. A. Hirsch, and J. Popkin, "A Quarterly Econometric Model of the United States: A Progress Report," *Survey of Current Business*, XLVI (May, 1966), 13-39.

[20] Such inequality pairs do occur for constant-dollar GNP with three and four quarter horizons and to a slight extent for personal consumption with two, four, and five quarter horizons and for the GNP price deflator with a two quarter horizon. In a follow-up study analyzing BEA (OBE) and Wharton model forecasts, Haitovsky and Treyz limit the applicability of their hypothesis to one-quarter forecasts [6].

11

THE STRUCTURE AND PROPERTIES OF THE MICHIGAN QUARTERLY ECONOMETRIC MODEL OF THE U.S. ECONOMY

BY SAUL H. HYMANS AND HAROLD T. SHAPIRO[1]

1. INTRODUCTION

THIS PAPER PRESENTS AN ANALYSIS of the latest version of the quarterly model of the U.S. economy used in the forecasting program of the Research Seminar in Quantitative Economics (RSQE) of the University of Michigan. A "Michigan Model" has been on the forecasting scene in the United States for more than twenty years, beginning with the Klein-Goldberger model, continuing through the many versions constructed under the direction of Professor Daniel B. Suits, e.g. [**15**], the DHL-III model constructed by the current authors [**8**], and now represented by the Michigan Quarterly Econometric Model (MQEM). Throughout these past two decades every Michigan model has been an operational model in use in a regular program of ex ante forecasting, and no Michigan model has ever been represented as anything more than an interim vehicle pending further testing and the results of ongoing research at RSQE.[2]

MQEM is a medium size, non-linear, quarterly econometric model designed primarily for short-term forecasting and policy analysis. The short-term nature of the model results from the basic structural characteristic that output is primarily expenditure-determined. The supply constraints present in the model operate on prices and through the effects of prices on expenditures (see Section 3 and 5 below). The model focuses on the determination of the principal variables in the National Income and Product Accounts along with related data on employment, productivity, and interest rates. There are 59 endogenous variables, 35 stochastic equations, and 24 identities.[3] Twelve of the endogenous variables form a recursive block in the sense that current quarter values can be calculated solely from predetermined variables or from successive substitution of "earlier" recursive variables. The most important exogenous variables are government expenditures in current prices, exports and foreign prices, agricultural prices, and unborrowed reserves.[4]

MQEM has been fitted to seasonally adjusted, quarterly data for the period 1954. 1–1970. 4. Eight of the stochastic equations have been fitted by the tech-

[1] We gratefully acknowledge the many contributions of Ms. Gail Blattenberger to the preparation of this paper.

[2] In this connection, the authors gratefully acknowledge the continuing research support of the National Science Foundation. The model being reported on here was completed under NSF Grant GS-36932X.

[3] The equations for personal taxes and corporate profits taxes are stochastic equations with coefficients which vary over time and are not estimated by any standard statistical procedures.

[4] In ex ante forecasts we frequently bypass unborrowed reserves and treat the treasury bill rate as exogenous.

nique of Instrumental Variables. Whenever this process required an instrument for a current endogenous variable, the instrument was based on a "quasi reduced form" estimate of the endogenous variable determined roughly in accordance with the causal-ordering technique of Fisher [**2**]. The remaining equations were fitted directly by Least Squares.[5]

Section 2 of the paper explains the block structure of the model and discusses the dynamic properties of individual equations. Section 3 considers dynamic characteristics of the model as a whole through the analysis of multiplier properties. The process of model validation is taken further in Section 4 which focuses on forecasting behavior. Concluding remarks and indications of current research directions are contained in Section 5.

2. BLOCK STRUCTURE AND EQUATION DYNAMICS

The structure of MQEM can be usefully discussed by considering it to be partitioned into the following six blocks of equations: Wages and Prices, Productivity and Employment, Expenditures, Income Flows, Interest Rates, and Output Composition. While the entire model is an integrated and interdependent system, the above categorization serves to break the system down into subsectors of equations which can be conveniently considered together. Table 1, organized in this block form, identifies the most important endogenous variables in each block and provides a succinct characterization of some important aspects of the structural equation corresponding to each variable.[6] The following discussion considers each of the principal blocks in turn.

A. Wages and Prices

The principal behavioral relationships in this block of ten equations serve to explain the basic wage rate and price level in the model, namely compensation per manhour and the implicit output deflator, both for the private nonfarm sector of the economy. These two "basic" variables then become the principal elements in the explanation of seven implicit deflators relating to various components of the Gross National Product Accounts.

Compensation per Manhour. The wage equation in the model is an expanded version of the Phillips-Lipsey [**11**] mechanism and explains the rate of change of the money wage over a two quarter interval. Wage changes respond to the level (in inverse form) and the rate of change of the unemployment rate (for males 20 and over) as well as to the rate of price inflation in the consumer sector. The short-run elasticity of wage changes with respect to price changes is about 2/5 so that the model contains a short-run Phillips Curve which is not particularly steep. In the longer run, however, the rate of growth of the money wage adjusts to reduce any deviation between the annual rate of growth of the *real* wage and 3.2%, the normal productivity standard. The effect of this adjustment process is to raise the price elasticity in the wage equation from about 2/5 in the short

5 A fuller discussion of these matters of estimation is contained in [**9**, (127–128)].

6 Space limitations prevent the listing of estimated equations in this paper. A listing of the equations of the current operating model is available on written request to RSQE.

TABLE 1

THE MQEM MODEL; MAIN BLOCKS AND PRINCIPAL ENDOGENOUS VARIABLES

Block and Endogenous Variables	Behavioral (*B*), Definitional (*D*), or Hybrid (*B* – *D*)[1]	Simultaneous (*S*) or Recursive (*R*) in Model	Estimated by Instrumental Variables (*I.V.*) or Direct Least Squares (*L.S.*)	Dependent Variable in Level (*L*) or Change (*Δ*) form[2]	Contains Lagged Dependent Variable	Fitted with Correction for First-Order Autocorrelation[3]
	Equation					
A. *Wages and Prices*						
Compensation per manhour	*B*	*R*	*L.S.*	*Δ*	Yes	Yes
Private nonfarm GNP deflator	*B*	*R*	*L.S.*	*L*	Yes	Yes
7 GNP component deflators	*B*	*R*	*L.S.*	*Δ*	Yes, 5 of 7	No
B. *Productivity and employment*						
Output per manhour	*B*	*S*	*I.V.*	*L*	Yes	No
Employment rate, males 20 and over	*B – D*	*S*	*L.S.*	*Δ*	No	No
C. *Expenditures*						
Consumption						
Autos	*B*	*R*	*L.S.*	*L*	Yes	No
Furniture and household equipment	*B*	*S*	*I.V.*	*L*	Yes	No
Other durables	*B*	*S*	*I.V.*	*L*	Yes	No
Nondurables	*B*	*S*	*I.V.*	*L*	Yes	No
Services	*B*	*S*	*I.V.*	*L*	Yes	No
Investment						
Business fixed	*B*	*R*	*L.S.*	*L*	Yes	No
Inventory	*B*	*S*	*I.V.*	*L*	Yes	No
Residential construction	*B*	*R*	*L.S.*	*L*	Yes	No
Imports	*B*	*S*	*I.V.*	*Δ*	Yes	No
D. *Income Flows*						
Private wages & salaries	*D*	*S*	*L.S.*	*Δ*	No	No
Profits	*B – D*	*S*	*I.V.*	*Δ*	No	No
Dividends	*B*	*S*	*L.S.*	*L*	Yes	No
E. *Interest Rates*						
Treasury bill rate	*B*	*S*	*L.S.*	*L*	Yes	No
Commercial paper rate	*B*	*S*	*L.S.*	*L*	Yes	No
Aaa rate	*B*	*S*	*L.S.*	*L*	Yes	No

[1] An estimated equation is considered "Definitional" if its form is motivated by a definition but at least one of the variables required by the definition is not contained in the model and must be represented by available proxy variables. A "Hybrid" equation is a "Definitional" equation in which an assumed behavioral relation has been substituted for one or more of the variables required by the definition.

[2] Some dependent variables are expressed in natural units, others in logarithms.

[3] Refers to whether the equation, with dependent variable in the form specified (and whether or not the lagged dependent variable appears), has been corrected for first-order autocorrelation of residuals.

run to about 3/4 in the long run (at any fixed level of the unemployment rate), thus yielding a Phillips Curve which grows steeper over time—but stops short of becoming vertical—in response to policies designed to maintain an unemployment rate below that which would correspond to zero price inflation.[7] The dynamic behavior of this price elasticity in adjusting to a permanent shift in the rate of inflation is not, however, monotonic. From its initial value of 2/5 the elasticity rises, reaches nearly unity after about a year and a half, and then proceeds via a damped cyclical path to its long-run equilibrium value of about 3/4.

Output Deflator, Private Nonfarm GNP. The hypothesis underlying the basic price equation in MQEM is that of a variable mark-up over efficient average cost as determined within the framework of a Cobb-Douglas production function. Operationally, the notion of efficient average cost is taken to mean standard unit labor cost, which we calculate as a two quarter average of the ratio of compensation per manhour to a productivity trend.[8] The mark-up factor is taken to vary with the strength of aggregate demand measured by the level of real GNP. This variable mark-up mechanism is considered to define the "desired" price level, whereas the actual price level is determined through a logarithmic Koyck adjustment relating desired price to the lagged actual price. The speed of adjustment in the Koyck mechanism is estimated to be about 50 percent per quarter.[9]

B. Productivity and Employment

Output Per Manhour, Private Nonfarm Sector. In the Michigan Model productivity growth is embodied in capital in the long run, but is responsive to changes in output—through work speed-ups, labor hoarding, and so on—in the short run. This leads to an equation of the form

$$\ln QMH = \alpha_0 \Delta \ln Q + \sum_{i=0}^{N} \beta_i \ln IBF_{-i} + \alpha_1 \ln QMH_{-1}, \tag{1}$$

where

QMH = output per manhour

Q = output

IBF = real business fixed investment.

The lagged dependent variable in equation (1) permits us to use a relatively short lag distribution on IBF to represent the accumulation of capital. Assuming $\Delta^2 \ln Q = 0$ (i.e., a constant rate of growth of output), equation (1) implies that, in the long run, normal productivity growth is given by

7 A simulation study [6] of the wages and prices block of MQEM yields (for the early 1970's) about 8 percent as the zero inflation unemployment rate, the so-called natural rate of unemployment [3], [**13**].

8 We also find, empirically, that short term movements in productivity affect the price level, though with a longer distributed lag and much smaller magnitude than in the case of standard unit labor cost.

9 The mathematics of this pricing framework, along with a comparative analysis of the price equations in several U.S. econometric models is contained in [7].

$$(2) \qquad \Delta \ln QMH = \frac{\Sigma \beta_i}{1 - \alpha_1} (\Delta \ln IBF) .$$

Our estimated productivity equation implies that $\Sigma\beta_i/(1 - \alpha_1) = .481$, so that normal annual productivity growth amounts to just under one half the annual rate of growth of *IBF*. Over the decade 1959-1969, real business fixed investment grew at an average annual rate of about 6.1 percent, implying a productivity growth rate of about 3 percent per year.

Employment Rates. The principal employment variable in the model is the employment rate for males 20 years of age and over. The two basic reasons for this choice are, i) there is little cyclical variability in the corresponding labor force group, thus permitting us to by-pass any labor force forecast in explaining this employment *rate*; and ii) the male 20 and over unemployment rate has seemed to perform better than the aggregate unemployment rate as an indicator of labor market tightness in the wage equation.[10] The model explains the employment rate by approximating the identity relating employment changes to changes in output, productivity and hours worked. Output and productivity are explained within MQEM. Cyclical changes in hours worked are implicitly represented to be a function of changes in output interacted with the unemployment rate so that a given rate of growth of output results in a smaller increase in employment at the peak of the cycle (low unemployment rates) when overtime hours are more easily available than additional workers.

The aggregate unemployment rate is approximated as a simple function of the male rate. It is calculated as an interesting statistic and plays no role in the dynamics of the model.

C. Expenditures

There are nine expenditure flows (all in 1958 dollars) explained in this block of the model. There are five consumption equations, three investment equations, and one import equation (see Table 1). These flows account for all of private real GNP except for exports.

Consumption Equations. All of the consumption equations can be viewed as derived from a rational distributed lag mechanism of the form

$$(3) \qquad C = \frac{A(L)}{B(L)} f(Y, r, P, \ldots) ,$$

where

C = a component of consumption expenditure

Y = some concept of consumer income

r = an interest rate (or interest rate differential)

P = a relative price

$A(L)$ and $B(L)$ = finite polynomial functions of the lag operator, L. In the

[10] See Perry [12] for a discussion of the instability of the Phillips Curve when the aggregate unemployment rate is used as the labor market variable.

case of consumer auto purchases, for example, the expression $A(L)f(Y, r, P, \ldots)$ takes the form (as fitted and excluding a dummy variable for auto strikes):

$$(4) \qquad A(L)f = .041 YPERM_{-1} + [.121 + .142 RLS_{-1} + .011 \Delta ICS_{-1}] YTRANS_{-1},$$

where

$YPERM$ = Permanent Income, a distributed lag on real Disposable Income net of Transfer Payments (billions of 1958 dollars)

RLS = A three quarter average of the spread (in percentage points) between long and short interest rates

ICS = Survey Research Center Index of Consumer Sentiment (1966 = 100)

$YTRANS$ = Transitory Income, the difference between Disposable Income and Permanent Income (billions of 1958 dollars)

Thus, if the consumer sentiment index is constant and long and short interest rates are equal, the (impact) coefficient on auto expenditures of Transitory Income is about three times as great as that of our measure of Permanent Income. Note, however, that interest rate effects and changes in consumer sentiment can cause substantial movements in the marginal propensity to spend on automobiles out of Transitory Income.

While we have been unable, in this framework, to isolate significant relative price effects for automobiles, relative prices do play an important role in the other two durables equations and in the equation for nondurables. Interest rate terms appear in every consumption equation except that for "other" durables. Our handling of transfer payments in the consumption sector requires some explanation. The fitted auto equation implies that in the long run an extra billion dollars of real income will raise auto expenditures by 0.112 billion 1958 dollars. But the auto equation excludes transfer payments from the income variable with the result that the long run MPC out of transfer income is 0.112 lower than out of non-transfer income. To prevent this effect from remaining in the model we have allocated these "unspent" transfer payments as additional spending on nondurables and services. Our experiments indicated that the resulting equations for nondurables and services were most satisfactory (by statistical criteria) when the 11.2 percent of transfer payments were allocated in the ratio of 7-to-3 to nondurables and services, respectively.

Tables 2–4 display the dynamic properties of the entire set of consumption equations. Table 2 shows the quarterly response of each consumption category and total consumption (C) to a permanent one billion dollar increase in the path of real disposable (non-transfer) income. For total consumer spending, the impact *MPC* is about three-tenths. In the second quarter the *MPC* cumulates to 0.53 as auto expenditures respond to the increase in income and by the second year the *MPC* has cumulated to 0.70, or about 92 percent of the steady-state *MPC* value of nearly 0.77.[11] Table 3 shows the quarterly response of each non-

[11] The average propensity to consume would be a good deal higher than 0.77 due to the presence of a trend term in the Services equation.

TABLE 2

QUARTERLY CHANGES IN CONSUMER SPENDING IN RESPONSE TO A PERMANENT ONE BILLION DOLLAR INCREASE IN REAL DISPOSABLE INCOME*
(RESPONSE IN BILLIONS OF 1958 DOLLARS)

Quarter	Nondurables	Services	Autos**	Furniture, etc.	Other Durables	Total *C*
1 (impact *MPC*)	.173	.029	0	.103	.014	.305
2	.249	.054	.152	.053	.018	.526
3	.283	.076	.170	.076	.022	.629
4	.298	.095	.195	.066	.024	.678
5	.304	.111	.188	.073	.026	.702
6	.308	.125	.176	.070	.027	.706
7	.309	.138	.156	.072	.028	.703
8	.309	.148	.146	.072	.028	.703
9	.310	.157	.136	.073	.029	.705
10	.310	.165	.130	.073	.029	.707
11	.310	.172	.125	.074	.029	.710
12	.310	.178	.122	.074	.029	.713
⋮	⋮	⋮	⋮	⋮	⋮	⋮
∞ (steady-state *MPC*)	.310	.217	.112	.098	.029	.766

* non-transfer disposable income.
** Evaluated at $\Delta ICS = 0$ and RLS at its sample mean value of 0.512.

TABLE 3

QUARTERLY CHANGES IN NON-AUTO COMPONENTS OF CONSUMER SPENDING IN RESPONSE TO A PERMANENT 50 BASIS POINT REDUCTION IN THE LONG TERM INTEREST RATE (RESPONSE IN BILLIONS OF 1958 DOLLARS)

Quarter	Nondurables	Services	Furniture etc.	Other Durables	Non-Auto *C*
1	0	0	0	0	0
2	.141	.191	.123	0	.455
3	.345	.261	.190	0	.796
4	.576	.500	.288	0	1.364
5	.678	.707	.251	0	1.636
6	.724	.886	.281	0	1.891
7	.743	1.042	.278	0	2.063
8	.753	1.177	.291	0	2.221
9	.757	1.293	.295	0	2.345
10	.758	1.394	.304	0	2.456
11	.759	1.482	.310	0	2.551
12	.760	1.558	.317	0	2.635
⋮	⋮	⋮	⋮	⋮	⋮
∞	.760	2.052	.699	0	3.511

TABLE 4

QUARTERLY CHANGES IN AUTO CONSUMPTION AND RESIDENTIAL CONSTRUCTION IN RESPONSE TO A PERMANENT 50 BASIS POINT INCREASE IN THE SPREAD BETWEEN LONG-TERM AND SHORT-TERM INTEREST RATES (RESPONSE IN BILLIONS OF 1958 DOLLARS)

Quarter	Autos*	Residential Construction
1	0	0
2	.147	.208
3	.343	.674
4	.599	1.145
5	.744	1.495
6	.870	1.715
7	.956	1.840
8	1.022	1.902
9	1.070	1.930
10	1.090	1.940
11	1.127	1.942
12	1.146	1.941
⋮	⋮	⋮
∞	1.208	1.936

* Response evaluated at $\Delta ICS = 0$ and $YTRANS$ equal to its sample mean value of 6.2 billion 1958 dollars.

auto consumption category to a maintained 50 basis point reduction in the long-term interest rate, and Table 4 shows the quarterly response of auto consumption to a maintained 50 basis point increase in *RLS*, the spread (long minus short) between long-term and short-term interest rates.

Residential Construction. The equation for residential construction expenditures is also of the form given in (4) with the function f taken to depend on disposable income, the vacancy rate, and *RLS*, the interest rate spread. Table 4 shows the quarterly response of residential building expenditures to a maintained 50 basis point increase in the interest rate spread, which is best considered as a measure of "intermediation."

Business Fixed Investment. Nonresidential, or "Business," fixed investment expenditures are explained via a distributed lag mechanism defined on the desired stock of capital. The latter is based on neoclassical capital theory as recently revitalized in the work of Jorgenson [**10**] and others. We take the desired stock, K^*, to be of the form:

$$K^* = \sum_{i=1}^{N_1} \alpha_i Q_{-i} + \sum_{i=1}^{N_2} \beta_i \frac{CMH}{UCC}_{-i}, \tag{5}$$

where,

CMH is conpensation per manhour, and
UCC is the user cost of capital defined as

$$(6) \qquad UCC = q\left[r + \delta + r\delta - \frac{c\delta}{1 - t}\right],$$

with

q = price of capital goods
r = interest rate
δ = depreciation rate
c = rate of investment tax credit
t = tax rate on profits.[12]

The separate distributed lags on output and relative input costs in (5) allow for possibly different expectation formation processes with respect to these two determinants of desired stock. The fitted investment function indicates that the two expectations processes are indeed quite different. In the case of *CMH/UCC* the distributed lag is of the inverted-*U* variety, while the lag distribution on the

TABLE 5

QUARTERLY CHANGES IN BUSINESS FIXED INVESTMENT IN RESPONSE TO PERMANENT CHANGES IN THE VARIABLES DETERMINING THE DESIRED STOCK (RESPONSE IN BILLIONS OF 1958 DOLLARS)

Quarter	Investment Response to One Billion (1958 Dollars) Permanent Increase in Output*	Investment Response to Permanent Increase in *CMH/UCC* of 0.125**
1	0	0
2	.060	.053
3	.137	.170
4	.196	.333
5	.227	.521
6	.238	.715
7	.235	.901
8	.224	1.065
9	.208	1.193
10	.189	1.270
11	.169	1.283
12	.152	1.271
⋮	⋮	⋮
∞	.142	1.261

* Output is measured by a tax-corrected non-service output variable. In 1970 the value of this output variable was about $435 billion (1958 dollars).

** In 1970 the value of the ratio *CMH/UCC* was about 4(3/4).

[12] This form of the user cost expression along with the form of the variable *CMH/UCC* in equation (5) arises from choosing K and MH (manhours) so as to maximize the profit expression

$$\Pi = (1 - t)[PQ - (CMH)(MH) - \delta qK - rqK] + cqI$$

subject to the constraints $Q = A(MH)^{\alpha}K^{\beta}$, and $K = (1 - \delta)K_{-1} + I$.

output variable has declining positive weights for five quarters followed by a U-shaped pattern of negative weights for seven quarters. A distributed lag of the kind found for the output variable is consistent with an expectations mechanism such as

$$(X^E - X_{-1}) = \alpha\left[\sum_{i=1}^{n_1} w_i X_{-i} - \sum_{i=1}^{n_2} v_i X_{-i}\right], \tag{7}$$

with

$$w_i, v_i > 0$$
$$w_i > v_i, \qquad \text{for } i = 1, \ldots, n_1$$

and

$$n_2 > n_1$$

but it is consistent with many other expectations mechanisms as well.

The dynamics of the business fixed investment equation may be seen from the results given in Table 5. A permanent increase of one billion (1958 dollars) in output raises real investment by \$.142 billion in the long run. The initial effect is small; it then builds to a peak of \$.238 billion in the sixth quarter and declines to \$.152 billion by the twelfth quarter. The response to a change in relative input costs (*CMH/UCC*) takes about twice as long to reach its maximum effect and exhibits far less over-shooting than does the response to an output change. It is useful to provide some perspective on the 0.125 increase in *CMH/UCC* used in Table 5. At 1970 levels of the components of *CMH/UCC*, repeal of the investment tax credit reduces *CMH/UCC* by about 0.13. The response values shown in Table 5 (with signs changed) are therefore very close to the estimated effects on investment of a repeal of the investment tax credit at about the time it was repealed in late 1969. Also at 1970 levels, a 50 basis point reduction in the long term interest rate would raise *CMH/UCC* by about 0.15, so that the response values in Table 5 are close to the estimated effects on investment of such a change in interest rates.

Inventory Investment. The inventory investment equation in MQEM is of the stock adjustment variety. *Intended* inventory investment, say I_i, is given by

$$I_i = \theta\alpha Q - \theta K_{-1}, \tag{8}$$

where αQ represents the desired stock of inventories, and θ is an adjustment rate. Unintended inventory investment, I_u, is taken to depend on the actual change in final sales, FS, thus

$$I_u = \beta_0 + \beta_1 \Delta FS, \tag{9}$$

with $\beta_1 < 0$. Total inventory investment is then obtained by summing equations (8) and (9):

$$I = \beta_0 + \theta\alpha Q + \beta_1 \Delta FS - \theta K_{-1}. \tag{10}$$

To determine the dynamic behavior of inventory investment, it is convenient to

TABLE 6

QUARTERLY CHANGES IN INVENTORY INVESTMENT AND INVENTORY STOCK IN RESPONSE TO A PERMANENT ONE BILLION DOLLAR INCREASE IN NON-SERVICE OUTPUT (RESPONSE IN BILLIONS OF 1958 DOLLARS)

Quarter	Investment	Stock
1	−.285	−.285
2	.624	.339
3	.173	.512
4	.275	.797
5	.169	.966
6	.161	1.127
7	.123	1.250
8	.104	1.354
9	.084	1.438
10	.069	1.507
11	.056	1.563
12	.046	1.609
⋮	⋮	⋮
∞	0	1.817

substitute the identities $FS = Q - I$ and $FS_{-1} = Q_{-1} - I_{-1}$ into equation (10), and then take first-differences to yield

$$(11) \qquad \Delta I = \frac{\theta\alpha + \beta_1}{1-\beta_1}\Delta Q - \frac{\beta_1}{1-\beta_1}\Delta Q_{-1} + \frac{\beta_1}{1-\beta_1}\Delta I_{-1} - \frac{\theta}{1-\beta_1}\Delta K_{-1}\,.$$

If $|\beta_1| > \theta\alpha$, then the initial effect of an increase in output will be to *reduce* inventory investment, thereby cutting back the impact multiplier in the model. If the *same* output change is maintained after the first period, then $\Delta Q = \Delta Q_{-1}$ and the first two terms on the right hand side of (11) can be combined to yield

$$(12) \qquad \Delta I = \frac{\theta\alpha}{1-\beta_1}\Delta Q + \frac{\beta_1}{1-\beta_1}\Delta I_{-1} - \frac{\theta}{1-\beta_1}\Delta K_{-1}\,.$$

In the second period of a permanent increase in output, ΔI_{-1} and ΔK_{-1} are both negative and therefore all the terms in (12) contribute to a sharp increase in inventory investment following the initial drop in the first quarter. In the long run the desired stock increase is attained so that ΔI converges to zero and the increase in inventory stock resulting from a permanent ΔQ is given by $\Delta K = \alpha\Delta Q$. The numerical details of this pattern of behavior of inventory investment and inventory stock, as implied by the fitted inventory equation, are shown in Table 6.

D. Income Flows

Private wages and salaries, corporate profits, dividend payments, and various tax flows are accounted for in this block of the model. In the structure of MQEM, personal income is determined by a series of subtractions from GNP so that the profit equation is about the most important in this block from the point of view of the dynamic behavior of the model.[13] The profit equation explains the change of corporate gross cash flow on the basis of the identity relating cash flow to revenue, the wage bill, and capital costs. Corporate revenue is taken to depend on current dollar GNP and capital costs are implicitly represented by a function of interest rates and investment expenditures. In the estimated equation, the marginal share of profits in current dollar GNP can be as high as 0.6 in the very short run (depending on the rate of inflation, the path of productivity behavior, etc.). Simulation results, however, have shown that the equation is consistent with the 10–15 percent average profit share which is observable in the data over long periods.

E. Interest Rates

In the current operating version of the model, both the long term Aaa interest rate and the 4–6 month prime commercial paper rate are explained via term structure relationships based on the 90-day treasury bill rate. The treasury bill rate itself is determined through an equation which contains variables representing the demand for and supply of credit. In the former category are i) the excess of business investment over retained earnings and capital consumption allowances, ii) expenditures on residential building, and iii) the excess of the consolidated government deficit over the net change in foreign official holdings of U.S. government liabilities. The supply of credit is represented by the increase in unborrowed reserves which is exogenous to the model and functions as the variable reflecting monetary policy.[14]

F. Output Composition

This last block of equations explains various sector outputs (or output indexes) used elsewhere in the model. These include the service component of GNP, the tax-corrected output variable which affects business fixed investment, the manufacturing index of industrial production, as well as capacity and capacity-utilization in manufacturing.

3. POLICY MULTIPLIERS

In the preceding section we attempted to provide some flavor of the structure of MQEM, including a discussion of some of the most important equations. We also presented tabular information on the dynamic characteristics of individual equations. These results reveal both that the model has the potential of reacting strongly to policy-induced shifts in expenditure levels and interest rates, and that

[13] Personal income and GNP are, of course, simultaneously determined. But personal income —in this version of the model—results from subtracting profits, indirect business taxes, and so on, from GNP rather than from adding up income components. Thus the profit equation is crucial to the determination of functional income shares.

[14] In those ex ante forecasting circumstances in which we feel that the Fed may be concentrating on an interest rate policy we forecast by rendering the treasury bill rate exogenous and can thereby infer the change in unborrowed reserves needed to attain an interest rate target. See Section 5 below for a discussion of current research on the monetary sector of the model.

such policy shifts may very well produce a pattern of cyclical response in aggregate output. We can pursue these matters directly by considering the results of a number of simulation experiments designed to reveal the dynamic multiplier properties of the model. The experiments were conducted by first running a forty quarter control simulation, and then changing a "policy parameter" and re-running the simulation. The multiplier results shown in subsequent tables report the deviations from the control path for a number of endogenous variables, with the deviations normalized as explained below. In general, the multipliers are based on a control simulation of the period 1958. 1–1967. 4, a ten year period which begins with a high rate of unemployment (6.8 percent for the year 1958). Because of the nonlinearities in the model, we also ran a number of multiplier experiments based on a control simulation of the period 1964.

TABLE 7

MULTIPLIERS, FISCAL POLICY EXPERIMENT #1 (F1): NONDEFENSE GOVERNMENT PURCHASES $5 BILLION (CURRENT DOLLARS) ABOVE CONTROL

	Deviations From Control	Deviations From Control Normalized by ΔG						
Quarter	Government Purchases in 1958 Prices (ΔG)	GNP (1958 Prices)	GNP (Current Prices)	Consumption (1958 Prices)	Business Fixed Investment (1958 Prices)	Inventory Investment (1958 Prices)	GNP Deflator (1958=100)	Treasury Bill Rate (%)
		High Unemployment Rate Period (1958. 1–1967. 4)						
1	5.48	.78	.70	.07	0	−.26	−.02	−.00
2	5.44	1.39	1.32	.17	.04	.28	−.02	.00
3	5.39	1.69	1.36	.28	.13	.41	−.07	.00
4	5.32	1.91	1.87	.41	.23	.42	−.01	.02
5	5.27	2.09	2.11	.53	.32	.41	−.00	.02
6	5.22	2.20	2.26	.59	.39	.41	.00	.03
7	5.15	2.20	2.21	.59	.43	.39	−.01	.04
8	5.08	2.14	2.27	.60	.45	.31	.02	.04
9	4.99	2.02	2.21	.56	.44	.24	.03	.04
10	4.89	1.86	2.11	.53	.41	.15	.04	.04
11	4.77	1.67	2.00	.48	.35	.07	.06	.04
12	4.68	1.44	1.84	.40	.27	−.01	.07	.04
16	4.42	.70	1.31	.06	−.02	−.25	.11	.02
20	4.26	.76	1.46	.04	−.09	−.16	.12	.02
24	4.12	1.17	1.97	.19	.03	.02	.12	.04
28	3.90	1.25	2.26	.21	.19	.05	.15	.06
32	3.60	.96	2.31	.09	.04	−.05	.20	.07
36	3.29	.64	2.36	−.02	−.11	−.14	.24	.07
40	3.06	.52	2.48	−.10	−.21	−.12	.27	.09

(*Continued on next page*)

TABLE 7 (*continued*)

	Deviations From Control	Deviations From Control Normalized by ΔG						
Quarter	Government Purchases in 1958 Prices (ΔG)	GNP (1958 Prices)	GNP (Current Prices)	Consumption (1958 Prices)	Business Fixed Investment (1958 Prices)	Inventory Investment (1958 Prices)	GNP Deflator (1958=100)	Treasury Bill Rate (%)
		Low Unemployment Rate Period (1964. 1–1973. 4)						
1	4.79	.79	.83	.08	0	−.26	−.00	−.00
2	4.77	1.44	1.50	.22	.04	.28	−.01	.00
3	4.70	1.76	1.85	.33	.13	.43	−.01	.01
4	4.65	1.96	2.12	.44	.24	.44	−.01	.02
5	4.58	2.09	2.35	.49	.34	.44	.01	.03
6	4.48	2.16	2.50	.53	.41	.41	.02	.04
7	4.35	2.15	2.61	.54	.46	.39	.03	.05
8	4.19	2.07	2.68	.52	.49	.30	.06	.05
9	4.05	1.91	2.70	.48	.47	.21	.08	.06
10	3.87	1.72	2.72	.44	.43	.10	.12	.06
11	3.66	1.50	2.76	.38	.36	.01	.16	.06
12	3.47	1.22	2.76	.30	.26	−.10	.20	.05
16	2.86	.17	2.78	−.11	−.18	−.44	.37	.04
20	2.60	.12	3.28	−.22	−.36	−.31	.43	.05
24	2.39	.47	4.25	−.21	−.22	−.05	.50	.10
28	2.20	.25	4.67	−.41	−.18	−.03	.59	.14
32	1.94	−.44	5.05	−.71	−.42	−.18	.72	.17
36	1.77	−1.02	5.28	−1.03	−.70	−.25	.82	.20
40	1.64	−1.05	5.68	−1.11	−.78	−.15	.89	.25

1–1973. 4, a period which begins with a substantially lower (and declining) rate of unemployment (5.2 percent for the year 1964). By running the same policy experiment for both a high and low unemployment rate period we can determine the practical importance of the nonlinearities in the model; in a number of interesting cases we report both sets of results.

In the area of fiscal policy, we conducted the following three experiments:

F1: The control path of nondefense federal purchases was raised by 5 billion (current) dollars. The results are reported in Table 7. The first column contains the deviations, by quarter, for the real value of government purchases (ΔG) resulting from the 5 billion current dollar shift and the endogenous movements in the government purchase deflator. The other deviations in the table are normalized by dividing through by the deviations in real government purchases. The normalized deviations can thus be interpreted as dynamic multipliers per billion dollars of real government purchases. The upper half of Table 7 contains the multipliers for

TABLE 8

MULTIPLIERS, FISCAL POLICY EXPERIMENT #2 (F2): NONDEFENSE GOVERNMENT PURCHASES $5 BILLION (CURRENT DOLLARS) ABOVE CONTROL; TREASURY BILL RATE FIXED ON CONTROL PATH

	Deviations From Control Normalized by ΔG			
Quarter	GNP (1958 Prices)	Consumption (1958 Prices)	Business Fixed Investment (1958 Prices)	GNP Deflator (1958=100)
1	.78	.07	0	−.02
2	1.39	.17	.04	−.02
3	1.68	.28	.13	−.07
4	1.90	.41	.23	−.01
5	2.10	.54	.32	−.00
6	2.24	.62	.39	.00
7	2.30	.64	.44	−.00
8	2.30	.67	.47	.02
9	2.25	.67	.48	.03
10	2.17	.67	.46	.04
11	2.07	.66	.43	.06
12	1.92	.62	.37	.07
16	1.28	.38	.15	.12
20	1.08	.29	.05	.15
24	1.29	.35	.10	.17
28	1.56	.45	.20	.20
32	1.67	.51	.26	.25
36	1.62	.54	.24	.33
40	1.48	.52	.17	.42

the high unemployment period, the lower half reports results for the low unemployment period.

F2: This experiment repeats F1 with the exception that the path of the Treasury Bill Rate is forced to remain as in the control run. This can be interpreted as fiscal policy accompanied by an accomodating monetary policy which prevents the fiscal policy from inducing changes in interest rates which feed back on expenditures. The results for the high unempolyment period are contained in Table 8; the normalization is identical to that in F1.

F3: This experiment repeats F1 with the exception that the increase in nondefense government purchases is "financed" by a permanent 5 billion (current) dollar upward shift in the personal tax function. The results, for the high unemployment period, are presented in Table 9 and are normalized by dividing through by the 5 billion (current) dollar change in both expenditures and taxes.

TABLE 9

MULTIPLIERS, FISCAL POLICY EXPERIMENT #3 (F3): NONDEFENSE GOVERNMENT PURCHASES AND PERSONAL INCOME TAX STRUCTURE EACH $5 BILLION (CURRENT DOLLARS) ABOVE CONTROL

Deviations From Control Path Normalized by the $5 billion Change			
Quarter	GNP (1958 Prices)	GNP (Current Prices)	Consolidated Government Surplus (Current Prices)
High Unemployment Rate Period (1958. 1–1967. 4)			
1	.60	.51	.23
2	.96	.88	.37
3	.95	.67	.28
4	.90	.84	.34
5	.87	.83	.33
6	.85	.83	.33
7	.82	.79	.31
8	.76	.79	.31
9	.69	.74	.29
10	.60	.68	.27
11	.51	.62	.24
12	.41	.56	.23
16	.20	.40	.19
20	.29	.51	.24
24	.40	.67	.29
28	.37	.71	.30
32	.26	.69	.29
36	.18	.68	.29
40	.17	.71	.30

Considering first the results of experiment F1 (see Table 7), we find that the fiscal policy multiplier for real GNP rises from an impact magnitude of nearly 0.8 to a peak of about 2.2 in the seventh quarter and then declines through a damped cyclical path. The less than unitary impact multiplier is the result of "unintended" decumulation of inventories. The near doubling of the multiplier in the second quarter results primarily from two factors: a sharp turn-around in inventory investment and an increase in consumption as auto expenditures respond with a lag. These effects are virtually the same in both the high and low unemployment rate experiments. By the end of the second year, however, a noticeable difference begins to emerge in the form of significantly more inflation being generated in the low unemployment rate experiment. There are three principal effects of this higher rate of inflation, all of which tend, in MQEM, to reduce the growth of real expenditures and output. First, the nominal tax structure shifts real resources out of the private sector. Second, the higher rate of inflation leads to a shift in the distribution of income towards profits. Finally, with the path of unborrowed reserves unchanged and nominal expenditures rising, the ratio of unborrowed reserves to current dollar expenditures declines, with a consequent increase in interest rates.

A comparison of the multipliers estimated under experiments F1 and F2 reveals that an accomodating monetary policy has a substantial effect on the long-run fiscal policy multiplier (compare Tables 7 and 8). The basic fiscal policy experi-

TABLE 10

MULTIPLIERS, MONETARY POLICY EXPERIMENTS: TREASURY BILL RATE 50 BASIS POINTS BELOW CONTROL

Quarter	GNP (1958 Prices)	GNP (Current Price)	Consumption (1958 Prices)	Business Fixed Investment (1958 Prices)	GNP Deflator (1958=100)
Deviations from Control					
1	0	0	0	0	0
2	.18	.18	.11	.02	.00
3	.66	.71	.27	.07	.01
4	1.58	1.62	.74	.16	.00
5	3.20	3.30	1.64	.36	.01
6	5.22	5.43	2.54	.66	.02
7	7.07	7.13	3.41	1.06	− .02
8	7.98	8.40	3.53	1.54	.05
9	8.34	8.93	3.86	1.99	.07
10	8.40	9.13	4.02	2.34	.09
11	8.20	9.09	4.10	2.55	.12
12	7.81	8.80	4.10	2.63	.13
16	5.32	7.45	3.60	2.15	.35
20	3.33	6.30	2.98	1.58	.50
24	2.92	6.33	2.56	1.63	.56
28	3.23	6.99	2.42	1.97	.58
32	3.22	7.46	2.25	2.19	.61
36	2.68	7.40	1.95	2.21	.65
40	1.89	6.80	1.38	2.15	.66
Low Unemployment Rate Period (1964. 1–1973. 4)					
1	0	0	0	0	0
2	.30	.32	.27	.02	− .00
3	1.20	1.29	.90	.07	− .00
4	2.66	2.82	1.75	.20	− .02
5	4.13	4.47	2.35	.43	− .02
6	5.39	5.90	2.87	.76	− .02
7	6.49	7.17	3.42	1.15	− .01
8	7.47	8.41	4.00	1.54	.00
9	8.25	9.55	4.46	1.92	.03
10	8.61	10.40	4.62	2.24	.09
11	8.64	11.04	4.72	2.49	.17
12	8.44	11.56	4.77	2.65	.26
16	5.81	12.50	4.15	2.47	.79
20	2.81	11.43	3.06	1.78	1.10
24	1.55	11.07	2.27	1.52	1.25
28	1.30	11.09	1.64	1.66	1.26
32	1.07	11.05	1.21	1.81	1.22
36	.65	10.33	.74	1.80	1.14
40	1.03	9.33	1.09	1.62	.95

ment (F1) results in the multiplier for real GNP declining in the long run to about 1/2, compared with a value of nearly 1(1/2) when monetary policy is accomodating (F2).

The third fiscal policy experiment on which we report (F3) is an approximation to a marginally balanced budget multiplier. The results (see Table 9) indicate that a policy of matched increases in government purchases and the level of the personal tax structure is stimulative and also leads to a rising government surplus due to endogenous tax recovery. The (balanced budget) multiplier for real GNP reaches a peak slightly above 0.9 after half a year and then declines through a damped cycle.

In conjunction, experiments F1 and F2 reveal that monetary policy—or, more accurately, interest rate policy—has significant leverage on the dynamic path of MQEM. To obtain a more direct measure of the quantitative impact of monetary policy, we conducted an additional experiment in which we estimate the effects of following a policy that succeeds in maintaining the 90-day Treasury Bill Rate on a path 50 basis points below that in the control solution. Table 10 contains, for a number of key aggregates, the deviations from control corresponding to such an easing of monetary policy. The top half of Table 10 contains the results for the high unemployment period and the bottom half contains the results for the low unemployment period. The easing of monetary policy has no impact on GNP in the initial quarter and only minimal impact in the second quarter. This, of course, is to be expected given the structure of MQEM, where all interest rate effects are lagged at least one quarter. The effects on aggregate demand, however, gather steam and by the end of the second year constant dollar GNP is almost $8 billion above the level in the control solution. The increase in real GNP reaches a peak of close to $8.5 billion in about two and a half years before declining in a damped cyclical fashion to its long-run value. As in earlier experiments, this stimulative policy generates considerably more inflation in a period already characterized by low unemployment rates. The extra dose of induced inflation, which begins to have a noticeable effect after two years, retards the growth of real output—in the manner already discussed in connection with experiment F1—and thus reduces the stimulative effect of the policy.

4. FORECASTING BEHAVIOR

A number of simulation experiments have been carried out to test the ex post forecasting properties of MQEM. These tests involved both static, or single-quarter, forecasts and dynamic, or multi-quarter, forecasts. In the latter case we experimented with relatively short simulations in which the forecasting horizon varied from two to eight quarters, and also with a longer run simulation spanning the entire period 1961. 1–1970. 4. Table 11 contains root mean squared error statistics relating to expost forecasting with MQEM over the period 1961. 1–1970. 4. In all cases these forecasting experiments use the model exactly as fitted, and the actual values of all exogeneous variables are used throughout.

The one-quarter forecasts are static forecasts in which the model is re-initialized

TABLE 11

ROOT MEAN SQUARED ERRORS FOR EX POST FORECASTS OF 1961. 1–1970. 4

Variables	Length of Forecast Horizon (In Quarters)						Full Period Simu-lation
	1	2	3	4	6	8	
Gross National Product (Billions of 58$'s)	2.74	3.35	4.23	5.24	6.44	6.94	9.02
Consumption (" " ")	1.93	2.39	3.05	3.46	3.78	3.71	4.37
Business Fixed Investment (" " ")	1.27	1.52	1.59	1.72	1.91	2.17	3.66
Residential Construction (" " ")	.74	1.09	1.37	1.44	1.31	1.43	1.67
Inventory Investment (" " ")	2.42	2.52	2.60	2.80	3.08	2.98	3.16
Imports (" " ")	.76	.98	1.15	1.27	1.47	1.56	1.69
Change in GNP (" " ")	2.74	3.48	3.91	4.44	4.82	3.88	3.74
Gross National Product (Billions of current Dollars)	2.95	3.71	4.88	6.37	7.77	8.22	10.52
Change in GNP (" " ")	2.95	3.78	4.50	5.60	5.38	3.95	3.99
Personal Income (" " ")	1.95	2.79	3.70	4.45	5.20	5.29	8.61
Corporate Profits (" " ")	1.90	2.48	3.17	3.77	4.76	5.58	6.62
GNP Deflator (1958=100.0)	.15	.19	.26	.33	.60	.97	2.17
Treasury Bill Rate (%)	.23	.25	.29	.33	.37	.27	.51
Unemployment Rate, Males 20 and over (%)	.17	.29	.35	.40	.49	.53	.58

each quarter so that actual values of lagged endogenous variables are always used in generating the one-period forecasts. Within this framework, the model is not permitted to compound its own forecasting errors. This is a somewhat artificial situation; but the results provide a useful benchmark from which to form an initial judgement about the adequacy of the model. It is apparent from these results that at least within this context the model operates well as a simultaneous unit. Real GNP is forecast with a root mean squared error (RMSE) of $2.7 billion, while in current prices the RMSE of GNP is just under $3 billion. On the basis of root mean squared error, unemployment rates are predicted within two-tenths of a percentage point, short-term interest rates within twenty-five basis points, and prices within two-tenths of a point on deflators scaled as 1958 = 100. It is not surprising, though it is comforting, that the model produces very small errors in one period forecasts. Beyond this, however, the extent to which the model can stay on track while generating its own lagged endogenous variables is of extreme importance. It is to be expected that forecasting accuracy will diminish as the time span of a forecast lengthens, but a model must "hold on" well for at least six to eight quarters if it is to be of any use as a vehicle for serious short-term forecasting and policy analysis.

Two-quarter forecasts are obtained by permitting the model to generate its own lagged endogenous variables for the second quarter of the forecast. The model first forecasts 1961. 1 and 1961. 2, using its own forecast of 1961. 1 as lagged "data" for the forecast of 1961. 2. The model is then re-initialized as of 1961. 1 and forecasts 1961. 2 and 1961. 3; the process is repeated through 1970.

3–1970. 4. In this fashion a time series of forecasts for 1961. 2–1970. 4 is obtained, with each being a two-quarter-ahead forecast. Table 11 contains the error statistics for these two-quarter dynamic forecasts. An analogous procedure was carried out for three-, four-, six-, and eight-quarter-ahead forecasts, with the results shown in Table 11. The final column in the table contains the error statistics for a single dynamic simulation of the entire 1961. 1–1970. 4 period.

The results of these multi-period forecasting experiments indicate that errors in predicting the level of real GNP and similar magnitudes do tend to cumulate as the forecasting horizon lengthens. This error build-up is not nearly so serious, however, with respect to *quarterly changes* in GNP, in either current or constant prices. As the forecasting horizon lengthens the model continues to reflect accurately the pace of economic activity as measured by *quarterly changes* in GNP. The same is true for most of the components of changes in GNP although these results are not presented in the table. It is important to understand how a short-term model such as MQEM can be characterized by a dynamic forecasting path in which errors in predicting the level of GNP tend to cumulate while the accuracy of the path of predicted quarterly changes shows little deterioration as the forecasting horizon lengthens. This simply reflects the fact that MQEM contains a preponderance of autoregressive effects in the explanation of most key endogenous variables. The dynamic behavior of the model is dominated by the phasing in of distributed lag response patterns and reactions to changing levels of exogenous variables; it is thus a rather complicated rate-of-change predictor.

The experiments reported on in this and the preceding section of the paper should be considered only a small part of the process of validating the model for use in the RSQE's ex-ante forecasting program. The greater the number and difficulty of tests which a model can be considered to have passed, the greater can be the confidence in the output of that model. We are currently conducting a more extensive series of tests—both inside and outside the sample period—designed to reveal further aspects of the model's strengths and weaknesses. Our judgement and experience is that MQEM is currently a valuable tool for use in ex ante forecasting and policy analysis, but a large menu of items designed to improve the model's usefulness and performance is also being accumulated as a result of our continuing testing. In the concluding section we shall sketch some of the more important aspects of our current research efforts in connection with the model.

5. CONCLUDING COMMENTS

There are a great many experiments which can and ought to be conducted on an econometric model in the process of attempting to "validate" that model for specific uses.[15] In Sections 3 and 4 we reported the results of a small number of important experiments; and we have conducted many others which space limi-

[15] For useful discussions of this issue, along with procedural suggestions, see [1], [14].

tations prevent us from discussing here, including attempts to simulate particular historical episodes such as cyclical turning points, high and low inflation periods, and so on. Beyond the results already discussed in some detail, we can at least tentatively draw the following additional conclusions from our experiments with MQEM: First, the model provides no evidence in support of the hypothesis that the American economy is subject to a self-perpetuating endogenous business cycle. The model quite clearly responds to exogenous shocks—whether policy-induced or not—by exhibiting a cyclical response mechanism. But the cyclical mechanism is highly damped and the model will not produce a sustained cyclical path in non-stochastic simulations with "smooth" exogenous variables.[16] Second, the model tends—in simulating historical episodes—to display a dynamic behavior which is less extreme than actual history. That is, periods of recession, high inflation, rapid growth, etc., are clearly reflected in the corresponding dynamic simulations, but generally with less amplitude (lower magnitude) than actually took place. To the extent that such episodes are generally to be regarded as aberrations, as breaks in the normal behavior of the system, the behavior of the model is understandable and, indeed, even appropriate. A model should neither be expected to forecast unique behavior patterns nor to have its estimated parameter values dominated by such episodes.[17]

In addition to tests designed to validate MQEM we also have a number of research efforts underway designed to expand the capabilities of the model itself. Under the direction of our colleague Professor Robert Holbrook a new monetary sector has been constructed and is now going through a series of tests and will shortly be incorporated into MQEM. We are also developing a six-sector disaggregation of output, employment and wage income as well as a three-sector disaggregation of business fixed investment with a consistent and interrelated treatment of both capital and labor demands. We also have begun the construction of a number of industry models and regional models designed to interact with MQEM in a meaningful way. A model of the furniture industry is near completion and econometric models of the State of Michigan and the automotive industry are underway. Finally, work is continuing on studies of optimal economic policy using MQEM as the principal experimental vehicle (see [5]).

As a final general point, we would like to emphasize a fact which our ex ante forecasting activity continually impresses upon us. No econometric model is any more than a tentative statement about the economy's interactive logic and it can never contain any more information than was fed into it in the process of construction. In many forecasting and policy uses this information is simply inadequate, and in some cases new events impinge on the economy which—even if only temporarily—break the logic which has been deduced from past events. Even if we had a model whose every error statistic was at least 50 percent less than those shown in Table 11, it would still take an economist who watches

[16] We judge this to be a basic conclusion which is also supported by the findings of the recent NBER Conference on Econometric Models of Cyclical Behavior [4].

[17] We can, of course, hope in the longer run to find more regularity to model in what we may now consider unique or aberrant episodes.

what goes on in the economy to communicate with the model and make sensible use of it for real-time forecasting and policy purposes.

University of Michigan

REFERENCES

[1] DHRYMES, PHOEBUS J., et al., "Criteria For Evaluation of Econometric Models," *Annals of Economic and Social Measurement*, I (July, 1972), 291-324.

[2] FISHER, FRANKLIN M., "The Choice of Instrumental Variables in the Estimation of Economy-Wide Econometric Models," *International Economic Review*, VI (September, 1965), 245-274.

[3] FRIEDMAN, MILTON, "The Role of Monetary Policy," *American Economic Review*, LVIII (March, 1968), 1-17.

[4] HICKMAN, BERT G., ed., *Econometric Models of Cyclical Behavior*, Bureau of Economic Research, Studies in Income and Wealth No. 36, (New York: National Bureau of Economic Research, 1972).

[5] HOLBROOK, ROBERT, "A Practical Method for Controlling A Large Nonlinear Stochastic System," *Annals of Economic and Social Measurement*, III (January, 1974), pp. 155–175.

[6] HYMANS, SAUL H., "The Inflation-Unemployment Trade-Off: Theory and Experience," in W.L. Smith and R.L. Teigen, eds., *Readings in Money, National Income, and Stabilization Policy*, 3rd edition (Homewood, Ill.: Richard D. Irwin, 1974), 160-174.

[7] ———, "Prices and Price Behavior in Three U.S. Econometric Models," in O. Eckstein, ed., *The Econometrics of Price Determination Conference*, October 30–31, 1970 (Washington, D.C.: Board of Governors of the Federal Reserve System, 1972).

[8] ——— AND HAROLD T. SHAPIRO, "The DHL-III Quarterly Econometric Model of the U.S. Economy," Research Seminar in Quantitative Economics, The University of Michigan, Ann Arbor, (1970).

[9] ——— AND ———, "The Michigan Quarterly Econometric Model of the U.S. Economy," in *The Economic Outlook for 1973*, (March, 1973), Research Seminar in Quantitative Economics, The University of Michigan.

[10] JORGENSON, DALE W., "Anticipations and Investment Behavior," in J. Duesenberry, et al., eds., *The Brookings Quarterly Econometric Model of the United States* (Chicago: Rand McNally & Co., 1965).

[11] LIPSEY, RICHARD G., "The Relation Between Unemployment and the Rate of Change of Money Wage Rates in the United Kingdon, 1862-1957, A Further Analysis," *Economica*, XXVII (February, 1960), 1-31.

[12] PERRY, GEORGE L., "Changing Labor Markets and Inflation," *Brookings Papers on Economic Activity*, III (1970), pp. 411–441.

[13] PHELPS, EDMUND S., "Phillips Curves, Expectations of Inflation and Optimal Unemployment Over Time," *Economica*, XXXIV (August, 1967), 254-281.

[14] SHAPIRO, HAROLD T., "Is Verification Possible? The Evalution of Large Econometric Models," *Journal of Agricultural Economics*, LV (May, 1973), 250-258.

[15] SUITS, DANIEL B., "Forecasting and Analysis with an Econometric Model," *American Economic Review*, LII (March, 1962), 104-132.

12

THE WHARTON LONG TERM MODEL: INPUT-OUTPUT WITHIN THE CONTEXT OF A MACRO FORECASTING MODEL

By R. S. Preston[1]

1. INTRODUCTION

Macro econometric model construction, although treating the underlying determinants of demand and income, has emphasized less the determinants of industry production and output. Most econometric models including the Wharton Model [**11**], the OBE Model [**10**], the MPS Model [**1**], the Michigan Model [**7**], and the Fair Model [**4**] lack detailed systematic treatment of the production sector. This does not imply the above mentioned econometric models have treated these areas in a way inadequate for their purpose. Models of income determination used for short term forecasting and policy analysis should emphasize the demand and income side; however longer term projections (5 to 10 years) are more interesting if industry detail becomes available for analysis.

Input-output data, although scarce compared to the availability of national income and product data, are an inportant source of industry detail that can be used to construct links between the demand side and production side of a macro model. These data provide a consistent accounting framework tracing the flow of intermediate inputs through the economy and the final delivery configuration which results. A static transactions table provides the detail needed to trace intermediate inputs and intermediate outputs at a given point in time. Translating the transactions table to a direct requirements coefficient table provides a first cut at a technical description of the intermediate inputs required to produce a given product. The inverse coefficient matrix provides an assessment of the impact that compositional shifts in final demand have on output levels, assuming the technical specifications for input configurations remain constant. An important aspect of modern input-output analysis is the development of techniques to model the adjustment of input coefficients in response to changing price and technology. Imbedding a flexible input-output table in a macro model framework is a further step that should be taken. This will result in a disaggregated general equilibrium framework making it possible to trace economic interplay between industrial sectors.

Providing a general equilibrium framework as a vehicle for policy analysis of longer run issues is important. Tracing the impact of alternative policies directly to demand categories is only a first step. Input-output in a macro

[1] The results reported in this paper are part of a continuing effort to design and construct a large scale macro econometric model to make detailed long run simulations of the U.S. economy. Many useful comments have resulted from discussions with L. R. Klein, B. G. Hickman, G. R. Schink and M. D. McCarthy.

framework can provide a highly structured and systematic way to trace the impact of alternative policies to a disaggregated level within the context of a general equilibrium framework.

The unique feature of the Wharton Long Term Annual and Industry Forecasting Model is the fully imbedded 63 sector input-output table.[2] However, the remaining structural detail has not been neglected. Traced out in summary form in Figure 1 are the major blocks and causal flows of the model. Driving the input-output sector are 49 final demand categories including 11 consumption equations and 29 fixed capital formation equations (disaggregated by industry).[3] Important also in the input-output sector are sectoral prices which aid in gauging the impact of price induced input substitution. The labor requirements sector is disaggregated by industry and includes 21 manufacturing and 6 non-manufacturing production functions. Labor requirements are obtained by renormalizing the production functions[4] on labor (or manhours)

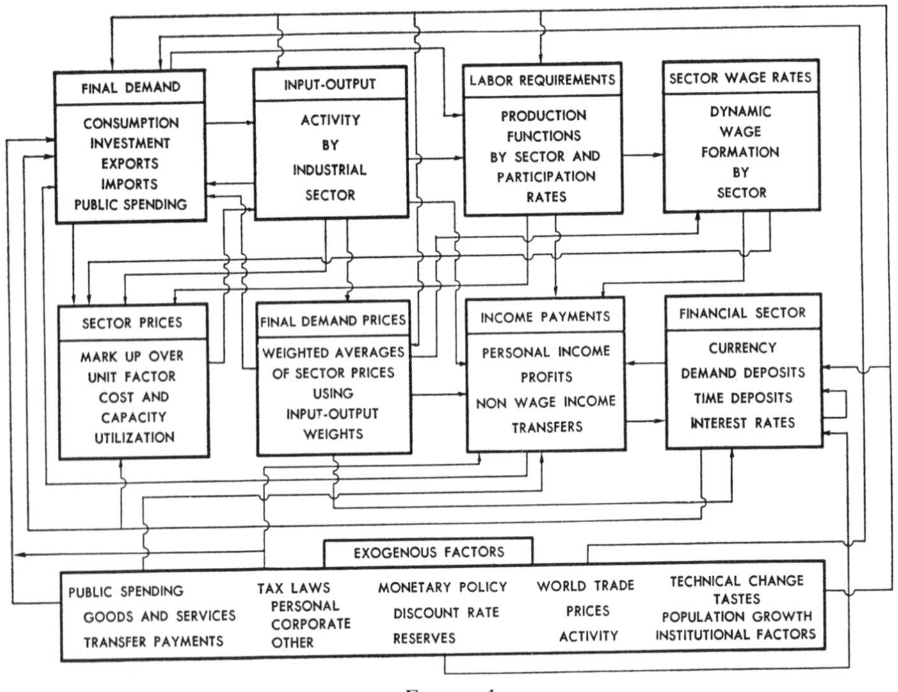

FIGURE 1

FLOW CHART OF THE WHARTON ANNUAL AND INDUSTRY FORECASTING MODEL

2 For a formal discussion of an earlier version of this model see Preston [**13**].

3 The investment functions are neoclassical in structure with output, price and user cost as major inputs. Estimation of polynomial lag distributions are used to assess the most appropriate dynamic response pattern. For a summary of the technique used see Preston [**13**].

4 Cobb-Douglas [**3**] production functions are estimated assuming cost minimization in equilibrium using a three step procedure. Separation of the speed of adjustment of manhours from that of employment is used to explain variations in weekly hours.

with capital stock, output and technical change remaining as right hand side variables.

The wage equations include not only Phillips Curve effects in the short run, but also lead/lag relationships between the various industrial sectors within the economy. Industries such as steel, autos, electrical machinery, petroleum, chemicals and textiles appear to be leaders, possibly because of strong unions setting the magnitude and tone of wage settlements. Followers appear insensitive to labor market conditions relying on results obtained in the heavily unionized sectors. Leaders appear to depend not only on cost of living indicators, but also on labor market conditions.

Elements of the production function, including the side conditions necessary for efficient factor use, form the basis for price determination at the industrial level. Mark-up over both unit labor cost and unit capital cost, capacity utilization variables and an assessment of long run dynamics provide the ingredients for price determination. Final demand prices are developed using the column problem from input-output theory. Sector input coefficients are used to weight sector prices to determine market prices for final demand categories. To close the system a demographic sector, a financial sector and various income identities are also included.

Moderately successful attempts have been made by Fisher, Klein and Shinkai **[5]**, Kresge **[9]**, Preston **[13]** and McCracken **[12]** in using input-output tables within a macro framework. These early attempts suggest that the use of input-output in a macro model framework requires treatment of both technical change and price induced substitution among industry inputs. Early efforts have not treated these problems directly, but have dealt with them through models of error adjustment. Results from Project LINK by Hickman and Lau **[6]**, which deal with the problem of changing coefficients in international trade share matrices, are directly applicable to a modified input-output framework resulting in direct treatment of the problem of coefficient change and price induced input substitution. In what follows we treat in detail the input-output sector of the model.

2. THE INPUT-OUTPUT SECTOR

Following the argument of Hickman and Lau **[6]** for each final spending category (g_j) assume a CES quantity index,

$$g_j = [\sum_{i=1}^{n} c_{ij} y_{ij}{}^{(\sigma_j - 1)/\sigma_j}]^{\sigma_j/(\sigma_j - 1)} \,. \tag{1}$$

σ_j is the elasticity of substitution between the net output (y_{ij}) of any two industries for the j-th final spending category. From the results of Armington **[2]**, cost minimizing quantities of output produced to satisfy a given level of final spending (g_j) are then

$$y_{ij} = c_{ij}^{\sigma_j} g_j^* \left(\frac{P_{ij}^y}{P_j^{g*}} \right)^{-\sigma_j} , \tag{2}$$

and

$$P_j^{g^*} = [\sum_{i=1}^{n} c_{ij}^{\sigma_j} P_{ij}^{y(1-\sigma_j)}]^{1/(1-\sigma_j)} \tag{3}$$

is a price index of the j-th final spending category where P_{ij}^y are sector output prices.

It follows that

$$P_j^{g^*} g_j^* = \sum_{i=1}^{n} P_{ij}^y y_{ij} = G_j \tag{4}$$

where G_j is the current dollar value of the j-th final spending category. The individual sectoral output demand funtions (2) are then written as

$$y_{ij} = c_{ij}^{\sigma_j} G_j P_{ij}^{y-\sigma_j} P_j^{g^*(\sigma_j-1)} . \tag{5}$$

In the base period, all prices are set equal to unity. Since

$$g_j \equiv \sum_{i=1}^{n} y_{ij} \tag{6}$$

then

$$y_{ij}^0 = c_{ij}^{\sigma_j} [\sum_{i=1}^{n} y_{ij}^0] = c_{ij}^{\sigma_j} g_j^0 , \tag{7}$$

where g_j^0 is base year final spending. Now, the ratio in the base year of the i-th industries net output to the j-th category of final spending is

$$c_{ij}^0 = y_{ij}^0 / g_j^0 = c_{ij}^{\sigma_j} . \tag{8}$$

Using (5) and (8) we obtain

$$y_{ij} = c_{ij}^0 G_j P_{ij}^{y-\sigma_j} P_j^{g*(\sigma_j-1)} \tag{9}$$

$$P_j^{g^*} = [\sum_{i=1}^{n} c_{ij}^0 P_{ij}^{y(1-\sigma_j)}]^{1/(1-\sigma_j)} . \tag{10}$$

Using (6), (9) can be rewritten as

$$G_j = g_j [\sum_{i=1}^{n} c_{ij}^0 P_{ij}^{y(1-\sigma_j)}] [\sum_{i=1}^{n} c_{ij}^0 P_{ij}^{y-\sigma_j}]^{-1} . \tag{11}$$

Using (11) and (9) we obtain

$$y_{ij} = c_{ij}^0 P_{ij}^{y-\sigma_j} [\sum_{k=1}^{n} c_{kj}^0 P_{kj}^{y-\sigma_j}]^{-1} g_j . \tag{12}$$

Linearizing (12) in the P_{ij}^y's by a Taylor series expansion around $P_{ij}^y = 1$ for all i and j gives the result

$$y_{ij} = c_{ij}^0 g_j + c_{ij}^0 g_j (-\sigma_j)(P_{ij}^y - 1) - c_{ij}^0 g_j (-\sigma_j) [\sum_{k=1}^{n} c_{kj}^0 (P_{kj}^y - 1)] . \tag{13}$$

Since $\sum_{k=1}^{n} c_{kj}^0 \equiv 1$, (13) reduces to

(14) $$y_{ij} = c_{ij}^0 g_j - \sigma_j(P_{ij}^y - \sum_{k=1}^{n} c_{kj}^0 P_{kj}^y) c_{ij}^0 g_j \, .$$

If we define the final spending price index,

$$P_j^g = \sum_{k=1}^{n} c_{kj}^0 P_{kj}^y \, ,$$

as a base year weighted average of industry sector prices, then (14) can be written as

(15) $$y_{ij} = c_{ij}^0 g_j - \sigma_j(P_{ij}^y - P_j^g) c_{ij}^0 g_j \, .$$

Note that since

$$\sum_{i=1}^{n} c_{ij}^0 = 1$$

and

$$P_j^g = \sum_{k=1}^{n} c_{kj}^0 P_{kj}^y$$

from (15) we obtain

$$\sum_{i=1}^{n} y_{ij} = g_j \, ,$$

independent of the choice of σ_j. If we linearize y_{ij} in terms of g_j around g_j^0, then

(16) $$y_{ij} = c_{ij}^0 g_j - \sigma_j y_{ij}^0 (P_{ij}^y - P_j^g) \, .$$

(16) gives a relationship between final spending and industry output which explicitly includes the effect of price induced input substitution.

Allowing for the partial adjustment hypothesis[5]

(17) $$y_{ij} = \delta_j y_{ij}^* + (1 - \delta_j)(y_{ij})_{-1} \, , \qquad 0 < \delta_j < 1 \, ,$$

assuming the original CES quantity index (1) to be a function of time, and assuming that P_{ij}^y is invariant with respect to final demand categories, Hickman and Lau [**6**] have obtained the following result which we use for purposes of estimation,

(18) $$y_{ij} - c_{ij}^0 g_j = -(\sigma_j y_{ij}^0 \beta_{ij}) - \sigma_j(1 - \delta_j) y_{ij}^0 (P_i^y - P_j^g) - \sigma_j y_{ij}^0 \alpha_{ij} t + \delta_j (y_{ij} - c_{ij}^0 g_j)_{-1} \, .$$

3. DATA

The data needed to estimate the coefficients of (18) are in part available from published sources and in part must be constructed. Estimates of P_i^y are directly

[5] Data used for purposes of estimation are not necessarily derived from a system in equilibrium, but one tending toward equilibrium.

observable as net output deflators by industry. Data on g_j are directly available from the national income accounts. Given an estimate of c^0_{ij}, the P^g_j are computed as

$$\sum_{i=1}^{n} \hat{c}^0_{ij} P^y_i = P^g_j \,. \tag{19}$$

A major effort is the derivation of data for c^0_{ij} and time series data on y_{ij}. Preston [**13**] has shown that the matrix $\{c^0_{ij}\}$ can be obtained as

$$\{c^0_{ij}\} = (I - A)^{-1} BH \,, \tag{20}$$

where A is the direct requirements matrix, B is a diagonal matrix (the elements on the main diagonal are the ratio of net value added to gross output, $b_{jj} = 1 - \sum_{i-1}^{n} a_{ij}$, $j = 1 \ldots n$) and H is a matrix which gives the percentage distribution of final deliveries for given final spending categories. Note that $\{c^0_{ij}\}$ is not necessarily a square matrix (it has as many rows as industries and as many columns as final spending categories.)

The 1963 Input-Output Table (13) gives an estimate of $\{c^0_{ij}\}$ (included are 63 industrial categories and 49 final demand categories). Once data for c^0_{ij} are obtained for year 1963, given data on the marginal totals g_j and $y_{i\cdot}$ where $y_{i\cdot}$ is real value added by industry (data directly available from the national income accounts), we assume for each year that the following will hold

$$y_{i\cdot} = \sum_{j=1}^{m} c_{ij} g_j \qquad \text{and} \qquad \sum_{i=1}^{n} c_{ij} = 1 \,. \tag{21}$$

Using a matrix balancing technique, estimates of $\{c^t_{ij}\}$ for years other than 1963 are derived.[6] With these estimates we can construct estimates of y^t_{ij} as $c^t_{ij} g^t_j$ for as many years as we have estimates of $\{c_{ij}\}$. This procedure is applied using the 1963 input-output table as a starting estimate. Estimates of y_{ij} are computed for the period 1952–1971.

4. REGRESSION RESULTS

Using a pooled time series cross section technique, regression estimates for the parameters of (18) are developed under the assumption that σ_j are invariant with respect to i. These pooled regressions are restricted to insure that the sum of the intercepts and trend coefficients for each final demand category equals zero, respectively. This preserves adding up,

$$\sum_{i=1}^{n} y_{ij} = g_j \,, \quad j = 1 \ldots m \,.$$

For each of 49 final demand categories a regression is computed pooling data for

[6] For a description of the general technique used see Kresge [**9**]. The iterative method provides for a choice of c^k_{ij} (c_{ij} at the k iteration) which minimizes $\sum_{j=1}^{n} (c^k_{ij} - c^{k-1}_{ij})^2$ subject to the constraint $\sum_{j=1}^{n} c^k_{ij} g_j = y_i$.

TABLE 1

ESTIMATES OF $\sigma_j(1 - \delta_j)$ AND δ_j BY FINAL SPENDING CATEGORY CONSUMPTION

Period of fit 1953–1971

	δ_j	$\sigma_j(1 - \delta_j)$
Autos and parts	.2688 (8.825)	−.1150 (.435)
Furniture and fixtures	.0137 (25.343)	−.3124 (4.291)
Other durable goods	.4648 (16.252)	−.0747 (2.103)
Food and beverages	.1139 (3.748)	−.5233 (13.639)
Clothing and shoes	.7041 (26.675)	−.3467 (9.123)
Gasoline and oil	.5380 (21.257)	−.2874 (10.973)
Other nondurables	.7603 (33.822)	−.3457 (8.774)
Housing services	.6413 (26.723)	−4.4268 (25.574)
Household operating services	.9407 (65.530)	−.6471 (11.962)
Transportation services	.9015 (80.034)	*
Other services	.6455 (24.695)	−.1276 (1.139)

* Obtained wrong sign or not significant.
Values in parentheses are t ratios.

each of 63 industries to obtain estimates of $\sigma_j(1 - \delta_j)$, δ_j and 63 trend and 63 intercept coefficients, one for each industry in the pool.

Tables 1 through 6 include selected results from all those obtained which represent a small fraction of the total number of coefficients estimated using the pooled cross section-time series constrained regression technique. However, these results bring out the important points. Tables 1, 2 and 3 give estimates of the speed of adjustment δ_j and the short run elasticity of substitution $\sigma_j(1-\delta_j)$ for each of 49 final demand categories.

In all cases but one the speed of adjustment δ_j is highly significant and falls between 0 and 1. For consumption goods the elasticity of substitution is negative. For one consumption category (transportation services) an insignificant coefficient is obtained and because of this, within the context of the general model, we suppress the coefficient and recompute the regression. For investment goods the substitution elasticity in many cases is either insignificant or of the wrong sign. This is the predominant result within manufacturing. For cases within manufacturing where we do obtain a statistically significant estimate of the substitution elasticity with the right sign, the estimates are close to 0. How-

TABLE 2

ESTIMATES OF $\sigma_j(1 - \delta_j)$ AND δ_j BY FINAL SPENDING CATEGORY
INVESTMENT

Period of fit 1953–1971

	δ_j	$\sigma_j(1 - \delta_j)$
Farm	.6469 (45.354)	*
Mining	.6098 (29.210)	−.0479 (3.728)
Primary iron and steel	.5969 (42.269)	*
Nonferrous metals	.5602 (31.531)	*
Electrical machinery	.7436 (38.361)	*
Nonelectrical machinery	.6755 (30.354)	*
Motor vehicles	.6629 (29.557)	−.0641 (1.858)
Aircraft	.7336 (31.972)	*
Other transport equipment	.7503 (40.614)	*
Stone, clay and glass	.5413 (20.607)	−.0273 (3.169)
Fabricated metals	.7364 (39.621)	*
Lumber	.4594 (14.749)	−.0503 (8.488)
Furniture	.6771 (31.431)	*
Instruments	.7020 (32.326)	*
Ordnance and miscellaneous	.7425 (25.549)	*
Food and beverage	.6786 (36.959)	*
Textile	.6203 (40.818)	*
Paper	.6481 (27.781)	*
Chemicals	.6789 (41.163)	*
Petroleum	.8127 (37.703)	−.0805 (1.482)
Rubber	.6847 (31.096)	*
Tobacco	.6501 (27.048)	*

(*Continued on next page*)

TABLE 2 (*Continud*)

Period of fit 1953–1971		
	δ_j	$\sigma_j(1 - \delta_j)$
Apparel	.7160 (35.524)	*
Leather	.6782 (28.677)	*
Printing and publishing	.6303 (26.161)	*
Transportation	.6421 (31.962)	*
Utilities	.9661 (61.794)	−.1541 (3.779)
Communications	.5498 (22.255)	−.6809 (14.963)
Commercial and other	.5407 (20.759)	−.5794 (6.374)

* Obtained wrong sign or not significant
Values in parentheses are *t* ratios

TABLE 3

ESTIMATES OF $\sigma_j(1 - \delta_j)$ AND δ_j BY FINAL SPENDING CATEGORY INVENTORIES, EXPORTS, IMPORTS, GOVERNMENT SPENDING

Period of fit 1953–1971		
	δ_j	$\sigma_j(1 - \delta_j)$
Inventories	.2769 (8.829)	*
Exports	.2321 (6.809)	−.5025 (5.825)
Imports	1.0251 (69.452)	−.2775 (3.056)
Federal nondefense	.5070 (18.611)	*
Federal defense	.7193 (35.873)	*
State and local-education	.6564 (26.884)	−.1041 (2.243)
State and local-health and welfare	.7112 (29.945)	−.0651 (4.660)
State and local-safety	.5305 (19.707)	−.1043 (11.503)
State and local-other	.8219 (59.266)	−.0156 (.466)

* Obtained wrong sign or not significant
Values in parentheses are *t* ratios

TABLE 4

SIGNIFICANT TREND COEFFICIENTS $(\alpha_{ij}\ \sigma_j)$* FINAL SPENDING ON FOOD AND BEVERAGE BY CONSUMERS

Period of fit 1953–1971

Industry	$\alpha_{ij}\sigma_j$
Farm	−.4563 (27.172)
Crude petroleum and natural gas	−.0122 (2.284)
Food and kindred products	−.0256 (4.535)
Paper and allied products	.0125 (2.346)
Chemicals	.0148 (2.736)
Railroads	−.1404 (18.942)
Motor freight	.0724 (12.464)
Telephone and telegraph	.0126 (2.362)
Electric, gas, water and sanitary	.0082 (1.537)
Wholesale trade	.3792 (27.778)
Retail trade	.0176 (2.264)
Real estate	.0315 (5.674)
Miscellaneous business services	.0322 (5.945)
Auto repair	.0129 (2.424)
Government industry	.0092 (1.727)

* Trend coefficients with nonsignificant t values are excluded from this list. However, they have been included in the pooled regression to preserve adding up. Values in parentheses are t ratios.

ever, for utilities, communications and commercial, we find considerably larger estimates of the elasticity. In comparing the results for consumption and investment goods with the remaining categories of final demand we find the following. The elasticity of substitution for both exports and imports appears with the right sign. For inventories we obtain an insignificant coefficient. The Federal sector shows very little price induced input substitution while the state and local sector shows significant price induced input substitution in the areas of education, health, welfare and safety.

These results suggest the following. Given a CES quantity index of final

TABLE 5

SIGNIFICANT TREND COEFFICIENTS $(\alpha_{ij}\sigma_j)$* FINAL SPENDING ON PLANT AND EQUIPMENT BY IRON AND STEEL

Period of fit 1953–1971	
Industry	$\alpha_{ij}\sigma_j$
Contract construction	−.0003 (14.213)
Primary iron and steel	−.0001 (5.446)
Nonelectrical machinery	.0003 (17.344)
Electrical machinery	.0001 (4.885)

* Trend coefficients with nonsignificant t values are excluded from this list. However they have been included in the pooled regression to preserve adding up. Values in parentheses are t ratios.

spending, the output demand functions which result, after assuming cost minimizing behavior on the part of producers in the delivery of a specific market basket of goods, yield estimated input substitution elasticities for consumption goods that are higher than for investment goods. The final demand categories of the consumer sector can be viewed as 11 different market baskets of goods. Producers wish to deliver these goods to the market place at minimum cost. Knowing input requirements, including the possibilities for substitution of inputs in the production of these goods, producers will respond by choosing input combinations which minimize cost for given market baskets. Our results suggest that producers have more flexibility in choosing inputs to satisfy consumption demand than they have in choosing inputs to satisfy investment demand. These remarks must be interpreted in light of the fact that the investment demand categories are more homogeneous than the consumption categories. We find that the remaining categories of final demand are more analogous to consumption than to investment. It appears that the character of producers' goods is more rigidly defined than the character of consumers' goods. Input requirements for producers' goods appear less malleable than input requirements for consumers' goods.

Tables 4, 5 and 6 include selected results for trend coefficients for three separate final demand categories. In each case trend coefficients with non-significant values are excluded from the reported list. However, these non-significant trend coefficients have been included in the pooled regression to preserve adding up. These results give an indication of the magnitude and direction of coefficient movement, independent of price induced input substitution. These movements should be associated with long run trends in technical change or changing tastes.

For the consumer demand category, food and beverages, we find a number of

TABLE 6

SIGNIFICANT TREND COEFFICIENTS ($\alpha_{ij}\ \sigma_j$)* FINAL SPENDING OF FURNITURE AND HOUSEHOLD EQUIPMENT BY CONSUMERS

Period of fit 1953–1971

Industry	$\alpha_{ij}\sigma_j$
Textile mill products	−.0045 (2.408)
Rubber and Plastic	.0037 (2.218)
Lumber	−.0036 (2.093)
Furniture and Fixtures	−.0231 (11.561)
Stone, clay and glass	−.0038 (2.221)
Primary iron and steel	−.0062 (3.638)
Fabricated metal products	−.0049 (2.875)
Electrical machinery	.0806 (18.000)
Miscellaneous manufacturing	−.0034 (2.006)
Railroads	−.0058 (2.902)
Retail trade	−.0153 (4.470)
Miscellaneous business service	.0039 (2.297)

* Trend coefficients with nonsignificant t values are excluded from this list. However, they have been included in the pooled regression to preserve adding up. Values in parentheses are t ratios.

significant coefficients with interesting connotations. The switch from rail transport to motor freight transport, in the agricultural sector, is evident from the declining trend coefficient for rail, contrasted with the increasing trend coefficient for motor freight. Increased fertilizer input in food production is evidenced by the positive trend coefficient for chemicals. The revolution in food packaging accounts for the positive trend coefficient associated with paper and allied products. The increased role of the middle man in food distribution is apparent in the declining coefficients associated with the farm and food processing sector, contrasted with increasing coefficients associated with the wholesale and retail trade sectors.

Consider the results of Table 5. Of 63 coefficients, only 4 are significant (contract construction, primary iron and steel, non-electrical machinery and electrical machinery). The added level of technology used in steel production

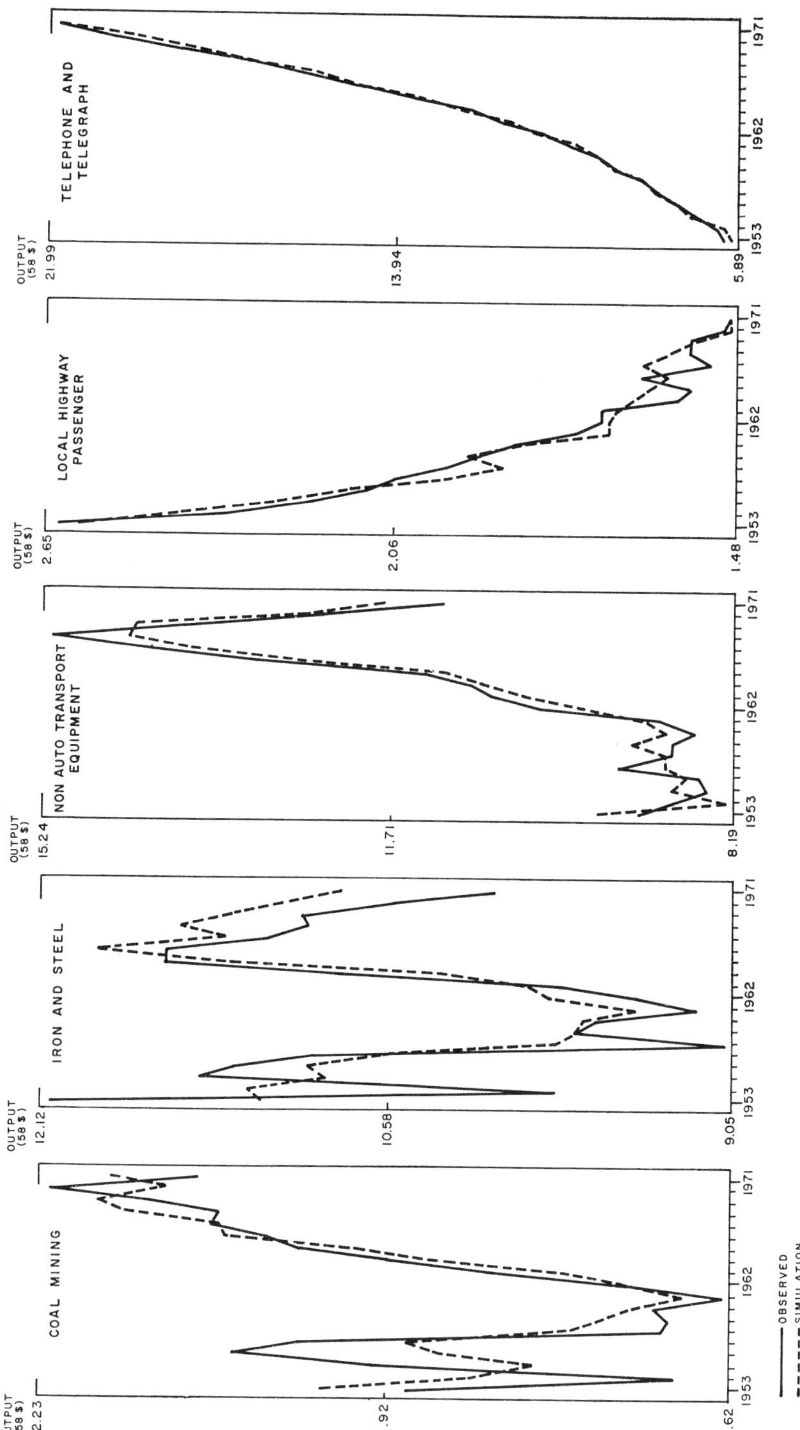

FIGURE 2
SELECTED SIMULATION RESULTS

(oxygen furnaces and continuous casting) has led to the machinery sector's playing a larger role in satisfying investments demand of the steel industry.

Returning to the consumer goods sector, examine the results of Table 6. The decline of almost all sector coefficients but electrical machinery and rubber and plastic products, is evidence of the explosion in electrical appliances for the home during the period 1952–1971. The increased use refrigeration, air conditioning and television is both the result of changing tastes and technology.

5. MULTIPLIER ANALYSIS AND SUBSYSTEM SIMULATION

We now turn to the simulation of the input-output subsystem and an analysis of the multiplier properties of the complete system. In simulating the output conversion sector of the model as a subsystem, we treat as exogenous final spending (g_j) and sector prices (P_i^y). Selected simulation results are recorded in Figure 2. These are representative of the general movements found throughout the 63 sectors. They are representative of areas where changing technology has been important in altering input requirements. Simulation results track changes in observed output, for both cycle and trend, quite closely.

A partial indication of the properties of the complete system are revealed in Tables 7–10. Thirteen separate multiplier calculations are set forth. Both the initial impact and long run response to variations in major policy variables are recorded. Results obtained for solutions (1)–(3) and (5)–(7) make an interesting comparison. The latter deals with corporate tax changes while the former deals with spending. A crowding out effect appears in solution (2) with both the impact on consumption and investment reduced in the long run. The reduction from the level of initial impact through time suggests that fiscal policy in the long run is ineffective. The crowding out effect is in direct contrast to the pattern for solutions (5)–(7). The pattern of little initial impact with a monotonic buildup results directly from the long lag distributions introduced in the investment sector and the detailed breakout of policy handles used in the derivation of the user cost variables. Note also that two thirds of the effect falls in the investment sector. The long run pattern for corporate tax policy is in direct contrast to the results obtained for personal tax policy. Here, most of the effect accrues to the consumption sector with the full effect building up by the second year. There appears to be little evidence of crowding out.

The results, obtained for the discount rate and nonborrowed reserve simulations, imply a pattern of monotonic buildup for investment, but at the expense of crowding out consumption. For investment, there is a monotonic buildup from the initial shock; however for consumption, the impact appears to be reduced after the third year.

The net effect of the thirteen policy scenarios on manufacturing output is recorded in Table 10. All of the dynamic patterns are similar to those obtained for aggregate GNP. It is interesting to note that proportionately more activity is generated in the manufacturing sector through the manipulation of corporate tax parameters, whereas manipulation of personal tax and monetary parameters

TABLE 7

WHARTON LONG TERM MODEL—MULTIPLIER ANALYSIS: GROSS NATIONAL PRODUCT

Solution ΔGNP	(1) +	(2) +	(3) +	(4) +	(5) +	(6) −	(7) −	(8) −	(9) +	(10) −	(11) −	(12) −	(13) +
Year													
1	1.38	1.98	.70	1.74	.07	.08	.15	3.70	4.83	2.29	.77	1.11	.96
2	1.42	1.91	.71	1.82	.25	.22	.53	6.07	5.07	3.29	.79	4.45	2.75
3	1.30	1.46	.64	1.59	.41	.35	.88	5.48	4.78	2.65	.72	4.90	3.04
4	1.26	1.22	.70	1.53	.57	.50	1.22	6.06	5.32	2.98	.80	3.64	2.25
5	1.36	1.20	.82	1.66	.77	.69	1.66	6.89	6.31	3.64	.97	2.42	1.48

Solution
(1) Change in real federal purchases by one billion dollars (goods only).
(2) Change in real federal purchases by one billion dollars (goods and services).
(3) Change in federal transfer payments by one billion dollars.
(4) Change in exports by one billion dollars.
(5) Change in investment tax credit by 50 basis points.
(6) Change in the effective corporate tax rate by 50 basis points.
(7) Change in depreciation tax lives by 10%.
(8) Change in the effective personal tax rate by 100 basis points.
(9) Change in the value of the standard deduction by 100 dollars.
(10) Change in the social insurance tax rate by 50 basis points.
(11) Change in the social insurance taxable base by 500 dollars.
(12) Change in the discount rate by 25 basis points.
(13) Change in non-borrowed reserves by one billion dollars.

TABLE 8

WHARTON LONG TERM MODEL—MULTIPLIER ANALYSIS: CONSUMPTION

Solution ΔC	(1) +	(2) +	(3) +	(4) +	(5) +	(6) −	(7) −	(8) −	(9) +	(10) −	(11) −	(12) −	(13) +
Year													
1	.33	.86	.60	.55	.02	.04	.05	4.11	4.14	1.96	.66	.49	.42
2	.41	.92	.65	.67	.08	.10	.17	5.45	4.60	2.81	.71	2.62	1.62
3	.36	.65	.62	.57	.14	.15	.29	5.40	4.59	2.61	.70	3.21	1.92
4	.33	.44	.65	.51	.19	.21	.41	5.90	4.94	2.84	.74	2.47	1.45
5	.37	.36	.72	.53	.26	.28	.56	6.48	5.55	3.26	.85	1.49	.82

Solution
(1) Change in real federal purchases by one billion dollars (goods only).
(2) Change in real federal purchases by one billion dollars (goods and services).
(3) Change in federal transfer payments by one billion dollars.
(4) Change in exports by one billion dollars.
(5) Change in investment tax credit by 50 basis points.
(6) Change in the effective corporate tax rate by 50 basis points.
(7) Change in depreciation tax lives by 10%.
(8) Change in the effective personal tax rate by 100 basis points.
(9) Change in the value of the standard deduction by 100 dollars.
(10) Change in the social insurance tax rate by 50 basis points.
(11) Change in the social insurance taxable bases by 500 dollars.
(12) Change in the discount rate by 25 basis points.
(13) Change in non-borrowed reserves by one billion dollars.

TABLE 9

WHARTON LONG TERM MODEL—MULTIPLIER ANALYSIS: INVESTMENT

Solution Δi	(1) +	(2) +	(3) +	(4) +	(5) +	(6) −	(7) −	(8) −	(9) −	(10) −	(11) −	(12) −	(13) +
Year													
1	.14	.24	.13	.28	.05	.04	.11	.69	.85	.40	.14	.23	.19
2	.15	.22	.12	.30	.18	.13	.38	1.12	.87	.61	.13	.97	.60
3	.11	.09	.09	.24	.29	.22	.64	.74	.66	.36	.10	1.20	.81
4	.12	.05	.10	.26	.42	.32	.90	.72	.80	.41	.12	1.26	.88
5	.15	.05	.13	.31	.57	.46	1.24	.78	.98	.56	.15	1.52	1.07

Solution
- (1) Change in real federal purchases by one billion dollars (goods only).
- (2) Change in real federal purchases by one billion dollars (goods and services).
- (3) Change in federal transfer payments by one billion dollars.
- (4) Change in exports by one billion dollars.
- (5) Change in investment tax credit by 50 basis points.
- (6) Change in the effective corporate tax rate by 50 basis points.
- (7) Change in depreciation tax lives by 10%.
- (8) Change in the effective personal tax rate by 100 basis points.
- (9) Change in the value of the standard deduction by 100 dollars.
- (10) Change in the social insurance tax rate by 50 basis points.
- (11) Change in the social insurance taxable base by 500 dollars.
- (12) Change in the discount rate by 25 basis points.
- (13) Change in non-borrowed reserves by one billion dollars.

TABLE 10

WHARTON LONG TERM MODEL—MULTIPLIER ANALYSIS: MANUFACTURING OUTPUT

Solution y_m	(1) +	(2) +	(3) +	(4) +	(5) +	(6) −	(7) −	(8) −	(9) +	(10) −	(11) −	(12) −	(13) +
Year													
1	.47	.69	.24	.68	.03	.03	.07	1.42	1.76	.84	.28	.46	.40
2	.47	.64	.23	.69	.12	.09	.25	1.63	1.72	1.02	.27	1.66	1.12
3	.41	.46	.20	.59	.19	.15	.40	1.28	1.53	.73	.23	1.77	1.17
4	.40	.39	.21	.57	.25	.21	.54	1.44	1.70	.82	.25	1.16	.80
5	.45	.41	.26	.64	.34	.29	.72	1.77	2.08	1.08	.32	.69	.51

Solution
- (1) Change in real federal purchases by one billion dollars (goods only).
- (2) Change in real federal purchases by one billion dollars (goods and services).
- (3) Change in federal transfer payments by one billion dollars.
- (4) Change in exports by one billion dollars.
- (5) Change in investment tax credit by 50 basis points.
- (6) Change in the effective corporate tax rate by 50 basis points.
- (7) Change in depreciation tax lives by 10%.
- (8) Change in the effective personal tax rate by 100 basis points.
- (9) Change in the value of the standard deduction by 100 dollars.
- (10) Change in the social insurance tax rate by 50 basis points.
- (11) Change in the social insurance taxable bases by 500 dollars.
- (12) Change in the discount rate by 25 basis points.
- (13) Change in non-borrowed reserves by one billion dollars.

have a proportionately greater effect in the nonmanufacturing sector. We would expect this result for corporate tax parameter variation, but the relative importance to, and impact on, the manufacturing sector of personal tax parameter and monetary policy variation is not as clear a priori.

Wharton EFA, Inc., Philadelphia

REFERENCES

[1] ANDO, ALBERT, "Equations in the MIT-PENN-SSRC Econometric Model of the United States," (mimeographed), University of Pennsylvania (January, 1973).

[2] ARMINGTON, P. S., "A Theory of Demand for Products Distinguished by Place of Production, "*International Monetary Fund Staff Papers*, XVI (March, 1969), 159-176.

[3] DOUGLAS, P. H., "Are There Laws of Production?" *American Economic Review*, XXXVIII (March, 1948), 1-41.

[4] FAIR, R. C., *A Short-Run Forecasting Model of the United States Economy* (Lexington, Mass.: D.C. Heath, 1970).

[5] FISHER, F. M., L. R. KLEIN, AND Y. SHINKAI, "Price and Output Aggregation in the Brookings Econometric Model," in J. S. Duesenberry, *et al.*, eds., *The Brookings Quaterly Econometric Model of the United States* (Chicago: Rand McNally and Co., 1965), 653-679.

[6] HICKMAN, B. G. AND L. J. LAU, "Elasticities of Substitution and Export Demands in a World Trade Model," paper prepared for the European Meeting of the Econometric Society, Budapest, (1972).

[7] HYMANS, S. H. AND H. T. SHAPIRO, *The DHL-III Quarterly Econometric Model of the U.S. Economy*, Research Seminar in Quantitative Economics, The University of Michigan, (1970).

[8] INPUT-OUTPUT STRUCTURE OF THE U. S. ECONOMY: 1963, Transactions Data for Detailed Industries, I (Washington, D. C.: U. S. Department of Commerce, 1969).

[9] KRESGE, D. T., "Price and Output Conversion: A Modified Approach," in J. S. Duesenberry, *et al.*, eds., *The Brookings Model: Some Further Results* (Chicago: Rand McNally and Co., 1969), 85-108.

[10] LIEBENBERG, M., A. A. HIRSCH, AND J. POPKIN, "A Quarterly Econometric Model of the United States: A Progress Report," *Survey of Current Business*, XLVI (May, 19966), 13-20.

[11] MCCARTHY, M. D., "The Wharton Quarterly Econometric Forecasting Model: MARK III. Studies in Quantitative Economics," No. 6, Economics Research Unit, Department of Economics, University of Pennsylvania, (1972).

[12] MCCRACKEN, M. D., "An Overview of Candide Model 1.0," Economic Council of Canada, Ottawa, (1972).

[13] PRESTON, R. S., "The Wharton Annual and Industry Forecasting Model," Economics Research Unit, Department of Economics, University of Pennsylvania, (1972).

13

THE HICKMAN-COEN ANNUAL GROWTH MODEL: STRUCTURAL CHARACTERISTICS AND POLICY RESPONSES

BY BERT G. HICKMAN, ROBERT M. COEN AND MICHAEL D. HURD[1]

1. INTRODUCTION

THIS PAPER DISCUSSES THE STRUCTURE and properties of the Hickman-Coen Annual Model of the U.S. economy. The model is designed to make conditional projections of the annual time paths of the major aggregative variables—actual and potential GNP; labor force, employment and unemployment; wages and prices—10 or more years into the future, under alternative assumptions about government policies and demographic and technological trends. It therefore incorporates those variables and processes which are most important for determining the movement of the economy over the long run, rather than emphasizing the minor (inventory-cycle) characteristics which primarily affect short-run stability.

The model combines elements of the Keynesian and neo-classical approaches to the determination of actual and potential output. The neo-classical strands are evident in the derivation of the factor demand equations from marginal productivity conditions incorporating relative factor prices and in the use of an explicit production function for potential output. The Keynesian constituents include an income-expenditure framework for the determination of effective demand in real terms and a specification that links the real and monetary sectors through interest rates. Money wages are proximately determined by changes in labor demand and wage expectations on a wage-adjustment hypothesis, whereas prices depend directly on long-run average cost and a markup which varies with the degree of capacity utilization.

The model is fitted to annual observations for the sample period 1924–40 and 1949–66. Where significant structural change has occurred, separate functions are estimated for prewar and postwar periods. It is a nonlinear system with a high proportion of logarithmic behavioral functions. The present version contains about 50 stochastic equations and 70 endogenous variables.

The principal novelties of the model include the introduction of interrelated demand functions for labor and capital; discrimination among concepts of potential, full employment, and capacity output; an integrated cost, production, and pricing framework; a long-run housing model featuring economic-demographic interactions in a disequilibrium framework; and an approach to wage determination utilizing elements of the search theory of unemployment rather than the Phillips curve approach commonly found in macroeconomic models.

[1] The authors gratefully acknowledge the assistance of Paul M. Harrigan, Andrea Kusko and Anthony K. Lima in preparing the computations for this paper. The research was supproted by the National Science Foundation under Grant No. GS41684.

We begin with a brief structural description of the model, pass on to an evaluation of ex-post prediction errors, and conclude with some multiplier analyses of fiscal and monetary policies in the short and long runs. The error and multiplier analyses are confined to the period after World War II. Similar studies of the prewar period will be reported in a later publication, together with ex-ante growth projections and other applications.

2. STRUCTURE OF THE MODEL

An overview of the model is presented in Table 1, which lists the principal equation blocs and endogenous variables. The first five blocs comprise the system of final demand equations, in which the principal arguments are real output and disposable personal income, relative prices, and interest rates. For given prices and interest rates, the income-expenditure loop is closed by the output, income, and tax-transfer blocs. Thus the first eight blocs together are basically a rather sophisticated and disaggregated version of the textbook multiplier-accelerator model. In itself this truncated system is inadequate for growth analysis, since it neglects supply constraints except in the housing sector.

The remainder of the model incorporates such constraints as they affect the growth of labor force, capital stock, potential output, and money supply. Real and monetary constraints are not treated as impenetrable ceilings, however, but rather as supply factors which interact with demand to determine the evolution of prices, production and employment.

Manpower constraints are modelled in the employment and labor force bloc, which contains equations for labor force participation and hours of work as functions of real wages, employment, and population. The labor input bloc consists entirely of a demand function for man-hours, with output and factor prices as the principal arguments. Together, these two blocs determine labor force, employment, unemployment, and hours worked as functions of population, output, and prices.

As mentioned earlier, wage changes depend primarily on changes in labor demand and wage expectations and prices are obtained as a variable markup on long-run average total cost. The money bloc contains a supply and demand model of the commercial banking sector to determine the money stock and Treasury bill rate as well as a term-structure model to relate short- and long-term interest rates. Finally, the utilization bloc contains equations to determine several measures of aggregate resource utilization. One or more feedback relations connects these blocs with each other and with the income, expenditure and employment system already described.

The foregoing overview of the model as a system built up from blocs incorporating the income and expenditure sides of the national accounts, production and employment relations, wage and price determination, and monetary factors is revealing in some aspects but not in others. In particular, it fails to highlight the unified view of firms' decision processes which connects the investment, employment, production and price equations. Enough space is available

TABLE 1

BLOC STRUCTURE OF HICKMAN-COEN MODEL

Bloc	Principal Endogenous Variables
1. CONS (Consumption)	1. Expenditures on automobiles; other durable goods; nondurable goods; services.
2. INV (Business investment)	2. Gross business fixed investment; stock of fixed business capital; inventory investment; inventory stock.
3. HOUS (Housing and residential construction)	3. Rent; nonfarm households; stock of nonfarm dwelling units; occupancy ratio; nonfarm housing starts; value per nonfarm housing start; residential construction expenditure.
4. GOVT (Government purchases of goods and services)	4. State and local government purchases of goods and services.
5. FORT (Foreign Trade)	5. Imports; exports.
6. OUT (Output)	6. GNP in current and constant prices; gross private nonresidential product in current and constant prices.
7. INC (Incomes)	7. Gross corporate profits; dividends; labor income; national income; personal income; disposable personal income.
8. TXTR (Taxes and transfers)	8. Unemployment compensation; unemployment contributions; contributions to social insurance; federal personal taxes; federal corporate taxes; indirect business taxes.
9. LBIN (Labor-input)	9. Private man-hours.
10. EMLF (Employment and labor force)	10. Labor force participation rate; average hours; labor force; employment; unemployment.
11. WAGE (money wages)	11. Change in aggregate wage rate.
12. PRIC (Product prices)	12. Implicit price deflators for: GNP; gross private nonresidential product; 12 final demand sectors.
13. MONY (Money stock and interest rates)	13. Currency; demand deposits; time deposits; commercial paper rate; average Moody's corporate bond rate.
14. UTIL (Resource utilization)	14. Levels and rates of utilization of capacity output; labor-optimizing output; full employment output; potential output. Full employment labor force; average hours at full employment; man-hours at full employment.

to summarize these relationships and also to comment on two other distinguishing features of the model—the wage equation and the housing sector—before turning to the simulation results.

2.1. *The production and factor demand functions.* Our approach stresses the interdependence of firms' decisions on labor and capital inputs. Imperfect competition is assumed in product markets, with product price set as a markup on average cost. For given product prices, output is demand-determined in the short run. Firms base their employment and investment decisions on output and factor prices in order to minimize production costs. The algebraic framework is as follows.

The production function is Cobb-Douglas:

$$(1) \qquad X_t = Ae^{\gamma t}(k_t K_{t-1})^{\alpha}(m_t M_t)^{\beta}, \qquad A, \alpha, \beta, \gamma > 0$$

where X_t is real output, k_t is an index of intensity of utilization of capital, K_t is observed capital stock in constant dollars at the end of period t, m_t is an index of intensity of utilization of labor, M_t is observed labor input in man-hours, and technical progress is assumed at the exponential rate γ. Under stationary[2] conditions, the measured inputs K_{t-1} and M_t would be fully adjusted to the desired or optimum levels K_t^* and M_t^*, and hence $k_t = k^* = 1$ and $m_t = m^* = 1$, where k^* and m^* are the long-run or normal utilization intensities. In the short-run, however, expectations lags and adjustment costs may cause k_t and m_t to diverge from normal, in which case the effective capital and labor inputs are $k_t K_{t-1}$ and $m_t M_t$.

Taking factor prices and output as exogenous insofar as investment and employment decisions are concerned, solution of the intertemporal cost minimization problem subject to (1) yields the following expressions for the desired inputs at normal intensities:

$$(2) \qquad M_t^* = \left[\left(\frac{\alpha}{\beta}\right)^{-\alpha} A^{-1}\right]^{(1/\alpha+\beta)} \left[\left(\frac{Q}{W}\right)_t^*\right]^{\alpha/(\alpha+\beta)} (X_t^*)^{1/(\alpha+\beta)} e^{-(\gamma/\alpha+\beta)t}$$

$$(3) \qquad K_t^* = \left[\left(\frac{\alpha}{\beta}\right)^{\beta} A^{-1}\right]^{(1/\alpha+\beta)} \left[\left(\frac{Q}{W}\right)_t^*\right]^{-\beta/(\alpha+\beta)} (X_t^*)^{1/(\alpha+\beta)} e^{-(\gamma/\alpha+\beta)t}.$$

In these expressions, the expected ratio of the rental price of capital (an implicit rental rate) to the money wage is denoted by $(Q/W)_t^*$ and the expected (long-run) output by X_t^*. Firms may not adjust immediately to variations in desired inputs, however, owing to adjustment costs. These costs are not explictly modelled, but are represented indirectly by the following partial adjustment hypotheses:

$$(4) \qquad \frac{M_t}{M_{t-1}} = \left(\frac{M_t^*}{M_{t-1}}\right)^{\lambda_1} \qquad 0 < \lambda_1 \leq 1$$

$$(5) \qquad \frac{K_t}{K_{t-1}} = \left(\frac{K_t^*}{K_{t-1}}\right)^{\lambda_2} \qquad 0 < \lambda_2 \leq 1.$$

Combining (2) and (4) with (3) and (5) yields our short-run factor demand functions:

$$(6) \quad M_t = \left\{\left[\left(\frac{\alpha}{\beta}\right)^{-\alpha} A^{-1}\right]^{(1/\alpha+\beta)} \left[\left(\frac{Q}{W}\right)_t^*\right]^{\alpha/(\alpha+\beta)} (X_t^*)^{(1/\alpha+\beta)} e^{-(\gamma/\alpha+\beta)t}\right\}^{\lambda_1} (M_{t-1})^{1-\lambda_1}$$

[2] The qualification is in order because the normal intensity indexes consistent with growth equilibrium exceed unity, as explained in [6].

$$(7) \quad K_t = \left\{ \left[\left(\frac{\alpha}{\beta} \right)^{\beta} A^{-1} \right]^{(1/\alpha+\beta)} \left[\left(\frac{Q}{W} \right)_t^* \right]^{-(\beta/\alpha+\beta)} (X_t^*)^{(1/\alpha+\beta)} e^{-(\gamma/\alpha+\beta)t} \right\}^{\lambda_2} (K_{t-1})^{1-\lambda_2}.$$

Finally, expected factor prices and expected output are specified as weighted geometric averages of current and past levels of those variables, with weights determined by the data.

As explained in [**5**], equations (6) and (7) were estimated jointly and constrained to yield unique values for the production parameters (α, β and γ) common to both derived demand functions. In the version of the model used herein, the parameters α and β were also constrained to yield constant returns to scale. Thus the production function itself is not directly estimated, but instead is inferred from the estimated factor demand equations. This formulation has two properties which are highly desirable in a long-run model. First, since the factor demand equations share the same production parameters, the growth rates of the inputs cannot diverge from the appropriate values to maintain a viable production relationship as output grows even over long time spans. Second, the factor demand functions allow for capital-labor substitution over the long-run in response to changes in relative factor prices.

2.2. *The capacity and labor utilization indexes.* In the model, capacity is a cost-based concept referring to the output that would be produced if the existing capital stock were operated with the optimal input of labor for existing techniques and factor prices. Solution of the long-run cost minimization problem with both capital and labor as variable factors yields the following expression for capacity output:

$$(8) \qquad X_t^c = A \left(\frac{\beta}{\alpha} \right)^{\beta} e^{\gamma t} \left[\left(\frac{Q}{W} \right)_t^* \right]^{\beta} (K_{t-1})^{\alpha+\beta}.$$

Expression (8) may also be obtained by substituting actual for desired capital stock in equation (3) and solving for output. It can be shown that X_t^c is the point on the long-run average cost curve for a firm with a capital stock of size K_{t-1}.

We define an index of capacity utilization as the ratio $(X/X^c)_t$, where X is actual and X^c is capacity output. This utilization ratio may be used to correct measured capital stock in the production function (1) for variations in intensity of use. In particular, it is shown in [**6**] that

$$(9) \qquad k_t = \left(\frac{X}{X^c} \right)_t^{(1/\alpha+\beta)}.$$

An analogous index for labor input can be constructed by conceiving of labor as the limiting factor and inverting equation (2) to yield the expression for labor-optimizing output:

$$(10) \qquad X_t^m = A \left(\frac{\beta}{\alpha} \right)^{-\alpha} e^{\gamma t} \left[\left(\frac{Q}{W} \right)_t^* \right]^{-\alpha} (M_t)^{\alpha+\beta}.$$

This leads to an index of labor utilization which can be used to correct measured man-hours in the production function:

$$m_t = \left(\frac{X}{X^m}\right)_t^{1/(\alpha+\beta)} . \tag{11}$$

Empirical estimates of production functions often use exogenous indexes of capacity utilization to correct capital stock for cyclical variations in the effective input of capital services, and similar adjustments are occasionally made for labor input. The novelty in our approach is that our indexes of capacity and labor utilization are inferred endogenously from the observed behavior of firms in adjusting measured inputs to the desired levels for long-run equilibrium. For a full discussion of these concepts and their rationale, the reader may consult [**6**].

2.3. *Potential and full-employment output.* We distinguish between two measures of output at full employment of the labor force. Potential is defined as that output which could be produced with existing technology if the full employment supply of man-hours were combined with the existing capital stock irrespective of cost considerations, and hence it is estimated from the production function. In contrast, full-employment output is related to costs and is defined as the output which would have to be demanded in order to induce entrepreneurs to hire the full employment labor supply at existing factor prices. For either concept, the "full employment" supply of man-hours is calculated from equations for average hours and labor force participation on the conventional assumption that full employment occurs when four per cent of the labor force is unemployed.

The equation for full employment output is obtained by solving the labor demand function (6) for output and substituting current full-employment man-hours (M^f) for actual man-hours:

$$X_t^f = A\left(\frac{\beta}{\alpha}\right)^{-\alpha}\left[\left(\frac{Q}{W}\right)_t^*\right]^{-\alpha} e^{\gamma t}(M_t^f)^{(\alpha+\beta)/\lambda_1}(M_{t-1})^{-((1-\lambda_1)(\alpha+\beta)/\lambda_1)} . \tag{12}$$

Potential output is determined from the production function (1) by inserting full employment man-hours and measuring both labor and capital inputs at their normal utilization intensities k^* and m^*:[3]

$$X_t^p = Ae^{rt}(k^*K_{t-1})^{\alpha}(m^*M_t^f)^{\beta} . \tag{13}$$

We base the estimate of potential output on the normal rates of capacity and labor utilization so that it changes over time only when available factor supplies and technology change, rather than varying from year to year as factors are used more or less intensively.

For details on labor force participation and average hours the reader is referred to [**3**] and [**4**]. The concepts of potential and full-employment output are

[3] As noted above, k^* and m^* exceed unity for a growing economy. The values of k^* and m^* are established by the method set forth in [**6**].

fully discussed in [**6**].

2.4. *Costs and prices,* We employ a variant of the markup hypothesis of price setting. Firms are assumed to base price on an estimate of normal or long-run average total cost,[4] but may vary the markup according to current demand pressures as measured by the rate of capacity utilization. Average cost is derived explicitly from the production function and factor prices by use of the following identity:

$$AC_t = A_0(Q_t)^{\alpha/(\alpha+\beta)}(W_t)^{\beta/(\alpha+\beta)}(X_t)^{(1-(\alpha+\beta))/(\alpha+\beta)}e^{-\gamma/(\alpha+\beta)t}\,. \tag{14}$$

The markup hypothesis is

$$\mu_t = \mu_0\left(\frac{X}{X^c}\right)_t^{\delta}. \tag{15}$$

Combining equations (14) and (15) and assuming partial adjustment of actual to desired price at the rate ε, yields the price equation:

$$P_t = \mu_0^{\varepsilon}\left(\frac{X}{X^c}\right)_t^{\delta\varepsilon}(AC)_t^{\varepsilon}(P_{t-1})^{1-\varepsilon}\,. \tag{16}$$

Equation (16) is used to predict the implicit price deflator for aggregate output in the model. Sectoral deflators for the various components of GNP are then linked to the aggregate deflator in auxiliary equations which also include capacity utilization and trend variables as proxies for systematic forces affecting relative prices.

2.5. *The wage equation.* The common justification for the Phillips curves which are found in most macroeconomic models is that wage changes depend on the excess demand for labor and that the unemployment rate is a proxy for excess demand. In our model it is specified that firms set wages in order to achieve the manpower level which minimizes costs of production. If manpower on hand is less than desired, firms will raise wages so that few or workers will quit and more job searchers will accept job offers. The wage increase necessary to achieve a particular manpower target depends on the perceived distribution of money wages, upon the pool of unemployed and upon the real wage: if people think that money wages are generally high, firms will have to offer high wages to reduce quits and increase job acceptances; if many people are unemployed, the flow into employment will be high given a fixed probability that each job searcher will accept employment; the real wage affects the flow into and out of the labor force and, therefore, affects the firms' wage offers. From these considerations a model is developed in which the level of money wages depends on the expected money wage, the difference between desired and actual man-hours, the ratio of the unemployed to the employed, and the expected real wage. To explain expected wages, adaptive expectations are assumed, but it is found

[4] As Hymans has shown [**11**], in the Cobb-Douglas case a markup on average total cost is formally equivalent to a markup on unit labor cost.

that expectations on the rate of change of wages rather than on the level of wages fit the data better.

The theory, estimation technique and results may be found in [**10**]; however, since the findings differ substantially from the findings of other researchers, they will be briefly summarized. The estimated equation is an equation in the rate of change of wages. The difference between desired and actual manhours is found to have considerable effect on wage changes; the unemployment rate has a modest and transitory effect. It appears, therefore, that there is no long-run relationship between wage inflation and unemployment, at least none that could be discovered in the single equation estimates. It still might be found, of course, that in complete model simulations something like a Phillips curve for wages or prices will be traced out; however, as will be seen later in this paper, the complete model solutions indicate only a temporary and rapidly diminishing tradeoff between unemployment and price inflation.

2.6. *Household formation and residential construction.* The housing sector is another example of specification for long-run analysis in the model. Most recent econometric work on the sector has concentrated on the short-term fluctuations of residential construction in the postwar economy, and there is a general concensus that the contra-cyclical pattern of home construction is due to variations in credit conditions. This factor finds a place in our model, since new housing starts depend partly on credit availability to builders, as proxied by a variable measuring the spread between short and long-term interest rates. We are more concerned, however, with the factors governing the long-run trends of household formation, the housing stock, and new construction. The current demand for dwelling space is a function of population and its age distribution, the ratio of housing rent to the consumer price index, and real income. The short-run supply depends on the standing stock of dwelling units and the same price ratio. Together demand and supply determine the occupancy rate (ratio of nonfarm households to dwelling units) and rental level on the existing housing stock, with due allowance for market disequilibrium. These variables in turn affect the flow of new housing starts, along with external cost determinants. Current starts augment the stock of dwelling units in the next period, which in turn affects occupancies and rents, and so on. Thus, in the long-run the housing stock depends on population and income growth, but the stock-adjustment process involves complex interactions between the housing market and construction industry and is subject to lengthy lags.

The submodel for housing includes four behavioral equations to determine respectively the number of households, the rent level, housing starts, and the average value per housing start. Several identities are necessary to define the dollar volume of new residential construction and to relate the number and value of new housing starts to the stock of dwelling units and its value in constant dollars. The complete housing model has been documented and simulated in [**8**] and [**9**].

3. PREDICTION ERRORS

The builder of a long-run model faces something of a dilemma when it comes to evaluation of forecast error. His model is designed primarily with an eye for its growth or trend properties, and yet part of the evidence on which the model may be judged is its tracking ability over the sample period. In our case, the parameters of the model were estimated on data spanning the Great Depression, the Korean and Vietnam Wars, and several peacetime cycles of varying severity. Moreover, the annual time unit, while entirely appropriate for a long-run model, permits only a crude approximation to the short-term dynamics of the business cycle. Despite these circumstances real GNP was predicted with an average error of 2.1 per cent during the postwar portion of the sample period (1951–1966) and of 2.4 per cent during the post-sample years 1967–1972. Both figures are for complete dynamic simulations with initial conditions beginning respectively in 1951 and 1967.

Comparable error statistics are shown for the components of real GNP and several other variables of interest in Table 2. The error in the implicit GNP

TABLE 2

PREDICTION ERRORS FOR DYNAMIC SIMULATIONS

Variable	RMSE[a]		RMSE/MEAN[b]	
	1951–66	1967–72	1951–66	1967–72
GNP	9.6	27.1	2.0	2.8
Real GNP	10.0	17.6	2.1	2.4
Real consumption	4.9	8.1	1.6	1.7
Real business fixed investment	4.0	3.6	8.2	4.7
Real residential construction	2.7	3.8	12.6	15.2
Real inventory investment	2.9	5.1	67.2	95.8
Real state and local purchases	0.8	2.8	1.9	3.8
Real exports	0.9	2.0	3.3	3.9
Real imports	0.8	2.2	3.4	4.6
Implicit price deflator (1958=100)	2.7	4.7	2.7	3.6
Civilian labor force	0.5	2.1	0.7	2.6
Employment	1.1	1.4	1.6	1.8
Unemployment rate (per cent)	1.1	1.1	22.2	24.8
Wage rate	0.1	0.2	2.3	6.1
Labor income	6.1	30.8	2.3	5.9
Corporate profits before taxes	6.9	36.5	13.0	42.9
Commercial paper rate (per cent)	0.3	2.2	9.1	35.9
Corporate bond rate (per cent)	0.2	2.8	6.0	37.8
Money stock (M_2)	5.1	31.6	2.3	5.5

[a] Root mean square error.
[b] Root mean square error as a ratio to the mean of the variable.

deflator is greater than for real GNP, but these errors are largely compensating insofar as nominal GNP is concerned. Relatively small errors for the labor force and employment result in a much larger error for the unemployment rate, which is predicted as their difference. The post-sample errors for interest rates, money stock and corporate profits are sharply higher than in the sample period, probably because of the inflationary environment after 1966.

Inventory investment is badly predicted. This is largely irrelevant for a long-run model, however, since inventory investment is a small fraction of GNP and accounts for little of the change in GNP over spans of three or more years. If inventory investment is treated as exogenous in the dynamic simulations, incidentally, the error in real GNP is reduced from 2.1 to 1.5 per cent in the sample period and from 2.4 to 1.7 in 1967–1972.

4. POLICY SIMULATIONS

Cause and effect are impossible to specify in the model owing to its simultaneous structure. An exogenous change in a policy instrument has indirect as well as direct effects on the endogenous variables. The principal channels for the direct effects can be identified from the model's structure, but the total effect of a policy change can only be obtained by simulation of the complete system.

The model contains many policy instruments. The fiscal instruments include federal purchases of goods and services, federal employment, tax rates pertaining to personal, corporate and indirect business taxes and to contributions for social insurance, the investment tax credit, and parameters for tax depreciation policy. Incremental federal expenditures for goods purchased from the private sector are a direct contribution to aggregate demand, as are incremental expenditures for federal employment. Tax changes affecting receipts from personal or indirect taxes or from social security contributions affect incomes (and in the case of indirect taxes, prices) directly and consumer and housing demands indirectly. Changes in the various tax parameters affecting corporate income will directly influence business fixed investment expenditures and dividend contributions to personal incomes.

The monetary instruments include unborrowed reserves, regulation Q, the rediscount rate, and the required reserve ratios against demand and time deposits. Changes in these instruments affect the supply side of the money market and induce changes in the money stock and interest rates.[5] The money stock is not an argument in any of the final demand functions of the model, but interest rates enter the behavioral equations for residential construction and expenditures on consumer durables.

It is important to note that neither nominal nor real interest rates enter the factor demand equations for fixed capital and labor. Both factor demands depend on the relative price of capital and labor, with the former represented by the rental price of capital and the latter by the money wage (equations (6) and

[5] See Scadding [**12**] on the specification and estimation of the monetary sector.

(7)). The rental price of capital in turn is a complex function of several variables:

$$Q = p_k(e^r - 1 + \delta)\frac{[1 - s - u(1 - ms)B]}{1 - u}, \tag{17}$$

where p_k is the price index of newly produced capital goods, δ is the real depreciation rate, s is the rate of tax credit for gross investment expenditure, u is the rate of direct taxation on business income, m is the proportion of the investment tax credit which must be deducted from the depreciable base of assets on which the credit is claimed, B is the discounted value of the stream of depreciation charges for tax purposes generated by a dollar of current investment, and r is the discount rate or cost of capital. The specification and measurement of r is crucial for an evaluation of the direct impact of monetary policy on business fixed investment. We have experimented with three alternative measures of r: the nominal after-tax rate of interest on private long-term bonds, the corresponding real rate of interest (the nominal rate corrected for the expected rate of price inflation), and a constant, after-tax required rate of return of 10 per cent. The last assumption yields smaller errors of prediction of investment alone and better performance of the entire model and hence has been adopted herein.[6] Since neither the nominal nor real rate of interest after taxes has approached 10 per cent during the postwar period, this means that business fixed investment has been invariant to the *direct* effects of monetary policy in the model. Monetarist economists have argued that business fixed investment has been unrestrained by high nominal interest rates in recent years because inflationary expectations have kept the real rate from rising appreciably with the nominal rate, but it is also consistent with observed behavior to adopt our assumption of a high required rate of return which has insulated business investment from monetary constraints and thrown the main burden of tight money on residential construction and consumer durables.

Only a limited number of policy simulations can be presented in this paper. We evaluate the effects of an independent increase of federal expenditures and an independent decrease in federal personal income taxes, in both cases with and without an accomodating monetary policy to prevent crowding out of other expenditures. We also assay the effects of an autonomous monetary stimulus in the form of an increase in unborrowed reserves.

Apart from the two cases of accomodating monetary actions accompanying fiscal policies, we do not analyze policy packages comprising simultaneous changes in several instruments. Nor do we investigate the effects of direct tax inducements for investment spending and capital-labor substitution. Finally, we consider only the effects of once-for-all changes in the levels of the instrument variables, as contrasted with differential growth rates in the instruments.

Multiplier results for twelve key variables are presented in Tables 3–5. They

[6] A similar assumption—a constant before-tax rate of return of 20 percent in the evaluation of investment opportunities—has been used by Hall and Jorgenson in a study of the effects of tax policy on investment behavior [7].

TABLE 3

FISCAL AND MONETARY MULTIPLIERS FOR HICKMAN-COEN MODEL, SELECTED VARIABLES

Year	GNP (Current Prices)					REAL GNP (1958 Prices)				
	ΔG 1	ΔG 2	ΔT 1	ΔT 2	ΔM	ΔG 1	ΔG 2	ΔT 1	ΔT 2	ΔM
1	2.73	2.87	1.47	1.51	2.90	1.64	1.76	.87	.95	1.68
2	2.51	3.07	1.91	2.27	4.00	.92	1.06	.76	.89	1.65
3	2.93	3.21	2.36	2.54	2.51	1.10	1.15	.95	.97	.64
4	3.54	3.53	2.85	2.85	.40	1.59	1.59	1.28	1.30	−.30
5	3.73	3.89	3.06	3.25	.44	1.65	1.75	1.36	1.46	.12
6	3.55	3.79	2.89	3.10	.73	1.64	1.73	1.32	1.38	.44
7	3.59	3.77	2.95	3.12	.81	1.71	1.77	1.37	1.43	.44
8	3.87	3.85	3.26	3.26	.34	1.90	1.88	1.59	1.57	.09
9	3.87	3.95	3.28	3.39	1.08	1.98	2.03	1.66	1.72	.70
10	3.90	3.91	3.38	3.40	.31	2.11	2.12	1.81	1.81	.10
11	4.09	4.02	3.60	3.59	.06	2.19	2.13	1.90	1.88	.05
12	4.30	4.22	3.83	3.84	.10	2.25	2.15	1.96	1.94	.14
13	4.33	4.27	3.90	3.91	−.12	2.28	2.22	2.03	2.00	−.08
14	4.35	4.46	4.16	4.12	−.17	2.38	2.29	2.15	2.08	−.02
15	4.24	4.12	3.90	3.86	−.14	2.13	2.04	1.90	1.85	.01
16	4.25	4.15	4.00	3.96	.16	1.92	1.88	1.79	1.76	.12
	Implicit Price Index (1958=100)					Unemployment Rate (Per Cent)				
1	.34	.36	.20	.19	.36	−.12	−.13	−.07	−.07	−.12
2	.44	.54	.30	.37	.62	−.11	−.13	−.07	−.09	−.15
3	.47	.53	.36	.40	.47	−.12	−.13	−.09	−.10	−.10
4	.50	.51	.40	.41	.17	−.15	−.16	−.12	−.13	−.03
5	.50	.52	.41	.44	.07	−.17	−.18	−.14	−.15	−.01
6	.45	.49	.38	.41	.09	−.17	−.18	−.14	−.15	−.04
7	.43	.46	.36	.39	.10	−.17	−.18	−.14	−.15	−.05
8	.42	.42	.36	.37	.04	−.19	−.18	−.15	−.15	−.02
9	.40	.40	.34	.35	.09	−.19	−.19	−.16	−.16	−.05
10	.36	.37	.32	.33	.04	−.20	−.20	−.17	−.17	−.02
11	.35	.36	.32	.32	.00	−.20	−.20	−.17	−.17	−.01
12	.36	.35	.33	.33	.01	−.20	−.19	−.17	−.17	−.02
13	.33	.33	.31	.32	−.01	−.19	−.19	−.17	−.17	.00
14	.33	.32	.31	.31	−.02	−.19	−.18	−.17	−.17	.00
15	.30	.29	.28	.28	−.02	−.17	−.16	−.16	−.15	.00
16	.31	.31	.28	.29	.00	−.15	−.15	−.14	−.14	−.01

TABLE 4

FISCAL AND MONETARY MULTIPLIERS FOR HICKMAN-COEN MODEL, SELECTED VARIABLES

Year	Potential Output (1958 Prices)					Potential Utilization (Per Cent)				
	ΔG 1	ΔG 2	ΔT 1	ΔT 2	ΔM	ΔG 1	ΔG 2	ΔT 1	ΔT 2	ΔM
1	.08	.06	−.01	.06	.02	.52	.56	.29	.29	.55
2	.15	.02	.12	.01	.26	.24	.33	.20	.28	.44
3	.16	.09	.12	.10	.16	.29	.32	.25	.27	.15
4	.21	.18	.15	.13	.12	.40	.41	.33	.34	−.12
5	.28	.28	.22	.15	.23	.39	.42	.32	.37	−.04
6	.34	.35	.21	.20	.10	.35	.38	.30	.32	.09
7	.37	.39	.30	.26	.08	.35	.36	.28	.31	.09
8	.47	.52	.36	.36	.18	.36	.35	.31	.31	−.02
9	.49	.56	.39	.38	.11	.37	.36	.31	.33	.15
10	.58	.54	.43	.41	.16	.36	.38	.33	.33	−.01
11	.66	.62	.48	.50	.18	.35	.35	.33	.32	−.03
12	.68	.74	.52	.55	.04	.35	.31	.32	.31	.02
13	.74	.76	.61	.58	.08	.33	.31	.31	.31	−.03
14	.83	.84	.63	.64	.12	.32	.30	.31	.30	−.03
15	.82	.88	.74	.73	.09	.26	.23	.23	.22	−.02
16	.84	.76	.83	.71	.05	.21	.21	.18	.20	.01
	Federal Surplus (Current Prices)					Net Exports (Current Prices)				
1	.07	.12	−.42	−.42	1.16	−.10	−.11	−.06	−.05	−.11
2	.00	.20	−.27	−.10	1.57	−.11	−.13	−.07	−.09	−.15
3	.09	.18	−.12	−.06	.91	−.11	−.13	−.09	−.10	−.11
4	.16	.13	−.06	−.08	.07	−.14	−.15	−.11	−.12	−.04
5	.20	.25	−.01	.05	.14	−.15	−.16	−.12	−.14	−.02
6	.10	.19	−.10	−.02	.27	−.16	−.17	−.13	−.14	−.04
7	.11	.17	−.09	−.03	.31	−.16	−.17	−.13	−.14	−.04
8	.19	.18	.01	.01	.15	−.16	−.16	−.13	−.13	−.02
9	.17	.20	.00	.04	.44	−.16	−.16	−.13	−.14	−.04
10	.17	.17	.03	.03	.16	−.16	−.17	−.14	−.14	−.02
11	.23	.21	.10	.10	.09	−.17	−.17	−.14	−.15	−.01
12	.29	.27	.17	.18	.13	−.17	−.16	−.15	−.15	−.01
13	.29	.28	.18	.20	.06	−.17	−.16	−.15	−.15	.00
14	.30	.28	.22	.21	.06	−.17	−.17	−.16	−.16	.00
15	.15	.12	.08	.08	.10	−.35	−.33	−.31	−.31	.01
16	.19	.18	.14	.15	.24	−.40	−.39	−.36	−.37	−.01

TABLE 5

FISCAL AND MONETARY MULTIPLIERS FOR HICKMAN-COEN MODEL, SELECTED VARIABLES

Year	Real Consumption (1958 Prices)					Real Business Fixed Investment (1958 Prices)				
	ΔG 1	ΔG 2	ΔT 1	ΔT 2	ΔM	ΔG 1	ΔG 2	ΔT 1	ΔT 2	ΔM
1	.30	.32	.65	.69	.40	.19	.21	.11	.11	.21
2	.28	.29	.86	.87	.59	.13	.18	.11	.13	.22
3	.31	.31	1.00	1.01	.31	.16	.20	.14	.16	.12
4	.51	.50	1.21	1.21	−.01	.23	.25	.18	.20	−.01
5	.62	.65	1.35	1.37	.07	.25	.28	.20	.24	.01
6	.67	.71	1.40	1.43	.14	.25	.28	.21	.24	.06
7	.74	.77	1.47	1.50	.21	.26	.29	.21	.24	.08
8	.87	.86	1.60	1.59	.06	.28	.30	.24	.26	.03
9	.91	.93	1.65	1.66	.26	.30	.31	.26	.28	.11
10	1.01	.99	1.74	1.73	.09	.31	.33	.28	.30	.03
11	1.11	1.06	1.83	1.82	.03	.32	.34	.29	.31	.01
12	1.18	1.14	1.91	1.89	.01	.33	.33	.30	.32	.04
13	1.22	1.17	1.96	1.92	−.06	.34	.34	.32	.34	.01
14	1.32	1.26	2.04	2.00	−.05	.35	.35	.34	.34	.01
15	1.31	1.26	2.05	2.00	−.05	.32	.32	.30	.31	.01
16	1.28	1.21	2.04	1.98	.02	.30	.31	.27	.30	.03
	Real Inventory Investment (1958 Prices)					Real Residential Construction (1958 Prices)				
1	.33	.36	.19	.19	.35	.01	.07	.12	.15	1.12
2	−.07	−.04	−.01	.06	.04	−.06	.08	.12	.22	1.49
3	.05	.01	.07	.02	−.15	−.03	.08	.13	.22	.82
4	.12	.10	.09	.09	−.23	.09	.11	.19	.21	.02
5	.05	.06	.04	.07	.00	.08	.12	.13	.18	.06
6	.01	.01	.02	.00	.10	.02	.08	.04	.09	.22
7	.03	.02	.01	.01	.03	.01	.05	.02	.05	.24
8	.04	.01	.05	.02	−.10	.05	.04	.04	.05	.17
9	.04	.05	.04	.05	.13	.04	.05	.03	.05	.33
10	.04	.06	.05	.04	−.11	.05	.04	.04	.04	.15
11	.02	.01	.03	.02	−.04	.06	.04	.04	.04	.07
12	.03	−.01	.03	.02	.04	.06	.04	.04	.04	.08
13	.01	.02	.01	.02	−.06	.06	.03	.04	.03	.05
14	.02	.02	.04	.02	−.02	.05	.03	.04	.03	.04
15	−.04	−.05	−.06	−.06	.01	.04	.02	.03	.01	.05
16	−.06	−.02	−.06	−.02	.03	.01	−.01	.01	−.01	.10

are based on a sample period control solution for 1951–66 and hence cover 16 years. The two columns headed ΔG refer to the effects of a permanent increase in the level of Federal spending of one billion dollars per year at current prices. Variant 2 assumes an accomodating monetary policy to keep interest rates constant in the face of higher expenditures, whereas variant 1 does not. Similarly, the columns headed ΔT show multipliers for a sustained cut in personal income tax receipts of one billion dollars per year at current prices, with (2) and without (1) an accomodating monetary policy. Finally, ΔM refers to an expansionary monetary policy consisting of a permanent increase in the level of unborrowed reserves of one billion dollars per year. Note that the multipliers for constant-price variables are measured relative to autonomous changes in current-price variables in these calculations. If the autonomous increments were converted to constant prices, the resulting multipliers for the "real" variables would be moderately higher, owing to induced price increases which reduce the real values of the nominal increments.

The impact (first-year) multipliers for nominal GNP range between 1.5 and 2.9 and those for real GNP between 0.9 and 1.8 (Table 3). The impact effects of the expenditure and money shocks are about the same, whereas the tax multipliers are only about half as large. Over the long-run, however, the tax multipliers build to a peak nearly equal to the expenditure multipliers, whereas the monetary multipliers diminish toward zero or negative values for real and nominal GNP. Cyclical fluctuations occur over the 16 year span in all cases, but with considerable variation in timing and amplitude according to type of shock.

According to the model, a sustained exogenous increase in federal expenditures or reduction in tax receipts can permanently reduce the level of unemployment, with most of the potential reduction accomplished within five years. An expansionary monetary policy will reduce unemployment temporarily, but after two or three years the unemployment rate reverts to approximately the original level.

The tradeoff between prices and unemployment differs in the short and long runs. In the case of the expansionary fiscal policies, the price level is raised permanently, but the rate of inflation—the rate of change of prices—which is largest in the first year, diminishes in each subsequent year and turns negative after five years. The expansionary monetary policy also reduces unemployment at the expense of some inflation during the first two years, but prices fall thereafter as the decline of unemployment is reversed, and they eventually return to the original level. Thus neither the price nor unemployment levels are altered in the long run by monetary policy.

Both potential output and its rate of utilization are increased by the expansionary fiscal policies assumed in the simulations (Table 4). Potential output increases only slightly at first, but it continues to grow throughout the period as the capital stock gradually rises owing to the sustained induced increase in business fixed investment (Table 5). Because the utilization rate also rises, the multiplier for actual output is greater than for potential. The average unemployment rate during 1951–66 was 4.8 per cent, and with this degree of slack the model implies that output gains occur from higher utilization as well as from higher growth of potential output itself.

Some rise in potential also occurs under monetary stimulus, but it is quite limited. This is because monetary policy does not permanently increase gross business fixed investment and capital stock growth in the model, for reasons already discussed.

The direct effect of easier money is to stimulate residential construction and purchases of consumer durable goods by lowering interest rates. Since these expenditures involve stock-adjustment processes, the stimulus to actual output is largely spent within three years (Tables 3 and 5), and thereafter the rate of utilization of potential output is usually lower in most years than if the policy change had not occurred (Table 4).

In the absence of an explicit government budget constraint, the sources of deficit finance are merely implicit in the model.[7] In the first simulation, the initial increase in Federal expenditure is implicitly financed by borrowing from the public or from excess reserves of commercial banks. As a result, interest rates rise and residential construction is deterred, offsetting part of the expansionary stimulus of Federal spending. In the second simulation, an accomodating monetary policy is assumed, in the sense that the Federal Reserve allows unborrowed reserves to increase enough to prevent interest rates from rising, and hence partly finances the increased government spending through creation of high-powered money. An accomodating monetary policy increases the GNP multiplier comparatively little, however, since the degree of "crowding out" of residential construction is small when interest rates are allowed to rise (Tables 3 and 5). A similar observation holds for fiscal stimulus through tax reduction, as may be seen by comparing the third and fourth simulations. "Crowding out" would probably be more substantial at present (1974) levels of interest rates than in the simulation period, however.

It is important to note that the ex-ante deficit for the case of increased Federal spending is converted to an ex-post surplus even during the first year (Table 4). When allowance is made for the rise of tax receipts induced by income expansion, then, deficit financing is essentially transitory for this case. A deficit-financed personal tax reduction, in contrast, results in ex-post deficits of diminishing magnitude for five or six years before an ex-post surplus is generated. Even in this case, however, the ex-post deficit each year is considerably smaller than the amount of the exogenous tax reduction.

The injection of additional unborrowed reserves by the central bank occurs entirely in the first year of the fifth simulation, presumably through an open market purchase. The Treasury more than recovers the amount disbursed by the Federal Reserve during the same year owing to the induced expansion of tax revenue, however, and continues to benefit from induced surpluses during

[7] See [2] on the desirability of including the government budget constraint in econometric models.

the subsequent years.

With regard to net exports, the various policies reduce the surplus or increase the deficit on foreign account to the extent that they raise income and imports (Table 4). Any induced changes in the monetary base stemming from foreign transactions is assumed to be offset in the simulations by appropriate Federal Reserve actions to control unborrowed reserves.

In summary, these policy simulations support elements of both the monetarist and non-monetarist views of the influence of fiscal and monetary policy, but favor the latter view more than the former.[8] The monetarist view that the growth path of real output cannot be lastingly affected by monetary policy is broadly confirmed by the model. The model also implies, however, that in the long-run (after ten years) the price level is also neutral with respect to a once-for-all change in the monetary base, contrary to monetarist thought.[9]

Within the structure of the model, the path of potential GNP is largely invariant to monetary policy because the latter does not directly affect business fixed capital formation, and the indirect stimulus to business investment from increased activity in the housing and consumption sectors is short-lived. Fiscal policy can have a lasting effect on potential output because it can induce sustained capital stock growth by permanently raising aggregate demand. (Fiscal actions directly affecting the rental price of capital provide another channel for affecting the growth paths of capital stock and potential output, but that topic remains for future investigation.) Thus the monetarist view that fiscal policy unaccompanied by monetary expansion can affect real GNP only for a short period is rejected in this model.

Finally, the trade-off between unemployment and inflation in these complete model simulations is consistent with the non-monetarist view. A trade-off does exist in the first few years, but the inflation rate diminishes rapidly and the price level actually declines after five years, although not back to the original level in the case of fiscal stimuli. In the case of a monetary stimulus, prices eventually revert to the original level, but so also does unemployment.

Stanford University
Northwestern University
Stanford University

REFERENCES

[1] Anderson, Leonall C., "The State of the Monetarist Debate," *Review* of the Federal Reserve Bank of St. Louis, LV (September, 1973), 2–8.

[2] Christ, Carl F., "Econometric Models of the Financial Sector," *Journal of Money, Credit and Banking*, III, Part II (May, 1971) 419–449.

[8] See [1] for a summary of the monetarist debate.

[9] This is because in the long-run the income velocity of money is sufficiently diminished (by the reduction of interest rates which results from an expansion of unborrowed reserves in the model) to offset the induced expansion of the money stock.

[3] COEN, ROBERT M., "Aggregate Labor Supply in the United States Economy," Memorandum No. 117, Center for Research in Economic Growth, Encina Hall, Stanford University, (August, 1971).

[4] ———, "Labor Force and Unemployment in the 1920's and 1930's: A Re-Examination Based on Postwar Experience," *The Review of Economics and Statistics*, LV (February, 1973), 46–55.

[5] ——— AND BERT G. HICKMAN, "Constrained Joint Estimation of Factor Demand and Production Functions," *The Review of Economics and Statistics*, LII (August, 1970), 287–300.

[6] ——— AND ———, "Aggregate Utilization Measures of Economic Performance," Memorandum No. 140, Center for Research in Economic Growth, Encina Hall, Stanford University, (February, 1973).

[7] HALL, ROBERT E. AND DALE W. JORGENSON, "Application of the Theory of Optimum Capital Accumulation," in Gary Fromm, ed., *Tax Incentives and Capital Spending* (Washington, D. C.: The Brookings Institution, 1971), 9-60.

[8] HICKMAN, BERT G., "What Became of the Building Cycle?" Paul A. David and Melvin W. Reder, eds., *Nations and Households in Economic Growth: Essays in Honor of Moses Abramovitz* (New York: Academic Press, 1974), 291-314.

[9] ———, MARY HINZ AND ROBERT WILLIG, "An Economic-Demographic Model of the Housing Sector," Memorandum No. 147, Center for Research in Economic Growth, Encina Hall, Stanford University, (April, 1973).

[10] HURD, MICHAEL D., "Wage Changes, Desired Manhours and Unemployment," Memorandum No. 155, Center for Research in Economic Growth, Encina Hall, Stanford University, (October, 1974).

[11] HYMANS, SAUL H., "Prices and Price Behavior in Three U. S. Econometric Models," in O. Eckstein, ed., *The Econometrics of Price Determination Conference*, October 30–31, 1970 (Washington, D. C.: Board of Governors of the Federal Reserve System, 1972).

[12] SCADDING, JOHN L., "An Annual Money Demand and Supply Model for the U. S.: 1924–1940/1949-1966," Memorandum No. 177, Center for Research in Economic Growth, Encina Hall, Stanford University, (October, 1974).

14

THE BROOKINGS QUARTERLY MODEL: AS AN AID TO LONGER TERM ECONOMIC POLICY ANALYSIS

By George R. Schink[1]

1. INTRODUCTION

All too often government economic policy decisions are made on the basis of what impacts can be expected before the next election. This constraint typically imposes a two or three year horizon on the analytical input into the governmental decision making process. The current energy crisis has forced policy makers into the new and, therefore, probably uncomfortable position of having to look several decades into the future to assess the relative merits of competing policy positions. In this paper, I hope to demonstrate the importance of looking beyond the next election and towards the next decade in reviewing policies designed to combat the current recession and/or inflationary problems. Two similar dollar value expansionary policies, a government expenditure increase and a personal tax reduction, are compared over a ten year horizon. As conventional wisdom would suggest, the government expenditure increase leads to a larger expansion over the first three years. Beyond the initial three year period, however, the effectiveness of the two policies reverses dramatically, with the government expenditure increase generating some perverse longer run impacts. Before considering these multiplier results, let us review the structure of the Brookings Quarterly Model.

2. STRUCTURE OF THE MODEL

Since the Brookings Model Project has not been regularly maintained since June 1972, this review of the model's structure is slanted towards the elements of the model which merit consideration for inclusion in other quarterly models. The analysis in this paper is carried out using the Brookings Condensed Model which is described in [7]. The condensed model contains 326 variables of which 200 are endogenous. The model includes 68 behavioral equations with 13 additional variables being defined in the input-output sector.

One valuable insight derived from the Brookings Model structure is related not to any specific sector specification but to the level of disaggregation or model size. The reason for constructing the Brookings Condensed Model was to permit an in-depth analysis of the gains and losses associated with disaggregation. Numerous within-sample and post-sample simulation experiments were conducted with the condensed and large versions of the Brookings Model which

[1] The author wishes to acknowledge the help of Gary Fromm, Lawrence R. Klein and David M. Rowe for advice and encouragement, Sonia Klein for a careful reading of this manuscript, and Andrea Best for her skillful typing.

are reported in [4] and [7].[2] The basic conclusion drawn from these studies is that disaggregation at the level contained in the large version of the Brookings Model leads to a significant improvement in overall model simulation and forecasting performance with the obvious additional benefit of increased detail. The newest version of the Wharton Model, the Mark IV, has adopted the basic disaggregation scheme incorporated in the large version of the Brookings Model and includes additional detail in the consumption, output originating, and foreign trade sectors.[3]

The Brookings Model is the only quarterly econometric model to date which uses an input-output technique to translate final demands into output originating by industrial sector and output originating sector deflators into final demand deflators.[4] The input-output method used in the Brookings Model has been improved substantially by Ross S. Preston in the context of an annual model, the Wharton Annual and Industry Model (see [5] and [6]). Use of the input-output matrix in the Brookings Quarterly Model has led to improved prediction of outputs originating by industrial sector and, thereby, better prediction of employment and sector prices. In addition, using the input-output matrix to translate sector deflators into final demand deflators has led to better overall price behavior predictions. Incorporation of an input-output matrix into an existing quarterly forecasting model should lead to better forecasting performance.

While the Brookings Model was the first to combine both input-output and other structural equations of the macro economy, later quarterly models have incorporated these features and in most cases have improved on the original specifications. One of the primary reasons for not keeping the Brookings Model project updated was the existence of numerous other quarterly model projects which had independent sources of support. Most of these other model projects, however, are funded for the purpose of making regular short-run forecasts and analyzing the current economic situation, which often leaves little time for basic research on alternative model sector specifications, problems of disaggregation, and methods of estimation. While work on these basic research problems continues at various research centers, one wonders whether the concept embodied in the Brookings Model project has outlived its usefulness.

3. MULTIPLIER EXPERIMENTS WITH THE CONDENSED MODEL

Multiplier experiments with large econometric models have given the economic community a new insight concerning the impacts of changes in government policy.[5] While the standard macroeconomic textbook expositions on the relative

[2] The large version of the Brookings Model contains 473 variables, of which 343 are endogenous. The large version of the model includes 107 behavioral equations with 25 additional variables being defined in the input-output sector. See [3] for a detailed description of the model.

[3] See [1] for a discussion of the model equations. The model contains almost 600 variables.

[4] The Wharton Mark IV Model, see [1], uses input-output coefficients to perform the latter translation.

[5] For a comparison of multiplier results obtained with several models, see G. Fromm and L. R. Klein [2].

impacts of spending versus tax policy changes were presented as over-simplifications of a complex process, they now appear to be at best misleading and often totally incorrect. Four ten-year multiplier experiments were run to examine in depth the relative merits of spending versus tax policy changes.[6]

3.1. *Increased government spending.* The government spending multiplier experiment involves a $3.5 billion increase in real government spending. This increase was allocated to the components of government spending in proportion to each component's existing expenditure share.[7] The proportional allocation includes a 0.3 million increase in government employment. The average increase in nominal government spend ing over the 40 quarters is approximately $5 billion. Table 1 presents the impacts of this multiplier experiment as well as an accommodating monetary policy experiment where nonborrowed reserves were increased by $0.5 billion in addition to the real government spending increase.[8]

Real GNP increases in the first quarter by $6.4 billion. The peak impact is attained in the fourth quarter ($9.8 billion) and is sustained through the sixth quarter. Introduction of the accommodating monetary policy produces an anomaly which requires some explanation. In particular, the increase in real GNP during the first two quarters is slightly less with an accommodating monetary policy than is the case when no monetary policy changes are made. This anomaly can be traced to a single equation in the Brookings Condensed Model; namely, the equation for single family housing starts. The primary interest rate variable in this equation is the mortage interest rate, but the three-month treasury bill rate enters this equation as a proxy for expected movements in the mortgage rate. If the bill rate decreases sharply, which occurs with the initial introduction of the accommodating monetary policy, single family housing starts are hypothesized to decrease slightly in anticipation of forthcoming declines in the mortgage interest rate. With an accommodating monetary policy, the peak impact on real GNP is not reached until the seventh quarter ($11.2 billion), but the increase in real GNP is greater than in the no accommodating monetary policy case from the third through twelfth quarters.

Over the longer run, the impacts on real GNP decline almost steadily. By the 28th quarter, the impact is reduced to only slightly more than the increase in real government expenditure. In the 40th quarter, the increase in real GNP is $0.3 billion less than the increase in real government expenditure in the no accommodating monetary policy case, and the real GNP increase is $0.1 billion more than the increase in real government expenditure with an accommodating monetary policy.

The impact on the GNP price deflator increases steadily throughout the 40

[6] These multiplier experiments were run over the period 1956 to 1965.

[7] In the Brookings Model, government expenditure is disaggregated by type of purchase into durables, nondurables, services, and construction as opposed to the federal and state and local breakdown used in most models.

[8] This accommodating monetary policy is somewhat arbitrary but serves to illustrate the non-neutrality of monetary policy.

TABLE

THE IMPACTS OF A $3.5 BILLION INCREASE
OVER A FORTY
QUARTER AFTER

	1	2	3	4	5	6	7	8	9
Real GNP	6.4	8.3	9.4	9.8	9.8	9.8	9.7	9.5	9.3
with accommodating monetary policy	6.1	7.9	9.5	10.6	10.9	11.1	11.2	11.1	10.8
Nominal GNP	6.1	8.4	10.0	11.1	11.9	12.7	13.5	14.0	14.4
with accommodating monetary policy	5.8	7.9	10.1	11.9	13.0	14.1	15.1	15.8	16.3
Unemployment rate (%)	−.37	−.67	−.83	−.86	−.83	−.78	−.74	−.72	−.72
with accommodating monetary policy	−.36	−.65	−.81	−.89	−.89	−.87	−.85	−.83	−.82
Real disposable income	3.2	3.9	4.6	5.0	5.1	5.2	5.3	5.0	4.9
with accommodating monetary policy	3.0	3.7	4.6	5.2	5.4	5.7	5.9	5.7	5.5
Real consumption	2.3	3.0	3.6	3.9	3.9	4.0	4.0	3.9	3.8
with accommodating monetary policy	2.2	2.9	3.6	4.0	4.2	4.4	4.5	4.4	4.3
Real nonresidential fixed investment	0.0	0.7	1.0	1.3	1.6	1.8	2.0	2.1	2.2
with accommodating monetary policy	0.0	0.6	1.0	1.4	1.9	2.2	2.5	2.8	2.9
Real residential investment	0.0	0.0	0.0	0.0	0.1	0.1	0.2	0.3	0.4
with accommodating monetary policy	−0.2	−0.2	0.2	0.5	0.4	0.4	0.5	0.5	0.5
Real inventory investment	0.7	1.4	1.6	1.6	1.3	1.0	0.7	0.5	0.3
with accommodating monetary policy	0.7	1.3	1.6	1.7	1.6	1.3	1.0	0.8	0.5
Nominal net exports	−0.1	−0.3	−0.4	−0.5	−0.6	−0.6	−0.7	−0.7	−0.7
with accommodating monetary policy	−0.1	−0.3	−0.4	−0.5	−0.6	−0.7	−0.7	−0.8	−0.8
Nominal personal income taxes	0.4	0.9	1.2	1.5	1.8	1.9	2.0	2.0	2.1
with accommodating monetary policy	0.4	0.9	1.2	1.5	1.9	2.1	2.2	2.2	2.3
GNP price deflator (1958=100)	0.1	0.2	0.3	0.4	0.6	0.8	0.9	1.0	1.2
with accommodating monetary policy	0.1	0.1	0.3	0.4	0.6	0.8	0.9	1.1	1.2

Note: All real variables are measured in billions of 1958 dollars and all nominal variables are measured in billions of dollars; other units as noted. The real government expenditure increase was allocated in proportion to existing expenditure shares among government

quarter period. The accommodating monetary policy permits substantially larger increases in real GNP with at most very minor increases in prices during the third through twelfth quarters. By the end of the 40 quarter period, the increase in the GNP price deflator is lower with the accommodating monetary policy even though real GNP is slightly higher.

The impact on nominal GNP increases almost steadily throughout the forty quarter period with the peak impact occurring during the fortieth quarter. The impact on nminal GNP falls slightly when the increase in real GNP declines sharply, but the steady increase in inflation eventually offsets the continuing

1

IN REAL GOVERNMENT EXPENDITURES
QUARTER PERIOD
CHANGE IN POLICY

10	11	12	16	20	24	28	32	36	37	38	39	40
9.1	8.9	8.5	7.0	5.1	4.2	3.8	3.5	3.6	3.4	3.4	3.4	3.2
10.5	9.9	9.1	6.6	4.5	3.9	3.8	3.8	4.0	3.8	3.8	3.8	3.6
14.9	15.2	15.5	16.5	16.3	16.8	18.2	19.4	21.5	22.0	22.8	23.7	24.4
16.7	16.8	16.7	16.6	15.9	16.2	17.5	18.7	20.6	21.0	21.7	22.6	23.2
-.71	-.69	-.67	-.57	-.41	-.35	-.32	-.30	-.31	-.30	-.30	-.30	-.29
-.80	-.76	-.71	-.52	-.35	-.29	-.27	-.27	-.28	-.27	-.27	-.27	-.27
4.8	4.6	4.3	3.3	1.6	0.4	-0.2	-0.9	-1.0	-1.3	-1.2	-1.1	-1.5
5.4	5.1	4.6	3.0	1.1	0.0	-0.5	-1.0	-1.0	-1.2	-1.1	-1.0	-1.3
3.8	3.8	3.7	3.3	2.4	1.9	1.6	1.2	1.1	0.9	1.0	1.0	0.8
4.3	4.2	3.9	3.1	2.1	1.7	1.5	1.2	1.2	1.0	1.1	1.1	0.9
2.1	2.0	1.8	1.2	0.6	0.2	0.1	0.1	0.3	0.3	0.3	0.3	0.3
2.9	2.8	2.5	1.5	0.6	0.2	0.1	0.3	0.4	0.4	0.4	0.4	0.5
0.5	0.5	0.6	0.4	0.1	-0.1	-0.3	-0.3	-0.3	-0.3	-0.3	-0.3	-0.3
0.5	0.5	0.5	0.3	0.0	-0.2	-0.3	-0.3	-0.3	-0.3	-0.3	-0.3	-0.3
0.1	0.0	-0.2	-0.4	-0.6	-0.4	-0.2	-0.1	0.0	0.0	0.0	0.0	0.0
0.2	0.0	-0.2	-0.7	-0.7	-0.4	-0.1	0.0	0.1	0.0	0.0	0.0	0.0
-0.7	-0.7	-0.7	-0.8	-0.7	-0.6	-0.6	-0.6	-0.5	-0.6	-0.5	-0.5	-0.5
-0.8	-0.8	-0.8	-0.8	-0.7	-0.6	-0.5	-0.5	-0.5	-0.5	-0.5	-0.5	-0.5
2.1	2.2	2.2	2.4	2.3	2.4	2.6	2.8	2.7	2.9	3.1	3.2	3.3
2.4	2.4	2.4	2.4	2.2	2.2	2.5	2.7	2.6	2.8	2.9	3.0	3.1
1.3	1.4	1.5	1.9	2.2	2.4	2.6	2.8	3.0	3.0	3.1	3.2	3.2
1.4	1.5	1.6	2.0	2.2	2.3	2.5	2.6	2.7	2.8	2.9	2.9	3.0

purchases of durables, nondurables, services, and construction. This proportional allocation included a 0.3 million increase in government employment. The accommodating monetary policy consists of a $0.5 billion increase in nonborrowed reserves.

declining impacts on real GNP.

The impacts on the unemployment rate reflect movements in real GNP fairly closely with several interesting exceptions. The largest decline in the unemployment rate occurs during the fourth quarter when no accommodating monetary policy is applied, but the decline in the unemployment rate begins to dissipate immediately, while the peak increase in real GNP is maintained for two additional quarters. With an accommodating monetary policy, the largest decline in the unemployment rate occurs during the fourth quarter, preceding the peak increase in real GNP by three quarters. By the thirty-second quarter, the decline in the unemployment rate is less when an accommodating monetary policy is applied even though the increase in real GNP is greater. These results indicate that an accommodating policy has a longer run impact on the composition of output as well as the level of output.

The peak increase in real disposable income and real consumption occurs during the seventh quarter with or without an accommodating monetary policy. The accommodating monetary policy, however, leads to a $0.6 billion larger increase in real disposable income and a $0.5 billion larger increase in real consumption at the peak. Following the peak increase, the impact on real disposable income declines steadily, turning negative by the twenty-eighth quarter. The impact on real consumption remains positive through the fortieth quarter but declines steadily. The impact on real consumption remains positive due to a continuing decline in the unemployment rate, which tends to sustain auto purchases, and a very slow adjustment process in the real services consumption equation. The eventual negative impact on real disposable income results primarily from an increase in the effective personal income tax rate which, in turn, results from the higher inflation rate.

The peak positive impact on real nonresidential fixed investment occurs during the ninth quarter, both with and without an accommodating monetary policy. Introduction of an accommodating monetary policy, however, leads to a $0.7 billion larger peak increase in real nonresidential fixed investment and larger increases from the fourth through sixteenth quarters. During the fortieth quarter the accommodating monetary policy leads to a $0.2 billion larger increase in real nonresidential fixed investment even though the increase in real GNP is only $0.4 billion.

Real residential investment exhibits a peak increase of $0.6 billion during the twelfth quarter when no accommodating monetary policy is applied. Introduction of the accommodating monetary policy leads to a peak increase of $0.5 billion in real residential investment but this peak value is reached by the fourth quarter.[9] During the first and second years, the accommodating monetary policy produces an increase in real residential investment of $0.1 billion and $0.3 billion, respectively. In the third year residential investment is the same with and without the accommodating monetary policy. The impact on real residential investment turns negative by the twenty-fourth quarter, as interest rates increase in response to expanded real activity and as real disposable income declines.

Real inventory investment reaches its peak increase by the third or fourth quarter and then decreases during the twelfth through thirty-second quarter. The net impact is a slight increase in inventory stocks with no significant movement thereafter. Nominal net exports are lower in every period as a result of both increased imports and decreased exports.

3.2. *Decreased personal income taxes.* The decreased personal taxes multiplier

[9] The initial decline in housing starts which was discussed above leads to the initial decline in real nonresidential investment.

experiment involves a $5.0 billion decrease in nominal personal income taxes. This kind of a tax decrease could be accomplished via an increase in the standard deduction or an increased dollar deduction per exemption. This $5.0 billion decrease in personal taxes is in general comparable to the $3.5 billion increase in real government expenditure, since the latter translates into approximately an average increase of $5.0 billion in nominal terms. Table 2 presents the impacts of this multiplier experiment as well as an accommodating monetary policy experiment where nonborrowed reserves were increased by $0.5 billion in addition to the nominal personal tax decrease.

Real GNP increases in the initial quarter by $5.1 billion as opposed to a $6.4 billion increase for the government spending increase. The peak impact occurs during the seventh quarter (an $8.5 billion increase) while the peak impact occurs during the fourth quarter (a $9.8 billion increase) for the government spending increase. Up to this point the standard macroeconomic textbook notions are preserved, but the relative impacts of the two policies reverse between the twelfth and sixteenth quarters. For the tax decrease, the positive impact on real GNP declines through the twenty-fourth quarter and then increases to $6.8 billion by the fortieth quarter. The impact on real GNP decreased steadily to only $3.2 billion by the fortieth quarter in the government expenditure increase experiment. If the accommodating monetary policy change is made in addition to the tax cut, the peak impact on real GNP of $10.1 billion occurs during the eighth quarter, which is $1.1 billion less and one quarter later than the peak impact for the real expenditure increase combined with an accommodating monetary policy.[10] The relative impacts of the tax and spending policies still reverse between the twelfth and sixteenth quarters when the accommodating monetary policy is applied. By the fortieth quarter, the tax cut combined with the accommodating monetary policy generates a $7.3 billion increase in real GNP as opposed to the $3.6 billion increase generated by the combined expenditure increase and accommodating monetary policy.

As was the case for the government expenditure increase multiplier experiment, the tax cut leads to a steadily increasing impact on the GNP price deflator throughout the forty quarter period. The price increases generated by the tax cut, however, are substantially less than those generated by the government expenditure increase. This lower inflation rate is illustrated most sharply by comparing the impacts of the tax cut and the expenditure increase on nominal and real GNP during the fortieth quarter. In the fortieth quarter, the tax cut leads to a $23.3 billion increase in nominal GNP, and a $6.8 billion increase in real GNP. On the other hand, the government expenditure increase generates a $24.4 billion increase in nominal GNP during the fortieth quarter and only a $3.2 billion increase in real GNP. When the accommodating monetary policy is combined with the tax cut, the impact on the GNP price deflator is essentially the same as the impacts without the monetary policy even though activity

[10] The decreased impact on real GNP during the first two quarters when an accommodating monetary policy is introduced results from the specification of the single unit housing starts equation discussed in conjunction with the increase in real government expenditure experiment.

TABLE

THE IMPACTS OF A $5 BILLION DECREASE
OVER A FORTY
QUARTER AFTER

	1	2	4	3	5	6	7	8	9
Real GNP	5.1	7.0	7.9	8.2	8.3	8.3	8.5	8.5	8.5
with accommodating monetary policy	4.8	6.6	8.0	9.1	9.4	9.7	10.0	10.1	10.0
Nominal GNP	4.8	6.8	8.0	8.8	9.4	10.1	10.8	11.4	11.8
with accommodating monetary policy	4.5	6.4	8.1	9.6	10.5	11.4	12.4	13.2	13.6
Unemployment rate (%)	−.16	−.38	−.53	−.59	−.59	−.56	−.55	−.54	−.54
with accommodating monetary policy	−.15	−.35	−.51	−.62	−.65	−.66	−.65	−.65	−.65
Real disposable income	7.0	7.8	8.3	8.6	8.7	8.9	9.0	9.0	8.8
with accommodating monetary policy	6.8	7.6	8.3	8.8	9.1	9.4	9.6	9.6	9.5
Real consumption	4.4	5.1	5.6	5.8	5.9	6.1	6.2	6.2	6.3
with accommodating monetary policy	4.3	4.9	5.5	6.0	6.2	6.5	6.7	6.8	6.7
Real nonresidential fixed investment	0.0	0.7	1.1	1.4	1.7	1.9	2.0	2.1	2.2
with accommodating monetary policy	0.0	0.7	1.1	1.5	2.0	2.3	2.6	2.8	2.9
Real residential investment	0.0	0.1	0.0	0.0	0.1	0.2	0.4	0.5	0.7
with accommodating monetary policy	−0.1	−0.1	0.3	0.5	0.4	0.5	0.6	0.8	0.9
Real inventory investment	0.9	1.6	1.8	1.6	1.3	1.0	0.8	0.5	0.3
with accommodating monetary policy	0.8	1.5	1.8	1.8	1.6	1.3	1.1	0.8	0.6
Nominal net exports	−0.3	−0.5	−0.6	−0.7	−0.8	−0.8	−0.8	−0.8	−0.8
with accommodating monetary policy	−0.3	−0.4	−0.6	−0.7	−0.8	−0.9	−0.9	−0.9	−0.9
Nominal personal income taxes	−4.8	−4.5	−4.2	−4.0	−3.8	−3.7	−3.6	−3.5	−3.5
with accommodating monetary policy	−4.8	−4.5	−4.2	−4.0	−3.7	−3.6	−3.4	−3.3	−3.2
GNP price deflator (1958 = 100)	0.0	0.1	0.1	0.2	0.4	0.5	0.6	0.7	0.8
with accommodating monetary policy	0.0	0.1	0.1	0.2	0.4	0.5	0.6	0.7	0.8

Note: All real variables are measured in billions of 1958 dollars and all nominal variables are measured in billions of dollars; other units as noted. The decrease in nominal personal

levels are higher.

While it is impossible to isolate all the factors leading to the lower inflation rate associated with the tax cut, one of the important factors is the relative impacts of the tax cut and expenditure increase on the unemployment rate. The tax cut leads to a maximum 0.59 percent decrease in the unemployment rate during the fourth quarter, while the government expenditure increase leads to a maximum decrease of 0.86 percent during the fourth quarter. The larger impact of the expenditure increases on the unemployment rate is due to the sharper generated increase in real GNP as well as the assumed 0.3 million in-

2

IN NOMINAL PERSONAL INCOME TAXES
QUARTER PERIOD
CHANGE IN POLICY

10	11	12	16	20	24	28	32	36	37	38	39	40
8.5	8.4	8.2	7.4	6.2	5.7	5.8	6.1	6.7	6.6	6.7	6.8	6.8
9.8	9.4	8.9	7.0	5.7	5.4	5.8	6.4	7.1	7.1	7.2	7.3	7.3
12.2	12.6	12.9	13.8	13.9	14.4	15.9	17.5	19.9	20.6	21.4	22.4	23.3
14.0	14.2	14.1	13.8	13.4	13.8	15.1	16.8	19.0	19.6	20.3	21.2	22.0
−.54	−.54	−.52	−.46	−.35	−.30	−.29	−.30	−.33	−.33	−.33	−.33	−.33
−.63	−.61	−.61	−.41	−.29	−.24	−.24	−.27	−.30	−.30	−.30	−.30	−.31
8.8	8.7	8.6	8.0	6.8	6.0	5.7	5.5	5.7	5.5	5.6	5.7	5.6
9.3	9.2	8.8	7.6	6.3	5.6	5.4	5.4	5.7	5.6	5.7	5.8	5.7
6.3	6.4	6.4	6.4	6.2	6.1	6.3	6.4	6.7	6.7	6.8	6.9	6.8
6.8	6.7	6.6	6.3	5.9	5.9	6.1	6.4	6.8	6.8	6.9	7.0	7.0
2.1	2.0	1.9	1.3	0.8	0.4	0.3	0.4	0.6	0.7	0.7	0.7	0.7
2.9	2.7	2.5	1.6	0.8	0.4	0.4	0.6	0.8	0.8	0.9	0.9	0.9
0.7	1.0	1.1	1.0	0.7	0.4	0.3	0.3	0.3	0.3	0.3	0.3	0.4
0.9	1.0	1.0	0.8	0.5	0.3	0.2	0.3	0.3	0.3	0.3	0.4	0.4
0.2	0.0	−0.1	−0.3	−0.4	−0.3	−0.1	0.0	0.1	0.1	0.1	0.1	0.1
0.3	0.1	−0.1	−0.6	−0.6	−0.3	−0.1	0.1	0.2	0.1	0.1	0.1	0.1
−0.9	−0.9	−0.9	−0.9	−0.8	−0.8	−0.8	−0.8	−0.8	−0.8	−0.8	−0.8	−0.8
−0.9	−1.0	−0.9	−0.9	−0.8	−0.7	−0.7	−0.7	−0.8	−0.8	−0.8	−0.8	−0.8
−3.4	−3.4	−3.3	−3.1	−3.1	−3.1	−2.9	−2.6	−2.5	−2.3	−2.2	−2.1	−1.9
−3.2	−3.1	−3.1	−3.2	−3.2	−3.2	−3.0	−2.7	−2.7	−2.5	−2.4	−2.3	−2.1
0.8	0.9	1.0	1.3	1.5	1.6	1.8	1.9	2.1	2.2	2.3	2.4	2.4
0.9	1.0	1.1	1.4	1.5	1.6	1.6	1.8	1.9	2.0	2.0	2.1	2.2

income taxes could be viewed as an increase in the standard deductions. The accommodating monetary policy consists of a $0.5 billion increase in nonborrowed reserves.

crease in government employment. The impact of the unemployment rate on wage rate is nonlinear, which implies a substantially stronger impact on wage rates for the government expenditure increase. These stronger impacts on wage rate are in turn reflected in a higher inflation rate.

The lower unemployment rate associated with the government expenditure increase is insufficient to explain the entire difference in the inflation rate. The remainder can be traced to shifts or distortions in the composition of output associated with the government expenditure increase, which on balance lead to a higher overall GNP price deflator. These shifts in the composition of output are responsible in part also for the reduction in the unemployment rate. Isolating the exact reasons for these shifts in the composition of output is impossible as this involves solving the model in one's head, but some are directly and indirectly related to the composition of the increase in government spending while others may be induced by shifting relative prices during the initial burst of inflation. Shifting the composition of government spending, especially eliminating the government employment component, could lead to a lower inflation rate.

The tax cut not only generates a substantially lower inflation rate than the government expenditure increase, but also a significantly different composition of final demand. Real disposable income increases in the initial period by $7.0 billion as a result of the tax cut, while the government expenditure increase generates only a $3.2 billion increase. For the tax cut, the peak increase in real disposable income of $9.0 billion occurs in the seventh quarter as compared to a $5.3 billion increase in the same quarter for the government expenditure increase. Introducing the accommodating monetary policy with the tax cut leads to a peak increase of $9.6 billion in real disposable income during the seventh quarter. The positive impact of the tax cut on real disposable income declines almost steadily from the seventh quarter through the twenty-eighth quarter but then stabilizes through the fortieth quarter at a value approximately equal to $5.6 billion. For the government expenditure increase, the impact in real disposable income declines steadily after the seventh quarter, turns negative at the twenty-eighth quarter, and is −$1.5 billion by the fortieth quarter. The differences in the paths of real disposable income between the seventh and fortieth quarters are not attributable to increases in the nominal personal income tax receipts, which increase by $1.7 billion under the tax cut and by $1.3 billion under the government expenditure increase. The most important causes are the higher inflation rate generated by the government expenditure increase.[11]

Real consumption does not reach its peak increase of $6.9 billion under the tax cut until the thirty-ninth quarter, while real disposable income peaks during the seventh quarter. During the seventh quarter, however, real consumption is $6.2 billion above its control path, reaches a $6.4 billion increase by the eleventh quarter, falls back to a $6.1 billion increase during the twenty-fourth quarter, and then continues up to its final peak. These relatively minor oscillations in real consumption are due to somewhat similar oscillations in the unemployment rate[12] and a very slow adjustment process in the real consumption of services equation.

The peak positive impact of $2.2 billion on real non-residential fixed investment under the tax reduction occurs during the ninth quarter, which is also the peak impact quarter when the accommodating monetary policy is applied. The accommodating monetary policy, however, produces an increase of $2.9 billion. Under the government expenditure increase, the peak impacts are identical both

[11] The effective personal income tax rate, however, is higher under the government expenditure increase.

[12] The unemployment rate variable enters the real consumption of autos equation.

in terms of size and timing with those generated by the tax cut, with and without the accommodating monetary policy. Over the entire forty quarter period, the tax cut generates more real non-residential fixed investment due to a slower and lesser decline after the peak impact.

Real residential investment increases to $1.1 billion above its control path in the twelfth quarter as a result of the tax reduction. The peak increase generated by the government expenditure increase is only $0.6 billion, also occurring during the twelfth quarter. For the tax cut, housing investment declines fairly sharply after the peak as is the case for the government expenditure increase, but the tax cut impact remains positive through the fortieth quarter. The continued positive impact on housing results from the impact on real disposable income remaining positive, but increasing interest rates limit the impact to a small positive value at the end of the forty quarter period.

Under the tax cut, the peak positive impact on real inventory investment of $1.8 billion occurs during the third quarter. After the third quarter, the impact declines, turning negative in the twelfth quarter, and continues downward through the twentieth quarter. The impact on real inventory investment becomes quite small by the twenty-eighth quarter and ends at $0.1 billion at the fortieth quarter. Nominal net exports experience a negative impact throughout. The peak impact of − $0.9 billion is attained during the tenth quarter (−$1.0 billion with an accommodating monetary policy in the eleventh quarter). The negative impact reaches − $0.7 billion by the fourth quarter and stabilizes at between − $0.7 billion and − $0.8 billion for the last half of the simulation period. The tax cut produces a larger negative impact on nominal net exports than does the government expenditure increase, primarily because of a higher demand for imports due to a higher level of real disposable income. Lower inflation under the tax cut, however, tends to offset the effects of higher income leading to a lesser reduction in exports and some abatement of the increase in imports.

3.3. *A summary comparison of the two policies over the decade.* While it is clear from the preceding tables that the tax cut produces more favorable economic conditions in the later years, the outlook on average for the entire decade is brought into clear focus by the results presented in Table 3. The tax cut begins to produce a higher level of real GNP during the fourth year and over the entire decade generates a $9.2 billion higher level of real GNP. The higher inflationary impact of the government expenditure increase is clearly illustrated by the nominal versus real GNP comparisons as well as the GNP price deflator comparisons. The government expenditure increase over the decade generates $22.1 billion more in terms of nominal GNP even though it generates $9.2 billion less in terms of real GNP. The government expenditure increase generates a substantially higher GNP price deflator in every year.

Increasing government expenditure leads to a lower rate of unemployment during all but the last two years, but one must bear in mind that the expenditure increase includes a 0.3 million increase in government employment. This

TABLE 3

COMPARISON OF THE IMPACTS OF CHANGES IN GOVERNMENT EXPENDITURE AND TAX POLICY OVER A TEN YEAR PERIOD

YEAR AFTER CHANGE IN POLICY

	1	2	3	4	5	6	7	8	9	10	SUM
Real GNP											
Expenditure increase	8.5	9.7	9.0	7.7	5.8	4.5	4.0	3.7	3.7	3.4	60.0
Tax decrease	7.1	8.4	8.4	7.8	6.7	5.9	5.7	6.0	6.5	6.7	69.2
Nominal GNP											
Expenditure increase	8.9	13.0	15.0	16.3	16.5	16.5	17.7	18.8	20.7	23.2	166.6
Tax decrease	7.1	10.4	12.4	13.6	13.9	14.1	15.3	16.8	19.0	12.9	144.5
GNP price deflator (1958=100)											
Expenditure increase	0.3	0.8	1.4	1.8	2.1	2.3	2.5	2.7	2.9	3.1	—
Tax decrease	0.1	0.6	0.9	1.2	1.5	1.6	1.7	1.9	2.1	2.3	—
Unemployment rate (%)											
Expenditure increase	−.68	−.77	−.70	−.61	−.47	−.37	−.32	−.31	−.30	−.30	—
Tax decrease	−.42	−.56	−.54	−.49	−.39	−.32	−.29	−.30	−.32	−.33	—
Real disposable income											
Expenditure increase	4.2	5.2	4.7	3.9	2.3	0.9	0.1	−0.6	−0.8	−1.3	18.6
Tax decrease	7.9	8.9	8.7	8.3	7.2	6.3	5.9	5.6	5.7	5.6	70.1
Real consumption											
Expenditure increase	3.2	4.0	3.8	3.5	2.7	2.1	1.8	1.4	1.2	0.9	24.6
Tax decrease	5.2	6.1	6.4	6.5	6.3	6.1	6.2	6.3	6.7	6.8	62.6
Nominal government deficit											
Expenditure increase	0.1	−0.7	−0.8	−1.0	−0.7	−0.7	−1.1	−1.5	−1.6	−2.0	−10.0
Tax decrease	2.2	1.3	0.9	0.7	0.7	0.7	0.3	−0.2	−0.4	−1.1	5.1

Note: All real variables are measured in billions of 1958 dollars and all nominal variables are measured in billions of dollars; other units as noted. The expenditure increase is a $3.5 billion increase in real government expenditures while the tax decrease is a $5 billion decrease in nominal personal income taxes. Both policy changes assume no compensating monetary policy change.

generates a reduction of about − 0.4 percent in the unemployment rate by itself.[13] Therefore, the impact on private employment generated by the tax cut is higher from the start.

The most perverse outcome associated with the government expenditure increase is its long run impact on real disposable income and thereby real consumption. The personal tax cut, as would be expected, generates a larger increase in real disposable income in every year. The eventual negative impact on real disposable income generated by the expenditure increase, however, would not be suggested by conventional wisdom. While the reasons for this perverse outcome were explored in detail above, the basic explanation is the higher inflation rate associated with the government spending increase. Over the decade, the personal tax cut generates $51.5 billion more real disposable income and $38.0 billion more real consumption.

The government expenditure increase does produce a more favorable nominal government deficit picture throughout the decade. The government spending increase essentially pays for itself from the beginning and generates a $10.0 billion surplus over the decade. This surplus results from both a modest reduction in transfers and a sharp increase in tax revenues. The sharp increase in taxes is in turn primarily a result of the strong impact on prices which increases nominal tax collections sharply. The government price deflator increases less

TABLE 4

LONG-RUN COMPARISON OF THE IMPACTS ON INVESTMENT OF CHANGES IN GOVERNMENT EXPENDITURE AND TAX POLICY

	Cumulative Impact		
	First 3 years	First 6 years	Sum over 10 years
Real nonresidential fixed investment			
Government expenditure increase	4.7	7.2	8.0
with an accommodating monetary policy	5.9	8.9	9.3
Personal tax decrease	4.8	7.9	9.9
with an accommodating monetary policy	6.0	9.6	12.1
Real residential investment			
Government expenditure increase	0.7	1.5	0.4
with an accommodating monetary policy	1.0	1.4	0.2
Personal tax decrease	1.2	3.6	4.9
with an accommodating monetary policy	1.7	3.6	4.7

Note: Both investment variables are measured in billions of 1958 dollars. The government expenditure increase is a $3.5 billion increase in real government expenditures while the personal tax decrease is a $5.0 billion decrease in nominal personal income taxes. The accommodating monetary policy consists of a $0.5 billion increase in nonborrowed reserves.

[13] Over the decade, the impact decreases from −0.45 to −0.35 percent.

quickly than the private price deflators, leading to an early surplus position. The tax cut does not produce a surplus until the eighth year and generates a $5.1 billion cumulative deficit over the decade.

Table 4 presents a comparison of the long run impacts on investment of the two policy changes with and without an accommodating monetary policy change. The tax cut and government expenditure increase produce nearly identical impacts on real nonresidential fixed investment over the first three years. The tax cut, however, produces substantially larger impacts by the end of six years and over the entire decade. In addition, the accommodating monetary policy produces a larger absolute increase in real nonresidential fixed investment over the decade when combined with the tax cut.

The personal tax decrease leads to a greater increase in real residential investment from the beginning, with the differential increasing over time. The decline in the cumulative impact of the government expenditure increase on residential investment between the sixth and tenth years results from the induced reduction in real disposable income. Introduction of an accommodating monetary policy produces a speedup in residential construction during the first three years but leads to essentially no additional investment by the end of six years and a slight decline in overall spending by the end of the decade. The latter result stems from a "crowding out" of residential investment by the increase in nonresidential investment. By the end of the decade, mortgage interest rates are higher with an accommodating monetary policy as a result of the induced increases in activity in general, and nonresidential fixed investment in particular. Due to the quicker response time of residential investment to changes in interest rates, housing investment is down slightly by the end of the decade.

4. CONCLUSIONS

One conclusion which should not be drawn from this paper is that tax policy changes are always better in the long run than government expenditure policy changes. As was indicated in the text above, a government expenditure policy could be developed which eliminated many if not all of the longer-run drawbacks associated with the particular policy considered in this paper. In addition, a combination of expenditure, tax, and monetary policies might generate the best features, short and long term, of the policies implemented separately. Balanced and diversified policies generally have the advantage of not localizing either gains or losses in particular sectors or with particular groups in the economy.

The basic conclusion which should be reached is that deriving policies which produce the most favorable outcome over the next two or three years can produce perverse longer term problems. The practice of ranking alternative policies on the basis of their short run impacts should be replaced by a careful analysis over both the short and long term.

Wharton Econometric Forecasting Associates, Philadelphia

REFERENCES

[1] ADAMS, F. G., LAWRENCE R. KLEIN, DAVID M. ROWE, AND VINCENT SU, *The Wharton Mark IV Quarterly Model* (Philadelphia: Wharton Econometric Forecasting Associates, Inc., unpublished).

[2] FROMM, GARY AND LAWRENCE R. KLEIN, "A Comparison of Eleven Econometric Models of the United States," *The American Economic Review*, LXIII, (May, 1973), 385–393.

[3] ———, ———, AND GEORGE R. SCHINK, "Short- and Long-Term Simulations with the Brookings Model," in Bert G. Hickman, ed., *Econometric Models of Cyclical Behavior*, Volume 1, Studies in Income and Wealth (New York: National Bureau of Economic Research, 1972).

[4] ———, AND GEORGE R. SCHINK, "Aggregation and Econometric Models," *International Economic Review*, XIV (February, 1973), 1–32.

[5] PRESTON, ROSS S., "The Wharton Long-Term Model: Input-Output within the Context of a Macro Forecasting Model," chapter 12 in this volume.

[6] ———, *The Wharton Annual and Industry Forecasting Model*, (Philadelphia: Economics Research Unit, University of Pennsylvania, 1972).

[7] SCHINK, GEORGE R., "An Evaluation of the Predictive Abilities of a Large Model: Post-Sample Simulations with the Brookings Model," in Gary Fromm and Lawrence R. Klein, eds., *The Brookings Model: Perspective and Recent Developments* (Amsterdam: North Holland, 1975).

15

JUDGING THE PERFORMANCE OF ECONOMETRIC MODELS OF THE U. S. ECONOMY

By Carl F. Christ[1]

INTRODUCTION

Econometric models of the U.S. economy have been developed to the point where forecasters who use them can forecast real and nominal GNP two or three quarters ahead with root mean square errors of less than one percent, and six quarters ahead with RMS errors of one to two percent. The best of them now usually do better than forecasters who do not use such models. Are the models then so reliable that we can believe what they say about the effects that particular fiscal or monetary policy actions will have, immediately and in the long run? And how can we learn the answer to such questions, either for today's models, or tomorrow's? That is what this paper is about. It draws heavily on the extensive and intensive work of the authors of the other papers in this symposium, and could not have been written without them.

My main contentions will be as follows. First, it is important to test econometric models as abstract representations of reality, as well as to test the forecasting performance of the people who use them. Second, testing of a model requires that the model be tried against data that occurred after the model was built, i.e., after the specifications were decided upon concerning which variables appear in each equation, which variables are endogenous and which exogenous, what is the functional form of each equation, what is the lag structure of each, what restrictions the parameters are to obey, etc. A common way to do this is to make forecasts for a period that is subsequent to the building of the model, and then examine the errors of those forecasts. Third, though the models forecast well over horizons of four to six quarters, they disagree so strongly about the effects of important monetary and fiscal policies that they cannot be considered reliable guides to such policy effects, until it can be determined which of them are wrong in this respect and which (if any) are right.

1. TESTING ECOMOMETRIC MODELS AND FORECASTERS

Every econometric model in this symposium is a system of equations intended to determine a vector of endogenous variables y_t at time t, in terms of a vector of exogenous variables x_t, vectors of lagged endogenous variables $y_{t-1}, \cdots, y_{t-L}$, a matrix of parameters A, and a vector of stochastic disturbances u_t. The system of equations can be symbolized by the following, where F is a (possibly nonlinear) vector function:

[1] This work was supported by a grant from the National Science Foundation to The Johns Hopkins University. Helpful comments were made by L. R. Klein and G. Fromm.

$$F(y_t, y_{t-1}, \cdots, y_{t-L}, x_t, A) = u_t \,. \tag{1}$$

The reduced form of the system, obtained by solving (1) for y_t, can be expressed as

$$y_t = G(y_{t-1}, \cdots, y_{t-L}, x_t, A) + v_t \tag{2}$$

where v_t is a stochastic disturbance vector depending on u_t and A. If (1) is nonlinear, so will (2) be; then (2) may have to be obtained by numerical methods rather than by explicit solution, and if (2) is not unique, spurious solutions must be rejected.

A model—once it has been specified by listing its endogenous variables, its exogenous variables, the functional form of each of its equations (including the lag structure), and any other restrictions upon its parameters—is an impersonal theoretical construct, that can and should be tested like any scientific theory, by comparing its implications against observed data. We use a sample of data ($t = 1, \cdots, T$) to obtain an estimate $\hat{A}$ of the parameters, and then see how closely the estimated equations (1) and (2) describe the values of the variables in the model during a chosen test period, which may be either the same sample period that was used for estimation, or a different (usually subsequent) period. In practice, this means substituting the estimate $\hat{A}$ into (1) and (2), and finding the values $\hat{u}_t$ and $\hat{v}_t$ that must be taken by the disturbance terms in the test period to maintain the equalities in the estimated equations (1) and (2). The more accurately the equations describe the data, i.e., the smaller are $\hat{u}_t$ and $\hat{v}_t$, in the test period, the more confidence we have in the model, *ceteris paribus*. More about this below.

It is worthwhile to distinguish between testing an econometric model, and testing a practical human forecaster who forecasts by means of an econometric model. The forecaster obtains, from some source extraneous to the model, ex ante forecasts of the exogenous variables x_t, and substitutes them into his estimate of the reduced form (2), and then calculates his forecasts of the future values of the endogenous variables y_t. Of necessity, his forecast period comes *after* the time when his model was specified, and *after* the sample period used to estimate its parameters. Sometimes, just before he is to announce a forecast, he may believe (based on recent events not explicitly included in the model) that the model is going to make (or has made) an incorrect forecast; in some cases he then may adjust one or more of the model's constant terms or slopes in a way that (in his judgment) is likely to improve the forecast. Therefore the correctness of such practical econometric forecasts is dependent in a complex way on the forecaster's ability to forecast the exogenous variables and to adjust the model in a subjective manner, as well as on the adequacy of the model itself.

In order to test an econometric model, as distinct from a forecaster who uses a model, it is of course necessary to make *no* subjective adjustments to the constant terms or slopes (adjustments made according to a pre-announced mechanical rule are acceptable, for the rule can be regarded as part of the model;

see the "PSS" forecasts in Hirsch *et. al.* [**12**]). It is also necessary to use *actual* values of exogenous variables, rather than ex ante forecasts thereof.

To test an econometric model of the U. S. economy, it is crucial to use a test period that occurs *after* the model has been specified. A test period that occurred before the model was specified does not provide a meaningful test. This is because, although economic theory plays an important part in building these models, it is not able to do the whole job alone; hence alternative functional forms and alternative lag structures are quite properly tried out against the data that are available at the time, and (again quite properly) any specification that does not describe those data with rather high R^2's is rejected right then. Therefore, any U. S. econometric model that is released by its builders will already have been shown to fit rather well the data that occurred before the model was specified.[2] Experience teaches that it is uncommon for such models to fit subsequent data as closely, and that the fit typically deteriorates as one moves to data occurring later and later after the time when the model was specified. This is a common finding, even after allowing for the deterioration in fit that would be expected as one extrapolates a correctly specified and properly estimated equation to data outside the sample period.[3] Testing a model by means of a test period that occurs after the model was built is the only way to discriminate between the (inferior) models that have been chosen to fit primarily the random and non-enduring features of the pre-model-building data, and the (superior) models that have been chosen to fit primarily the systematic and enduring features of the economy.

These crucial tests, using a test period that occurs after the building of the model, are most commonly made by first estimating the model (1) using the pre-model-building data, and then using the reduced form (2) to make conditional forecasts for the post-model-building test period, given actual values of the exogenous variables for the test period and actual initial values of the lagged endogenous variables at the beginning of the test period. This is the type of forecast to which most emphasis will be given in this paper. Such forecasts (whether they use actual or ex ante exogenous values) are often called post-sample forecasts, which indeed they are, but it is more important that they are forecasts of data from the post-model-building period, for reasons noted above. (In particular, it is not sufficient to divide the pre-model building period into two parts, and estimate the model from the earlier part, and then use the latter part as a post-sample test period: this yields a pre-model-building test period, and hence does not provide the crucial test that is needed.) Root mean square errors (RMSE's) for post-model-building forecasts are presented and discussed below.

[2] This conclusion applies even if the explicit screening procedure described in the text is not used in building the model, because the model builder knows a great deal about recent economic events in his country, and designs the model with them in mind.

[3] One makes the required allowance by means of the standard error of forecast, proposed by Hotelling [**13**] and extended to econometric model forecasts by Brown [**4**] and by Goldberger, Nagar, and Odeh [**10**].

2. POLICY SIMULATION

If and when an econometric model of the economy has been shown to be a reliable predictor of post-model-building data, it can be relied upon to tell us the time-paths of the multiplier effects of alternative government policies that appear in the model. The usual vehicle for obtaining such multipliers is the *policy simulation.* It is constructed by comparing two dynamic simulations computed from the model over the same time period, one of which uses actual values of all the exogenous variables, and the other of which uses the same set of exogenous values *except* that, at some chosen instant, the time-path of one of the policy variables is given a step-wise increase or decrease and thereafter follows a path that is a fixed distance above or below the actual path. The resulting paths of the endogenous variables in the two simulations differ by amounts that are attributed to the policy change. Multipliers are then computed, showing the effect on an endogenous variable divided by the step-change in the policy variable, after the lapse of one quarter, two quarters, etc.

Even if an econometric model is not yet shown to be a reliable predictor, dynamic simulations based on it are of great interest, for they show what the model implies about the time-paths of the multiplier effects of policy changes. Such multipliers will be discussed below.

3. ROOT MEAN SQUARE ERRORS OF THE MODELS' FORECASTS

Table 1 lists the models in this symposium,[4] and shows for each the number of equations, stochastic equations, and exogenous variables; the sample period used to estimate it; the types of forecasts for which root mean square errors are presented by the authors; and the types of policy simulations that are presented.

Table 2 shows the root mean square errors of post-sample forecasts of nominal and real GNP, and of the GNP deflator, that are presented in the symposium, for forecasts one quarter ahead, two quarters ahead, and so on up to eight quarters ahead. Almost all the forecasts deteriorate as the horizon lengthens. The semi-naive forecasts made by the "ARIMA" (auto-regressive integrated moving average) method, based only on past values of the variable that is being forecast, are uniformly the poorest. Apart from them, the largest RMSE for any variable and length of horizon is about twice the smallest. The forecasts in the American Statistical Association-NBER survey of regular forecasters are about as good as the median of the econometric forecasters for nominal GNP and for short-horizon price level forecasts, and better than most of the econometric forecasts for real GNP and for 4- and 5-quarters-ahead price level forecasts. The Wharton III forecasts, which are *subjectively adjusted* and based on *ex ante* exogenous variable values, are the best of the econometric forecasts for nominal GNP, and

[4] Tables 1–4 and the ensuing discussion omit RMSE's and policy simulations for the Brookings, MPS, and Wharton annual models because papers presenting them did not reach me before press time.

TABLE 1

MODEL SIZES, SAMPLE PERIODS, TYPES OF FORECASTS FOR WHICH ROOT MEAN SQUARE ERRORS ARE PRESENTED, AND TYPES OF POLICY SIMULATIONS PRESENTED

Line	Model (Quarterly unless otherwise stated)	Number of			Sample Period	RMSE's of forecasts		Policy Simulations				
						Within sample	Post sample	Fiscal			Monetary	
		Stoch Eqs.	Eqs.	Exog Vari-ables		Exog variable values used		Gov. Pur-chases	Taxes	Bal-anced Budget	Unbor-rowed Reserved	Treas bill rate
a	b	c	d	e	f	g	h	j	k	l	m	n
1	BEA	67	117		54.1–71.4	—	actual and ex ante	×	×			
2	Fair[1]	14	19	20	56.1–73.2	actual	actual and ex ante					
3	DRI[2]	477	698	184	61.1–72.4	actual	ex ante	×	×		×	
4	MQEM	35	59	63	54.1–70.4	actual	—	×		×		×
5	St. Louis[1,3]	5	9	3	53.1–68.4	—	actual					
6	Wharton III[2]	68	191	92	53.3–70.1	actual	ex ante	×	×	×	×	
7	Wharton III[2] anticipations	79	202		53.3–70.1	actual	—	×	×		×	
8	Liu-Hwa[3] monthly	51	131	27	54Ja–71Dc	actual	actual	×	×		×	
9	Hickman-Coen annual	50	70		24–40, 49–66	actual	actual	×	×		×	

[1] The Fair and St. Louis models are re-estimated before each forecast.
[2] For some equations the sample period was different from the typical period shown in column f.
[3] The papers on the St. Louis and Liu-Hwa models do not give RMSE's, but the authors kindly supplied them to me.

nearly the best for real GNP and the price level. The BEA EAF3 forecasts, which are also *subjectively adjusted* and based on *ex ante* exogenous values, are very good for short-horizon forecasts, but deteriorate rather rapidly as the horizon lengthens. The (*unadjusted*) Fair model that uses *actual* exogenous values is about third best, especially for nominal GNP and the price level. On the other hand, two other *unadjusted* or *mechanically adjusted* models using *actual* exogenous values (St. Louis and BEA PSS) are in many cases the poorest. The Fair model does better when using *actual* exogenous values than when using *ex ante* ones. On the other hand, the *subjectively adjusted* BEA model does worse when using *actual* than when using *ex ante* exogenous values (compare the EPF and EAF3 forecasts). We return to this below. The DRI model, which uses *ex ante* exogenous values, does quite well with real and nominal GNP one quarter ahead, but gets worse rapidly for longer horizons. The Liu-Hwa forecasts (*unadjusted*, and based on *actual* exogenous values) are good, but their horizon is too short (eight months, or about three quarters) to be very revealing. The Hickman-Coen forecast errors were not shown separately for different horizons.

In general, it appears that *subjectively adjusted* forecasts using *ex ante* exogenous values are better than the others. It is no surprise that subjective adjustment helps. It may surprise some that the use of actual exogenous values does not help, and sometimes hinders. But there is likely to be some interaction, in the sense that if a forecaster feels that the preliminary forecast turned out by his model is unreasonable, he may both adjust the model and change his ex ante forecast of the exogenous variables, in order to obtain a final forecast that he thinks is more reasonable. This suggests that when unadjusted models are used, *actual* exogenous values should yield better forecasts than ex ante values. The two sets of forecasts from the Fair model bear this out. It also suggests that if *subjectively adjusted* models are used, *ex ante* exogenous values should yield better forecasts than actual values. A comparison of the EAF3 and EPF forecasts from the BEA model beares this out.

To test econometric models, free from the subjective judgment of the human forecasters who use them, we want to see the RMSE's of forecasts made without subjective adjustment, and with actual exogenous values. Such RMSE's are present in some but not all of the papers in this symposium. Fortunately, they have been computed for all the models that are represented in the NBER/NSF Model Comparison Seminar. The first report presenting them is Fromm and Klein **[8]**, and the second one is Fromm and Klein **[9]**, to appear in the *Annals of Economic and Social Measurement*. The authors have kindly given me permission to make use of these forthcoming results. They are graphed in Figures 1, 2, and 3, respectively, for nominal GNP, real GNP, and the GNP deflator. For reference, the ASA/NBER forecasts are included also. The forecast periods are not identical, but all begin no earlier than 1965.4 and end no later than 1972.4. A comparison of Table 2 with the graphs indicates once again that econometric model forecasts can be improved by the use of subjective judgment.

The forecasts deteriorate rapidly as the forecast horizon is lengthened, with

TABLE 2

RMSE'S (ROOT MEAN SQUARE ERRORS) OF POST-SAMPLE FORECASTS OF NOMINAL GNP, REAL GNP, AND THE GNP DEFLATOR

Line	Forecaster	Forecast Period	Forecast Type[1]	Exog. Variable Values	Adjustments to Model[2]	RMSE's (Root Mean Square Errors)[9] of Post-Sample Forecasts							
						Number of Quarters Ahead							
						1	2	3	4	5	6	7	8
a	b	c	d	e	f	g	h	j	k	l	m	n	p
	Part I: GNP in Billions of Current Dollars												
1	ASA-NBER[3,5]	70.3–73.2	—	—	—	4.9	7.9	11	13	16			
2	ARIMA[4]	〃	—	—	—	11	19	27	27	46	58		
3	BEA (EAF3)	〃	A	ex ante	subj	3.2	7.0	8.4	13	16	15		
4	BEA (EPF)	〃	C	actual	subj	6.4	8.9	14	16	14	14		
5	BEA (PSS)	〃	D	actual	mech	8.7	13	13	12	17	20		
6	Fair[5]	〃	B	ex ante	none	5.3	11	16	18	22			
7	Fair[5]	〃	D	actual	none	5.1	7.2	8.5	11	12			
8	DRI	69.4–73.4	A	ex ante	subj	4.3	7.9	12	15	18	18	21	26
9	St. Louis[6]	69.1–73.3	D	actual	none	8.2	12	16	18	22	26	28	27
10	Wharton III	71.2–74.1	A	ex ante	subj	4.8	6.2	6.7	7.5	9.5	10	12	9.5
11	Liu-Hwa[6,7]	72Ja–Dc	D	actual	none	5.4	6.5	4.2					
12	Hickman-Coen	67–72										27[8]	
	Part II: GNP in Billions of 1958 Dollars												
13	ASA-NBER[3,5]	70.3–73.2	—	—	—	3.5	3.7	6.1	7.9	8.8			
14	ARIMA[4]	〃	—	—	—	8.7	13	17	23	29	36		
15	BEA (EAF3)	〃	A	ex ante	subj	2.5	4.7	5.2	8.2	9.3	7.2		

16	BEA (EPF)	〃	C	actual	subj	5.4	8.3	12	15	13	9.2		
17	BEA (PSS)	〃	D	actual	mech	7.9	11	11	11	15	17		
18	Fair[5]	〃	B	ex ante	none	6.1	9.5	10	13	7.5			
19	Fair[5]	〃	D	actual	none	4.4	6.6	7.8	11	10			
20	DRI	69.4–73.4	A	ex ante	subj	3.1	5.6	7.8	7.7	10	9.1	9.1	1.3
21	St. Louis[6]	69.1–73.3	D	actual	none	6.4	11	11	15	17	20	23	25
22	Wharton III	71.2–74.1	A	ex ante	subj	3.2	4.9	5.7	6.9	8.8	9.7	10	8.9
23	Liu-Hwa[6,7]	72Ja–Dc	D	actual	none	6.2	7.8	7.4					
24	Hickman-Coen	67–72										18[8]	
	Part III: GNP Deflator (1958: 100)												
25	ASA-NBER[3,5]	70.3–73.2	—	—	—	.6	1.1	1.3	1.1	1.0			
26	ARIMA[4]	〃	—	—	—	.8	1.3	2.1	2.8	3.0	3.8		
27	BEA (EAF3)	〃	A	ex ante	subj	.5	.8	1.4	1.9	1.7	1.1		
28	BEA (EPF)	〃	C	actual	subj	.5	1.0	1.3	1.5	1.7	2.0		
29	BEA (PSS)	〃	D	actual	mech	.6	.6	.6	.7	1.0	1.4		
30	Fair[5]	〃	B	ex ante	none	.8	1.1	1.3	1.5	1.4			
31	Fair[5]	〃	D	actual	none	.7	1.0	1.2	1.2	1.1			
32	St. Louis[6]	69.1–73.3	D	actual	none	.6	1.1	1.4	1.7	2.0	2.3	2.6	2.6
33	Wharton III	71.2–74.1	A	ex ante	subj	.5	.8	1.2	1.3	1.4	1.5	1.5	1.5
34	Liu-Hwa[6,7]	72Ja–Dc	D	actual	none	.7	.8	.8					
35	Hickman-Coen	67–72											

[1] Forecasts of types A and B use ex ante exogenous variable values.
Forecasts of types C and D use actual exogenous variable values.
Forecasts of types A and C use subjective adjustments to the model.
Forecasts of types B and D use either no adjustments to the model, or adjustments made by a mechanical rule stated in advance.
See columns e and f.

[2] Abbreviations are as follows:
"subj" =subjective

"mech" = by a mechanical rule stated in advance.

3 Forecast errors from the ASA/NBER Survey of Regular Forecasters, as reported by Fair [**7**].

4 ARIMA stands for auto-regressive integrates moving average forecasts, using only the lagged values of the variable being forecast, according to a Box-Jenkins technique described in Hirsch *et al*. [**12**]. It is a semi-naive method.

5 Fair gives mean absolute errors. I have multiplied them by 1.22, 1.26, and 1.26 respectively for Parts I, II, and III to transform them approximately to RMSE's.

6 Anderson and Carlson [**2**] and Liu and Hwa [**15**] do not present RMSE's but the authors kindly supplied to me the RMSE's shown here.

7 Liu and Hwa [**15**] use a monthly model. The RMSE's shown for 1, 2, and 3 quarters ahead are their RMSE's for the middle month of each quarter, i.e., 2, 5, and 8 months ahead.

8 Hickman and Coen [**11**] present only one post-sample RMSE for each variable; it is for forecasts of annual data during 1967–72, based on a dynamic simulation beginning with initial conditions for 1967.

9 Fair [**7A**] and McNees [**16**] examine the errors of post-sample forecasts made with ex ante values of exogenous variables, by several model builders, for periods different from the ones reported in this Table. Tee average errors reported by those authors differ, sometimes rather substantially, from the RMSE's shown here for DRI and Wharton forecasts. Those authors show the DRI, Michigan, and Wharton forecasts about equal when ex ante exogenous values are used.

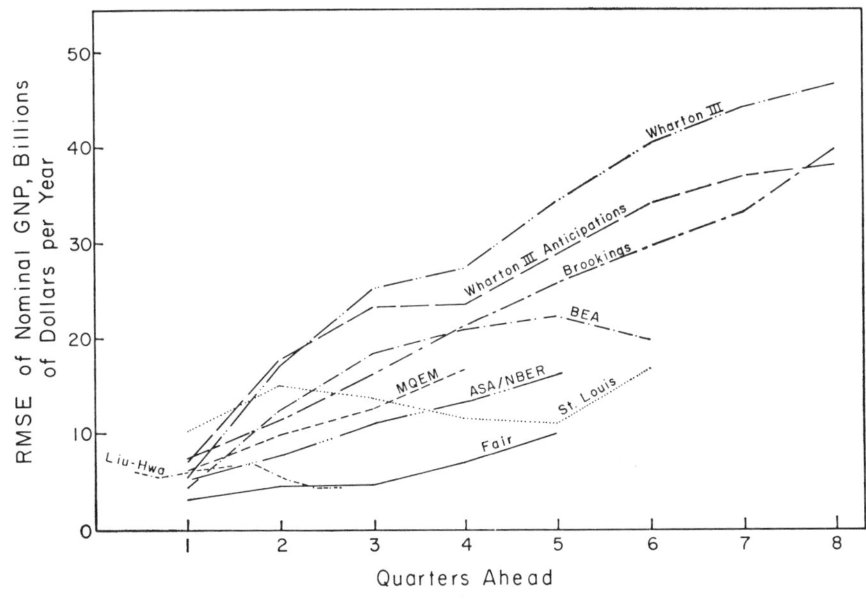

FIGURE 1

ROOT MEAN SQUARE ERRORS OF POST-SAMPLE FORECASTS OF NOMINAL GNP USING ACTUAL EXOGENOUS VARIABLE VALUES AND NO SUBJECTIVE ADJUSTMENTS. SOURCE: FROMM AND KLEIN [9], TABLE 1.

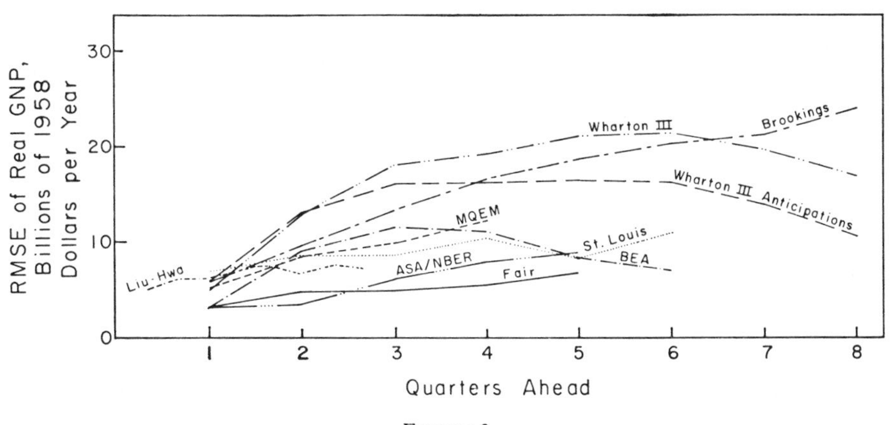

FIGURE 2

ROOT MEAN SQUARE ERRORS OF POST-SAMPLE FORECASTS OF REAL GNP USING ACTUAL EXOGENOUS VARIABLE VALUES AND NO SUBJECTIVE ADJUSTMENTS. SOURCE: FROMM AND KLEIN [9], TABLE 1.

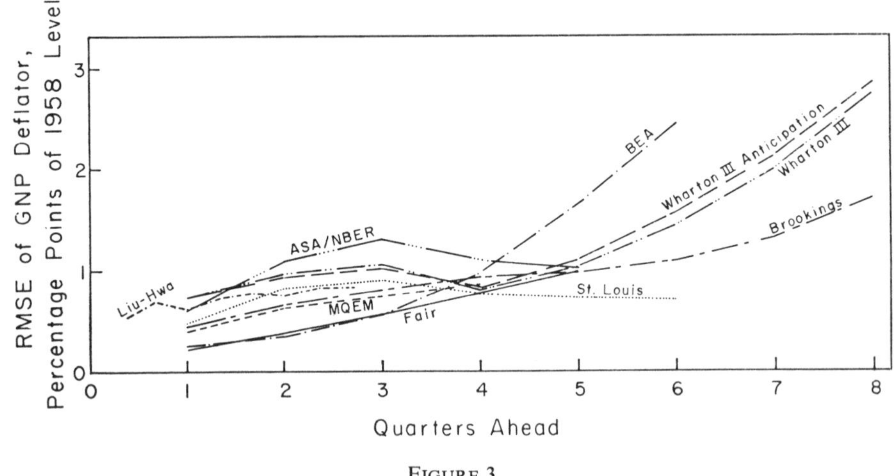

FIGURE 3

ROOT MEAN SQUARE ERRORS OF POST-SAMPLE FORECASTS OF THE GNP DEFLATOR USING ACTUAL EXOGENOUS VARIABLE VALUES AND NO SUBJECTIVE ADJUSTMENTS. SOURCE: FROMM AND KLEIN [9], TABLE 3.

few exceptions. Typically the RMSE doubles or trebles as we go from one quarter ahead to 5 quarters ahead. This makes it clear, if indeed it was not clear already, that these econometric models are at best only approximations to the economy as it existed when they were built and estimated; they do not state fundamental immutable laws of human behavior.

There are substantial differences in the forecasting abilities of the models unassisted by judgment, as shown in the graphs. All have RMSE's for real and nominal GNP that are 1% or less for one quarter ahead, and 3% or less for five or six quarters ahead. The Fair model looks relatively good here, and so does the St. Louis model after one or two quarters, but remember that each treats as exogenous certain variables that convey a lot of information about income and employment, and are difficult to forecast ex ante. For the Fair model the chief such variables are consumer and business anticipations, financial variables related to the housing market, and potential output. For the St. Louis model they are high-employment Federal expenditures, and potential output. This helps explain both their good performance and the fact that their errors do not grow very much as the horizon grows. The Michigan model sometimes takes the Treasury bill rate as exogenous, which gives it some advantage.

To make a comparison of models without giving an advantage to a model that treats a hard-to-forecast variable as exogenous, one can compare models via unadjusted forecasts that use ex ante values of the exogenous variables. Unfortunately, the only model for which such forecasts are presented in this symposium is Fair's, so no such comparisons can be made here.

4. POLICY SIMULATIONS YIELDED BY THE MODELS

Government-purchases multipliers (without accommodating monetary policy) are presented for the models in this symposium in Table 3, and monetary policy multipliers in Table 4. Similar multipliers for real and nominal GNP are presented in Fromm and Klein [9]. For real GNP they are shown in Figures 4 and 5.[5]

All the quarterly models in Table 3 agree fairly closely on fiscal multipliers for GNP, both real and nominal, for about the first two years after the fiscal policy change: the two-year government purchases multiplier is put between 1.9 and 2.8 for nominal GNP, and between 1.4 and 2.4 for real GNP. All the quarterly models in Fromm and Klein [9] agree approximately with these results, except for the St. Louis model which puts the five-quarter (and later) fiscal multipliers close to zero. But after two years, the agreement begins to evaporate.

Consider nominal GNP first. The MPS model shows a substantial decline in the fiscal multiplier from 3.1 at seven quarters to 1.8 at 20 quarters, when the policy simulation was stopped. The other models show fiscal multipliers still increasing at 40 quarters, some with small cycles and some without, except possibly the Fair and Liu-Hwa models, whose policy simulations do not go that far.

Consider real GNP next. Here the disagreement is even more spectacular. Three models show substantial negative government-purchases multipliers after a time: −0.5 at 20 quarters for MPS, −3 at 40 quarters for Wharton III, and −23 at 40 quarters for BEA! Four models show declines in the government-purchases multiplier from its peak, amounting to ten percent in one case and about 66 percent in the others, by the end of the policy simulation: Wharton III anticipations model and Wharton annual model at 20 quarters, and the Brookings and DRI models at 40 quarters. The Michigan model's multiplier falls to zero at 40 quarters. The Hickman-Coen multiplier is still rising after 40 quarters. The Hickman-Coen multiplier is still rising after 40 quarters, but turns down at 56 quarters and is still falling at 64 quarters.

This is a strikingly varied set of results concerning the long-run effect of an increase in government purchases.

Consider now the effects of a $1 billion increase in annual government purchases on prices, shown in Table 3. All the models find the effect to be less than one percent, but they do not agree very well. The Hickman-Coen model shows the effect peaking after 16 quarters, but the others show it still increasing at the end of the policy simulation, 16 to 40 quarters after the policy change.

Consider now the response over time to an easing of monetary policy, as shown in Table 4. There is very serious disagreement here, and it begins immediately after the policy change. Most models do agree that both real and nominal GNP will be increased, but the DRI model shows a negative effect on both from about 20 to 40 quarters after the change, and the Hickman-Coen model shows a small negative effect on both at 52 to 56 quarters and a small

[5] For the MPS model the results graphed in Figure 4 were computed by Albert Ando, while those in Figures 1–3 and 5 were computed by the Model Comparison Seminar.

TABLE 3

FISCAL MULTIPLIER EFFECTS OF A $1 BILLION INCREASE IN NOMINAL[1] GOVERNMENT PURCHASES UPON NOMINAL GNP, REAL GNP, AND THE GNP DEFLATOR, WITHOUT ACCOMMODATING MONETARY POLICY

Line	Model	Simulation Period	Fiscal Multipliers[2] as a Function of Time Elasped												
a	b	c	d	e	f	g	h	j	k	l	m	n	p	q	r
	Part I: Nominal GNP in Billions of Dollars														
			Number of Quarters Elapsed												
			1	4	8	12	14	16	20	28	40	56	64		
1	BEA[3]	66.1–70.4	.9	2.2	2.8	$\overline{3.1}$		$\underline{2.9}$	2.9*						
2	DRI[1]	63.1–72.4	1.5	2.3	$\overline{2.5}$	2.3	$\underline{2.3}$	2.4	2.6	3.3	3.7*				
3	MQEM	58.1–67.4	.7	1.9	$\overline{2.3}$	1.8		$\underline{1.3}$	1.5	2.3	2.5*				
4	MQEM	64.1–73.4	.8	2.1	2.7	2.8		2.8	3.3	4.7	5.7*				
5	Wharton III[4]	62.1–65.4	1.3	1.8	2.2	$\overline{2.5}$	$\underline{2.5}$	2.5*							
6	Liu-Hwa	61Ja–67Dc	.6	1.5	1.9	2.4	2.6*								
7	Liu-Hwa	68Ja–71Dc	.6	1.3	1.8	2.3	2.4*								
8	Hickman-Coen	51–66		$\overline{2.7}$	$\underline{2.5}$	2.9		3.5	$\overline{3.7}$	$\underline{3.6}$	3.9	$\overline{4.4}$	4.3		
	Part II: Real GNP in Billions of 1958 Dollars														
			Number of Quarters Elapsed												
			1	4	6	8	12	14	16	20	24	28	40	56	64
9	BEA[3]	66.1–70.4	.8	$\overline{1.7}$	1.5	1.4	.7		.2	−.3					
10	DRI[1]	63.1–72.4	1.5	2.2	2.2	$\overline{2.2}$	1.8	1.7	$\underline{1.7}$	1.8	2.1	$\overline{2.3}$	1.8		
11	MQEM	58.1–67.4	.8	1.9	$\overline{2.2}$	2.1	1.4		$\underline{.7}$	.8	1.2	$\overline{1.2}$	.5		

12	MQEM	64.1–73.4	.8	2.0	$\overline{2.2}$	2.1	1.2		.2	$\underline{.1}$	$\overline{.5}$	.2	−1.0		
13	Wharton III[4]	62.1–65.4	1.3	2.0	2.2	2.4	$\overline{2.5}$	2.3	2.2	1.6					
14	Wharton III anticipations	62.1–66.4	1.1	1.7	1.8	$\overline{1.8}$			1.7	1.6					
15	Liu-Hwa	61Ja–67Dc	.6	1.5	1.7	$\overline{1.7}$	1.6	1.6							
16	Liu-Hwa	68Ja–71Dc	.5	1.1	$\overline{1.1}$	1.1	1.1	1.0							
17	Hickman-Coen	51–66		$\overline{1.6}$		$\underline{.9}$	1.1		1.6	$\overline{1.6}$	$\underline{1.6}$	1.7	2.1	$\overline{2.4}$	1.9

Part III: GNP Deflator (1958 : 100)

			Number of Quarters Elapsed												
			1	4	8	12	16	20	28	40	56	64			
18	BEA[3]	66.1–70.4	0	.04	.20	.34	.41	.45*							
19	MQEM	58.1–67.4	−.02	−.01	.02	.07	.11	.12	.15	.27*					
20	MQEM	64.1–73.4	0	−.01	.06	.20	.37	.43	.59	.89*					
21	Wharton III[4]	62.1–65.4	−.02	−.14	−.10	.05	.30*								
22	Hickman-Coen	51–66		.34	.44	.47	$\overline{.50}$	.50	.43	.36	.33	.31			

[1] For the DRI model's fiscal simulation, the increase in government purchases was in real terms.

[2] An asterisk * means the multiplier was still growing at the end of the simulation. An overline ‾ or an underline _ denotes a peak or a trough in the multiplier, respectively.

[3] This is the BEA simulation that kept the unemployment rate at 4%.

[4] This is the Wharton III simulation that increased <u>non</u>defense purchases.

TABLE 4

MONETARY POLICY: EFFECTS OF A $1 BILLION INCREASE IN UNBORROWED RESERVES, OR A CUT OF 50 BASIS POINT IN THE TREASURY BILL RATE, ON NOMINAL GNP, REAL GNP, AND THE GNP DEFLATOR

Line	Model	Simulation Period	Policy Variable[1]	Monetary Policy Effects[2] as a Function of Time Elapsed											
a	b	c	d	e	f	g	h	j	k	l	m	n	p	q	r
	Part I: Nominal GNP in Billions of Dollars														
				Number of Quarters Elapsed											
				1	4	8	10	12	14	16	20	32	36	56	64
1	DRI	63.1–72.4	RU	0	7	$\overline{11}$	9	7	5	3	−1	−2	−3		
2	MQEM	58.1–67.4	TBR	0	1.6	8.4	$\overline{9.1}$	8.8		7.4	$\underline{6.3}$	$\overline{7.5}$	7.4		
3	MQEM	64.1–73.4	TBR	0	2.8	8.4	10	12		$\overline{13}$	11	11	10		
4	Wharton III	62.1–65.4	RU	1.3	4.2	6.8	7.6	$\overline{8.1}$	7.9	7.5					
5	Wharton III	65.1–68.4	RU	1.0	3.2	5.3	6.2	6.7	7.0	7.2*					
6	Liu-Hwa	61Ja–67Dc	RU	0	2.2	14	21	27	31*						
7	Liu-Hwa	68Ja–71Dc	RU	0	2.2	13	20	24	28*						
8	Hickman-Coen	51–66	RU		2.9	$\overline{4.0}$		2.5		$\underline{.4}$	.4	.3	$\overline{1.1}$	−.2	.2*
	Part II: Real GNP in Billions of 1958 Dollars														
				Number of Quarters Elapsed											
				1	4	8	10	12	14	16	24	28	36	56	64
9	DRI	63.1–72.4	RU	0	7	$\overline{9}$	8	6	2	0	$\underline{-4}$	−3	−2*		
10	MQEM	58.1–67.4	TBR	0	1.6	8.0	$\overline{8.4}$	7.8		5.3	$\underline{2.9}$	$\overline{3.2}$	2.7		
11	MQEM	64.1–73.4	TBR	0	2.7	7.5	$\overline{8.6}$	8.4		5.8	1.6	1.3	$\underline{.6}$		

12	Wharton III	62.1–65.4	RU	1.4	4.5	7.2	8.0	$\overline{8.4}$	8.0	7.8					
13	Wharton III	65.1–68.4	RU	1.1	3.4	5.2	5.7	$\overline{6.0}$	5.8	5.6					
14	Wharton III anticipations	62.1–66.4	RU	.7	1.7	2.6		$\overline{2.9}$		2.7					
15	Liu-Hwa	61Ja–67Dc	RU	0	2.2	13	17	20	22*						
16	Liu-Hwa	68Ja–71Dc	RU	0	1.8	10	14	15	16*						
17	Hickman-Coen	51–66	RU		$\overline{1.7}$	1.7		.6		–.3	.4	.4	$\overline{.7}$	$\underline{–.1}$	.1*

Part III: GNP Deflator (1958 : 100)

				Number of Quarters Elapsed											
				1	3	4	8	16	20	28	32	36	40	56	64
18	MQEM	58.1–67.4	TBR	0	.01	0	.05	.35	.50	.58	.61	.65	.66*		
19	MQEM	64.1–73.4	TBR	0	0	–.02	0	.79	1.10	$\overline{1.26}$	1.22	1.14	.95		
20	Wharton III	62.1–65.4	RU	–.04	–.20	–.12	–.18	–.09							
21	Wharton III	65.1–68.4	RU	0	–.01	–.01	–.01	0							
22	Hickman-Coen	51–66	RU			.36	$\overline{.62}$	.17	$\underline{.07}$	$\overline{.10}$	$\underline{.04}$	$\overline{.09}$	.04	$\underline{–.02}$	0*

[1] RU = unborrowed reserves
TBR = Treasury bill rate

[2] An asterisk * means the effect was still increasing at the end of the simulation. An overline ¯ or underline _ denotes a peak or a trough in the effect, respectively.

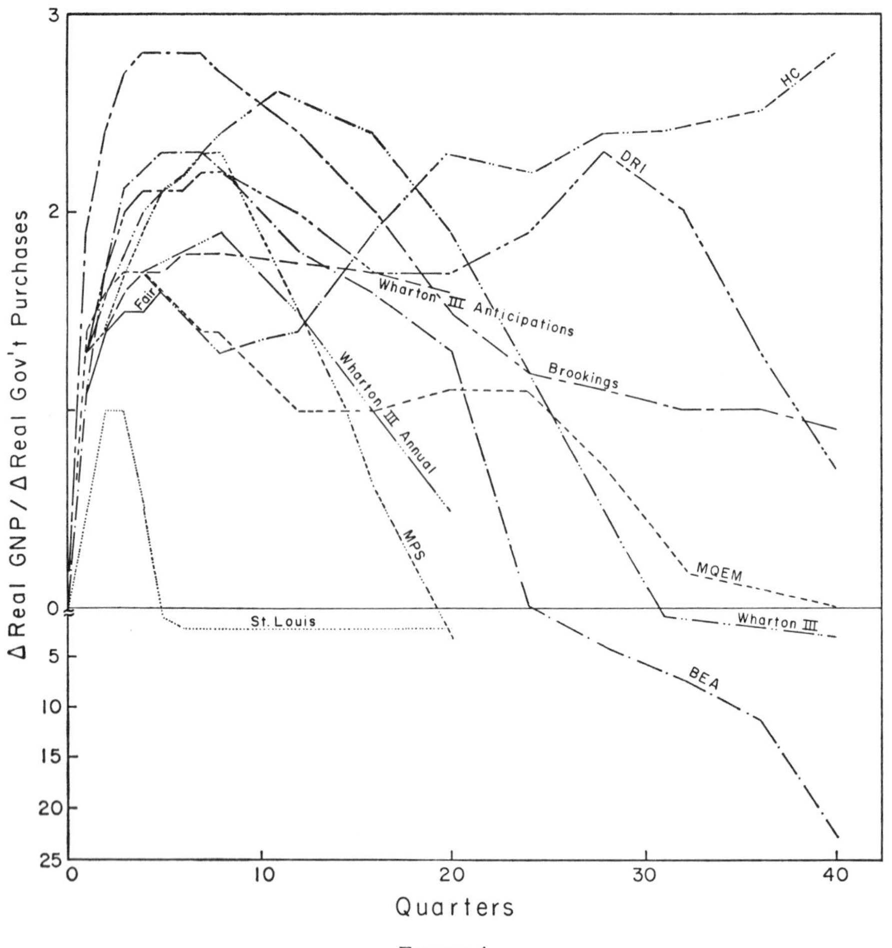

FIGURE 4

DYNAMIC MULTIPLIER EFFECTS OF A MAINTAINED $ 1 BILLION INCREASE IN REAL GOVERNMENT PURCHASES UPON REAL GNP WITHOUT ACCOMODATING MONETALY POLICY AS A FUNCTION OF TIME ELAPSED. SOURCE: FROMM AND KLEIN [9], TABLE 5.

negative effect on real GNP at 16 quarters. The amounts of increase obtained by the other models differ by factors of three and four after eight to 12 quarters, and more after that. Some models show a monotonically increasing effect over time, and some show cycles. The four models whose monetary policy effects are reported in Fromm and Klein [9] but not in Table 4 are equally at variance with each other and with the rest. The MPS model shows very large effects of a $1 billion step increase in unborrowed reserves, rising to $36 billion for nominal GNP and to $16 billion for real GNP at the end of 20 quarters. The Wharton annual model shows similar effects, except that its effect on real GNP

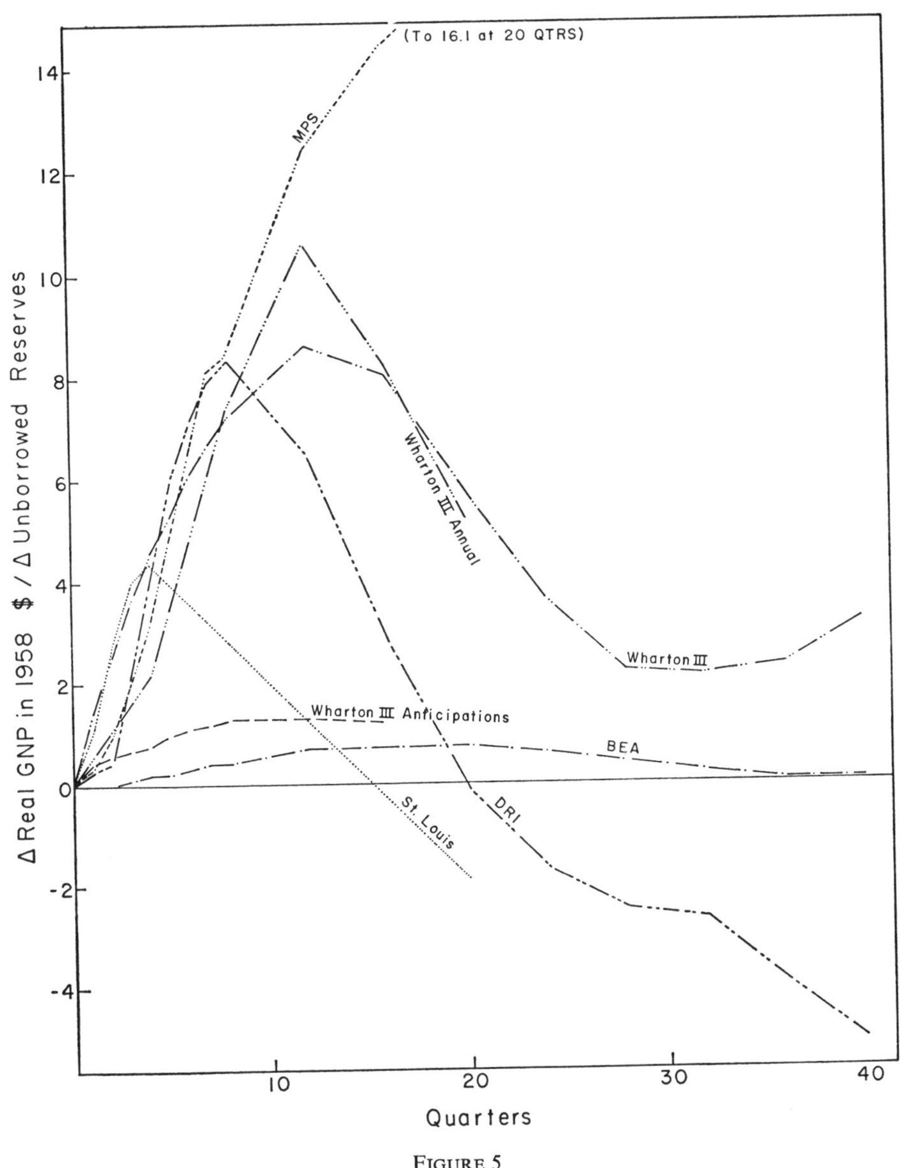

FIGURE 5

DYNAMIC MULTIPLIER EFFECTS OF A MAINTAINED $1.0 BILLION INCREASE IN UNBORROWED RESERVES UPON REAL GNP AS A FUNCTION OF TIME ELAPSED (EXCEPT FOR ST. LOUIS MODEL, WHERE THERE IS A $1 BILLION INCREASE IN M_1). SOURCE: FROMM AND KLEIN [9], TABLE 8.

turns down at about 12 quarters. According to the St. Louis model, the effect on nominal GNP rises to about $5 billion after four quarters and stabilizes there, while the effect on real GNP follows the nominal effect for about four quarters and then turns down, becoming slightly negative at 16 and 20 quarters. The BEA model shows the effect on nominal GNP rising throughout 40 quarters, and the effect on real GNP being near zero for five quarters, rising to $0.7 billion at 16 quarters, and returning to zero at 36 to 40 quarters.

The models differ almost as much on the effect of an easing of monetary policy on the price level, as shown in Table 4. The Wharton III model shows virtually no effect (at least for 16 quarters), the Hickman-Coen model shows an interim increase but no effect remaining at 64 quarters, and the Michigan model shows a positive effect, still increasing at the end of the 1958–67 policy simulation period, but decreasing at the end of the 1964–73 period.

The models disagree very strongly about the effects that follow from important fiscal and monetary policy actions. This is probably due in part to the use of different simulation periods. We face great uncertainty about this vital matter, until we can determine which of the models are wrong about it, and which (if any) are right. It would be valuable to have post-model-building RMSE statistics over much longer horizons than the eight quarters shown in Table 2 and the graphs, and policy simulations over periods having identical starting dates. Failing this, it will be difficult to make the important choice among models that have similar multiplier paths over short periods but extremely different paths over long periods.

An important aspect of the evaluation of an econometric model is the analysis of the economic theory contained in its equations. It is desirable to relate the theoretical structure of each model to the results it yields, including the character of the time-paths predicted by the model for the effects of important policy changes. That is too large an undertaking to be carried out in this paper. It will certainly be the subject of much future research. Each of the papers in this symposium has made a valuable contribution toward this end.[6]

5. SUGGESTIONS FOR TESTING MODELS AND FORECASTERS

For the future, the following types of computations would be helpful in testing and comparing the performance of econometric models, and the forecasting prowess of those who use them. Some of these computations are already being published by some model builders.

Errors of forecasts for periods that occur after the building of the model.

Errors of forecasts over longer horizons that have typically been used so far: at least eight quarters, and preferably much longer. Of course, a model cannot be evaluated in this way until several years after it is built.

Residuals of structural equations in post-model-building periods, to determine which structural equations stand up over time and which do not.

RMSE's (root mean square errors) of forecasts and residuals that are based on

(a) true exogenous values, and again ex ante exogenous values.

[6] Since I have criticized some macro-econometric models for not taking account of the government budget restraint, it is a pleasure to agree with Ando [3] that the simplified version of the MPS model presented there contains the government budget restraint implicitly.

(b) subjective adjustments to the model, and again no adjustments.
(c) a model that has been re-estimated using all data right up to the beginning of the forecast period, and again a model that has not been re-estimated.
(d) preliminary data as available at the beginning of the forecast peried, and again final revised data.

Policy simulations for periods of 20 years in order to find which policies have cyclical effects and which have monotonic effects, and whether the policy multipliers appear to converge eventually, and if so, to what values.

Comparisons of policy multipliers over time and between models, and the attempt to find which models yield the most reliable multipliers over long periods. For this purpose, the abovementioned RMSE's over longer forecasting horizons will help.

Stochastic as well as exact policy simulations, to determine whether exact simulations are a reliable guide in a world where nonstochastic equations do not perfectly describe events. Starting dates for simulations should be identical.

Performance in predicting turning points for the period after the model was built.[7] This includes an assessment of whether actual turing points are correctly predicted, and also of whether the model predicts the occurrence of turning points that do not actually occur.

The Johns Hopkins University

REFERENCES

[1] ADAMS, F. GERARD AND VIJAYA G. DUGGAL, "Anticipations Variables in an Econometric Model: Performance of the Anticipations Version of Wharton Mark III," chapter 1 in this volume.
[2] ANDERSON, LEONALL C. AND KEITH CARLSON, "St. Louis Model Revisited," chapter 3 in this volume.
[3] ANDO, ALBERT, "Some Aspects of Stabilization Policies, the Monetarist Controversy, and the MPS Model," chapter 7 in this volume.
[4] BROWN, T. M., "Standard Error of Forecast of a Complete Econometric Model," *Econometrica*, XXII (April, 1954), 178–192.
[5] DUGGAL, VIJAYA G., LAWRENCE R. KLEIN, AND MICHAEL D. MCCARTHY, "The Wharton Model Mark III: A Modern IS–LM Construct," chapter 8 in this volume.
[6] ECKSTEIN, OTTO, EDWARD W. GREEN, AND ALLEN SINAI, "The Data Resources Model: Uses, Structure and Analysis of the U. S. Economy," chapter 9 in this volume.
[7] FAIR, RAY, "An Evaluation of a Short-Run Forecasting Model," chapter 2 in this volume.
[7A] MCNEES, STEPHEN K., "The Predictive Accuracy of Econometric Forecasts," *New England Economic Review* (September/October, 1973), 3–27.
[8] FROMM, GARY AND LAWRENCE R. KLEIN, "A Comparison of Eleven Econometric Models of the United States," *American Economic Review*, LXIII (May, 1973), 385–393.

[7] Adams and Duggal [**1**] discuss the performance of the Wharton III anticipations model at turning points, but only within the sample, where the performance can be expected to be better than for post-sample and post-model-building periods.

[9] ——, AND ——, "The NBER/NSF Model Comparison Seminar: An Analysis of Results," chapter 18 in this volume.

[10] GOLDBERGER, ARTHUR S., A. L. NAGAR, AND H. S. ODEH, "The Covariance Matrices of Reduced-Form Coefficients and of Forecasts for a Structural Econometric Model," *Econometrica,* XXIX (October, 1961), 556–573.

[11] HICKMAN, BERT G., MICHAEL D. HURD, AND ROBERT M. COEN, "The Hickman-Coen Annual Growth Model: Structural Characteristics and Policy Responses," chapter 13 in this volume.

[12] HIRSCH, ALBERT A., BRUCE T. GRIMM, AND GORTI V. L. NARASIMHAM. "Some Multiplier and Error Characteristics of the BEA Quarterly Model," chapter 10 in this volume.

[13] HOTELLING, HAROLD, "Problems of Prediction," *American Journal of Sociology,* XLVIII (1942–43), 61–76.

[14] HYMANS, SAUL H. AND HAROLD T. SHAPIRO, "The Structure and Properties of the Michigan Quarterly Econometric Model of the U.S. Economy," chapter 11 in this volume.

[15] LIU, TA-CHUNG AND ERH-CHENG HWA, "A Monthly Econometric Model of the U.S. Economy," chapter 4 in this volume.

[16] FAIR, RAY C., "Forecasts from the Fair Model and a Comparison of the Recent Forecasting Records of Seven Forecasters," Princeton University Econometric Research Program, July, 1973 (duplicated).

16

ASYMPTOTIC THEORY AND LARGE MODELS

By J. D. Sargan

1. INTRODUCTION

My contribution to this symposium is little related to the rest since I am an outsider looking into the large model building activity. There are very difficult problems in estimating and testing large models, particularly the problem of multiple choice, making the conventional Neyman-Pearson theory of significance testing inappropriate. There is some unease among the profession about the results achieved from the use of large models in forecasting, and although one can interpret the progress made as learning from experience, yet there is considerable doubt about how this learning can be done efficiently. Particularly the modification to models, made as a result of the experience of predicting from them, is in present practice a matter of art rather than science. On this I would like to make only two points. If some *ad hoc* procedure in necessary to obtain good predictions from a model, such as adjusting the constant terms on the equations of the model to fit recent current values, this is an indication of some misspecification of its stochastic properties, and the model should be estimated with appropriately modified assumptions about the stochastic process generating the errors. In the same way, if it is possible in the prediction period to forecast an important part of the errors on the structural equations, this would equally be very useful in improving the estimation of the model. The objection may be raised that it would be difficult to avoid cheating. To avoid this it would seem legitimate, after preliminary estimates of the usual kind to give general ideas about the order of magnitude of the coefficients and the error variances, preferably before looking at detailed residuals for each time period, for the econometrician to consider the impact in each period of all those influences, of which he might take account in a prediction period, and so to produce his forecasts of the error on each equation throughout the sample period. Of course an immediate check on the correlation and regression coefficient of the estimated error on the subjective forecast error would throw light on the usefulness of the subjective forecast. But there would be no problem in fitting these forecasts into the model and the likelihood function, so as to improve the estimates of the model. A second point of somewhat less importance is the use of the mean square error as a criterion for the accuracy of the predictions. If a series of predictions from the same estimated model is used, we can split the mean square error into two independent parts, one the contribution of the errors in the estimated coefficients, the second the variance of the actual errors on the reduced form equations in the prediction period. If the second moment of the errors in the estimates of the reduced form coefficients is infinite, then the probability of the occurrence of very large errors in the whole set of predictions is relatively high. Since the argument for the non-existence of the moments is a very general one, depending only on the singularity of the relationship between the structural and reduced form coefficients of the model for values of the estimates which have non-zero probability density, it applies to most estimators, including all single equation estimators of the structural equations (notably O. L. S.), and to 3SLS, but not to FIML (see **[6]**). However it would not be too difficult to modify the estimators so that this problem is avoided, and it requires considerable study to evaluate its practical impact. For the rest of this paper I wish to discuss the difficulty of making any theoretical approach to the distribution of simultaneous estimators in large models.

2. ASYMPTOTIC THEORY AND LARGE MODELS

In discussing simultaneous equation estimators we start from asymptotic theory because it is simple. Exact finite sample theory is difficult. Attempts to improve on asymptotic results may be crude and difficult to make rigorous. Yet asymptotic theory usually seems to be adequate, somewhat surprisingly since if one considers the general arguments, used, for example, by Mann and Wald **[5]**, it seems that a sample of size 1000 or so might be required for a good asymptotic approximation. In practice even quite small samples seem to agree well with asymptotic theory. Of course, a comparison of the asymptotic moments with the finite sample moments, or with the Nagar series approximation to the sample moments might give some indication of the size of sample required to give a good asymptotic approximation. A more direct and easily interpretable indication is probably given by using the Edgeworth approximations, although both this and the Nagar approach are themselves dependent on the sample size being sufficiently large. From this type of comparison it appears superficially that the size of sample required to reduce the maximum difference between the cumulative distribution function and the corresponding asymptotic approximate distribution function to a given level would increase quite strongly with the number of variables in the model and indeed that with more complicated estimators it might increase more than proportionately with the size of the model. This is a vague statement, but its impact is that conventional asymptotic theory, considering the limiting distribution as the sample size tends to infinity and the model remains constant, is quite irrelevant to the "inadequate sample size" situation.

This means that it is very difficult to say anything about the statistical properties of the estimators, since obviously exact finite sample theory is impossibly difficult, and Monte Carlo studies are computer time and memory consuming; and since the space of parameters is many dimensional, it is very difficult to draw general conclusions from such studies. However it seems possible to use asymptotic limiting theory by considering sequences of stochastic models, such that the dimensions of the matrices increase with the sample size. Indeed there is no difficulty in conceiving of this type of asymptotic theory. Already we are familiar with "small σ asymptotics" as a useful method of approximation, where, in effect, a sequence of stochastic models is under consideration.

Specifically suppose that we define three infinite matrices B_∞, with elements b_{ij}, all integers i and $j \geq 1$; C_∞, with elements c_{ij} all integers i and $j \geq 1$; and a positive definite infinite matrix Ω_∞, with elements ω_{ij}, all integers i and $j \geq 1$. Consider also two sequences of integers $n(T)$, $m(T)$, increasing in T, and define B_T as the $n(T) \times n(T)$ matrix whose elements are b_{ij}, $1 \leq i, j \leq n(T)$, C_T as the $n(T) \times m(T)$ matrix whose elements are c_{ij}, $1 \leq i \leq n(T)$, $1 \leq j \leq m(T)$, and Ω_T as the $n(T) \times n(T)$ whose elements are ω_{ij}, $1 \leq i, j \leq n(T)$. We consider the sequence of models defined by

$$B_T y_t + C_T z_t = u_t\,, \qquad t = 1, \ldots, \mathrm{T},$$

where z_t is a non-stochastic vector defined as taken from the columns of an infinite matrix Z_∞, with elements z_{it}, all positive integers i and t, which are uniformly bounded, i.e., $|z_{it}| \leq b_z$, all i and t. u_t is a vector of structural equation errors such that $E(u_t) = 0$, and $E(u_t u_t') = \Omega_T$.

The matrices B_∞, C_∞, Ω_∞ can be interpreted as representations of linear operators in Hilbert Spare see [**4**, **2**]. The B_T, C_T, Ω_T are restrictions or sections of these operators, obtained in effect by considering the applications of the operators to vectors restricted to lying in finite dimensional subspaces. We are particularly interested in cases where one can argue about the limiting distributions of estimators of the Jorgenson-Brundy type [**3**], where an estimate of the reduced form coefficient is obtained by making a preliminary estimate of the structural form coefficients. Thus we will need to consider the continuity of the relationship between reduced form coefficients and structural coefficients. This can be considered by first assuring that the linear operator $P_\infty = -B_\infty^{-1}C_\infty$ is well defined, and then considering conditions under which it can be said that

$$\lim_{T\to\infty} P_T = -\lim_{T\to\infty} (B_T^{-1}C_T) = P_\infty\,.$$

The following three assumptions seem reasonable in the context.

ASSUMPTION 1. In any given row of B, there are no more than p elements which are non-zero. In any row of C there are no more than q elements which are non-zero.

This seems a plausible assumption to make, capturing an essential feature of most large scale econometric models, that only a small proportion of the total number of variables in the model appear in any one equation. We now specialize the assumption further. Suppose we are primarily concerned with one set of equations, and we consider the number of this set to remain finite as $T \to \infty$. We assume that there is only one standardizing restriction in each equation taking the form $b_{ii} = 1$, all i. By renumbering the equations and endogenous variables we ensure that this set of equations are the first N equations. Now consider the other endogenous variables which occur in the first N equations. By Assumption 1, the number of these is a maximum of $(p - 1)N$. However it seems likely that this would be a considerable overestimate, since we are likely to have taken our original N equations, so that each contains more than one of the first N endogenous variables, and also there is a considerable overlap in the other endogenous variables that they contain. Taking the number of these endogenous variables, to be N_1^*, consider next the N_1^* equations which explain them. Suppose N_2^* is the number of extra endogenous variables contained in these N_1^* equations, and so on, so that at each stage we select N_r^* equations as those equations explaining the endogenous variables, which occur in the previous $N_{(r-1)}^*$ equations, and which have not been explained by previous equations. Note that we have that

$$N_r^* \leq (p-1)N_{(r-1)}^* ,$$

from Assumption 1. However, it does not seem unreasonable to require that N_r^* has an upper bound. This is equivalent to the following:

ASSUMPTION 2.
(a) $b_{ij} = 0$, if $j > i + P$ for some $P > 0$.
(b) $c_{ij} = 0$, if $j > qi$.

Assumption 2a can be construed verbally as requiring that the model is almost recursive. This has been noted as a feature of large econometric models by many authors. Assumption 2b is merely a matter of reordering the exogenous variables so that the variables that occur in the equation (1) have the lowest indices and so on.

ASSUMPTION 3.
(a) $\sum_{j=1}^{\infty} |b_{ij}| \leq d + 1 < 2$ for all i,
(b) $|c_{ij}| < d^*$, for some d^*, all i and j.

Assumption 3a is perhaps rather overstrong but convenient. Noting that $b_{ii} = 1$, it is equivalent to requiring that

$$\sum_{j \neq i} |b_{ij}| \leq d < 1$$

for all i. This is a Hadamard condition ensuring that if we write

$$B_T = I_T - B_T^* ,$$

then B_T^* has all its latent roots within the unit circle.[1] There are several reasons for exploring the consequences of this assumption. As a piece of casual empiricism it has frequently been found that Gauss-Seidel methods of solving for the predicted values of the endogenous variables work rather well in large econometric models. This would not be found if B_T^* had large explosive roots. A rather more specialized theoretical argument would argue that the simultaneity in econometric models almost invariably arises from the neglect of short lags,

[1] In this paper we define the sup norm for a finite dimensional or infinite dimensional matrix as follows:

$$\|A\| = \sup |a_{ij}| ,$$

where the single vertical lines denote the modulus. If the elements of A satisfy $\sum_j |a_{ij}| \leq d$, all i, and z is an arbitrary vector, then $\|Az\| \leq d\|z\|$.

so that a more correct specification of the form of the model would have short lags of the form $y_{j(t-\delta_i)}$ in the i-th equation if $j \neq i$. Models of this general type have been discussed by, for example, Bear [**1**], and it has been found that a necessary condition, that the model should be robust to ignoring the lags, is that B_T^* have stable latent roots. It is not difficult to slightly generalize by converting it to a "dominant diagonal" type of condition by rescaling the endogenous variables, but this is easily done, and Assumption 3a is rather simpler to present in the proofs below. Define

$$N_1 = N + N_1^* .$$

THEOREM 1. *On the above assumptions, if P_T^* denotes the first N_1 rows of P_T, and P_∞^* the first N_1 row of P_∞, then both P_T^* and P_∞^* exist and*

$$\lim_{T\to\infty} P_T^* = P_\infty^* .$$

PROOF. Considering $B_\infty^* = I_\infty - B_\infty$, and $B_\infty^* J_\infty$, where J_∞ is any infinite matrix, taking any column of the latter expression we note that from Assumption 1 the sums defining the product matrix have not more than p non-zero elements, and so are always convergent. Thus $B_\infty^* J_\infty$ is a well-defined product matrix, and in particular $(B_\infty^*)^r$ is well defined for any r. Also note that if $(B_\infty^*)^r = Q_{r\infty}$ and $B_T^{*r} = Q_{rT}$, then

$$q_{r\infty ij}^* = q_{rTij}^* = 0, \qquad \text{if } j > i + rP.$$

Considering now the j-th column of $P_\infty, P_T, C_\infty, C_T$, and denoting them by $p_\infty, p_T, c_\infty, c_T$ respectively we consider

$$p_\infty = - \sum_{r=0}^{\infty} (B_\infty^*)^r c_\infty ,$$

and

$$p_T = - \sum_{r=0}^{\infty} (B_T^*)^r c_T .$$

Using Assumption 3 and the Cauchy convergence criterion each infinite series converges, and we have from the preceding argument that if $H_{N_1T}, H_{N_1\infty}$ have each N_1 rows, containing a unit matrix in the first N_1 columns, and zeroes elsewhere then

$$H_{N_1\infty}(B_\infty^*)^r = (Q_r \vdots 0)$$

where Q_r has $N_1 + rP$ columns. Considering in succession $H_{N_1T}(B_T^*)^r$ for $r = 1, 2, 3, \ldots$, and using

$$(Q_r \vdots 0) = (Q_{r-1} \vdots 0)B_\infty^* = (Q_{r-1} \vdots 0)(B_T^* \vdots 0)$$

it follows easily that we can also write that

$$H_{N_1T}(B_T^*)^r = (Q_r \vdots 0) ,$$

where now the number of columns in the last zero matrix is $n(T) - N_1 - rP$. Thus if

$$(1) \qquad r \leq (n(T) - N_1)/P$$

we have

$$H_{N_1T}(B_T^*)^r c_T = H_{N_1\infty}(B_\infty^*)^r c_\infty .$$

Then defining r_T as the largest integer satisfying (1), and

$$p_{\infty 1} = H_{N_1\infty} p_\infty ,$$

$$p_{T1} = H_{N_1T} p_T ,$$

we have

$$p_{T1} - p_{\infty 1} = - \sum_{r=r_T+1}^{\infty} (H_{N_1T}(B_T^{*r})c_T - H_{N_1\infty}(B_\infty^*)^r c_\infty) .$$

Using the sup norm for the vectors, and the corresponding norm for the matrices from Assumption 3 each term in the sum is $0(d^r)$, and so the sum is $0(d^{r_T}) = 0(d^{n(T)/P})$. End of Proof.

We are now interested in defining the systematic parts of the first N_1 endogenous variables. On the usual definitions (except for the transposition of the matrix, each systematic part corresponds to a row of the matrix,

$$\tilde{Y}_T = -H_{N_1T} B_T^{-1} C_T Z_T$$

where Z_T is made up of the first $m(T)$ rows, and the first T columns of Z_∞.

Now taking some particular z_t vector (a column of Z_∞) and considering each element of $C_\infty z_t$ we see that from Assumptions 1 and 3b the element is well defined and uniformly bounded. Further more making use of an expression similar to that of Theorem 1 we see that

$$\tilde{Y}_\infty = -H_{N_1\infty} B_\infty^{-1} C_\infty Z_\infty$$

is well defined and uniformly bounded.

THEOREM 2. *On Assumptions 1, 2, and 3*

$$\lim_{T\to\infty} (\tilde{Y}_T - \tilde{Y}_\infty) = 0 .$$

PROOF. From Assumption 2b we can take it that $m(T) \leq qn(T)$. Now defining z_t as before and z_{tT} to be the vector made up of the first $m(T)$ elements of z_i, it follows from 2b that the i-th element of $C_T z_{tT} - C_\infty z_t$ is zero if $i < m(T)/q$. Repeating the arguments of Theorem 1 it follows that

$$\| \tilde{Y}_T - \tilde{Y}_\infty \| = 0(d^{m(T)/qP}) .$$

End of Proof.

Now following the results established by Jorgenson and Brundy [3] there is no difficulty in showing that if Z_T^* is the set of M variables which occurs in the first N equations and $\tilde{Y}_{\infty T}$ is the sub-matrix of $\tilde{Y}_{\infty}$ which forms the first T columns of $\tilde{Y}_{\infty}$, then the variables $\tilde{Y}_{\infty T}$, Z_T^* form an asymptotically efficient set of instrumental variables for estimating the first N_1 equations of the model in the following sense.

If $\hat{\Omega}^*$ is some arbitrary consistent estimator of the $N \times N$ principal sub-matrix Ω^* of Ω_∞ and we write

$$TR_T = \begin{pmatrix} \tilde{Y}_{\infty T} Y_T^{*1} & \tilde{Y}_{\infty T} Z_T^{*1} \\ Z_T^* Y_T^{*1} & Z_T^* Z_T^{*1} \end{pmatrix}$$

where Y_T^* is the matrix formed from the first N_1 rows of Y_T, and if B^* is the submatrix of B_∞ obtained by taking its first N rows and first N_1 columns, C^* is the submatrix of C_∞ obtained by taking its first N rows and M columns, and $A = (B^*; C^*)$, vec A is the $N(N_1 + M)$ vector made up of N subvectors each a transposed row of A, $\hat{A}$ represents the instrumental variable estimators and S is a matrix of $N(N_1 + M)$ columns and a number of rows equal to the number of unconstrained elements in the first N equations, such that in each row all the elements are zero, except for a single unit occurring where the corresponding unconstrained element occurs in vec A, then the instrumental variable estimators are defined by

$$S(\hat{\Omega}^{*-1} \otimes R_T) \operatorname{vec} \hat{A} = 0 . \tag{2}$$

The asymptotic efficiency follows from considering the effect of adding an arbitrary set of Z_T^{**} selected from Z_T, to the $\tilde{Y}_{\infty T}$, Z_T^* as instrument variables.

Then defining

$$\tilde{Z}_T = \begin{pmatrix} \tilde{Y}_{\infty T} \\ Z_T^* \\ Z_T^{**} \end{pmatrix},$$

and

$$X_T = \begin{pmatrix} Y_T^* \\ Z_T^* \end{pmatrix},$$

and

$$TR_T^* = (X_T \tilde{Z}_T^1)(\tilde{Z}_T \tilde{Z}_T^1)^{-1} (\tilde{Z}_T X_T^1)$$

we consider the instrumental variables estimates $\hat{A}^*$ defined by

$$S(\hat{\Omega}^{*-1} \otimes R_T^*) \operatorname{vec} \hat{A}^* = 0 . \tag{3}$$

We now introduce the following general assumption.

ASSUMPTION 4.

$$\lim_{T \to \infty} \sum_{t=1}^{T} z_{it} z_{jt} / T = m_{ij}$$

exists for all i and j, and the matrix $M_\infty = (m_{ij})$ is bounded and strictly positive definite, in the sense that, if M_T is the $m(T) \times m(T)$ principal submatrix, all the latent roots of M_T have a positive lower and upper bound uniformly as $T \to \infty$.

Using this assumption there is no dificiculty in showing that

(a) if $P_{e\infty} = \begin{pmatrix} P_\infty \\ I_M 0 \end{pmatrix}$, then $\operatorname{plim}_{T\to\infty} R_T = \operatorname{plim}_{T\to\infty} R_T^* = \bar{R} = P_{e\infty} M_{e\infty}^{P\prime}$, and

(b) if the identification condition is satisfied that $S(I \otimes P_{e\infty})$ is of full rank, then $\sqrt{T}\ \text{vec}\,(\hat{A}^* - A)$ and $\sqrt{T}\ \text{vec}\,(\hat{A} - A)$ have the same asymptotic variance matrix $(S(\Omega^{*-1} \otimes \bar{R})S')^{-1}$. However a more interesting problem is to consider a further set of estimators given by taking preliminary estimates of (B_T, C_T), $(\hat{B}_T, \hat{C}_T)$ and using these to generate $\hat{Y}_T = -H_{N_1T}\hat{B}_T^{-1}\hat{C}_T Z_T$. We now consider estimates given by

$$(4) \qquad S(\Omega^{*-1} \otimes \hat{R}_T)\ \text{vec}\,\tilde{A} = 0$$

where

$$T\hat{R}_T = \begin{pmatrix} \hat{Y}_T Y_T^{*1} & \hat{Y}_T Z_T^{*1} \\ Z_T^* Y_T^{*1} & Z_T^* Z_T^{*1} \end{pmatrix}.$$

The preliminary estimate of $(\hat{B}_T, \hat{C}_T)$ and the corresponding $\hat{\Omega}^*$ can be based on arbitrarily chosen sets of instrument variables. The following assumption will be used.

Assumption 5. For some α, β such that $0 < \alpha, \beta < 1/2$, and $\alpha + \beta > 1/2$, and some positive f and g,

(a) $\lim_{T\to\infty} (m(T)(P(T^{\alpha-1}(\sum_{t=1}^{T} u_{it}z_{jt}) \geq f))) = 0$ uniformly in i and j.

(b) $\lim_{T\to\infty} (n(T)P(T^\beta |\hat{b}_{ij} - b_{ij}| \geq g)) = 0$

$\lim_{T\to\infty} (n(T)P(T^\beta |\hat{c}_{ij} - c_{ij}| \geq g)) = 0$ uniformly in i and j.

These assumptions seem reasonable if both $n(T)$ and $m(T)$ are proportional to some power of T. Assumption 5a will then be satisfied, for example, if the errors are normally distributed with uniformly bounded variance, given Assumption 4, for any $\alpha < 1/2$. Condition 5b is not very strong. It would, for example, be satisfied from the Chebychev inequality, if suitable moments exist and are of the correct order of magnitude in T. If the number of instrumental variables used in making these preliminary estimates is sufficiently large we can prove that 5b is satisfied except for the uniformity in i and j.

Theorem 3. *On Assumptions 1, 2, 3, 4, 5,* $\text{vec}\,(\tilde{A} - \hat{A}) = 0(T^{-1/2})$. *The estimators $\tilde{A}$ and $\hat{A}$ are asymptotically equivalent.*

Proof. We prove that both estimators have the same asymptotic distribution. Now

$$S(\hat{\Omega}^{*-1} \otimes \hat{R}_T)\ \text{vec}\,A = S(\hat{\Omega}^{*-1} \otimes I)/T(\text{vec}\,A(X_T\hat{Y}_T^1 : X_T Z_T^{*1}))$$

so that

$$S(\hat{\Omega}^{*-1} \otimes \hat{R}_T) \operatorname{vec}(\tilde{A} - A) = S(\hat{\Omega}^{*-1} \otimes I)/T(\operatorname{vec}(U_T^* Y_T^1 : U_T^* Z_T^{*1}))$$

where the $U_T^* = AX_T$ is the $N \times T$ matrix of errors on the first N equations. Now writing $\sqrt{T} \operatorname{vec}(\tilde{A} - A) = S^1 \Delta^* A$, noting that $\Delta^* A$ is a vector equal to the scaled up errors on the unconstrained elements of A, we have

$$\begin{aligned}
&[S(\hat{\Omega}^{*-1} \otimes \hat{R}_T)S^1]\Delta^* A \\
&\quad = S(\hat{\Omega}^{*-1} \otimes I) \operatorname{vec}(U_T^* \hat{Y}_T^1 : U_T^* Z_T^{*1})/\sqrt{T} \\
&\quad = S(\hat{\Omega}^{*-1} \otimes I) \operatorname{vec}(U_T^* Y_{\infty T}^1 : U_T^* Z_T^{*1})/\sqrt{T} \\
&\qquad + S(\hat{\Omega}^{*-1} \otimes I) \operatorname{vec}(U_T^* Z_T^1)(\hat{P}_T^1 - P_T^1) + (P_T^1 - P_\infty^1))/\sqrt{T}
\end{aligned}$$

where

$$\hat{P}_T = -H_{N_1 T} \hat{B}_T^{-1} \hat{C}_T ,$$

$$P_T = -H_{N_1 T} B_T^{-1} C_T ,$$

and

$$P_{\infty T} = -H_{N_1^\infty} B_\infty^{-1} C_\infty .$$

In order to prove the theorem it is only necessary to prove

(a) $\operatorname{plim}_{T\to\infty} \hat{R}_T = \hat{R}$,

(b) $\operatorname{plim}_{T\to\infty} \operatorname{vec}(U_T^* Z_T^1 (P_T^1 - P_{\infty T}^1))/\sqrt{T} = 0$, and

(c) $\operatorname{plim}_{T\to\infty} (\operatorname{vec} U_T^* Z_T^1 (\hat{P}_T^1 - P_T^1)/\sqrt{T}) = 0$.

In the following section I give the details of the proofs of (c), and (b), omitting the proof of (a), since this is similar and simpler than the proofs of (b) and (c).

We have

$$\begin{aligned}
\hat{P}_T - P_T &= -H_{N_1 T} \hat{B}_T^{-1} (\hat{C}_T - C_T - (\hat{B}_T - B_T) B_T^{-1} C_T) \\
&= -H_{N_1 T} \hat{B}_T^{-1} (\psi_T + \hat{C}_T - C_T) ,
\end{aligned}$$

where

$$\psi_T = (\hat{B}_T - B_T) P_T .$$

Now if p_{kT} is the k-th column of P_T, c_{kT} is the k-th column of C_T.

$$p_{kT} = -\sum_{k=0}^{\infty} (B_T^*)^r c_{kT} . \tag{4}$$

Since in the i-th row of $(B_T^*)^r$ all elements such that $j > i + rP$ are zero,

$$c_{jk} = 0 \qquad \text{if } k > qj ,$$

the contribution of the r-th term of (4) to p_{ikT} is zero if

$$k > q(i + rP)$$

or if

$$r < (k - qi)/qP .$$

Now defining r_{ik} as the integer, such that

$$r_{ik} \leq (k - qi)/qP < r_{ik} + 1,$$

we have that, for $r \geq r_{ik}$, the modulus of the r-th term is less than $d^r d^*$. Thus

$$|p_{ikT}| \leq d^{r_{ik}} d^*/(1 - d) \leq d^{(k-qi)/qP} d^*/d(1 - d) .$$

On the other hand from

$$p_{kT} = B_T^* p_{kT} + c_{kT} ,$$

we have

$$\|p_{kt}\| \leq d\|p_{kt}\| + d^* ,$$

or

$$|p_{ikT}| \leq d^*/(1 - d) ,$$

for all i and k.

Thus we can write

(5) $\quad (p_{ikT}) \leq d^*/(1 - d)$, all i and k, $\leq (d^* d((^{k-qi)/qP}))/d(1 - d)$ if $\ k \geq qi + P$.

Taking an arbitrary d_u such that $d < d_u < 1$, and defining

$$\delta = (d_u - d)/p,$$

we can choose T_0, such that $T^\beta \delta \geq g$ if $T \geq T_0$.

Now consider the probability that at least one of the inequalities listed in Assumption (5) is satisfied for the model of order T. Using Bonferroni's inequality, this probability is less than the sum of the separate probabilities for each inequality. The number of the coefficients b_{ij}, c_{ij} under consideration is less than $n(T)(p + q)$ from Assumption 1, and the limit in Assumption 5b are uniform in i and j so that the probability that any one of the coefficients satisfies the inequalities listed under (5b) tends to zero as $T \to \infty$. Similarly the number of variables $\sum_{t=0}^{T} u_{it} z_{jt}$ is $m(T)N$ and so the probability that any of the inequalities listed under 5a is satisfied tends to zero as $T \to \infty$.

On the other hand if none of the inequalities listed in Assumption 5 is satisfied, then if $T > T_0$,

$$\sum_j |\hat{b}_{ij}| < d_u < 1, \qquad \text{for all } j.$$

Define

$$\hat{B}_T^* = I_T - \hat{B}_T .$$

Consider now ψ_{ijT}, where

$$\psi_T = (\hat{B}_T - B_T) P_T ,$$

and taking account of

$$\hat{b}_{ij} - b_{ij} = 0 \qquad \text{if } j > i + P .$$

Then, in view of (5) and Assumption 5b we can write

$$(6) \qquad \begin{aligned} T^{\beta} |\psi_{ij}| &\leq d^* gp/(1 - d) && \text{for all } i \text{ and } j \\ &\leq (d^* gp d^{(j-qi)/qP})/d^2(1 - d) , && \text{if } j \geq q(i + 2P) . \end{aligned}$$

Consider

$$T^{\beta} H_{N_1 T} B_T^{-1} \psi_j = T^{\beta} \sum_{r=0}^{\infty} H_{N_1 T} \hat{B}_T^{*r} \psi_j ,$$

where ψ_j is the j-th column of ψ_T.

Now writing $H_{N_1 T} \hat{B}_T^{*r} = (\hat{Q}_r : 0)$, $\hat{Q}_r$ has not more than $N_1 + rP$ columns. Thus if $j \geq q(N_1 + (r + 2)P)$, $\hat{Q}_r$ multiplies a sub-vector of ψ_j whose maximal modulus element is less than

$$(d^* gp d^{(j - q(N_1 + rP))/qP})(d^2(1 - d)) .$$

Thus defining r_0 as the integer such that

$$r_0 \leq (j - q(N_1 + 2P))/qP < r_0 + 1 ,$$

we have that

$$T^{\beta} H_{N_1 T} \hat{B}_T^{-1} \psi_j = T^{\beta} \sum_{r=0}^{r_0} H_{N_1 T} \hat{B}_T^{*r} \psi_j + T^{\beta} \sum_{r=r_0+1}^{\infty} H_{N_1 T} \hat{B}_T^{*r} \psi_j$$

and note that in the first r_0 terms we have for the sup norm

$$\begin{aligned} \left\| \sum_{r=0}^{r_0} T^{\beta} H_{N_1 T} \hat{B}_T^{*r} \psi_j \right\| &\leq \sum_{r=0}^{r_0} (d_u^r d^{(j - q(N_1 + rP))/qP} d^* gp/d^2(1 - d) \\ &\leq d^{(j - qN_1)} (d_u/d)^{r_0 + 1} - 1) d^* gp/(d_u - d) d(1 - d) \\ &\leq d^{(j - qN_1)} ((d_u/d)^{(j - q(N_1 + P))/qP} d^* gp/(d_u - d) d(1 - d) \\ &= d_u^{(j - qN_1)} d^* gp/d_u(d_u - d)(1 - d) . \end{aligned}$$

For the remaining terms we have

$$\begin{aligned} \left\| \sum_{r=r_0+1}^{\infty} T^{\beta} H_{N_1 T} \hat{B}_T^{*r} \psi_j \right\| &\leq \sum_{r=r_0+1}^{\infty} d_u^r (d^* gp/(1 - d)) \\ &= d_u^{r_0+1} d^* gp/(1 - d)(1 - d_u) \\ &\leq d_u^{(j - q(N_1 + 2P))/qP} d^* gp/(1 - d)(1 - d_u) . \end{aligned}$$

Thus

$$\| T^{\beta} H_{N_1 T} \hat{B}_T^{-1} \psi_j \| \leq d_u^{j/qP} k_1 ,$$

where k_1 is a constant independent of j. Consider in the same way

$$H_{N_1 T} \hat{B}_T^{-1} (\hat{c}_{jT} - c_{jT})$$

where $\hat{c}_{jT} - c_{jT}$ is the j-th column of $\hat{C}_T - C_T$, and note that $\hat{c}_{ij} - c_{ij} = 0$ if $j \geq qi$. Thus

$$T^{\beta}H_{N_1T}\hat{B}_T^{-1}(\hat{c}_{jT}-c_{jT}) = \sum_{r=0}^{\infty} T^{\beta}H_{N_1T}\hat{B}_T^{*r}(\hat{c}_{jT}-c_{jT}),$$

and writing

$$H_{N_1T}\hat{B}_T^{*r} = (\hat{Q}_r : 0)$$

as before where $\hat{Q}_r$ has $N_1 + rP$ columns it follows that

$$H_{N_1T}\hat{B}_T^{*r}(\hat{c}_{jT}-c_{jT}) = 0$$

unless $j \geq q(N_1 + rP)$. So defining r_0 as before

$$\begin{aligned}\|T^{\beta}H_{N_1T}\hat{B}_T^{-1}(\hat{c}_{jT}-c_{jT})\| &= \left\| \sum_{r=r_0+3}^{\infty} T^{\beta}H_{N_1T}\hat{B}_T^{*r}(\hat{c}_{jT}-c_{jT}) \right\| \\ &\leq d_u^{r_0+3}g/(1-d_u) \\ &\leq d_u^{(j-qN_1)/qP}g/(1-d_u).\end{aligned}$$

Then

$$\|T^{\beta}H_{N_1T}\hat{B}_T^{-1}(\psi_j + (\hat{c}_{jT}-c_{jT}))\| \leq kd_u^j$$

where

$$k = k_1 + d_u^{-N_1/P}g/(1-d_u).$$

Finally

$$\begin{aligned}&T^{\alpha+\beta-1}(U_T^*Z_T^1)(\hat{P}_T^1 - P_T^1) \\ &\quad = \sum_{j=1}^{m(T)} (T^{\alpha-1}U_T^*Z_{jT})((\psi_j^1 + (\hat{c}_{jT}-c_{jT})^1\hat{B}_T^{1-1})H_{N_1T}^1T^{\beta})\end{aligned}$$

so that

$$\|T^{\alpha+\beta-1}(U_T^*Z_T^1)(\hat{P}_T^1 - P_T^1)\| \leq fk/(1-d_u).$$

It follows that

$$\operatorname*{plim}_{T\to\infty} T^{-1/2}(U_T^{*1}Z_T^1)(\hat{P}_T^1 - P_T^1) = 0.$$

In a similar way from Theorem 1 we deduce that

$$\|P_T - P_{\infty T}\| = 0(d^{m(T)/qP}).$$

Thus

$$\|T^{\alpha-1}U_T^*Z_T^1(P_T^1 - P_{\infty T}^1)\| \leq k_2d^{m(T)}/q^Pm(T)f,$$

and so

$$\operatorname*{plim}_{T\to\infty} (T^{-1/2}(U_T^*Z_T^1)(P_T^1 - P_{\infty T}^1)) = 0.$$

End of Proof.

3. GENERAL CONCLUSIONS

From the last theorem we conclude that for a wide category of simultaneous equation models the results of asymptotic sampling theory are still a good approximation even in very large models. One extension, which would be comparatively simple to make is to allow the variables Z_T to include lagged endogenous variables. The assumptions used here could no doubt be weakened, but I conjecture that it is necessary for these results, that all the latent roots (the spectrum) of the B_T^* matrix should be within the unit circle. Even this criterion for the validity of asymptotic theory cannot be considererd directly for realistic non-linear models, but it might be worthwhile to test for the satisfaction of the criterion linearized versions of existing estimates of large econometric models. It may indeed be found that only a small proportion of actual models satisfy such weakened conditions. (Note that with dynamic models with simple distributed lags use of a shorter unit time period makes it more likely that the latent roots condition will be satisfied.) Within the group of models satisfying these conditions, we can draw the standard conclusions about the relative advantages of different estimators. Thus OLS estimates have biases which are independent of sample size, and a relatively small variance, Iterated instrumental variable estimates have relatively small biases in large samples, and relatively larger variance. In sufficiently large samples one expects the MSE of the instrumental variable estimator to be smaller than of OLS.

However as with most asymptotic results a major problem is to evaluate how large a sample is required to obtain a reasonable approximation. One possibility is to use Nagar type approximations for the bias and variances making the assumption that if the resulting differences from the asymptotic moments are small, then the difference between the exact moment and the asymptotic moment is also small. This still leaves the problem of an excessive number of dimensions in the parameter space to be explored. A possible starting point is to take an estimated model and explore one dimensional variations on it (e.g., by scaling the B_T^* matrix by an arbitrary scalar).

This paper has concentrated on the iterated instrumental variable type estimator since it is well defined in the inadequate sample size situation. In the Appendix I give a result on the definition of an inadequate sample size for the FIML estimator.

London School of Economics

APPENDIX

A1. *The FIML estimator with inadequate sample size.* In a paper given at the 1969 Winter Meetings of the Econometric Society, Lawrence R. Klein mentioned that FIML estimators were only well defined if the total number of variables in the model was less than the sample size. The arguments produced for this statement [1] have not been universally agreed to be convincing. However on looking at the problem I found that Klein was correct as shown by the following two theorems.

The model to be considered will be written

$$Ax_t = By_t + Cz_t = u_t, \qquad t = 1, \ldots, T,$$

where B is $n \times n$, and C is $n \times m$, where the model is assumed to be identified by zero restricitions, and one standardizing restriction per equation. We consider the FIML estimates in the case where the covariance matrix is unrestricted (except that it is positive definite) and there are no identities, and where $T < m + n$. Using X for the data matrix of x_t, we then have that this is of rank less than $m + n$ so that $\exists\, \alpha$ such that

$$X\alpha = 0 .$$

The concentrated log-likelihood function can then be written

$$L = T \log |det\ B| - \frac{1}{2} T \log det(AX'XA') .$$

If we can find A_0 satisfying the restrictions such that

(I) $$\det B_0 \neq 0$$

and

(II) $$\lambda' A_0 = \alpha' ,$$

then the first term of L is finite and the second term is infinite, so that the likelihood has no maximum. If we can also show that there are an infinite set of A_0 satisfying these conditions, then the estimator can be considered to be unidentified.

THEOREM A1. *If at least* $(T - n - 1)$ *of the* z_t *variables are linearly independent for all* $t = 1, \ldots, T$, *and the reduced form errors have every conditional distribution absolutely continuous then the probability that (I) and (II) are satisfied is one.*

PROOF. Write

$$\alpha' = (\beta' : \gamma') , \qquad \lambda_i b_{0ij} = \mu_{ij} , \qquad \lambda_i c_{0ij} = \nu_{ij} .$$

Then (II) can be written

(IIA) $$\sum_{i=1}^{n} \mu_{ij} = \beta_j$$

(IIB) $$\sum_{i=1}^{n} \nu_{ij} = Y_j .$$

Obviously we require that (III) any element of μ_{ij}, ν_{ij} equals zero, when the corresponding element of b_{ij}, c_{ij} is restricted to be zero. We also require that (IV) $\mu_{ij} \neq 0$ if the corresponding b_{ij} is standardized to a non-zero value. If we can find μ_{ij} satisfying these conditions, and if $b_{ij(i)}$ is standardized to equal d_i in the i-th equation, then define

$$\lambda_i = \frac{\mu_{ij(i)}}{d_i} ,$$

and then

$$b_{0ij} = \frac{\mu_{ij}}{\lambda_i} . \tag{1}$$

Finally take ν_{ij} for each j satisfying III and IIB; for example, we could take ν_{ij} equal for all i, such that c_{ij} is not restricted to be zero. Then take

$$c_{0ij} = \frac{\nu_{ij}}{\lambda_i} . \tag{2}$$

and conditions (II) are all satisfied.

To satisfy (I) suppose we can find a square $n \times n$ matrix h_{ij}, such that det $H \neq 0$, and $\sum_{i=1}^{n} h_{ij} \neq 0$, all j, otherwise h_{ij} satisfies conditions similar to conditions (III) and (IV). We can obtain such an H matrix by starting from $\bar{B}$, the true B matrix, and progressively modifying the h_{ij} to satisfy the above conditions. No change is required in the j-th column if $\sum_i h_{ij} \neq 0$. If $\sum_i h_{ij} = 0$, change one non-zero element of h_{ij} so as to make $\sum_{i=1}^{n} h_{ij} \neq 0$; but ensure that det H remains non-zero, and that all the elements corresponding to standardized coefficients remain non-zero. An alternative choice, which is relatively simple, is available in the case where the standardized coefficients all occur on the diagonal of the B matrix, for in this case we can take $H = I$.

Now if $T > n - 1$, we take $T - n + 1$ linearly independent columns of the Z matrix and call the sub matrix Z_1. Then we determine β from the condition

$$Y\beta + Z_1\gamma_1 = 0 .$$

Using the Cramer representation of the solution for β and γ_1, we find that any element of β is zero with probability zero, so that we consider the case where β is strictly non-zero. Similarly if $T \leq n - 1$, we determine $n - T$ of the elements of β to have arbitrary non-zero values and then determine the remaining elements of β from

$$Y\beta = 0 .$$

Again using the Cramer representation we see that β is strictly non-zero with probability one; and we can take $\gamma = 0$.

We now choose ϕ_j so that $\phi_j \sum_i h_{ij} = \beta_j$. ϕ_j is then well-defined and non-zero. Then take $\mu_{ij} = \phi_j h_{ij}$. Then all the conditions on μ_{ij} are satisfied. Since

$$b_{0ij}\phi_j = h_{ij}/\lambda_i ,$$

we have

$$\det B_0 = \det H \, \Pi\phi_j / \Pi\lambda_i \neq 0 .$$

Then the C_0 matrix is chosen from (2). Note that the H matrix is only constrained to keep certain functions of H non-zero, so that there are an infinite set of H values which satisfy these non-zero conditions. Thus the estimator is unidentified. End of Proof.

In fact we can be more specific about the samples for which the likelihood function has no maximum. Define a set of n_1 endogenous variables as a partially recursive set if by reordering the variables so that they form the first n_1 endogenous variables, and reordering the equations appropriately we can write

$$B = \begin{pmatrix} B_1 & B_2 \\ 0 & B_3 \end{pmatrix},$$

where B_1 is $n_1 \times n_1$ and B_3 is $(n - n_1) \times (n - n_1)$.

We define a set of endogenous variables which is such that the corresponding elements of β are all zero, to be a zero coefficient set, where

$$Y\beta + Z\gamma = 0 .$$

THEOREM A2. *If every vector satisfying* $X\alpha = 0$, *defines a zero coefficient set, which contains no partially recursive set, then the maximum likelihood estimator is unidentified.*

PROOF. Since det $\bar{B} \neq 0$, if we consider the expansion det $B = \sum \pm b_{ij} b_{2j'} \dots b_{nk}$, where $(ij \dots k)$ is some permutation of $(12 \dots n)$, at least one of the terms in the sum must have all its elements not zero-restricted. Choose one such term, and reorder the endogenous variables so that these elements now lie on the diagonal of B. Thus we have that every element on the diagonal is not restricted to be zero. We now preserve this feature, by applying the same reordering to the endogenous variables and to the equations, whenever we need to reorder.

First reorder, so that if the number of zero elements in β is n^*, then the first n^* endogenous variables correspond to these zero elements. Now consider the upper left-hand principal minors of B of dimension less than or equal to n^* in turn, starting with minors of dimension n^*, then of dimension $n^* - 1, n^* - 2$, and so on. When considering the principal minor of dimension $r \leq n^*$, we note that since the first r variables do not form a partially recursive set, we must be able to find a b_{ij}, $j \leq r$, $i > r$, such that b_{ij} is not restricted to be zero. Then interchange the j-th column with the r-th column, and the j-th row with the r-th row. After the case $r = 2$ has been dealt with, it will be found that for every $r \leq n^*$ b_{rr} is not restricted to be zero, and for some $i > r$ b_{ir} is not restricted to be zero. We now show how it is possible to choose μ_{ij} so that it satisfies (I), (IIA), (III) and (IV).

We consider the columns of μ_{ij} in sequence, for $j = 1, 2, \dots, n$, choosing them so as to make the successive top left-hand principal minors non-singular. Denote the top left-hand principal minor determinant of order r by D_r. Suppose that we have chosen the first $r - 1$ columns so that conditions (IIA), (III) and (IV) are satisfied for all $j \leq r - 1$, and $D_j \neq 0$, $j \leq r - 1$. Choose all μ_{ir}, $i < r$, which are not restricted to be zero, so that they take arbitrary non-zero values.

If there are more than one μ_{ir}, $i > r$, which is not restricted to be zero, then choose for all except one of these μ_{ir} arbitrary non-zero values. Now it remains to choose μ_{rr} and μ_{kr}, where $k > r$ is the row of the element which we have left to be chosen. Then D_r does not depend upon μ_{kr}, but is a linear function of μ_{rr}. The coefficient of μ_{rr} is D_{r-1} which by assumption is non-zero. There is a unique value of μ_{rr}, μ_{rr}^* which makes $D_r = 0$. Now, if $n \leq n^*$, (IIA) gives

$$\sum_{i=1}^{n} \mu_{ir} = 0\,.$$

Since all μ_{ir} except μ_{rr} and μ_{kr} are fixed we can regard this as determining μ_{kr} in terms of μ_{rr}. So we can determine μ_{rr} so that $\mu_{rr} \neq 0$, $\mu_{kr} \neq 0$, $D_r \neq 0$. Note that since we need only choose μ_{rr} to avoid three values, an infinite set of possible μ_{rr} can be chosen at this stage.

If $n > n^*$, we proceed as before but now choose all μ_{ir}, $i \neq r$, arbitrarily non-zero and choose μ_{rr} so that $\mu_{rr} \neq 0$, $D_r \neq 0$, and $\sum_{i=1}^{n} \mu_{ir} \neq 0$. Then we can rescale all μ_{ir} by a suitable non-zero scale factor so that $\sum_{i=1}^{n} \mu_{ir} = \beta_r$. Thus we ensure that at each stage (IIA), (III), (IV) are satisfied and that $D_r \neq 0$. When $r = n$, we then have that the $n \times n$ matrix μ_{ij}, satisfies (I), (IIA), (III), and (IV), so that as in Theorem A1 we can rescale to determine λ and B_0.

As noted earlier there is an infinite set of alternative μ_{ij} that satisfies the conditions. Provided that two alternative choices of μ_{ij} are made so that the rows of the μ_{ij} are non-proportional then the resulting B_0 will be different. This is clearly possible, so that the FIML maximum is not identified. End of Proof.

REFERENCE TO APPENDIX

Klein, Lawrence R., "Forecasting and Policy Evaluation Using Large Scale Econometric Models: The State of the Art," in M. D. Intriligator, ed., *Frontiers of Quantitative Economics* (Amsterdam: North Holland, 1971).

REFERENCES

[1] Bear, D.V.T., "The Matrix Multiplier and Distributed Lags," *Econometrica*, XXXI (July, 1963), 514–529.

[2] Dunford, N. and J. T. Schwartz, *Linear Operators* (New York: Interscience Publishers, 1963).

[3] Jorgenson, D. W. and J. M. Brundy, "Efficient Estimation of Simultaneous Equations by Instrumental Variables," *Review of Economics and Statistic*, LIII (August, 1971), 207–224.

[4] Macduffee, C. C., *The Theory of Matrices* (New York: Chelsea Publishing Co., 1956).

[5] Mann, H.B. and A. Wald, "On the Statistical Treatment of Linear Stochastic Difference Equations," *Econometrica*, XI (January, 1943), 173–200.

[6] Sargan, J. D., "The Tails of the FIML Estimates of the Reduced Form Coefficients," unpublished manuscript, 1973.

17

BIRTH CONTROL IN AN ECONOMETRIC SIMULATION

By Daniel B. Suits, Ward Mardfin, Srawooth Paitoonpong and Teh-Pei Yu

In forecasting with econometric models, economists ordinarily pay relatively little attention to the influence of birth and death rates or other demographic variables which are generally shoved aside under the heading of "long-run" factors, negligible for the purpose at hand or at most contributing to a constant trend. Current birth rates, for example, are neglected on the ground that they have relatively little influence on the economy until the number of people of working age is affected some 15 or 16 years later. In fact, however, demographic factors exercise influence on the economy that is important even in the short run. For example, changes in birth rates alter female labor-force participation rates and hence affect the size of the labor force long before they alter the population old enough to work. Likewise, changes in family size and age composition alter per capita income associated with any given total output and have immediate implications for consumption functions, total demand, capital formation, and other key economic magnitudes.

When we turn from forecasting to simulation and policy analysis, the case for including demographic elements in econometric models becomes even stronger. Even the argument of the 16-year lag between birth rate and population of working age loses force when simulations are extended over 20 or 25 years, whereas such short-run effects as changes in labor-force participation and investment rates compound over longer periods into factors of sizeable magnitude.

Demographic factors are even more important when simulation is employed as a tool of policy analysis or optimization. Policy analysis is certainly one-sided and incomplete when birth rates are neglected as either part of the output to be evaluated, or as one of the available policy instruments. Such neglect certainly precludes comparison of birth control with alternative investment projects, and in any case contributes to the bias of developers toward hardware and showy projects. (Probably the greatest political drawback to birth control as an instrument of policy is that there is nothing to hang a sign on. Omitting demographic facts of life from econometric simulation confines them even deeper into limbo.)

This is not to say that demographic factors have been entirely neglected. A considerable literature has grown up in recent years dealing with various aspects of the impact of the economy on birth and death rates and on their effects, in turn, on economic events. Without attempting to be exhaustive, we mention Adleman [**1**], Blandy [**2**], Freedman [**7**], Gregory [**8**], Janowitz [**10**] and [**11**], and Rosenberg [**12**]. In addition, demographic factors have been included in a number of simulation models in which parameters are supplied primarily on a theoretical basis. The oldest substantial study was Coale and Hoover [**3**]; other theoretical models have been compiled by Denton and Spencer [**4**], Enke [**6**] and Zaidan [**21**].

To the best of our knowledge, however, there has been no complete econometric model in which birth and death rates are included as important endogenous variables in the economic process, and it is our purpose here to make a beginning in that direction. For a number of reasons, unfortunately, the task of incorporating birth and death rates in a large complex econometric model is a formidable one. Therefore, rather than embark immediately on the immense research effort that would be required, we have decided to begin in a modest way by putting together a relatively small model of the economic growth process in which birth and death rates are incorporated as part of the central core. Section 1 of this paper presents the structure of the model and discusses the equations of its final statistical form. In section 2, we use the model to simulate development of a nation as it grows from *GNP* of $100 per capita to $5,000 or more. This simulation is then compared with actual experience in a number of countries.

Section 3 is devoted to simulation of alternative growth policies. By comparing the development path followed under the stimulus of a birth control program to what would be expected in its absence, we attempt to estimate the economic value of averting births. In addition, by comparing birth control with an investment program that would generate the same economic gain, we estimate the trade-off between birth control and capital formation. Results show that economic values ascribable to birth control lie somewhere between $760 and $2,000 per birth averted, depending on discount rate applied. As a trade-off, each birth averted has the same economic pay-off as the investment of an additional $500 to $1,000 (again, depending on discount rate) in gross capital formation. These results can be compared with conclusions reached by other researchers, and we show that after differences in technique and definition are allowed for, our results are in reasonable agreement with most of those arrived at in earlier estimates derived from somewhat different points of view.

In the concluding section, we discuss a number of improvements needed in the model for future research.

2. THE MODEL

The model employed is a revision and expansion of one published several years ago by Sommers and Suits [**15**], modified to permit explicit investigation of the impact of birth control programs. It consists of 11 equations:

$$B_t = F_1(GNP_t/N_t, S, I) + u_{1t}, \tag{1}$$

$$D_t = F_2(GNP_t/N_t) + u_{2t}, \tag{2}$$

$$GCF_t/GNP_t = F_3(GNP_t/N_t, B_t, D_t) + u_{3t}, \tag{3}$$

$$r_t = F_4(GCF_t/GNP_t, B_t, D_t) + u_{4t}, \tag{4}$$

$$\Pi_t = \Pi_{t-1}(1 + r_t), \tag{5}$$

(6) $$(L/N)_{Ft} = F_6(GNP_t/N_t, B_t) + u_{6t},$$

(7) $$(L/N)_{Mt} = F_7(GNP_t/N_t, B_t) + u_{7t},$$

(8) $$(L/N)_t = 1/2(L/N)_{Ft} + 1/2(L/N)_{Mt},$$

(9) $$GNP_t/N_t = \Pi_t(L/N)_t,$$

(10) $$N_t = N_{t-1} + (B_t - D_t)N_{t-1}/1{,}000,$$

(11) $$GNP_t = (GNP_t/N_t)N_t.$$

Equation (1) relates B_t, crude birth rate per 1,000 population in year t, to gross national product per capita (GNP_t/N_t) and to two dummy variables designating the ethnic composition of the population. S has value 1 for all Spanish and Portuguese-speaking nations; I has value 1 for all Islamic nations. Otherwise S and I are zero.

Equation (2) relates D_t, crude death rate per 1,000 population to *GNP* per capita.

Equation (3) expresses GCF_t/GNP_t, the ratio of gross capital formation to *GNP*, as a function of *GNP* per capita and birth and death rates. Equation (4) indicates that r_t, the annual growth rate of output per worker during year t, depends on the rate of capital formation and birth and death rates. Equation (5) is the identity by which Π_t, output per worker in year t, is derived from output per worker the preceding year via its growth rate.

In equation (6), the ratio of female labor force to female population $(L/N)_{Ft}$ is made to depend on per capita *GNP* and birth rate, while equation (7) does the same for the male ratio, $(L/N)_{Mt}$. In (8) the ratio of total labor force to total population, $(L/N)_t$ is defined as the average of ratios for males and females. (Although male and female populations are not exactly equal, this is a sufficiently accurate approximation for our purposes.) Equation (9) defines *GNP* per capita as equal to the product of output per worker and ratio of labor force to population, while equation (10) updates total population N_t by adding births and subtracting deaths from last year's population. This neglects net migration as a factor in population growth, but is, again, a sufficiently accurate approximation for our purposes.

Equations (10) and (11) play no direct role in simulations, but are required to estimate the economic value of birth-control programs. Variables u_1, u_2, u_3, u_4, u_6 and u_7 represent the random influence of all factors omitted from the respective equations.

The regression equations were fitted by two-stage least squares to data for a cross-section of 70 countries taken as of 1970. Information on birth and death rates, and on ratios of labor force to population were drawn from the United Nations [**17**]. Data on *GNP* per capita and on the ratio of *GCF* to *GNP* were taken from the compilation in Suits [**16**] and were originally drawn primarily from IMF sources. Rates of growth in output per worker were calculated from productivity time series covering 25 nations, most of which were already fully industrialized, as published by ILO [**9**].

Experimentation with the data showed, as might be expected, that few of the equations could be closely fitted by linear regressions. A scatter of birth and death rates plotted against *GNP/N*, for example, revealed no systematic change in rates until *GNP* per capita exceeded about $500. Beyond $500, both birth and death rates declined sharply with rising *GNP/N* until the latter reached about $1,000. Beyond this, the change was again small. For this reason, equations (1) and (2) were fitted as piece-wise linear approximations by the use of two dummy variables. D_1 has value 0 until *GNP/N* reaches $500, and has value 1 thereafter; D_2 has value 0 until *GNP/N* reaches $1,000 and has value 1 thereafter. The resulting equations were

$$(1)\quad B_t = 39.87 + \underset{(2.33)}{3.18S} + \underset{(3.00)}{5.29I} - \underset{(.006)}{.0407}(GNP_t/N_t - \$500)D_1 + \underset{(.007)}{.0397}(GNP_t/N_t - \$1{,}000)D_2$$

$$(2)\quad D_t = 14.50 - \underset{(.003)}{.0123}(GNP_t/N_t - \$500)D_1 + \underset{(.003)}{.0123}(GNP_t/N_t - \$1{,}000)D_2\,.$$

Figures in parentheses are standard errors of second-stage coefficients. The estimated coefficients bear out what appeared in the scatter: sharp decline in rates as income per capita rises from $500 to $1,000, and little change thereafter. With $R^2 = .72$, equation (1) proved to have the highest coefficient of multiple determination of any of the equations fitted. Death rates vary much less systematically with *GNP* per capita and are more subject to other factors, as indicated by a coefficient of multiple determination of .33.

Taken together, equations (1) and (2) represent the demographic transition from a situation of low death rate, high birth rate and rapid population growth

TABLE 1

DEMOGRAPHIC TRANSITION AS CALCULATED FROM EQUATIONS (1) AND (2)
(RATES ARE PER 1,000 OF POPULATION)

GNP per capita	Birth rate	Death rate	Population growth rate
500 or below	39.87	14.50	25.37
600	35.80	13.27	22.63
700	31.73	12.04	19.69
800	27.66	10.81	16.85
900	23.59	9.58	14.01
1000	19.52	8.35	11.17
2000	18.52	8.35	10.17
3000	17.52	8.35	9.17
4000	16.52	8.35	8.17
5000	15.52	8.35	7.17

characteristic of poor nations today to the situation of low birth and death rates and slow population growth characteristic of industrialized nations. As shown in Table 1, nations with *GNP* per capita below $500 exhibit birth rates that average about 40 per thousand of population but death rates of only about 14.5, resulting in population growth rates slightly over 2.5 percent per year. The rapid decline in birth rates as income grows from $500 to $1,000, however, cuts population growth rates in half despite falling death rates. Changes are substantially slower as nations grow still richer, but by the time *GNP* per capita reaches $5,000, population growth has been reduced to an average of only .7 percent per year.

Equation (3), is likewise curvilinear, and was approximated by a piece-wise linear relationship in the same fashion as (1) and (2). For the sake of symmetry, we maintained the same breaking points as in the other equations. The result was

$$(3) \qquad GCF_t/GNP_t = 29.84 + \underset{(.0058)}{.0097}(GNP_t/N_t) - \underset{(.0103)}{.0040}(GNP_t/N_t - \$500)D_1 - \underset{(.0055)}{.0099}(GNP_t/N_t - \$1{,}000)D_2 - \underset{(.2099)}{.5892}(B_t - D_t)$$

The fit was fairly close with $R^2 = .46$.

The negative coefficients on the higher-income terms indicate that the rate of increase in investment ratio tends to decline as income rises, and since the sum of the three coefficients is negative, the ratio itself declines as income exceeds $1,000 per capita. Although the size of the standard errors is disappointing, an F-test of the two negative income terms taken together reveals a highly significant contribution to the regression. The declining savings rate at high income means, of course, that simulation with the model yields a maximum attainable income of about $7,000 per capita. When we begin at *GNP*/*N* of $100, however, it takes 200 years to reach this maximum, and since our evaluation of development programs involves heavy discounting, events beyond the first 75 or 100 years count for very little. Thus we feel that (3) is a useful approximation by which to study the early stages of economic growth in poor nations. It is plainly less well adapted for the analysis of the problems of industrial nations.

The last term in (3) poses a different kind of problem. It is negative, as expected, indicating that investment ratios are lower where population growth is most rapid, even given *GNP* per capita. In the course of trial simulation, however, the absolute magnitude of the coefficient proved to be so large that declining birth rates were accompanied not only by a rising fraction of *GNP* devoted to capital formation, but by so large a rise that per capita consumption was reduced. This response was unrealistically large, and would greatly exaggerate the economic stimulation provided by a birth control program. Because of this, we cut the parameter back to $-.2$ when using equation (3) in our final simulations. This involved reducing the coefficient by nearly two standard deviations, but we felt this necessary to avoid a substantial built-in bias in favor of birth control. A compensating change was made in the constant term.

Equation (4), the relationship of productivity growth to capital formation and population increase was fitted by a homogeneous linear equation

$$(4) \qquad r_t = \underset{(.037)}{.192}(GCF_t/GNP_t) - \underset{(.021)}{.035}(B_t - D_t) .$$

The negative influence of population growth involves two factors. For one, rapid population growth shifts the composition of capital formation toward housing and similar population-related facilities and away from productive equipment. For another, the more rapidly population grows, the more any given addition to capital must be devoted to capital widening: providing the new workers with the same tools and equipment available to their predecessors, rather than to capital deepening: raising the average quantity of capital per worker.

There is a certain ambiguity in the concept of multiple correlation as applied to a homogeneous equation. For our purposes here we have defined

$$\text{“}R^2\text{”} = 1 - \frac{\Sigma(r - \hat{r})^2}{\Sigma(r - \bar{r})^2} .$$

That is, as 1 minus the ratio of mean squared error to variance of r. The goodness of fit thus defined for (4) is “R^2” $= .58$.

In one respect, (4) leaves something important to be desired. Growth in output per worker generally consists of rising productivity per worker-hour combined with declining average annual number of hours worked per worker. It would improve and greatly enrich our results if these two components could be treated separately, but necessary data are unavailable.

Before arriving at the final form for equation (6), we experimented with a number of alternatives, including various forms of logistic. Although the results were promising, none fitted nearly as well as the logarithmic form finally adopted:

$$(6) \qquad ln\,(L/N)_{Ft} = 3.4633 + \underset{(.094)}{.1003}\, ln\,(GNP_t/N_t) - \underset{(.246)}{.3489}\, ln\, B_t .$$

Ratio of labor force to population responds to birth rates in two ways. A fall in birth rate raises the fraction of population that are old enough to work. Even given labor-force participation rates, then, this raises the fraction of the population at work. In addition, however, declining birth rates increase female labor force participation by freeing women for work outside the home. In view of this double effect, the standard error on the birth-rate term in (6) is disappointingly large, but we are satisfied that this is largely due to the substantial correlation between birth rate and *GNP* per capita shown in equation (1).

A similar equation was fitted for the male labor force:

$$(7) \qquad ln\,(L/N)_{Mt} = 3.6913 + \underset{(.0438)}{.0542}\, ln\,(GNP_t/N_t) - \underset{(.1144)}{.0032}\, ln\, B .$$

This equation showed a very poor fit with $R^2 = .05$ and not statistically significant. This is only to be expected. Male labor-force participation varies little with per capita income, except for the very young and very old. Moreover, male labor force ratios are affected by birth rates only via their influence on age composition. Since (7) proved so poorly measured, for purposes of simulation, we supressed it and assigned a constant value of 0.5 to the male labor-force ratio.

The remaining equations are definitions and, of course, were employed in the forms indicated above.

2. SIMULATION OF ECONOMIC GROWTH

In simulating growth with the econometric model, we began with a nation of 10 million people and \$100 per capita. The system of equations implied the other initial values, shown in the first line of Table 2. With these as initial conditions, the dynamic system generated values year by year over time. Results are shown by decades in the remaining lines of the table.

Labor-force ratios rise slowly until birth rates begin to decline as *GNP* passes \$500 in about the 66th year. Thereafter, the female labor-force ratio rises sharply. At the same time, death rates begin to drift downward to stabilize at 8.4 per thousand as *GNP* per capita passes \$1,000 in about the 84th year. Population growth slows from its high initial rate of 2.55 percent per year at the outset to reach 2/3 of 1 percent at the end of the period shown, but total population reaches more than twelve times its initial level at the end of the growth period. This corresponds to an average of about 1.8 percent per annum.

The ratio of gross capital formation to *GNP* rises to reach a maximum about the 84th year, after which it declines sharply. Toward the end of the period, investment ratios fall to unrealistic levels and the simulation was terminated.

Output per worker triples during the first fifty years in response to rapid capital accumulation combined with slower population growth, and increases more than five times again during the second fifty years. As investment ratios drop toward the end of the simulation, the rate of productivity increase slows.

As a result of rising productivity and increasing labor-force ratios, *GNP* per capita follows an ogive growth path. Growth is slow at the outset, averaging about 2.3 percent annual increase over the first fifty years. During the second fifty years, growth rates accelerate to average 3.7 percent annually, but slow again in keeping with stabilization of labor-force ratios and declining growth of productivity. By the end of the 240 years of simulated growth, *GNP* per capita has risen from its initial level of \$100 to reach \$5,602, a level about 20 percent above that observed for the U. S. in 1970.

2.1. *Comparison of the simulation with observed growth.* Since long-run growth data are available for several industrialized nations, it is interesting to compare observed economic growth with what is calculated in the simulation. This was done by converting *GNP* per capita for each nation to U. S. dollars at 1970 prices. The resulting levels for 1870 and 1970 were then located on the simulation path and the corresponding simulation dates were recorded. The difference

TABLE 2

SIMULATION OF 140 YEARS OF ECONOMIC DEVELOPMENT

Year	Labor-force ratio (percent)			Output per worker (dollars)	*GNP* per capita (dollars)	Birth rate	Death rate	Population (millions)	*GNP* (bil $)	*GCF/GNP* (percent)
	Male	Female	Total			(per 1000)				
0	50	14.0	32.0	312	100	39.87	14.5	10	1.00	15.8
10	50	14.3	32.2	388	127	39.87	14.5	12.85	1.60	16.1
20	50	14.6	32.3	483	156	39.87	14.5	16.50	2.58	16.4
30	50	15.0	32.5	606	197	39.87	14.5	21.20	4.17	16.8
40	50	15.3	32.7	767	250	39.87	14.5	27.24	6.82	17.3
50	50	15.7	32.8	981	322	39.87	14.5	43.85	11.28	17.9
60	50	16.1	33.1	1240	410	39.87	14.5	57.61	17.96	18.8
70	50	16.9	33.5	1691	566	37.9	13.9	57.61	32.59	20.3
80	50	19.5	34.8	2370	823	28.1	11.0	70.65	58.16	23.0
90	50	23.3	36.6	3606	1321	19.3	8.4	79.93	105.60	24.4
100	50	24.6	37.3	5360	1999	18.6	8.4	88.78	177.45	21.7
110	50	25.9	37.8	7549	2865	17.7	8.4	97.87	280.42	18.3
120	50	27.2	38.6	9953	3844	16.8	8.4	106.91	410.92	14.5
130	50	28.5	39.3	12234	4799	15.8	8.4	115.64	554.99	10.6
140	50	29.5	39.7	14099	5602	15.0	8.4	123.99	694.56	7.3

TABLE 3

COMPARISON OF SIMULATED WITH ACTUAL LONG-RUN GROWTH, SELECTED INDUSTRIAL NATIONS, 1870–1970

	1870		1970		
	GNP/N	Simulation year	*GNP/N*	Simulation year	Calculated number of years
Federal Republic of Germany	$530	68	$3,739	119	51
France	566	70	3,403	116	46
Italy	295	47	1,987	100	53
U. K.	490	65	2,503	106	41
U. S. (1875)	650	74	4,769	130	56

between these dates was then taken as the calculated number of years required for the same growth to have occurred along the simulation curve. For example, 1870 *GNP* per capita in the Federal Republic of Germany was estimated at $530, which is attained on the simulation path about year 68. The estimated 1970 figure of $3,739 is reached on the path about year 119. This indicates that the economic growth that required 100 years in reality, corresponds to only about 51 years on the simulation path. For purposes of these comparisons, data for *GNP* per capita were taken from U. S. Bureau of the Census [**19**]. The results in Table 3 show that Germany is quite typical of the industrial nations shown. Growth actually accomplished over the 100 year period corresponds to what would require only about half that many years along the simulation path.

Although we have no way to appraise the magnitude of the difference, it is no surprise to find that the actual growth of nations has been substantially slower than the simulation would indicate. The simulation generates a steady-growth path, and entails no allowance for the ten years of world wars and the prolonged periods of severe economic depression that characterized the century. In addition, since the model was fitted to a modern cross-section, the simulation represents the development path under modern technical conditions. The embodiment of modern technology in new capital permits a present-day developing country to grow by giant steps. In contrast, the past growth of industrialized nations occurred in the context of massive innovation.

To explore this matter further, growth of the same nations over the decade 1960–1970 as shown by U. N. data [**18**] was compared with the simulation path in the same fashion. Restriction of the period to a single decade minimizes the influence of technical change on the result. Moreover, the decade in question was one of generally high prosperity and, despite the Vietnam war, and trouble in the Middle East, was relatively peaceful on a world-wide basis. As shown in the top portion of Table 4, the simulated time required to accomplish the same growth as that exhibited by the industrialized nations was uniformly longer than the 10 years actually observed, ranging from 11 years for the U. K. to 25 years for the Federated German Republic.

TABLE 4

COMPARISON OF SIMULATED WITH ACTUAL GROWTH, SELECTED NATIONS, 1960–1970

	GNP/N	Simulation year	*GNP/N*	Simulation year	Calculated number of years
Industrialized Nations					
Federal Republic of Germany	$1,560	94	3,739	119	25
France	1,585	94+	3,403	115+	20
Italy	845	80+	1,987	100+	20
U. K.	1,660	95	2,503	106	11
U. S.	3,350	115	4,769	130	15
Poorer Nations					
Argentina	820	80	1,078	85	5
Bolivia	130	12	206	32	10
Brazil	273	43	391	57	14
Chile	386	57	684	75	8
Costa Rica	485	65	544	69	4
Egypt	169	24	216	34	10
Ecuador	285	45+	280	45−	−1
Gabon	373	56	670	75	19
Ivory Coast	235	51	347	53	2
S. Korea	200	31	260	41	10
Madagascar	133	13	133	13	0
Morocco	202	31−	203	31+	1
Pakistan	217	34	259	41	7
Philippines	216	34	259	41	7
Senegal	250	40	217	34	−6
Tunisia	269	43	270	43	0
Uruguay	815	80−	820	80+	1
Zambia	240	38	386	57	19

Some part of this long simulation time is doubtless attributable to the sharp decline in the investment ratio produced by equation (3) at high levels of *GNP* per capita. A similar comparison made for a number of poorer nations over the same decade reveals that in most cases the 10-year growth actually achieved represented gains that would have been made in considerably shorter time along the simulation path. Of the 18 nations examined in the lower portion of Table 4, about a third achieved growth for which simulated times range from 7 to 14 years. For two—Gabon and Zambia—the decade resulted in growth that would have taken 19 years via the simulation path. But growth of the remainder corresponded to little or no simulation growth, or to actual decline over the decade. On the average, therefore, the poorer nations examined grew more slowly than the simulation path would predict. It is not clear, however, how much of this result is attributable to serious bias in the model, for examination of the slowest-growing nations reveals that many of them suffered from severe organizational and political difficulties, natural disasters, and other handicaps to economic development that do not appear in the model. Policy simulation, after all, is an effort to ascertain the effect of specified measures if they were adopted and pursued. It sheds no light on whether a nation will, in fact, adopt a given policy. Nevertheless, we believe that the comparisons indicate substantial room for improvement in the model, and the following policy analysis should be evaluated with this in mind.

3. EFFECT OF BIRTH CONTROL ON DEVELOPMENT

At first sight, Table 2 appears to accord a very minor role to demographic factors in the growth process. During the first sixty years of growth, no change in birth or death rates is discernible while *GNP* per capita increases fourfold. There is, to be sure, a modest rise in labor-force participation during this time, but even at the end of the 140 year period the ratio of total labor force to population is only about 25 percent higher that it was at the beginning. The gain in *GNP* per capita attributable to this factor over the entire period is, therefore, somewhat smaller than the overall gain from all factors recorded for the first decade alone.

But the impression that demographic factors are negligible is misleading on at least three counts. In the first place, any contribution of birth control to the economy is in addition to what would be obtained anyhow, and this is especially true among poor nations that are trapped in the stage where fertility is unresponsive to economic change. In the second place, only the most direct ramifications of demographic factors are identifiable in the table. A change in birth rate that might have a very small initial impact is subject to a substantial multiplier and can generate much larger overall improvement. Finally, no account has yet been taken of the cost of such demographic modification as reduced birth rates. Even a program that produces only modest economic gains can yield a handsom pay-off if it doesn't cost much to impliment.

An improved notion of the role of demographic factors can be had by comparing the results of Table 2 with a second simulation for an identical society which has reduced its birth rate. Although the final result requires the comparison of two complete simulations each extending over the entire development period, we can get a preliminary idea of the outcome by comparing results after only one year. We begin with two societies in year 0, each with 10 million population, \$1 billion *GNP*, and so on, as before. The only respect in which they differ is that the crude birth rate of 40 per thousand in one society results in 400,000 births, while in the other society, ten percent, or 40,000 of these births have been averted. The situation of the societies as of one year later is recorded in Table 5. The first column gives results as simulated in the absence of birth control and the second column shows what happens when 40,000 births have been averted. The difference between the two columns is the gain due to

TABLE 5

SIMULATION OF THE EFFECTS OF A BIRTH CONTROL PROGRAM: FIRST YEAR

	After one year with:		Increase due to birth control
	No birth control	40,000 births averted	
Population	10,253,700	10,213,700	−40.000
Labor force	3,281,200	3,295,400	14,200
Output per worker (dollars)	319.2228	320.1402	.9147
GNP (millions of $)	1,047.43	1,055.00	7.57
Consumption (do)	881.31	879.05	−2.26
Investment (do)	166.12	175.95	9.83
Per capita (dollars)			
GNP	102.1514	103.2920	1.1406
Consumption	85.9504	86.0652	.1148
Investment	16.2010	17.2268	1.0258

birth control and is recorded in the last column.

As seen in the first line of the table, prevention of 40,000 births, other things equal, means a population 40,000 smaller than it would otherwise have been. Despite the smaller population, however, the labor force is larger, primarily because of the effect of reduced births on female labor-force participation. This increase in labor force is reenforced by higher productivity per worker, mainly the result of increased investment per capita, and the combined effect is a $7,500,000 gain in gross national product. Representing the increase in *GNP* by

$$\Delta GNP = \Pi \Delta L + L \Delta \Pi + \Delta \Pi \Delta L ,$$

we can analyse the growth of *GNP* into a gain of roughly $4.5 million from larger labor force, almost $3 million associated with higher productivity, and a small additional gain from interaction of the two. Combined with smaller population, the growth of *GNP* yields real per capita *GNP* about $1.14 greater than would otherwise have been the case.

The productivity gain is generated by the sharp increase in gross capital formation which exceeds in magnitude the rise in *GNP*. This occurs because reduced population leads to lower total consumption despite a small rise in consumption per head.

No matter how we look at it, it is clear that prevention of 40,000 births has given rise to substantial economic gains. At a minimum, the gain could be measured by the $7.5 million rise in *GNP*, which divided by 40,000 births yields an increase of about $188 per birth prevented. But this does not take into account that the additional output is distributed over a smaller population than would otherwise have been the case. A better measure of the gain can be had by calculating the difference between the *GNP* emerging from the birth control measure and the level that would be required to provide the smaller population with the same *GNP* per capita that would have been experienced in the absence of any birth control program. That is, in the absence of birth control, *GNP* would have amounted to about \$102.15 per capita, so to provide this average to the 10,213,700 people found in the population where birth-control measures have been put in effect would require *GNP* of only about \$1,043 million. The difference between this figure and the \$1,055 available under birth control indicates a gain of \$12 million as the value of the birth control program. (Thus measured, the gain is equal to the difference in *GNP* per capita multiplied by population. This is the measure suggested by Enke [**6**].) In other words, prevention of 40,000 births results in a *GNP* large enough to provide the population with the same average level of real goods and services per capita that they would have obtained anyhow, with \$12 million left over to do with as they like. Measured on this basis, the value of the birth control program is clearly about \$300 per birth prevented.

This is still a minimum estimate, of course, because to the extent that the extra output is applied to investment—and in our simulation about 80 percent of it is—further gains will be made in subsequent years, attributable to these same 40,000 births even if no further prevention of births occurs. To take such future gain into account, the value of a birth control program is defined as the present value of all future gains arising from the program, calculated by comparing annually the simulated growth paths of two societies, one pursuing, the other not pursuing the program. Formally, let GNP_t^* and N_t^* represent, respectively, *GNP* and population of a society t years after initiation of a birth control program, and let $(GNP/N)_t$ represent the *GNP* per capita that would have become available in that same year t in the absence of any program. At discount rate i, then, the value V_B of birth control is given by

$$V_B = \sum_0^{\infty} [GNP_t^* - (GNP/N)_t N_t^*]e^{-it} . \tag{12}$$

Although V_B could readily be calculated for a program that reduced births by 40,000 for exactly one year, a simulation in which birth rates returned immediately to their uncontrolled levels is unrealistic. In the first place, effort invested in birth control education is likely to have residual effects for some time after the program has been discontinued. In the second place, it would be uneconomical for a nation to invest in the training of technical workers, the establishment of clinical facilities and similar costs merely for a one-year, one-shot effort. A more realistic simulation should involve a program of longer duration and for this purpose we decided to simulate a program of birth control that would alter the parameters of the birth-rate equation in such fashion as to avoid 40,000 births annually for a period of 15 years. In the 16th year the parameters were restored to their original values and the simulation continued. Accordingly, equation (1) was modified by addition of the term

$$[1{,}000(-40{,}000)/N_t]D_3$$

to the right hand side to obtain

TABLE 6

CALCULATION OF THE VALUE OF AVOIDING 40,000 BIRTHS ANNUALLY FOR FIFTEEN YEARS

Year	N^* (millions)	GNP^*/N^* (dollars)	GNP/N (dollars)	$GNP^*_t - (GNP/N)_t N^*_t$ (millions of dollars)	Accumulated V_B to date at 10% (millions of dollars)	20%
1975	10.00	100	100	0	0	0
1976	10.21	103	102	11.60	10.50	9.50
1977	10.43	106	104	15.32	23.04	19.77
1978	10.66	109	107	19.05	37.19	30.32
1979	10.89	111	109	23.33	52.68	40.63
1980	11.12	114	112	27.39	69.29	50.71
1985	12.40	129	125	47.88	163.01	93.00
1990	13.84	146	139	93.72	262.75	116.02
1995	15.69	162	156	99.28	336.68	132.92
2000	17.78	182	175	129.37	394.49	138.83
∞	—	—	—	—	630.85	144.26

$$(1') \qquad B_t = 39.87 + 3.18S + 5.29I - .0407(GNP_t/N_t - 500)D_1 + .0397(GNP_t/N_t - 1{,}000)D_2 - 1{,}000(40{,}000/N_t)D_3 .$$

The variable D_3 is a dummy whose values correspond to the presence ($D_3 = 1$) or absence ($D_3 = 0$) of birth control effect on the birth rate. When the program is in force, the term holds the simulated birth rate just enough below the rate that would otherwise rule to avoid 40,000 births in year t, while leaving all other parameters of the system unaltered. For our simulation, therefore, D_3 was assigned the value 1 for $t = 1$ through 15, and the value 0 for all t exceeding 15. V_B was calculated by comparing the results of this simulation with a second simulation in which $D_3 = 0$ for all t.

Some key results of our calculation are given in Table 6 where 1975 is taken as $t = 0$. Beginning in 1975 with $1 billion *GNP* and 10 million population, the birth control program generates a gain of $11 million in 1976 exactly as earlier. In 1977, however, an additional gain of $15.32 million is realized. This 1977 contribution is larger than that of 1976 because some influence from the 40,000 births prevented in 1976 continues to be felt in 1977 and this continued effect is combined with the effect of the 40,000 additional births prevented in 1977. Put in another way, the prevention of 40,000 births in 1976 pushes the economy on to a higher development path along which it would continue even if birth rate parameters were restored to their initial values. Prevention of an additional 40,000 births in 1977, therefore, pushes the economy onto a still higher growth path. Each year the program continues, the economy rises to a higher growth path until by 1990 it reaches a path to which it has been raised by the cumulative influence of 15 years of birth control. Although the program is terminated at the this point ($D_3 = 0$), the difference between this path and the lower path that would otherwise have been followed persists year after year and continues to make a contribution to the value of the program. Detailed comparison of the two simulations reveals that by the end of the fifteen years, the birth control program has pushed the society onto a growth path that is two years ahead of what would have been attained in the absence of the program.

The last two columns of Table 5 show how V_B accumulates. The value is, of course, heavily influenced by the discount rate employed; at 10 percent, all future gains expected from the birth control program accumulate to a 1975 value of $630.85 million. At the heavier 20 percent discount rate, the present value is only $144.26 million.

3.1. *Value per birth averted.* The results are more readily understandable and more easily compared with earlier findings if they are translated into value per birth prevented. This is done as follows. Since the birth control program in question consists of a steady stream of 40,000 births averted annually for a period of 15 years, let us translate its present value into an equivalent 15-year steady stream of annual earnings. At the 10 percent discount rate, a present value of $630.85 million is equivalent to a 15-year steady stream of $81.68 million annually, or the equivalent of slightly more than $2,000 for each birth averted in a steady stream for 15 years. (Alternatively, the same result can be arrived at by dividing the $630.85 million present value of the birth-control program by the "present value" of the 15-year stream of 40,000 annual births. The latter procedure can also be followed in the generally more realistic cases where the number of births averted varies over time.)

At the heavier 20 percent discount rate, the birth-control program works out to the equivalent of a 15-year steady stream of $30.37 million, or about $760 per birth averted.

These results suggest somewhat greater value to birth prevention than those reached by earlier workers. In his earliest work in this field, Enke [**5**] estimated $384 as the value per birth averted in an economy of $100 *GNP* per capita when he used a 10 percent discount rate, and at $212 when discounting at 20 percent. These estimates, however, included only the present value of consumption released by the averted births, and included no allowance for any gain from increased female labor-force participation nor from expanded capital formation or the increased effectiveness of investment associated with slower population growth.

In later work, based on simulation with a more complete theoretical model developed at TEMPO, Enke [**6**] arrived at results that appear to be very close to those presented here. Differences in the kind of birth control program used, and in the way his results were presented preclude accurate comparison of his results with ours, but working very roughly from some of his published figures (Enke [**6**, Table 1, (805)] we arrive at an estimated range of values from about $1,500 to $2,500 per birth prevented, when a 10 percent discount rate is employed. This is almost exact agreement with our results.

Zaidon [**22**], taking into account not only the discounted value of consumption saved but also some part of the contribution of birth reduction to higher productivity, arrived at an estimate for Egypt that ranged from \$327 to \$971 per birth prevented. The range was generated by differences in assumption and in discount rate employed. Not only are these figures somewhat below our estimates, but they apply to Egypt when per capita *GNP* was about 50 percent higher than the \$100 level used in our simulation. Since, in our simulations, this difference in income would be accompanied by greater gains from birth control, our results and those of Zaidon differ somewhat more than shown merely by comparison of the figures.

Simon [**13**], publishing before Enke's simulation results had become available, argued that the determination of how much a nation could afford to invest in birth control depended not on the total value of the program as we have measured it, but only on that part of the value that spills over onto nonparticipating families. He argued that a substantial part of the value is privately captured by those families who reduce their birth rates. For example, the value of consumption saved by not having children accrues automatically to the remaining members of the families who hold down the number of their children. Thus, he claimed, value of birth control to the public at large arises only from actual increases in gross national product, not from merely spreading a given *GNP* over fewer consumers. Couching Simon's conception in the formal terms employed earlier, we can define S_B, that part of the value of a birth control program arising from increased *GNP*, as

$$S_B = \sum_{0}^{\infty} (GNP_t^* - GNP_t)e^{-it} . \tag{13}$$

That is, the spill-over portion of total value would be defined as the present value of annual differences between *GNP* under the birth-control regime and what would otherwise have been available.

Using a 30-year simulation with the Coale-Hoover model and a 15 percent discount rate, Simon estimated this spill-over value at only about \$114 per birth averted in India. To compare this result with ours, we calculated the value of S_B from our simulation. At a discount rate of 20 percent, the spill-over portion of our 15-year birth control program proved to be only about \$930,000. This is the equivalent of a 15-year steady stream of \$120,000 annually, or only about \$3 per birth averted. When the discount rate was reduced to 15 percent, we arrived at a negative present value for the spill-over benefit. The reason for the negative figure is that under our simulation, total *GNP* generated by the birth-control program exceeds what would otherwise be available only during the first 8 years of the program. Thereafter, differences in *GNP* per capita are insufficient to make up for the reduction of population so contributions to S_B are negative. The 20 percent discount rate places a sufficiently small weight on later years to maintain a positive total, but present value is negative when later years are more heavily weighted by the 15 percent rate.

Actually, comparison between Simon's results and ours are even less favorable than the figures imply, for as we have seen, part of any increase in total *GNP* results from rising female labor-force participation and most of this, too, is privately captured by those women who join the labor force as a result of having fewer children.

3.2. *Comparison of birth control with other forms of investment.* Regardless of how measured, prospective pay-off has little meaning until compared with costs of the program. Costs of birth control are of two sorts: there is an annual direct cost of birth control methods to families who have decided to adopt them, and there are costs to education, field work, clinics and other facilities needed to acquaint people with the desirability of limiting population growth and to provide them with the technical knowledge necessary to do so. Once a decision to adopt birth control has been reached, direct costs of even the most expensive of generally accepted methods are far below the value estimated for our program. Enke [**5**], for example, estimated the direct cost of using the pill at $90 per birth prevented, and this is probably the most expensive method. But even with all costs considered, birth control is not very expensive. Simon [**14**] arrived at a maximum total cost of less than $100 per birth avoided in a nation of $100 *GNP* per capita, including in his estimate all costs of information, dispensing, propaganda and incentive payments to families joining the program. In view of these figures, it appears that a poor nation can expect returns somewhere between seven and twenty times outlays made for birth control. As others have noted, this is a remarkably favorable payment compared to what would be expected from other forms of investment.

Our simulation model, however, makes it possible to go beyond this stage and to make a direct comparison between birth-control and resources invested in gross capital formation by calculating how much additional capital formation would be needed to obtain the same gain provided by the birth-control program. Since (12) above can be used to calculate the value of any shift in the parameters of the model, we modified equation (3) so as to raise the amount annually invested in gross capital formation by K dollars above the level that would otherwise obtain each year for 15 years. That is, (3) became

$$(3') \quad GCF_t/GNP_t = 29.84 + .0097(GNP_t/N_t) - .0040(GNP_t/N_t - 500)D_1 - .0099(GNP_t/N_t - 1000)D_2 + (K/GNP_t)D_3 .$$

As in (1′), D_3 is a dummy variable assigned the value 1 in years 1 to 15, and the value 0 in all years beyond 15. Results of a simulation in which any fixed value is assigned to K can then be compared to one in which the value of K is zero throughout and V_B calculated exactly as for birth control. We then proceeded to run successive simulations with different values of K until, by successive approximations, we reached a value of K which produced the same V_B as that already determined for the 15-year birth-control program.

At the 10 percent discount rate, we found we could generate V_B equal to the same $630.85 million present value obtained from birth control by assigning the value $K = \$19.48$ million. In other words, at the 10 percent discount rate, a steady 15-year stream of $19.48 million annually invested in additional gross capital formation would yield the same economic gain as a steady 15-year stream of 40,000 births averted annually. At this rate, each birth averted is the equivalent of about $487 in resources devoted to gross capital formation.

When we repeated the experiment with discount rate set at 20 percent, we found that a substantially larger amount of extra annual investment was required to bring the value up to what could be obtained from birth control. The interesting reason for the larger figure is that the effects of birth control—especially holding down the number of dependents and raising the female labor-force ratio—occur somewhat earlier than do productivity gains reaped from augmented investment. The heavier the discount applied, therefore, the greater the extra investment needed to generate a present value equal to that available from the faster-acting birth control program. According to our estimates, the amount of extra investment needed to match the value of birth control at 20 percent discount rate is almost exactly double what would be needed at 10 percent.

4. NEED FOR A MORE ELABORATE MODEL

Although the influence of discount rate on the investment equivalent of birth control was unexpected, it appears entirely reasonable. The immediate impacts of birth rate reduction are smaller population and larger labor force, and nothing in the investment process pays off this rapidly. But while we are convinced that the phenomenon is valid, its magnitude as represented by the simulation is largely accidental, for in compiling the model we paid no specific attention to the timing differences between effects of birth rate and investment. Accurate measurement of these timing differences—which, as we have seen, can make a profound difference in how we view the pay-offs of different policies—demands further elaboration of the model, particularly of the demographic sections.

Most important, crude birth rates should be replaced by more accurate measures of fertility. One alternative is to replace them by total fertility or gross reproduction rates, and some work has been done along these lines. For example, a theoretical model employing total fertility rate has been published by Denton and Spencer [**4**], while Janowitz [**11**] has applied cross-section data to explore the relationship of gross reproduction rate to economic variables. A still better approach, however, would be to replace crude birth and death rates in the model by a matrix of age-specific birth and survival rates, with each individual rate expressed as a function of appropriate economic variables. A study of such functions was published a decade ago by Adleman [**1**].

Incorporating such a matrix in the model would not only improve the estimate of the trade-off between birth-control and capital formation, it would also yield superior insight into the impact of economic factors on population. In particular, since such a matrix, would generate a complete age distribution for the population, it would permit us to replace equations (6) and (7) by matrices of age and sex-specific labor-force participation rates, with individual rates expressed as functions of economic variables and, for females, of age-specific birth rates. Among others results, this would greatly facilitate the assessment of how the value of any given birth control program is divided between what is privately capturable by participants and what spills over onto the public at large.

There is, of course, room for improvement in other parts of the model. We have noted that the investment function (3) generates an unrealistically large decline in investment ratios at high levels of *GNP* per capita, and was unrealistically responsive to changes in birth rate. A more careful formulation of the function that would follow the observable decline in investment ratio, but which would extrapolate more realistically at high levels of income would surely improve results.

Still further improvement could be made if productivity gains were expressed as a function of average level of education, and education costs were taken into account as part of investment. This might be done in terms of age-specific school attendence rates applied to the age distribution of the population as generated by the demographic matrix. It would also be useful if productivity per worker could be separated into its two components, average annual hours per worker and output per worker-hour. Insufficient data exist to do this on a cross-section basis, but it might be possible to employ functions fitted to time-series drawn from long-term U. S. history to obtain at least plausible working relationships.

In its present form, however, our model is sufficient to demonstrate the important role of demographic factors, even over relatively short spans of time. Considering the large number of unknowns that we have to contend with, it is questionable whether demographic factors in a model will contribute very much to its year-to-year (not to say quarter-to-quarter) forecasting accuracy. But our model underscores, once again, the great pay-off available from investment in birth control both in absolute terms and in comparison with other forms of investment, and these may well be controling consideration in policy selection.

Michigan State University
University of Hawaii

REFERENCES

[1] ADELMAN, IRMA, "An Econometric Analysis of Population Growth," *American Economic Review*, LIII (June, 1963), 314–339.

[2] BLANDY, R., "Population and Employment Growth: An Introductory Empirical Exploration," *International Labor Review*, CVI (October, 1972), 347–366.

[3] COALE, ANSLEY J. AND EDGAR M. HOOVER, *Population Growth and Economic Development in Low Income Countries* (Princeton: Princeton University Press, 1958).

[4] DENTON, FRANK T., AND BYRON G. SPENCER, "A Simulation Analysis of the Effects of Population Change on a Neoclassical Economy," *Journal of Political Economy*, LXXXI (March/April, 1973), 356–375.

[5] ENKE, STEPHEN, "The Economic Aspects of Slowing Population Growth," *The Economic Journal*, LXXVI (March, 1966), 44–56.

[6] ———, "Economic Consequences of Rapid Population Growth," *The Economic Journal*, LXXXI (December, 1971), 800–811.

[7] FREEDMAN, DEBORAH S., "The Relation of Economic Status to Fertility," *American Economic Review*, LIII (June, 1963), 414–426.

[8] GREGORY, P. *et al.*, "A Simultaneous Equation Model of Birth Rates in the U.S.," *Review of Economics and Statistics*, LIV (November, 1972), 374–380.

[9] International Labor Office, *Yearbook of Labor Statistics* (Geneva: I.L.O., various editions).
[10] Janowitz, Barbara S., "An Econometric Analysis of Fertility Rates," *Journal of Development Studies,* IX (April, 1973), 425–431.
[11] ———, "The Effects of Demographic Factors on Age Composition and the Implications for Per Capita Income," *Demography,* X (November, 1973), 507–515.
[12] Rosenberg, W., "A Note on the Relationship of Family Size and Income in New Zealand," *Economic Record,* XLVII (September, 1971), 399–409.
[13] Simon, Julian, "The Value of Avoided Births to Underdeveloped Countries," *Population Studies,* XXIII (March, 1969), 61–68.
[14] ———, "Family Planning Prospects in Less Developed Countries and a Cost-Benefit Analysis of Various Alternatives," *The Economic Journal,* LXXX (March, 1970), 58–71.
[15] Sommers, Paul M. and Daniel B. Suits, "A Cross-section Model of Economic Growth," *Review of Economics and Statistics,* LIII (May, 1971), 121–128.
[16] Suits, Daniel B., *Principles of Economics,* 2nd edition (New York: Harper and Row, 1973).
[17] United Nations, *Demographic Yearbook* (New York: United Nations, various editions).
[18] ———, *Statistical Yearbook* (New York: United Nations, various editions).
[19] U. S. Bureau of the Census, *Long-term Economic Growth* (Washington, D. C.: U. S. Government Printing Office, 1966).
[20] Veneris, Yiannis P., Frederick Sebold, and Richard Harper, "The Impact of Economic, Technological, and Demographic Factors on Aggregate Birth Rates," *Review of Economics and Statistics,* LXV (November, 1973), 493–497.
[21] Zaidon, George, "Population Growth and Economic Development," *Studies in Family Planning,* XLII (May, 1969), 1–6.
[22] ———, *The Costs and Benefits of Family Planning Programs,* World Bank Occasional Staff Papers No. 12 (Baltimore: Johns Hopkins Press, 1971).

18

THE NBER/NSF MODEL COMPARISON SEMINAR: AN ANALYSIS OF RESULTS

BY GARY FROMM AND LAWRENCE R. KLEIN

INTRODUCTION

FOR THREE YEARS, the leading American model builders (macroeconometric) and proprietors have been meeting regularly in a seminar for the purposes of designing and implementing uniform applications. Basically, the people intimately concerned with model building and maintenance have been dissatisfied with attempts by third party scholars to use the data underlying the models or generated by the models for their own research purposes—often in the form of model testing. Large scale models are such complicated and delicate mechanisms that they require very careful handling by people who fully understand them. While there is some advantage in having the objectivity of third-party researchers at work on the problem, there have been so many unfortunate cases of improper use of materials that the seminar participants have gathered together for their own study of the problem. Through the interaction of group research with group discipline, and the participation of third-party scholars, it is hoped to achieve the requisite objectivity of comparisons without sacrificing model integrity.

The principal interests of model proprietors in the seminar work have been focused thus far on error and multiplier analysis. In separate studies, such things as frequency response characteristics, sub-sector performance, specialized policy simulations, optimal control simulations, and other applications have been studied. In the seminar, we have limited our research to analyses that can readily be made across models, for comparative purposes.[1]

The participating models and proprietors are:

Bureau of Economic Analysis Model (BEA), A. A. Hirsch, Bruce Grimm, and G. V. L. Narasimham
Brookings Model, G. Fromm, L. R. Klein, and G. Schink
University of Michigan (MQEM) Model, S. Hymans and H. Shapiro
Data Resources Inc. (DRI) Model, O. Eckstein, E. Green, and A. Sinai
Fair Model, Princeton and Yale Universities, R. Fair
Federal Reserve Bank of St. Louis Model (FRB, St. Louis), L. Andersen and K. Carlson
M.I.T., Pennsylvania, S.S.R.C. Model (MPS), A. Ando and R. Rasche
Wharton Model (Mark III and Anticipations Version), M. D. McCarthy, L. R. Klein, F. G. Adams, G. R. Green, and V. Duggal
Stanford University (H-C Annual) Model, B. Hickman and R. Coen

[1] For comparisons of the structure of these models, see G. Fromm, [**12**].

Reprinted from *Annals of Economic and Social Measurement,* 5/1 (1976).

Wharton Annual Model, R. S. Preston
Cornell University (Liu-Hwa Monthly) Model, T. C. Liu and E. C. Hwa

A principal feature of the present approach to model comparison and testing is the attempt to achieve as much uniformity as seems possible in this area of research. Our collection contains large and small models; annual, quarterly, and monthly models; short and long horizon simulations. It would be both undesirable and unusual if all models were nearly alike.

Still, there are strong similarities among many of the models. With the exception of the monetarist approach of the St. Louis model, all the systems follow a Keynesian framework in which expenditures depend on income and other variables and production or income is a function of expenditures and factor costs. However, there is considerable variation in detailed specifications and the relative importance accorded financial–real sector interactions in expenditure and portfolio decisions. A limited set of characteristics of the models may be found in Table 1.

TABLE 1
SUMMARY OF SELECTED CHARACTERISTICS OF MODELS

Model	Time Frame	Scale[a]	Disaggregation of Production[b]	Endogenous Financial–Real Interaction[c]
BEA	Quarterly	Medium	Limited	Weak
Brookings	Quarterly	Very Large	Medium	Medium
MQEM	Quarterly	Small	Limited	Weak
DRI-74	Quarterly	Very Large	Medium (Recursive)	Medium
Fair	Quarterly	Small	Limited	None
St. Louis	Quarterly	Very Small	None	Strong
MPS	Quarterly	Large	Limited	Strong
Wharton	Quarterly	Large	Medium	Medium
H–C	Annual	Medium	Limited	Weak
Wharton Annual	Annual	Very Large	High	Medium
Liu–Hwa	Monthly	Medium	Limited	Medium

[a] Based on number of equations: very small = 9 or less; small = 10–49; medium = 50–119; large = 120–199; very large = 200 or more.
[b] Based on sector detail: limited = 2–5 sectors; medium = 6–20 sectors; high = 21 or more sectors.
[c] Based on qualitative judgments on pervasiveness of financial variables in real sector equations and real variables in financial sector equations.

Therefore, the challenging issue is to make comparative sense of standardized applications of differentiated models.

The directives to model proprietors were to:

1. simulate dynamically from fixed initial conditions

1961.1–1967.4	quarterly
1961.1–1967.12	monthly
1961–1967	annually

2. simulate dynamically from fixed initial conditions beyond sample values
3. calculate fiscal multipliers for changes in non-defense spending or personal income taxes with and without accommodating monetary policies.

In the error calculations for individual variables, we asked for mean-squared error, the variance of error, and the bias computed from the formula,

$$\text{MSE}=\frac{1}{T}\sum_{t=1}^{T}(\hat{X}_t-X_t)^2=\frac{1}{T}\sum_{t=1}^{T}[(\hat{X}_t-X_t)-(\bar{\hat{X}}-\bar{X})]^2+(\bar{\hat{X}}-\bar{X})^2$$

$$\text{MSE}=\text{VARIANCE}+\text{BIAS}^2$$

$$\hat{X}_t=\text{forecast value of } X$$

$$X_t=\text{observed value of } X$$

$$\bar{\hat{X}}=\text{mean of } \hat{X}=\frac{1}{T}\sum_{t=1}^{T}\hat{X}_t$$

$$\bar{X}=\text{mean of } X=\frac{1}{T}\sum_{t=1}^{T}X_t$$

In the case of the historical sample period, we standardized the calculations to the period 1961–67, if possible. In some instances, the samples terminated prior to 1967, and the exercise was accordingly translated or truncated. For the extrapolations beyond the sample period, the starting date for the simulations was right after the end of the sample and therefore not uniform across all models. Data limitations made the spans of the extrapolation period differ for each model. Generally, we looked for 8 period lengths of solution for each simulation exercise, with a period being a month, quarter, or year. Some models are not structured to run dynamically that long and others are cut short for diverse reasons. Therefore, all simulations are not of equal length, either for solution span or period covered for the different solutions.

The list of variables simulated is:

GNP, nominal
GNP, real, 1958 prices
GNP, implicit price deflator, 1958:100
Unemployment rate
Consumer expenditures, nominal
Consumer expenditures, real, 1958 prices
Nonfarm investment, nominal
Nonfarm investment, real, 1958 prices
Nonfarm inventory investment, nominal

Nonfarm inventory investment, real, 1958 prices
Residential construction, nominal
Residential construction, real, 1958 prices
Short-term interest rate
Long-term interest rate
Nonfarm wage rate
Hours worked per week
Corporate profits before tax and IVA
Money supply (M1)
Employee compensation, nominal
Personal income, nominal.

The small models (Fair and St. Louis) had no information for several of these variables. In other cases, some variables were obtainable from the models; some were not.

Some of the variables in this list, which is merely an extract from the larger list of variables in several of the models, are connected through identities. The first three variables satisfy

$$\frac{\text{GNP (nominal)}}{\text{GNP (real)}} = \text{GNP (deflator)}.$$

All three variables are stochastic, but only two *independent* pieces of information about stochastic performance can be inferred from the error statistics associated with them. Tabulations are given for all three, but they should not be independently interpreted. Also, profits come from a national income–national product identity in some models; in others there are direct profit equations, and the statistical discrepancy is the "residual." In the profits case as well, interpretation should be adjusted to the fact that all the components of income may not be independently estimated.

As a study group we set out with high standards for uniformity; but, as in any practical application, we had to allow many compromises. In the end, we achieved about as much uniformity as we could hope to get from 12 teams of independent scholars—especially in economics.

Error Analysis

Before we look into the details of the several models' performance, let us make some overall conclusions of the basis of error analysis.

1. There are substantial disparaties among the different variables studied for simulation error. Smooth, slow-moving variables are more accurately simulated than are variables with high variance and large period-to-period fluctuation. Among the components of GNP, the largest element by far is consumption, but on an absolute basis, the errors associated with relatively small magnitudes like fixed investment and inventory investment

are as large as the consumption errors. Similarly, on the income side, the errors associated with profits are as large as those associated with wages, although the latter variable is much larger. Also the error in simulating the relatively slow-moving long-term interest rate is much smaller than the error in simulating the short-term interest rate. Some of the general comments about performance are contradicted for some of the models. These general observations refer to predominant model performance.

2. Simulation error grows with the length of the simulation period; the error in one-period simulations is smaller than the error in two-period simulations which, in turn, is smaller than the error in three-period simulations, etc.[2] There are a few exceptions that can be explained by some peculiarities or smallness of sample.
3. There are effectively two regimes—one within sample and one in extrapolation. Within-sample simulations look very favorable. The error statistics for this group of simulations are about as low as we could expect to realize with "noisy" economic data. If error statistics were actually this small in realistic applications, policy makers would have little to worry about, as far as forecasting precision is concerned. Extrapolation error is, on the other hand, nearly two or three times as large as within-sample simulation error. When one does not have the confines of samples that contain only data to which the model has been "fitted," one is subject to a much wider margin of error. Extrapolation error is just on the borderline of being usable for policy application. There is definitely room for improvement, although empirical models with this observed degree of imprecision have proved to be useful in decision-making processes.
4. For central variables like real and nominal GNP, the errors in simulating first differences are smaller than the errors in simulating levels. This is indicative of a significant bias component, which gets "differenced out." In most cases, error accumulation is moderate for simulated first differences.

Table 2 gives results for each model for real and nominal GNP (with first differences, as well), both inside and outside sample periods. The main conclusions (1–4) stated above can be seen in this and the succeeding tables. Consider the BEA Model for a start. The GNP error grows from approximately $2.0 billion to about $8.0 or $9.0 billion in 6 quarters; but in first difference form the growth is only from about $2.0 to $4.0 billion. In some models the first difference errors are essentially flat. Also, the increase of extrapolation error over within-sample error is noticeable in every case. It is hard to characterize this

[2] These remarks should not be confused with those relevant to error of time-cumulated aggregates; thus the error of one-period change in some variables may be less than the error of total change over many periods, where the latter can be calculated as the sum of all intermediate one-period changes. This kind of cumulation over longer periods of time is used in the paper by Leonall C. Andersen and Keith M. Carlson, "St. Louis Model Revisited." It was also used in some early error calculations for the Wharton Model. See L. R. Klein and M. K. Evans. [**10**].

growth, but it would not be an understatement to say that error doubles or triples in extrapolation.

The number of extrapolation periods is extremely limited; therefore, firm statements about extrapolation periods cannot be made. More experience will have to be gained with this measure. All models have not been able to provide extrapolation simulations, and the one, two, or three observations for the longest extrapolations were sometimes very close, giving a misleading implication of improved forecast accuracy with lengthening horizon in the case of the Wharton Model (first differences) and the Liu–Hwa Model.

There are more striking similarities than differences across models. In the short run, GNP prediction errors for one or two quarters (2–6 months for Liu–Hwa) look very much the same, given the error of measurement of GNP itself in most models. Much larger differences show up in extrapolation, although in change form similarity prevails again. The small models, the Fair Model and the St. Louis Model, seem to have rather small GNP errors even in extrapolation, but this may have been a very favorable sample period for them. New economic programs (NEP), shortages, and other rough economic events of later years have been hard on model performance for these two systems. It should be stressed that the Fair model changes every quarter in extrapolation. The updating of coefficients is something like the system of "constant adjustments" made in *ex ante* forecasting, which serves to keep most of the other models much closer to actual values in *ex ante* forecasting than would be suggested by the extrapolation error calculations in Tables 2–5.

The figures in Table 3 show that consumption errors are of the order of magnitude of GNP errors; they have about the same percentage error as GNP error. Among other leading components of GNP, inventory error is quite large, but it does not grow very much with projection horizon or between within-sample and extrapolation periods. It fluctuates pretty much like an unexplained random variable with a zero mean. It defies systematic explanation in tight-fitting equations and appears in model simulation to be like a disturbance of the system as a whole.

Housing investment and business capital formation have similar error patterns and sizes. They do not grow as much as the consumption error over the simulation horizon, but they have much larger percentage errors than does consumption. In dollar magnitude, the three types of investment (I, II, and IH) contribute more towards total GNP error than does consumption.

In extrapolation, the models got caught up in a highly inflationary environment. The price level error grows considerably with the extrapolation horizon, as does the wage rate projection. The RMSE for the wage rate was remarkably stable over the interpolation simulation horizon. For most models, the short interest rate is subject to larger error than is the long rate. There are only isolated exceptions to this rule for certain periods in a few models.

On the income side of the national income account figures, there is a similar classification of stable and volatile items, giving rise to a dispersion of error

TABLE 2

SIMULATION OF GNP IN TWELVE MODELS, ROOT—MEAN—SQUARE—ERROR (BILLIONS OF DOLLARS)

		periods ahead—Within Sample								long run
		1	2	3	4	5	6	7	8	
BEA	GNP$	2.39	4.68	6.57	7.81	8.95	9.99			13.65
	Δ	2.39	3.86	4.15	4.21	4.24	4.50			4.95
	real GNP	1.97	3.99	5.68	6.94	8.12	8.94			9.53
	Δ	1.97	3.28	3.68	3.78	3.76	3.98			4.46
Brookings	GNP$	4.08	5.38	5.83	5.85	5.78	5.72	5.66	5.80	
	Δ	4.08	3.29	3.37	3.49	3.72	3.66	3.64	3.66	
	real GNP	3.70	4.66	5.01	5.13	5.19	5.25	5.32	5.57	
	Δ	3.70	2.96	3.13	3.26	3.43	3.38	3.37	3.33	
MQEM	GNP$	3.25	4.72	7.11	8.15	9.15	9.91	10,32	10.08	6.51
	Δ	3.25	5.18	7.51	6.48	6.96	7.21	6.94	6.37	4.29
	real GNP	2.97	4.83	7.11	8.27	9.35	10.14	10.55	10.35	9.48
	Δ	2.97	5.24	6.91	6.20	6.67	6.91	6.63	5.91	4.09
DRI	GNP$	4.73	5.82	6.02	6.29	5.78	5.87	6.21	6.33	5.24
	Δ	4.73	4.25	4.28	4.33	4.47	4.52	4.40	4.41	4.34
	real GNP	3.97	4.91	4.78	4.60	4.74	5.58	5.96	6.23	6.30
	Δ	3.97	3.58	3.59	3.57	3.89	3.89	3.79	3.88	3.67
Fair	GNP$	2.80	4.12	4.49	4.50	4.00				
	Δ	2.80	3.13	3.47	3.50	3.76				
	real GNP	2.81	4.14	4.32	4.22	3.61				
	Δ	2.81	3.81	3.15	3.33	3.51				
St. Louis	GNP$	3.16	4.51	5.52	6.34	6.93	7.55	8.51	9.60	19.41
	Δ	3.16	3.16	3.16	3.16	3.16	3.16	3.16	3.16	3.16
	real GNP	2.88	4.09	4.77	4.98	4.68	4.33	4.43	4.72	4.34
	Δ	2.88	2.90	2.91	2.92	3.02	3.03	2.90	2.92	2.96
MPS	GNP$	2.65	3.73	5.31	5.27	6.77	7.06	7.36	7.12	10.60
	Δ	2.65	3.62	3.95	3.89	3.91	4.01	4.03	4.08	
	real GNP	2.76	3.60	4.11	4.23	5.46	6.00	6.32	6.38	8.20
	Δ	2.76	3.36	3.45	3.52	3.43	3.60	3.45	3.49	
Wharton (Mark III)	GNP$	2.89	4.60	6.14	6.81	7.20	7.29	7.30	7.16	10.01
	Δ	2.89	4.20	4.07	4.15	4.07	4.09	4.12	4.12	4.16
	real GNP	3.21	4.23	4.65	4.64	4.89	5.12	5.35	5.73	11.93
	Δ	3.21	3.57	3.46	3.68	3.70	3.71	3.70	3.75	4.82
Wharton Anticipations	GNP$	2.82	4.11	5.49	6.18	6.53	6.60	6.67	6.60	12.14
	Δ	2.82	4.03	3.89	3.97	3.92	4.01	4.00	3.96	4.80
	real GNP	2.98	3.65	3.89	3.96	4.36	4.76	5.19	5.70	12.83
	Δ	2.98	3.37	3.27	3.50	3.57	3.64	3.59	3.59	5.12
H–C Annual	GNP$	13.54	13.11	12.74	17.65	16.80	16.69			9.57
	Δ	13.54	10.49	11.23	11.42	10.47	11.18			10.20
	real GNP	9.20	12.77	12.31	13.09	15.50	14.16			10.00
	Δ	9.20	12.18	10.80	11.19	11.22	11.13			10.50
Wharton Annual	GNP$	4.96	5.74	10.33	14.32	23.57				21.76
	Δ	4.96	4.27	6.39	9.96	12.71				14.06
	real GNP	6.20	7.08	6.37	8.84	10.87				7.21
	Δ	6.20	7.41	8.44	10.52	10.32				9.97
Liu–Hwa (monthly)	GNP$	2.53	2.67	2.95	3.43	3.73	3.82	4.29	4.84	11.66
	Δ	2.53	2.46	2.50	2.44	2.62	2.46	2.48	2.47	2.73
	real GNP	2.23	2.54	2.83	3.31	3.39	3.85	3.62	4.27	11.47
	Δ	2.23	2.48	2.47	2.50	2.60	2.52	2.53	2.49	2.72

periods ahead—Extrapolation								
1	2	3	4	5	6	7	8	Notes
4.30	12.47	18.21	20.78	21.13	19.72			Serial correlations of residuals are used in simulation as estimated in the sample; no other adjustments except for the GM strike, 1964. Extrapolation period is 1969:1–1971:2.
4.30	11.31	6.40	4.04	4.09	4.43			
3.51	9.05	11.54	11.02	8.42	6.83			
3.51	7.93	3.38	3.48	5.56	6.81			
6.74	11.36	16.08	20.94	25.69	29.54	33.18	39.77	No adjustments made to model as estimated for within sample simulation. Period is 1959:1–1965:4. Extrapolation period is 1966:1–1970:4. Extrapolation solution adjusted for average error in last 4 sample periods.
6.74	7.61	8.32	7.94	8.44	7.11	7.08	8.01	
5.86	9.64	13.40	16.41	18.78	20.45	21.24	24.22	
5.86	6.30	6.90	6.47	6.84	5.75	5.81	6.34	
6.04	9.88	12.45	16.49					No adjustments made to model as estimated for within sample simulation. Extrapolation period is 1968:1–1970:4. Extrapolation solution adjusted for average error at end of sample period.
6.04	8.07	8.60	9.35					
5.16	8.38	9.95	12.09					
5.16	6.78	7.45	7.92					
								Model re-estimated in 1974. Within sample simulation, 1962:1–1968:4. Extrapolation not possible with this new version.
2.91	4.35	4.52	6.77	9.89				No adjustment made to model as estimated within sample period, 1962:1–1967:4, but observed values of anticipation variables used as exogenous input. Strike quarters (1964:4, 1965:1, 1965:2) deleted. Coefficients re-estimated every period for extrapolation, 1965:4–1969:4.
2.91	3.76	4.32	4.50	4.49				
3.12	4.74	4.71	5.40	6.61				
3.11	3.15	3.23	3.03	2.98				
10.29	14.88	13.83	11.69	11.15	16.11			No adjustments made to model as estimated for within or outside sample simulations. Extrapolation period is 1970:1–1971:4.
10.29	10.89	11.56	12.62	13.13	10.75			
6.81	8.54	8.36	10.25	8.33	10.86			
6.81	7.04	7.62	8.18	7.77	5.33			
								Serial correlations of residuals are used in simulation as estimated in the sample; no other adjustments.
5.71	17.04	25.09	27.25	34.14	40.35	43.99	46.57	Revised to agree with standard case in Adams and Duggal. No adjustments made to model as estimated for within- or outside-sample simulations. Extrapolation period 1970.2–1972.4.
5.71	14.05	10.41	7.40	8.26	6.90	4.43	4.95	
5.02	12.93	17.96	19.35	21.24	21.55	19.73	17.03	
5.02	9.67	6.71	5.00	5.14	3.72	3.57	3.45	
7.07	17.66	23.16	23.49	28.60	34.02	36.79	38.01	No adjustments made to model as estimated for within sample simulations. All anticipatory variables endogenously generated, except for lags. Extrapolation period, 1970:2–1972:4.
7.07	12.39	8.34	6.58	7.14	6.35	4.01	4.03	
5.80	13.00	16.14	16.07	16.56	16.21	14.01	10.65	
5.80	8.80	5.49	5.08	4.87	3.56	3.74	3.66	
								No adjustments made to model as estimated for within sample simulations, 1956–66, *by year.* Exports, farm inventories and farm residences assumed to be exogenous. Inadequate sample for annual extrapolation.
								No adjustments made to model as estimated for within sample simulations, 1961–1967, *by years.* Inadequate sample for annual extrapolation.
5.94	5.44	5.92	6.28	6.50	5.09	3.98	4.24	No adjustments made to model as estimated for within or outside sample simulations, sample, 1961:01–1967:12, outside sample 1972:01–1972:12.
5.94	5.80	6.88	5.87	5.65	5.75	5.58	5.63	
5.29	6.19	6.19	7.88	7.76	6.66	7.67	7.38	
5.29	5.53	5.34	5.91	6.15	5.22	5.76	5.74	

TABLE 3

SIMULATIONS OF GNP COMPONENTS IN ELEVEN MODELS, ROOT—MEAN—SQUARE—ERROR (BILLIONS OF DOLLARS)

		periods ahead—within sample							
		1	2	3	4	5	6	7	8
BEA	C$	1.91	2.58	3.08	3.76	4.59	5.24		
	real C	1.89	2.47	3.08	3.84	4.54	4.98		
	I$	1.09	1.84	2.47	3.09	3.63	4.08		
	real I	0.96	1.62	2.17	2.68	3.12	3.47		
	II$	2.25	3.05	3.32	3.43	3.59	3.79		
	real II	2.12	2.86	3.10	3.19	3.33	3.53		
	IH$	0.57	0.77	0.97	0.96	0.94	1.01		
	real IH	0.52	0.64	0.81	0.82	0.82	0.87		
Brookings	C$	2.44	2.77	2.97	2.91	2.88	2.88	2.70	2.74
	real C	2.29	2.58	2.70	2.63	2.61	2.67	2.59	2.72
	I$	0.59	0.84	1.01	1.16	1.19	1.22	1.27	1.43
	real I	0.52	0.78	0.93	1.05	1.11	1.16	1.22	1.37
	II$	1.77	2.26	2.29	2.30	2.41	2.45	2.53	2.59
	real II	1.75	2.23	2.26	2.28	2.39	2.43	2.51	2.57
	IH$	0.53	0.90	0.95	0.93	0.91	0.96	1.00	1.01
	real IH	0.44	0.75	0.77	0.74	0.75	0.80	0.84	0.84
MQEM	C$	1.97	3.05	4.17	5.13	5.80	6.30	6.67	6.80
	real C	2.15	3.20	4.41	5.45	6.08	6.52	6.90	6.88
	I$	1.03	1.73	2.34	2.82	3.22	3.45	3.56	3.37
	real I	0.94	1.52	2.04	2.42	2.70	2.84	2.85	2.68
	II$								
	real II	2.33	2.45	2.57	2.47	2.70	2.93	2.88	2.90
	IH$	0.67	0.91	1.22	1.25	1.27	1.39	1.54	1.60
	real IH	0.59	0.76	1.01	1.05	1.09	1.17	1.28	1.32
DRI	C$	3.35	3.82	3.88	4.17	4.06	4.09	4.06	3.89
	real C	3.06	3.42	3.28	3.10	3.20	3.48	3.65	3.69
	I$	1.62	1.84	2.15	2.20	2.28	2.41	2.51	2.65
	real I	1.40	1.53	1.85	1.94	2.03	2.17	2.29	2.41
	II$	2.08	2.42	2.48	2.56	2.59	2.63	2.74	2.87
	real II	1.91	2.21	2.27	2.35	2.38	2.44	2.55	2.67
	IH$	0.68	1.01	1.38	1.65	1.88	2.19	2.37	2.33
	real IH	0.57	0.80	1.11	1.35	1.59	1.87	2.00	1.93
Fair	C$	1.96	2.33	2.79	2.98	3.17			
	real C								
	I$	0.37	1.17	1.14	1.15	1.11			
	real I								
	II$	2.56	3.43	3.35	3.42	2.96			
	real II								
	IH$	0.56	0.88	1.09	1.12	1.15			
	real IH								
MPS	C$	2.12	2.81	3.24	3.36	3.91	4.42	4.82	4.79
	real C	2.01	2.90	3.80	3.88	4.66	5.15	5.50	5.60
	I$	0.99	1.21	1.34	1.47	1.59	1.68	1.74	1.79
	real I	1.02	1.28	1.51	1.68	1.88	1.98	2.01	1.99
	II$	2.01	2.09	2.14	2.19	2.49	2.48	2.56	2.55
	real II	2.11	2.19	2.25	2.32	2.63	2.62	2.72	2.70
	IH$	0.43	0.63	0.83	0.80	0.81	0.91	1.08	1.22
	real IH	0.49	0.71	0.94	0.89	0.90	1.00	1.21	1.38
Wharton Mark III	C$	1.92	2.53	3.30	3.87	4.23	4.52	4.66	4.80
	real C	2.00	2.46	2.76	2.88	3.00	3.16	3.25	3.22
	I$	1.95	2.23	2.42	2.47	2.51	2.52	2.53	2.52
	real I	1.82	1.97	2.05	2.08	2.14	2.22	2.30	2.37
	II$	3.45	3.64	3.74	3.68	3.72	3.72	3.78	3.86
	real II	3.32	3.50	3.58	3.51	3.53	3.53	3.57	3.65
	IH$	1.84	1.89	2.02	2.14	2.17	2.21	2.24	2.27
	real IH	1.57	1.57	1.67	1.79	1.87	1.95	2.01	2.03

long run	periods ahead—extrapolation							
	1	2	3	4	5	6	7	8
9.05	4.61	9.12	13.41	16.20	18.46	20.09		
5.91	4.26	7.21	9.41	10.02	9.81	9.16		
5.55	2.01	2.32	2.59	4.02	4.85	4.57		
4.10	1.61	1.92	1.84	2.53	2.81	2.28		
3.70	2.59	5.41	6.95	6.45	4.60	2.22		
3.44	2.18	4.50	5.84	5.42	3.86	1.96		
1.59	1.74	3.82	4.44	4.09	3.55	3.09		
1.63	1.14	2.49	2.85	2.51	2.08	1.66		
	5.80	8.45	11.56	13.62	15.50	16.95	17.24	18.56
	5.16	7.19	9.56	10.98	11.73	12.35	11.61	12.04
	3.12	3.79	4.44	5.37	6.66	8.14	9.72	11.31
	2.57	3.37	4.19	5.03	5.97	6.85	7.58	7.94
	3.68	4.68	5.01	5.47	5.05	5.03	4.53	4.23
	3.37	4.27	4.49	4.90	4.48	4.46	3.94	3.66
	1.06	2.38	3.20	3.76	3.20	3.60	3.91	4.63
	0.80	1.83	2.48	2.93	2.97	2.82	2.93	3.30
4.22	4.46	6.87	8.18	10.06				
7.00	4.07	6.54	7.60	8.32				
2.94	2.42	3.54	3.92	5.24				
2.31	2.09	2.12	3.11	4.30				
2.39	2.75	2.52	2.78	2.97				
1.53	0.85	1.23	1.46	1.49				
1.34	0.67	0.97	1.16	1.02				
3.51								
3.81								
2.83								
2.60								
2.83								
2.63								
2.29								
1.92								
	3.27	3.97	4.59	6.15	7.97			
	1.63	1.84	2.05	2.54	3.01			
	3.81	4.77	4.92	4.63	4.84			
	1.06	2.03	3.00	3.67	4.44			
7.12								
4.97								
2.68								
3.21								
3.34								
3.16								
1.60								
1.53								
4.97	5.87	10.43	14.82	17.33	21.64	25.40	28.32	30.36
6.51	2.89	5.04	7.21	8.51	9.31	9.25	8.53	6.97
3.52	4.46	3.41	2.18	1.35	3.50	6.21	8.13	8.83
3.26	2.03	1.65	2.13	2.59	3.58	4.79	5.30	5.17
5.08	4.53	8.85	12.15	12.70	14.20	14.85	14.55	14.76
4.73	3.74	7.38	10.08	10.52	11.62	12.01	11.57	11.50
2.40	4.02	3.62	5.32	7.91	8.80	9.17	9.51	9.68
2.13	3.27	3.29	4.39	6.00	6.59	6.88	7.18	7.39

Notation: C = consumer expenditure
I = nonfarm gross investment in plant and equipment
II = nonfarm inventory investment
IH = residential construction

TABLE 3 (continued)

		periods ahead—within sample							
		1	2	3	4	5	6	7	8
Wharton Anticipations	C$	1.87	2.30	2.92	3.48	3.85	4.19	4.37	4.55
	real C	1.85	2.11	2.26	2.40	2.61	2.88	3.09	3.11
	I$	1.21	1.48	1.96	2.32	2.39	2.33	2.50	2.57
	real I	1.12	1.33	1.74	2.04	2.10	2.07	2.29	2.43
	II$	2.30	3.60	3.80	3.72	3.84	3.91	4.15	4.28
	real II	2.88	3.46	3.65	3.55	3.66	3.72	3.97	4.09
	IH$	0.53	1.03	1.65	2.00	2.21	2.43	2.55	2.60
	real IH	0.49	0.82	1.35	1.67	1.89	2.15	2.33	2.39
H–C Annual	real C	5.11	6.58	6.60	6.98	8.38	7.79		
	real I	3.39	4.57	4.69	4.75	5.03	4.96		
	real II	2.34	3.10	3.11	3.11	3.16	3.18-		
	real IH	1.34	1.92	2.00	2.37	2.49	2.44		
Wharton Annual	C$	2.34	2.66	6.67	10.90	17.99			
	real C	2.98	3.47	3.14	4.08	5.54			
	I$	1.39	2.32	2.72	1.94	2.89			
	real I	1.59	2.37	2.66	2.52	3.85			
	II$	1.93	2.59	2.54	2.74	2.97			
	real II	1.80	2.43	2.37	2.66	2.89			
	IH$	1.44	1.20	2.60	3.78	4.16			
	real IH	1.31	1.00	2.09	2.87	2.68			
Liu-Hwa (Monthly)	C$								
	real C	1.67	1.81	1.97	2.26	2.12	2.50	2.21	2.35
	I$								
	real I	2.33	2.32	2.53	2.35	2.29	2.40	2.55	2.13
	II$								
	real II	2.45	2.60	2.83	2.94	2.84	3.01	2.91	3.27
	IH$								
	real IH	0.40	0.51	0.51	0.65	0.66	0.74	0.73	0.88

magnitude. Profit error is large relative to the level of profits. The Wharton and BEA Modeals are exceptional in the extrapolation simulation.

Money supply is a stock variable and therefore slower-moving than components of GNP or personal income. Errors seem to grow only moderately and in some models do not show such large amplification between extrapolation and within-sample periods. Some models, however, bypass the endogenous treatment of money supply.

The analytical purpose behind this detailed investigation of model comparison is to look for insights into ways of improving upon model performance. Models that are simulated here without any adjustments in extrapolation do worse, and residual variables (unemployment, profit) are better projected in systems that build direct estimates of these variables. Actual forecasts would, in fact, make initial corrective adjustments so that errors would be much smaller in such cases than in the unadjusted extrapolations.

It is not intended to try to infer from this cross-model comparison any best model. No model truly dominates on the basis of the ground rules laid down here. Some are better on one variable; others on different variables. The dif-

long run	periods ahead—extrapolation							
	1	2	3	4	5	6	7	8
5.59	5.38	9.33	13.16	15.06	18.64	21.66	23.68	24.68
6.46	2.46	4.16	5.87	6.71	6.75	6.04	4.72	2.55
4.52	1.93	2.11	2.68	3.25	2.63	3.62	6.01	6.36
3.88	2.29	2.80	2.03	1.02	0.96	2.50	3.73	3.49
6.50	6.20	6.01	9.82	10.57	12.26	11.93	10.66	10.31
6.07	5.09	5.05	8.18	8.80	10.09	9.74	8.56	8.08
3.57	2.72	1.12	2.85	4.57	5.98	6.50	7.07	7.25
3.14	1.80	1.66	2.87	3.94	4.89	5.30	5.71	5.87
4.93								
4.00								
2.93								
2.70								
16.08								
4.52								
2.50								
3.20								
2.89								
2.76								
4.14								
2.47								
4.34	3.60	3.25	3.36	2.86	3.28	4.38	3.31	3.72
3.10	1.27	1.31	1.39	1.40	1.43	1.40	1.21	1.20
4.60	5.60	5.79	6.53	6.92	6.67	6.64	7.23	7.20
2.34	0.53	0.78	0.90	1.14	1.16	1.19	1.01	1.29

ferences between models are often so small that they are not significant when errors of measurement are taken into account. An improvement in something like GNP simulation would have to be persistently more than $1.0 billion in order to be worth considering, and even that sum is clouded by measurement error. The Wharton anticipations version shows persistently lower errors than does Mark III, but the difference is quite small, at most $0.5 billion. This apparent improvement in error performance is suggestive but by no means definitive.

The Liu–Hwa model, after 8 months has about the same GNP error as many of the models after two quarters, over the sample period. In extrapolation, the Liu–Hwa errors are smaller but the sample is too small to be clearly indicative. One of the brightest hopes for substantial improvement, however, may be in the use of monthly data.

The annual models, after 2 years, show errors that are comparable with quarterly models after 8 quarters. The error of nominal GNP continues to grow after 2 years for the Wharton Annual model, but real GNP errors are quite stable for longer simulations. The Hickman–Coen model simulations are in some

TABLE 4

SIMULATIONS OF MARKET VARIABLES IN TWELVE MODELS, ROOT—MEAN—SQUARE—ERROR

periods ahead—extrapolation								
1	2	3	4	5	6	7	8	Notes
0.25	0.34	0.57	0.98	1.65	2.44			P is measured on a base of 100, Un in percent, rs in percent, rL in percent, w in $ thousands/year, h in hours (40 hours standard)
0.35	0.86	1.23	1.39	1.40	1.26			Notation: P = GNP deflator
0.87	1.07	1.16	1.19	1.19	1.14			Un = Unemployment rate
0.42	0.52	0.60	0.68	0.75	0.79			rs = Commercial paper rate
0.04	0.06	0.10	0.13	0.15	0.17			rL = Bond yield
0.15	0.18	0.19	0.22	0.27	0.32			w = Wage rate h = Hours worked
0.42	0.65	0.80	0.91	0.96	1.08	1.30	1.70	
0.26	0.51	0.81	1.02	1.16	1.26	1.14	1.21	
0.43	0.48	0.50	0.52	0.54	0.60	0.70	0.77	rs is the treasury bill rate in percent; rL the treasury bond rate in percent, w in $/hr., and h in hours.
0.28	0.40	0.45	0.51	0.54	0.61	0.69	0.76	
0.02	0.02	0.03	0.04	0.05	0.07	0.08	0.10	
0.17	0.22	0.23	0.30	0.33	0.33	0.31	0.30	
0.39	0.61	0.75	0.86					
0.23	0.52	0.65	0.79					w is an index of private nonfarm compensation/man hour, 1967:100.
0.54	0.53	0.59	0.66					
0.23	0.32	0.38	0.43					
0.44	0.58	0.71	0.83					
0.21	0.39	0.57	0.76	0.97				
0.36	0.68	0.90	1.08	1.23				
0.48	0.81	0.90	0.76	0.71	0.70			
0.22	0.23	0.29	0.36	0.34	0.30			
1.15	1.30	1.36	1.35	1.52	1.41			
0.50	0.52	0.45	0.32	0.34	0.37			
								w is measured in cents h is measured in hours/person/week
0.72	0.96	1.04	0.80	1.02	1.41	1.99	2.73	w is measured in $ thousands/yr for the manufacturing sector; h is measured in hours (40 hour standard) for the manufacturing sector.
0.52	1.11	1.63	2.00	2.42	2.83	3.10	3.29	
0.77	1.10	1.33	1.51	1.57	1.70	1.86	1.93	
0.23	0.35	0.39	0.49	0.56	0.64	0.75	0.89	
0.07	0.09	0.11	0.11	0.16	0.22	0.27	0.32	
0:72	0.95	1.01	0.81	1.10	1.54	2.11	2.82	
0.52	1.08	1.53	1.84	2.18	2.51	2.72	2.83	
0.78	1.12	1.36	1.52	1.57	1.69	1.84	1.90	
0.23	0.35	0.40	0.50	0.57	0.64	0.75	0.88	
0.07	0.09	0.11	0.11	0.16	0.22	0.26	0.30	
								w is measured in $/hr. h is measured in 1,000 hrs/person/yr.

		periods ahead—within sample								long run
		1	2	3	4	5	6	7	8	
BEA	P	0.21	0.33	0.41	0.50	0.55	0.59			1.37
	Un	0.22	0.25	0.31	0.32	0.32	0.34			0.45
	rs	0.19	0.22	0.24	0.23	0.20	0.20			0.21
	rL	0.13	0.17	0.21	0.20	0.21	0.23			0.29
	w	0.03	0.04	0.05	0.05	0.05	0.06			0.11
	h	0.14	0.18	0.21	0.22	0.24	0.24			0.25
Brookings	P	0.20	0.32	0.39	0.44	0.46	0.46	0.48	0.47	
	Un	0.25	0.34	0.38	0.38	0.39	0.40	0.40	0.41	
	rs	0.22	0.22	0.25	0.25	0.25	0.26	0.26	0.26	
	rL	0.10	0.10	0.13	0.16	0.17	0.17	0.18	0.20	
	w	0.01	0.01	0.02	0.02	0.01	0.01	0.01	0.01	
	h	0.11	0.11	0.11	0.11	0.12	0.12	0.12	0.12	
MQEM	P	0.16	0.26	0.36	0.47	0.57	0.65	0.73	0.81	1.13
	Un	0.16	0.32	0.44	0.51	0.53	0.54	0.56	0.54	0.37
	rs	0.20	0.26	0.31	0.37	0.42	0.47	0.50	0.51	0.43
	rL	0.11	0.17	0.21	0.23	0.25	0.27	0.29	0.31	0.34
	w	0.27	0.29	0.43	0.52	0.63	0.73	0.81	0.89	0.43
	h									
DRI	P	0.21	0.34	0.44	0.53	0.57	0.57	0.54	0.57	0.77
	Un	0.20	0.24	0.26	0.27	0.27	0.31	0.33	0.34	0.33
	rs	0.39	0.50	0.52	0.57	0.61	0.61	0.58	0.57	0.59
	rL	0.15	0.22	0.25	0.25	0.23	0.21	0.18	0.18	0.25
	w	0.30	0.40	0.50	0.60	0.60	0.50	0.40	0.40	0.60
	h									
Fair	P	0.18	0.29	0.35	0.37	0.37				
	Un	0.21	0.33	0.43	0.51	0.52				
St. Louis	P	0.19	0.31	0.38	0.45	0.55	0.68	0.82	0.98	3.10
	Un	0.23	0.27	0.32	0.35	0.34	0.24	0.17	0.19	0.33
	rs	0.34	0.36	0.34	0.33	0.36	0.40	0.44	0.50	0.55
	rL	0.16	0.17	0.16	0.16	0.16	0.16	0.19	0.22	0.41
MPS	P	0.21	0.26	0.37	0.47	0.60	0.64	0.64	0.66	1.61
	Un	0.35	0.44	0.48	0.49	0.53	0.60	0.67	0.69	0.44
	rs	0.15	0.17	0.15	0.14	0.16	0.16	0.17	0.15	0.23
	rL	0.11	0.13	0.13	0.15	0.14	0.14	0.12	0.10	0.15
	w	1.06	1.23	2.03	2.31	2.72	2.84	2.79	2.66	4.56
	h	0.11	0.13	0.14	0.15	0.16	0.17	0.16	0.17	0.19
Wharton Mark III	P	0.28	0.31	0.37	0.49	0.62	0.71	0.81	0.92	1.17
	Un	0.21	0.39	0.52	0.57	0.61	0.63	0.65	0.66	0.91
	rs	0.27	0.34	0.36	0.38	0.40	0.41	0.41	0.42	0.42
	rL	0.14	0.22	0.24	0.24	0.28	0.31	0.33	0.35	0.37
	w	0.02	0.02	0.02	0.03	0.03	0.03	0.03	0.03	0.02
Wharton Anticipations	P	0.29	0.31	0.36	0.48	0.60	0.69	0.78	0.88	1.05
	Un	0.21	0.38	0.50	0.56	0.60	0.63	0.65	0.66	1.05
	rs	0.25	0.33	0.36	0.38	0.40	0.41	0.41	0.41	0.41
	rL	0.14	0.22	0.24	0.25	0.28	0.31	0.34	0.36	0.35
	w	0.02	0.02	0.02	0.03	0.03	0.03	0.03	0.03	0.02
H–C Annual	P	1.20	1.95	2.36	2.89	3.36	3.39			2.32
	Un	0.88	1.15	1.07	0.92	1.19	1.17			1.06
	rs	0.45	0.42	0.47	0.50	0.56	0.49			0.30
	rL	0.21	0.27	0.33	0.30	0.43	0.44			0.24
	w	0.04	0.06	0.08	0.09	0.11	0.12			0.05
	h	0.01	0.02	0.02	0.02	0.02	0.02			0.01

TABLE 4 (continued)

		periods ahead—within sample								long
		1	2	3	4	5	6	7	8	run
Wharton Annual	P	0.70	0.64	1.52	2.74	3.89				2.99
	Un	0.63	0.97	1.20	1.60	1.92				1.33
	rs	0.14	0.14	0.24	0.38	0.46				0.34
	rL	0.19	0.32	0.42	0.56	0.63				0.54
	w	0.04	0.03	0.05	0.10	0.14				0.11
Liu-Hwa Monthly	P	0.29	0.31	0.36	0.36	0.42	0.47	0.46	0.41	2.36
	Un	0.26	0.35	0.43	0.50	0.59	0.62	0.69	0.69	0.75
	rs	0.12	0.15	0.18	0.19	0.18	0.25	0.25	0.22	0.25
	rL	0.05	0.08	0.12	0.14	0.15	0.15	0.18	0.16	0.55
	w	0.02	0.02	0.02	0.02	0.02	0.03	0.03	0.02	0.05
	h	0.21	0.21	0.22	0.22	0.21	0.22	0.23	0.24	0.44

cases a bit larger than other model errors for one or two years, but this model's errors stabilize rapidly and do not grow in the third and later years of simulation horizon.

The root mean squared error was decomposed, as remarked previously, into a variance and a bias component. The bias component is quite large for some of the main aggregates. That is why the first difference transformation produces markedly smaller errors than for levels of GNP. Other main aggregates such as total consumption or wage payments also have large bias components. Volatile magnitudes such as inventory investment do not have large bias components. In the later, hyperinflationary, period of 1973–74 the tendency to underestimate the price level more than price change is also indicative of a large bias component.

Dynamic Policy Multipliers

Examinations of complete-system solution errors within and beyond sample periods over which parameters are estimated, such as those conducted, are useful for indicating how models perform in unconditional prediction. Given actual values of exogenous variables, such tests reveal whether models yield aggregate economic magnitudes sufficiently close to reality that the results may be used as reliable inputs for subsequent analysis and policy decisions. However, error statistics generally do not reveal much information about responsiveness of models to shifts in policy variables or parameters. That is, they are of limited value for evaluating conditional forecasting.

For this reason there is keen interest in dynamic multipliers resulting from alternative monetary and fiscal policy actions. This is particularly true during the past few years—when there have been massive shifts in government expenditures, taxes, and monetary policy due to the Vietnamese war and the battle to

periods ahead—extrapolation								
1	2	3	4	5	6	7	8	Notes
								w is measured in $/hr in the manufacturing sector.
0.54	0.69	0.61	0.73	0.76	0.75	0.82	0.82	
0.30	0.54	0.93	1.00	1.04	1.41	1.17	1.06	
0.27	0.35	0.39	0.39	0.40	0.42	0.42	0.43	w is measured in $ thousands/yr and h in hours (40 hour standard)
0.07	0.11	0.13	0.18	0.19	0.22	0.24	0.22	
0.03	0.03	0.04	0.04	0.03	0.04	0.04	0.04	
0.20	0.20	0.15	0.19	0.12	0.13	0.12	0.13	

contain inflation. There has been much debate about desired spending and monetary expansion rates. Some differences in prescriptions have come from differences in goals; others have arisen due to controversy about magnitudes of multipliers.

Discrepancies between multiplier values across models can be attributed to a number of factors, the relative importance of which is yet to be determined. They are listed here in no particular order. First, lack of standardization of variables treated exogenously probably is a major contributor to discrepancies. For example, a model that has an exogenous foreign sector normally will have, other things being equal, higher GNP-foreign sector government expenditure multipliers than a model that makes imports and exports functions of domestic and foreign incomes and prices. Similarly, expenditure multipliers are downward biased when state and local government outlays are taken to be exogenous. Many other such examples could be given, including those from the financial-monetary sector.

Another cause for discrepancies are differences in periods over which multipliers are calculated. Given non-linear relationships between real output (or capacity utilization or unemployment rates) and prices, increments in nominal or constant dollar fiscal stimulus will reveal different multiplier responses at various stages of the economy's growth cycle. At high utilization rates and near the peak of the cycle (when potential output gaps are small), real multipliers will be lower than when capacity is less fully utilized. Timing patterns also are affected; real responses are faster and price increases slower at low rather than high utilization rates.

Aside from the degree of exogeneity of a model and the initial conditions at the time exogenous shifts are introduced, the magnitudes of such changes may influence the sizes of multipliers. With a completely linear model, multipliers depend only on the lag structure and parameters which attach to endogenous and exogenous variables.

For example, in matrix notation, a linear system might take the form:

$$A + BY_t + \sum_{j=1}^{p} B_j Y_{t-j} + CZ_t = 0$$

where,

Y = endogenous variables, y_i, $i = 1 \ldots n$

Y_{t-j} = lagged endogenous variables, $y_{i,t-j}$, with lags $j = 1 \ldots p$

Z = exogenous variables, z_k, $k = 1 \ldots m$

A, B, B_j, C = matrices of constant coefficients of orders $1 \times n$, $n \times n$, $n \times p$, and $n \times m$, respectively

The solution of the system is given by:

$$Y_t = -B^{-1}A - B^{-1} \sum_{j=1}^{p} B_j Y_{t-j} - B^{-1}CZ_t$$

Impact multipliers, first period changes in an element of the column vector Y_t with respect to changes in an element of A or Z_t are, respectively,

$$\frac{dy_{it}}{da_j} = b^{ij}$$

and

$$\frac{dy_{it}}{dz_{kt}} = \sum_{q=1}^{n} b^{iq} C_{qk}$$

where b^{ij} and b^{iq} are the (i,j) and (i,q) elements of B^{-1}. Multi-period impacts of Z_t would depend on summed products of elements of B^{-1}, B_j and C.

However, most econometric models are, to a significant degree, non-linear in variables. For instance, nominal values often are derived in inflating real quantities. Therefore, unless linear approximations are used (which may lead to substantially biased multiplier estimates), numerical methods must be employed to obtain solutions of models and their multipliers.

Finally, the causal nature of models greatly affects multipliers. Reduced form systems generally have vastly different multiplier properties than models which exhibit more complete structural linkages.

The caveats apply to the results shown in Tables 5–8, which report dynamic multipliers over a ten-year interval. Solution periods range from starting near the onset of recessions to the middle of booms. Amounts of exogenous change in non-defense government expenditures vary from \$5 billion constant (1958) dollars to \$1 billion in current dollars. Tax and monetary shifts are similarly disparate. Thus, lack of standardization hampers intermodel comparisons.

Despite such differences, however, with the exception of the FRB St. Louis Model, there is a fair amount of agreement among quarterly models. Nominal

GNP–non-defense government expenditure multipliers are around two after four quarters and then generally continue to rise, with slight fluctuation, thereafter. Results for the annual models and Liu–Hwa monthly model are consistent with this pattern.

Much of the sustained multiplier increase is due to pressures on prices, which appear to accelerate as simulation periods are lengthened. Prices continue to rise despite declines in rates of increase or falls in absolute levels of real output, drops in capacity utilization, and higher unemployment rates. Few of the models contain price anticipation variables and, where they are included, it is doubtful that they are strong enough to account for this phenomenon.

These and related effects are mirrored in the results for constant dollar multipliers (Δreal GNP/Δreal expenditures). Conventional textbook expositions generally depict real expenditure multipliers approaching positive asymptotes. But, most of the models here show such multipliers reaching a peak in two or three years and then declining (see Table 5). Multipliers for the MPS model decline to negative values quite early, but not as early as the St. Louis Model. At the end of five to ten years, some of the models show that continued sustained fiscal stimulus has ever-increasing perverse effects.

For models in which the stimulus is introduced in nominal terms, the decline in real expenditure multipliers, in part, is attributable to decreasing the amount of real input. That is, the expenditure increase declines in real terms as prices rise. A concomitant effect of the rise in prices is to lower real values of all other exogenous nominal dollar expenditures or transfers. Moreover, in models where government transfers such as current dollar social security payments are endogenous, insufficient allowance probably is made for Congressional actions to raise benefit levels as inflation erodes real living standards. Thus, when nominal exogenous stimuli are used in solutions of models, unless upward adjustments in outlays are made for endogenous increases in prices, real stimulus falls and multipliers, as conventionally calculated, will tend to decline after a period of time.

There are also other effects at work. These may be illustrated by the Brookings and Wharton Annual model simulations, wherein government expenditure inputs are stated in real terms. Here, too, real expenditure multipliers rise to a peak and then begin to fall. While there probably are some multiplier feedbacks on some exogenous expenditures and transfers from prices, the primary cause of the fall-offs in multipliers after two years in these models most likely is due to capacity constraints and reductions in rates of increase of business fixed and inventory investment. Only in the Fair model does the real multiplier fail to drop. This model has only a short solution horizon and some nonresponsive anticipatory variables. Although the real multiplier drops in the H–C Annual model, this becomes apparent only after 14 years.

Economic theory also suggests that declines in real multipliers could be caused by financial stringency if monetary authorities do not curtail rising interest rates by expanding bank reserves so as to support ever higher financial transactions and investment demands. As can be seen by comparing results

TABLE 5

SIMULATION OF FACTOR INCOME PAYMENTS AND MONEY SUPPLY IN TEN MODELS, ROOT—MEAN—SQUARE—ERROR (BILLIONS OF DOLLARS)

		periods ahead—within sample								long run
		1	2	3	4	5	6	7	8	
BEA	PI	1.96	3.23	4.14	4.80	5.52	6.31			11.41
	W	1.79	2.88	3.55	3.66	3.66	4.09			7.77
	PR	2.44	3.04	4.06	4.82	5.39	5.84			6.86
	MI	0.81	1.38	1.71	1.83	1.94	2.15			3.29
Brookings	PI	1.72	2.39	2.61	2.65	2.43	2.45	2.33	2.50	
	W	1.79	2.63	2.98	3.09	2.95	3.03	3.00	3.05	
	PR	2.34	3.13	3.38	3.55	3.70	3.79	3.82	3.76	
	MI	0.61	1.02	1.29	1.49	1.64	1.74	1.76	1.80	
MQEM	PI	1.86	3.11	4.85	6.07	6.90	7.56	8.28	8.33	4.57
	PR	1.99	2.34	3.09	3.44	4.00	4.36	4.72	5.06	6.01
DRI	PI	4.01	4.64	5.14	5.56	5.03	4.83	4.56	4.40	4.62
	PR	2.17	2.55	2.77	3.12	3.44	3.90	4.11	4.24	4.08
	MI	1.12	1.22	1.33	1.41	1.47	1.49	1.57	1.60	1.30
MPS	PI	2.00	2.66	4.30	4.73	5.72	6.34	6.62	6.51	7.94
	W	1.89	2.47	3.73	4.20	5.18	5.77	5.91	5.77	6.57
	PR	2.63	3.07	3.31	3.03	3.26	3.00	3.01	2.98	3.77
	MI	0.62	1.00	1.34	1.53	1.63	1.66	1.68	1.69	1.64
Wharton Mark III	PI	1.66	2.77	3.88	4.40	4.51	4.63	4.60	4.85	6.74
	W	1.37	2.56	3.66	4.17	4.30	4.37	4.21	4.31	6.92
	PR	2.80	3.05	3.07	3.08	3.47	3.64	3.82	4.00	4.34
	MI	0.77	1.17	1.45	1.64	1.74	1.85	1.96	2.06	2.58
Wharton Anticipations	PI	1.59	2.61	3.65	4.14	4.21	4.30	4.23	4.45	8.39
	W	1.37	2.48	3.51	3.98	4.07	4.12	3.89	3.95	8.53
	PR	2.84	2.98	2.92	2.93	3.31	3.51	3.77	3.98	4.39
	MI	0.78	1.18	1.44	1.62	1.74	1.87	2.00	2.11	2.29
H-C Annual	PI	8.61	8.89	8.63	10.85	11.26	11.33			4.83
	W	7.64	7.81	6.45	8.67	9.57	9.30			6.05
	PR	5.04	4.45	4.78	6.49	5.29	5.35			6.87
	MI	3.16	3.36	3.72	4.16	4.05	4.30			2.44
Wharton Annual	PI	2.47	4.49	9.98	14.11	21.04				18.86
	W	2.46	4.74	9.93	14.13	19.67				17.91
	PR	2.92	3.11	3.44	3.89	3.95				3.37
	MI	2.08	2.76	2.63	2.75	3.37				1.23
Liu-Hwa Monthly	PI	3.86	4.11	4.31	4.32	4.58	4.53	4.27	5.24	7.41
	W	2.02	2.18	2.42	2.65	2.61	2.75	2.91	2.97	8.08
	PR	1.62	2.53	2.91	3.41	3.21	3.88	3.72	3.94	5.72
	MI	0.74	0.91	0.97	1.28	1.08	1.54	1.48	1.84	2.94

shown in Tables 6 and 7, an accommodating monetary policy of constant interest rates tends to raise long-term expenditure multipliers but does not alter the basic pattern of movement to a peak and then decline.

Multipliers for decreases in personal taxes are shown in Table 8. In the first few years, nominal GNP-tax multipliers rise more slowly than nominal GNP-expenditure multipliers, but surpass the latter in the BEA and MQEM models after seven years. Real GNP-tax multipliers in all the models peak after two to three years, but are significantly lower (by 0.3 to 0.9) than real GNP-expendi-

periods ahead—extrapolation								
1	2	3	4	5	6	7	8	Notes
2.68	9.44	15.73	19.33	21.81	22.93			Notation: PI = Personal Income
4.00	12.32	19.59	23.60	25.90	26.65			W = Employee compensation
3.17	5.48	4.55	4.17	3.57	4.46			PR = Corporate Profits before tax
2.36	4.59	6.66	8.24	9.47	10.44			MI = Currency and demand deposits
3.43	6.20	9.63	12.67	16.04	19.15	21.50	25.38	Demand deposits without the addition of
3.22	6.24	9.63	12.91	15.86	18.97	20.88	24.36	currency are used for MI Currency is
3.82	5.70	7.82	10.26	12.68	14.17	15.81	17.50	separately tabulated.
1.23	2.49	3.80	5.31	7.13	9.28	11.59	14.16	
4.87	7.22	7.86	10.92					
4.06	5.20	5.24	5.22					
13.13	22.30	29.54	33.29	41.49	49.16	55.61	61.56	
10.08	18.39	25.14	28.61	36.41	43.84	50.02	55.91	
6.91	9.28	9.00	7.95	7.63	6.82	6.72	7.46	
2.32	2.01	2.28	3.28	4.87	5.86	7.20	8.64	
13.40	22.14	28.60	31.57	38.93	45.76	51.16	55.82	
10.12	18.09	24.21	26.96	34.00	40.55	45.67	50.27	
7.39	9.53	8.25	6.77	6.26	5.46	6.13	7.88	
2.52	2.21	2.14	2.97	4.50	5.32	6.41	7.67	
7.83	8.75	11.96	10.00	7.24	14.67	9.61	10.22	
3.77	3.79	4.46	3.61	3.63	3.56	3.21	3.54	
5.84	5.54	4.25	5.44	5.80	4.29	5.49	5.07	
2.21	1.90	2.83	1.92	2.71	2.12	2.33	2.55	

ture multipliers. This is not unexpected. The differences between expenditure and tax multipliers need not necessarily equal unity. They do so only in simplistic balanced-budget models that exclude a multiplicity of leakages and income-expenditure feedbacks. (For a proof, see G. Fromm and P. Taubman; for examples of policy simulations with balanced budget strategies, see V. Duggal.)[3]

[3] G. Fromm and P. Taubman, [**14**]; V. Duggal, [**8**].

Aside from first-round effects in multiplier calculations, government expenditure changes (of a constant average mix) probably are more powerful than personal income tax changes over a period of a few years because shifts in government outlays tend to be more intensive in generating private investment than comparable amounts of personal income tax increase or reduction. This advantage persists in the Brookings, DRI, Wharton Anticipation, H–C Annual, and Wharton Annual models but disappears in the BEA, MQEM, MPS, and Wharton Standard models. In fact, real GNP-real tax multipliers are higher (for some models, less negative) for the latter models after from three to seven years. This occurs because non-linear impacts of capacity constraints and price effects are different in these than in the former models.

There are even more striking disparities between models in multiplier responses to shifts in monetary policy. With the exception of the FRB St. Louis Model (in which demand deposits and currency are augmented), an exogenous increase of either $0.5 billion or $1.0 billion in unborrowed reserves is introduced in each model. As can be seen in Table 9, this has virtually no short-run or long-run effect on nominal GNP in the BEA model and an ever-increasing one (at least over five years) in the MPS and Wharton Annual models.[4] In the DRI, Wharton standard, and H–C Annual models, the nominal GNP-nominal money multiplier peaks after two to three years and then begins to decline in a cycling path.

Real GNP-nominal money multipliers reflect these same patterns over the first few years, but because of rises in prices, multipliers are lower thereafter. Prices apparently rise fastest in the DRI and FRB St. Louis models, since real GNP-nominal money multipliers become negative after four or five years.

Prospects

This summary report marks the end of a second phase of comprehensive analysis of American econometric models.[5] In the first phase a number of U.S. models were examined in detail for cyclical content (1969), followed soon after by a similar examination of price determination in 1970.[6] These two investigations—both conferences—looked carefully into cross-model comparisons for specific characteristics. The seminar on model comparisons looked at a wider variety of model properties in a cross-section analysis. What remains for future research in this area?

[4] In more recent (updated and revised) versions of the BEA model, money multipliers are significantly stronger.

[5] It is encouraging to learn that the format of our research discussions and project planning are attractive to model builders in other environments. Japanese model proprietors have held a similar conference; Canadian model builders have attended our seminars as guests; and European model builders have considered holding similar comparative meetings. All the participants in the U.S. seminars have felt that much was gained in the information exchanges in these model comparison seminars.

[6] B. G. Hickman [**15**]; Otto Eckstein [**9**].

New topics for discussion have enlarged our agenda as follows:

Turning point analysis
Ex ante error analysis
Error decomposition
Comparative policy simulation
Added information through model combination

Models perform less well in the neighborhood of critical turning points than along sustained monotonic paths of expansion or decline. Much is to be learned about model performance in seeing whether direction and magnitude of change at peaks and troughs is correctly simulated. A step in turning point research has already been taken by Adams and Duggal and reported in their analysis of the Wharton Model (anticipation version). There was prior consideration of this matter in the 1969 conference. Now that the U.S. economy is in the midst of a major recession, we are having an unusual opportunity to examine extreme turning points in great detail. When the cycle has completed its course, it will be a good time to look back and see what has been learned about turning point performance.

The seminar has concentrated attention primarily on sample period and *ex post* extrapolation error. A number of individual model proprietors have been making their own examinations of *ex ante* forecast error. Additionally, some outsiders have tried to make independent assessments of forecast error. As these parties often lack the familiarity with the models that only the proprietors can acquire in daily use, some of these error calculations encounter the pitfalls pointed out in Howrey, Klein, and McCarthy's paper. Accordingly, the participants in the seminar on model comparisons are designing an internal study for the analysis of *ex ante* forecast errors.

Errors are studied only partly for their own sake; they are most useful as a guide to model improvement by showing where deficiencies occur. To be most helpful in this respect, errors should be decomposed into the parts due to (1) coefficient uncertainty, (2) residual disturbances, (3) errors in forecast input values (initial conditions and exogeneous variables), (4) misspecifications of the equation system. The analysis of error is being designed so as to bring these different sources into display for separate measurement.

Although we have not achieved as much model uniformity as we wanted for the calculations discussed in this summary paper, we have come far in this direction. Cross-model comparison has been done only for multiplier and historical error analysis, but the seminar is now embarking on a new investigation of alternative policy analysis particularly for the historical phase, 1965–75. Comparable changes in monetary, fiscal, and trade policies, as compared with those actually followed in this period, are being introduced into the several models to see if there is any consensus as to what public authorities might have or should have done to have avoided or mitigated the inflation-recession condi-

TABLE 6

DYNAMIC MULTIPLIERS: GROSS NATIONAL PRODUCT/GOVERNMENT NONDEFENSE EXPENDITURES

Quarters of change	BEA	Brook-ings	MQEM	DRI-74	Fair	FRB St. Louis	MPS	Wharton Mark III		H–C Annual	Wharton Annual	Liu–Hwa Monthly
								Standard	Anticipations			
ΔGNP/ΔG (current dollars)												
1	1.1	1.8	1.4	1.5	1.1	0.6	1.2	1.2				0.7
2	1.5	2.3	1.6	1.9	1.4	1.1	1.7	1.5				1.1
3	1.7	2.7	1.7	2.2	1.5	1.2	2.1	1.7				1.4
4	1.9	2.8	1.8	2.3	1.6	0.7	2.5	1.8		2.7	1.5	1.6
5	1.9	2.8	1.8	2.3	1.7	0.1	2.8	1.9				1.7
6	1.9	2.9	1.8	2.4		0.1	3.0	2.0				1.8
7	1.9	2.9	1.8	2.5		0.1	3.1	2.1				1.9
8	1.9	2.9	1.8	2.5		0.1	3.0	2.2		2.6	2.3	2.0
12	1.9	3.0	1.8	2.5		0.1	2.2	2.4		2.9	2.7	2.4
16	2.1	3.1	2.0	2.3		0.1	1.8	2.6		3.5	3.3	
20	2.5	3.0	2.6	2.5		0.1		2.5		3.7	3.9	
24	2.9	3.1	3.2	2.9				2.3		3.6		
28	3.1	3.3	3.8	3.4				2.3		3.6		
32	3.1	3.4	4.0	3.5				2.3		3.9		
36	3.2	3.7	4.1	3.6				2.8		3.9		
40	3.3	3.8	4.3	4.0				3.9		3.9		
ΔGNP58/ΔG58 (constant dollars)												
1	1.1	1.8	1.4	1.3	1.1	0.5	1.2	1.3	1.1			
2	1.7	2.4	1.6	1.7	1.4	1.0	1.5	1.6	1.4			
3	2.1	2.7	1.7	2.0	1.5	1.0	1.9	1.8	1.6			
4	2.2	2.8	1.7	2.1	1.5	0.5	2.2	2.0	1.7	1.6	1.7	
5	2.3	2.8	1.6	2.1	1.6	−0.1	2.3	2.1	1.7			
6	2.3	2.8	1.5	2.1		−0.2	2.4	2.2	1.8			
7	2.3	2.8	1.4	2.2		−0.2	2.4	2.3	1.8			
8	2.2	2.7	1.4	2.2		−0.2	2.2	2.4	1.8	1.1	1.9	
12	1.8	2.4	1.0	2.0		−0.2	0.7	2.6		1.4	1.5	
16	1.6	2.0	1.0	1.7		−0.2	−0.5	2.4	1.7	1.8	1.0	
20	1.3	1.5	1.1	1.7		−0.2		1.9	1.6	1.9	0.5	
24	0.03	1.2	1.1	1.9				1.2		1.8		
28	−3.8	1.1	0.7	2.3				0.3		2.0		
32	−7.4	1.0	0.2	2.0				−0.8		2.3		
36	−11.2	1.0	0.1	1.3				−1.9		2.3		
40	−23.2	0.9	−0.0	0.7				−3.0		2.4		

TABLE 7

DYNAMIC MULTIPLIERS: GROSS NATIONAL PRODUCT/GOVERNMENT EXPENDITURES WITH COMPENSATING MONETARY POLICY

Quarters of change	BEA	Brook-ings	MQEM	DRI-74	Fair	FRB St. Louis	MPS	Wharton Mark III Standard	Wharton Mark III Anticipations	H–C Annual	Wharton Annual	Liu–Hwa Monthly
ΔGNP/ΔG (current dollars)												
1	0.9			1.4			1.2	1.3				
2	1.5			1.8			1.7	1.6				
3	2.0			2.1			2.2	1.9				
4	2.3			2.3			2.6	2.0		2.9	1.6	
5	2.4			2.3			3.0	2.2				
6	2.5			2.5			3.4	2.4				
7	2.5			2.7			3.7	2.5				
8	2.5			2.7			3.9	2.6		3.1	2.5	
12	2.3			2.8			4.4	3.0		3.2	3.2	
16	2.5			2.7			6.0	3.0		3.5	4.1	
20	3.0			2.7				2.8		3.9	5.0	
24	3.5			2.7				2.6		3.8		
28	3.9			2.9				2.4		3.8		
32	4.0			3.3				2.5		3.9		
36	4.1			3.8				3.0		4.0		
40	4.2			4.0				4.2		3.9		
ΔGNP58/ΔG58 (constant dollars)												
1	0.9			1.2			1.1	1.4	1.2			
2	1.5			1.7			1.6	1.8	1.6			
3	1.9			1.9			2.0	2.1	1.8			
4	2.2			2.0			2.3	2.3	2.0	1.7	1.7	
5	2.3			2.1			2.5	2.5	2.1			
6	2.4			2.2			2.7	2.6	2.2			
7	2.3			2.3			2.9	2.8	2.3			
8	2.2			2.4			2.9	2.9	2.3	1.3	2.1	
12	1.7			2.3			2.4	3.2	2.2	1.5	2.0	
16	1.4			2.1			2.4	3.0	1.9	1.8	1.8	
20	1.3			1.9				2.4		2.0	1.5	
24	0.6			1.7				1.6		2.0		
28	−1.1			1.5				0.5		2.1		
32	−2.7			1.4				−0.6		2.2		
36	−5.7			1.5				−1.7		2.4		
40	−9.4			1.1				−2.6		2.5		

TABLE 8

DYNAMIC MULTIPLIERS: GROSS NATIONAL PRODUCT/PERSONAL TAXES

Quarters of change	BEA	Brook-ings	MQEM	DRI-74	Fair	FRB St. Louis	MPS	Wharton Mark III Standard	Wharton Mark III Anticipations	H–C Annual	Wharton Annual	Liu–Hwa Monthly
ΔGNP/—ΔTP (current dollars)												
1	0.4	1.0	0.6	0.9			0.4	0.4				0.1
2	0.8	1.4	1.1	1.2			0.9	0.7				0.2
3	1.1	1.6	1.2	1.2			1.2	0.9				0.4
4	1.3	1.8	1.2	1.3			1.5	1.0		1.5	0.8	0.6
5	1.5	1.9	1.3	1.2			1.9	1.2				0.7
6	1.7	2.0	1.3	1.3			2.2	1.3				0.8
7	1.8	2.2	1.3	1.3			2.5	1.4				0.9
8	1.8	2.3	1.4	1.3			2.7	1.5		1.9	1.8	1.0
12	1.8	2.6	1.7	1.2			3.4	1.7		2.4	2.2	1.2
16	1.8	2.8	2.1	0.9			3.7	1.5		2.9	3.9	
20	2.2	2.8	2.6	1.0				1.2		3.1	5.9	
24	2.7	2.9	3.3	1.2				0.7		2.9		
28	3.2	3.2	4.9	1.9				0.4		3.0		
32	3.3	3.5	5.6	3.2				0.4		3.3		
36	3.3	4.0	6.7	4.1				0.7		3.3		
40	3.5	4.7	7.6	4.6				1.6		3.4		
ΔGNP58/—ΔTP58 (constant dollars)												
1	0.4	1.0	0.6	0.9			0.4	0.5	0.4			
2	0.7	1.3	1.1	1.2			0.8	0.8	0.6			
3	1.0	1.5	1.1	1.2			1.1	1.0	0.7			
4	1.2	1.6	1.2	1.3			1.3	1.2	0.8		1.0	
5	1.3	1.6	1.1	1.3			1.6	1.3	0.9			
6	1.4	1.4	1.1	1.3			1.8	1.5	1.0			
7	1.4	1.6	1.1	1.3			2.0	1.6	1.0			
8	1.4	1.6	1.1	1.2			2.1	1.7	1.1		1.4	
12	1.1	1.6	1.1	0.9			2.2	1.9	1.0		0.9	
16	0.8	1.5	1.2	0.6			1.8	1.6	0.9		0.5	
20	0.5	1.3	1.1	0.5				1.1			0.2	
24	0.3	1.2	0.9	0.7				0.6				
28	-0.2	1.2	1.1	0.9				0.3				
32	-0.4	1.3	0.6	0.9				0.1				
36	-0.7	1.4	0.8	0.3				0.2				
40	-1.0	1.5	0.9	0.2				0.6				

TABLE 9

Dynamic Multipliers: Gross National Product/Unborrowed Reserves or Money Stock

Quarters of change	BEA	Brook-ings	MQEM	DRI-74	Fair	FRB St. Louis	MPS	Wharton Mark III: Standard	Wharton Mark III: Anticipations	H–C Annual	Wharton Annual	Liu–Hwa Monthly
ΔGNP/ΔM (current dollars)												
1	0.0			0.3		1.2	0.4	1.3				0.0
2	0.0			0.6		2.9	1.1	2.4				0.1
3	0.1			2.0		4.5	2.2	3.4				0.6
4	0.2			4.3		5.3	3.6	4.1		1.5	1.8	1.5
5	0.2			6.2		5.1	5.4	4.8				2.7
6	0.3			7.4		5.1	7.4	5.5				4.3
7	0.5			8.3		5.1	9.5	6.3				5.9
8	0.5			8.8		5.1	11.4	6.8		1.3	7.6	7.4
12	0.8			7.9		5.1	17.4	8.2		0.9	16.0	14.0
16	0.9			4.9		5.1	24.7	8.0		0.1	25.8	
20	1.1			2.4		5.1	36.1	5.9		0.1	43.6	
24	1.3			0.6				3.6		0.2		
28	1.5			−0.1				1.7		0.2		
32	1.5			1.9				1.4		0.1		
36	1.5			1.8				2.1		0.3		
40	1.8			0.4				4.5		0.1		
ΔGNP58/ΔM (constant dollars/current dollars)												
1	0.0			0.3		1.1	0.3	1.4	0.4			0.0
2	0.0			0.5		2.7	1.0	2.6	0.6			0.1
3	0.1			1.9		4.0	2.0	3.6	0.7			0.6
4	0.2			4.1		4.4	3.2	4.5	0.8		2.2	1.4
5	0.2			5.9		4.0	4.8	5.2	1.0			2.7
6	0.3			7.1		3.6	6.4	6.0	1.1			4.5
7	0.4			7.9		3.2	8.1	6.6	1.2			5.7
8	0.4			8.3		2.8	8.4	7.2	1.3		7.4	7.0
12	0.7			6.5		1.2	12.4	8.6	1.3		10.6	10.0
16	0.7			2.8		−0.4	14.5	8.0	1.2		8.2	
20	0.7			−0.1		−1.9	16.1	5.7			5.2	
24	0.6			−1.7				3.6				
28	0.4			−2.5				2.2				
32	0.2			−2.7				2.1				
36	0.0			−4.0				2.3				
40	0.0			−5.1				3.2				

Notes to Tables 6–9

BEA Model: Period 1962–71. Increase of $1 billion in federal non-defense expenditures; proportion due to compensation of government employees based on 1962–71 actual data. $1 billion (1958 dollars) decrease in personal taxes. Increase of $0.5 billion in unborrowed reserves.

Brookings Model: Period 1956.1–1965.4. Increase of $5 billion (1958 dollars) in government expenditures; decrease of $5 billion in personal taxes. Tax multiplier computed as ratio to deflated and undeflated values of $5.0 billion, respectively.

MQEM Model: Period 1962.1–1971.4. $1 billion increase in nondefense expenditures; decrease of $1 billion in personal taxes.

DRI-74 Model: Period 1961.1–1970.4. Increase of $5 billion (1958 dollars) in federal non-defense expenditures. Decrease of $5 billion in personal taxes. Increase of $1.0 billion in unborrowed reserves.

Fair Model: Period 1962.1–1963.1. $1 billion increase in non-defense expenditures; anticipations variables are exogenous. No tax variables in model.

FRB St. Louis Model: Period 1962.1–1966.4. $5 billion increase in non-defense expenditures. Increase of $0.5 billion in MI.

MPS Model: $1 billion increase in exports without accommodating monetary policy and $1 billion decrease in personal taxes. Increase of $0.5 billion in unborrowed reserves.

Wharton Mark III Model: Period 1965.1–1974.4. Increase of $1 billion in non-defense expenditures with average associated change in government wage bill and employment; decrease of $1 billion in personal taxes. Increase of $0.5 billion in unborrowed reserves.

H–C Annual Model: Period 1951–66. Increase of $1 billion in non-defense expenditures. Interest rates are endogenous. Decrease of $1 billion in personal taxes. Increase of $0.5 billion in unborrowed reserves.

Wharton Annual Model: Period 1962–66. Increase of $5 billion (1958 dollars) in non-defense expenditures with average associated change in government wage bill and employment; decrease of $1 billion in personal taxes. Increase of $0.5 billion in unborrowed reserves.

Liu–Hwa Model: Period 1961.01–1964.06. Increase of $1 billion in non-defense spending. Decrease of $1 billion in personal taxes. Increase of $1 billion in unborrowed reserves.

---

tion in which we now find ourselves (1974–75). These will be presented in another seminar symposium.[7]

The different models in this large seminar collection all view the working of the economy through somewhat different mechanisms—different approximations to reality. Each has some special characteristics, and each has some unusual insight. A combination of model results may prove to be more effective than any one set in interpreting movements in the economy. A study to seek improved or "optimal" combinations of model results is presently being initiated.

These are only some of the findings and lines of research that could be pursued by this unusual seminar of model builders. As ever, there is much to be done, much more scope for standardization, and much room for improvement—both in model structure and results.

National Bureau of Economic Research
University of Pennsylvania

[7] Results were reported at the December 1975 meetings of the American Economic Association.

REFERENCES

[1] ANDERSON, L. C. AND K. M. CARLSON, "A Monetarist Model for Economic Stabilization," *Federal Reserve Bank of St. Louis Review,* LII (April, 1970), 7–25.

[2] ANDO, ALBERT, "Equations in the MIT-PENN-SSRC Econometric Model of the United States," (mimeographed), University of Pennsylvania (January, 1973).

[3] ———, AND F. MODIGLIANI, *The MPS Econometric Model: Its Theoretical Foundation and Empirical Findings,* forthcoming.

[4] COEN, ROBERT M., "Labor Force and Unemployment in the 1920's and 1930's: A Re-Examination Based on Postwar Experience," *The Review of Economics and Statistics,* LV (February, 1973), 46–55.

[5] DE LEEUW, FRANK AND EDWARD GRAMLICH, "The Federal Reserve—MIT Econometric Model," *Federal Reserve Bulletin,* LIV (Washington, D.C.: Board of Governors of the Federal Reserve System, January, 1968), 11–40.

[6] DHRYMES, PHOEBUS L., *et. al.,* "Criteria for Evaluation of Econometric Models," *Annals of Economic and Social Measurement* (July, 1972), 291–324.

[7] DUESENBERRY, J. S., G. FROMM, L. R. KLEIN, AND E. KUH, eds., *The Brookings Quarterly Econometric Forecasting Model of the United States* (Chicago: Rand McNally and Co., 1965).

[8] DUGGAL, V., "Fiscal Policy and Economic Stablization," *The Brookings Model: Perspective and Recent Developments,* eds., G. Fromm and L. R. Klein (Amsterdam, North Holland, 1975).

[9] ECKSTEIN, OTTO, ed., *Econometrics of Price Determination,* (Washington, D.C.: Federal Reserve Board, 1972).

[10] EVANS, MICHAEL K. AND LAWRENCE R. KLEIN, *The Wharton Econometric Forecasting Model* (Philadelphia: Economics Research Unit, Wharton School of Finance and Commerce, University of Pennsylvania, 1968).

[11] FAIR, RAY C., *A Short-Run Forecasting Model of the United States Economy* (Lexington, Mass.: D.C. Heath and Co., 1970).

[12] FROMM, G., "Implications to and from Economic Theory in Models of Complex Systems," *American Journal of Agricultural Economics,* LV (May 1973), 259–71.

[13] ———, LAWRENCE R. KLEIN, AND GEORGE R. SCHINK, "Short- and Long-Term Simulations with the Brookings Model," in Bert G. Hickman, ed., *Econometric Models of Cyclical Behavior, Volume I,* Studies in Income and Wealth (New York: National Bureau of Economic Research, 1972).

[14] ———, AND P. TAUBMAN, *Policy Simulations with an Econometric Model* (Amsterdam: North-Holland, 1967).

[15] HICKMAN, BERT, ed., *Economic Models of Cyclical Behavior* (N.Y., National Bureau of Economic Research, 1972).

[16] HIRSCH, ALBERT A., M. LIEBENBERG, AND G. R. GREEN, "The BEA Quarterly Econometric Model," *Bureau of Economic Analysis Staff Paper No. 22,* U.S. Department of Commerce (July, 1973).

[17] HYMANS, SAUL H., AND HAROLD T. SHAPIRO, "The DHL-III Quarterly Econometric Model of the U.S. Economy," Research Seminar in Quantitative Economics, The University of Michigan, Ann Arbor, (1970).

[18] LIEBENBERG, M., A. A. HIRSCH, AND J. POPKIN, "A Quarterly Econometric Model of the United States: A Progress Report," *Survey of Current Business,* XLVI (May, 1966), 13–39.

[19] LIU, TA-CHUNG AND ERH CHENG HWA, "A Monthly Econometric Model of the U.S. Economy," chapter 4 in this volume.

[20] MCCARTHY, MICHAEL D., "The Wharton Mark III Econometric Model of the United States," Economics Research Unit, University of Pennsylvania, 1972.

[21] PRESTON, R. S., "The Wharton Annual and Industry Forecasting Model," Economics Research Unit, Department of Economics, University of Pennsylvania, 1972.